Photo Credits:
Jeffrey Aranita 63, 415.
COMSTOCK: 179.
EARTH SCENES: Richard Shiell 239.
Robert I. Faulkner 379.
THE IMAGE BANK: Joseph Drivas 99;
         Steven Hunt 1, 455; John Martin 203;
         Michel Tcherevkoff 331.
NAWROCKI STOCK PHOTO:
         John Kornick 303.
         Steve Niedorf 127.
THE STOCK MARKET:
         Masahiro Sano 153, 353.
TSW/ Chicago: Ed Pritchard 271.
VIESTI ASSOCIATES, Inc.: Dan Barba 31.

Design: Grace Kao, Kelly Kao.

Home Office: 9 Pine Street, New York, NY 10005
ISBN: 0-8215-1678-7
 23456789/06 05 04 03 02

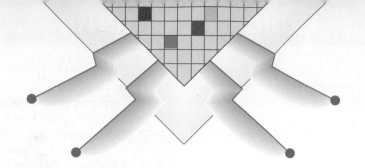

NEW EDITION

New Progress in
Mathematics

An innovative approach including *two* options:

- Pre-Algebra
- Algebra

Rose Anita McDonnell

Catherine D. LeTourneau

Anne Veronica Burrows

with

Dr. Elinor R. Ford

Sadlier-Oxford
A Division of William H. Sadlier, Inc.

Table of Contents

Introduction: Problem Solving

Chapter 1

Whole Numbers and Decimals

Chapter 2

Fractions

USE THESE STRATEGIES:
Use a Graph
Write an Equation
Use a Formula
Make a Table
Multi-Step Problem
Use Simpler Numbers

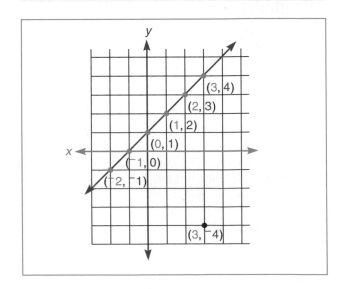

Chapter 15

Polynomials and Rational Expressions

Chapter 16

Linear and Quadratic Relations

End of Book Material

Dear Student,

Mastery in problem solving is dependent on critical thinking.
To think critically, it is essential for you to organize your thoughts.
Here are a set of steps that will help you do just that.

1	2	3	4	5
IMAGINE	**NAME**	**THINK**	**COMPUTE**	**CHECK**
Create a mental picture.	List the facts and the questions.	Choose and outline a plan.	Work the plan.	Test that the solution is reasonable.

When working to solve a problem, these steps help you to form a plan that will lead you to choose one or more of these problem-solving strategies:

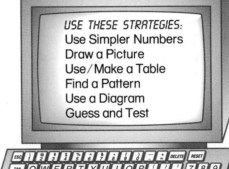

USE THESE STRATEGIES:
Use Simpler Numbers
Draw a Picture
Use / Make a Table
Find a Pattern
Use a Diagram
Guess and Test

USE THESE STRATEGIES:
Hidden / Extra Information
Write an Equation
Combining Strategies
More than One Solution
Logical Reasoning
Interpret the Remainder

USE THESE STRATEGIES:
Use a Graph
Make an Organized List
Use a Model / Drawing
Multi-Step Problem
Use a Formula
More than One Equation

1 IMAGINE

Create a mental picture.

As you read a problem, create a picture in your mind. Make believe you are there in the problem. This will help you think about:
- what facts you will need;
- what the problem is asking;
- how you will solve the problem.

After reading the problem, draw and label a picture of what you imagine the problem is all about.

2 NAME

List the facts and the questions.

Name or list all the facts given in the problem. Be aware of *extra* information not needed to solve the problem. Look for *hidden* information to help solve the problem. Name the question or questions the problem is asking.

3 THINK

Choose and outline a plan.

Think about how to solve the problem by:
- looking at the picture you drew;
- thinking about what you did when you solved similar problems;
- choosing a strategy or strategies for solving the problem.

4 COMPUTE

Work the plan.

Work with the listed facts and the strategy to find the solution. Sometimes a problem will require you to add, subtract, multiply, or divide. Two-step problems require more than one choice of operation or strategy. It is good to *estimate* the answer before you compute.

5 CHECK

Test that the solution is reasonable.

Ask yourself:
- "Have you answered the question?"
- "Is the answer reasonable?"

Check the answer by comparing it to the estimate. If the answer is not reasonable, check your computation. You may use a calculator.

Problem-Solving Strategy: Making a Table

Problem: A local chemical plant wants to promote "Earth Day." So it offers environmental clean-up jobs to local youth. Each young person could earn $13.40 for each lot cleaned of aluminum cans and paper and $16.60 for packaging properly the debris collected in every three lots. In how many different ways can a young person earn $90?

Job Combinations		
Cleanup	Packaging 3 lots	Cleanup
$13.40	$16.60	$13.40
+	+	+
Cleanup	Packaging 3 lots	Packaging 3 lots
$13.40	$16.60	$16.60
+...	+...	+...
$90	$90	$90

 1 IMAGINE   Draw and label a picture of the possible job combinations and the goal, to earn $90.

2 NAME

Facts: $13.40 — Lot cleaned
$16.60 — 3 lots packaged
$90   — Possible total earnings

Question: Which combination(s) will earn $90?

3 THINK   This is a "combination" problem. Use the "Making a Table" strategy so you can clearly see which combinations will give you $90. Use your *Imagine* picture to help you arrange your table so that:

Job Amount × Number of Jobs (n) = Total Earned

Job	Job Amount	Number of Jobs =	Total Earned
Cleanup	$13.40	x	$
Packaging	$16.60	y	$
Combination of Clean & Package	$30.00	z	$
			$90.00

By looking at the table it is clear that $30 is a factor of 90.
So, establish an equation: 1 Cleanup job + 1 Package job = $30
$$\$30 \times n = \$90$$

 4 COMPUTE

$30n = \$90$
$n = \$90 \div \$30$
$n = 3 \longleftarrow$

So, 3 combinations of cleaning and packaging will earn a young person $90.

 5 CHECK

Cleaning $13.40 × 3 = $40.20
Packaging $16.60 × 3 = $49.80   ⟶ Total = $90.00

x

Problem-Solving Strategy: Finding a Pattern

Problem: In the first year of an 8-year space mission, a spaceship crew visits 14 space colonies. In the second year they make 19 visits and in the third, 24. At this rate, how many colonies will they visit during the 8-year mission?

1 IMAGINE Sketch a picture of the crew's 8-year mission.

2 NAME

Facts: 1st year — 14 colonies ⎫
           2nd year — 19 colonies ⎬ Rate of visits
           3rd year — 24 colonies ⎭ increasing
           ⋮   ⋮

Questions: 8th year — _?_ Colonies visited
             Total   — _?_ Colonies visited

3 THINK To find the total number of colonies visited, examine the increasing rate or number of colonies visited each year. Look for a pattern to find the rate of change.

Year	1	2	3	4	5	6	7	8
Visits Made	14	19	24					

+5 +5
+10   +10

Each year the crew visited 5 *more* colonies.
Use the rate or pattern of +5 to find the number of visits made each year. Complete the table above.

Add to find the total visited in the 8 years.

4 COMPUTE By adding 5 to the 14 in year one and each year following, the answers are: 14, 19, 24, 29, 34, 39, 44, 49.

To add quickly, examine:

Ones: Each one's digit is a 4 or 9. There are 4 fours and 4 nines.
$4(4 + 9)$ = sum of ones column = $4 \times 13 = 4(10 + 3) = 52$

Tens: Sum can be expressed as:
$2(10 + 20 + 30 + 40) = 2 \times 100 = 200$ or 20 tens

Ones (52) + Tens (20 tens = 200) = 252 Total colonies visited

5 CHECK Does 252 seem like a reasonable answer? Check your sum by using the addition algorithm on your calculator.

Problem-Solving Strategy: Write an Equation

Problem: What three consecutive odd numbers have a sum of 171?

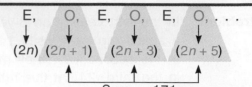

1 IMAGINE	Draw three *consecutive* odd numbers that when added equal 171.

2 NAME

Facts:

Name an even number:	$2n$
Name an odd number:	$2n + 1$
Name the next consecutive odd number:	$2n + 3$
Name the next consecutive odd number:	$2n + 5$
Sum of 3 consecutive odds:	171

Question: What are the three consecutive odd addends whose sum is 171?

3 THINK

$(2n)$ is an even number because any number multiplied by 2 makes an even number.
$(2n + 1)$ is an odd number because one more than any even number makes an odd number.
Add the 3 *consecutive* odd numbers pictured above.

$$(2n + 1) + (2n + 3) + (2n + 5) = 171$$

Collect all the "$2n$" terms and all the whole-number terms.

$$(2n + 2n + 2n) + (1 + 3 + 5) = 171 \longrightarrow 6n + 9 = 171$$

4 COMPUTE

Solve:
$$6n + 9 = 171$$
$$6n + 9 - 9 = 171 - 9$$
$$6n + 0 = 162$$
$$6n = 162$$
$$\frac{6}{6}n = \frac{162}{6} \longrightarrow n = 27$$

If $n = 27$, then the three consecutive odd numbers are:

$(2n + 1) = 2(27) + 1 = 54 + 1 = 55$
$(2n + 3) = 2(27) + 3 = 54 + 3 = 57$
$(2n + 5) = 2(27) + 5 = 54 + 5 = 59$

> The three consecutive odd numbers whose sum is 171 are: 55, 57, 59

5 CHECK

Add: $55 + 57 + 59 \stackrel{?}{=} 171$
$55 + 57 + 59 = 171$

Problem-Solving Strategy: Extra Information

Problem: A freighter is steaming up the Amazon River at 8 miles per hour. The Amazon is navigable for 2300 miles by ocean-going ships. How long will it take the freighter to travel 908 miles?

1 IMAGINE Draw and label a picture showing the speed of the boat and the distance to be traveled.

2 NAME *Facts:* 2300 mi—navigable length of river
908 mi—distance freighter must travel
8 mph—freighter's rate of speed

Question: __?__ hr: time needed to travel the distance

3 THINK To find the time, use this formula:

distance = rate × time   OR $d = rt$

Substitute given values in this equation:

$d = rt$

$908 = 8t$

> Why was $d \neq 2300$?
>
> 2300 was the distance the river was navigable. But the question asked how long it would take for the freighter to go 908 miles. Do not use 2300 miles. It is "extra" information.

4 COMPUTE $908 = 8t$ is same as $8t = 908$

$$\frac{8t}{8} = \frac{908}{8}$$

$t = 113.5$ or $113\frac{1}{2}$ hours

5 CHECK It sounds reasonable that at 8 miles per hour it would take the freighter $113\frac{1}{2}$ hours to go 908 miles.

Check the solution by substituting 113.5 for (t):

$8t = 908 \longrightarrow 8(113.5) = 908$
$908 = 908$ Answer checks.

Problem-Solving Strategy: Multi-Step Problems/Combining Strategies

Problem: A roll of film costs $4.50 plus tax. The cost of developing each roll is $7.50 plus tax. The sales tax is 6%. How many rolls of film can a tourist buy and have developed given a $55 budget?

1 IMAGINE Draw and label a picture of the costs involved.

Film $4.50

Developing $7.50

Tax 6%

Cost of 1 roll ?

2 NAME *Facts:*   Film—$4.50 a roll
Development—$7.50 a roll
Sales tax—6% of total

Question: ? rolls bought and developed for $55

3 THINK This is a multi-step problem. Usually there are several ways to solve such problems.

Use estimation to think about one of these ways:

1 Roll + 1 Development + Sales Tax = Total Cost
about $4 +   about $7 + Sales Tax $\approx$ $12

If 1 roll costs about $12, then 4 rolls cost about $48.
So, 5 rolls would cost about $60, which is too much.

One solution is to estimate the cost of 4 rolls,
and see how close the total cost comes to $55.

$[(4 \times \$4.50) + (4 \times \$7.50)] + (0.06 \times \text{Total cost 4 rolls}) \stackrel{?}{=} \$55$

4 COMPUTE $[\$18 + \$30] + [0.06 \text{ of } (\$18 + \$30)] = \underline{\ ?\ }$
$\$48 + (0.06 \times \$48) = \$48 + \$2.88 = \$50.88$

Since $50.88 is almost $55, there is not enough money to purchase another roll. So, the answer is 4 rolls.

5 CHECK Use another way to solve the problem. See if you get the same answer. Find the total cost of 1 roll and development.

$(\$4.50 + \$7.50) + [0.06 \times (\$4.50 + \$7.50)] = \$12.72$

Divide $55 by $12.72, the total cost of 1 roll, to find how many rolls can be bought.

$\$55 \div \$12.72 = 4.32 \text{ rolls} \approx 4 \text{ rolls}$ Answer checks.

1 Whole Numbers And Decimals

In this chapter you will:

- Read and write whole numbers and decimals
- Round and compare whole numbers and decimals
- Add and subtract whole numbers and decimals
- Multiply and divide whole numbers and decimals
- Use number properties as shortcuts in computation
- Solve problems: logical reasoning
- Use technology: input-output

Do you remember?

Our numeration system has two important features:

It is based on 10.

It is a place-value system. Each place or position in the number represents a different value or power of ten.

$$3 \times 10 = 30$$

$$27,432,637$$

$$3 \times 10,000 = 30,000$$

More Than Meets the Eye

RESEARCHING TOGETHER

Look at the digital clock. Scientists tell us that the face has 28 different lights and a colon. What time is it when the fewest number of lights are lit? When the largest number are lit?

$$15:08$$

In one day, how many times does at least one 9 show?

1

Reading and Writing Whole Numbers and Decimals

In our base-ten numeration system, the value of each place in a decimal numeral is a power of ten.

Commas separate the periods.

Each *period* is colored differently.

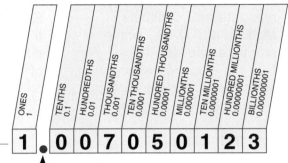

1	2	1,	5	2	0,	4	0	3,	0	7	6,	9	8	0

TRILLIONS   BILLIONS   MILLIONS   THOUSANDS   ONES

Read this number in periods.

121,520,403,076,980 is read: 121 trillion, 520 billion, 403 million, 76 thousand, 980

Now read this number.

1.007050123 is read:

1 *and* 7 million, 50 thousand, 123 billionths

1	.	0	0	7	0	5	0	1	2	3

Decimal point is always read: *and*

A number can be written or expressed in different ways:

Standard form or standard numeral: 706.0083

Place value with numerals: 700 + 6 + 0.008 + 0.0003

Place value with words: 7 hundreds + 6 ones + 8 thousandths + 3 ten thousandths

Expanded form:

706.0083 = (7 × 100) + (6 × 1) + (8 × 0.001) + (3 × 0.0001)

Read each number. Write it in expanded form.

1. 84,219

2. 46,386

3. 4,000,000

4. 16,000,000

5. 9,627,900

6. 3,274,158

7. 6,721,809,050

8. 49,002,726,300

9. 7,643,000,000,000

Read each number. Give the value of the circled digit.

10. 2 7 . 2 0 ⑥ 3 4 1

11. 1 8 . ⑦ 0 6 4 1

12. 1 0 7 2 . 4 ⑥ 0 7

13. 7 . 9 2 4 0 0 ②

14. ① 8 . 0 0 5 0 0 1

15. 0 . ④ 8 2 0 5

16. ④ 2 2 . 0 8 7 0 1

17. 0 . 2 7 6 3 5 9 ②

18. 1 . 0 0 7 0 ② 3

Write in standard form.

19. $(9 \times 10{,}000) + (5 \times 100) + (3 \times 1)$ **20.** $(6 \times 100{,}000) + (3 \times 1000) + (7 \times 1)$

21. $(4 \times 1{,}000{,}000) + (9 \times 1000) + (8 \times 10)$ **22.** $(2 \times 1{,}000{,}000{,}000) + (5 \times 1000)$

23. $(6 \times 10) + (1 \times 0.001) + (5 \times 0.0001)$ **24.** $(7 \times 1) + (9 \times 0.01) + (2 \times 0.00001)$

25. $(8 \times 0.1) + (7 \times 0.0001)$ **26.** $(3 \times 0.0001) + (4 \times 0.000001)$

Short Word Names

Short word names are often used in writing numbers.

    65 million means 65,000,000
    3.2 billion means 3,200,000,000

Write the standard numeral.

27. 3 million   **28.** 9 billion   **29.** 81 trillion   **30.** 79 billion

31. 1.5 million   **32.** 2.5 billion   **33.** 3.75 billion   **34.** 1.8 trillion

Write the number that is named by the *scrambled* digits in exercises 35–43.

35. 4 tenths
7 millionths
8 ones
5 ten thousandths

36. 3 hundred thousandths
4 tenths
7 hundreds
9 hundredths

37. 2 hundredths
7 thousandths
4 millionths
5 tenths

38. 9 hundreds
9 ones
8 hundred thousandths
7 ten thousandths

39. 2 tenths
4 ten thousandths
7 hundredths
5 billionths

40. 4 millionths
6 tens
0 hundredths
1 thousandth

41. $500 + 0.02 + 30$ **42.** $0.008 + 0.4 + 7000$ **43.** $0.0009 + 0.6 + 20 + 7$

44. Write the *greatest* number using the digits 1, 2, 3, and 4 each once.

45. Write the *least* number using the digits 0, 1, 2, 3, 4, and 5 each once.

46. What is the *greatest* 8-digit whole number?

47. What is the *least* 6-digit decimal?

48. Which of these numbers is 3,000,000 *less than* 5,550,678?

    a. 5,250,678   **b.** 2,550,678

    c. 5,520,678   **d.** 5,477,678

49. Which of these numbers is 0.0007 *greater than* 1.32111605?

    a. 1.32811605   **b.** 1.32111675

    c. 1.32810605   **d.** 1.32181605

1-2 Comparing and Ordering Whole Numbers and Decimals

To compare whole numbers:

- Compare the digits in the greatest place-value position.
- If they are the same, compare the next digits to the *right*.

> means "is greater than."
< means "is less than."

Compare: **902,267** __?__ **902,867**

902,267 < 902,867 because 2 hundred < 8 hundred

To compare decimals:

- Write the numbers vertically, aligning on the decimal points.
- Rewrite with zeros if needed.
- Compare as with whole numbers.

Compare: **0.12302** __?__ **0.1321**

0.1 2 3 0 2
0.1 3 2 1 0   ← Write zero.

0.12302 < 0.1321 because 2 hundredths < 3 hundredths

Compare: **0.125** __?__ **0.1250**

0.1 2 5 0   ← Write zero.
0.1 2 5 0

0.125 = 0.1250 because 125 thousandths
is the same as 1250 ten thousandths

To order whole numbers or decimals:

- Write the numbers vertically, aligning on the decimal points. (Write any necessary zeros.)
- Now compare the value of the digits.
- Arrange the numbers in the order specified (least to greatest, greatest to least).

Order from least to greatest: 10.142, 10.1423, 10.1421

1 0.1 4 2 0   Since each number is the same except for the
1 0.1 4 2 3   ten-thousandths place, compare these values:
1 0.1 4 2 1   Since 0.142<u>0</u> < 0.142<u>1</u> < 0.142<u>3</u>,
                    then 10.1420 < 10.1421 < 10.1423.
     So, from least to greatest: 10.142, 10.1421, 10.1423

Given 627,309.147085, name the place of these digits:

1. 9   **2.** 4   **3.** 6   **4.** 2   **5.** 1   **6.** 5   **7.** 8   **8.** 3

Now name the digit in the:

9. hundreds place   **10.** tens place   **11.** hundred-thousandths place

12. thousandths place   **13.** hundredths place   **14.** ten-thousandths place

Compare. Use <, =, or >.

15. 27,631,486 __?__ 72,631,486   **16.** 46,906,113 __?__ 46,906,131

17. 519,261,403 __?__ 51,926,140   **18.** 6,900,386 __?__ 69,003,860

19. 70,461,314 __?__ 70,461,314   **20.** 82,061,924 __?__ 82,601,924

21. 0.1002 __?__ 0.1003   **22.** 0.371 __?__ 0.376   **23.** 0.221 __?__ 0.22

24. 0.333 __?__ 0.33   **25.** 0.06 __?__ 0.006   **26.** 4.02706 __?__ 4.2706

27. 0.0072 __?__ 0.0702   **28.** 24.079 __?__ 24.709   **29.** 3.92061 __?__ 3.092061

Order these numbers from greatest to least.

30. 8,673,419; 8,773,419; 8,773,491   **31.** 60,961,721; 60,969,721; 60,901,721

32. 201,617,554; 201,677,554; 201,717,554   **33.** 0.64987; 0.64988; 0.0698

34. 1.377; 1.379; 1.037   **35.** 4.606; 46.069; 49.006

36. 8.3765; 8.7356; 8.537   **37.** 0.0021; 0.0201; 0.00201

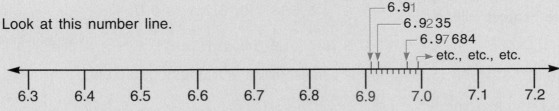

Density of Decimals

Look at this number line.

┌─ 6.91
│ ┌─ 6.9235
│ │ ┌─ 6.97684
│ │ │ → etc., etc., etc.

6.3 6.4 6.5 6.6 6.7 6.8 6.9 7.0 7.1 7.2

An *infinite* number of decimals can be found, or exist, between any two decimals.

Write two decimals that exist between each of these decimal pairs.

38. 0.320, 0.330   **39.** 0.45, 0.49   **40.** 0.0047, 0.051

41. 0.0009, 0.0014   **42.** 0.000003, 0.000009   **43.** 0.0102, 0.01

Solve.

A caliper is set to measure a width of 0.00246.
Which of these measures can pass through the gauge? Explain.

44. 0.00146   **45.** 0.02046   **46.** 0.20406

47. 0.00246   **48.** 0.000246   **49.** 0.02460

CALCULATOR ACTIVITY

50. What is the smallest decimal your calculator can display? (What is the smallest decimal a microcomputer can display?)

51. What is the greatest number your calculator can display?

1-3　Rounding Whole Numbers and Decimals

To round a number to a certain place, look at the digit to the *right* of that place.

- If the digit is 5 or greater, round the number up by increasing the digit being rounded by 1.

- If the digit is less than 5, round the number down by leaving the digit being rounded unchanged.

> 5 or greater: Round up.
> Less than 5:
> Leave unchanged.

- Replace the remaining digits with zeros.

Look at this place-value chart.

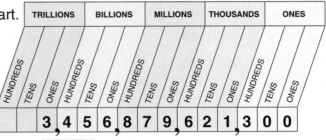

Round 3,456,879,621,300
to the nearest trillion.

3,456,879,621,300 rounded to the nearest trillion is 3,000,000,000,000.

Round 539,672,100
to the nearest million.

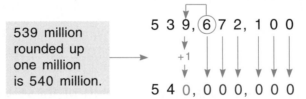

> 539 million rounded up one million is 540 million.

539,672,100 rounded to the nearest million is 540,000,000.

Round decimals as whole numbers are rounded. Look at this place-value chart.

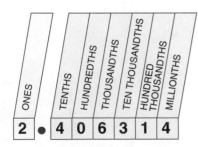

Round 2.406314
**to the nearest
hundred thousandth.**

4 < 5

2.4 0 6 3 1 ④

2.4 0 6 3 1 Ø　Drop final zero.

2.406314 rounded
to the nearest hundred thousandth is 2.40631.

6 > 5

2.4 0 ⑥3 1 4

Round 2.406314
to the nearest hundredth.　2.4 1 Ø Ø Ø Ø　≈ 2.4 1

2.406314 rounded to the nearest hundredth is 2.41.

Round 19,607,258,321,860 to each of these places.

1. hundreds
2. thousands
3. billions
4. millions
5. trillions
6. ten thousands
7. hundred thousands
8. ten trillions
9. hundred billions

Round 246.8031459 to each of these places.

10. ones
11. tenths
12. thousandths
13. millionths
14. hundred thousandths
15. hundreds

Round to the nearest million.

16. 9,204,781
17. 24,201,367
18. 10,205,964
19. 27,428,300
20. 14,224,810
21. 5,827,051
22. 27,930,416
23. 106,907,632

Round to the nearest thousandth.

24. 2.3604
25. 8.0295
26. 7.6491
27. 10.2877
28. 3.25761
29. 21.00827
30. 4.42998
31. 6.32450

Read this graph. It shows amounts of money, rounded to the nearest million, spent annually on advertising. The actual dollar amounts for each item are scrambled among the numbers in exercises 32–36.

Advertising Costs				
Product	**Amount in Millions of Dollars**			
soups				230
computers				231
credit cards				229
gasoline			199	
cosmetics			198	
	$100	$150	$200	$250

In each exercise find the name of the product to which the given dollar amount corresponds.

32. $230,450,000
33. $228,508,900
34. $198,499,200
35. $230,813,400
36. $198,860,700

CHALLENGE

37–41. Round each dollar amount in exercises 32–36 to the nearest hundred thousand. Express each, using a decimal and a *short word name*.

1-4 Adding Whole Numbers and Decimals

To add whole numbers:

- Write the numbers vertically so that place values align.
- Add from right to left, starting with the ones column.

Add: 24,027 + 498 + 6,154

> Estimate using the greatest place of the least addend.

Estimate: 24,000 + 400 + 6,100 = 30,500

```
        1                    1 1                    1 1               1     1 1            1      1 1
   2 4, 0 2 7           2 4, 0 2 7           2 4, 0 2 7           2 4, 0 2 7           2 4, 0 2 7
        4 9 8                4 9 8                4 9 8                4 9 8                4 9 8
 +  6, 1 5 4          +  6, 1 5 4          +  6, 1 5 4          +  6, 1 5 4          +  6, 1 5 4
           9                   7 9                6 7 9            0 6 7 9          3 0, 6 7 9
```

Regroup:

19 ones =	17 tens =	No regrouping	10 thousands =	No regrouping
1 ten	1 hundred		1 ten thousand	
9 ones	7 tens		0 thousands	

To add decimals:

- Write the numbers vertically, aligning on the decimal points.
- Compute as with whole numbers.

Add: 0.936 + 0.014 + 0.28

Estimate: 0.93 + 0.01 + 0.28 = 1.22

```
    0.9 3 6                  1  1 1
    0.0 1 4              0.9 3 6
  + 0.2 8                0.0 1 4
  _____            + 0.2 8 0
                       _____
                         1.2 3 0
```

> Write a zero as a placeholder.

Estimate. Then compute.

1. 716,213
        +162,076

2. 152,036
        + 27,842

3. 2,519,751
        + 702,153

4. 87,027,809
        + 1,974,312

5. 65,721
         7,364
        + 7,845

6. 14,862
        67,295
        + 5,827

7. 14,170
         9,528
        13,944
        +20,050

8. 62,314
        50,418
         9,687
        +10,892

Find the sum.

9.	10.	11.	12.
86,769	850,647	411,840	6,891,348
162,076	7,364	6,086,538	67,294
950,789	801,007	263,108	233,434
8,524	7,845	2,955	5,827
+ 65,721	+ 56,865	+ 14,682	+3,241,609

13. $4,063,762 + 9,217,834 + 10,962,871 + 9,831,592$

14. $16,863,219 + 1,263,177 + 40,106,273 + 703,814$

Compute.

15. $1.072 + 2.117$ **16.** $3.109 + 2.57$ **17.** $13.08 + 8.33$ **18.** $0.793 + 9.825$

Estimating Sums by Rounding

To estimate a sum, round to:

- The *greatest* place-value position.

or

- The *desired* place-value position.

$$4,\boxed{7}36,510 \longrightarrow 5,000,000$$
$$8,\boxed{2}13,621 \longrightarrow 8,000,000$$
$$+2,\boxed{4}65,863 \longrightarrow 2,000,000$$
Estimated Sum $\longrightarrow$ $15,000,000$

Round to:	nearest whole number		Round to:	nearest tenth
$3 . \boxed{5}$	$\longrightarrow$	4	$3 . 5$ $\longrightarrow$	$3 . 5$
$1 . \boxed{4}8$	$\longrightarrow$	1	$1 . 4\boxed{8}$ $\longrightarrow$	$1 . 5$
$+16 . \boxed{1}07$	$\longrightarrow$	$+16$	$+16 . 1\boxed{0}7$ $\longrightarrow$	$+16 . 1$
		21		$21 . 1$

Estimate the sum.

19. Round to millions.	20. Round to hundred thousands.	21. Round to thousands.
6,759,083	7,921,834	31,424
4,621,836	8,500,140	36,821
9,024,159	9,217,800	24,833
+8,217,415	+4,724,831	+63,214

22. Round to tenths.	23. Round to thousandths.	24. Round to ones.
6.34	0.4735	15.76
7.09	1.1362	8.31
+1.85	+4.8196	+ 1.827

25. Round to nearest dime.	26. Round to nearest dollar.	27. Round to nearest cent.
$85.98	$607.53	$1.088
+ 17.55	+ 24.99	+ 2.157

Subtracting Whole Numbers and Decimals

To subtract whole numbers:

- Write the numbers vertically so that place values align.
- Subtract from right to left, starting with the ones column.

Subtract: **30,681 – 18,405**

> For a close estimate use 30,000 – 18,000 = 12,000

$$\begin{array}{r} 7\ 11 \\ 30,6\cancel{8}\cancel{1} \\ -18,4\,0\,5 \\ \hline 6 \end{array}$$

Regroup:
81 = 7 tens 11 ones

$$\begin{array}{r} 7\ 11 \\ 30,6\cancel{8}\cancel{1} \\ -18,4\,0\,5 \\ \hline 7\ 6 \end{array}$$

No regrouping

$$\begin{array}{r} 7\ 11 \\ 30,6\cancel{8}\cancel{1} \\ -18,4\,0\,5 \\ \hline 2\ 7\ 6 \end{array}$$

$$\begin{array}{r} 2\ 10 \quad 7\ 11 \\ 3\cancel{0},6\cancel{8}\cancel{1} \\ -18,4\,0\,5 \\ \hline 2\ 2\ 7\ 6 \end{array}$$

3 ten thousands 0 thousands =
2 ten thousands 10 thousands

$$\begin{array}{r} 2\ 10 \quad 7\ 11 \\ \cancel{3}\cancel{0},6\cancel{8}\cancel{1} \\ -1\,8,4\,0\,5 \\ \hline 1\ 2,2\ 7\ 6 \end{array}$$

No regrouping

To subtract decimals:

- Write the numbers vertically, aligning on the decimal points.
- Compute as with whole numbers.

Subtract: **11.5 – 9.07** ⟶

Estimate: **11 – 9 = 2**

$$\begin{array}{r} 4\ 10 \\ 1\,1\,.\,\cancel{5}\,\cancel{0} \\ -\quad 9\,.\,0\,7 \\ \hline 2\,.\,4\,3 \end{array}$$

Zero as a placeholder

Estimate. Then compute.

1. 6,083,725
    –   71,213

2. 87,129,546
    – 1,016,403

3. 2,473,596
    –   427,829

4. 513,862
    –147,576

5. 300,000
    –134,213

6. 2,090,000
    –1,903,040

7. 3,001,840
    – 236,108

8. 9,050,789
    – 850,647

9. 5,216,921 – 1,926,813

10. 2,567,843 – 567,890

11. 809,521,576 – 396,544,207

12. 300,792 – 106,354

13. 49.73
    –21.4

14. 87.952
    –47.83

15. 0.821
    –0.7346

16. 51.62
    –27.419

17. 57.12
    – 7.965

18. 2.53
    –0.589

19. 1.032
    –0.459

20. 3.107
    –1.658

21. 10 – 8.53

22. 13 – 0.126

23. 7.01 – 1.85

24. 50.3 – 7.26

Estimating Differences by Rounding

To estimate a difference, round to:

- The *greatest* place-value position.

or

- The *desired* place-value position.

$$6\,\textcircled{5}, 4\,2\,1 \longrightarrow 7\,0,0\,0\,0$$
$$-2\,\textcircled{3}, 6\,8\,9 \longrightarrow -2\,0,0\,0\,0$$
Estimated Difference $\longrightarrow$ $5\,0,0\,0\,0$

Round to:	nearest tenth
$0.6236 \longrightarrow$	0.6
$-0.3760 \longrightarrow$	-0.4
	0.2

Round to:	nearest hundredth
$0.6236 \longrightarrow$	0.62
$-0.3760 \longrightarrow$	-0.38
	0.24

Estimate the difference.

25. Round to thousands.
$$78{,}742$$
$$-19{,}053$$

26. Round to millions.
$$8{,}156{,}028$$
$$-6{,}892{,}001$$

27. Round to ten thousands.
$$142{,}056$$
$$-\ 38{,}549$$

Estimate the difference to the nearest whole number. Then find the exact answer.

28.
$$6.72$$
$$-3.861$$

29.
$$5.003$$
$$-2.675$$

30.
$$476.8$$
$$-\ 59.79$$

31.
$$64.53$$
$$-\ 7.796$$

Estimate the difference to the nearest tenth. Then find the exact answer.

32. $15 - 6.24$ **33.** $19 - 11.09$ **34.** $7 - 3.25$ **35.** $0.309 - 0.192$

36. $8.52 - 3.07$ **37.** $7.03 - 0.998$ **38.** $6.078 - 2.84$ **39.** $6.59 - 0.7683$

Find the missing sum or addend.

40. $\underline{\ ?\ } + 17 = 35.6$ **41.** $4.8 + \underline{\ ?\ } = 11.36$ **42.** $10.6 + \underline{\ ?\ } = 21.57$

43. $\underline{\ ?\ } - 6 = 13.5$ **44.** $16.1 - \underline{\ ?\ } = 5.9$ **45.** $3.08 - \underline{\ ?\ } = 1.8$

Find the missing digits.

46.
$$27.513$$
$$-10.?\,?\,?$$
$$17.506$$

47.
$$50.054$$
$$-05.5\,?\,?$$
$$?\,?.510$$

48.
$$7.?\,0\,?$$
$$+?.098$$
$$9.4\,?\,7$$

49.
$$3.?\,0\,?$$
$$+?.095$$
$$?\,2.2\,?\,2$$

MAKE UP YOUR OWN...

50. Who is faster? You or a partner?

Imagine an unexpected gift of $50 to each. Open a catalog and quickly estimate mentally the cost of three items you could buy.

Then calculate the exact purchase amount and change you would receive.

1-6 Multiplying Whole Numbers and Decimals

To multiply whole numbers:

$207 \times 1573 = \underline{\quad ?\quad}$

- First estimate:

  $200 \times 1500 = 300,000$

- Multiply by ones, by tens, and so on.

- Add the partial products.

$$
\begin{array}{r}
1\ 5\ 7\ 3 \\
\times\ \ 2\ 0\ 7 \\
\hline
1\ 1\ 0\ 1\ 1 \longleftarrow 7 \times 1573 \\
3\ 1\ 4\ 6\ 0\ 0 \longleftarrow 200 \times 1573 \\
\hline
3\ 2\ 5,6\ 1\ 1 \longleftarrow \text{Sum of Partial Products}
\end{array}
$$

To multiply decimals:

$9 \times 4.2 = \underline{\quad ?\quad}$

- First estimate:

  $9 \times 4 = 36$

- Multiply as with whole numbers.

- Find the total number of decimal places in *both* factors.

- Count off from the right this number of places in the product. Place the decimal point there.

$$
\begin{array}{r}
4.2 \longleftarrow \text{1 decimal place} \\
\times\ \ 9. \longleftarrow \text{0 decimal places} \\
\hline
3\ 7.8 \longleftarrow \text{1 decimal place to the left}
\end{array}
$$

$0.002 \times 0.04 = \underline{\quad ?\quad}$

$$
\begin{array}{r}
0.0\ 4 \longleftarrow \text{2 decimal places} \\
\times\ \ 0.0\ 0\ 2 \longleftarrow \text{3 decimal places} \\
\hline
0.0\ 0\ 0\ 0\ 8 \longleftarrow \text{5 decimal places to the left needed}
\end{array}
$$

Insert 4 zeros to fill the 5 decimal places.

Estimate. Then multiply.

1. $\begin{array}{r} 8642 \\ \times\ \ 16 \\ \hline \end{array}$	**2.** $\begin{array}{r} 4212 \\ \times\ \ 51 \\ \hline \end{array}$	**3.** $\begin{array}{r} 8060 \\ \times\ \ 24 \\ \hline \end{array}$	**4.** $\begin{array}{r} 1900 \\ \times\ \ 37 \\ \hline \end{array}$	**5.** $\begin{array}{r} 7315 \\ \times\ \ 42 \\ \hline \end{array}$
6. $\begin{array}{r} 4160 \\ \times\ 307 \\ \hline \end{array}$	**7.** $\begin{array}{r} 4003 \\ \times\ 206 \\ \hline \end{array}$	**8.** $\begin{array}{r} 5100 \\ \times\ 908 \\ \hline \end{array}$	**9.** $\begin{array}{r} 7503 \\ \times\ 805 \\ \hline \end{array}$	**10.** $\begin{array}{r} 6940 \\ \times\ 403 \\ \hline \end{array}$

Compute.

11. $\begin{array}{r} 0.926 \\ \times\ \ 0.8 \\ \hline \end{array}$	**12.** $\begin{array}{r} 5.01 \\ \times\ 0.9 \\ \hline \end{array}$	**13.** $\begin{array}{r} 3.603 \\ \times\ \ 0.7 \\ \hline \end{array}$	**14.** $\begin{array}{r} 0.205 \\ \times\ 0.15 \\ \hline \end{array}$	**15.** $\begin{array}{r} 6.18 \\ \times 0.45 \\ \hline \end{array}$
16. $\begin{array}{r} 5.7 \\ \times 0.03 \\ \hline \end{array}$	**17.** $\begin{array}{r} 2.06 \\ \times 0.08 \\ \hline \end{array}$	**18.** $\begin{array}{r} 0.16 \\ \times 0.208 \\ \hline \end{array}$	**19.** $\begin{array}{r} 0.002 \\ \times\ 1.03 \\ \hline \end{array}$	**20.** $\begin{array}{r} 1.009 \\ \times\ 2.06 \\ \hline \end{array}$

Estimating Products

To estimate the product, round factors
to the greatest place-value position.

3 2 × 6 8 2 7   0 . 3 7 2 × 0 . 4 5 1

3 0 × 7 0 0 0 = 2 1 0 , 0 0 0   0 . 4   × 0 . 5   = 0 . 2 0
Estimated Product   Estimated Product

3 2 × 6 8 2 7 = 2 1 8 , 4 6 4   0 . 3 7 2 × 0 . 4 5 1 = 0 . 1 6 7 7 7 2
Actual Product   Actual Product

Estimate by rounding; then multiply.

21. 46 × 365   **22.** 28 × 3921   **23.** 42 × 8211

24. 25 × 47,526   **25.** 49 × 16,178   **26.** 62 × 402,079

27. 10.8 × 6.03   **28.** 3.06 × 7.904   **29.** 26.5 × 9.31

30. 3.156 × 4.78   **31.** 7.02 × 1.363   **32.** 0.76 × 1.14

Solve.

33. The highest price paid for a ruby ring was $227,300 per carat.
The ruby weighed 15.97 carats. How much did the ruby cost?

34. A tree loses 158.76 L of water a day through its leaves.
At this rate, how many liters of water would the tree lose in a week?

35. Felicia's math textbook is 1.5 cm thicker than the
accompanying workbook. The workbook is 0.9 cm thick.
How thick is the textbook?

36. The cafeteria tables are 1.28 m longer than the length of the
student desks. The student desks are 0.75 m long. How long
would four cafeteria tables be, placed end to end?

37. A shelf is 1 meter (100 cm) long. How much room is left
on the shelf if 27 books, each 3.2 cm thick, are placed
on the shelf side by side?

38. Which costs more, 7.2 tons of maple wood at $795.25 per ton
or 9.31 tons of pine wood at $598.50 per ton?

CHALLENGE   **Solve.** [Hint: Compute within each ( ) first.]

39. 5(0.15 + 2.75)   **40.** 6(4.2 + 3.85)   **41.** 7(8.7 − 3.12)

42. 9(0.82 − 0.115) **43.** 0.3(7.6 + 1.25)   **44.** 0.6(3.3 + 1.17)

45. 1.1(6.4 − 1.55) **46.** 2.2(1.08 − 0.99) **47.** (6 + 3) × (6 − 3)

48. (7 + 4) × (7 − 4) **49.** (5 + 1.2) × (5 − 1.2) **50.** (8 − 1.5) × (8 + 1.5)

1-7 Dividing by a Whole Number

Find the quotient: 36,995 ÷ 183 = __?__

To divide whole numbers:

- Estimate to find the first digit of the quotient.

  36,995 ÷ 183

  40,000 ÷ 200 = 200   Try 2 in the quotient.

- Multiply: 2 × 183 = 366
- Subtract: 369 − 366 = 3
- Bring down 9.

- Estimate again with the partial dividend of 39.

  39 ÷ 183

  40 ÷ 200 < 1   Write 0 in the quotient.

- Bring down 5.

- Estimate again with the partial dividend of 395.

  395 ÷ 183

  400 ÷ 200 = 2   Try 2 in the quotient.

- Multiply: 2 × 183 = 366
- Subtract: 395 − 366 = 29   29 < 183

So, 36,995 ÷ 183 = 202 R29

> Decide where the quotient begins.
>
> 183)36,995   183 > 36
>
> 183)36,995   183 < 369
>
> The quotient begins in the hundreds place.

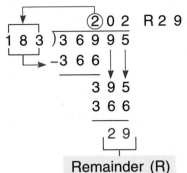

Remainder (R)

To divide a decimal by a whole number:

- Place the decimal point in the quotient directly above the decimal point in the dividend.
- Divide as with whole numbers.

3.76 ÷ 4 = __?__

```
    0.9 4
4 ) 3.7 6
   -3 6
    ‾‾‾
      1 6
      1 6
```

0.6 ÷ 15 = __?__

```
      0.0 4
1 5 ) 0.6 0
```

Write zeros when needed.

$\dfrac{\text{quotient}}{\text{divisor })\text{dividend}}$	dividend ÷ divisor = quotient	$\dfrac{\text{dividend}}{\text{divisor}}$ = quotient
$\begin{array}{r} 0.0\,3 \\ 12\,)\overline{0.3\,6} \end{array}$	0.3 6 ÷ 1 2 = 0.0 3	$\dfrac{0.3\,6}{1\,2} = 0.0\,3$

Compute.

1. 27)2889
2. 45)11,295
3. 38)76,152
4. 40)14,480

5. 86)34,467
6. 21)105,026
7. 201)20,502
8. 111)34,299

9. 13,617 ÷ 17
10. 8528 ÷ 41
11. 152,635 ÷ 38
12. 59,430 ÷ 54

13. 25,720 ÷ 341
14. 78,152 ÷ 621
15. 37,250 ÷ 502
16. 98,605 ÷ 450

17. $4\overline{)2.4}$ **18.** $3\overline{)5.1}$ **19.** $12\overline{)0.84}$ **20.** $15\overline{)0.75}$

21. $25\overline{)7}$ **22.** $24\overline{)15}$ **23.** $96\overline{)234.24}$ **24.** $89\overline{)1.0947}$

25. $56\overline{)114.24}$ **26.** $69\overline{)13.869}$ **27.** $51\overline{)50.082}$ **28.** $72\overline{)115.2}$

Find the quotient. Round to the nearest hundredth.

29. $21.95 \div 43$ **30.** $6.21 \div 15$ **31.** $32.8 \div 7$ **32.** $78.2 \div 9$

33. $63.2 \div 25$ **34.** $98.7 \div 20$ **35.** $9.17 \div 18$ **36.** $32.5 \div 102$

Solve.

37. The printer took 8 minutes to print a Happy Birthday banner. The banner was 18 pages long. How many minutes does it take to print 1 page of the banner?

38. Harry used his calculator to solve 25 division problems. He completed the problems in 112 seconds. How long did it take to complete one problem? (Round to the nearest tenth of a second.)

39. A telephone book of 1926 pages has 626,420 listings. Approximately how many listings are on one page?

40. The telephone switchboard at the Pentagon can handle over 200,000 calls per day. If the calls arrive at a constant rate, about how many calls arrive each hour?

41. Cindy used 18.34 m of telephone wire to make 7 bracelets in her arts-and-crafts class. How much wire was used for each bracelet?

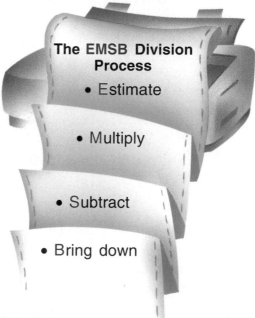

The EMSB Division Process
- Estimate
- Multiply
- Subtract
- Bring down

CRITICAL THINKING Match exercises 42–47 with their products.

42. $0.1 \times 0.09 \times 1.5 \times 0.04 = \underline{\ ?\ }$ **a.** 0.0054

43. $0.02 \times 0.003 \times 0.09 = \underline{\ ?\ }$ **b.** 0.00000054

44. $2.7 \times 0.01 \times 0.2 = \underline{\ ?\ }$ **c.** 0.000054

45. $0.18 \times 3.0 \times 0.0001 = \underline{\ ?\ }$ **d.** 0.054

46. $0.15 \times 2.0 \times 0.9 \times 0.2 = \underline{\ ?\ }$ **e.** 0.00054

47. $0.03 \times 0.012 \times 0.5 \times 0.003 = \underline{\ ?\ }$ **f.** 0.0000054

48. Order the products a.–f. from least to greatest.

49. Explain how you can name other factors of 0.54.

1-8 Dividing by a Decimal

To divide by a decimal:

- Change the divisor to a whole number by multiplying by a power of 10.
- Multiply the dividend by the same power of ten.
- Divide as with whole numbers.

Shortcut
Move the decimal point in the dividend to the right the same number of places as in the divisor.

$7.58 \div 2.4 =$ ___?___

$2.4.\overline{)7.5.8}$

Move each decimal point one place.

$2.4 \times 10 = 24$
$7.58 \times 10 = 75.8$

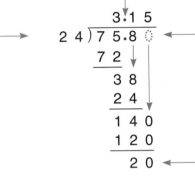

Write zeros when needed.

If you keep getting a remainder, round the quotient.

3.15 rounds to 3.2, so $7.58 \div 2.4 \approx 3.2$.

Compare the dividend and the divisor to decide if the quotient is greater than 1 or less than 1.

Dividend > Divisor
$7 \div 1.4 = 5$

Dividend < Divisor
$1.4 \div 7 = 0.2$

Tell what power of 10 to use to change the divisor to a whole number.
Place the decimal point in the quotient.

1. $\dfrac{6.03}{0.3} = 201$

2. $\dfrac{14.7}{0.07} = 21$

3. $\dfrac{0.625}{0.5} = 125$

4. $\dfrac{0.144}{1.2} = 12$

5. $0.4\overline{)0.02} = 5$

6. $1.1\overline{)0.77} = 7$

7. $0.08\overline{)16} = 2$

8. $1.5\overline{)450} = 3$

9. $2.8 \div 0.07 = 4$

10. $0.72 \div 0.9 = 8$

11. $0.62 \div 0.02 = 31$

12. $15 \div 0.25 = 6$

Compute mentally.

13. $0.005\overline{)0.45}$

14. $0.012\overline{)0.48}$

15. $0.06\overline{)7.2}$

16. $0.4\overline{)0.012}$

17. $2.13 \div 0.003$

18. $0.54 \div 0.009$

19. $0.018 \div 0.6$

20. $0.0028 \div 0.7$

Compute. Check quotients using a calculator.

21. $2.7\overline{)9.72}$ **22.** $8.3\overline{)51.46}$ **23.** $0.017\overline{)0.1207}$ **24.** $0.48\overline{)3.12}$

25. $1.6\overline{)7.808}$ **26.** $7.2\overline{)63.504}$ **27.** $0.33\overline{)0.7425}$ **28.** $0.45\overline{)0.9135}$

Find the quotient to the nearest hundredth.

29. $7.1\overline{)53.6}$ **30.** $3.6\overline{)4.94}$ **31.** $0.009\overline{)0.07}$ **32.** $0.48\overline{)1.22}$

33. $0.72\overline{)5}$ **34.** $43\overline{)21.59}$ **35.** $2.9\overline{)58.74}$ **36.** $0.73\overline{)0.24}$

Estimate the quotient. Round each number to its greatest place-value position.

37. $18\overline{)389}$ **38.** $62\overline{)2878}$ **39.** $1.7\overline{)65.95}$ **40.** $9.8\overline{)19.65}$

41. $308 \div 6.35$ **42.** $10.32 \div 0.86$ **43.** $79.1 \div 43.2$ **44.** $22.4 \div 4.3$

45. Which is greater: 2 divided by 25 or 0.2 divided by 0.25?

46. Which is less: 2.5 divided by 5 or 5 divided by 2.5?

Find the missing number.

47. $3 \times \square = 9 \times 5$ **48.** $\square \times 6 = 8 \times 9$ **49.** $\square \times 0.2 = 6 \times 0.4$

50. $1.2 \times \square = 0.6 \times 0.8$ **51.** $\square \times 0.05 = 0.1 \times 30$ **52.** $0.4 \times \square = 20 \times 0.18$

53. $\square \times 20 = 0.4 \times 4$ **54.** $30 \times \square = 0.2 \times 0.9$ **55.** $\square \times 25 = 50 \times 0.003$

Solve.

56. A paper clip manufacturer produces jumbo paper clips, which are 3.4 times longer than standard paper clips. The jumbo paper clip is 105 mm long. How long is the standard paper clip? (Round to the nearest hundredth.)

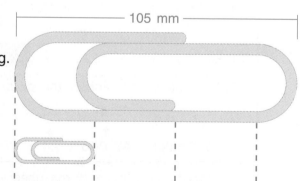

105 mm

57. A machine produces about 25,000 paper clips in 1 hour. About how many clips are produced per minute? Per second?

58. Would 32 standard paper clips, placed end to end, be longer or shorter than a meter (1000 mm)?

59. The factors of 0.000012 can be $0.2 \times 0.2 \times 0.2 \times 0.5 \times 0.003$. Work together and list other factors that when multiplied will be equal to 12 millionths.

1-9 Estimating with Whole Numbers and Decimals

Front-End Estimation with Adjustment

Compute the *front* digits; then adjust using the *back* digits.

**54,740 + 267 + 23,130 ≈ ? **

Front Back

$$\left.\begin{array}{r} 54,740 \\ 267 \\ +23,130 \end{array}\right\} \text{about } 1{,}000$$

Estimate: 77,000 + 1,000 = 78,000

**11,892 – 4560 ≈ ? **

Front Back

$$\left.\begin{array}{r} 11,892 \\ -4,560 \end{array}\right\} \text{about } 300$$

Estimate: 7,000 + 300 = 7,300

**3.6 + 7.15 + 9.24 ≈ ? **

Front Back

$$\left.\begin{array}{r} 3.6 \\ 7.15 \\ +9.24 \end{array}\right\} \text{about } 1.0$$

Estimate: 19.00 + 1.0 = 20

**6.308 – 2.221 ≈ ? **

Front Back

$$\left.\begin{array}{r} 6.308 \\ -2.221 \end{array}\right\} \text{about } 0.1$$

Estimate: 4.000 + 0.1 = 4.1

Clustering

When several addends *"cluster"* about a certain value, multiply that value by the number of addends.

**342 + 361 + 354 + 347 = ? **

Estimate: |350 + 350 + 350 + 350|
→ 4 × 350 = 1400

**9.32 + 8.7 + 9.13 = ? **

Estimate: |9 + 9 + 9|
→ 3 × 9 = 27

Compatible Numbers

Adjust the divisor and/or the dividend to easily divisible or compatible numbers.

**|47,448| ÷ |23| = ? **

Estimate: 48,000 ÷ 24 = 2000

**14.78 ÷ 0.3 = |147.8| ÷ |3| = ? **

Estimate: 150 ÷ 3 = 50

Understanding the patterns used when multiplying and dividing by powers of ten is very useful in estimation and mental math.

23 × 10 = 230	0.9 × 10 = 9	52,000 ÷ 10 = 5200	1.2 ÷ 10 = 0.12
23 × 100 = 2300	0.9 × 100 = 90	52,000 ÷ 100 = 520	1.2 ÷ 100 = 0.012

Compute mentally.

1. 7 × 8000
2. 500 × 400
3. 0.9 × 200
4. 90 × 0.03
5. 820 ÷ 10
6. 0.6 ÷ 100
7. 50 ÷ 1000
8. 70 ÷ 1000

Compare. Use <, =, or >.

9. 300×70 __?__ 30×700

10. 5×500 __?__ 50×50

11. 30×150 __?__ 4.5×1000

12. 400×700 __?__ 2.8×1000

13. 0.1×47.2 __?__ 100×0.472

14. 0.369×10 __?__ 0.01×369

Estimate the sum or difference.

15.
```
  6,799,083
    431,288
+   651,237
```

16.
```
   58,329
   41,665
+  10,583
```

17.
```
   3.27
   1.68
+  5.29
```

18.
```
   0.305
   1.264
+ 1.739
```

19.
```
   86,431
  -45,199
```

20.
```
   7963
 -  458
```

21.
```
   18.93
  -16.87
```

22.
```
   0.9
 -0.631
```

23. $31,200 + 28,960 + 32,090 + 29,490 + 30,870$

24. $8.96 + 11.02 + 9.65 + 9.38 + 10.6 + 12.3$

Estimate the product or quotient.

25. 750×41

26. $16,178 \times 49$

27. 10.8×6.3

28. 34.5×6.9

29. $8528 \div 41$

30. $21,493 \div 52$

31. $23.75 \div 8$

32. $73.1 \div 9$

33. $6805 \div 11$

34. $31,214 \div 15$

35. $8.43 \div 1.23$

36. $48.6 \div 6.1$

Use an estimation strategy to spot unreasonable answers. Write R for reasonable answers and U for unreasonable answers. Do not compute.

37. $1728 + 2215 + 8821 \approx 12,800$

38. $5.7 + 5.1 + 4.2 + 4.8 \approx 16$

39. $29,315 - 16,920 \approx 12,400$

40. $35.16 - 9.078 \approx 26.1$

41. $371 \times 48.3 \approx 185,000$

42. $983 \times 0.97 \approx 990$

43. $0.49 \times 2.35 \approx 1.16$

44. $29,876 \div 24 \approx 1200$

45. $63,215 \div 9.3 \approx 700$

46. $4.52 \div 1.53 \approx 3$

CALCULATOR ACTIVITY

How creative can you be?
Create division problems with whole numbers that fit the descriptions given below. (The first one is done.)

47. A 4-digit number is divided by a 2-digit number. The remainder is 10.

| 26 | × | 82 | = | 2132 | + | 10 | = | 2142 |

Problem: $2142 \div 26 =$ __?__

48. A 5-digit number is divided by a 3-digit number. The remainder is 100.

49. A 4-digit number is divided by a 3-digit number. The remainder is 9.

50. A 6-digit number is divided by a 3-digit number. The remainder is 20.

51. Is there only one division problem for each description? Explain.

1-10 Number Properties and Computational Shortcuts

Number properties and the rules for the operations of addition and multiplication can be used to make computation easier. Let *a*, *b*, and *c* be any numbers.

▶ Commutative Property

of Addition	of Multiplication
$a + b = b + a$	$a \times b = b \times a$
$2 + 3.5 = 3.5 + 2$	$0.4 \times 12 = 12 \times 0.4$

▶ Associative Property

of Addition	of Multiplication
$a + (b + c) = (a + b) + c$	$a \times (b \times c) = (a \times b) \times c$
$1.3 + (8 + 2) = (1.3 + 8) + 2$	$4 \times (2.5 \times 7) = (4 \times 2.5) \times 7$

▶ Identity Property

of Addition	of Multiplication
$a + 0 = 0 + a = a$	$a \times 1 = 1 \times a = a$
$7.9 + 0 = 0 + 7.9 = 7.9$	$0.8 \times 1 = 1 \times 0.8 = 0.8$

Identity element for addition   Identity element for multiplication

▶ Zero Property of Multiplication

$a \times 0 = 0 \longrightarrow 6.27 \times 0 = 0$

▶ Distributive Property

$a (b + c) = (a \times b) + (a \times c)$
$0.5 (3 + 7) = (0.5 \times 3) + (0.5 \times 7)$

These properties can be used when rearranging addends
and factors to find computational shortcuts.

79 + 36 + 21 + 82 + 64 = ? ⟶ This sum can be rewritten as:

= 79 + 21 + 36 + 64 + 82 ⟶ Order of addends changed
(Commutative Property for Addition)

(79 + 21) + (36 + 64) + 82 ⟶ Grouped for easier addition
(Associative Property for Addition)

100   +   100   + 82 = 282

1.5 + 2.7 − 1.5 = ?
1.5 − 1.5 + 2.7
(1.5 − 1.5) + 2.7

Identity element
for addition ⟶ 0 + 2.7 = 2.7

(7.2 × 0.6) + (7.2 × 0.4) = ?
7.2 × (0.6 + 0.4)

7.2 × 1 = 7.2

Identity element
for multiplication

20

Identify the number property used. Solve for *n*.

1. $6.2 + n = 6.2$ **2.** $5.1 + 8 = n + 5.1$

3. $(7 + 6.2) + 1.8 = 7 + (6.2 + n)$

4. $3.8 \times n = 0$ **5.** $7 + (3 + n) = (7 + 3) + 1.2$ **6.** $7.02 \times n = 7.02$

7. $5 \times (2.4 \times n) = (5 \times 2.4) \times 6.7$

8. $6 (3 + n) = 6 \times 3 + 6 \times 1.1$

Solve. Identify any number properties used.

9. $26 + 34 + 18 + 66 + 24 = 26 + 24 + 34 + 66 + 18 = (26 + 24) + (34 + 66) + 18$

10. $(23 \times 0.5) \times 12 = 23 \times (0.5 \times 12)$

11. $46 + 29 + 11 - 29 = 46 + 11 + 29 - 29 = (46 + 11) + (29 - 29)$

12. $10 \times (152 + 368) = (10 \times 152) + (10 \times 368)$

13. $(41.3 \times 0.3) + (41.3 \times 0.7) = 41.3 \times (0.3 + 0.7)$

14. $9.27 + 8.24 + 0.73$ **15.** $(2.6 \times 12) + (4.4 \times 12)$

16. $87 \times 5 \times 8.2$ **17.** $57 + 82 + 42 + 21 + 117$

18. $(144 \times 7) + (144 \times 3)$ **19.** $1.5 \times 2.84 \times 4$

20. $(73 \times 0.06) + (73 \times 0.94)$ **21.** $526 + 414 - 312 + 800 - 526$

22. $2.5 \times 81 \times 6$ **23.** $6.7 \times [5.72 - (2.63 + 2.09)]$

Closure Property

When the members of a set of numbers are added and their sum is also a member of the set, that set of numbers is said to be closed under addition. This is called the **closure property of addition**.

Add even numbers: $2 + 6 = 8$
After trying several examples, the sums are always even. We say that the set of even numbers is *closed* under addition.

Add odd numbers: $1 + 3 = 4$
Just one example shows that the sum is even, not odd.
We say that the set of odd numbers is *not closed* under addition.

 CRITICAL THINKING   **True or false? Explain.**

24. The even numbers are closed under multiplication.

25. The odd numbers are closed under multiplication.

26. The multiples of 5 are closed under addition.

27. The numbers 0 and 1 are closed under addition.

28. The numbers 0 and 1 are closed under multiplication.

29. The whole numbers are closed under subtraction.

30. The whole numbers are closed under division.

TECHNOLOGY

Brain Work   Computer Work

These problems can be solved either with your brain,
the human computer, or with your electronic computer.

In order to perform mathematical operations on the computer, it is important
to know these BASIC symbols for frequently used mathematical operations.

Meaning	Math Symbol	BASIC Symbol	Meaning	Math Symbol	BASIC Symbol
Add	$+$ $5 + a$	$+$ $5 + A$	power	6^n 6^2	$\uparrow$ or $\wedge$ $6\uparrow2$ or $6\wedge2$
Subtract	$-$ $b - 16$	$-$ $B - 16$	is greater than	$>$ $4 > c$	$>$ $4 > C$
Multiply	$\times$ 5×7	$*$ $5 * 7$	is less than	$<$ $8 < d$	$<$ $8 < D$
Divide	$\div$ $m \div 3$	$/$ $M / 3$	is not equal to	$\neq$ $x \neq y$	$<>$ $X<>Y$

Write these BASIC expressions as mathematical expressions and simplify.

1. $5*7$ **2.** $8\uparrow2$ **3.** $(15/13)\uparrow3$ **4.** $(5+7)*(12-4)$ **5.** $2\uparrow3+3\uparrow2$

6. $8-2+3$ **7.** $8*2+3$ **8.** $8/2*3$ **9.** $3*(5-1)/2$ **10.** $2\uparrow5/4\uparrow2$

Write these mathematical expressions as BASIC expressions and simplify.

11. 8×7 **12.** $216 \div 12$ **13.** 5^4 **14.** $(5+3) \times (8-2)$ **15.** $2^4 + 4^2$

16. $7 + 9 \times 7$ **17.** $5(12-3)-4$ **18.** $2^3(5+7)$ **19.** $6^2 \div 3^2$ **20.** $9 \times 12 \div 6$

21. Type the following program.
Remember to press ENTER or RETURN at the end of each line.

```
10 PRINT "HELLO, I'M YOUR FRIEND, THE COMPUTER."
20 PRINT "SEE HOW MUCH MATH I KNOW!"
30 PRINT "100 X 3 = ";100*3
40 PRINT "12 SQUARED = ";12↑2
50 END
```

Now type "RUN" and press ENTER/RETURN. What is the output?
Type CLS (or, on some machines, type "HOME"). Now run the program again.
The program will be stored in the computer's memory unless it is erased.
Write a program to print and simplify the expressions in exercises 1–20.

INPUT, FOR-NEXT, and IF-THEN Statements

Examine this BASIC program which uses PRINT, INPUT, and the FOR-NEXT loop.

PROGRAM
```
10 PRINT "WHAT IS YOUR NAME?"
20 INPUT A$
30 FOR N = 1 TO 5
40 PRINT "HELLO";A$
50 NEXT N
60 END
```

$ is the *string variable* (or character variable). It is used when a word is expected as input.

OUTPUT
```
WHAT IS YOUR NAME?
? KAREN BROWN


HELLO KAREN BROWN
HELLO KAREN BROWN
HELLO KAREN BROWN
HELLO KAREN BROWN
HELLO KAREN BROWN
```

The name typed in by the user.

Give the output for each program below. Input the value given.

22.
```
10 PRINT "WHAT IS YOUR AGE
   IN YEARS?"
20 INPUT H
30 PRINT "YOUR AGE IN DAYS
   IS AT LEAST "; 365*H
40 END

(INPUT VALUES 13 OR 14)
```

23.
```
10 PRINT "WHAT MULTIPLES
   DO YOU WISH?"
20 INPUT N (INPUT VALUE 7)
30 PRINT "THE FIRST 13
   MULTIPLES OF "; N
40 FOR M = 0 TO 12
50 PRINT M*N,
60 NEXT M
70 END
```

24. Write a program that asks for the length and width of a rectangle and which then outputs the area of that rectangle.

The **IF-THEN** command causes the CPU to process a comparison.
If the comparison is *true*, the instructions following THEN are executed.
If the comparison is *not true*, the next command in the program is executed. For example:

```
10 PRINT "3 TIMES A NUMBER PLUS 2 EQUALS 14."
20 PRINT "WHAT IS THE NUMBER?"
30 INPUT A
40 LET N = 3*A+2
50 IF N = 14 THEN GOTO 80
60 PRINT "SORRY, THAT IS INCORRECT. TRY AGAIN."
70 GOTO 20
80 PRINT "CONGRATULATIONS,"; A; "IS CORRECT!"
90 END
```

Look at the IF-THEN statement in line 50. If the value entered in line 30 satisfies the conditions stated in line 10 and computed in line 40, then the **GOTO** command in line 50 directs the program to line 80. If the value entered is incorrect, the program continues on to the next line, then back to line 20 through the use of the GOTO statement in line 70.

Change the lines in the program above to solve each of these equations.

25. 5 less than twice a number is 17.

26. 30 is 2 times the sum of 5 and a number.

27. A number doubled equals 52.

28. One more than half a number equals 7.

1-12 Problem Solving: Logical Reasoning

Problem: Three local soccer teams chose names and sponsors. The team captains were Sam, Joyce, and Andy. The available names were: Lions, Tigers, and Bears. The teams could be sponsored by Bill's Bakery, Paulita's Pizza, or Vinnie's Videos. Help the captains remember their sponsors and team names, given these clues:

Clue I: Sam and the captain who is sponsored by the pizzeria are neighbors.

Clue II: Andy's team name and sponsor begin with the same letter.

Clue III: There is a tiger on the uniform of the captain who lives next to Joyce.

Teams	Sponsors
S – L, T, or B	BB, PP, or VV
J – L, T, or B	BB, PP, or VV
A – L, T, or B	BB, PP, or VV

1 IMAGINE Draw a picture of the 3 captains and the different ways they can be associated with 3 teams and 3 sponsors. Use initials to represent each.

2 NAME *Facts:*

Captains	— Sam, Joyce, and Andy
Teams	— Lions, Tigers, and Bears
Sponsors	— Bill's Bakery, Paulita's Pizzeria, and Vinnie's Videos
Three clues	— Given above

Question: Can you find each captain's team and sponsor?

3 THINK Make a chart to represent all the possibilities you found during your *Imagine* step.

	Lions	Tigers	Bears	Bill's B.	Paulita's P.	Vinnie's V.
Sam	NO	YES	NO	NO	NO	YES
Joyce	YES	NO	NO	NO	YES	NO
Andy	NO	NO	YES	YES	NO	NO

4 COMPUTE Use the clues one at a time to write "Yes" in the appropriate boxes. Write "No" in boxes that are eliminated.

Clue I: Since the sponsor of Sam's team is not Paulita's Pizzeria, put No in the appropriate box.

Clue II: This clue reveals that Andy must play soccer for the Bears, sponsored by Bill's Bakery. Fill in the appropriate Yes's and No's. Notice that on the chart there is now only one possible sponsor for Sam's team. Fill in the appropriate boxes. This means that Joyce's team must be sponsored by Paulita's Pizzeria. Fill in these boxes.

Clue III: This clue reveals that Sam and Joyce must be neighbors. Since Sam wore a Tiger uniform, he must play on that team. Now fill in the rest of the boxes on the chart.

5 CHECK Check the results against the original clues to make sure that they are true.

Solve, using logical reasoning.

1. In the second row of Professor Digit's math class there are five students: Bob, Ted, Carol, Marie, and Anna. Professor Digit has arranged them alphabetically by their last names, which are Shaw, Browne, Friel, Lee, and Cook. List the full names of the students and their seating order (front to back) given that: no two boys or girls sit in consecutive seats; Marie is glad that Ted is not in front of her; Anna's initials are the first two letters of the alphabet.

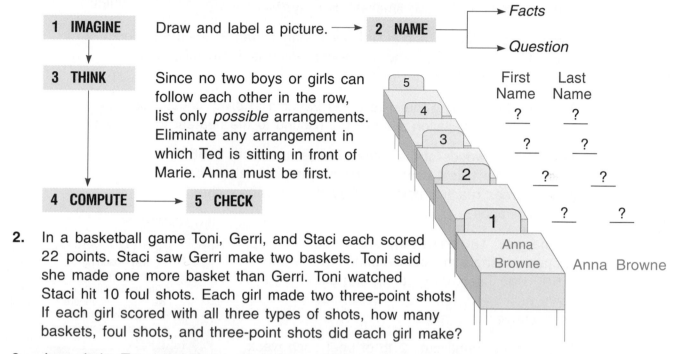

1 IMAGINE   Draw and label a picture. ⟶ **2 NAME** ⟶ *Facts*

⟶ *Question*

3 THINK   Since no two boys or girls can follow each other in the row, list only *possible* arrangements. Eliminate any arrangement in which Ted is sitting in front of Marie. Anna must be first.

4 COMPUTE ⟶ **5 CHECK**

2. In a basketball game Toni, Gerri, and Staci each scored 22 points. Staci saw Gerri make two baskets. Toni said she made one more basket than Gerri. Toni watched Staci hit 10 foul shots. Each girl made two three-point shots! If each girl scored with all three types of shots, how many baskets, foul shots, and three-point shots did each girl make?

3. Jane, Lois, Tom, and Kurt each enjoy a different math operation: +, −, ×, or ÷. Each also has a favorite property: commutative, associative, identity, or inverse. Match each person with his or her favorite math operation and property, given that: Tom and the girl who likes addition both like the properties beginning with I's; Kurt is a whiz at tables in any order; Jane is better at adding opposites than the boy who likes division.

4. Carl, Fred, Ed, Stan, and Dan play basketball. Two play forward, two play guard, and one is the center. Tell which position each boy plays, given that: Ed and the other guard are brothers; the boys whose names rhyme play different positions; Ed and Dan are related; the center's name and position begin with the same letter.

5. In the Botanical Park's flower garden there is one section each of tulips, pansies, mums, and hyacinths. Each section is a different color: red, yellow, white, or pink. Name the order (front to back) and the color of the flowers in the garden, given that: the pansies and hyacinths are at opposite ends of the garden; the white flowers are in front of the pansies; the red flowers follow the pink flowers; the tulips are not white.

1-13 Problem Solving: Applications

Solve.

1. The curator of the jungle exhibit reported that the weights of the 4 newborn monkeys were: 2.3 kg, 2.36 kg, 2.35 kg, and 2.29 kg. List these weights from heaviest to lightest. What is the difference in the weights of the two smallest monkeys?

2. The Amazon River is about 130 miles longer than 3 times the length of the Mississippi River. The Mississippi River is 1290 miles long. What is the length of the Amazon?

3. A certain tropical rain forest receives 254 cm of precipitation per year. What is the precipitation per month? (Round to the nearest thousandth.)

4. The giant redwoods of the United States are about 1.85 times taller than the tallest canopy trees of a tropical rain forest. If these trees reach a height of 200 ft, how tall are the giant redwoods?

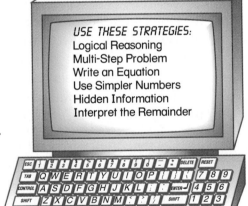

5. As many as 180 trees may live on one hectare of jungle in South America. If 5 500 000 hectares of jungle are cut down each year, how many trees may be destroyed in a month?

USE THESE STRATEGIES:
Logical Reasoning
Multi-Step Problem
Write an Equation
Use Simpler Numbers
Hidden Information
Interpret the Remainder

6. Drew's pet piranha eats 2 lb of beef each week. At a cost of $1.89 per pound, what does Drew pay to feed his fish for 4 weeks?

7. On a recent expedition a scientist planned to use porters to move 728.5 lb of equipment. Each porter could carry no more than 35 lb. How many porters did the scientist have to hire to move the equipment?

8. Approximately one third of the 215 exhibits in the school district science fair dealt with tropical plants. About how many exhibits was this?

9. The figures for the average daily relative humidity over a 5-day period in the jungle were 95%, 94.5%, 98%, 95.5%, and 98.5%. List these figures in increasing order.

10. A certain rain forest receives 160 cm of rain over a 200-day period. If the rate of precipitation is constant during this time, how many centimeters of rain fall in one day?

11. The science museum of a city allotted $400,000 for research on the tropical rain forest ecosystem. The director spent $80,000 on computer hardware and $85,650 on research equipment. The rest was set aside to finance research expeditions. How much money was available for research expeditions? If each expedition costs $120,000, how much money must the museum raise to finance two expeditions?

12. An exhibit of tropical birds includes the pygmy parrot, which is 8 cm long, and the macaw, which is 11.5 times longer. What is the length of the macaw?

13. A scientific expedition to the Amazon rain forest found that it could travel 30 miles a day by boat and 14 miles a day by land. In one 9-day period the expedition traveled 4 days by boat and 5 days by land. How much farther did it travel by boat than by land during that time?

14. The local museum charges an admission fee of $3.50 for students and $5.75 for adults. How much will it cost for 25 students and 6 adults to enter the museum?

15. Each week the zoo spends $120.50 to feed its monkeys, $32.20 to feed its birds, and $17.35 to feed its snakes. How much does it cost to feed these animals in a year?

16. Meg, Jo, Beth, and Amy are eighth graders. Each has as a pastime one of the following: dancing, reading, sports, or music. Their hair colors are: red, blonde, brown, and black.

    Use the following clues to find the hair color and pastime of each girl.

    - Beth's hair color does not begin with the same letter as her name.

    - The dancer has red hair.

    - Jo has the darkest and Amy the lightest hair color.

    - One girl's name and pastime begin with the same letter.

    - Amy and the girl who likes sports are sisters.

More Practice

Read each number. Give the value of the underlined digit.

1. 6 <u>4</u>, 3 9 2 **2.** 3 <u>7</u> 1, 9 0 6, 2 4 8 **3.** 9, 0 3 5, 7 6 1, <u>4</u> 2 8

4. 3 5 . <u>6</u> 1 7 9 **5.** 0 . 6 3 4 0 <u>8</u> 9 5 **6.** 5 . 0 0 <u>3</u> 8 9 6

Compare. Use <, =, or >.

7. 64,900,100 __?__ 64,899,999 **8.** 4,082,076 __?__ 482,076

9. 0.1583 __?__ 0.5183 **10.** 0.0764 __?__ 0.07640

Round 426,137,508,347 to each of these places.

11. hundred **12.** million **13.** hundred thousand **14.** ten billion

Round 147.3051698 to each of these places.

15. tenth **16.** hundredth **17.** millionth **18.** ten thousandth

Use an estimation strategy to solve.
Then find the exact answer.

19. 31,508 + 65,453 + 85,047 **20.** 750,038 + 64,762 + 8,746

21. 7.425 + 5.093 **22.** 0.6483 + 8.4205 + 3.0645

23. 4,304,729 − 851,924 **24.** 706,126,515 − 487,508,329

25. 64.85 − 37.4 **26.** 41.73 − 17.328

27. 35 × 54,437 **28.** 62 × 206,048

29. 20.7 × 4.02 **30.** 6.248 × 5.69

31. 45,684 ÷ 243 **32.** 265,530 ÷ 501

33. 36.74 ÷ 4 **34.** 20.54 ÷ 0.79

Solve. Identify the property used.

35. 56 + 19 + 22 − 19 = 56 + 22 + 19 − 19 = (56 + 22) + (19 − 19)

36. 2.5 × 3.96 × 4 **37.** 6.29 + 4.78 + 0.71

38. Kevin can read 47 pages in one hour. How many pages can he read in 20 hours?

39. A hardware company produces 24 billion nails a year. About how many nails does it produce per month? per week?

*See *Still More Practice*, p. 497.

Math Probe

CRYPTARITHMS: The Mystery of "Hidden" Numbers

A *cryptarithm* (sometimes called an *alphameric*) is a puzzle made by substituting letters for digits.

Example:
$$\begin{array}{r} U \\ +\,I \\ \hline US \end{array}$$

U must be 1 because a 2-digit sum of two single-digit numbers lies between, but does not include, 9 and 19.

$$\begin{array}{r} U \\ +\,I \\ \hline US \end{array} \longrightarrow \begin{array}{r} 1 \\ +\,I \\ \hline 1S \end{array} \longrightarrow \begin{array}{r} 1 \\ +\,9 \\ \hline 10 \end{array}$$

The letter I must be 9 because 1 + 9 = 10. 9 is the only addend that will give a 2-digit sum. S must be 0.

Remember: The value of the letter remains the same throughout the puzzle but may change from puzzle to puzzle.

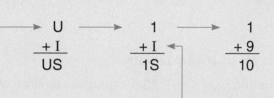

What are the numbers?

$$\begin{array}{r} DIETS \\ -\ FAD \\ \hline FOOD \end{array}$$

Try these.

1.
$$\begin{array}{r} BB \\ +\,BB \\ \hline ABE \end{array}$$

2.
$$\begin{array}{r} DIETS \\ -\ FAD \\ \hline FOOD \end{array}$$

3. ON × ON = SON

4. TO × TO = TOO

5.
$$\begin{array}{r} SEND \\ +\,MORE \\ \hline MONEY \end{array}$$

6.
$$\begin{array}{r} ME \\ \times\ ME \\ \hline SHE \\ WEE \\ \hline MINE \end{array}$$

7.
$$\begin{array}{r} MNOMOPN \\ +\ MNOOMNP \\ \hline SNOOMRMM \end{array}$$

8. THIS + IS + VERY = EASY

9. Try to make up a cryptarithm of your own.

10. Make up a cryptarithm, using your name.
Find the sum of your first and last name. Now find the product.

Check Your Mastery

Read each number. Give the value of the underlined digit. See pp. 2–3

1. 5̲ 4, 6 2 7
2. 2 6 0, 7 1 5, 3 5̲ 9
3. 7, 2 4 6̲, 9 3 1,5 0 8
4. 1 5 . 3̲ 2 4 6
5. 0 . 4 6 7 1 0 3̲ 5
6. 2 . 1 0̲ 0 6 2 7

Compare. Use <, =, or >. See pp. 4–5

7. 35,800,500 _?_ 35,799,499
8. 6,019,201 _?_ 6,019,201
9. 0.2383 _?_ 0.3238
10. 0.1937 _?_ 0.18571

Round 327,451,674,582 to each of these places. See pp. 6–7

11. ten
12. ten thousand
13. hundred million
14. billion

Round 326.4501789 to each of these places.

15. hundredth
16. hundred thousandth
17. millionth
18. tenth

Compute. See pp. 8–17

19. 52,652 + 34,629 + 46,168
20. 3.675 + 4.205
21. 5,801,336 − 462,539
22. 62.37 − 13.283
23. 27 × 42,725
24. 30.5 × 5.16
25. 404,650 ÷ 980
26. 50.05 ÷ 0.68

Use estimation to solve. Then find the exact answer. See pp. 18–19

27. 310,900 + 89,329 + 5,804
28. 6.4578 + 0.3916 + 2.2896
29. 416,208,313 − 109,315,212
30. 48.63 − 26.5
31. 53 × 104,108
32. 4.826 × 8.07
33. 64,476 ÷ 398
34. 67.2 ÷ 48

Solve. Identify the property used. See pp. 20–21

35. 38 + 21 + 54 − 21 = 38 + 54 + 21 − 21 = (38 + 54) + (21 − 21)
36. 1.5 × 6.54 × 6
37. 3.31 + 2.85 + 0.69

Solve. See pp. 8–19

38. Clare can type 52 words in one minute. How many words can she type in 30 minutes?

39. A paper factory produces 36 billion reams of paper a year. About how many reams of paper does it produce per month? per week?

In this chapter you will:

- Rename fractions as mixed numbers
- Find the prime factorization of numbers
- Find the GCF and LCM using prime factorization
- Rename fractions as decimals
- Compare and order fractions
- Add and subtract fractions and mixed numbers
- Multiply and divide fractions and mixed numbers
- Simplify complex fractions
- Solve problems: finding hidden facts

Do you remember?

A number has many fraction names:

$$3 = \frac{3}{1}, \frac{6}{2}, \frac{9}{3}, \frac{12}{4}, \ldots$$

The list is infinite.

$$\frac{3}{4} = \frac{3}{4}, \frac{6}{8}, \frac{9}{12}, \frac{12}{16}, \ldots$$

RESEARCHING TOGETHER

Speed Math

The Ride-a-Mile Bicycle Company presented their new models at a bike show. Racing models were either silver or blue.
Every silver bike was a racing model.
Half the blue bikes were racing models.

$\frac{1}{3}$ of the bikes were racing models.

There were 40 blue bikes and 30 silver bikes. How many bicycles were neither silver nor blue?
(Clue: Use a Venn diagram.)

2-1 Fractions and Mixed Numbers

Students charted the weather for 14 days.
5 of the days were rainy.

$\frac{5}{14}$ of the days were rainy.

Fractions can be shown on a number line.
This number line is divided into fourteenths.
The dot marks the point for $\frac{5}{14}$.

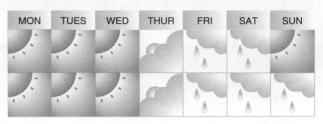

$\frac{5}{14}$ rainy days

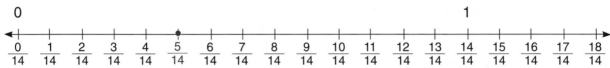

$2\frac{3}{4}$ is a **mixed number.** It has a whole number part and a fraction part.

To change a mixed number to a fraction: $2\frac{3}{4} = \frac{?}{4}$

- Multiply the whole number by the denominator.

- Add the numerator.

- Place the result over the denominator.

$$2\frac{3}{4} = \frac{(4 \times 2) + 3}{4} = \frac{11}{4}$$

To change a fraction greater than 1 to a mixed number:

- Divide the numerator by the denominator.

$$\frac{28}{5} \longrightarrow 5\overline{)28}\ ^{5\ R3} \longrightarrow 5\frac{3}{5}$$

- Place the remainder over the denominator.

$$\frac{19}{3} \longrightarrow 3\overline{)19}\ ^{6\ R1} \longrightarrow 6\frac{1}{3}$$

Name the fraction or mixed number shown by the shaded part.

1.

2.

3.
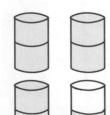

4.

Name the fraction or mixed number shown by the dot.

5. ‹—|—|—|—|—|—|—|—•—|—→
    0   1   2   3

6. ‹—|—|—•—|—|—|—|—|—→
    0   1   2

Place each on a number line.

7. $3\frac{3}{4}$　**8.** $1\frac{1}{2}$　**9.** $\frac{1}{4}$　**10.** $\frac{13}{4}$　**11.** $\frac{11}{8}$　**12.** $\frac{9}{9}$

Solve mentally. Change each to a fraction. Use a calculator for exercises 31–36.

13. $5\frac{1}{8}$　**14.** $4\frac{1}{10}$　**15.** $1\frac{7}{12}$　**16.** $10\frac{4}{7}$　**17.** $4\frac{3}{4}$　**18.** $3\frac{2}{3}$

19. $5\frac{1}{2}$　**20.** $3\frac{7}{9}$　**21.** $3\frac{3}{4}$　**22.** $9\frac{5}{6}$　**23.** $5\frac{2}{3}$　**24.** $7\frac{2}{9}$

25. $2\frac{5}{12}$　**26.** $2\frac{4}{5}$　**27.** $12\frac{2}{3}$　**28.** $4\frac{7}{10}$　**29.** $1\frac{1}{16}$　**30.** $4\frac{1}{12}$

31. $30\frac{9}{11}$　**32.** $26\frac{2}{5}$　**33.** $21\frac{4}{7}$　**34.** $112\frac{4}{5}$　**35.** $98\frac{45}{73}$　**36.** $111\frac{15}{16}$

Change each to a mixed number.

37. $\frac{7}{5}$　**38.** $\frac{13}{3}$　**39.** $\frac{21}{6}$　**40.** $\frac{19}{4}$　**41.** $\frac{17}{8}$　**42.** $\frac{21}{9}$

43. $\frac{113}{8}$　**44.** $\frac{56}{6}$　**45.** $\frac{59}{3}$　**46.** $\frac{57}{6}$　**47.** $\frac{91}{10}$　**48.** $\frac{85}{11}$

49. $\frac{64}{9}$　**50.** $\frac{83}{3}$　**51.** $\frac{77}{9}$　**52.** $\frac{85}{8}$　**53.** $\frac{78}{25}$　**54.** $\frac{72}{15}$

Write each answer as a mixed number.

55. $5\overline{)138}$　**56.** $3\overline{)128}$　**57.** $4\overline{)782}$　**58.** $6\overline{)439}$　**59.** $3\overline{)112}$　**60.** $7\overline{)205}$

61. $8\overline{)1036}$　**62.** $2\overline{)1243}$　**63.** $7\overline{)1026}$　**64.** $4\overline{)1537}$　**65.** $6\overline{)4037}$　**66.** $9\overline{)5291}$

Change the mixed number to a fraction.

67. An airplane traveled for $4\frac{1}{2}$ hours.

68. A kitchen floor has an area of $99\frac{3}{4}$ square feet.

69. Mr. Lopez ordered $15\frac{5}{8}$ yards of drapery.

70. Divide 5 sheets of 9-in. × 12-in. colored paper into fourths in 5 different ways.

2-2 Equivalent Fractions

Equivalent fractions, like $\dfrac{4}{12}$ and $\dfrac{1}{3}$, name the same point on a number line.

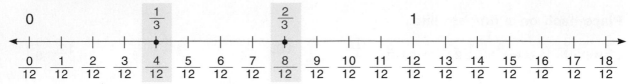

To find equivalent fractions, use the identity element for multiplication (1), and:

- Multiply the numerator and the denominator by the same number.

$$\dfrac{1}{3} \quad \dfrac{\times 3}{\times 3} = \dfrac{3}{9}$$

$$\dfrac{1}{3} \quad \dfrac{\times 5}{\times 5} = \dfrac{5}{15}$$

So, $\dfrac{1}{3} = \dfrac{3}{9} = \dfrac{5}{15}$

OR

Other names for one

- Divide the numerator and the denominator by the same number.

$$\dfrac{6}{12} \quad \dfrac{\div 3}{\div 3} = \dfrac{2}{4}$$

$$\dfrac{6}{12} \quad \dfrac{\div 6}{\div 6} = \dfrac{1}{2}$$

So, $\dfrac{6}{12} = \dfrac{2}{4} = \dfrac{1}{2}$

A fraction is in simplest form when the numerator and the denominator have no common factors except 1.

$$\dfrac{4}{12} = \dfrac{1}{3} \quad \longleftarrow \text{Simplest Form}$$

To find the simplest form of a fraction, divide both the numerator and the denominator by their **greatest common factor (GCF).**

Factors of 8: 1, 2, 4, 8
Factors of 12: 1, 2, 3, 4, 6, 12
So, 4 is the greatest common factor (GCF).

$$\dfrac{8}{12} \quad \dfrac{\div 4}{\div 4} = \dfrac{2}{3} \quad \longleftarrow \text{Simplest Form}$$

Copy and complete. Write equivalent fractions.

1. $\dfrac{1}{8} = \dfrac{2}{16} = \dfrac{?}{24} = \dfrac{?}{32}$

2. $\dfrac{1}{5} = \dfrac{2}{10} = \dfrac{3}{?} = \dfrac{4}{?}$

3. $\dfrac{2}{7} = \dfrac{4}{14} = \dfrac{?}{?} = \dfrac{?}{?}$

4. $\dfrac{3}{4} = \dfrac{6}{8} = \dfrac{?}{?} = \dfrac{?}{?}$

5. $\dfrac{5}{6} = \dfrac{10}{12} = \dfrac{?}{?} = \dfrac{?}{?}$

6. $\dfrac{3}{10} = \dfrac{6}{20} = \dfrac{?}{?} = \dfrac{?}{?}$

Complete to find the equivalent fractions.

7. $\dfrac{15}{20} \dfrac{\div 5}{\div 5}$

8. $\dfrac{20}{40} \dfrac{\div 2}{\div 2}$

9. $\dfrac{9}{21} \dfrac{\div 3}{\div 3}$

10. $\dfrac{12}{30} \dfrac{\div 3}{\div 3}$

11. $\dfrac{14}{28} \dfrac{\div 2}{\div 2}$

12. $\dfrac{25}{50} \dfrac{\div 5}{\div 5}$

13. $\dfrac{24}{36} \dfrac{\div 6}{\div 6}$

14. $\dfrac{27}{33} \dfrac{\div 3}{\div 3}$

15. Which of these equivalent fractions are in simplest form?

Complete the equivalent fractions.

16. $\dfrac{4}{7} = \dfrac{?}{14}$

17. $\dfrac{12}{36} = \dfrac{6}{?}$

18. $\dfrac{6}{27} = \dfrac{2}{?}$

19. $\dfrac{3}{21} = \dfrac{?}{42}$

20. $\dfrac{5}{6} = \dfrac{?}{30}$

21. $\dfrac{1}{7} = \dfrac{3}{?}$

22. $\dfrac{3}{8} = \dfrac{9}{?}$

23. $\dfrac{18}{36} = \dfrac{?}{18}$

Write each fraction in simplest form.

24. $\dfrac{8}{56}$

25. $\dfrac{4}{48}$

26. $\dfrac{8}{32}$

27. $\dfrac{18}{36}$

28. $\dfrac{10}{40}$

29. $\dfrac{42}{49}$

30. $\dfrac{20}{50}$

31. $\dfrac{12}{30}$

32. $\dfrac{32}{40}$

33. $\dfrac{15}{25}$

34. $\dfrac{16}{24}$

35. $\dfrac{4}{32}$

36. $\dfrac{6}{30}$

37. $\dfrac{15}{45}$

38. $\dfrac{6}{18}$

39. $\dfrac{8}{16}$

40. $\dfrac{18}{42}$

41. $\dfrac{10}{90}$

42. $\dfrac{25}{75}$

43. $\dfrac{22}{88}$

44. $\dfrac{27}{54}$

45. $\dfrac{3}{27}$

46. $\dfrac{4}{100}$

47. $\dfrac{18}{56}$

48. $\dfrac{14}{49}$

Write each fraction in simplest form.

49. Two cities on a map are $\dfrac{10}{16}$ of an inch apart.

50. A piece of lumber measures $7\dfrac{6}{8}$ inches.

51. Lisa spent $12\dfrac{10}{60}$ hours on her science project.

52. Darren filled $6\dfrac{14}{20}$ bins with hay.

CRITICAL THINKING

53. Explain how multiplying the numerator and the denominator of a fraction by the same number uses the identity element of multiplication.

54. Is it possible to find equivalent fractions by adding the same number to the numerator and the denominator? Explain, using examples.

2-3 Factors, Prime and Composite Numbers

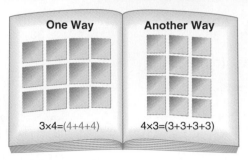

One Way

$3 \times 4 = (4+4+4)$

Another Way

$4 \times 3 = (3+3+3+3)$

The Yearbook Committee had to decide how to arrange the photos of its 12 members in a rectangle for a 1-page spread.

The **factors** of 12 are: 1, 2, 3, 4, 6, and 12.

Factors of a product: the whole numbers that are multiplied to find that product.

Now study these different ways that 12 items can be arranged to form a rectangle. ⟶

1 × 12	or	12 × 1
2 × 6	or	6 × 2
3 × 4	or	4 × 3

The **factors** of 7 are: 1 and 7.

So, 7 items can be arranged in two ways to form a rectangle. ⟶

| 1 × 7 | or | 7 × 1 |

Prime number: a whole number greater than one that has exactly two factors, itself and 1.

Composite number: a whole number, other than 0, that has *more than* two factors.

7 is a prime number. (Factors: 1 and 7)
12 is a composite number. (Factors: 1, 2, 3, 4, 6, 12)
0 and 1 are neither prime nor composite numbers.

List all the factors of each product.*

1. 36
2. 40
3. 100
4. 66
5. 80
6. 57
7. 72
8. 41
9. 24
10. 125

True or false? Explain.

11. 1 is a factor of every whole number.
12. The number 25 has exactly 3 factors.
13. 2 is a prime number.
14. The number 4 has exactly 2 factors.
15. The number 6 has exactly 3 factors.
16. 3 is a composite number.

Tell whether each number is prime or composite.*

17. 56
18. 21
19. 31
20. 19
21. 13
22. 217
23. 150
24. 101
25. 400
26. 141

CRITICAL THINKING   Find the prime numbers that complete these statements.

27. $6 = \underline{?} + \underline{?}$
28. $10 = \underline{?} + \underline{?}$
29. $24 = \underline{?} + \underline{?}$
30. $18 = \underline{?} + \underline{?}$
31. $30 = \underline{?} + \underline{?}$
32. $36 = \underline{?} + \underline{?}$

2-4 Prime Factorization

Every composite number (4, 6, 8, 9, . . .) can be written
as a product of two or more prime numbers.

Prime factorization of a number is a way of showing a number
as the product of prime numbers.

To find the prime factors of a number, use *one* of these methods.

Way One

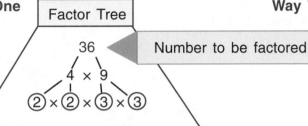

Factor Tree

36

4 × 9

②×②×③×③

Remember to continue factoring
until only primes remain.

Way Two

Number to be factored

Division by Primes		
		Think:
36 ÷	2	= 18
18 ÷	2	= 9
9 ÷	3	= 3
3 ÷	3	= 1
Remember to continue dividing until the quotient is 1.		

The prime factorization of 36 is: 2 × 2 × 3 × 3.

In exponential form: $36 = 2^2 \times 3^2$

Use either method to find the prime factorization of each number.

1. 90
2. 30
3. 63
4. 70
5. 56
6. 45
7. 72
8. 40
9. 84
10. 18
11. 12
12. 360
13. 27
14. 50
15. 160

Write the prime factorization of each number, using exponents.*

16. 40
17. 9
18. 75
19. 15
20. 52
21. 64
22. 80
23. 32
24. 24
25. 96
26. 66
27. 12
28. 48
29. 125
30. 280

Choose the correct composite number.

31. $2^3 \times 3^2$ a. 72   b. 70   c. 45   d. 75
32. $7^3 \times 5$ a. 343   b. 1715   c. 1517   d. 435
33. $2^5 \times 7$ a. 234   b. 244   c. 224   d. 254
34. $5^3 \times 11$ a. 2315   b. 1375   c. 2015   d. 1275

CALCULATOR ACTIVITY

35. Use a calculator to find the prime factorization of:
   a. 32,840   b. 96,425

*See page 498 for more practice.   37

2-5 Greatest Common Factor

Prime factorization can be used to find the **greatest common factor (GCF)** of two or more numbers. The GCF is useful in expressing fractions in simplest form.

▶ **Find the GCF of 18 and 24.**

The prime factorization of 18 is: 2 × 3 × 3.

The prime factorization of 24 is: 2 × 2 × 2 × 3.

The common factors of 18 and 24 are: 2 and 3.

The GCF of 18 and 24 is: 2 × 3 or 6.

> Sometimes the only GCF of two or three numbers is 1.

▶ **Find the GCF of 16, 28, and 60.**

The prime factorization of 16 is: 2 × 2 × 2 × 2.

The prime factorization of 28 is: 2 × 2 × 7.

The prime factorization of 60 is: 2 × 2 × 3 × 5.

The common factors of 16, 28, and 60 are: 2 and 2.

The GCF of 16, 28, and 60 is: 2 × 2 or 4.

Write the GCF of the numbers.

1. 10 = 2 × 5
    18 = 2 × 3 × 3

2. 15 = 3 × 5
    20 = 2 × 2 × 5

3. 63 = 3 × 3 × 7
    27 = 3 × 3 × 3

4. 14 = 2 × 7
    42 = 2 × 3 × 7

5. 21 = 3 × 7
    25 = 5 × 5
    39 = 3 × 13

6. 42 = 2 × 3 × 7
    60 = 2 × 2 × 3 × 5
    75 = 3 × 5 × 5

Use prime factorization to find the GCF of the numbers.*

7. 30 and 45
8. 36 and 54
9. 20 and 35
10. 32 and 48
11. 69 and 72
12. 36 and 56
13. 72 and 90
14. 42 and 60
15. 27 and 36
16. 12, 18, and 30
17. 9, 15, and 24
18. 36, 48, and 54

CHALLENGE

Look at the fractions on this number line.

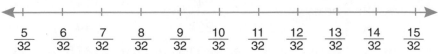

$$\frac{5}{32} \quad \frac{6}{32} \quad \frac{7}{32} \quad \frac{8}{32} \quad \frac{9}{32} \quad \frac{10}{32} \quad \frac{11}{32} \quad \frac{12}{32} \quad \frac{13}{32} \quad \frac{14}{32} \quad \frac{15}{32}$$

19. Name a fraction between any two fractions.

20. Can you name more than one fraction between any two fractions? How many are there? Explain.

2-6 Least Common Multiple

Least common multiple (LCM): the smallest number that is a common multiple (product) of two or more numbers.

The least common multiple is the **least common denominator (LCD)**.

Here are two ways to find the LCM or LCD.

To find the LCM or LCD of two numbers, you can list the nonzero multiples of each number.

Find the LCM or LCD of 9 and 12.

Multiples of 9:   9, 18, 27, 36, 45

Multiples of 12:   12, 24, 36, 48, 60

The smallest multiple common to both numbers is 36.

36 is the LCM and the LCD of 9 and 12.

Another way to find the LCM or LCD of two or more numbers is to use prime factorization.

Find the LCM of 4, 6, and 8.

The prime factorization of 4 is: 2×2

The prime factorization of 6 is: 2×3

The prime factorization of 8 is: $2 \times 2 \times 2$

The LCM of 4, 6, and 8 is: $24 = 2 \times 2 \times 2 \times 3$

> Notice that the LCM has no extra factors.

Use either method to find the LCM of these numbers.*

1. 40 and 65

2. 15 and 6

3. 8 and 12

4. 9 and 26

5. 6 and 10

6. 60 and 12

7. 60, 30, and 18

8. 12, 16, and 18

9. 4, 9, and 10

10. 21, 25, and 35

11. 150, 45, and 30

12. 60, 35, and 70

CHALLENGE

Twin primes are pairs of prime numbers that *differ by two*. For example, 3 and 5 are twin primes. So are 5 and 7.

13. List the other pairs of twin primes between 1 and 100.

*See page 498 for more practice.

2-7 Renaming Fractions as Decimals

Every fraction or mixed number is **equivalent to** or can be renamed as a decimal.

▶ **To rename a fraction as an equivalent decimal:**

■ If the denominator of the fraction can be renamed easily as a power of ten:

- Change the denominator to a power of ten.

$$\frac{3}{4} = \frac{?}{10^n}$$ 10, 100, 1000, . . . are powers of ten.

$$\frac{3}{4} = \frac{?}{100}$$

- Change the equivalent fraction to a decimal.

$$\frac{3}{4} = \frac{?}{100} \longrightarrow \frac{3 \times 25}{4 \times 25} = \frac{75}{100}$$

$$\frac{3}{4} = \frac{75}{100} = 0.75$$

■ If the denominator of the fraction cannot be renamed easily as a power of ten:

- Divide the numerator by the denominator.
- Express the quotient as a terminating or as a repeating decimal.

$$\frac{5}{8} = \underline{?} \rightarrow 8\overline{)5.0\ 0\ 0}^{\ 0.6\ 2\ 5}$$

A terminating decimal has a remainder of zero.

$$\frac{3}{16} = \underline{?} \rightarrow 16\overline{)3.0^{14}0^{12}0^{8}0}^{\ 0.1\ 8\ 7\ 5}$$

$$\frac{1}{3} = \underline{?} \rightarrow 3\overline{)1.0\ 0\ 0}^{\ 0.3\ 3\ 3}$$

In a repeating decimal the same digit or series of digits repeats.

$$\frac{1}{7} = \underline{?} \rightarrow 7\overline{)1.0^{3}0^{2}0^{6}0^{4}0^{5}0^{1}0^{3}0}^{\ 0.1\ 4\ 2\ 8\ 5\ 7\ 1\ 4 \ldots}$$

$$\frac{1}{3} = 0.\overline{3}$$

Write a bar over the digit or series of digits that repeats.

$$\frac{1}{7} = 0.\overline{142857}$$

▶ **To rename a mixed number as a decimal:** $2\frac{1}{15} = \underline{?}$

■ Change the mixed number to a fraction. $\longrightarrow 2\frac{1}{15} = \frac{31}{15}$

■ Then divide. $\longrightarrow \frac{31}{15} \longrightarrow 15\overline{)3\ 1.^{1}0^{10}0^{10}0}^{\ 2.0\ 6\ 6} = 2.0\overline{6} \longrightarrow 2\frac{1}{15} = 2.0\overline{6}$

Use a power of ten to change each to a decimal.

1. $\frac{4}{5}$ 2. $\frac{1}{4}$ 3. $\frac{1}{8}$ 4. $\frac{9}{20}$ 5. $\frac{7}{8}$ 6. $\frac{11}{25}$

7. $\frac{13}{20}$ 8. $\frac{16}{25}$ 9. $\frac{11}{50}$ 10. $\frac{49}{50}$ 11. $\frac{6}{25}$ 12. $\frac{13}{25}$

13. $2\frac{1}{4}$ 14. $3\frac{7}{10}$ 15. $11\frac{1}{100}$ 16. $4\frac{11}{20}$ 17. $5\frac{1}{2}$ 18. $6\frac{2}{5}$

Rewrite each repeating decimal, using the bar.

19. 0.212121... **20.** 0.305305305... **21.** 0.18888...

22. 2.3575757... **23.** 1.01010101... **24.** 8.4565656...

Change each to a terminating or a repeating decimal. (Hint: Look for shortcuts.)

25. $\frac{3}{8}$ **26.** $\frac{3}{5}$ **27.** $\frac{7}{10}$ **28.** $\frac{1}{40}$ **29.** $\frac{2}{3}$ **30.** $\frac{5}{8}$

31. $\frac{2}{5}$ **32.** $\frac{7}{8}$ **33.** $\frac{2}{9}$ **34.** $\frac{5}{24}$ **35.** $\frac{3}{20}$ **36.** $\frac{1}{16}$

37. $\frac{4}{21}$ **38.** $\frac{5}{9}$ **39.** $\frac{3}{10}$ **40.** $\frac{2}{11}$ **41.** $\frac{9}{40}$ **42.** $\frac{6}{24}$

43. $4\frac{2}{5}$ **44.** $3\frac{1}{8}$ **45.** $5\frac{1}{7}$ **46.** $6\frac{1}{3}$ **47.** $1\frac{1}{5}$ **48.** $2\frac{3}{11}$

49. $8\frac{1}{6}$ **50.** $1\frac{7}{8}$ **51.** $4\frac{4}{13}$ **52.** $7\frac{1}{12}$ **53.** $3\frac{4}{7}$ **54.** $9\frac{1}{2}$

55. $6\frac{1}{9}$ **56.** $3\frac{3}{7}$ **57.** $1\frac{4}{11}$ **58.** $3\frac{4}{9}$ **59.** $6\frac{1}{5}$ **60.** $4\frac{1}{8}$

Change the fraction to a decimal.

61. $\frac{3}{4}$ of Earth's surface is covered by water.

62. Acid rain destroyed $\frac{27}{50}$ of the forest.

63. $\frac{17}{20}$ of the students visited the aquarium.

64. The ice froze to a thickness of $1\frac{2}{3}$ ft.

65. Five eighths of the oil spill was removed.

SUPPOSE **THAT...**

66. $\frac{1}{4} = 0.25$, $\frac{2}{4} = 0.50$, so $\frac{3}{4} = $ ___?___

67. $\frac{1}{5} = 0.2$, $\frac{2}{5} = 0.4$, $\frac{3}{5} = 0.6$, so $\frac{4}{5} = $ ___?___

68. $\frac{1}{20} = 0.05$, $\frac{2}{20} = 0.10$, so $\frac{3}{20} = $ ___?___, $\frac{4}{20} = $ ___?___, and $\frac{5}{20} = $ ___?___

69. $\frac{1}{50} = 0.02$, $\frac{2}{50} = 0.04$, so $\frac{3}{50} = $ ___?___, $\frac{4}{50} = $ ___?___, and $\frac{5}{50} = $ ___?___

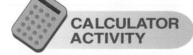 **CALCULATOR ACTIVITY** **Rename each fraction as a decimal. Decide when to use a calculator and when to rename the fraction mentally.**

70. $\frac{3}{20}$ **71.** $\frac{7}{72}$ **72.** $\frac{12}{15}$ **73.** $\frac{4}{27}$ **74.** $\frac{81}{900}$ **75.** $\frac{7}{25}$

76. $\frac{7}{13}$ **77.** $\frac{150}{200}$ **78.** $\frac{7}{66}$ **79.** $\frac{13}{90}$ **80.** $\frac{5}{40}$ **81.** $\frac{11}{60}$

Find the decimal equivalents; then order from least to greatest.

82. $\frac{5}{9}$, $\frac{17}{30}$, $\frac{11}{18}$ **83.** $\frac{3}{11}$, $\frac{2}{9}$, $\frac{8}{33}$ **84.** $\frac{7}{9}$, $\frac{5}{7}$, $\frac{11}{15}$

Comparing and Ordering Fractions

To compare fractions with *like denominators,* compare their numerators.

$$\frac{7}{12} > \frac{5}{12} \quad \text{because } 7 > 5 \qquad\qquad \frac{2}{9} < \frac{4}{9} \quad \text{because } 2 < 4$$

To compare fractions with *unlike denominators,* change them into equivalent fractions with a common denominator. Then compare their numerators.

Compare: $\frac{4}{5}$ __?__ $\frac{3}{7}$

- Find the LCD. (See page 39.)

  LCD of 5 and 7 is 35. 5: 5, 10, 15, 20, 25, 30, 35, . . .

  7: 7, 14, 21, 28, 35, . . .

- Change to equivalent fractions.

  $$\frac{4}{5} = \frac{?}{35} \longrightarrow \frac{4}{5} \times \frac{7}{7} = \frac{28}{35}$$

  $$\frac{3}{7} = \frac{?}{35} \longrightarrow \frac{3}{7} \times \frac{5}{5} = \frac{15}{35}$$

- Compare the numerators.

  $$28 > 15 \longrightarrow \frac{28}{35} > \frac{15}{35} \text{ OR } \frac{4}{5} > \frac{3}{7}$$

Another way to compare:
Change each fraction
to a decimal and compare.

$$\frac{3}{5} \text{ __?__ } \frac{7}{9} \longrightarrow 0.6 \text{ __?__ } 0.\overline{7}$$

$$0.6 < 0.\overline{7} \longrightarrow \frac{3}{5} < \frac{7}{9}$$

To order fractions from least to greatest or greatest to least, find their common denominators and compare numerators.

Order from greatest to least: $\frac{7}{9}, \frac{2}{3}, \frac{5}{6}$

$$\frac{7}{9} = \frac{14}{18}, \quad \frac{2}{3} = \frac{12}{18}, \quad \frac{5}{6} = \frac{15}{18}, \quad \text{so } \frac{5}{6} > \frac{7}{9} > \frac{2}{3}$$

Find the LCD for each pair of fractions. Then compare them.

1. $\frac{1}{7}$ __?__ $\frac{1}{6}$

2. $\frac{1}{5}$ __?__ $\frac{1}{2}$

3. $\frac{1}{8}$ __?__ $\frac{1}{4}$

4. $\frac{1}{4}$ __?__ $\frac{1}{6}$

5. $\frac{1}{12}$ __?__ $\frac{1}{30}$

6. $\frac{1}{9}$ __?__ $\frac{1}{6}$

7. $\frac{1}{14}$ __?__ $\frac{1}{28}$

8. $\frac{1}{10}$ __?__ $\frac{1}{8}$

9. $\frac{1}{25}$ __?__ $\frac{1}{30}$

10. $\frac{1}{25}$ __?__ $\frac{1}{10}$

11. $\frac{1}{16}$ __?__ $\frac{1}{18}$

12. $\frac{1}{7}$ __?__ $\frac{1}{21}$

Compare. Use <, =, or >.

13. $\frac{2}{5}$? $\frac{1}{5}$ 14. $\frac{3}{7}$? $\frac{5}{7}$ 15. $\frac{4}{5}$? $\frac{4}{7}$ 16. $\frac{2}{9}$? $\frac{3}{7}$

17. $1\frac{4}{7}$? $\frac{8}{14}$ 18. $1\frac{1}{5}$? $\frac{9}{10}$ 19. $\frac{1}{3}$? $\frac{2}{7}$ 20. $\frac{4}{5}$? $\frac{7}{8}$

21. $3\frac{3}{6}$? $3\frac{12}{24}$ 22. $\frac{4}{7}$? $\frac{3}{5}$ 23. $2\frac{8}{9}$? $2\frac{9}{10}$ 24. $\frac{4}{11}$? $\frac{5}{9}$

25. $\frac{5}{8}$? $\frac{3}{4}$ 26. $\frac{9}{32}$? $\frac{11}{16}$ 27. $\frac{3}{5}$? $\frac{7}{20}$ 28. $\frac{2}{3}$? $\frac{8}{9}$

29. $\frac{7}{10}$? $\frac{4}{5}$ 30. $\frac{1}{4}$? $\frac{2}{5}$ 31. $\frac{2}{3}$? $\frac{1}{2}$ 32. $\frac{3}{9}$? $\frac{1}{3}$

33. $\frac{6}{12}$? $0.58\overline{3}$ 34. $\frac{10}{11}$? $0.\overline{54}$ 35. $\frac{4}{9}$? $0.\overline{5}$ 36. $\frac{1}{6}$? $0.1\overline{6}$

Order from greatest to least.

37. $\frac{2}{3}, \frac{1}{5}, \frac{3}{4}$ 38. $\frac{1}{7}, \frac{2}{3}, \frac{1}{6}$ 39. $\frac{2}{7}, \frac{4}{5}, \frac{5}{6}, \frac{1}{3}$

40. $\frac{3}{5}, \frac{5}{6}, \frac{2}{3}, \frac{9}{10}$ 41. $2\frac{3}{7}, 1\frac{5}{8}, 1\frac{4}{9}, \frac{8}{9}$ 42. $4\frac{2}{5}, \frac{1}{3}, 2\frac{4}{7}, \frac{5}{6}$

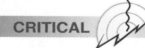

CRITICAL   THINKING

Predict which fraction in each pair is closer to $\frac{1}{2}$. Check your predictions with a calculator.

43. $\frac{5}{9}$ or $\frac{4}{7}$ 44. $\frac{5}{8}$ or $\frac{9}{14}$ 45. $\frac{4}{9}$ or $\frac{7}{15}$

46. $\frac{21}{40}$ or $\frac{16}{30}$ 47. $\frac{14}{25}$ or $\frac{15}{29}$ 48. $\frac{24}{49}$ or $\frac{25}{48}$

Solve.

49. $\frac{3}{8}$ of Jenny's music collection consists of tapes and $\frac{4}{9}$ of the collection are CD's. Does she have more tapes or more CD's?

50. Mario spent $\frac{3}{7}$ of July's allowance and $\frac{2}{5}$ of August's allowance on CD's. During which month did he spend more?

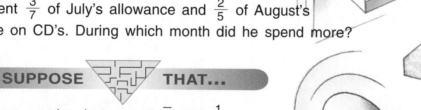

SUPPOSE   THAT...

51. 0.52 is one number between $0.\overline{5}$ and $\frac{1}{2}$. Name another number between $0.\overline{5}$ and $\frac{1}{2}$.

52. $\frac{19}{60}$ is one number between $0.\overline{3}$ and $\frac{3}{10}$. Name another number between $0.\overline{3}$ and $\frac{3}{10}$.

53. Explain why you can find more than one number between these numbers.

2-9 Adding Fractions and Mixed Numbers

Of Eric's stamps, $\frac{3}{10}$ are from North America, $\frac{1}{10}$ are from South America, and $\frac{1}{5}$ are from Europe. What fractional part of his collection consists of stamps from North or South America?

> **To add fractions with *like denominators*:**

- Add the numerators.
- Write the sum over the common denominator.
- Express the sum in simplest form.

$$\frac{3}{10} + \frac{1}{10} = \frac{4}{10} = \frac{2}{5}$$ 　Simplify.

$\frac{2}{5}$ of Eric's stamps are from North or South America.

What fractional part of his collection consists of stamps from North America or Europe? ⟶ $\frac{3}{10} + \frac{1}{5} = \underline{\;?\;}$

> **To add fractions with *unlike denominators*:**

- Change the fractions to equivalent fractions that have a common denominator.
- Add. Then express the sum in simplest form.

$\frac{1}{2}$ of Eric's stamps are from North America or Europe.

$$\frac{3}{10} = \frac{3}{10}$$
$$+\frac{1}{5} = +\frac{2}{10}$$
$$\overline{}\; \frac{5}{10} = \frac{1}{2}$$

Simplify.

> **To add mixed numbers:**

- Add the fractional parts as above.
- Add the whole-number parts. Express the sum in simplest form.

$4\frac{3}{8} + 12\frac{7}{8} = \underline{\;?\;}$

Estimate: $4 + 12 = 16$

$$\begin{array}{r} 4\frac{3}{8} \\ +12\frac{7}{8} \\ \hline 16\frac{10}{8} \end{array}$$ ⟶ $\frac{10}{8} = 1\frac{2}{8} = 1\frac{1}{4}$

Regroup and simplify.

$16 + 1\frac{1}{4} = 17\frac{1}{4}$

$10\frac{1}{4} + 17\frac{3}{5} = \underline{\;?\;}$

Estimate: $10 + 17 = 27$

$$\begin{array}{r} 10\frac{1}{4} = 10\frac{5}{20} \\ +17\frac{3}{5} = +17\frac{12}{20} \\ \hline 27\frac{17}{20} \end{array}$$

No regrouping needed.
Fraction is in simplest form.

Write the sum in simplest form.

1. $\dfrac{3}{16} + \dfrac{5}{16}$ 2. $\dfrac{2}{9} + \dfrac{4}{9}$ 3. $\dfrac{3}{10} + \dfrac{2}{10}$ 4. $\dfrac{3}{5} + \dfrac{1}{5}$

5. $\dfrac{1}{9} + \dfrac{2}{9}$ 6. $\dfrac{7}{12} + \dfrac{3}{12}$ 7. $\dfrac{6}{21} + \dfrac{8}{21}$ 8. $\dfrac{1}{8} + \dfrac{5}{8}$

9. $\dfrac{1}{6} + \dfrac{3}{4}$ 10. $\dfrac{1}{3} + \dfrac{2}{9}$ 11. $\dfrac{1}{4} + \dfrac{3}{8}$ 12. $\dfrac{2}{5} + \dfrac{1}{2}$

13. $\begin{array}{r} 10\frac{1}{4} \\ + \ 7\frac{3}{4} \\ \hline \end{array}$ 14. $\begin{array}{r} 19\frac{2}{5} \\ + \ 7\frac{3}{5} \\ \hline \end{array}$ 15. $\begin{array}{r} 6\frac{4}{7} \\ +2\frac{5}{7} \\ \hline \end{array}$ 16. $\begin{array}{r} 1\frac{5}{8} \\ +3\frac{7}{8} \\ \hline \end{array}$ 17. $\begin{array}{r} 2\frac{1}{12} \\ +2\frac{3}{4} \\ \hline \end{array}$

18. $\begin{array}{r} 9\frac{3}{4} \\ +7\frac{3}{8} \\ \hline \end{array}$ 19. $\begin{array}{r} 2\frac{2}{3} \\ +4\frac{5}{9} \\ \hline \end{array}$ 20. $\begin{array}{r} 7\frac{5}{6} \\ +4\frac{1}{3} \\ \hline \end{array}$ 21. $\begin{array}{r} 11\frac{1}{2} \\ + \ 6\frac{1}{3} \\ \hline \end{array}$ 22. $\begin{array}{r} 15\frac{1}{5} \\ + \ 9\frac{3}{4} \\ \hline \end{array}$

23. $\begin{array}{r} 5\frac{1}{2} \\ +5\frac{4}{5} \\ \hline \end{array}$ 24. $\begin{array}{r} 6\frac{4}{9} \\ +7\frac{5}{6} \\ \hline \end{array}$ 25. $\begin{array}{r} 3\frac{1}{4} \\ +7\frac{2}{3} \\ \hline \end{array}$ 26. $\begin{array}{r} 17\frac{2}{5} \\ + \ 8\frac{2}{3} \\ \hline \end{array}$ 27. $\begin{array}{r} 1\frac{5}{7} \\ +4\frac{2}{3} \\ \hline \end{array}$

Solve.

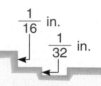

$\dfrac{1}{16}$ in. $\dfrac{1}{32}$ in.

Exercise 28

28. A wood carver is carving a pattern for a special stamp issue. He begins by cutting into the wood $\frac{1}{16}$ of an inch. In the deepest section of the pattern, he cuts down an additional $\frac{1}{32}$ of an inch. At its deepest, how far down is the wood cut?

29. A wood carver whittles musical instruments from pieces of wood. He uses $2\frac{3}{8}$ inches of wood to make a whistle and $3\frac{5}{8}$ inches to make a harmonica. How much wood does he use to make both instruments?

MAKE UP YOUR OWN...

30. Write a word problem in which the two addends are fractions and the sum is a whole number.

31. Write a word problem in which the two addends are mixed numbers and the sum is a whole number.

MENTAL 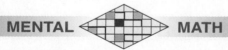 MATH

Compute each. Use what you have learned about the commutative and associative properties.

32. $\dfrac{1}{4} + \dfrac{3}{8} + \dfrac{3}{4}$ 33. $\dfrac{2}{5} + \dfrac{1}{10} + \dfrac{1}{5}$ 34. $\dfrac{2}{7} + \dfrac{1}{21} + \dfrac{1}{3}$

35. $\dfrac{1}{6} + \dfrac{1}{2} + \dfrac{1}{3}$ 36. $\dfrac{1}{2} + \dfrac{3}{10} + \dfrac{1}{5}$ 37. $\dfrac{1}{3} + \dfrac{1}{8} + \dfrac{1}{6}$

2-10 Subtracting Fractions and Mixed Numbers

Tanya's three plants were grown in soils using different fertilizers. In one month plant A grew $\frac{15}{16}$ of an inch, plant B grew $\frac{11}{16}$ of an inch, and plant C grew $\frac{5}{8}$ of an inch. What was the difference between the growth of plants A and B?

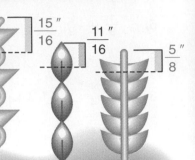

A   B   C

▶ **To subtract fractions with *like denominators*:**

- Subtract the numerators.
- Write the difference over the common denominator.
- Express the difference in simplest form.

$$\frac{15}{16} - \frac{11}{16} = \frac{4}{16} = \frac{1}{4}$$

Simplify.

The difference between the growth of plants A and B was $\frac{1}{4}$ of an inch.

What was the difference between the growth of plants A and C? ⟶ $\frac{15}{16} - \frac{5}{8} = \underline{\ ?\ }$

▶ **To subtract fractions with *unlike denominators*:**

- Change the fractions to equivalent fractions with a common denominator.
- Subtract.
- Express the difference in simplest form.

$$\begin{array}{rcl} \frac{15}{16} &=& \frac{15}{16} \\ -\frac{5}{8} &=& -\frac{10}{16} \\ \hline && \frac{5}{16} \end{array}$$

The difference between the growth of plants A and C was $\frac{5}{16}$ of an inch.

▶ **To subtract mixed numbers:**

- Subtract the fractional parts as above.
- Subtract the whole-number parts.
- Express the sum in simplest form.

$$\begin{array}{rcl} 9\frac{2}{7} &=& 8\frac{9}{7} \\ -5\frac{4}{7} &=& -5\frac{4}{7} \\ \hline && 3\frac{5}{7} \end{array}$$

Cannot subtract $\frac{4}{7}$ from $\frac{2}{7}$. Regroup.

$$14\frac{3}{9} - 3\frac{1}{6} = \underline{\ ?\ }$$

Estimate: $14 - 3 = 11$

$$\begin{array}{rcl} 14\frac{3}{9} &=& 14\frac{6}{18} \\ -3\frac{1}{6} &=& -3\frac{3}{18} \\ \hline 11\frac{3}{18} &=& 11\frac{1}{6} \end{array}$$

Write the difference in simplest form.

1. $\frac{3}{17} - \frac{2}{17}$

2. $\frac{6}{15} - \frac{2}{15}$

3. $\frac{2}{21} - \frac{1}{21}$

4. $\frac{9}{11} - \frac{3}{11}$

5. $\frac{5}{6} - \frac{3}{6}$

6. $\frac{5}{12} - \frac{1}{12}$

7. $\frac{7}{10} - \frac{2}{5}$

8. $\frac{5}{6} - \frac{1}{3}$

9. $\frac{12}{21} - \frac{1}{7}$

10. $\frac{15}{21} - \frac{5}{7}$

11. $\frac{8}{10} - \frac{2}{5}$

12. $\frac{4}{5} - \frac{1}{7}$

Copy and complete the regrouping.

13. $2\frac{1}{8} = 1\frac{?}{8}$ **14.** $7\frac{1}{3} = 6\frac{?}{3}$ **15.** $4\frac{2}{3} = 3\frac{?}{3}$ **16.** $6\frac{2}{5} = 5\frac{?}{5}$

Write the difference in simplest form.

17. $\begin{array}{r} 5\frac{7}{8} \\ -2\frac{3}{8} \\ \hline \end{array}$ **18.** $\begin{array}{r} 3\frac{5}{7} \\ -1\frac{2}{7} \\ \hline \end{array}$ **19.** $\begin{array}{r} 4\frac{3}{4} \\ -2\frac{1}{2} \\ \hline \end{array}$ **20.** $\begin{array}{r} 16\frac{7}{9} \\ -8\frac{2}{3} \\ \hline \end{array}$ **21.** $\begin{array}{r} 13\frac{4}{5} \\ -9\frac{3}{10} \\ \hline \end{array}$

22. $\begin{array}{r} 2\frac{2}{7} \\ -1\frac{5}{14} \\ \hline \end{array}$ **23.** $\begin{array}{r} 8\frac{1}{9} \\ -2\frac{1}{6} \\ \hline \end{array}$ **24.** $\begin{array}{r} 10\frac{1}{12} \\ -6\frac{3}{8} \\ \hline \end{array}$ **25.** $\begin{array}{r} 12\frac{1}{3} \\ -7\frac{4}{9} \\ \hline \end{array}$ **26.** $\begin{array}{r} 13\frac{1}{10} \\ -3\frac{4}{15} \\ \hline \end{array}$

Rounding Fractions and Mixed Numbers

- *Round down* fractions less than $\frac{1}{2}$.

  $\frac{2}{9}$ rounds to 0. $2\frac{5}{12}$ rounds to 2.

  > Less than $\frac{1}{2}$: $\frac{4}{9}, \frac{5}{12}, \frac{7}{15}$
  > The numerator is less than the denominator divided by 2.

- *Round up* fractions equal to $\frac{1}{2}$ or greater than $\frac{1}{2}$.

  $\frac{7}{12}$ rounds up to 1. $3\frac{9}{17}$ rounds to 4.

  > Greater than $\frac{1}{2}$: $\frac{6}{11}, \frac{9}{14}, \frac{11}{20}$
  > The numerator is more than the denominator divided by 2.

When you know how to round fractions and mixed numbers, you can estimate before you compute.

$9\frac{1}{15} + 4\frac{17}{18} \approx$ **?** $\begin{array}{r} 9\frac{1}{15} \approx 9 \\ +4\frac{17}{18} \approx +5 \\ \hline 14 \end{array}$ $6\frac{7}{9} - \frac{2}{5} \approx$ **?** $\begin{array}{r} 6\frac{7}{9} \approx 7 \\ -\frac{2}{5} \approx -0 \\ \hline 7 \end{array}$

Estimate by rounding to the nearest whole number.

27. $\frac{1}{9} + \frac{16}{17}$ **28.** $1\frac{3}{7} + 3\frac{11}{20}$ **29.** $\frac{8}{9} - \frac{1}{15}$ **30.** $5\frac{8}{17} - 2\frac{2}{25}$

31. $7\frac{3}{49} + 4\frac{2}{19}$ **32.** $6\frac{13}{24} + 4\frac{5}{12}$ **33.** $10\frac{13}{21} - 3\frac{1}{14}$ **34.** $12\frac{3}{28} - 10\frac{9}{10}$

CHALLENGE

To add or subtract fractions having denominators that are relatively prime (GCF = 1) quickly, try using cross products.

Add: $\frac{1}{5} + \frac{1}{4} \longrightarrow \frac{1}{5} \overset{4+5}{\underset{\times}{\times}} \frac{1}{4} = \frac{9}{20}$ | Subtract: $\frac{2}{3} - \frac{1}{7} \longrightarrow \frac{2}{3} \overset{14-3}{\underset{\times}{\times}} \frac{1}{7} = \frac{11}{21}$

35. $\frac{1}{6} + \frac{1}{5}$ **36.** $\frac{2}{5} - \frac{1}{4}$ **37.** $\frac{3}{4} + \frac{2}{3}$ **38.** $\frac{6}{7} - \frac{1}{5}$ **39.** $\frac{2}{11} + \frac{1}{3}$

Multiplying Fractions and Mixed Numbers

One room in a school is set aside as a computer lab.

$\frac{3}{4}$ of the computer terminals are used for word processing.

Of these, $\frac{2}{5}$ have color screens.

What part of the computer terminals have color screens?

Find $\frac{2}{5}$ of $\frac{3}{4}$ or $\frac{2}{5} \times \frac{3}{4}$

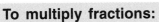

▶ To multiply fractions:

- Multiply the numerators.
- Multiply the denominators.
- Express in lowest terms.

$\frac{2}{5} \times \frac{3}{4} = \frac{6}{20} = \frac{3}{10}$ ⟶ $\frac{3}{10}$ of the computer terminals have color screens.

Of the 20 computer terminals in the picture, how many are used for word processing (WP)?

▶ To multiply whole numbers and mixed numbers:

- Change them to fractions.
- Then multiply the fractions.

$\frac{3}{4} \times 20 = \underline{\quad?\quad}$

$\frac{3}{4} \times \frac{20}{1} = \frac{60}{4} = 15$

Study this example.

$1\frac{1}{6} \times 2\frac{1}{2} = \underline{\quad?\quad}$

$\frac{7}{6} \times \frac{5}{2} = \frac{35}{12} = 2\frac{11}{12}$

15 of the terminals are used for word processing.

▶ Cancellation: a shortcut for multiplication

Divide the same number into one of the numerators and one of the denominators. Cancel as many times as you can.

$3\frac{1}{3} \times 2\frac{2}{5} = \underline{\quad?\quad}$

$3\frac{1}{3} \times 2\frac{2}{5} = \frac{10}{3} \times \frac{12}{5}$

First estimate.

$3 \times 2 = 6$

Divide by 5. ⟶ $= \frac{\overset{2}{\cancel{10}}}{3} \times \frac{12}{\underset{1}{\cancel{5}}}$

Then divide by 3. ⟶ $= \frac{\overset{2}{\cancel{10}}}{\underset{1}{\cancel{3}}} \times \frac{\overset{4}{\cancel{12}}}{\underset{1}{\cancel{5}}} = \frac{8}{1} = 8$

Multiply. Cancel where possible.

1. $\frac{3}{5} \times \frac{3}{8}$

2. $\frac{3}{7} \times \frac{4}{7}$

3. $\frac{2}{5} \times \frac{5}{9}$

4. $\frac{4}{10} \times \frac{5}{7}$

5. $\frac{2}{9} \times \frac{6}{14}$

6. $\frac{9}{20} \times \frac{4}{15}$

7. $\frac{2}{3} \times 9$

8. $16 \times \frac{1}{4}$

9. $8 \times \frac{1}{4}$

10. $12 \times \frac{2}{3}$

11. $\frac{1}{6} \times 10$

12. $\frac{2}{3} \times 24$

13. $30 \times \frac{2}{15}$

14. $\frac{6}{35} \times 7$

15. $\frac{3}{5} \times \frac{20}{21}$

16. $\frac{9}{14} \times \frac{7}{12}$

17. $1\frac{2}{3} \times 3\frac{1}{8}$

18. $4\frac{1}{3} \times 2\frac{1}{4}$

19. $7\frac{1}{4} \times 3\frac{1}{5}$

20. $2\frac{1}{7} \times 2\frac{2}{3}$

21. $5\frac{5}{8} \times 5\frac{1}{3}$

22. $2\frac{1}{2} \times 3\frac{1}{4}$

23. $6\frac{2}{5} \times 2\frac{3}{8}$

24. $\frac{1}{6} \times 8\frac{1}{5}$

25. $8\frac{3}{4} \times 1\frac{3}{7}$

26. $\frac{3}{4} \times 2\frac{3}{7}$

27. $7\frac{1}{4} \times 16$

28. $3\frac{5}{6} \times 12$

29. $2\frac{1}{12} \times \frac{3}{5}$

30. $6 \times 12\frac{2}{3}$

31. $2\frac{5}{7} \times 12\frac{3}{5}$

32. $8\frac{1}{4} \times 6$

Multiply. Cancel where possible.

33. $\frac{2}{5} \times \frac{5}{2} \times 3$

34. $\frac{2}{5} \times \frac{10}{12} \times \frac{1}{4}$

35. $\frac{9}{10} \times \frac{5}{6} \times \frac{2}{3}$

36. $\frac{7}{8} \times \frac{4}{7} \times \frac{2}{3}$

37. $8\frac{1}{4} \times 6\frac{1}{11} \times 4$

38. $2\frac{1}{4} \times 8\frac{3}{5} \times 1\frac{1}{9}$

Compute. (Remember the order of operations: multiply first; then add or subtract.)

39. $\frac{2}{3} \times \frac{6}{7} + 1\frac{1}{14}$

40. $\frac{4}{5} \times \frac{1}{6} + \frac{2}{5}$

41. $\frac{7}{8} + \frac{1}{4} \times \frac{1}{2}$

42. $\frac{5}{6} - \frac{1}{2} \times \frac{1}{4}$

43. $1\frac{1}{3} + 2\frac{1}{5} \times 1\frac{1}{9}$

44. $3\frac{1}{3} - 1\frac{1}{4} \times \frac{1}{12}$

Estimate. Round factors to whole numbers.

45. $2\frac{1}{2} \times 1\frac{7}{8}$

46. $1\frac{1}{3} \times 3\frac{4}{5}$

47. $3\frac{6}{7} \times 5\frac{1}{4}$

48. $2\frac{1}{9} \times 4\frac{2}{3}$

49. $11\frac{8}{9} \times 1\frac{5}{9}$

50. $6\frac{1}{10} \times 7\frac{3}{5}$

51. $8\frac{2}{3} \times 9\frac{1}{3}$

52. $7\frac{1}{9} \times 8\frac{2}{5}$

Solve.

53. Eighteen of the eighth graders are in the computer lab. One half of them are girls. How many are girls?

54. Sixteen computer terminals are in use. One eighth of them are being used to input data. How many terminals are being used to input data?

55. The student council sold cupcakes to raise funds for computer software. They sold $25\frac{1}{2}$ dozen at $3 a dozen. How much money did they raise?

56. In a class of 28 students $\frac{5}{7}$ have home computers. How many of the students do *not* have home computers?

CUPCAKE SALE

2-12 Dividing Fractions, Complex Fractions, and Mixed Numbers

Reciprocals are two numbers whose product is 1.

$$\frac{3}{4} \times \frac{4}{3} = 1 \longrightarrow \frac{3}{4} \text{ and } \frac{4}{3} \text{ are reciprocals.}$$

$$6 \times \frac{1}{6} = 1 \longrightarrow 6 \text{ and } \frac{1}{6} \text{ are reciprocals.}$$

$$1\frac{1}{2} \times \frac{2}{3} = 1 \longrightarrow 1\frac{1}{2} \text{ and } \frac{2}{3} \text{ are reciprocals.}$$

Zero does *not* have a reciprocal.

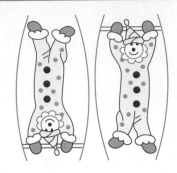

▶ **To divide fractions:**

- Compare the dividend and the divisor to decide if the quotient is greater than 1 or less than 1.

- Multiply by the reciprocal of the divisor.

$$\frac{3}{4} \div \frac{1}{8} = \; ? \qquad \frac{3}{4} > \frac{1}{8} \text{ quotient} > 1$$

$$\frac{3}{4} \div \frac{1}{8} = \frac{3}{4} \times \frac{8}{1} \quad \longleftarrow \text{Reciprocal of } \frac{1}{8}$$

$$\frac{3}{\overset{}{\underset{1}{4}}} \times \frac{\overset{2}{8}}{1} = \frac{3}{1} \times \frac{2}{1} = \frac{6}{1} = 6$$

▶ **To divide mixed numbers:**

- First change them to fractions.

- Then multiply by the reciprocal of the divisor.

$$1\frac{2}{5} \div 2\frac{1}{10} = \; ? \qquad 1\frac{2}{5} < 2\frac{1}{10} \text{ quotient} < 1$$

$$\frac{7}{5} \div \frac{21}{10} = \frac{7}{5} \times \frac{10}{21}$$

$$\underbrace{\qquad}_{\text{Reciprocals}}$$

$$= \frac{\overset{1}{7}}{\underset{1}{5}} \times \frac{\overset{2}{10}}{\underset{3}{21}} = \frac{2}{3} \quad \text{simplest form}$$

A **complex fraction** has a fraction in the numerator, the denominator, or both.
To simplify complex fractions, divide the numerator by the denominator.

$$\frac{\frac{3}{8}}{\frac{1}{5}} \longrightarrow \frac{3}{8} \div \frac{1}{5} = \frac{3}{8} \times \frac{5}{1} = \frac{15}{8} = 1\frac{7}{8}$$

$$\frac{8}{\frac{4}{5}} \longrightarrow \frac{8}{1} \div \frac{4}{5} = \frac{\overset{2}{8}}{1} \times \frac{5}{\underset{1}{4}} = 10 \qquad \frac{1\frac{2}{3}}{4\frac{1}{6}} \longrightarrow \frac{5}{3} \div \frac{25}{6} = \frac{\overset{1}{5}}{\underset{1}{3}} \times \frac{\overset{2}{6}}{\underset{5}{25}} = \frac{2}{5}$$

Write the reciprocal.

1. $\frac{7}{8}$ 2. $\frac{4}{5}$ 3. 7 4. 3 5. $\frac{1}{10}$ 6. $\frac{1}{4}$

7. $\frac{9}{7}$ 8. $\frac{4}{3}$ 9. $1\frac{2}{5}$ 10. $2\frac{2}{3}$ 11. $2\frac{4}{5}$ 12. $3\frac{2}{3}$

Write the quotient in simplest form.

13. $\frac{2}{3} \div \frac{3}{3}$ **14.** $\frac{4}{5} \div \frac{8}{8}$ **15.** $\frac{1}{5} \div \frac{2}{7}$ **16.** $\frac{2}{3} \div \frac{5}{7}$

17. $\frac{4}{11} \div \frac{8}{15}$ **18.** $\frac{8}{21} \div \frac{2}{5}$ **19.** $\frac{6}{14} \div \frac{2}{7}$ **20.** $\frac{3}{5} \div \frac{6}{10}$

21. $\frac{2}{7} \div \frac{5}{6}$ **22.** $\frac{2}{3} \div \frac{1}{8}$ **23.** $\frac{5}{6} \div \frac{2}{3}$ **24.** $\frac{1}{8} \div \frac{5}{16}$

25. $14 \div \frac{2}{3}$ (Hint: Rewrite 14 as $\frac{14}{1}$.)   **26.** $25 \div \frac{5}{6}$ **27.** $18 \div \frac{1}{4}$

28. $48 \div \frac{6}{7}$ **29.** $10 \div \frac{1}{2}$ **30.** $24 \div \frac{1}{6}$ **31.** $2\frac{5}{8} \div \frac{3}{16}$

32. $7\frac{1}{2} \div \frac{3}{10}$ **33.** $9\frac{1}{6} \div \frac{11}{12}$ **34.** $8\frac{3}{4} \div 2\frac{1}{2}$ **35.** $18 \div 2\frac{1}{4}$

36. $4\frac{1}{6} \div 6\frac{2}{3}$ **37.** $\frac{1}{8} \div 1\frac{5}{16}$ **38.** $3\frac{1}{5} \div 8$ **39.** $2\frac{2}{3} \div 16$

40. $3\frac{3}{5} \div 4\frac{2}{7}$ **41.** $12 \div 8\frac{1}{2}$ **42.** $9\frac{1}{6} \div 5$ **43.** $7\frac{1}{4} \div 2\frac{1}{8}$

Simplify. (Hint: Express whole numbers and mixed numbers as fractions.)

44. $\dfrac{\frac{4}{9}}{\frac{1}{3}}$ **45.** $\dfrac{\frac{3}{5}}{\frac{7}{10}}$ **46.** $\dfrac{\frac{2}{5}}{\frac{1}{4}}$ **47.** $\dfrac{\frac{6}{7}}{\frac{1}{2}}$ **48.** $\dfrac{\frac{2}{7}}{\frac{2}{7}}$

49. $\dfrac{6}{\frac{1}{2}}$ **50.** $\dfrac{2}{\frac{1}{3}}$ **51.** $\dfrac{\frac{1}{2}}{7}$ **52.** $\dfrac{1\frac{1}{5}}{3\frac{1}{10}}$ **53.** $\dfrac{2\frac{1}{3}}{1\frac{4}{5}}$

Solve.

54. Eva cuts lead strips to make stained-glass windows. She has a $3\frac{3}{4}$-foot strip of lead and cuts it into 5 equal pieces. How long is each piece of lead?

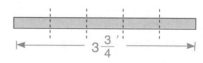

$3\frac{3}{4}$

Exercise 54

55. Mr. Thorn works $7\frac{1}{2}$ hours a day installing stained-glass windows. If each window takes $1\frac{1}{4}$ hours to install, how many can he install in 1 day?

56. An artist has 60 pieces of stained glass. He uses $\frac{3}{5}$ of them to make 2 matching windows. How many pieces of stained glass are in each window?

Compute. (Hint: Divide first; then add or subtract.)

57. $\frac{7}{8} \div \frac{1}{4} + 3$ **58.** $12\frac{1}{4} - \frac{6}{7} \div \frac{3}{14}$ **59.** $2\frac{1}{2} \div 5 + 1\frac{1}{4}$

60. $6\frac{2}{3} \div \frac{5}{6} - 1\frac{1}{5}$ **61.** $3 \div 10\frac{1}{2} + \frac{6}{7}$ **62.** $5 \div \frac{9}{10} - 3\frac{1}{8}$

63. $1\frac{1}{8} + 8\frac{3}{4} \div \frac{7}{9}$ **64.** $8\frac{7}{10} - 1\frac{4}{5} \div \frac{3}{11}$ **65.** $12 \div \frac{3}{15} - 9$

2-13 Estimating Fractions

Front-End Estimation: Compute the whole-number parts and then adjust using the fraction part.

Use this strategy when adding or subtracting mixed numbers.

Add: $6\dfrac{7}{9} + 3\dfrac{1}{17} \approx \underline{\ ?\ }$

$$\left.\begin{array}{r} 6\ \dfrac{7}{9} \\ +\ 3\ \dfrac{1}{17} \end{array}\right\} \text{about } 1$$

Estimate: $9 + 1 = 10$

Subtract: $7\dfrac{12}{13} - 4\dfrac{11}{12} \approx \underline{\ ?\ }$

$$\left.\begin{array}{r} 7\ \dfrac{12}{13} \\ -\ 4\ \dfrac{11}{12} \end{array}\right\} \text{about } 0$$

Estimate: $3 + 0 = 3$

Clustering: When several addends "cluster" about a certain value, multiply that value by the number of addends.

Use this strategy when adding fractions or mixed numbers.

Add: $\dfrac{4}{9} + \dfrac{10}{21} + \dfrac{6}{13} + \dfrac{6}{11} + \dfrac{7}{12} \approx \underline{\ ?\ }$

Estimate: $\dfrac{1}{2} + \dfrac{1}{2} + \dfrac{1}{2} + \dfrac{1}{2} + \dfrac{1}{2} = 5 \times \dfrac{1}{2} = \dfrac{5}{2} = 2\dfrac{1}{2}$

Add: $1\dfrac{8}{9} + 2\dfrac{1}{10} + 2\dfrac{1}{7} \approx \underline{\ ?\ }$

Estimate: $2 + 2 + 2 = 3 \times 2 = 6$

Compatible Numbers: Adjust the factors to numbers that are easily divisible by each other.

Use this strategy when multiplying fractions or mixed numbers.

Multiply: $\dfrac{1}{8} \times 25 \approx \underline{\ ?\ }$

Estimate: $\dfrac{1}{8} \times 24 = 3$

Multiply: $4\dfrac{1}{7} \times \dfrac{1}{15} \approx \underline{\ ?\ }$

Estimate: $4 \times \dfrac{1}{16} = \dfrac{1}{4}$

or

$5 \times \dfrac{1}{15} = \dfrac{1}{3}$

When dividing mixed numbers, sometimes it is useful to adjust the divisor and/or dividend to whole numbers that divide easily.

$$13\dfrac{1}{9} \div 7\dfrac{2}{3} \approx \underline{\ ?\ } \longrightarrow 14 \div 7 = 2$$

Estimate each sum and difference.

1. $8\frac{1}{16} + 3\frac{1}{20}$

2. $7\frac{4}{9} + 8\frac{9}{20}$

3. $10\frac{9}{10} + 5\frac{3}{47}$ 4. $12\frac{7}{8} + 9\frac{10}{11}$

5. $5\frac{20}{21} - 3\frac{7}{8}$

6. $9\frac{1}{7} - 3\frac{2}{17}$

7. $11\frac{5}{6} - 2\frac{3}{41}$ 8. $17\frac{22}{23} - 6\frac{3}{7}$

9. $\frac{9}{10} + 1\frac{1}{16} + \frac{7}{8} + \frac{14}{15} + 1\frac{2}{19} + 1\frac{1}{12}$ 10. $9\frac{3}{4} + 9\frac{9}{10} + 10\frac{1}{9} + 10\frac{2}{15}$

Estimate each product and quotient.

11. $\frac{1}{7} \times 15$

12. $\frac{1}{9} \times 28$

13. $\frac{1}{12} \times 35$

14. $\frac{1}{20} \times 39$

15. $\frac{2}{3} \times 17$

16. $\frac{3}{4} \times 21$

17. $\frac{5}{6} \times 35$

18. $\frac{7}{8} \times 63$

19. $\frac{1}{5} \times \frac{11}{3}$

20. $\frac{1}{7} \times \frac{15}{19}$

21. $\frac{1}{9} \times \frac{17}{25}$

22. $\frac{1}{10} \times \frac{21}{50}$

23. $24\frac{5}{11} \div 7\frac{1}{12}$

24. $11\frac{1}{3} \div 1\frac{6}{7}$

25. $38\frac{1}{5} \div 5\frac{3}{7}$

26. $41\frac{1}{7} \div 3\frac{11}{13}$

Mental Computation

Sometimes the distributive property can be used to multiply mentally a mixed number by a fraction.

$$\frac{1}{5} \times 10\frac{1}{2} \longrightarrow \frac{1}{5} \times \left(10 + \frac{1}{2}\right) \longrightarrow \left(\frac{1}{5} \times 10\right) + \left(\frac{1}{5} \times \frac{1}{2}\right) = 2\frac{1}{10}$$
$$\underbrace{}_{2} \quad + \quad \underbrace{}_{\frac{1}{10}}$$

$$\frac{3}{4} \times 24\frac{4}{5} \longrightarrow \frac{3}{4} \times \left(24 + \frac{4}{5}\right) \longrightarrow \left(\frac{3}{4} \times 24\right) + \left(\frac{3}{4} \times \frac{4}{5}\right) = 18\frac{3}{5}$$
$$\underbrace{}_{18} \quad + \quad \underbrace{}_{\frac{3}{5}}$$

Solve mentally.

27. $\frac{1}{3} \times 9\frac{1}{2}$

28. $\frac{1}{2} \times 4\frac{1}{3}$

29. $\frac{1}{7} \times 14\frac{2}{3}$

30. $\frac{1}{9} \times 27\frac{2}{5}$

31. $\frac{2}{5} \times 10\frac{1}{2}$

32. $\frac{3}{8} \times 24\frac{1}{3}$

33. $\frac{4}{5} \times 15\frac{1}{8}$

34. $\frac{5}{6} \times 18\frac{1}{10}$

35. $\frac{5}{8} \times 32\frac{2}{3}$

36. $\frac{2}{3} \times 9\frac{6}{7}$

37. $\frac{7}{9} \times 9\frac{3}{14}$

38. $\frac{9}{10} \times 20\frac{1}{3}$

Solve.

Exercise 40

39. A salt crystal grows $\frac{3}{16}$ of an inch a month. At this rate, about how much will the crystal grow in $2\frac{1}{3}$ years?

40. A chemist uses $\frac{3}{4}$ of $2\frac{1}{10}$ gallons of a salt solution in an experiment. Approximately how many gallons of salt solution is left after the experiment?

1 gal   1 gal $\frac{1}{10}$ gal

Problem: The traffic department estimates that no more than 365 cars can cross the Memorial Bridge every 10 minutes. If the estimate is correct, what is the maximum number of cars that can cross the bridge in $1\frac{1}{2}$ hours?

Time: 10 min
365ᵗʰ car

1 IMAGINE Sketch a picture of what is happening.

2 NAME

Facts: 365 cars every 10 *minutes*

Question: __?__ cars in $1\frac{1}{2}$ *hours*

3 THINK You are asked to find how many cars can cross in $1\frac{1}{2}$ *hours,* but you are given how many cross in 10 *minutes.* Whenever different measures are given, look for a "hidden" fact.

"Hidden" in the ten minutes is how many cars crossed in 1 hour. Study this:

$$60 \text{ minutes} = 1 \text{ hour}$$
$$\text{so, } 6 \text{ ten minutes} = 1 \text{ hour}$$
$$\text{and } 3 \text{ ten minutes} = \frac{1}{2} \text{ hour}$$
$$\text{Therefore, } (6 + 3) \text{ ten minutes} = 1 \text{ hour} + \frac{1}{2} \text{ hour}$$
$$\text{OR, } 9 \text{ ten minutes} = 1\frac{1}{2} \text{ hours}$$

Now create an equation to show how to find how many cars, *C,* crossed in $1\frac{1}{2}$ hours if 365 cars cross in 10 minutes.

$$C = 9 \times 365$$

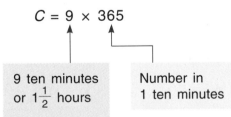

9 ten minutes or $1\frac{1}{2}$ hours

Number in 1 ten minutes

4 COMPUTE $C = 9 \times 365$
$C = 3285$ cars in $1\frac{1}{2}$ hours

5 CHECK Is it reasonable that over three thousand cars will cross in $1\frac{1}{2}$ hours if 365 cross in 10 minutes? Check your multiplication computation by division.

$$3285 \div 9 \overset{?}{=} 365$$
$$365 = 365$$

Use the strategy of finding "hidden facts" to solve.

1. A shoe store shelf is 8.5 feet long. If stacks of shoe boxes 7.5 inches wide are tightly placed side by side, how many stacks of shoe boxes fit across a shelf?

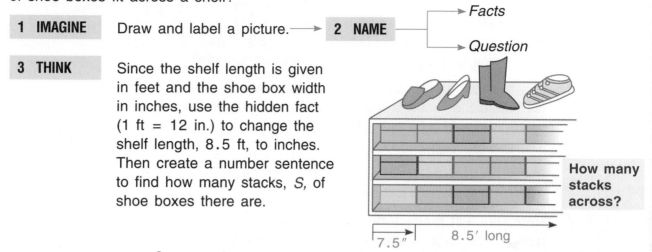

| **1 IMAGINE** | Draw and label a picture. ⟶ | **2 NAME** | ⟶ Facts
⟶ Question |

3 THINK   Since the shelf length is given in feet and the shoe box width in inches, use the hidden fact (1 ft = 12 in.) to change the shelf length, 8.5 ft, to inches. Then create a number sentence to find how many stacks, *S*, of shoe boxes there are.

How many stacks across?

$S = \underline{\ ?\ }$ inches (shelf length) ÷ 7.5 inches (each box)
(Hint: Remember only *whole* stacks of shoe boxes will fit on shelf.)

4 COMPUTE ⟶ **5 CHECK**

2. The Mustangs made 11 foul shots and 19 baskets, while the Lions made 19 foul shots and 14 baskets. Which team won? What was the final score?

3. When Sandy is sleeping, her heart rate is 64 beats per minute. If she slept for $9\frac{1}{4}$ hours last night, how many times did her heart beat while she was sleeping?

4. If it rained on $\frac{3}{10}$ of the days in April and 12 days in March, which month had the most rainy days? If it rained 7 days in May, how many rainy days were there in these three months altogether?

5. Mr. Dow lives 16 miles from his workplace. If he drives to work five days a week and his car gets 19.2 miles to the gallon, how much gas does he use in one week commuting to and from work?

6. If a valley glacier moves at a rate of 0.32 cm per day, how far will it move in the year 1996?

7. Dr. Sarn has ordered a patient to drink ten 8-ounce glasses of water every day. How many pints of water will this patient drink in one week?

8. Mr. Smith's heart beats 3780 times in one hour. If his daughter's heart rate is 90 beats per minute, how many times slower is Mr. Smith's heart beat than his daughter's?

9. A computer printer can print out at the speed of 125 lines per minute. If it takes two hours to print the research project of Professor Geos, how many lines long is his report?

2-15 | Problem Solving: Applications

Solve.

1. The playing speed of some records is 45 rpm (revolutions per minute). Others play at $33\frac{1}{3}$ rpm. How many rpm separate these two playing speeds?

2. A piano keyboard has 88 keys. Of the keys $\frac{9}{22}$ are black and the rest are white. How many black and white keys are on a piano keyboard?

3. The first three strings on Roy's guitar are 0.028, 0.032, and 0.040 inches wide. Express each of these measurements as a fraction.

4. Ramona must practice her guitar $3\frac{1}{2}$ hours each week. She practiced $\frac{3}{4}$ hour on Monday, $\frac{5}{6}$ hour on Tuesday, and $\frac{2}{3}$ hour on Wednesday. How much longer must she practice this week to fulfill her obligation?

5. The pie graph at the right shows the makeup of a modern jazz ensemble. If there are 24 musicians in the ensemble, how many musicians are there in each section?

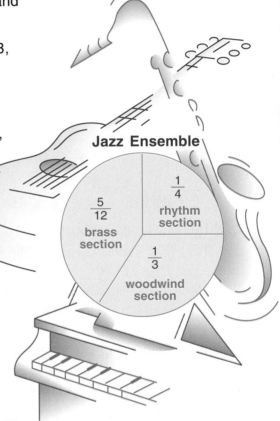

Jazz Ensemble

$\frac{5}{12}$ brass section

$\frac{1}{4}$ rhythm section

$\frac{1}{3}$ woodwind section

6. Terese discovered that the width of the keys making up an octave on her piano keyboard is $6\frac{1}{2}$ in. The keyboard of her piano has $7\frac{1}{3}$ octaves. How long is her piano keyboard? (Express your answer in inches.)

7. The width of the keys making up an octave on an English piano is $6\frac{3}{8}$ inches. On a German piano the width is $6\frac{1}{4}$ inches. How much smaller is the width of an octave on the German piano?

8. The G above middle C on a standard piano keyboard vibrates $1\frac{1}{2}$ times faster than middle C. If middle C vibrates at 128 cycles per second, how fast does the G above it vibrate?

9. An orchestra tunes to a pitch called "Concert A." Concert A vibrates half as fast as the A an octave higher. If the latter vibrates at 880 cycles per second, how fast does Concert A vibrate?

10. A concert grand piano is 9 feet long. A baby grand piano is $3\frac{5}{6}$ feet shorter. How long is a baby grand piano?

11. The pitch of a violin ranges from 200 to 3000 cycles per second. A viola is $\frac{1}{5}$ lower in pitch than a violin. What is the pitch range of a viola?

12. It takes an instrument maker $93\frac{1}{3}$ hours to make a guitar by hand. If the instrument maker works at a constant rate, how many hours must he or she spend on a guitar each day in order to finish it in 20 days?

13. Melvin practiced tuba for $\frac{1}{8}$ of a day. Two thirds of this time he practiced at school. What part of a day did he practice at school?

14. DJ Duke played one record for $2\frac{1}{3}$ minutes and another for $3\frac{1}{6}$ minutes. For how many minutes did he play both records?

15. A tractor trailer weighing 26,500 pounds empty is loaded with three pianos each weighing $530\frac{5}{8}$ pounds. After delivering two pianos, how much does the truck and its remaining contents weigh?

16. One pipe from a pipe organ is $24\frac{2}{3}$ feet high. A second pipe is $8\frac{3}{4}$ feet high. How many feet shorter is the second pipe?

17. On September 1 *Mel's Music* gave both piano and guitar lessons. Thereafter, piano lessons were offered every third day and guitar lessons every fourth day. How many times during the month were both piano and guitar lessons given on the same day?

USE THESE STRATEGIES:
Use a Graph
Multi-Step Problem
Write an Equation
Use Simpler Numbers
Hidden Information
Extra Information
Organized List

Each member of the school chorus sings one of the four voice parts represented by this graph. Use the graph to complete exercises 18–21.

18. How many students participate in chorus?

19. What part of the chorus sing:
a. soprano?   **b.** alto?
c. tenor?   **d.** bass?

20. There are $\frac{3}{4}$ as many students in the chorus as there are in the orchestra. How many students are in the orchestra?

21. Half of the students in the orchestra are eighth graders. One third of the students in chorus are also eighth graders. How many eighth graders are in orchestra or chorus?

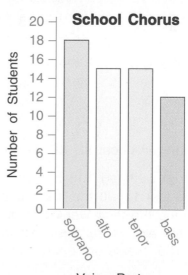

School Chorus

Number of Students

Voice Parts

More Practice

Write each fraction in simplest form.

1. $\frac{6}{9}$ **2.** $\frac{12}{24}$ **3.** $\frac{15}{45}$ **4.** $\frac{4}{16}$ **5.** $\frac{16}{100}$

Tell whether each number is prime or composite.

6. 21 **7.** 149 **8.** 13 **9.** 81 **10.** 41

Write the prime factorization of each number using exponents.

11. 72 **12.** 8 **13.** 48 **14.** 98 **15.** 175

Use prime factorization to find the GCF of the numbers.

16. 12 and 16 **17.** 84 and 120 **18.** 72 and 80

Find the LCM of the numbers.

19. 6 and 7 **20.** 9 and 27 **21.** 4, 8, and 12

Change each to a terminating or repeating decimal.

22. $\frac{2}{5}$ **23.** $\frac{5}{8}$ **24.** $\frac{9}{24}$ **25.** $1\frac{3}{11}$ **26.** $5\frac{1}{3}$

Compare. Use <, =, or >.

27. $\frac{3}{8}$? $\frac{5}{8}$ **28.** $\frac{9}{10}$? $\frac{4}{5}$ **29.** $3\frac{4}{7}$? $3\frac{7}{9}$ **30.** $\frac{5}{6}$? $0.8\overline{3}$

Use estimation to solve. Then find the exact answer, and express in simplest form.

31. $\frac{3}{10} + \frac{1}{5}$ **32.** $\frac{7}{8} - \frac{3}{4}$ **33.** $\frac{5}{12} + \frac{1}{4}$ **34.** $\frac{9}{10} - \frac{1}{2}$

35. $\begin{array}{r} 4\frac{1}{3} \\ + 2\frac{1}{4} \\ \hline \end{array}$ **36.** $\begin{array}{r} 12\frac{4}{7} \\ + 3\frac{2}{5} \\ \hline \end{array}$ **37.** $\begin{array}{r} 9\frac{7}{10} \\ - 6\frac{3}{4} \\ \hline \end{array}$ **38.** $\begin{array}{r} 10\frac{1}{2} \\ - 4\frac{5}{8} \\ \hline \end{array}$

39. $\frac{2}{5} \times \frac{5}{8}$ **40.** $\frac{7}{10} \times \frac{5}{6}$ **41.** $\frac{6}{7} \div \frac{3}{5}$ **42.** $\frac{1}{9} \div \frac{2}{3}$

43. $2\frac{3}{4} \times \frac{2}{3}$ **44.** $7\frac{1}{4} \times 2\frac{3}{8}$ **45.** $6\frac{1}{2} \div 4$ **46.** $6\frac{1}{3} \div 2\frac{1}{6}$

Solve.

47. Four pens cost $3.50. What will a dozen pens cost?

48. Karen weighed 108 lb. She has been on a low-fat diet for the past three weeks. She lost $1\frac{1}{4}$ lb the first week. During the second week she lost $2\frac{1}{2}$ lb. During the third week she gained $\frac{3}{4}$ lb. What was her net loss or gain at the end of the three weeks?

Math Probe

Patterns of Repeating Decimals

1. Look at these repeating decimals.

$\frac{1}{9} = 0.\overline{1}$ $\frac{3}{9} = 0.\overline{3}$ $\frac{5}{9} = 0.\overline{5}$ $\frac{7}{9} = \underline{\ ?\ }$

$\frac{2}{9} = 0.\overline{2}$ $\frac{4}{9} = 0.\overline{4}$ $\frac{6}{9} = 0.\overline{6}$ $\frac{8}{9} = \underline{\ ?\ }$

$\frac{9}{9} = \underline{\ ?\ }$

Can you guess these decimals?

2. Can you see the pattern here?
Copy and complete.

$\frac{1}{99} = 0.\overline{01}$ $\frac{4}{99} = \underline{\ ?\ }$ $\frac{17}{99} = \underline{\ ?\ }$ $\frac{82}{99} = \underline{\ ?\ }$

$\frac{2}{99} = 0.\overline{02}$ $\frac{5}{99} = \underline{\ ?\ }$ $\frac{58}{99} = \underline{\ ?\ }$ $\frac{91}{99} = \underline{\ ?\ }$

$\frac{3}{99} = 0.\overline{03}$ $\frac{7}{99} = \underline{\ ?\ }$ $\frac{74}{99} = \underline{\ ?\ }$ $\frac{99}{99} = \underline{\ ?\ }$

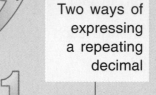

$\frac{1}{9} = 0.1111...$

Two ways of expressing a repeating decimal

$\frac{1}{9} = 0.\overline{1}$

3. Can you guess these? Check with a calculator.
Copy and complete.

$\frac{1}{999} = \underline{\ ?\ }$ $\frac{41}{999} = \underline{\ ?\ }$ $\frac{123}{999} = \underline{\ ?\ }$ $\frac{179}{9999} = \underline{\ ?\ }$

$\frac{2}{999} = \underline{\ ?\ }$ $\frac{75}{999} = \underline{\ ?\ }$ $\frac{5}{9999} = \underline{\ ?\ }$ $\frac{203}{9999} = \underline{\ ?\ }$

$\frac{13}{999} = \underline{\ ?\ }$ $\frac{152}{999} = \underline{\ ?\ }$ $\frac{12}{9999} = \underline{\ ?\ }$ $\frac{1234}{9999} = \underline{\ ?\ }$

4. Notice these patterns. Predict answers. Check with a calculator.

$\frac{1}{11} = 0.\overline{09}$ $\frac{7}{11} = \underline{\ ?\ }$ $\frac{1}{3} = 0.\overline{3}$ $\frac{2}{3} = 0.\overline{6}$

$\frac{2}{11} = 0.\overline{18}$ $\frac{5}{11} = \underline{\ ?\ }$ $\frac{1}{30} = 0.0\overline{3}$ $\frac{2}{30} = \underline{\ ?\ }$

$\frac{3}{11} = \underline{\ ?\ }$ $\frac{8}{11} = \underline{\ ?\ }$ $\frac{1}{300} = 0.00\overline{3}$ $\frac{2}{300} = \underline{\ ?\ }$

$\frac{4}{11} = \underline{\ ?\ }$ $\frac{10}{11} = \underline{\ ?\ }$ $\frac{1}{3000} = \underline{\ ?\ }$ $\frac{2}{3000} = \underline{\ ?\ }$

5. Find some other fractions that produce repeating decimal patterns.

Check Your Mastery

Write each fraction in simplest form. See pp. 32–35

1. $\frac{4}{6}$ 2. $\frac{24}{28}$ 3. $\frac{11}{33}$ 4. $\frac{12}{24}$ 5. $\frac{45}{50}$

Tell whether each number is prime or composite. See p. 36

6. 17   7. 30   8. 47   9. 125   10. 71

Write the prime factorization of each number using exponents. See p. 37

11. 54   12. 19   13. 125   14. 107   15. 432

Use prime factorization to find the GCF of the numbers. See p. 38

16. 15 and 42   17. 36 and 60   18. 63 and 91

Find the LCM of the numbers. See p. 39

19. 6 and 15   20. 24 and 40   21. 6, 9, and 12

Change each to a terminating or repeating decimal. See pp. 40–41

22. $\frac{3}{8}$ 23. $\frac{2}{5}$ 24. $\frac{7}{11}$ 25. $2\frac{5}{24}$ 26. $4\frac{2}{3}$

Compare. Use <, =, or >. See pp. 42–43

27. $\frac{4}{7}$? $\frac{3}{7}$ 28. $\frac{2}{3}$? $\frac{5}{6}$ 29. $5\frac{5}{9}$? $5\frac{1}{3}$ 30. $\frac{5}{8}$? 0.625

Order from least to greatest.

31. $\frac{2}{3}, \frac{3}{5}, \frac{3}{4}, \frac{1}{6}$ 32. $\frac{9}{8}, \frac{3}{2}, \frac{5}{4}, \frac{7}{16}$ 33. $\frac{5}{6}, \frac{5}{12}, \frac{1}{20}, \frac{7}{10}$

Compute. See pp. 44–51

34. $\frac{7}{10} + \frac{1}{5}$ 35. $3\frac{2}{3} + 4\frac{3}{4}$ 36. $\frac{5}{6} - \frac{1}{6}$ 37. $8\frac{5}{12} - 5\frac{1}{6}$

38. $\frac{3}{5} \times \frac{5}{9}$ 39. $6\frac{2}{3} \times 3\frac{5}{9}$ 40. $\frac{7}{15} \div \frac{4}{9}$ 41. $2\frac{1}{3} \div 6$

Use estimation to solve. See pp. 52–53
Then find the exact answer, and express in simplest form.

42. $\frac{3}{4} + \frac{7}{8}$ 43. $11\frac{1}{4} + 1\frac{5}{6}$ 44. $\frac{11}{12} - \frac{1}{3}$ 45. $15\frac{8}{9} - 9\frac{2}{3}$

46. $\frac{4}{11} \times \frac{7}{8}$ 47. $1\frac{1}{2} \times \frac{6}{7}$ 48. $\frac{5}{12} \div \frac{3}{4}$ 49. $4\frac{3}{4} \div 2\frac{1}{8}$

Solve. See pp. 44–53

50. Three pairs of socks cost $7.50. What will a dozen pairs of socks cost?

51. David weighed $125\frac{1}{2}$ lb. He has been on a low fat diet for the past three weeks. He lost $2\frac{1}{2}$ lbs the first week. During the second week he gained $\frac{3}{4}$ lb. During the third week he lost $4\frac{1}{4}$ lbs. What was his net loss or gain at the end of the three weeks?

Cumulative Review

Choose the correct answer.

1. 0.005680 is how much greater than 0.0004359?

   a. 0.0524410
   b. 0.0052541
   c. 0.0052551
   d. 0.0052441

2. The prime factorization of 36 is:

   a. $2^3 \times 3^3$
   b. $2^2 \times 3^2$
   c. $3^3 \times 2^2$
   d. $2^3 \times 3^2$

3. What is the next fraction in the sequence $\frac{1}{3}, \frac{2}{9}, \frac{4}{27}, \frac{8}{81}$?

   a. $\frac{16}{54}$
   b. $\frac{10}{243}$
   c. $\frac{16}{162}$
   d. $\frac{16}{243}$

4. Which numbers are in order from greatest to least?
   a. 1.2, 1.02, 1.210
   b. 1.210, 1.2, 1.02
   c. 1.210, 1.2, 1.211
   d. 1.02, 1.2, 1.210

5. 13 is the rounded sum of $8\frac{1}{3}$ and:

   a. $4\frac{4}{9}$
   b. $5\frac{7}{9}$
   c. $4\frac{2}{9}$
   d. $4\frac{11}{12}$

6. 0.75 is another way of expressing the sum of:

   a. 0.4 and 0.55
   b. $\frac{1}{2}$ and 0.25
   c. 0.33 and 4.2
   d. 0.5 and 0.05

7. Which fractions are in order from least to greatest?

   a. $\frac{2}{9}, \frac{1}{4}, \frac{3}{8}, \frac{2}{3}, \frac{5}{6}$
   b. $\frac{1}{4}, \frac{2}{9}, \frac{2}{3}, \frac{3}{8}, \frac{5}{6}$
   c. $\frac{5}{6}, \frac{2}{9}, \frac{1}{4}, \frac{2}{3}, \frac{3}{8}$
   d. $\frac{1}{6}, \frac{1}{8}, \frac{2}{9}, \frac{3}{10}, \frac{4}{12}$

8. The product of $\frac{2}{3}$ and the sum of $\frac{1}{2}$ and $\frac{1}{5}$ is:

   a. $\frac{4}{21}$
   b. $\frac{7}{15}$
   c. $\frac{7}{10}$
   d. $\frac{2}{15}$

9. 3.2605 rounded to the nearest hundredth is 0.14 less than:
   a. 3.27
   b. 3.34
   c. 3.12
   d. 3.4

10. The product of $\frac{5}{8}$ and $\frac{2}{3}$ is how much less than 1?

    a. $\frac{7}{12}$
    b. 3
    c. $\frac{12}{15}$
    d. $\frac{5}{12}$

11. The reciprocal of $\frac{5}{9}$ is 3 times greater than:

    a. 5
    b. $\frac{3}{5}$
    c. $\frac{5}{3}$
    d. $\frac{1}{3}$

12. The product of 0.204 and 0.8137 is how much less than 1?
    a. 0.659948
    b. 0.8340052
    c. 0.1659984
    d. 0.1659948

13. The sum of $\frac{5}{12}$ and what number is less than $\frac{1}{2}$?

    a. 0.375
    b. 0.083
    c. 0.651
    d. 0.084

14. If $3(0.4 + 0.07)$ is equal to 6 times a number, what is the number?

    a. 0.235
    b. 14.1
    c. 2.35
    d. 1.41

Compute.

15. $\begin{array}{r} 457.096 \\ +398.812 \end{array}$

16. $\begin{array}{r} 4.206 \\ \times\ 2.68 \end{array}$

17. $\begin{array}{r} 45.106 \\ -24.047 \end{array}$

18. $111\overline{)0.3885}$

19. $0.00944 \div 0.004$

20. $0.009 \div 0.5$

21. $2\frac{1}{4} + 4\frac{1}{3}$

22. $7\frac{4}{9} + 7\frac{5}{6}$

23. $9\frac{6}{7} - \frac{2}{3}$

24. $7\frac{1}{12} - 6\frac{3}{8}$

25. $\frac{3}{4} \times 1\frac{3}{7}$

26. $\frac{1}{8} \div 1\frac{3}{16}$

Use <, =, or > to compare.

27. $28,425,046\ \underline{\ ?\ }\ 28,425,406$

28. $(0.2146 - 0.1046)\ \underline{\ ?\ }\ 0.10192$

Round to the nearest thousandth.

29. 23.08290

30. 3.10807

31. 10.86705

32. 15.02518

Write the prime factorization for each number, using exponents.

33. 45

34. 604

35. 176

36. 2187

Express each number as a decimal.

37. $1\frac{3}{8}$

38. $2\frac{5}{16}$

39. $1\frac{5}{9}$

40. $2\frac{5}{7}$

Solve.

41. Mark counted 2,465 pennies from the penny walk. Jill counted 1044 more than Mark. How many pennies were counted altogether?

42. The bill for sports was $1246.08 for uniforms, $358.95 for trophies, and $856.82 for supplies. To the nearest whole number, what was the total bill?

43. In a school of 1259 students, $6266.25 was raised. If 564 students each pledged $5.75, what was the average pledge by the remaining students?

44. If Nick bought $\frac{1}{4}$ pound of apricots and Adam bought 12 ounces of raisins, how many ounces of fruit did the two boys buy?

45. There are 36 students in the eighth grade. Twice as many students like math as do science. If $\frac{1}{3}$ like science, how many like math?

46. If $10\frac{1}{2}$ pizzas are eaten by 28 junior high students, what is the average amount eaten by one student?

+10 BONUS

47. Imagine that your grandparents have given you $2400 for your birthday. You plan to save $\frac{1}{3}$. You want to spend $\frac{1}{8}$ of the amount on a new sound system, and $\frac{1}{6}$ of the money on clothes for school and skiing. Another $\frac{1}{4}$ must be used for school tuition and books. Compute the dollar amount for each designation. What fractional part of the original $2400 remains?

3 | Equations, Inequalities, and Integers

In this chapter you will:

- Write and evaluate mathematical or algebraic expressions and sentences
- Solve addition, subtraction, multiplication, and division equations
- Find solutions to inequalities
- Solve problems: using equations
- Use technology: calculator keys

Moving the Earth

"Give me a place to stand, and I'll move the earth," this mathematician said. Who was it? What was meant by that remark? Find out all you can about this ancient mathematical genius. Write and illustrate this story.

Do you remember?

Expresses an equality: =

Expresses an inequality:

≠ : is not equal

> : is greater than

< : is less than

≥ : is greater than or equal to

≤ : is less than or equal to

Addition and subtraction are related operations.

$$7 + 9 = 16 \qquad n + 9 = 16$$
$$16 - 9 = 7 \qquad 16 - 9 = n$$

Multiplication and division are related operations.

$$7 \times 8 = 56 \qquad 7 \cdot n = 56$$
$$56 \div 8 = 7 \qquad 56 \div 7 = n$$

3-1 Order of Operations

Order of Operations: rules that show the order in which several given mathematical computations must be done. These rules are:

- Compute exponents first.
- Do multiplications or divisions first, working from *left* to *right*.
- Then do additions or subtractions, working from *left* to *right*.

Order of Operations	
1.	( ) before [ ]
2.	Exponents
3.	" × " or " ÷ " left to right
4.	" + " or " − " left to right

$$20 \div 5 \times 3$$
$$4 \quad \times 3 = 12$$

$$17 - 9 + 5$$
$$8 \quad + 5 = 13$$

$$21 - 6 \times 3 \div 9 + 2^2$$
$$21 - \quad 18 \quad \div 9 + 4$$
$$21 - 2 \quad + 4$$
$$19 \quad + 4 = 23$$

If there are grouping symbols in an expression, do the computation inside the grouping symbols first, beginning with the innermost symbols.

$$(8 - 5) \times 2 - 3 \times (10 - 9)$$
$$3 \quad \times 2 - 3 \times \quad 1$$
$$6 \quad - \quad 3 \quad = 3$$

$$[15 + (6 \times 2)] \div 3$$
$$[15 + \quad 12] \quad \div 3$$
$$27 \quad \div 3 = 9$$

Sometimes the times sign is omitted just before or just after a grouping symbol.

$$2(3 + 6) \text{ means } 2 \times (3 + 6)$$
$$(27 \div 3) 5 \text{ means } (27 \div 3) \times 5$$

Remember:
$$\frac{9 + 9}{8 - 2}$$
$$\frac{18}{6} = 3$$
The fraction line is a grouping symbol. Simplify the numerator and denominator first.

Simplify.

1. $16 - 18 \div 3$
2. $7 + 6 \times 2$
3. $15 \div 3 \times 2$
4. $16 - 8 + 1$
5. $3^2 + 12 \div 6$
6. $5^2 - 10 \div 5$
7. $60 \times 3 \div 2^2$
8. $77 + 3 - 2$
9. $8 \times 9 \div 3^2$
10. $7 + 7 \div 7 \times 7$
11. $7 - 7 \times 7 \div 7$
12. $(7 \times 7) + 7 \div 7$
13. $(7 + 7) \div 7 + 7$
14. $(7 - 7) \div 7 + 7$
15. $7 + (7 + 7) \times 7$

Simplify.

16. $(13 + 2) \times 3 - [(12 \div 4) + (8 \times 3)]$　**17.** $[(20 - 3) \times 4] + \{[5 \times (6 + 10)] \div (2 - 1)\}$

18. $(108 \div 9) \times 2 + (144 - 73)$　**19.** $[(16 + 0) \times 18] + [2 \times (3 - 3)]$

20. $1 + \{[(9 - 8) \times 7] \div 7\}$　**21.** $[3 + (16 \div 2)] - 10$

22. $[1120 - (10 \times 11) + 2] \div 4$　**23.** $94 + \{[(20 \times 10) - (225 \div 9)] \times 2\}$

24. $(24 - 10)8 \div 2^2$　**25.** $11 + (13 - 12) - 12$

26. $10^2 - (36 + 3) + 83$　**27.** $208 - 7(44 \div 2^2)$

28. $(17 \times 2)8 - 199$　**29.** $(204 \div 4) \div 17 - 3$

30. $[4 + (8 \times 2)] + 1^2$　**31.** $17 + 3 \times 2 - 56 \div 7$

32. $85 \div 5 + 12 - 7 \times 2$　**33.** $7^2 \div 7 + 4 \times 20 - 7$

Complete each expression to make it true. (The first one is done.)

34. $8[(6 - 3) \times 2] + 4 = 2 + 50$　**35.** $98 - [2(7 + 3)] \div 5 = 2 \underline{\ \ \ }$

36. $[48 - 4(17 - 9)] \div 8 = 2 \underline{\ \ \ }$　**37.** $[7 - (3 \times 2)] + 99 - 4 = 2 \underline{\ \ \ }$

38. $[16 + 4(18 \div 2)] \div 26 = 2 \underline{\ \ \ }$　**39.** $104 + [56 - 2(9 + 3)] - 18 = 2 \underline{\ \ \ }$

40. $97 - [10 + 5(3 + 2)] \div 5 = 2 \underline{\ \ \ }$　**41.** $\{[7 \times 5 - 5(2 \times 3) + 3] + 4\} \div 3 = 2 \underline{\ \ \ }$

Rewrite the expression using ( ) and [ ] to make each sentence true.

42. $144 \div 8 - 2 + 5 \times 2 = 34$　**43.** $144 \div 8 - 2 + 5 \times 2 = 4$

44. $144 \div 8 - 2 + 5 \times 2 = 26$　**45.** $144 \div 8 - 2 + 5 \times 2 = 58$

46. $144 \div 8 - 2 + 5 \times 2 = 6$　**47.** $144 \div 8 - 2 + 5 \times 2 = 9$

Write a mathematical expression. (Use grouping symbols.)

48. 275 family admission tickets were sold before 10 A.M. 26 were returned for refund. 102 family admission tickets were sold after 10 A.M.

49. 462 people visited the park in the morning. 45 people left in the afternoon. 252 people visited the park in the evening.

50. Early-bird admission tickets cost $8.50 each. After 10 A.M., tickets cost $10 each. Find the total amount of ticket sales for the park if 246 early-bird tickets and 624 regular tickets were sold.

Exercise 49

462 entered A.M.

45 left

252 entered evening

65

3-2 Mathematical or Algebraic Expressions

Variable: a letter used in a mathematical statement to represent a number.
In these expressions x is the variable.

$$x + 14 \qquad 2x \qquad 2x + 3 \qquad \frac{x^2}{4}$$

A **mathematical, or algebraic, expression** uses one or more variables
and the operation symbols, like $+$, $-$, $\times$, or $\div$.

Word Phrase	Mathematical Expression
8 more than a number	$n + 8$
15 more than 2 times a number	$2 \times n + 15$ or $2n + 15$ — It is common practice to omit the multiplication sign.
twice as many players	$2p$
$13 less than her pay	$p - \$13$
5 times his savings divided evenly among 3 people	$5s \div 3$ or $\dfrac{5s}{3}$
the length of a side squared	s^2
twice the width added to twice the length	$2\ell + 2w$ — 2 variables

Write a mathematical expression. (Choose a letter for each variable.)

1. 5 more than a number

2. twice as many children

3. a temperature minus 4°

4. 22 subtracted from a length

5. 10 times a weight

6. a number divided by 7

7. half a number added to 15

8. h multiplied by 9

9. 15 decreased by z

10. two thirds of k

11. the sum of a and b

12. the sum of 4 and y

13. 10 less than c

14. 12 more than d

15. j divided by 6

16. the product of 7 and r

17. the quotient of 20 and a

18. 5% of h

19. 3 less than twice q

20. u increased by 7

21. o increased by p

22. 6 less than t

23. 54 divided by x

24. add 5, $f,$ and g

Write a mathematical, or algebraic, expression. (The first one is done.)

25. 3 times the difference between 2 and a number ──────→ $3(2 - n)$

26. 7 more than 2 times an amount of money

27. 6 less than twice a number

28. 2 less than the quotient of $a \div b$

29. the sum when 3 doubled is added to a number

30. the difference when 5 squared is subtracted from a number

31. the quotient when twice a number is divided by 7

32. the product when 12 is multiplied by the sum of $10 + x$

33. two less than 10 more than a number

34. two fifths of three less than a number

**For each statement let p be the variable.
State what p represents. Then write a
mathematical expression for the statement.**
(The first one is done.)

35. The stock market went up 4 points from yesterday's
total. Let p represent yesterday's total points.
Statement: $p + 4$

36. This year's profits are $300 more than last year's.

37. The population of Bayville doubled in 20 years.

38. The new stadium holds 3000 more people than
the old stadium.

39. Gasoline prices have increased by 7% since
last year.

40. The temperature has dropped 23° since sunset.

41. Seven eighths of the people at the concert stayed
for the encore.

42. Twenty more than twice as many students
graduated this year than last year.

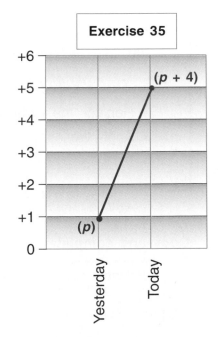

Exercise 35

Write a word phrase for each.

43. $2b + 1$ **44.** $(a + b) \div 3$ **45.** $4x - 10$ **46.** $4x + 2y$

47. $9x(3)$ **48.** $5y - 7$ **49.** $3b \div 2$ **50.** $4 + 3a$

3-3 Evaluating Mathematical or Algebraic Expressions

To evaluate a mathematical, or algebraic, expression:

- Replace the variable with a number.
- Simplify the expression.

These digital clocks show the time in cities that are in different time zones.

6:00	**7:00**	**8:00**	**9:00**
Seattle	**Phoenix**	**Chicago**	**New York**

If t represents the time in Seattle, ⟵ If it is 4 P.M. in Seattle,
then: it is 6 P.M. in Chicago
$\quad t + 1$ represents the time in Phoenix, because: $t + 2 \longrightarrow 4 + 2 = 6$
$\quad t + 2$ represents the time in Chicago,
$\quad t + 3$ represents the time in New York.

The value of each expression depends on t, the time in Seattle.

If t represents the time in Chicago,
then: $t - 2$ represents the time in Seattle.

To evaluate expressions with more than one operation:

- Replace the variable with a number.
- Apply the rules for order of operations.

Let $a = 7 \quad b = 6 \quad c = 5$

$(a - b)^2 \times c \longrightarrow (7 - 6)^2 \times 5 \longrightarrow (1)^2 \times 5 \longrightarrow 1 \times 5 = 5$

Copy and complete the chart.

	Phoenix time t	New York time $t + 2$	Chicago time $t + 1$	Seattle time $t - 1$
1.	6 P.M.	6 + 2 = 8 P.M.		
2.	9 P.M.			
3.	1 P.M.			
4.	12 Noon			
5.	10 A.M.			
6.	8 P.M.			

Evaluate when *a* = 15, *b* = 22, *c* = 14, *d* = 17, *r* = 100, *s* = 25.

7. $b + 6$ **8.** $c + 10$ **9.** $r - 19$ **10.** $d - 8$ **11.** $6s$

12. $7a$ **13.** $\dfrac{126}{c}$ **14.** $\dfrac{85}{d}$ **15.** $\dfrac{1}{2}c$ **16.** $\dfrac{1}{5}s$

17. $r \div 20$ **18.** $r - 51$ **19.** $40d$ **20.** $7s$ **21.** $10 + r$

Find the value when *a* = 4, *b* = 3, *c* = 1.

22. $6a + 3$ **23.** $8b - 24$ **24.** $(a + b) - 5$ **25.** $a + (b - c)$

26. $5a - (b + c)$ **27.** $7a(b + c)$ **28.** $(b - c)a$ **29.** $(10^2 - a) \div c$

Find the value when *r* = 10, *s* = 8, *t* = 3.5.

30. $6t - 5$ **31.** $6r - 4t$ **32.** $5s - \dfrac{8t}{4}$

33. $\dfrac{8r}{s} - s$ **34.** $2t + r$ **35.** $(12 + r) - (r + s)$

36. $t(r + s)$ **37.** $rs - t$ **38.** $s(4t + r)$

Find the value when *x* = 20, *y* = 4, *w* = 1.

39. $(x - w)y$ **40.** $2^2 + 2(y + w)$ **41.** $x - 3y + 2$

42. $y + 6w - 3^2$ **43.** $\dfrac{3(x - y)}{8}$ **44.** $\dfrac{3y + 8}{x}$

Rico practiced guitar for half of Tom's practice time (T) plus 10 minutes. $\left(R = \dfrac{T}{2} + 10\right)$ Steve practiced for 3 times Tom's practice time minus 18 minutes. $(S = 3T - 18)$

45. Who practiced longer if Tom practiced for 20 minutes?

46. Who practiced longer if Tom practiced for 40 minutes?

If n is a variable representing the position of a number in a sequence, find the number in the indicated position for the given rule.

	Sequence	Rule	Position	Number	
47.	2, 4, 6, 8, ...	$2n$	25th	?	← Think: 2×25
48.	5, 6, 7, 8, ...	$n + 4$	17th	?	
49.	5, 11, 17, 23, ...	$6n - 1$	100th	?	

3-4 | Mathematical or Algebraic Sentences

An English sentence can be written as a **mathematical,** or **algebraic, sentence** by using one or more variables, the operation symbols, like +, −, ×, or ÷, and the relation signs, like =, ≠, >, <, ≥, or ≤.

English Sentence	Mathematical Sentence
Seven added to a number is ten.	$n + 7 = 10$
One less than six times a number is 27.	$6n - 1 = 27$ $6 \times n = 6n$ or $6 \cdot n$ "·" means multiply.
The number of books on a shelf divided by three is less than 9 books.	$\dfrac{c}{3} < 9$
Lonnie's height is equal to or greater than Ken's height of 62 inches.	$h \geq 62$
The weight of a package is not equal to 34 pounds.	$p \neq 34$

Equation: an algebraic sentence expressing an equality.
    It uses an equals (=) sign.

Eight times a number is 48. ——→ $8n = 48$ ←— Equation

Inequality: an algebraic sentence expressing an unequal relationship.
    It uses one of these symbols: ≠, >, or <.

Two more pens is less than 10. ——→ $p + 2 < 10$ ←
A ton does not equal 1900 pounds. ——→ $t \neq 1900$ ←   Inequalities

An algebraic sentence using the symbol ≥ or ≤ is also an inequality.

The book weighs four pounds or less. ——→ $w \leq 4$ ←

Write a mathematical sentence.

1. A number multiplied by 6 is 42.
2. 5 less than a number is 14.
3. One third of a number is 10.
4. The sum of a number and 6 is 14.
5. The product of a number and 3 is 18.
6. The quotient of a number and 5 is 10.
7. The difference between a number and 6 is less than 20.
8. The product of a number and 7 is not 50.
9. The difference between a number and 17 is not 18.
10. When 7 is added to a number, the result is greater than 6.

Write a mathematical sentence. Identify it as an equation or an inequality.

11. The quotient of a number divided by 3 is not 17.

12. Three times a number divided by 2 is 30.

13. The sum of 17 and a number is 34.

14. The difference between 28 and a number is greater than 10.

15. 8 increased by a number is greater than or equal to 20.

16. Three fourths of a number is less than or equal to 24.

17. 4 more than the product of a number and 6 is 40.

18. 3 less than the product of a number and 5 is less than 32.

Write a mathematical sentence to describe each problem situation.

19. A box holds 24 pairs of gloves. Kareem has 26 pairs of gloves. How many pairs of gloves will not fit in the box?

20. The length of a rectangular box is twice the width. If the length is 32 inches, how wide is the box?

21. Ceara is two years younger than her brother. If Ceara is ten, how old is her brother?

22. The shortest side of a triangle is 9 cm. The longest side is 15 cm. The sum of the sides is 36 cm. Find the missing side.

23. The length of a ruler is at least 12 inches.

24. Tomas is at most fourteen years old.

25. If a plane travels 350 mph, how far will it travel in 5 hours? (Hint: Let d = distance traveled.)

26. The area of circle A is at least two times greater than the area of circle B. If the area of circle B is 36 square inches, what is the area of circle A?

$=$	$3 = 3$
$<$	$2 < 3$
$>$	$3 > 2$
$\neq$	is not equal to $5 \neq 6$
$\geq$	is greater than or equal to $x \geq 6$
$\leq$	is less than or equal to $y \leq 7$

MAKE UP YOUR OWN...   **Write a word problem for each.**

27. $n + 4 = 16$

28. $t - 20 \neq 16$

29. $4p < 16$

30. $5x - 3 \geq 12$

31. $3s + 2 \leq 11$

32. $\dfrac{w}{2} > 98$

SKILLS TO REMEMBER   **Complete. Use <, =, or >.**

33. $13.5 + 0.81 \underline{\ ?\ } 14.3$

34. $2000 - 108 \underline{\ ?\ } 892$

35. $7.02 \div 1.8 \underline{\ ?\ } 0.4$

36. $\dfrac{3}{8} \cdot 1\dfrac{1}{9} \underline{\ ?\ } \dfrac{1}{2}$

37. $2\dfrac{1}{5} - \dfrac{3}{4} \underline{\ ?\ } 1\dfrac{2}{5}$

38. $8\dfrac{2}{3} \div 8\dfrac{3}{5} \underline{\ ?\ } 1$

3-5 Evaluating Mathematical or Algebraic Sentences

Given the value of the variable, a mathematical or algebraic sentence can be evaluated by:

- Substituting the given number value for the variable.
- Simplifying the sentence.

Let $r = 6$. Then:

$2r + 4 = 16 \longrightarrow (2 \times 6) + 4 = 16 \longrightarrow 16 = 16$

$r - 1 > 4 \longrightarrow 6 - 1 > 4 \longrightarrow 5 > 4$

$2r \neq 10 \longrightarrow (2 \times 6) \neq 10 \longrightarrow 12 \neq 10$

TRUE STATEMENTS

Sometimes a value will be substituted for the variable that will make the statement false.

Let $x = 7$. Then:

$x + 3 = 9 \longrightarrow 7 + 3 = 9$, but $7 + 3 \neq 9$

$2x + 5 = 20 \longrightarrow (2 \times 7) + 5 = 20$, but $14 + 5 \neq 20$

$\dfrac{x}{2} - 1 = 2 \longrightarrow \dfrac{7}{2} - 1 = 2$, but $3\frac{1}{2} - 1 \neq 2$

FALSE STATEMENTS

To evaluate sentences with *more than one* operation:

- Substitute a number for the variable.
- Apply the rules for order of operations.

Let $a = 12$, $b = 3$, $c = 5$, and d and e be any whole numbers:

$(a - b) \times c = d \longrightarrow (12 - 3) \times 5 = 9 \times 5 = d \longrightarrow d = 45$

$\dfrac{(a + b)}{c} < e \longrightarrow \dfrac{(12 + 3)}{5} = \dfrac{15}{5} = 3 \longrightarrow \dfrac{12 + 3}{5} < 4, 5, 6, \ldots \longrightarrow e > 3$

State whether each is a true or a false statement for the given value of each variable.

1. $n + 8 > 9$ when $n = 2$

2. $p - 16 < 5$ when $p = 20$

3. $\dfrac{3}{4}y = 12$ when $y = 16$

4. $\dfrac{1}{2}f = 7$ when $f = 12$

5. $4m + 3 = 14$ when $m = 3$

6. $7h - 2 < 26$ when $h = 4$

7. $2(r + 4) = 18$ when $r = 5$

8. $4(b - 5) < 12$ when $b = 8$

9. $\dfrac{c + 4}{2} = 5$ when $c = 6$

10. $\dfrac{m}{2} + 2 \geq 6$ when $m = 8$

11. $4(b - 5) < 12$ when $b = 8$

12. $\dfrac{c + 4}{2} = 5$ when $c = 6$

Let $r = 10$, $t = 6$, $d = 2$. Find a whole-number value for n that will make each a true mathematical sentence.

13. $2(r + t) - d = n$

14. $(r - t) - 2d = n$

15. $(r - t) - 2d < n$

16. $(r - t) - 2d \geq n$

17. $\dfrac{r}{d} + t = n$

18. $\dfrac{r}{d} + t > n$

19. $3(r - d) + t = n$

20. $\dfrac{4(r + d)}{6} = n$

21. $\dfrac{4(r + d)}{6} - 3 = n$

Let $a = 6$, $b = 2$, and $c = 3$. Find a whole-number value for n that will make each a true mathematical sentence.

22. $(a - b) + c < n$

23. $a \times b \times c \neq n$

24. $3(a + b) - c > n$

25. $4(a - b) + c < n$

26. $\dfrac{a}{b} + c = n$

27. $\dfrac{6c}{a} \times 2 < n$

Complete each so that it makes a true sentence.
Use whole numbers, variables, or the symbols =, ≠, >, <, ≥, or ≤.

28. $\dfrac{3t}{?} = t$

29. $r + 7 - (4 + 3) = \underline{\;?\;}$

30. $9 + m - 9 \underline{\;?\;} m$

31. $5(a + b) = 5a + \underline{\;?\;}$

32. $6x + 6y = \underline{\;?\;} (x + y)$

33. $\dfrac{4p}{(5 - ?)} = p$

34. $5(r - 6) = 5r - \underline{\;?\;}$

35. $3x + \underline{\;?\;} = 3x$

36. $q - 9 + 3^2 = \underline{\;?\;}$

37. $y \times 1 \underline{\;?\;} y$

CRITICAL THINKING **True or false? Correct the false statements.**
(Hint: Substitute different values for the variables.)

38. $n^2 \times 1 = n^2$ for all values of n

39. $b + 0 = b$ for all values of b

40. $\dfrac{n}{n} = 1$ for all values of n except zero

41. $2(n - m) > 0$ for all values of m

42. $n \times n = 2n$ for all values of n

43. $(a \times 1) + 0 = 0$ for all values of a

44. $y \times y \times y = 3y$ for all values of y

45. $\dfrac{0}{c} = c$ for all values of c

46. $a(b + c) = (a \times b) + (a \times c)$ for all values of a, b, and c

47. $a + b \neq b + a$ for all values of a and b

48. $x + (y + z) \neq (x + y) + z$ for all values of x, y, and z

49. If $(a + b) = c$, then $(c - b) = a$ for all values of a, b, and c.

50. If $(a \times b) = c$, then $(c \div b) = a$ for all values of a, b, and c.

3-6 Addition and Subtraction Equations

Equation: a mathematical statement of equality.
Both sides of an equation name the same number.

To solve an equation, find the number to substitute for the variable that makes the mathematical statement true.

Think about a balance scale.
It suggests a way to solve equations.

Addition Equation: Solve: $x + 6 = 9$

- *Subtract* the number added to x from *both* sides of the equation.

$$x + 6 - 6 = 9 - 6$$

- Simplify. The solution is 3.

$$x = 3 \quad \text{Solution}$$

- To check, substitute 3 for x.

$$x + 6 = 9$$
$$3 + 6 = 9$$
$$9 = 9$$

Subtraction Equation: Solve: $x - 7 = 11$

- *Add* the number subtracted from x to *both* sides of the equation.

$$x - 7 + 7 = 11 + 7$$

- Simplify. The solution is 18.

$$x = 18 \quad \text{Solution}$$

- To check, substitute 18 for x.

$$x - 7 = 11$$
$$18 - 7 = 11$$
$$11 = 11$$

> Addition and subtraction are inverse operations. One "undoes" the other.

---

1. In an addition or subtraction equation, solve by adding or subtracting:
   a. 6 from both sides.
   b. a number and its opposite.
   c. the same number from both sides.
   d. zero.

2. Which of these should be solved by adding 9 to both sides?
   a. $9s$
   b. $18 - t = 9$
   c. $x + 9 = 18$
   d. $x - 9 = 18$

3. Which of these should be solved by subtracting 2 from both sides?
   a. $x + 2 = 32$
   b. $x - 2 = 32$
   c. $\dfrac{x}{2} = 32$
   d. $2x = 32$

4. Which of these shows that subtraction "undoes" addition?
   a. $z + 5 = 15$, so $z = 15 - 5$
   b. $z - 7 = 17$, so $z = 17 + 7$

5. Which of these shows that addition is the inverse operation of subtraction?
   a. $d - 4 = 8$, so $d = 8 + 4$
   b. $d + 4 = 8$, so $d = 8 - 4$

Solve.

6. $x + 8 = 11$ **7.** $r + 7 = 11$ **8.** $h - 16 = 94$

9. $s + 29 = 46$ **10.** $s - 27 = 59$ **11.** $29 + b = 100$

12. $t + 100 = 101$ **13.** $a - 9 = 2$ **14.** $t - 43 = 10$

15. $r - 201 = 0$ **16.** $1 + b = 1$ **17.** $s - 48 = 172$

18. $x - 88 = 100$ **19.** $y - 7 = 208$ **20.** $24 + c = 72$

21. $55 + x = 101$ **22.** $8 + r = 16$ **23.** $a + 79 = 485$

24. $t - 10 = 0$ **25.** $z - 1.1 = 9.9$ **26.** $d + 1.2 = 2.5$

Select the correct answer; then solve.

27. A number increased by 12 is 57.

    a. $57 + 12 = a$ **b.** $a + 12 = 57$ **c.** $a - 57 = 12$

28. A number decreased by 6 is 5.

    a. $a - 6 = 5$ **b.** $6 - 5 = a$ **c.** $11 - 5 = 6$

29. A number added to 14 is 36.

    a. $36 + 14 = x$ **b.** $x - 36 = 14$ **c.** $14 + x = 36$

Solve.

30. When 14 eighth graders got on the school bus, there was a total of 42 students on the bus. How many were on the bus before the eighth graders came?

31. The number of absentees at Drake Junior High School on Friday was 42. The total attendance that day was 914. How many students are enrolled at Drake Junior High School?

32. A shipment of canned goods contained 56 damaged items. There were 2824 cans in good condition. How many cans were shipped in all?

 **CALCULATOR ACTIVITY**

Find the value of each expression when $a = 5$, $b = 2$, and $c = 4$. Then copy and complete the puzzle. The numbers in connecting boxes should total 1200.

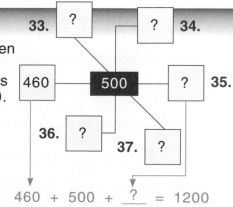

33. $13a(b + c) - 15$ **34.** $11abc \div (3c - 10)$

35. $(3a - 4b)38 - (a^2 + 1)$

36. $\dfrac{(188 + 25c)}{b + c} \times ab$ **37.** $\dfrac{8112}{ac + 3b} + (2c + a)$

$460 + 500 + \underline{\ ?\ } = 1200$

3-7 Multiplication and Division Equations

Addition and subtraction are *inverse* operations.

To "undo" adding 3, subtract 3.

Similarly, multiplication and division are *inverse* operations.

To "undo" multiplying by 3, divide by 3.

Multiplication Equation:

Solve: $8n = 32$

- Divide both sides of the equation by 8. $\dfrac{8n}{8} = \dfrac{32}{8}$
- Simplify. The solution is 4. $n = 4$ Solution
- To check, substitute 4 for n.

$$8n = 32$$
$$8(4) = 32$$
$$32 = 32$$

Multiplication and division are inverse operations. One "undoes" the other.

Division Equation:

Solve: $\dfrac{x}{5} = 7$

- Multiply both sides of the equation by 5. $\dfrac{x}{5} \times 5 = 7 \times 5$
- Simplify. The solution is 35. $x = 35$ Solution
- To check, substitute 35 for x.

$$\dfrac{x}{5} = 7$$
$$\dfrac{35}{5} = 7$$
$$7 = 7$$

1. Which of these equations would you solve by multiplying both sides by 2?

   a. $x + 2 = 25$ **b.** $2x = 18$ **c.** $\dfrac{x}{2} = 3$

2. Which of these equations would you solve by dividing both sides by 6?

   a. $x - 6 = 10$ **b.** $6x = 24$ **c.** $\dfrac{x}{6} = 36$

3. Which equation would you solve by multiplying both sides by 9?

   a. $27x = 81$ **b.** $x + 5 = 45$ **c.** $\dfrac{x}{9} = 2$

4. Which equation would you solve by dividing both sides by 20?

   a. $20x = 120$ **b.** $x = 60$ **c.** $\dfrac{x}{8} = 80$

Solve. (The first two are done.)

5. $\dfrac{x}{7} = 8 \longrightarrow \dfrac{x}{7} \times 7 = 8 \times 7 \longrightarrow x = 56$ **6.** $5x = 10 \longrightarrow \dfrac{5x}{5} = \dfrac{10}{5} \longrightarrow x = 2$

7. $4a = 16$ **8.** $8s = 32$ **9.** $\dfrac{r}{5} = 75$ **10.** $\dfrac{t}{4} = 10$

11. $16r = 96$ **12.** $36x = 108$ **13.** $\dfrac{b}{15} = 120$ **14.** $\dfrac{x}{19} = 10$

Solve.

15. $3c = 42$ **16.** $4a = 0$ **17.** $8 = 24d$ **18.** $48 = \dfrac{y}{3}$

19. $\dfrac{a}{12} = 11$ **20.** $11 = \dfrac{z}{8}$ **21.** $8s = 14.4$ **22.** $18x = 10.8$

23. $x \div 5 = 165$ **24.** $\dfrac{t}{4} = 14$ **25.** $\dfrac{b}{1.2} = 7$ **26.** $\dfrac{a}{11} = 8.8$

Choose the correct equation; then solve.

27. 9 times a number is equal to 72.

    a. $9n = 72$ **b.** $\dfrac{9}{n} = 72$ **c.** $72n = 9$

28. Divide some number by 14. The quotient is 6.

    a. $\dfrac{14}{b} = 6$ **b.** $\dfrac{b}{14} = 6$ **c.** $14 \div 6 = b$

29. A number divided by 10 is equal to 15.

    a. $n \div 15 = 10$ **b.** $n \cdot 10 = 15$ **c.** $n \div 10 = 15$

30. When 128 is divided by a number, the quotient is 8.

    a. $128 \div 8 = n$ **b.** $\dfrac{n}{128} = 8$ **c.** $\dfrac{128}{n} = 8$

31. The product of two factors is 225. One factor is 5. What is the other?

    a. $\dfrac{5}{x} = 225$ **b.** $5x = 225$ **c.** $5 + x = 225$

Solve.

32. Ushers divided the concert programs into 5 equal stacks. Each stack had 7426 programs. How many programs were there in all?

33. For the class party each student contributed $2.00. The total contributed was $54. How many students contributed?

Exercise 34

34. A piece of wood was cut into 12 equal pieces. The wood was originally 420 cm long. How long was each piece of wood?

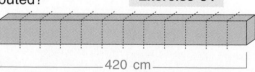

420 cm

Equations with More Than One Operation

In an equation that has more than one operation, *reverse* the order of operations to solve:

- Undo additions or subtractions first.
- Undo multiplications or divisions next.

Solve: $3x + 1 = 13$	
$3x + 1 - 1 = 13 - 1$	Undo addition first. Subtract 1 from both sides.
$3x = 12$	Simplify.
$\dfrac{3x}{3} = \dfrac{12}{3}$	Undo multiplication. Divide both sides by 3.
$x = 4$ Solution	Simplify. The solution is 4.
Check: $(3 \times 4) + 1 = 13$	Substitute to check.
$12 + 1 = 13$	
$13 = 13$	

Solve: $\dfrac{x}{4} - 2 = 3$	
$\dfrac{x}{4} - 2 + 2 = 3 + 2$	Undo subtraction first. Add 2 to both sides.
$\dfrac{x}{4} = 5$	Simplify.
$\dfrac{x}{4} \times 4 = 5 \times 4$	Undo division. Multiply both sides by 4.
$x = 20$ Solution	Simplify. The solution is 20.
Check: $\dfrac{20}{4} - 2 = 3$	Substitute to check.
$5 - 2 = 3$	
$3 = 3$	

For each equation choose the order of operations (a–f) to solve.

1. $2x + 1 = 57$

2. $14x - 42 = 56$

3. $\dfrac{r}{17} + 21 = 31$

4. $3x - 2 = 19$

5. $\dfrac{m}{4} - 3 = 1$

6. $3x + 2 = 20$

7. $\dfrac{s}{12} - 3 = 5$

8. $5x - 10 = 15$

9. $\dfrac{a}{4} + 12 = 26$

10. $\dfrac{t}{7} - 4 = 2$

a. Add; then multiply.

b. Add; then divide.

c. Multiply; then add.

d. Subtract; then multiply.

e. Subtract; then divide.

f. Divide; then subtract.

Solve.

11. $4a + 3 = 15$

12. $7b + 11 = 95$

13. $20 + 3t = 95$

14. $15 + 5n = 40$

15. $9 + 7n = 16$

16. $13 + 10p = 103$

17. $11y - 31 = 90$

18. $5b - 3 = 12$

19. $16n - 10 = 54$

20. $3x + 11 = 17$

21. $\dfrac{t}{9} - 6 = 32$

22. $\dfrac{y}{6} - 1 = 7$

23. $\dfrac{a}{4} - 7 = 10$

24. $16 + \dfrac{y}{2} = 21$

25. $5x - 7 = 38$

Choose the correct equation; then solve.

26. 4 times a number minus 3 is 21.

   a. $4(n - 3) = 21$ **b.** $4n - 3 = 21$ **c.** $4n + 3 = 21$

27. 5 more than 4 times a number is 37.

   a. $37 + 4n = 5$ **b.** $4n + 5 = 37$ **c.** $37 + 5 = 4n$

28. 4 times a number divided by 5, increased by 60, is 68.

   a. $\dfrac{4n}{5} = 68$ **b.** $4n \times 5 = 68$ **c.** $\dfrac{4n}{5} + 60 = 68$

Solve.

29. Four times a number minus 8 is 28.

30. Anna used 34 grams of iron filings in her second experiment. This is 16 grams more than twice the number of grams used in the first. How many grams were required for the first experiment?

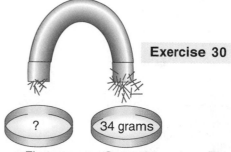

Exercise 30

First   Second

31. A number divided by 6 when added to 12 is 100.

Solve. Use the associative and commutative properties to collect like terms; for example:

$3x + 2x + 4 = 19 \longrightarrow \underbrace{(3x + 2x)}_{5x} + 4 = 19 \longrightarrow 5x + 4 - 4 = 19 - 4 \longrightarrow \dfrac{5x}{5} = \dfrac{15}{5} \longrightarrow x = 3$

32. $n + 3 + 2n = 12$

33. $7c - 2c - 1 = 19$

34. $3n - 10 - 2n = 1$

35. $6t + 2 - 3t = 14$

36. $5a + 2a - 8 = 13$

37. $4 + 2d + 4d = 28$

38. $7 + 5d - 1d = 35$

39. $7y + 10 + 2y = 91$

40. $8y - 3 - 6y = 7$

3-9 Equations with Grouping Symbols

Solve for *n*: 5(*n* – 3) = 40

To solve an equation with parentheses, use *one* of these two methods:

I Distributive Property $a(b + c) = ab + ac$

Distribute 5 across (*n* – 3).	$5(n - 3) = 40$
Multiply each term by 5. ⟶	$5n - 15 = 40$
Add 15. ⟶	$5n - 15 + 15 = 40 + 15$
Divide by 5. ⟶	$\dfrac{5n}{5} = \dfrac{55}{5}$
	$n = 11$ Solution

II Inverse Operations

Since (*n* – 3) was multiplied by 5,	$5(n - 3) = 40$
do the *inverse,* divide by 5. ⟶	$\dfrac{5(n - 3)}{5} = \dfrac{40}{5}$
	$n - 3 = 8$
Add 3. ⟶	$n - 3 + 3 = 8 + 3$
	$n = 11$ Solution
Check. ⟶	$5(n - 3) = 40$
	$5(11 - 3) = 40$
	$(5 \times 11) - (5 \times 3) = 40$
	$55 - 15 = 40$
	$40 = 40$

Solve each equation by using the distributive property.

1. 3(*a* + 5) = 36   **2.** 2(*x* + 3) = 30   **3.** 9(*y* + 1) = 9

4. 20(3 + *k*) = 100   **5.** 6(*r* – 2) = 72   **6.** 7(*c* – 1) = 56

7. 15(*m* – 10) = 600   **8.** 8(*n* + 5) = 64   **9.** 12(*b* + 3) = 84

Solve each equation by using inverse operations.

10. 2(*y* + 9) = 50   **11.** 3(*x* + 6) = 45   **12.** 9(*k* – 6) = 81

13. 4(*s* – 5) = 12   **14.** 12(*t* – 4) = 36   **15.** 6(*y* – 8) = 24

16. 10(*c* + 3) = 90   **17.** (*b* + 5)25 = 400   **18.** (*m* – 12)7 = 140

Solve each equation.

19. $10(4 + x) = 200$

20. $16(a + 5) = 96$

21. $(t - 7)8 = 88$

22. $4(n + 10) = 60$

23. $3(x - 8) = 3$

24. $(k - 9)4 = 0$

Fraction Bars in Equations

The *fraction bar* acts as a *grouping symbol*.

Solve: $\dfrac{n + 2}{3} + 11 = 15$ Think: $\dfrac{(n + 2)}{3} + 11 = 15$

Use inverse operations to solve such equations.

Subtract 11. $\longrightarrow$ $\dfrac{n + 2}{3} + 11 - 11 = 15 - 11$

Multiply by 3. $\longrightarrow$ $\dfrac{n + 2}{3} \times 3 = 4 \times 3$

Subtract 2. $\longrightarrow$ $n + 2 - 2 = 12 - 2$

$$n = 10 \quad \text{Solution}$$

Check. $\longrightarrow$ $\dfrac{n + 2}{3} + 11 = 15$ $\longrightarrow$ $\dfrac{10 + 2}{3} + 11 = 15$

$$\dfrac{12}{3} + 11 = 15$$

$$4 + 11 = 15$$

$$15 = 15$$

Solve each equation.

25. $\dfrac{a - 1}{5} + 5 = 10$

26. $\dfrac{b + 7}{2} + 6 = 11$

27. $\dfrac{2t + 1}{3} - 3 = 2$

28. $\dfrac{3x - 1}{2} + 7 = 14$

29. $\dfrac{n + 3}{4} - 6 = 3$

30. $\dfrac{c - 5}{7} - 2 = 0$

31. $\dfrac{4d + 1}{3} - 4 = 3$

32. $\dfrac{6r - 3}{7} + 2 = 5$

33. $\dfrac{5y - 2}{3} + 10 = 16$

Write an equation and solve.

34. The product of 5 and the difference between a number and 7 is 75. What is the number?

35. When 10 is added to half the sum of a number and 8, the result is 30. What is the number?

Set: a collection of objects called *elements* or *members*. A set is named by a capital letter, and the names of its members are placed between braces.

$A = \{2, 4, 6, 8\}$ ⟶ Reads: "*A* is the set whose members are 2, 4, 6, and 8" or "the set of even numbers between 1 and 10."

Finite set has a *countable* number of members.

$D = \{3, 6, 9, 12\}$ ⟶ Reads: "*D* is the set of first four nonzero multiples of 3."

Infinite set is a set that has *no end* to the number of its members.

$E = \{0, 4, 8, 12, \ldots\}$ ⟶ Reads: "*E* is the set of all multiples of 4."

Three dots represent the infinity of the numbers.

Empty set is a set having *no members*. Its symbol is "ϕ".

$\phi = \{$all walking guppies$\}$

$\phi = \{$all odd numbers divisible by two$\}$

These sets have *no members.*

Subset is a part of a set. Its symbol is $\subset$.

If $A = \{2, 4, 6, 8\}$, then one subset, S, is: $S = \{4, 6\}$ or $\{4, 6\} \subset A$

Inequality: a mathematical sentence expressing an unequal relationship and using one of these symbols: $\neq, <, >, \leq,$ **or** $\geq$.

$$x - 5 \neq 7 \qquad\qquad y + 3 \geq 16$$

Replacement set, *R*, is the set of numbers from which replacements for the variable in an inequality may be taken.

Three dots indicate numbers are omitted.

$R = \{1, 2, 3, \ldots, 10\}$
If $x > 4$, and R is the set of whole numbers from 1 to 10, then only $x = 5, 6, 7, 8, 9, 10$ will make the inequality true.
If $R = \{0, 1, 2, 3, \ldots\}$, or R is the set of whole numbers, x can be any whole number greater than 4.

Solution set, *S*, is a subset of the replacement set, *R*. It is the set of numbers taken from the replacement set that makes the inequality true.

Describe these sets in words.

1. $F = \{2, 4, 6, 8, \ldots\}$ 2. $G = \{6, 8, 10, \ldots\}$ 3. $H = \{21, 22, 23, 24, 25\}$

4. $K = \{11, 13, 15, 17, 19, 21\}$ 5. $J = \{100, 101, 102, \ldots, 199\}$

List the members of the set of :

6. multiples of 6.

7. whole numbers between 10 and 20.

8. whole numbers.

9. multiples of 4 that are less than 50.

10. multiples of 5 that are less than 30.

11. odd numbers greater than 5.

12. even numbers less than or equal to 10.

Complete. (The first one is done.)

	Inequality	Replacement Set	Solution Set
13.	$m > 3$	$\{0, 1, 2, 3, 4\}$	$\{4\}$
14.	$x \leq 4$	$\{0, 1, 2, 3, 4\}$	
15.	$9 < r$	$\{5, 6, 7, \ldots, 25\}$	
16.	$11 \neq z$	$\{5, 6, 7, 8, 9\}$	
17.	$y \geq 21$	$\{20, 25, 30, \ldots, 50\}$	
18.	$f \neq 7$	$\{100, 99, 98, \ldots, 1\}$	
19.	$19 \neq d$	$\{17, 19, 21, \ldots, 33\}$	
20.	$26 \leq t$	$\{100, 200, 300, \ldots\}$	
21.	$3 \geq c$	$\{0, 1, 2, \ldots, 10\}$	
22.	$h \neq 13$	$\{12, 14, 16, 18, 20\}$	
23.	$w \leq 29$	$\{50, 40, 30, \ldots, 10\}$	
24.	$p > 70$	$\{1, 2, 3, \ldots, 180\}$	
25.	$b > 6$	$\{0, 1, 2, 3\}$	
26.	$a + 5 < 12$	$\{0, 1, 2, 3, \ldots, 10\}$	
27.	$a - 5 = 15$	$\{0, 5, 10, \ldots, 50\}$	

Use the solution sets in exercises 13–27 to answer the following.

28. Which sets are subsets of the whole numbers?

29. Which sets are subsets of the set of multiples of ten?

30. Which sets are subsets of the set of even numbers?

31. Which sets are subsets of the set of odd numbers?

32. Which sets are subsets of multiples of five?

33. Are there any empty sets?

34. Are there any infinite sets?

Formula: a mathematical sentence that gives a simplified way of solving particular problems. Each variable represents some part of the problem.

$A = \ell w$ ⟶ A: area; ℓ: length; w: width

$P = 2(\ell + w)$ ⟶ P: perimeter; ℓ: length; w: width

$d = rt$ ⟶ d: distance; r: rate of speed; t: time

A train travels 120 mph. If the rail distance between two cities is 300 miles, how long does it take the train to travel this distance?

To solve a problem using formulas:

$d = rt$

- Write the formula that will solve the problem.

  300 miles = (120 mph) t

- Substitute the numbers given in the problem.

  $300 = 120t$ ⟶ $120t = 300$

- Solve for the unknown variable.

  $t = \dfrac{300}{120}$ ⟶ $t = 2\frac{1}{2}$ hr Solution

If a plane traveled 1375 miles in 5 hours, how fast did it go per hour?

$$d = rt$$

$1375 = r(5)$ ⟶ $1375 = 5r$ ⟶ $5r = 1375$

$r = \dfrac{1375}{5}$ ⟶ $r = 275$ miles per hour, or 275 mph Solution

What kind of problem does each formula solve? Tell the meaning of each variable.

1. $A = \frac{1}{2} bh$
2. $P = 4s$
3. $V = \ell wh$
4. $A = \pi r^2$
5. $C = \pi d$
6. $C = 2\pi r$
7. $A = s^2$
8. $I = prt$

Solve for the missing variable.

9. $A_, = \frac{1}{2} bh$ when $b = 10'$ and $h = 15'$
10. $P = 4s$ when $s = 5'$
11. $V = \ell wh$ when $\ell = 6'$, $w = 3'$, and $h = 9'$
12. $C = \pi d$ when $d = 35'$
13. $A = s^2$ when $A = 225$ square yards
14. $A = \pi r^2$ when $r = 7'$
15. $V = e^3$ when $e = 6'$
16. $P = 4s$ when $P = 36'$
17. $V = \ell wh$ when $V = 100$ cubic feet, $w = 2'$, and $h = 5'$
18. $A = \frac{1}{2} bh$ when $A = 200$ square feet and $h = 10'$

Write a formula for each.

19. Commission = Total Sales times Rate of Commission
20. Discount = List Price times Rate of Discount
21. Tax = Marked Price times Rate of Tax
22. Rate of Discount = Discount divided by List Price
23. To find the principal, given the interest, rate, and time.

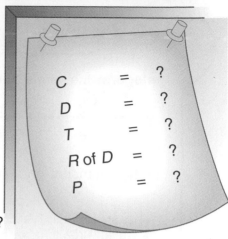

C = ?
D = ?
T = ?
R of D = ?
P = ?

Solve, using formulas.
(Hint: Remember the five problem-solving steps.)

24. How long will it take $2500 to earn $400 at 4% per year?

25. A pool 75 feet long and 60 feet wide contains 54,000 cubic feet of water. What is its depth?

26. An aquarium 15 feet long and 3 feet wide contains 360 cubic feet of water. Find its depth.

27. The outside rim of a cylindrical can measures 13.2 inches. What is the radius of the lid of the can? (Use $\frac{22}{7}$ for π.)

28. A triangular field has a base of 65 rods and an altitude of 124 rods. How many square rods does the field cover?

29. A triangle contains 1020 square rods. If the base is 40 rods, what is its altitude?

30. A square board is 1.2 feet long. Find its area in square yards.

31. The perimeter of a square tile is 28.8 inches. What is its area?

32. The edge of a cube is 10 m. Find its volume.

33. If a circular track has a diameter of 1.5 miles, what is its circumference?

CRITICAL **THINKING**

Solve. Use what you have learned about solving equations.

Example: $P = 2(\ell + w)$, so $\ell = \dfrac{P}{2} - w$

34. $V = \ell wh$, so $w = $?   35. $A = \frac{1}{2} bh$, so $b = $?   36. $P = 4s$, so $s = $?

37. $I = prt$, so $t = $?   38. $C = \pi d$, so $d = $?   39. $A = \ell w$, so $w = $?

40. A label states that a plastic dish can withstand temperatures to 75°C. The dishwasher manual states that the drying cycle temperature is 160°F. Should the dish be put in the dishwasher? (Use: $\frac{9}{5}$ C + 32 = F.)

Not above 75°C

3-12 | Integers

Integers: the whole numbers and their opposites.

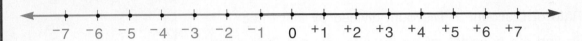

Of two numbers on a number line, the number *to the right* has the greater value.

$^+1 > {}^-3$: positive 1 *is greater than* negative 3.

Use a number line to order integers.

From least to greatest $^+4$, 0, $^-11$, $^+1$, $^-2$ is $^-11$, $^-2$, 0, $^+1$, $^+4$.

Every integer has an *opposite* that is the same distance
from 0 on the number line but is in the opposite direction.

The opposite of $^+7$ is $^-7$. ⟶ $^-(^+7) = {}^-7$

The opposite of $^-5$ is $^+5$. ⟶ $^-(^-5) = {}^+5$

Name the letter that matches each integer on the number line.

1. $^+3$	2. $^+12$	3. $^-9$

4. $^+15$ 5. $^-21$ 6. $^-15$

Arrange in order from least to greatest.

7. $^+5$, $^-6$, $^-4$, $^+1$ 8. 0, $^-3$, $^-20$, $^+7$, $^+9$ 9. $^-8$, $^+3$, $^+8$, $^-10$, $^-5$

10. $^+18$, 0, $^-10$, $^-15$ 11. $^+2$, $^-11$, $^-2$, $^-16$, $^+12$ 12. $^-21$, $^+12$, $^+14$, $^-30$, $^-7$

Write the opposite of each integer.

13. $^+2$ 14. $^+11$ 15. $^-9$ 16. $^-2$ 17. $^+15$ 18. $^+53$

19. $^-15$ 20. $^-1$ 21. 0   22. $^+42$ 23. $^-81$ 24. $^-100$

25. $^+42$ 26. $^+19$ 27. $^-21$ 28. $^-12$ 29. $^+31$ 30. $^+17$

31. Which integers in exercises 13–30 are whole numbers?

Write an integer for each.

32. $^-(^+3)$ **33.** $^-(^-6)$ **34.** $^-(^-4)$ **35.** $^-(^+8)$ **36.** $^-(^+2)$

37. $^-(^-5)$ **38.** $^-(^-9)$ **39.** $^-(^+7)$ **40.** $^-(^+1)$ **41.** $^-(0)$

Compare. Write < or >.

42. $^+3$ __?__ $^+9$ **43.** $^+26$ __?__ $^+10$ **44.** 0 __?__ $^+6$ **45.** $^+3$ __?__ 0

46. $^-6$ __?__ $^+3$ **47.** $^+7$ __?__ $^-9$ **48.** $^+5$ __?__ $^-4$ **49.** $^-8$ __?__ $^+7$

50. $^-10$ __?__ $^-1$ **51.** $^-15$ __?__ $^-20$ **52.** $^-7$ __?__ 0 **53.** 0 __?__ $^-14$

Absolute Value

The **absolute value** of a number is the distance that number is from zero on the number line.

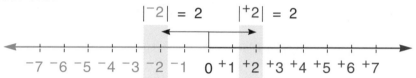

$$|^-2| = 2 \qquad |^+2| = 2$$

The absolute value of $^-2$ is: $|^-2| = 2$ ← distance from zero

The absolute value of $^+2$ is: $|^+2| = 2$ ← distance from zero

The absolute value of 0 is: $|0| = 0$ ←

Compare. Write <, =, or >.

54. $|^-5|$ __?__ $|^+5|$ **55.** $|^+8|$ __?__ 8 **56.** $|^-15|$ __?__ $^-15$

57. $|4-4|$ __?__ $|0|$ **58.** $|3+7|$ __?__ $|^-10|$ **59.** $|^+2|$ __?__ $|^-2|$

CRITICAL   THINKING

True or false? Explain.

60. Zero is an integer.

61. Zero is a whole number.

62. The opposite of the opposite of $^+5$ is $^+5$.

63. The opposite of the opposite of $^-12$ is $^-12$.

64. All whole numbers are integers.

65. All integers are whole numbers.

66. All integers are positive.

67. All whole numbers are positive.

68. The opposite of the absolute value of $^-3$ is $^-3$.

69. The opposite of the absolute value of $^+5$ is $^-5$.

3-13 Operations with Integers

Addition of Integers

Like Signs (+, + OR −, −)
- Find the sum.
- Use the sign of the addends.

$$^-6 + {}^-11 = {}^-17$$

Unlike Signs (+, −)
- Find the difference.
- Use the sign of the addend having greater absolute value.

$$^+14 + {}^-9 = {}^+5$$

Subtraction of Integers

The same as adding the opposite of the subtrahend

$$^+7 - {}^+10 = \underline{\ ?\ } \longrightarrow {}^+7 + {}^-10 = {}^-3$$

Multiplication of Integers

Like Signs (+, + OR −, −)
- Product is positive.

$$^-6 \times {}^-7 = {}^+42$$

Unlike Signs (+, −)
- Product is negative.

$$^+5 \times {}^-8 = {}^-40$$

Division of Integers

Like Signs (+, + OR −, −)
- Quotient is positive.

$$^+30 \div {}^+6 = {}^+5$$

Unlike Signs (+, −)
- Quotient is negative.

$$^-45 \div {}^+9 = {}^-5$$

Add.

1. $^+3 + {}^+4$
2. $^-1 + {}^-6$
3. $^+6 + {}^-4$
4. $^-1 + {}^+7$

5. $^-5 + {}^+3$
6. $^-8 + {}^+1$
7. $^+9 + {}^-10$
8. $^+3 + {}^-11$

9. $^+2 + {}^-2$
10. $^-7 + 0$
11. $0 + {}^+12$
12. $^-8 + {}^+8$

Subtract.

13. $^+4 - {}^+8$
14. $^-2 - {}^-6$
15. $^+8 - {}^-3$
16. $^+9 - {}^-12$

17. $^-10 - {}^-6$
18. $^+9 - {}^+4$
19. $^-6 - {}^+15$
20. $^-3 - {}^+11$

21. $^+5 - {}^+11$
22. $^+16 - {}^-7$
23. $0 - {}^-13$
24. $0 - {}^+26$

25. $^-16 - {}^-20$
26. $^+16 - {}^+30$
27. $^-11 - {}^-11$
28. $^+14 - {}^-14$

88

Multiply.

29. $^+7 \times {}^+11$ **30.** $^+6 \times {}^+8$ **31.** $^-3 \times {}^-6$ **32.** $^-2 \times {}^-12$

33. $^-7 \times {}^+6$ **34.** $^-4 \times {}^+12$ **35.** $^+8 \times {}^-7$ **36.** $^+9 \times {}^-4$

37. $^-5 \times {}^-5$ **38.** $^-7 \times {}^+7$ **39.** $^-9 \times 0$ **40.** $0 \times {}^+13$

Divide.

41. $^-108 \div {}^-12$ **42.** $^+60 \div {}^+3$ **43.** $^+72 \div {}^+12$ **44.** $^-96 \div {}^-8$

45. $\dfrac{^-36}{^-4}$ **46.** $\dfrac{^-96}{^-12}$ **47.** $\dfrac{^-30}{^+15}$ **48.** $\dfrac{^+48}{^-6}$

49. $\dfrac{^+63}{^-7}$ **50.** $\dfrac{^-84}{^+7}$ **51.** $\dfrac{^-200}{^+25}$ **52.** $\dfrac{^+175}{^-25}$

Solve each addition or subtraction equation. (The first two are done.)

53. $n + {}^+3 = {}^-7 \longrightarrow n + {}^+3 - {}^+3 = {}^-7 - {}^+3 \longrightarrow n = {}^-10$

54. $a - {}^-6 = {}^+5 \longrightarrow a - {}^-6 + {}^-6 = {}^+5 + {}^-6 \longrightarrow a = {}^-1$

55. $^+4 + c = {}^+12$ **56.** $^-6 + r = {}^-8$ **57.** $^-3 + d = {}^+2$

58. $e + {}^+7 = {}^-3$ **59.** $h - {}^+2 = {}^+11$ **60.** $m - {}^+4 = {}^+9$

61. $y - {}^-3 = {}^-7$ **62.** $x - {}^-5 = {}^-16$ **63.** $b - {}^-8 = {}^+5$

Solve each multiplication or division equation. (The first two are done.)

64. $^-5n = {}^+20 \longrightarrow \dfrac{^-5n}{^-5} = \dfrac{^+20}{^-5} \longrightarrow n = {}^-4$

65. $\dfrac{t}{^+7} = {}^-3 \longrightarrow \dfrac{t}{^+7} \times {}^+7 = {}^-3 \times {}^+7 \longrightarrow t = {}^-21$

66. $^+11s = {}^-66$ **67.** $^-5d = {}^+45$ **68.** $^+13a = 0$ **69.** $^-14b = {}^-14$

70. $\dfrac{h}{^-4} = {}^-20$ **71.** $\dfrac{n}{^+8} = {}^+15$ **72.** $\dfrac{c}{^+10} = 0$ **73.** $\dfrac{r}{^-9} = {}^-9$

Solve.

74. Jan's checking account has a balance of $^-\$35$. If she deposits $115 in her account, what is the new balance?

75. A number is multiplied by $^+2$, then multiplied by $^-3$. The result is $^+12$. What is the number?

76. A number is divided by $^-5$, then divided by $^+5$. The result is $^-1$. What is the number?

Fast Fractions

Operations with fractions can be quick and accurate by using the special keys on a fraction calculator.

When a student enters 12 ÷ 5 on a calculator, the display shows 2.4.

Fraction calculators can show the quotient in a different way.

 This key is called the *integer divide* key. The key gives the result of a division problem as an integer or whole number and a remainder.

KEY-IN

 press **5** **=**

DISPLAY READS

Quotient   Remainder

12 ÷ 5 is 2 Remainder 2.

 This key is used to express a fraction as a ratio of the numerator to the denominator.

KEY-IN

8 press **/** **9**

DISPLAY READS

 8/9

The ratio 8:9 = $\frac{8}{9}$ as a fraction.

 The *simplify* key is used to express a fraction in lowest terms or simplest form. A fraction calculator will simplify a fraction step by step or all at once.

KEY-IN

8 **/** **40** press **Simp** **=**   *DISPLAY* 4/20 press **Simp** **=**   *DISPLAY* 2/10 press **Simp** **=**   *DISPLAY* 1/5

or

KEY-IN

8 **/** **4** **0** press **Simp** **8** **=**   *DISPLAY* 1/5

└─Greatest Common Factor

$\frac{8}{40} = \frac{1}{5}$ in lowest terms.

 This key will display an improper fraction as a mixed number.

KEY-IN

5 **0** **/** **1** **9** **A b/c** **=**   *DISPLAY* 2 U 12/19

$\frac{50}{19} = 2\frac{12}{19}$ as a mixed number.

 This key enters the whole number part of a mixed number.
Add $4\frac{5}{12} + \frac{3}{8}$

KEY-IN

4 **Unit** **5** **/** **1** **2** **+** **3** **/** **8** **=** 4 U 19/24

$4\frac{5}{12} + \frac{3}{8} = 4\frac{19}{24}$ Sum

Express each ratio as a fraction in simplest form.

1. 12:15
2. 140:84
3. 72:32
4. 104:78

5. Express the fractions in exercises 2–4 as mixed numbers.

6. Use a different type of calculator to complete exercises 1–4. Describe the results. (Hint: Key in 12 ÷ 15)

Compute. (Express improper fractions as mixed numbers.)

7. $\frac{5}{24} + \frac{6}{15}$

8. $11\frac{5}{7} + 9\frac{3}{4}$

9. $\frac{19}{25} - \frac{2}{7}$

10. $1\frac{4}{9} - \frac{16}{21}$

11. $\frac{17}{20} + 1\frac{8}{9}$

12. $2\frac{8}{11} + 1\frac{4}{5}$

13. $\frac{5}{6} \div 3\frac{10}{11}$

14. $10\frac{2}{3} \div 6\frac{1}{5}$

Use the integer division key to complete exercises 15–18.

15. 58 ÷ 3
16. 70 ÷ 9
17. 41 ÷ 18
18. 122 ÷ 11

19. Use the ⎡÷⎤ key to complete exercises 15–18. Compare your results.

Solve.

20. Find the value of $\frac{2}{3} + \frac{6}{7}$ in simplest terms.

21. Add $\frac{8}{9} + \left(\frac{3}{4} + \frac{1}{2} \right)$.

22. A video tape that plays for 90 minutes will play $\frac{90}{60}$ hours. Express this as a mixed number in simplest terms.

23. The driveway which measures $18\frac{2}{3}$ ft by $6\frac{4}{5}$ ft is to be repaved. What is the area of the surface to be repaved?

24. What is the total weight of 4 packages weighing $3\frac{2}{3}$ lb, $5\frac{1}{4}$ lb, $6\frac{7}{8}$ lb, and $4\frac{5}{8}$ lb?

25. Ted, Hank, and Lucy each picked $1\frac{2}{3}$ bushels of apples an hour for $3\frac{1}{10}$ hours. How many bushels did they pick altogether?

26. A bank pays interest annually on a CD at the rate of $6\frac{1}{4}$%. Find to the nearest cent, the interest for one year on an investment of $890.

Problem: Althea worked on her computer project four times as long as Bernie worked on hers. If together they worked a total of 15 hours, how long did each girl spend on her own project?

1 IMAGINE

Draw and label a picture of Althea's (A) and Bernie's (B) work.

2 NAME

Facts: Bernie: h hours on project
               Althea: 4 times Bernie's hours, h
               Total time: 15 hours

Question: How much time did each spend on her project?

3 THINK

Look at the drawing:
     h = hours Bernie spent
     $4h$ = Althea's hours, which were 4 times Bernie's hours
$h + 4h = 15$

Can you solve this equation?

4 COMPUTE

$h + 4h = 15$

$5h = 15$ Divide both sides by 5.

$\dfrac{5h}{5} = \dfrac{15}{5}$

$h = 3$ hours   (time Bernie spent)

$4h = 4 \cdot 3 = 12$ hours   (time Althea spent)

> First combine *like* terms.
> $h + 4h = 5h$

5 CHECK

If 15 hours were spent by both Bernie and Althea, is it reasonable that Bernie spent 3 hours and Althea spent 12 hours? Check your computations by substituting 3 for h in the equations.

$$h + 4h \stackrel{?}{=} 15$$
$$3 + (4 \cdot 3) \stackrel{?}{=} 15$$
$$15 = 15$$

Solve by writing and solving an equation.

1. Ti has 12 coins. He has some quarters, 4 nickels, and one less dime than nickels. How many of each type of coin does he have? How much money does he have in coins?

1 IMAGINE	Draw and label a picture. ⟶	2 NAME ⎯⎯⟶ Facts
		⎯⎯⟶ Question

3 THINK	Let q represent the number of quarters. Write an equation to represent the sum of the coins.

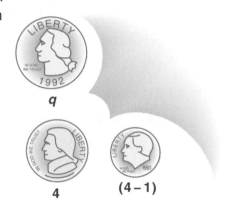

quarters + nickels + dimes = 12

$$q + 4 + (4-1) = 12$$
$$q + 4 + 3 = 12$$
$$q + 7 = 12$$

Solve this equation to find the number of quarters. Then compute the total amount of money in coins.

4 COMPUTE	⟶	5 CHECK

Total number of coins = ___?___
Total money = ___?___

2. The sum of a number and 14 is 20. What is the number?

3. The sum of seven and three times a number is sixteen. Find the number.

4. The difference between twenty-four and a number is fifteen. Find the number.

5. Four times a number increased by seven is fifty-five. What is the number?

6. Seven more than half a number is nine. What is the number?

7. A jet plane is traveling at 600 mph. At this rate, how long will a trip of 4800 miles take?

8. One number is 6 times another. The greater number is 1680. What is the lesser number?

9. One less than twice a number is 21. Find the number.

10. The length of a rectangle is twice its width. The length is 18 cm. Find the area.

11. One class has 9 fewer boys than girls. Together there are thirty-three students. What is the number of boys in the class? The number of girls?

12. A team scored 8 more points during the second half than during the first half. The team scored 62 points in all. How many points did they score in each half of the game?

3-16 Problem Solving: Applications

Choose the correct equation. Solve.

1. Four less than twice a number is $^-16$. Find the number.

   a. $4 < 2(^-16)n$ **b.** $4 - 2n = \,^-16$ **c.** $2n - 4 = \,^-16$

2. What number added to $^-16$ is half $^-4$?

   a. $n + \,^-4 = \,^-16$ **b.** $^-16 + n = \dfrac{^-4}{2}$ **c.** $\dfrac{^-16 + n}{2} = \,^-4$

3. Half the sum of a number and $^-6$ is $^-4$. What is the number?

   a. $2(n + \,^-6) = \,^-4$ **b.** $\dfrac{^-6n}{2} = \,^-4$ **c.** $\dfrac{n + \,^-6}{2} = \,^-4$

4. The product of $^-4$ and what number doubled is $^-16$?

   a. $^-4(2n) = \,^-16$ **b.** $^-4(n^2) = \,^-16$ **c.** $^-4 + 2n = \,^-16$

5. One fourth of what number when decreased by 6 is $^-16$?

   a. $\dfrac{n}{4} + 6 = \,^-16$ **b.** $\dfrac{n}{4} - 6 = \,^-16$ **c.** $\dfrac{n - 6}{4} = \,^-16$

6. The difference between a number and 6 when divided by $^-4$ equals $^-16$. Find the number.

   a. $\dfrac{n - 6}{^-4} = \,^-16$ **b.** $\dfrac{n + 6}{^-4} = \,^-16$ **c.** $\dfrac{6 - n}{4} = \,^-16$

7. Rico practiced guitar for 10 minutes more than half the time Tom practices. If Rico practices 25 minutes, how long does Tom practice?

8. Each day Shannon exercises 24 minutes less than twice as long as Marlene exercises. If Shannon exercises for 36 minutes, how long does Marlene exercise?

9. If a circular track has a circumference of 5500 yards, what is its diameter? (Use $\dfrac{22}{7}$ for π.)

10. Mr. Sandi's weekly earnings are $85 less than twice his wife's earnings. If Mr. Sandi earned $525 last week, how much money did his wife earn?

11. Jenny has three more than twice the number of compact discs as Joshua. If Jenny has 27 compact discs, how many discs does Joshua own?

12. The school band has 6 members in the percussion section. The brass section is three times larger than the percussion section, and the rest of the band members make up the woodwind section. The band has 39 members altogether. How many members make up the woodwind section?

13. The sum of two numbers is twenty-six. The larger number is six more than four times the smaller number. What are the numbers? (Hint: Let n represent the smaller number and $4n + 6$ represent the larger number.)

14. The difference between two numbers is nineteen. Find the numbers if the smaller number is 2 less than half the larger.

Write and solve each equation.

15. The difference between $^-8$ and a number is $^-15$. Find the number.

16. What number when subtracted from 11 equals $^-20$?

17. Sixteen decreased by a number is $^-13$. What is the number?

18. What number less than $^-29$ is $^-34$?

19. Thirteen minus a number is $^-15$. Find the number.

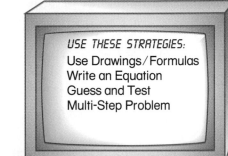

USE THESE STRATEGIES:
Use Drawings/Formulas
Write an Equation
Guess and Test
Multi-Step Problem

20. The width of a rectangle is 5 inches less than the length. If the perimeter is 38 inches, find both dimensions. (Hint: Let n represent the length and $n - 5$ represent the width. Substitute both expressions in the formula $P = 2\ell + 2w$.)

21. The longer side of a parallelogram is 4 cm greater than the shorter side. If the perimeter is 32 cm, what is the length of each side? (Remember: A parallelogram is a quadrilateral.)

22. What are the lengths of each side of this kite if the perimeter is 44 cm?

23. The sum of three consecutive numbers is 78. What is the largest number? (Hint: Let n represent the largest, $n - 1$ the next, and $n - 2$ the smallest.)

24. The sum of four consecutive numbers is $^-14$. Find the numbers.

25. What is the length of the shortest side of this triangle?

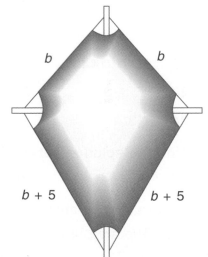

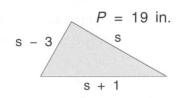

P = 19 in.

CHALLENGE

26. Six times a number equals the sum of that number and $^-20$. What is the number?

95

More Practice

Simplify.

1. $117 \div 9 - 5$ 2. $329 + 6 \times 7$ 3. $12 \times 60 - 29$

4. $628 - 7(528 \div 6)$ 5. $[(12 \times 45) + 504] \div 36$

Write a mathematical or algebraic expression.

6. 4 times the sum of 5 and a number   7. 15 less than 3 times the money

8. the quotient when 4 squared is divided by a number

Evaluate when $s = 3$, $t = 5$, $u = 12$, $x = 6$, $y = 1$, and $z = 10$.

9. $10s - 3t$ 10. $3 + 4(x + y)$ 11. $u + 3(z + t)$ 12. $\dfrac{2(u + x)}{s}$

Write a mathematical sentence to describe the problem situation. Solve.

13. The length of a rectangular box is three times its width. If the width is 28 in., how long is the box?

State whether each is a true or false statement for the given value of each variable.

14. $c + 6 > 13$ when $c = 4$ 15. $4(x + 2) \leq 24$ when $x = 4$

Solve.

16. $6b = 144$ 17. $\dfrac{d}{64} = 9$ 18. $y - 8 = 0$ 19. $32 + x = 109$

20. $\dfrac{b}{6} - 9 = 3$ 21. $3d + 1 = 76$ 22. $35 - 3y = 26$ 23. $15 + \dfrac{a}{5} = 20$

24. $7(3 + n) = 147$ 25. $(c - 12)9 = 0$ 26. $13(d + 6) = 195$

Find the solution set. Replacement set: $\{1, 2, 3, 4, 5\}$.

27. $p > 3$ 28. $c < 6$ 29. $4 \geq d - 1$ 30. $a + 1 \leq 4$

Solve using formulas.

31. The area of a square garden is 225 square yd. What is the length of the garden?

32. How long will it take \$3200 to earn \$320 interest at 5% per year?

Write an integer for each.

33. $^-(^+7)$ 34. $^-(^-2)$ 35. $^-(^+12)$ 36. $^-(^-21)$

Solve.

37. $^+5 + {^+7}$ 38. $^+9 - {^-6}$ 39. $^-15 - {^-21}$ 40. $^+13 - {^+8}$

41. $^+6 \times {^-8}$ 42. $^+64 \div {^-8}$ 43. $\dfrac{^+150}{^+25}$ 44. $^-9 \times {^-4}$

Math Probe

ABSOLUTE VALUE? — |ABSOLUTELY!!|

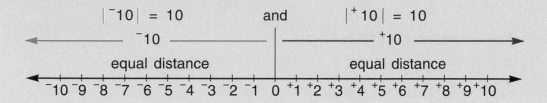

$|^-10| = 10$ and $|^+10| = 10$

$^-10$ $^+10$

equal distance   equal distance

$^-10\ ^-9\ ^-8\ ^-7\ ^-6\ ^-5\ ^-4\ ^-3\ ^-2\ ^-1\ 0\ ^+1\ ^+2\ ^+3\ ^+4\ ^+5\ ^+6\ ^+7\ ^+8\ ^+9\ ^+10$

To solve equations in which the variable is *within* absolute value, study this example:

Solve: $|x + 2| = 6$ ⟶ Think: $|?| = 6$

> What numbers are 6 units from 0?

Since both $^+6$ and $^-6$ are six units from zero, two equations must be solved.

$|^+6| = 6$ $|^-6| = 6$

$x + 2 = {}^+6$ $x + 2 = {}^-6$

$x + 2 \boxed{-2} = 6 \boxed{-2}$ ⟨ Subtract 2 from both sides. ⟩ $x + 2 \boxed{-2} = {}^-6 \boxed{-2}$

$x = 4$ $x = {}^-8$

$|4 + 2| = |^+6| = 6$ ⟨ Check. So, $x = {}^+4; {}^-8$. ⟩ $|^-8 + 2| = |^-6| = 6$

Use this method to solve these equations.

1. $|x + 5| = 11$ 2. $|x - 4| = 2$ 3. $|x - 7| = 12$

4. $|3x| = 9$ 5. $|5x| = 25$ 6. $|\frac{x}{3}| = 8$

7. $|\frac{x}{4}| = 3$ 8. $|2x + 4| = 14$ 9. $|3x + 9| = 12$

10. $|\frac{x}{2} + 6| = 1$ 11. $|\frac{x}{3} - 2| = 3$ 12. $|4x - 8| = 16$

Be careful of equations of this type: $|x| + 2 = 6$

Notice that *only the variable* is within the absolute value symbol.

To solve this equation:

- Transform the equation, leaving $|x|$ alone on one side of the equation. $|x| + 2 - 2 = 6 - 2$
- THINK: $|x| = 4$. So, there are two solutions, $^+4$ and $^-4$.

Use this method to solve these equations.

13. $|x| \times 7 = 63$ 14. $|x| + 1 = 5$ 15. $3|x| - 1 = 5$

Check Your Mastery

Simplify See pp. 64–65

1. $91 + 9 \times 5$
2. $144 \div 6 - 4$
3. $15 \times 30 - 50$
4. $336 - 8(247 \div 13)$
5. $[(23 \times 14) + 310] \div 79$

Write a mathematical or algebraic expression. See pp. 66–67

6. 3 times the sum of 7 and a number
7. 12 more than twice the money
8. the product when 2 is multiplied by four times a number

Evaluate when $s = 4$, $t = 6$, $u = 10$, $x = 1$, $y = 7$, and $z = 0$. See pp. 68–69

9. $7t - 4u$
10. $4 + 5(s + t)$
11. $y + 2(x + z)$
12. $\dfrac{2(u + t)}{s}$

Write and solve a mathematical sentence to describe this. See pp. 70–71

13. The width of a rectangular box is one half its length. If the length is 32 in., how wide is the box?

State whether each is a true or false statement for the given value of each variable. See pp. 72–73

14. $d - 7 \le 6$ when $d = 11$
15. $3(4 + x) > 31$ when $x = 6$

Solve. See pp. 74–81

16. $3f = 39$
17. $\dfrac{e}{72} = 8$
18. $z + 16 = 42$
19. $54 - x = 0$
20. $\dfrac{c}{4} - 3 = 1$
21. $63 - 4t = 55$
22. $4g - 26 = 10$
23. $20 + \dfrac{a}{7} = 26$
24. $3(5 + a) = 63$
25. $(c - 34)7 = 469$
26. $11(b + 2) = 165$

Find the solution set. Replacement set: $\{0, 1, 2, 3, 4\}$. See pp. 82–83

27. $e > 3$
28. $d \le 3$
29. $4 > 3s$
30. $2b - 1 \ge 3$

Solve using formulas. See pp. 84–85

31. The perimeter of a square garden is 56 ft. What is the area of the garden?
32. How long will it take $2500 to earn $450 interest at 6% per year?

Write an integer for each. See pp. 86–87

33. $^-(^-6)$
34. $^-(^+4)$
35. $^-(^-17)$
36. $^-(^+34)$

Solve. See pp. 88–89

37. $^+8 + {}^-4$
38. $^+9 - {}^+7$
39. $^-13 - {}^-16$
40. $^+20 - {}^+12$
41. $^-7 \times {}^+7$
42. $^+56 \div {}^-7$
43. $\dfrac{^+250}{^+50}$
44. $^-6 \times {}^-8$

45. A player loses 8 points four times; then gains 60 points. If the winning score is 50, how many more points does the player need?

4 Rational Numbers

In this chapter you will:

- Identify and compare rational numbers
- Identify properties of rational numbers
- Add and subtract rational numbers
- Solve addition and subtraction equations with rational numbers
- Multiply and divide rational numbers
- Solve multiplication and division equations with rational numbers
- Solve problems: equations with rational numbers

Do you remember?

To solve equations with whole numbers, use *inverse operations*.

$$d + 5 = 9$$
$$d + 5 \boxed{- 5} = 9 \boxed{- 5}$$
$$d = 4$$

$$8x = 48$$
$$\frac{8x}{\boxed{8}} = \frac{48}{\boxed{8}}$$
$$x = 6$$

$$\frac{n}{7} = 1$$
$$\frac{n}{7} \boxed{\times 7} = 1 \boxed{\times 7}$$
$$n = 7$$

Another Bridge to Cross

This mathematician could not seem to stop thinking! He thought so much he developed a whole new area of mathematics called *topology*. Who was he? Find out about one of his puzzles called "The Seven Bridges of Königsberg." With friends, create your own interesting puzzle. Ask others to solve it.

Rational Numbers

▶ **Rational numbers:** any numbers that can be written in the fractional form $\frac{a}{b}$, where a and b are integers and b is not equal to ($\neq$) 0.

▶ **Some subsets of rational numbers:** whole numbers, integers, positive and negative fractions, and terminating and repeating decimals.

Identify to which subset each of these belongs:

$$0, \quad {}^{+}\frac{1}{4}, \quad {}^{+}5\frac{1}{2}, \quad {}^{-}17, \quad {}^{-}0.75, \quad {}^{-}\frac{1}{2}, \quad {}^{-}0.\overline{3}, \quad {}^{-}\frac{8}{2}$$

Rational numbers can be shown on a number line:

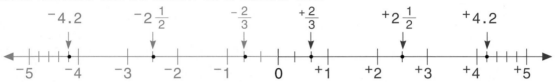

Like integers, every rational number has an **opposite** that is the *same distance* from 0 but is in the *opposite direction*.

Opposites: ${}^{-}4.2$ and ${}^{+}4.2$ $\qquad {}^{-}\frac{2}{3}$ and ${}^{+}\frac{2}{3}$ $\qquad {}^{-}2\frac{1}{2}$ and ${}^{+}2\frac{1}{2}$

Of two numbers on a number line, the number *to the right* has the greater value.

$${}^{+}2\frac{1}{2} > {}^{-}1: \quad \text{positive } 2\frac{1}{2} \text{ is greater than negative 1.}$$
$${}^{-}4.2 < {}^{-}2: \quad \text{negative } 4.2 \text{ is less than negative 2.}$$

Write the opposite of each rational number. Tell which rational numbers are also integers.

1. ${}^{+}9.14$
2. ${}^{+}25.1$
3. ${}^{-}\frac{9}{2}$
4. ${}^{-}\frac{1}{2}$
5. ${}^{-}2.8$

6. ${}^{-}0.7$
7. ${}^{+}4\frac{1}{5}$
8. ${}^{+}1\frac{2}{3}$
9. $\frac{0}{3}$
10. ${}^{-}\frac{15}{3}$

11. ${}^{-}100$
12. ${}^{+}2$
13. ${}^{-}\frac{5}{8}$
14. 0
15. ${}^{-}4.0\overline{1}$

16. ${}^{+}33.\overline{3}$
17. ${}^{-}5.\overline{75}$
18. ${}^{-}1$
19. ${}^{+}2.\overline{6}$
20. ${}^{+}5\frac{1}{9}$

21. ${}^{+}5\frac{1}{2}$
22. ${}^{+}81\frac{1}{2}$
23. ${}^{+}42.\overline{1}$
24. ${}^{-}\frac{3}{8}$
25. ${}^{+}\frac{21}{7}$

26. ${}^{-}1\frac{1}{2}$
27. ${}^{+}2.3$
28. ${}^{+}\frac{6}{3}$
29. ${}^{-}0.2$
30. ${}^{-}\frac{9}{4}$

Draw a number line and locate each rational number.

31. ${}^{+}3\frac{1}{2}$
32. ${}^{-}2\frac{1}{3}$
33. ${}^{+}\frac{3}{4}$
34. ${}^{-}0.5$
35. ${}^{+}4.75$

36. ${}^{-}\frac{1}{4}$
37. ${}^{+}\frac{7}{8}$
38. ${}^{-}1\frac{1}{2}$
39. ${}^{-}0.25$
40. ${}^{+}1.4$

Compare. Write <, =, or >.

41. $^+8$? $^-2$ **42.** $^-3$? $^+10$ **43.** 0 ? $^+6.1$ **44.** $^+3.5$? 0

45. $^+10$? $^+10.3$ **46.** $^+0.8$? $^-\frac{4}{5}$ **47.** $^+2.5$? $^+2\frac{1}{2}$ **48.** $^-2.3$? $^-3.2$

49. $^-\frac{3}{5}$? $^-0.4$ **50.** $^-0.\overline{1}$? $^-\frac{1}{9}$ **51.** $^-\frac{3}{4}$? $^+0.\overline{75}$ **52.** $^-\frac{1}{4}$? $^-0.2$

Write each set of numbers in order from least to greatest.

53. $^-2.5,\ ^-3,\ 0,\ ^+1\frac{1}{2},\ ^-0.3,\ ^-\frac{9}{2},\ ^+3\frac{3}{4}$ **54.** $^-1\frac{1}{4},\ ^+3.25,\ ^-3\frac{1}{2},\ ^+4,\ ^-4,\ ^-\frac{11}{2}$

55. $^+2.75,\ ^-0.5,\ ^-3,\ 0,\ ^+1\frac{1}{3},\ ^-\frac{9}{4}$ **56.** $0,\ ^-3\frac{2}{3},\ ^+1,\ ^-\frac{8}{4},\ ^-\frac{10}{3},\ ^+2.25$

Write true (T) or false (F). Explain.

57. $^-3.14$ is a rational number but not an integer.   **58.** $^+1$ is a rational number.

59. $^+2$ is an integer but not a rational number.   **60.** Any integer is a rational number.

61. $^-14$ is an integer and a rational number.   **62.** Any rational number is an integer.

63. $^+2\frac{1}{2}$ is an integer and a rational number.   **64.** 0 is an integer.

Write a rational number for each expression.

65. a gain of $9.25   **66.** a deposit of $132.50   **67.** down $3\frac{1}{8}$ points

68. a loss of $25.90   **69.** $10.5°$ below zero   **70.** 2.3 km underwater

MENTAL MATH   (The first two are done.)

71. $^-(^-\frac{1}{2}) = $? $\longrightarrow$ The opposite of $^-\frac{1}{2}$ is $^+\frac{1}{2}$.

72. $^-[^-(^+12)] = $? $\longrightarrow$ The opposite of the opposite of $^+12$ is $^+12$.

73. $^-[^-(^-3)] = $?   **74.** $^-[^-(^+1.5)] = $?   **75.** $^-(^+9\frac{1}{3}) = $?

76. $^-[^-(0)] = $?   **77.** $^-[^-(^-1\frac{3}{4})] = $?   **78.** $^-(^-2.1) = $?

CRITICAL THINKING   **Complete. Write: *all, some,* or *no.***

79. ? integers are rational numbers.   **80.** ? integers are whole numbers.

81. ? positive numbers are integers.   **82.** ? fractions are rational numbers.

83. ? repeating decimals are whole numbers.   **84.** ? terminating decimals are rational numbers.

85. ? rational numbers are whole numbers.

Properties of Rational Numbers

All rational numbers have the *same* properties as whole numbers. These properties apply to *both* positive and negative rational numbers.

Addition	Property	Multiplication

Commutative

For any numbers *a*, *b*:

$$a + b = b + a$$
$$^-3 + 5 = 5 + ^-3$$
$$2 = 2$$

For any numbers *a*, *b*:

$$a \times b = b \times a$$
$$^-6 \times 3 = 3 \times ^-6$$
$$^-18 = ^-18$$

Associative

For any numbers *a*, *b*, *c*:

$$(a + b) + c = a + (b + c)$$
$$(^-5 + 2) + ^-4 = ^-5 + (2 + ^-4)$$
$$^-7 = ^-7$$

For any numbers *a*, *b*, *c*:

$$(a \times b) \times c = a \times (b \times c)$$
$$(^-3 \times 2) \times ^-5 = ^-3 \times (2 \times ^-5)$$
$$30 = 30$$

Identity

For any number *a*:

$$a + 0 = 0 + a = a$$
$$^-1.3 + 0 = 0 + ^-1.3 = ^-1.3$$

Identity element for addition: 0

For any number *a*:

$$a \times 1 = 1 \times a = a$$
$$\frac{^-3}{4} \times 1 = 1 \times \frac{^-3}{4} = \frac{^-3}{4}$$

Identity element for multiplication: 1

Inverse

For any number *a*:

$$a + {}^-a = 0$$
$$^-7 + {}^-(^-7) = 0$$

For any number *a* (except for zero):

$$a \times \frac{1}{a} = 1$$
$$^-6 \times \frac{1}{^-6} = 1$$

Distributive

For any numbers *a*, *b*, *c*: $a \times (b + c) = (a \times b) + (a \times c)$

$$^-6 \times (3 + ^-5) = (^-6 \times 3) + (^-6 \times ^-5) \longrightarrow 12 = 12$$

1. Check the above number properties by substituting these values for *a*, *b*, and *c*.

   $$a = {}^+5 \qquad b = {}^-3 \qquad c = {}^+4$$

2. Is the commutative property true for subtraction? Explain.

3. Is the associative property true for division? Explain.

4. For any number *a*: $a \times 0 = \underline{\ ?\ }$. Check the zero property of multiplication by substituting $^-3$ for *a*.

Name the property.

5. $^+6 + {}^-8 = {}^-8 + {}^+6$

6. $^+14 + {}^-14 = 0$

7. $^-2\frac{1}{2} \times {}^+1 = {}^-2\frac{1}{2}$

8. $^+3\,({}^-6 + {}^+8) = ({}^+3 \times {}^-6) + ({}^+3 \times {}^+8)$

9. $^+2\,({}^-4 \times {}^+5) = ({}^+2 \times {}^-4) \times {}^+5$

10. $({}^-4 + {}^+7) + {}^-3 = {}^-3 + ({}^-4 + {}^+7)$

11. $\frac{1}{9} \times ({}^-3 \times {}^+6) = ({}^-3 \times {}^+6) \times \frac{1}{9}$

12. $^-8 + ({}^+7 + {}^-4) = ({}^-8 + {}^+7) + {}^-4$

13. $^-7 \times {}^-\frac{1}{7} = 1$

Find _n_. Name the property used. (The first one is done.)

14. $^-4.2 \times n = {}^-4.2 \longrightarrow n = 1$ Identity property of multiplication.

15. $^+\frac{3}{4} + n = {}^+\frac{3}{4}$

16. $\frac{2}{3} \times (n + {}^-2) = (\frac{2}{3} \times {}^+5) + (\frac{2}{3} \times {}^-2)$

17. $^-5 \times {}^+\frac{1}{10} = {}^+\frac{1}{10} \times n$

18. $({}^-4 + 0.5) + {}^-5 = {}^-4 + (0.5 + n)$

19. $^-\frac{1}{2} + n = 0$

20. $^+\frac{1}{3} \times ({}^-2 \times {}^+\frac{3}{4}) = (n \times {}^-2) \times {}^+\frac{3}{4}$

21. $^+2.5 + 0 = n + {}^+2.5$

22. $^-\frac{1}{3} \times n = 1$

23. $(0.5 \times {}^-3) + (0.5 \times {}^-5) = n\,({}^-3 + {}^-5)$

Name the opposite of each rational number. (The first two are done.)

24. $^-\frac{3}{5} \longrightarrow {}^+\frac{3}{5}$ is the opposite because $^-\frac{3}{5} + {}^+\frac{3}{5} = 0$

25. $^+1.7 \longrightarrow {}^-1.7$ is the opposite because $^+1.7 + {}^-1.7 = 0$

26. $^-2\frac{1}{3}$

27. $^-0.5$

28. $^+4.\overline{3}$

29. $^-1\frac{1}{5}$

30. $^+5.08$

31. $^-3.1$

32. 0

33. $^+4.\overline{6}$

CHALLENGE

Name the reciprocal of each rational number.
(The first one is done.)

34. $^-0.5 \longrightarrow$ Think: $^-0.5 \times \underline{\ ?\ } = 1$

$^-0.5 = {}^-\frac{5}{10} = {}^-\frac{1}{2} \longrightarrow$ The reciprocal of $^-\frac{1}{2}$ is $^-\frac{2}{1}$.

35. $^-1.1$

36. $^+2.4$

37. $^+1.5$

38. $^-1\frac{1}{3}$

39. $^-\frac{3}{4}$

40. $^+2\frac{1}{2}$

41. $^+3\frac{1}{3}$

42. $^-6\frac{1}{4}$

43. **Check exercises 26–42 on a calculator.** (Remember: $a + {}^-a = 0$ and $a \times \frac{1}{a} = 1$.)

SKILLS TO REMEMBER   **Solve for _n_.**

44. $7.2 + 1.03 = n$

45. $6 - 1.08 = n$

46. $11 + 8.6 - 7 = n$

47. $8\frac{1}{5} + 1\frac{3}{4} = n$

48. $2 - 1\frac{5}{8} = n$

49. $\frac{1}{3} + 4\frac{1}{2} - 2 = n$

4-3 Adding Rational Numbers

▶ **To add rational numbers with *like signs*:**

- Find the sum of the numbers.
- Use the sign of the addends.

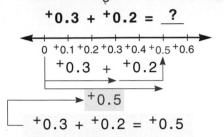

$^+0.3 + {}^+0.2 = \underline{}$

$^+0.3 + {}^+0.2 = {}^+0.5$

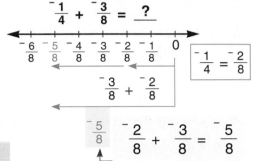

$\dfrac{^-1}{4} + \dfrac{^-3}{8} = \underline{}$

$\dfrac{^-1}{4} = \dfrac{^-2}{8}$

$\dfrac{^-2}{8} + \dfrac{^-3}{8} = \dfrac{^-5}{8}$

▶ **To add rational numbers with *unlike signs*:**

- Find the *difference* of the numbers.
- Use the sign of the addend farther from zero (one with *greater* absolute value).

$^-2 + {}^+4 = \underline{}$

$^-2 + {}^+4 = {}^+2$

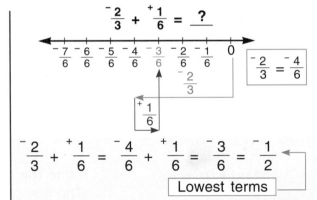

$\dfrac{^-2}{3} + \dfrac{^+1}{6} = \underline{}$

$\dfrac{^-2}{3} = \dfrac{^-4}{6}$

$\dfrac{^-2}{3} + \dfrac{^+1}{6} = \dfrac{^-4}{6} + \dfrac{^+1}{6} = \dfrac{^-3}{6} = \dfrac{^-1}{2}$

Lowest terms

Add.

1. $^+8 + {}^+4$
2. $^+7 + {}^+6$
3. $^-6 + {}^-4$
4. $^-5 + {}^-8$

5. $^-9 + {}^+7$
6. $^+3 + {}^-5$
7. $^+9 + {}^-7$
8. $^+6 + {}^-9$

9. $^+1.2 + {}^+0.7$
10. $^+3.5 + {}^+1.3$
11. $^+7.8 + {}^-7.2$
12. $^+1 + {}^-6.2$

13. $^-0.6 + {}^+0.5$
14. $^+0.4 + {}^-0.6$
15. $^-1.3 + {}^+1.3$
16. $^-2.1 + {}^+2.1$

17. $^+0.9 + {}^-2.1$
18. $^-1.7 + {}^-1.7$
19. $^-3 + {}^+0.3$
20. $^+20 + {}^-5.04$

21. $0 + {}^+2.8$
22. $^-3.5 + 0$
23. $^-0.06 + {}^+0.19$
24. $^+0.2 + {}^-0.04$

25. $^-3.2 + {}^+3.2$
26. $^+7.01 + {}^-5.1$
27. $^-2.4 + {}^+2.06$
28. $^-1.1 + {}^+2.1$

29. $^-3.2 + {}^+10$
30. $^-20 + {}^+11.9$
31. $^-16.4 + {}^-30$
32. $^+30 + {}^-0.3$

33. $^-9.9 + {}^-9.9$
34. $^+7.45 + {}^-8.09$
35. $^-6.03 + {}^-3.97$
36. $^-45 + {}^+60.5$

Find each sum.

37. $^+\frac{1}{3} + ^-\frac{1}{3}$ 38. $^-\frac{1}{7} + ^-\frac{5}{7}$ 39. $^-\frac{2}{9} + ^-\frac{3}{9}$ 40. $^+1 + ^-\frac{1}{5}$

41. $^+\frac{1}{4} + ^-1$ 42. $^+\frac{2}{5} + ^-\frac{2}{5}$ 43. $^-\frac{5}{11} + ^+\frac{3}{11}$ 44. $^+1\frac{1}{6} + ^-1\frac{1}{6}$

45. $^+3 + ^-2\frac{1}{4}$ 46. $^+\frac{3}{5} + ^-\frac{1}{5}$ 47. $^-2\frac{1}{2} + ^-3\frac{1}{4}$ 48. $^-1\frac{3}{8} + ^+3\frac{1}{2}$

49. $^+1\frac{1}{8} + ^-6$ 50. $^-3\frac{1}{8} + ^+3\frac{1}{5}$ 51. $^+6\frac{4}{5} + ^+1\frac{1}{10}$ 52. $^+4\frac{2}{3} + ^-5\frac{8}{9}$

Solve each equation.

53. $^-16 + ^+16 = s$ 54. $^-21 + ^-40 = d$ 55. $^-35 + ^+50 = r$

56. $^+12 + ^-19 = a$ 57. $^+16 + ^-27 = n$ 58. $^-11 + ^-15 = b$

59. $^-5.2 + ^-8.7 = c$ 60. $^-0.75 + ^+0.25 = h$ 61. $^+2.4 + ^-1.3 = x$

62. $^-2.1 + ^+1.4 = m$ 63. $^+4\frac{3}{7} + ^-5\frac{1}{7} = e$ 64. $^-10 + ^+7\frac{3}{4} = z$

65. $^+3\frac{1}{8} + ^-5\frac{3}{4} = k$ 66. $^-5\frac{1}{6} + ^+2\frac{2}{3} = t$ 67. $^+6\frac{1}{2} + ^-7\frac{1}{3} = v$

Add. (Hint: Look for properties.)

68. $^-19 + ^+16 + ^-1 = b$ 69. $^+3 + ^-4 + ^+7 = a$ 70. $^+15 + ^-8 + ^+5 = e$

71. $^+42 + ^-8 + ^-42 = f$ 72. $^-2 + ^+13 + ^-8 = d$ 73. $^-7 + ^+11 + ^+7 = c$

74. $^-7.01 + ^+6.5 + ^+7.01 = z$ 75. $^+1.1 + ^-11 + ^-3.1 = y$

76. $^-2\frac{3}{4} + ^+7\frac{1}{2} + ^+2\frac{3}{4} = h$ 77. $^+12.5 + ^-12.5 + ^-12.5 = c$.

Choose the correct answer.

78. Add $^-15.3$ to 17.1.   **a.** 32.4   **b.** 1.8   **c.** $^-1.8$

79. Find the sum of $^+0.6$ and $^-0.21$.   **a.** 0.39   **b.** 39   **c.** $^-0.39$

80. Find a number that is $^-25\frac{3}{4}$ more than $9\frac{5}{16}$.   **a.** $16\frac{7}{16}$ **b.** $35\frac{1}{16}$ **c.** $^-16\frac{7}{16}$

Solve.

81. The temperatures from 9 until noon were reported as: $^-1.5°C$, $^-0.4°C$, $^+2.1°C$, and $^+6.7°C$. What was the net change in temperature?

82. Last month Skip deposited $125.50 in his checking account. He wrote checks for $50 and $27.60. What was the net result of these transactions?

83. The changes in stock over a five-day period were: $^+1\frac{1}{2}$, $^+\frac{7}{8}$, $^-\frac{3}{4}$, $^-1\frac{1}{8}$, and $^+1\frac{5}{8}$. Find the net change for the week.

84. A scuba diver descended 30.3 meters below the ocean surface, rose 16.6 meters, and then descended 7.1 meters. How far below the ocean surface is the diver?

85. In a game one player lost 22 points, gained 38 points, then lost 15 points. Another player gained 15 points, lost 37 points, then gained 18 points. What was the score of the player who lost?

4-4 Subtracting Rational Numbers

To subtract a rational number, *add its opposite*.

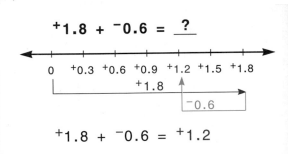

$$^+7 - {}^-3 = \underline{}$$
$$^+7 + {}^+3 = {}^+10$$
opposite

$$^+1.8 - {}^+0.6 = \underline{}$$
$$^+1.8 + {}^-0.6 = \underline{}$$
opposite

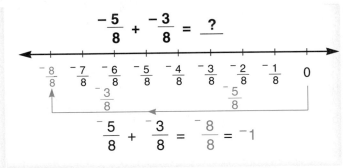

$$\frac{^-5}{8} - \frac{^+3}{8} = \underline{}$$
$$\frac{^-5}{8} + \frac{^-3}{8} = \underline{}$$
opposite

$$^+1.8 + {}^-0.6 = \underline{}$$

$$^+1.8 + {}^-0.6 = {}^+1.2$$

$$\frac{^-5}{8} + \frac{^-3}{8} = \underline{}$$

$$\frac{^-5}{8} + \frac{^-3}{8} = \frac{^-8}{8} = {}^-1$$

What number is $^-1\frac{1}{2}$ subtracted from $^-2\frac{1}{3}$?

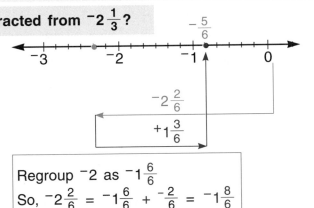

$$^-2\frac{1}{3} - {}^-1\frac{1}{2} = n$$
$$^-2\frac{1}{3} + {}^+1\frac{1}{2} = n$$
LCD = 6
$$^-2\frac{2}{6} + {}^+1\frac{3}{6} = n$$
$$^-1\frac{8}{6} + {}^+1\frac{3}{6} = \frac{^-5}{6}$$

Regroup $^-2$ as $^-1\frac{6}{6}$

So, $^-2\frac{2}{6} = {}^-1\frac{6}{6} + \frac{^-2}{6} = {}^-1\frac{8}{6}$

Subtract.

1. $^-7 - {}^+6$
2. $^+5 - {}^-11$
3. $^+4 - {}^+9$
4. $^-7 - {}^+15$

5. $0 - {}^-13$
6. $0 - {}^+19$
7. $^-8 - {}^+15.2$
8. $^+4.5 - {}^-6.2$

9. $^+3.1 - {}^+3.1$
10. $^-9.3 - {}^-9.3$
11. $^+5.2 - {}^+7.5$
12. $^-3.4 - {}^-4.7$

13. $^+6.08 - {}^+1.9$
14. $^-7.5 - {}^-3.8$
15. $^-2.03 - {}^-5.4$
16. $^+3.6 - {}^+2.12$

17. $^-0.64 - {}^+1.8$
18. $^+0.17 - {}^-3.9$
19. $0 - {}^-2.25$
20. $0 - {}^+1.09$

21. $^-2.4 - {}^+2.4$
22. $^+11.4 - {}^-2.9$
23. $^-9.8 - {}^-10.08$
24. $^+6.1 - {}^+10$

25. $^-20 - {}^-2.2$
26. $^+16.4 - {}^-0.6$
27. $^+13.05 - {}^+17.9$
28. $^-2.1 - {}^-20.01$

29. $^+16.16 - {}^-61.61$
30. $^-0.09 - {}^-1.401$
31. $^-1.082 - {}^+3.09$
32. $^+0.069 - {}^+3$

Find the difference.

33. $\dfrac{-7}{8} - \dfrac{+1}{4}$

34. $\dfrac{+7}{10} - \dfrac{+3}{10}$

35. $\dfrac{+1}{8} - \dfrac{+3}{4}$

36. $\dfrac{+2}{3} - \dfrac{+5}{6}$

37. $\dfrac{-7}{8} - \dfrac{+1}{3}$

38. $\dfrac{+4}{5} - \dfrac{-1}{4}$

39. $^-3\dfrac{5}{8} - {}^-1\dfrac{1}{2}$

40. $6\dfrac{7}{12} - {}^+4\dfrac{2}{3}$

41. $^+5\dfrac{2}{5} - {}^+7\dfrac{1}{4}$

42. $^-4\dfrac{1}{7} - {}^-5\dfrac{2}{5}$

43. $^+2\dfrac{3}{4} - {}^-4\dfrac{1}{3}$

44. $^-4\dfrac{1}{2} - {}^-2\dfrac{5}{9}$

Add or subtract to solve each equation.

45. $^+2 - {}^+5 = h$

46. $^-16 - {}^+7 = r$

47. $^-8 - {}^-13 = m$

48. $^+3 + {}^-6.8 = a$

49. $^-8 + {}^-11.7 = d$

50. $^+2.2 - {}^+7.1 = c$

51. $^-4.3 - {}^-1.08 = t$

52. $^-14 - {}^+2.25 = k$

53. $^+17 - {}^-9.17 = b$

54. $0 - {}^-7\dfrac{2}{5} = x$

55. $^+2.4 + {}^-2\dfrac{1}{5} = f$

56. $^+1\dfrac{1}{2} - {}^-1.5 = e$

57. $^-2\dfrac{5}{8} + {}^+0.75 = n$

58. $^-10.2 + {}^+3\dfrac{1}{4} = s$

59. $^-1.6 - {}^-2\dfrac{1}{3} = y$

Simplify the expressions. Use the rules for order of operations. (The first is done.)

60. $^+2 - ({}^-8 + {}^-7) = n \longrightarrow {}^+2 - ({}^-15) = n \longrightarrow {}^+2 + {}^+15 = n \longrightarrow {}^+17 = n$

61. $^+7 + ({}^-6 - {}^+4) = n$

62. $^-9 - ({}^+8 - {}^-3) = n$

63. $^-6 - ({}^-3.5 + {}^-4) = n$

64. $^+5 - ({}^-2.4 + {}^+6.5) = n$

65. $(^-8 - {}^-3) + ({}^+9 - {}^-1.5) = n$

66. $(^-2.1 + {}^+2.1) - {}^-6.3 = n$

Solve.

67. A deep-sea diver found sunken treasure at a depth of $^-108\dfrac{1}{2}$ ft. She rose $35\dfrac{3}{4}$ ft to where she had left her camera. At what depth was her camera?

68. Stock shares fell from $^+2\dfrac{1}{2}$ to $^-1\dfrac{3}{4}$. Find the decrease. (Represent this decrease as a negative rational number.)

69. Kurt's checking balance is $\$17.50$. He writes a check for $\$21.25$. When the amount of this check is entered into the bank's computer, what balance will the computer indicate?

CHALLENGE

70. The sum of two integers is 5. Their difference is 13. Find the two integers.

71. The sum of two integers is $^-9$. Their difference is 5. Find the two integers.

Equations with Addition and Subtraction

Solve addition and subtraction equations involving positive and negative numbers as you solve equations involving other whole numbers.

▶ **To solve an addition equation:** *Subtract the same number* from both sides of the equation.

Solve: $p + {}^-7 = {}^+10.2$

$p + {}^-7 - {}^-7 = {}^+10.2 - {}^-7$ ◀────── Subtract $^-7$ from both sides of the equation.

$p + {}^-7 + {}^+7 = {}^+10.2 + {}^+7$

$p + 0 = {}^+17.2$ **Check:** Substitute $^+17.2$ for p.

$p = {}^+17.2$ $p + {}^-7 = {}^+10.2$

$^+17.2 + {}^-7 = {}^+10.2 \longrightarrow {}^+10.2 = {}^+10.2$

▶ **To solve a subtraction equation:** *Add the same number* to both sides of the equation.

Solve: $n - {}^-8 = {}^+9\frac{1}{4}$ ┌── Add $^-8$ to both sides of the equation.

$n - {}^-8 + {}^-8 = {}^+9\frac{1}{4} + {}^-8$ ◀─┘

$n - 0 = {}^+9\frac{1}{4} + {}^-8$ **Check:** Substitute $^+1\frac{1}{4}$ for n.

$n = {}^+1\frac{1}{4}$ $n - {}^-8 = {}^+9\frac{1}{4}$

$^+1\frac{1}{4} - {}^-8 = {}^+9\frac{1}{4}$

$^+1\frac{1}{4} + {}^+8 = {}^+9\frac{1}{4} \longrightarrow {}^+9\frac{1}{4} = {}^+9\frac{1}{4}$

Choose the correct mathematical expression for each.

1. 5 more than a number
   a. $n - {}^+5$ b. $^+5 - n$ c. $n + {}^+5$ d. $n + {}^-5$

2. 3.1 added to p
   a. $p - {}^-3.1$ b. $p + {}^+3.1$ c. $^-3 - p$ d. $p + {}^-3.1$

3. $^-8\frac{1}{2}$ decreased by r
   a. $r - {}^-8\frac{1}{2}$ b. $^-8\frac{1}{2} + r$ c. $^-8\frac{1}{2} - r$ d. $r + {}^-8\frac{1}{2}$

4. the difference between y and 11.5
   a. $y + {}^-11.5$ b. $y - {}^-11.5$ c. $y + {}^+11.5$ d. $y - {}^+11.5$

5. the sum of x and $^-\frac{2}{3}$
   a. $^-\frac{2}{3} - x$ b. $x + {}^+\frac{2}{3}$ c. $x + {}^-\frac{2}{3}$ d. $^+\frac{2}{3} + {}^-x$

Evaluate each expression.

6. $x - {}^+3$ when $x = {}^-4$

7. $3 - k$ when $k = {}^-7$

8. $b + {}^-6$ when $b = {}^+15$

9. ${}^+5 - n$ when $n = {}^+12.8$

10. $m + m$ when $m = {}^-2.3$

11. $a - {}^+7$ when $a = {}^-6.4$

12. $h + {}^-10$ when $h = {}^+7\frac{2}{5}$

13. $r - {}^-\frac{1}{6}$ when $r = 0$

14. ${}^+1 - y$ when $y = {}^-\frac{3}{4}$

15. ${}^-9 - k$ when $k = {}^-3\frac{3}{8}$

Write a mathematical sentence. Solve it.

16. When ${}^-18$ is added to x, the result is ${}^+35$.

17. When ${}^-20$ is subtracted from x, the result is ${}^-2.5$.

18. When x is added to ${}^-\frac{1}{4}$, the result is ${}^-2$.

19. When ${}^-2.3$ is added to x and ${}^-4.1$ is subtracted from the sum, the result is ${}^+10$.

20. When ${}^-5.8$ is subtracted from ${}^+6.2$ and x is added to the difference, the result is ${}^+2.4$.

21. The sum of x, ${}^-\frac{4}{5}$, ${}^-1\frac{3}{10}$, and ${}^+4\frac{1}{5}$ is ${}^-2$.

Solve.

22. $n + {}^-6 = {}^-11$

23. $r + {}^+3 = {}^-8$

24. $x + {}^-2 = {}^+7$

25. $a + {}^+1.7 = {}^+8.6$

26. $n + {}^-4.4 = {}^-9.2$

27. $t + {}^+6.7 = 0$

28. $s + {}^-1.5 = 0$

29. $x - {}^+6 = {}^-13$

30. $n - {}^-20 = {}^+15$

31. $y - {}^+7.2 = {}^+3.5$

32. $f - {}^-6.1 = {}^-4.3$

33. $d - {}^-4.1 = {}^+5.9$

34. $c - {}^-\frac{3}{4} = {}^+2\frac{1}{8}$

35. $p + {}^+\frac{4}{5} = {}^+1\frac{1}{10}$

36. $h + {}^-\frac{2}{3} = {}^-2\frac{4}{9}$

37. $f + {}^-1\frac{5}{6} = {}^+4\frac{1}{3}$

38. $m - {}^-9\frac{3}{10} = {}^+5\frac{1}{4}$

39. $b - {}^+6\frac{4}{9} = {}^+7\frac{2}{3}$

40. ${}^-7.2 + r = {}^-8\frac{1}{2}$

41. ${}^+2\frac{1}{3} + d = {}^+1.2$

42. $y - {}^-6\frac{1}{4} = {}^+2.1$

Solve.

43. After receiving a rebate of $6 for every item purchased, the final cost for a blender was $40.95, $15 for a toaster, and $28.39 for a coffee pot. What was the original price of each item?

(Hint: Let $p = $ the original price of an item. Then $p + {}^-6$ is the cost after the rebate.)

4-6 Multiplying Rational Numbers

The product of two rational numbers with the *same sign* is positive.

$^+9 \times {}^+6 = \underline{\ ?\ }$
same signs
$^+9 \times {}^+6 = {}^+54$

$-\frac{1}{3} \times -\frac{2}{5} = \underline{\ ?\ }$
same signs
$-\frac{1}{3} \times -\frac{2}{5} = {}^+\frac{2}{15}$

$^-0.1 \times {}^-0.37 = \underline{\ ?\ }$
same signs
$^-0.1 \times {}^-0.37 = {}^+0.037$

Multiplication Rules		
+, +	→	+
−, −	→	+
+, −	→	−
−, +	→	−

The product of two rational numbers with *different signs* is negative.

$^+5 \times {}^-6 = \underline{\ ?\ }$
different signs
$^+5 \times {}^-6 = {}^-30$

$-\frac{3}{4} \times {}^+\frac{1}{5} = \underline{\ ?\ }$
different signs
$-\frac{3}{4} \times {}^+\frac{1}{5} = -\frac{3}{20}$

$^+0.7 \times {}^-1.3 = \underline{\ ?\ }$
different signs
$^+0.7 \times {}^-1.3 = {}^-0.91$

$^-2\frac{1}{2}$ multiplied by $\frac{4}{5} = \underline{\ ?\ }$

$^-2\frac{1}{2} \times {}^+\frac{4}{5} = n$
different signs

$n = \dfrac{{}^-5}{2} \times \dfrac{{}^+4}{5}$

$n = \dfrac{{}^-\overset{1}{\cancel{5}}}{\underset{1}{\cancel{2}}} \times \dfrac{{}^+\overset{2}{\cancel{4}}}{\underset{1}{\cancel{5}}}$

$n = {}^-2$

OR

$n = \dfrac{{}^-20}{10}$

$n = {}^-2$

Find the product.

1. $^-2 \times {}^-12$
2. $^+7 \times {}^+11$
3. $^-7 \times {}^+6$

4. $^+9 \times {}^-4$
5. $^-1 \times {}^+2.2$
6. $^+1.5 \times {}^-0.2$

7. $0 \times {}^-5.7$
8. $^-6.2 \times {}^-1$
9. $^-16 \times {}^-0.5$

10. $^-4.2 \times {}^-1.8$
11. $^+50 \times {}^-1.4$
12. $^-3.7 \times {}^-0.14$

13. $^-15 \times {}^+\frac{3}{5}$
14. $^-100 \times {}^+\frac{1}{2}$
15. $-\frac{2}{3} \times {}^-36$

16. $-\frac{2}{5} \times {}^+\frac{5}{6}$
17. $^+\frac{1}{2} \times {}^+\frac{3}{5}$
18. $-\frac{7}{8} \times -\frac{16}{21}$

19. $^-1\frac{1}{6} \times {}^+2\frac{2}{5}$
20. $^+3\frac{1}{3} \times {}^-1\frac{1}{5}$
21. $^+1\frac{3}{5} \times {}^-7\frac{1}{2}$

22. $^-3\frac{3}{4} \times {}^+2\frac{2}{5}$
23. $^-2\frac{1}{4} \times {}^-2\frac{2}{3}$
24. $^+6\frac{3}{7} \times 0$

25. $^+4\frac{1}{5} \times {}^-3\frac{2}{7} \times {}^-2\frac{1}{2}$
26. $^-6\frac{1}{4} \times {}^+7\frac{1}{5} \times {}^-2\frac{1}{2}$
27. $^-8\frac{7}{9} \times 0 \times {}^-4\frac{1}{3}$

Evaluate.

28. $3n$ when $n = {}^-21$ **29.** ${}^-5m$ when $m = {}^-14$ **30.** ${}^+2p$ when $p = {}^-1.2$

31. ${}^-4s$ when $s = {}^-1.5$ **32.** ${}^+3.2t$ when $t = 0$ **33.** ${}^-10v$ when $v = {}^-0.25$

34. ${}^+20d$ when $d = \frac{{}^-3}{4}$ **35.** ${}^+\frac{1}{7}e$ when $e = {}^-28$ **36.** $\frac{{}^-2}{3}f$ when $f = {}^-1$

37. ${}^-4p$ when $p = {}^+\frac{1}{2}$ **38.** ${}^+\frac{3}{4}x - 2$ when $x = {}^-8$

Complete.

39. The product of two positive numbers is a __?__ number.

40. The product of a positive number and a negative number is a __?__ number.

41. The product of two negative numbers is a __?__ number.

42. When three factors are negative, the product is __?__ .

43. The product of a number and ${}^-1$ changes the number into its __?__ .

Choose the correct answer. (Use the rules for order of operations.)

44. ${}^+3 \times ({}^-5 + {}^-4)$ **a.** ${}^+19$ **b.** ${}^-27$ **c.** ${}^-19$ **d.** ${}^+27$

45. ${}^-2.5 + ({}^-5 \times {}^-7)$ **a.** ${}^+32.5$ **b.** ${}^-37.5$ **c.** ${}^-32.5$ **d.** ${}^+37.5$

46. $({}^-7 + {}^+3) - ({}^-5 \times {}^-2)$ **a.** ${}^+6$ **b.** ${}^+14$ **c.** ${}^-14$ **d.** ${}^-6$

47. $({}^+1.7 \times {}^-2) + ({}^+1.7 - {}^+1.7)$ **a.** ${}^-6.8$ **b.** ${}^+3.4$ **c.** ${}^+6.8$ **d.** ${}^-3.4$

48. $({}^-8 \times {}^-0.2 \times {}^+1) + {}^-2$ **a.** ${}^+0.4$ **b.** ${}^-3.6$ **c.** ${}^-0.4$ **d.** ${}^+3.6$

49. $({}^+\frac{4}{5} + \frac{{}^-1}{2}) \times ({}^+1 - {}^-2\frac{1}{3})$ **a.** ${}^+1$ **b.** ${}^+\frac{2}{5}$ **c.** ${}^-1$ **d.** $\frac{{}^-2}{5}$

Solve.

50. What is the product when ${}^-1\frac{1}{4}$ is doubled?

51. What is twice the sum of ${}^-2\frac{3}{5}$ added to ${}^+1\frac{1}{2}$?

52. What is half the difference of ${}^-1.7$ subtracted from ${}^+2.3$?

53. What is twice the difference of ${}^-2.01$ subtracted from ${}^-1.02$?

54. What is three times the sum of ${}^-1.5 + {}^+3\frac{1}{2}$?

55. What is half the sum of ${}^-1\frac{1}{4}$, ${}^+2.3$, and ${}^-3\frac{1}{4}$?

56. When placed in liquid nitrogen a chemical changes in temperature ${}^-4.8°C$ every second. What is the overall change in temperature after a half-minute?

57. During a 2-week drought the water table level changed ${}^-0.35$ m every day. What was the final change in the water table level?

111

4-7 Dividing Rational Numbers

▶ **The quotient of two rational numbers with the *same sign* is positive.**

$$^+27 \div {}^+9 = \underline{\ ?\ }$$
same signs
$$^+27 \div {}^+9 = {}^+3$$

$$\frac{^-3}{4} \div \frac{^-3}{4} = \underline{\ ?\ }$$
same signs
$$\frac{^-3}{4} \div \frac{^-3}{4} = {}^+1$$

$$^+3.2 \div {}^+0.4 = \underline{\ ?\ }$$
same signs
$$^+3.2 \div {}^+0.4 = {}^+8$$

Division Rules
Like signs ⟶ +   (+, +), (−, −)
Unlike signs ⟶ −   (+, −), (−, +)

▶ **The quotient of two rational numbers with *different signs* is negative.**

$$^-54 \div {}^+6 = \underline{\ ?\ }$$
different signs
$$^-54 \div {}^+6 = {}^-9$$

$$\frac{^+3}{8} \div \frac{^-1}{2} = \underline{\ ?\ }$$
different signs
$$\frac{^+3}{\overset{}{\underset{4}{8}}} \times \frac{^-\overset{1}{2}}{1} = \frac{^-3}{4}$$

$$^-2.1 \div {}^+7 = \underline{\ ?\ }$$
different signs
$$^-2.1 \div {}^+7 = {}^-0.3$$

▶ **Multiplication and division are *related* operations; one undoes the other.**

$$^+5.1 \times {}^+4 = {}^+20.4$$
$$^+20.4 \div {}^+4 = {}^+5.1$$

$$^-5.1 \times {}^+4 = {}^-20.4$$
$$^-20.4 \div {}^+4 = {}^-5.1$$

$$^+5.1 \times {}^-4 = {}^-20.4$$
$$^-20.4 \div {}^-4 = {}^+5.1$$

$$^-5.1 \times {}^-4 = {}^+20.4$$
$$^+20.4 \div {}^-4 = {}^-5.1$$

Copy and complete.

1. $^+56 \div {}^-8 = \underline{\ ?\ }$ because $^-8 \times \underline{\ ?\ } = {}^+56$

2. $^-2.4 \div {}^-4 = \underline{\ ?\ }$ because $^-4 \times \underline{\ ?\ } = {}^-2.4$

3. $\frac{^-1}{2} \div \frac{^+1}{2} = \underline{\ ?\ }$ because $^+\frac{1}{2} \times \underline{\ ?\ } = {}^-\frac{1}{2}$

4. $0 \div {}^-7 = \underline{\ ?\ }$ because $^-7 \times \underline{\ ?\ } = 0$ ◀── What happens when you divide zero by a negative number?

5. $0 \div {}^+\frac{3}{4} = \underline{\ ?\ }$ because $^+\frac{3}{4} \times \underline{\ ?\ } = 0$ ◀── By a positive number?

Divide. Express the quotient in lowest terms.

6. $\dfrac{^+63}{^+7}$ 7. $\dfrac{^-48}{^-6}$ 8. $\dfrac{^-21}{^+3}$ 9. $\dfrac{^-60}{^+5}$ 10. $\dfrac{^+81}{^-9}$

11. $\dfrac{^-1.5}{^-0.3}$ 12. $\dfrac{^+3.2}{^+0.8}$ 13. $\dfrac{^+0.54}{^-0.6}$ 14. $\dfrac{^-0.72}{^+0.8}$ 15. $\dfrac{^+4.55}{^+0.05}$

16. $\dfrac{^+6.39}{^-0.03}$ 17. $\dfrac{^-3.02}{^-0.2}$ 18. $\dfrac{^-30}{^-120}$ 19. $\dfrac{^+8}{^+40}$ 20. $\dfrac{^-11}{^+88}$

21. $\dfrac{^-18}{^+72}$ 22. $\dfrac{^-80}{^-640}$ 23. $\dfrac{^+5\frac{1}{2}}{^-6\frac{1}{4}}$ 24. $\dfrac{^+12\frac{1}{3}}{\frac{^-37}{3}}$ 25. $\dfrac{\frac{^-201}{2}}{^+\frac{1}{2}}$

112

Find the quotient.

26. $^-4.2 \div {}^-0.6$ **27.** $^-5.7 \div {}^-0.3$ **28.** $^+4.8 \div {}^+0.8$ **29.** $^-6.1 \div {}^+6.1$

30. $^+3.8 \div {}^-0.1$ **31.** $^-6.1 \div {}^+10$ **32.** $^+7.2 \div {}^-10$ **33.** $^-0.32 \div {}^+0.4$

34. $^+0.54 \div {}^-0.9$ **35.** $^+63 \div {}^+0.07$ **36.** $^-36 \div {}^-0.04$ **37.** $^+5.6 \div {}^-0.7$

38. $\frac{^-4}{5} \div \frac{^-2}{3}$ **39.** $\frac{^+5}{6} \div \frac{^+1}{2}$ **40.** $\frac{^-3}{4} \div \frac{^-3}{10}$ **41.** $\frac{^+2}{3} \div {}^-6$

42. $\frac{^-3}{8} \div {}^+9$ **43.** $^-2\frac{1}{3} \div {}^+2\frac{1}{3}$ **44.** $^+5\frac{1}{4} \div {}^-1\frac{1}{2}$ **45.** $^-8\frac{1}{8} \div {}^-3\frac{3}{4}$

Multiply or divide.

46. $^-4 \times {}^+12$ **47.** $^-6 \times {}^-5$ **48.** $^-15 \div {}^+3$ **49.** $^-44 \div {}^-8$

50. $^-3.4 \times {}^-1.7$ **51.** $^+7.2 \times {}^-1.2$ **52.** $^-6.3 \div {}^+1.8$ **53.** $^-1.05 \div {}^-2.1$

54. $\frac{^+5}{6} \div \frac{^+1}{2}$ **55.** $\frac{^-7}{12} \div \frac{^+3}{4}$ **56.** $^+4\frac{2}{3} \div {}^-1\frac{1}{6}$ **57.** $^+7\frac{1}{7} \div {}^-6\frac{1}{4}$

Solve. (Use the rules for order of operations.)

58. $(^-5 \times {}^+6) \div (^-13 + {}^+10) = \underline{\ ?\ }$ **59.** $(^-2.4 + {}^-1.6) \times {}^+2.1 = \underline{\ ?\ }$

60. $(^-3.6 \div {}^+9) + {}^+4 = \underline{\ ?\ }$ **61.** $(\frac{^-1}{2} \times \frac{^+4}{5}) \div {}^-2 = \underline{\ ?\ }$

62. $(^+3 + {}^-4.5 + {}^-1.5) \times {}^-5 = \underline{\ ?\ }$ **63.** $(^+2.1 \div {}^-3) - (^-1.4 \div {}^-7) = \underline{\ ?\ }$

64. $(\frac{^-2}{3} \times {}^-9) + (\frac{^-4}{5} \times {}^+10) = \underline{\ ?\ }$ **65.** $(^+3\frac{1}{4} + {}^-5\frac{1}{2}) \div (^-9 - {}^-4) = \underline{\ ?\ }$

66. Which two examples have the same answer?

   a. $^-3 \times {}^-4$ **b.** $^-2 \times {}^+6$ **c.** $\dfrac{^-3 \times {}^-4}{^+1}$ **d.** $\dfrac{^-2 \times {}^-6}{^-1}$

67. Which answer is different from the others?

   a. $^+8 \times {}^-3 \times {}^-1$ **b.** $^-6 \times {}^-1 \times {}^+4$ **c.** $\dfrac{^+2 \times {}^-12}{^+1}$ **d.** $\dfrac{^-3 \times {}^+8}{^-1}$

Solve.

68. The product of what number and $^+25$ is $^-60$?

69. $^-1.2$ divided by what number equals $^-30$?

70. The quotient of what number divided by $^-0.9$ is $^+3.6$?

71. A number is multiplied by $^+5$, then multiplied by $^-0.2$. The result is $^-16$. What is the number?

72. A number is divided by $\frac{^-1}{3}$, then divided again by $\frac{^-1}{3}$. The result is $^-2$. What is the number?

◄═════ **MAKE UP YOUR OWN** ═════►

73. Write a multiplication problem like exercise 71. Then solve it.

74. Write a division problem like exercise 72. Then solve it.

Solving Multiplication and Division Equations

Multiplication and division equations with positive and negative rational numbers are solved just like those with whole numbers.

▶ **To solve a multiplication equation,** *divide* both sides by the same number.

$$5n = {}^-45$$

Divide both sides by $^+5$. ⟶ $\dfrac{5n}{5} = \dfrac{^-45}{5}$

$$n = {}^-9$$

Check: $5n = {}^-45$

Substitute $^-9$ for n. ⟶ $5(^-9) = {}^-45$

$${}^-45 = {}^-45$$

$${}^-7c = {}^-8.4$$

Divide both sides by $^-7$. ⟶ $\dfrac{^-7c}{^-7} = \dfrac{^-8.4}{^-7}$

$$c = {}^+1.2$$

Check: $^-7c = {}^-8.4$

Substitute $^+1.2$ for c. ⟶ $^-7(^+1.2) = {}^-8.4$

$${}^-8.4 = {}^-8.4$$

▶ **To solve a division equation,** *multiply* both sides by the same number.

Multiply both sides by $^+1.5$.

$$\dfrac{b}{1.5} = {}^-30$$

⟶ $\dfrac{b}{1.5} \times 1.5 = {}^-30 \times 1.5$

$$b = {}^-45$$

Check: $\dfrac{b}{1.5} = {}^-30$

Substitute $^-45$ for b. ⟶ $\dfrac{^-45}{1.5} = {}^-30$

$${}^-30 = {}^-30$$

Multiply both sides by $^-3$.

$$\dfrac{r}{^-3} = 1\dfrac{1}{6}$$

⟶ $\dfrac{r}{^-3} \times {}^-3 = {}^+1\dfrac{1}{6} \times {}^-3$

$$r = {}^+\dfrac{7}{\overset{6}{\underset{2}{\cancel{6}}}} \times \dfrac{^-\overset{1}{\cancel{3}}}{1} = {}^-3\dfrac{1}{2}$$

Check: $\dfrac{r}{^-3} = 1\dfrac{1}{6}$

Substitute $^-3\dfrac{1}{2}$ for r. ⟶ $\dfrac{^-3\frac{1}{2}}{^-3} = 1\dfrac{1}{6}$ ⟶ $^+1\dfrac{1}{6} = {}^+1\dfrac{1}{6}$

Complete each statement. Then solve the equations.

1. $^-1.2n = {}^+1$ is a multiplication equation. To solve, __?__ both sides by __?__.

2. $\dfrac{x}{4} = {}^+2\dfrac{2}{5}$ is a division equation. To solve, __?__ both sides by __?__.

Write an equation. Solve it.

3. One third of a number, t, is equal to negative twenty.

4. Three fourths times a number, r, is equal to sixteen.

5. Negative two and five tenths times a number, n, is equal to negative thirty.

6. A number, e, divided by negative five is equal to negative three and one half.

7. The product of $^-3\dfrac{1}{3}$ and a number is equal to positive 20.

8. The quotient when a number is divided by $^-11$ is $^+23.1$.

Solve.

9. $3x = {}^-42$

10. $9y = {}^-99$

11. $^-4t = {}^-64$

12. $7n = {}^+84$

13. $^-0.5s = {}^+3.5$

14. $^-0.45m = {}^-0.27$

15. $^-5.6p = {}^-50.4$

16. $^+1.45c = {}^-0.87$

17. $^-0.8a = {}^+0.56$

18. $-\dfrac{2}{3}d = {}^+\dfrac{2}{9}$

19. $^+\dfrac{1}{2}x = {}^-2\dfrac{1}{4}$

20. $-\dfrac{2}{5}e = {}^+2\dfrac{1}{10}$

21. $\dfrac{h}{^-15} = {}^+6$

22. $\dfrac{a}{^+10} = {}^-9$

23. $\dfrac{r}{^-8} = {}^-56$

24. $\dfrac{v}{^+5} = {}^-30$

25. $\dfrac{d}{^-0.1} = {}^-16$

26. $\dfrac{b}{^-0.4} = {}^+12$

27. $\dfrac{w}{^-2.2} = {}^-3.5$

28. $\dfrac{b}{^+5.1} = {}^-2.16$

29. $\dfrac{x}{^+0.38} = {}^-15$

30. $\dfrac{t}{^-4} = {}^+\dfrac{5}{8}$

31. $\dfrac{y}{^+9} = {}^-1\dfrac{1}{2}$

32. $\dfrac{z}{^-3} = {}^+1\dfrac{4}{5}$

Which equation has a different solution from the others?

33. **a.** $d + 8 = {}^-2$ **b.** $\dfrac{s}{5} = {}^-2$ **c.** $r - {}^-6 = {}^+4$ **d.** $^-1.5a = {}^+15$

34. **a.** $^-6 = \dfrac{d}{3}$ **b.** $^-1 = \dfrac{u}{^-18}$ **c.** $t - {}^+20 = {}^-38$ **d.** $x + 7 = {}^-11$

35. **a.** $^-3m = {}^+4.5$ **b.** $\dfrac{d}{^+0.3} = {}^-5$ **c.** $e - {}^-4 = {}^+5.5$ **d.** $z + 6 = {}^+4.5$

36. **a.** $^+\dfrac{2}{3}k = {}^-1$ **b.** $y + 8 = {}^+6.5$ **c.** $\dfrac{b}{^-2} = {}^+0.75$ **d.** $c - 2.1 = 2.4$

Variables as Divisors

Sometimes the variable may appear as the divisor in an equation.
You can use the cross-products rule to solve the equation.

Solve: $\dfrac{^-36}{n} = {}^+2\dfrac{2}{5}$

$\dfrac{^-36}{n} \diagdown\!\!\!\!\diagup \dfrac{^+12}{5}$

$^+12n = {}^-36 \times 5$

$n = {}^-15$

Solve: $\dfrac{^+4.8}{a} = {}^-0.3$

$\dfrac{^+4.8}{a} \diagdown\!\!\!\!\diagup \dfrac{^-0.3}{1}$

$^-0.3a = {}^+4.8$

$a = {}^-16$

Solve each equation.

37. $\dfrac{^+18}{r} = {}^-1\dfrac{1}{9}$

38. $\dfrac{^-48}{m} = {}^-2\dfrac{2}{3}$

39. $\dfrac{^-3\frac{1}{2}}{s} = {}^-1\dfrac{3}{4}$

40. $\dfrac{^+0.84}{c} = {}^-5.6$

41. $\dfrac{^+4.4}{n} = {}^+0.8$

42. $\dfrac{^-18.5}{t} = {}^+7.4$

To find the least common multiple (LCM) of equations with fractional rational numbers, find the **LCM** of the denominators.

LCM of: $1\frac{1}{2}x + 2\frac{5}{6} = {}^{-}1\frac{2}{3}$ is 6 because 6 is the LCM of 2, 6, and 3.

The LCM of decimal rational numbers is always a power of ten that represents the *greatest* number of decimal places in any term of the equation.

LCM of: **1.12c + 2.06 = 9.9 is __?__**

Greatest decimal place is in 1.12c and in 2.06 ⟶ LCM = 10 × 10 = 100

▶ **Solve for x:** $1\frac{1}{2}x + 2\frac{5}{6} = {}^{-}1\frac{2}{3}$

- Change terms to improper fractions.

$$\frac{3}{2}x + \frac{17}{6} = \frac{{}^{-}5}{3}$$

- Find the LCM of 2, 6, and 3.

LCM (2, 6, 3) : 6

- Multiply by the LCM.

$$6\left(\frac{3}{2}x + \frac{17}{6} = \frac{{}^{-}5}{3}\right)$$

$$= \left(\overset{3}{\cancel{6}} \times \frac{3}{2}\right)x + \left(\overset{1}{\cancel{6}} \times \frac{17}{\cancel{6}}\right) = \left(\overset{2}{\cancel{6}} \times \frac{{}^{-}5}{\cancel{3}}\right)$$

- Solve by using inverse operations. (The inverse of + 17 is − 17, and the inverse of × 9 is ÷ 9.)

$$= \quad 9x + 17 = {}^{-}10$$

$$= 9x + 17 - 17 = {}^{-}10 - 17$$

$$9x = {}^{-}27$$

$$\frac{9}{9}x = \frac{{}^{-}27}{9} \longrightarrow x = {}^{-}3$$

- Check by substituting the value found in the original equation.

$$1\frac{1}{2}x + 2\frac{5}{6} = {}^{-}1\frac{2}{3}$$

$$\left(1\frac{1}{2}\right)\left({}^{-}3\right) + 2\frac{5}{6} = {}^{-}1\frac{2}{3}$$

$${}^{-}4\frac{1}{2} + 2\frac{5}{6} = {}^{-}1\frac{2}{3} \longrightarrow {}^{-}1\frac{2}{3} = {}^{-}1\frac{2}{3}$$

▶ **Solve for c: 1.12c + 2.06 = 9.9** (LCM is 100. Multiply each term by 100.)

$$100(1.12c + 2.06 = 9.9) = (100 \times 1.12c) + (100 \times 2.06) = (100 \times 9.9)$$

$$112c + 206 = 990 \longrightarrow 112c = 990 - 206$$

$$112c = 784 \longrightarrow c = \frac{784}{112} \longrightarrow c = 7$$

Check: 1.12(7) + 2.06 = 9.9 ⟶ 7.84 + 2.06 = 9.9 ⟶ 9.9 = 9.9

Name the LCM for each equation. Then solve.

1. $^-1.5 + 0.3r = ^-4.2$

2. $0.8d + 0.4 = ^-5.2$

3. $0.12a + 0.56 = ^-0.28$

4. $4t - 0.07 = ^-0.55$

5. $0.06n + ^-0.3 = ^-0.21$

6. $0.15b - 1 = ^-5.5$

7. $3a + ^-1\frac{1}{2} = ^-5\frac{1}{4}$

8. $\frac{m}{8} - 2\frac{1}{2} = ^-4$

9. $2\frac{1}{2}h + \frac{^-3}{4} = ^+1\frac{1}{2}$

Choose an equivalent equation. Then solve.

10. $1.4x + 3.5 = 31.5$ **a.** $14x + 35 = 31.5$ **b.** $14x + 35 = 315$

11. $0.25n - 3 = ^-1.25$ **a.** $25n - 300 = ^-125$ **b.** $25n - 3 = ^-125$

12. $^-0.3d + ^-2.8 = ^-4$ **a.** $^-3d + ^-28 = ^-4$ **b.** $^-3d + ^-28 = ^-40$

13. $\frac{r}{^-3} + 2\frac{1}{4} = ^-1\frac{3}{4}$ **a.** $^-4r + 27 = ^-21$ **b.** $r + 27 = ^-21$

14. $^-1\frac{1}{4}m - ^+\frac{1}{6} = ^+2\frac{1}{3}$ **a.** $^-15m - 2 = ^+28$ **b.** $^-15m - 2 = ^-28$

15. $\frac{e}{2} - 3\frac{1}{5} = ^+2\frac{4}{5}$ **a.** $5e - 16 = 14$ **b.** $5e - 32 = 28$

16. $\frac{2}{3}z - ^-\frac{1}{2} = ^-3\frac{1}{2}$ **a.** $4z - ^-3 = ^-21$ **b.** $4z - ^-3 = ^-7$

Simplify by Combining Like Terms

$\boxed{7n + 2n} + 8 = ^-28$

$9n + 8 = ^-28$

$9n + 8 - 8 = ^-28 - 8$

$9n = ^-36$

$n = ^-4$

| Like terms contain the same variable. |

$\boxed{5d - 3d} - 3 = ^+4.2$

$2d - 3 = ^+4.2$

$2d - 3 + 3 = ^+4.2 + 3$

$2d = ^+7.2$

$d = ^+3.6$

Combine like terms; then solve.

17. $6b - 2b + 6 = ^-10$

18. $5t + 2t - 1 = ^-36$

19. $2r - 4 + 3r = ^+2.5$

20. $3n + 1.2 + 4n = ^-0.9$

21. $6g + 11 - 2g = 31$

22. $4s - 3 - 2s = ^-1.4$

23. $7m + 1.5 - 8m = ^-2.1$

24. $9h - 3.2 - 10h = 6$

25. $2c + 1\frac{1}{3} - 4c = ^-4$

26. $5y - \frac{1}{2} - 8y = ^+5\frac{1}{2}$

27. $1.2x - 7 + 1.8x = 20$

28. $1\frac{1}{4}a + 6 - \frac{1}{4}a = 8$

CHALLENGE   Solve these equations with grouping symbols.

29. $3(n + 2) - 2n = 9$

30. $^-4(6 + a) + 2a = 12$

31. $^-2(5 - c) + 3c = 5$

32. $\dfrac{3m + 7m + 8}{2} = 9$

33. $\dfrac{5c - 3c + 1}{3} = 5$

34. $\dfrac{6b - 8b + 4}{^-3} = 2$

35. $\dfrac{2(n + 3)}{2} = 4$

36. $\dfrac{2m + 11 - 3m}{3} = ^-1$

37. $\dfrac{3x + 4 - 2x}{^-3} = 5$

Problem: Yesterday a certain stock opened at $^+12\frac{3}{8}$ points. At the close of the day the stock was at $^+10\frac{3}{4}$ points. What rational number represents the change in the stock's value during the day? Indicate whether the change is negative or positive.

1 IMAGINE Picture the starting and final values of the stocks on a number line showing 10 through 13 with quarters between.

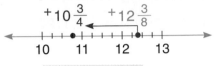

stock dropped

2 NAME *Facts:* Begins: $^+12\frac{3}{8}$

Ends: $^+10\frac{3}{4}$

Question: How had the value of the stock changed during the day?

3 THINK Look at the picture of the stock falling.
Now write a word sentence showing what happened.
Since stock dropped, this is:

Opening Value – Closing Value = Change
$$12\frac{3}{8} \quad - \quad 10\frac{3}{4} \qquad = \text{Change}$$

Now write an equation for change, C.
$$C = 12\frac{3}{8} \quad - \quad 10\frac{3}{4}$$
$$C = 1\frac{5}{8} \text{ amount of change, not direction of change}$$

But since stock dropped, change is a negative value, $^-1\frac{5}{8}$:
$$C = {}^-1\frac{5}{8}$$

4 COMPUTE Solve the equation for C.
$$^+12\frac{3}{8} + C = {}^+10\frac{3}{4}$$
$$^+12\frac{3}{8} - {}^+12\frac{3}{8} + C = {}^+10\frac{3}{4} - {}^+12\frac{3}{8}$$
$$C = {}^+10\frac{3}{4} + {}^-12\frac{3}{8}$$
$$C = {}^-1\frac{5}{8}$$

5 CHECK Substitute $^-1\frac{5}{8}$ for C in the original equation.
$$^+12\frac{3}{8} + C = {}^+10\frac{3}{4}$$
$$^+12\frac{3}{8} + {}^-1\frac{5}{8} \stackrel{?}{=} {}^+10\frac{3}{4}$$
$$^+10\frac{3}{4} = {}^+10\frac{3}{4}$$

Solve by writing an equation.

1. A chemist listed the temperature at which 5 samples froze:
$^-3.5°C$, $^-3.2°C$, $^-3°C$, $^-2.8°C$, and $^-1.5°C$.
What was the average temperature of the samples?

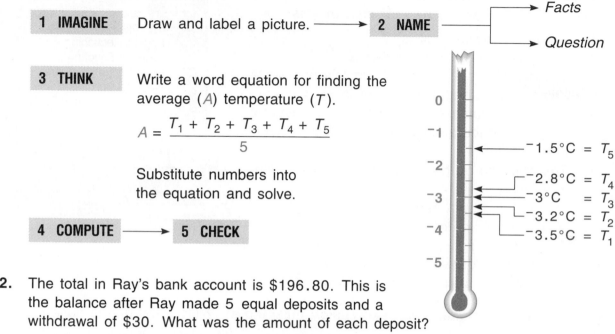

| 1 IMAGINE | Draw and label a picture. → | 2 NAME |

Facts

Question

| 3 THINK | Write a word equation for finding the average (A) temperature (T). |

$$A = \frac{T_1 + T_2 + T_3 + T_4 + T_5}{5}$$

Substitute numbers into the equation and solve.

| 4 COMPUTE | → | 5 CHECK |

$^-1.5°C = T_5$

$^-2.8°C = T_4$
$^-3°C\ \ \ = T_3$
$^-3.2°C = T_2$
$^-3.5°C = T_1$

2. The total in Ray's bank account is $196.80. This is the balance after Ray made 5 equal deposits and a withdrawal of $30. What was the amount of each deposit?

3. If Vera's watch loses 75 seconds each day, how much time does it lose in a week? (Express your answer in minutes.)

4. A man had $585.50 in his savings account. He deposited $50, withdrew $65.75, deposited $170, withdrew $90.20, and withdrew $35. How much did he then have in his account?

5. The price of a certain stock decreased $18.60 per share over 30 days. What was the average daily decrease?

6. Twice a certain number decreased by 10 is $^-1\frac{1}{3}$. What is the number?

7. The low temperatures for five days were:
$^-3°C$, $^+6°C$, $^-1°C$, $^+10°C$, and $^-3°C$.
What was the average low temperature for those five days?

8. Six times a certain number decreased by $^-13$ is $^-16.4$. Find the number.

9. TECHNO stock fell in price by the same amount for each of three straight days. On the fourth day the price rose $^+2\frac{1}{2}$ points. If at the end of the fourth day the stock was valued at $^+1\frac{3}{8}$, by how much had the price fallen on each of the first three days?

10. A number is divided by 3 and then decreased by $^-1$. The result is 6.5. What is the number?

Problem Solving: Applications

Complete each statement.

Write: *positive, negative, zero,* or *meaningless*.

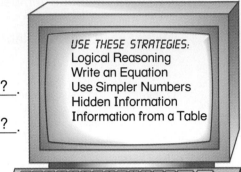

USE THESE STRATEGIES:
Logical Reasoning
Write an Equation
Use Simpler Numbers
Hidden Information
Information from a Table

1. A number minus itself is __?__.
2. Zero minus a positive number is __?__.
3. A positive number minus a negative number is __?__.
4. Zero minus a negative number is __?__.
5. A negative number minus a positive number is __?__.
6. The sum of the absolute value of two numbers is always __?__.
7. The opposite of the absolute value of a number is always __?__.
8. Zero divided by a negative number is __?__.
9. Any number divided by itself is __?__.
10. A negative number divided by zero is __?__.
11. The quotient of two negative numbers is __?__.
12. A positive number divided by zero is __?__.

What value of *b* makes each expression meaningless? (The first one is done.)

13. $^-1.5 \div (^+4 - b)$ Think: $^+4 - ^+4 = 0$ and division by zero is meaningless.
So, $b = ^+4$ makes the expression meaningless.

14. $\dfrac{^+2}{^-8 - b}$ 15. $\dfrac{^-8}{^+1.2 + b}$ 16. $\dfrac{^+6.4}{^-3.2 + b}$ 17. $\dfrac{^-3}{b - ^+2.5}$

Choose the correct answer.

18. If $^-\frac{4}{5} m = 0$, then $^-\frac{4}{5} + m = $ __?__.   **a.** $^-\frac{5}{4}$ **b.** $^-\frac{4}{5}$ **c.** 0

19. If $\dfrac{1}{\frac{d}{3}} = \dfrac{^-1}{7}$, then $d = $ __?__.   **a.** $^+\frac{1}{27}$ **b.** $^+21$ **c.** $^-21$

20. Take 15 hundredths from 16 thousandths. The result is:
    a. $^-0.01$ **b.** $^-0.145$ **c.** $^-0.134$

21. The opposite of $^-10$ decreased by the reciprocal of $^-10$ is:
    a. $^-9\frac{1}{10}$ **b.** $^+10\frac{1}{10}$ **c.** $^-1\frac{1}{10}$

22. Multiply 2 thousandths by 3 tenths and subtract 3 hundredths from the product. The result is:
    a. $^-0.0012$ **b.** $^-0.0294$ **c.** $^-0.006$

23. Divide negative one half by 3 and add 10 to the quotient. The result is:
    a. $^+9\frac{5}{6}$ **b.** $^-10\frac{1}{6}$ **c.** $^+8\frac{1}{2}$

24. From 8 tenths take 1 and 4 hundredths. Then divide by negative 3 tenths. The result is:
    a. $^+2$ **b.** $^-8$ **c.** $^+0.8$

25. The value of a stock decreased by $\frac{3}{8}$ point daily over a 4-day period.

    a. Use a rational number to express the overall change in the stock's value.

    b. If the stock was at $7\frac{1}{4}$ points before it decreased in value, what is its value now?

26. Marta is $3\frac{1}{2}$ years younger than her brother. Together the sum of their ages is $27\frac{1}{2}$. How old is each one now?
(Hint: Let b = brother's age and $b - 3\frac{1}{2}$ = Marta's age.)

27. Jeremy is 14 years old. This is $4\frac{1}{2}$ years more than half his sister's age. How old is his sister?

28. Swenson's batting average was 0.271. Watson had 53 hits in 200 times at bat. Find a rational number expressing the difference between Watson's average and that of Swenson.

29. During a drought the water-table level changed $^-0.35$ m per day. If the drought lasted 2 weeks, express the overall change in the water-table level using a rational number.

A consumer reporter tested four different fabrics to find the amount each would shrink when washed. Use the table to complete exercises 30–32.

Fabric	A	B	C	D
Change in length	$-1\frac{3}{8}''$	$\frac{^-15}{16}''$	$-1\frac{1}{4}''$	$\frac{^-7}{8}''$

30. Order the fabrics from the one that will shrink least to the one that will shrink most.

31. How many inches more did sample A shrink than sample D?

32. How many inches less did sample B shrink than sample C?

Variables on Both Sides of an Equation

Two less than four times a number is equal to three added to three times a number. What is the number?

- Write an equation.
- Add the opposite of 3a to both sides. (This brings the variable to one side.)
- Solve and check the equation.

$$
\begin{aligned}
4a - 2 &= 3a + 3 \\
-3a &= -3a \\
\hline
a - 2 &= 3 \\
a - 2 + 2 &= 3 + 2 \\
a &= 5
\end{aligned}
$$

Write and solve each equation.

33. A number added to 6 is equal to 30 less than four times the number. What is the number?

34. Twice the sum of some number and $^-4$ is equal to the product of the number and 6. What is the number?

35. Half the sum of a number and 15 is equal to the opposite of the number doubled. Find the number.

36. Twice a number subtracted from 23 is equal to 3 more than half the number. What is the number?

More Practice

Write the opposite of each rational number.

1. $^+3.16$
2. $^+4.36$
3. $^-\frac{8}{3}$
4. $^-\frac{1}{4}$
5. $^-1.\overline{9}$
6. $^-4.8$
7. $\frac{0}{6}$
8. $^+5\frac{2}{7}$
9. $^+3\frac{1}{9}$
10. $^-0.6$

Compare. Write <, =, or >.

11. $^-\frac{1}{3}$ __?__ $^-0.2$
12. $^-2.3$ __?__ $^-3.2$
13. $^-\frac{4}{5}$ __?__ $^-\frac{3}{5}$
14. $^+9$ __?__ $^+9.3$
15. $^+4$ __?__ $^-7$
16. 0 __?__ $^-3$

Name the property.

17. $(^-3 + 2) + ^-6 = ^-3 + (2 + ^-6)$
18. $^-3 \times ^-\frac{1}{3} = 1$
19. $^-2 \times 4 = 4 \times ^-2$
20. $^-\frac{6}{7} \times 1 = 1 \times ^-\frac{6}{7} = ^-\frac{6}{7}$
21. $^-4 \times (2 + ^-3) = (^-4 \times 2) + (^-4 \times ^-3)$

Compute.

22. $^+4 + ^+11\frac{1}{3}$
23. $^-0.4 + ^-2$
24. $0 - ^-6.5$
25. $^-18.7 - ^-14.3$
26. $^-5 \times ^-7$
27. $^+0.4 \times ^-6$
28. $^-\frac{1}{3} \times ^-\frac{1}{3}$
29. $^+\frac{3}{4} \times ^-\frac{1}{4}$
30. $0 \div ^-6.1$
31. $^-9 \div ^-1.2$
32. $^-80 \div ^+10$
33. $^+\frac{4}{6} \div ^-\frac{1}{4}$

Solve the equation.

34. $r + ^+9 = ^+6$
35. $x + ^+15 = ^-6$
36. $p + ^-3 = ^+8\frac{1}{2}$
37. $y + ^+4.2 = ^+1.8$
38. $z - ^+3.1 = ^-4.1$
39. $t + ^+0.8 = ^+0.11$
40. $^+3x - ^-5 = ^+5$
41. $^-7r + ^+3 = ^-45$
42. $^-2c + ^+8 = ^-15$
43. $\frac{x}{3} - ^+2 = ^+4$
44. $\frac{r}{^-2} + ^+4 = ^-12$
45. $\frac{b}{^-3} + ^-7 = ^-18$
46. $3(x - ^+4) = ^+15$
47. $^+8(t + 5) = ^+72$
48. $\frac{2d + ^+8}{^+4} = ^+5$

Write an equation and solve.

49. Nine less than 7 times a number is 75. Find the number.

50. A number divided by 4 is 3 more than 13. Find the number.

True or false? Explain.

51. The sum of a number and its opposite is always zero.

52. The difference of two negative numbers is always negative.

53. The quotient of two numbers with opposite signs is always negative.

54. The product of two numbers is positive. The factors must have been positive.

POLYOMINOES

A **polyomino** is a formation made up of a number of squares, with each square sharing at least one complete side with another.

These are polyominoes. ⟶

These are *not* polyominoes. ⟶

One polyomino is *the same as* another if it can be flipped or turned to match the other. These polyominoes are all the same because:

This ⟶   flips to form this, ⟶   which turns to form this, ⟶   which flips to form this. ⟶

A polyomino is *named* by the number of squares in its formations.

- A **domino** is made up of 2 squares.
  There is only 1 possible arrangement of 2 squares. ⟶

- A **triomino** is made up of 3 squares.
  There are two possible arrangements of 3 squares. ⟶

- A **tetromino** is made up of 4 squares.

- A **pentamino** is made up of 5 squares.

Discover these polyominoes!
Trace along graph-paper lines to help you draw the formations.

1. There are 5 possible (different) *tetrominoes*. Draw them. (Remember: Any tetromino that flips or turns to match another is the same as the other. So both count as just 1.)

2. How many *pentaminoes* are there? Draw them all!

Make another complete set of pentaminoes on colored paper, using 1-inch squares. Cut out the pentaminoes.

3. Arrange all the pentaminoes to form a 6-inch by 10-inch rectangle.

4. Rearrange them all into a 4-inch by 15-inch rectangle.

5. Without folding the pentaminoes, try to imagine which of them can be folded along the lines to make an open box. Now test your guesses by folding.

Check Your Mastery

Write each set of numbers in order from least to greatest. See pp. 100–101

1. $^-1\frac{1}{3}$, $^+1.33$, $^-1\frac{1}{4}$, $^+2$, $^-1$, $^+1$
2. 0, $^-5\frac{1}{4}$, $^+5$, $^-4.5$, $^+2.5$

Name the property. Then solve. See pp. 102–113

3. $^-5.3(4 - 4)$
4. $^-10(^-2.1 + 5)$
5. $^-2\frac{1}{4} \times \frac{^-4}{9}$

Compute.

6. $^-9 + {^+5.2}$
7. $^-10 + {^-7.5}$
8. $^-8 - {^-3\frac{1}{4}}$
9. $^+5 - {^+10.2}$
10. $^-6 \times {^+8\frac{1}{3}}$
11. $^-8 \times {^+5\frac{1}{2}}$
12. $^-44 \div {^+1.1}$
13. $^+27 \div {^-1.8}$

Solve the equation. See pp. 104–117

14. $x - {^+3} = {^-5}$
15. $y + {^-8} = {^+4}$
16. $r - {^-5} = {^+9.7}$

17. $4y = {^-33.2}$
18. $\frac{r}{^-3} = {^-9}$
19. $2t + {^+10} = {^+22}$

20. $^-6q = {^-24.6}$
21. $\frac{x}{^-4} = {^+8\frac{1}{2}}$
22. $^-5r + {^-1} = {^+1}$

23. $25y - {^+200} = {^-150}$
24. $^-0.3d + {^-1.8} = {^-5}$
25. $12x + {^+30} = {^+26.4}$

26. $\frac{1}{2}x + \frac{1}{6} = \frac{^-7}{3}$
27. $\frac{2}{3}r - \frac{^-1}{2} = {^-4\frac{1}{2}}$
28. $3t - {^-4} = {^-25}$

29. $2(x + 4) = {^+10}$
30. $\frac{5x - 3}{3} = {^+8}$
31. $\frac{3x + 2}{2} = {^+7}$

32. $4(r - 5) = {^+12}$
33. $\frac{6t + 2}{8} = {^+4}$
34. $5(q + {^+9}) = {^+90}$

Solve. See pp. 100–117

35. The temperature during a 5-day period was $^-8°$C, $^+4°$C, $^-1°$C, $^+1°$C, and $^-2°$C. What was the average temperature for that period?

36. A woman had $1270 in her checking account. She deposited $190, wrote checks for $25 and $110, deposited $180, wrote a check for $45, and deposited $150. How much did she then have in her account?

37. Jeff had a total of $415 in his savings account. After making 3 equal withdrawals of $40, how much was left in the account?

38. On Tuesday the cost of a certain stock opened at $^+45\frac{1}{4}$ points. At day's end the stock was at $^+51\frac{1}{2}$. What rational number represents the change?

Cumulative Review

Choose the correct answer.

1. 8 divided by the product of 3 and the sum of $4 + (^-2)$ is equal to:

   a. $1\frac{1}{3}$ b. $\frac{1}{4}$

   c. $\frac{1}{5}$ d. $\frac{1}{6}$

2. What is the sum of $x(y - z)$ and $x(y + z)$ when $x = 4$, $y = 5$, and $z = {}^-1$?

   a. 48
   b. 32
   c. 24
   d. 40

3. What property is used in solving $4(x + 3y) = 4x + 12y$?

   a. Associative
   b. Identity
   c. Commutative
   d. Distributive

4. What number when divided by one half is twelve less than three times the number?

   a. 24
   b. $^-12$
   c. 12
   d. 18

5. A number is multiplied by 0.04; then by 0.008. The result is 32. What is the number?

   a. 8000   b. 4000
   c. 100,000   d. 10,000

6. What rule is used to simplify $^-5 - 4 = {}^-9$?

   a. $a - b = b - a$
   b. $a - b = a + b$
   c. $a - b = a - (^+b)$
   d. $a - b = a + (^-b)$

7. The reciprocal of 4.8×10^{-1} is:

   a. $2.08\overline{3}$ b. 0.48
   c. 0.048 d. 0.408

8. If $x - 11 = 14$, what is the value of x?

   a. 25
   b. $^-25$
   c. 125
   d. $^-125$

9. 5 more than half a number equals 3 more than the number. Find the number.

   a. 5   b. 6
   c. 4   d. 8

10. What is the difference when 8^2 is subtracted from 12?

   a. $^-20$ b. $^-52$
   c. 20   d. 52

11. What is the solution set for $3t - 5 > 7$?

   a. $\{4, 3, 2, 1, \ldots\}$
   b. $\{3, 2, 1, \ldots\}$
   c. $\{5, 6, 7, 8, \ldots\}$
   d. $\{4, 5, 6, \ldots\}$

12. What is the value of $3 + (2x - y) + z$, when $x = \frac{1}{2}$, $y = \frac{2}{3}$, and $z = 0$?

   a. $\frac{2}{3}$ b. $\frac{1}{3}$
   c. $2\frac{2}{3}$ d. $3\frac{1}{3}$

13. What is twice the sum of $^-1\frac{1}{2}$ and 0.04?

   a. $^-2.92$ b. $^-1.2$
   c. $^-1.5$ d. $^-2.5$

14. What is the number if $\frac{4}{5}$ of it is the square root of 256?

   a. 16   b. 20
   c. 24   d. 32

Add.

15. $^+0.04 + ^+0.26$ **16.** $^+0.5 + ^-0.05$ **17.** $^-2.17 + ^+1.32$ **18.** $^-0.03 + ^-3.0$

Subtract.

19. $^+3.5 - ^+2.1$ **20.** $^-8.4 - ^-8.4$ **21.** $^+0.1 - ^+0.01$ **22.** $^-1.02 - ^-2.01$

Multiply.

23. $\dfrac{^-3}{7} \times \dfrac{^-8}{9}$ **24.** $^-0.4 \times \dfrac{^+4}{9}$ **25.** $^-5\dfrac{2}{3} \times ^+3\dfrac{2}{9}$ **26.** $\dfrac{^-2}{5}\left(^-3.5 - ^-3\dfrac{1}{2}\right)$

Divide.

27. $\dfrac{^-5}{12} \div \dfrac{^+15}{8}$ **28.** $^+3\dfrac{4}{5} \div ^-2.5$ **29.** $^+3\dfrac{1}{4} \div 0$ **30.** $^-8\dfrac{3}{8} \div ^-1\dfrac{3}{4}$

Simplify.

31. $^+2 + ^+8 - (^-4 \times ^+3)$ **32.** $^-4 - (^-2 + ^+5) \times ^-1$

33. $(^-1.2 + ^+1.2) - ^-1.2$ **34.** $(^-7 - ^-2) + (^+8 - ^-0.5)$

Solve.

35. $^-3n + ^+4 = ^-8$ **36.** $\dfrac{^+4}{9}n + ^+5 = ^-3$ **37.** $\dfrac{x}{^-3} + ^+6 = 0$

38. $\dfrac{^-7}{8}n - ^-1.2 = ^+5.2$ **39.** $^+5x - ^+0.05 = ^+1.95$ **40.** $\dfrac{^-2}{3}t - ^+1.6 = ^-10.4$

Solve.

41. If a group of scouts walked 3.2 km in an hour, how long did it take them to reach camp, 26.4 km away?

42. Susan had $85.60 in her savings account. She withdrew $12.35 but later deposited $15.75. How much did she have in her account then?

43. The sports banquet committee collected $3750. If an athlete and parent paid $25 jointly to attend, how many people were at the banquet?

44. How many 8-in. tiles are needed to cover a circular floor having a 15-ft radius?

45. A school received 35 cases that held a total of 415 books. One case contained 5 less books than the others. How many books were in that case?

46. Mark lives 4.5 kilometers from the athletic field. Jim lives 2.1 kilometers farther away than Karen, whose home is twice as far from the field as Mark's. How far from the field does Jim live?

+10 BONUS

47. Create a board game that involves "plus and minus" scoring. (For example, if in "The Wilderness Game" you reach a mountain top, you score +20. If you land on a "Danger Zone" square, you lose 10.) Design the game board and write a set of rules for your game.

Write th

9. (9

10. (8

11. (3

12. (5

13. (7

14. (4

15. (6

Write in

16. 1.

20. 35

24. 8,

28. W

a.

29. W

a.

30. W

a.

Compl

31. S

32. S

33. S

34. S

In this chapter you will:

- Work with positive and negative exponents
- Work with scientific notation with large and small numbers
- Multiply and divide in scientific notation
- Find patterns to complete sequences
- Use divisibility rules
- Work with logic problems
- Solve problems: using simpler numbers
- Use technology: flowcharts

Do you remember?

24 is *divisible* by 2 because
$$24 \div 2 = 12 \text{ R } 0$$
24 is *divisible* by 3 because
$$24 \div 3 = 8 \text{ R } 0$$
24 is *divisible* by 4 because
$$24 \div 4 = 6 \text{ R } 0$$
24 is *not divisible* by 5 because
$$24 \div 5 = 4 \text{ R } 4$$
24 is *divisible* by 6 because
$$24 \div 6 = 4 \text{ R } 0$$

RESEARCHING TOGETHER

Exponential Monkey Business

By mistake, two monkeys have escaped from the lab on the new planet Ziga. Pretty soon Ziga's monkey population begins to grow exponentially. Make a graph to show that exponential growth. Find out: Will this growth continue indefinitely? Will the monkeys take over Ziga? Make another graph showing what will happen.

5-5 Divisibility

Here are some rules to check for divisibility:

Number is Divisible By	Rule	Example
2	If the ones digit is divisible by 2, the number is divisible by 2.	2768 $8 \div 2 = 4$ 2768 is divisible by 2.
3	If the sum of the digits is divisible by 3, the number is divisible by 3.	728,031 $7 + 2 + 8 + 0 + 3 + 1 = 21$ $21 \div 3 = 7$ 728,031 is divisible by 3.
4	If the tens and ones digits together are divisible by 4, the number is divisible by 4.	4,205,124 $24 \div 4 = 6$ 4,205,124 is divisible by 4.
5	If the ones digit is 0 or 5, the number is divisible by 5.	27,965 and 114,370 are divisible by 5.
8	If the hundreds, tens, and ones digits together are divisible by 8, the number is divisible by 8.	5,618,352 $352 \div 8 = 44$ 5,618,352 is divisible by 8.
9	If the sum of the digits is divisible by 9, the number is divisible by 9.	458,982 $4 + 5 + 8 + 9 + 8 + 2 = 36$ $36 \div 9 = 4$ 458,982 is divisible by 9.
10	If the ones digit is 0, the number is divisible by 10.	9,027,530 is divisible by 10.

By inspection, name the divisors (2, 3, 4, 5, 8, 9, 10) for each number.

1. 348 **2.** 621 **3.** 1348 **4.** 2448 **5.** 3480

6. 7254 **7.** 6210 **8.** 6216 **9.** 4134 **10.** 6345

Complete each. (Use the rules for divisibility.)

11. $5225 \div \underline{\ ?\ } = 1045$ **12.** $3411 \div \underline{\ ?\ } = 379$ **13.** $4024 \div \underline{\ ?\ } = 503$

14. $7101 \div \underline{\ ?\ } = 2367$ **15.** $1110 \div \underline{\ ?\ } = 111$ **16.** $3112 \div \underline{\ ?\ } = 1556$

Copy and complete the chart. Which numbers are divisible by 2? by 3? by 4? by 5? by 8? by 9? by 10?

	Number	Divisible By						
		2	3	4	5	8	9	10
17.	723,112	Yes	No	Yes	?	?	?	?
18.	560,025							
19.	802,750							
20.	754,008							
21.	2,407,320							
22.	9,620,416							
23.	7,213,843							
24.	15,407,105							
25.	23,170,140							

CRITICAL THINKING   **True or false?** Use your chart to check.

26. If a number is divisible by 10, it is divisible by 5.

27. All numbers that are divisible by 9 are divisible by 3.

28. All numbers that are divisible by 2 are divisible by 4.

29. All numbers that are divisible by 4 are divisible by 8.

30. A number that is divisible by 2 is an even number.

31. A number that is divisible by 10 is divisible by 2.

32. No number can pass all the divisibility tests.

33. A number that does not pass any of the divisibility tests is prime.

34. A number that is divisible by 2 and by 3 is also divisible by 6.

Use a calculator to check for divisibility by 6.

35. 728

36. 936

37. 1420

38. 24,526

39. 120,552

40. 936,008

41. 1,572,421

42. 16,306,540

43. Complete the divisibility rule for 6.

   _?_ numbers that are divisible by _?_ are divisible by 6.

44. What is the least number that is divisible by all the numbers from 1 to 10?

45. Look up a divisibility rule for 11. Which number, 1171 or 1309, is divisible by 11?

5-6 | Patterns and Sequences

Sequence: a list of numbers written in order.

Term: the name given to each number in the sequence.

To find the terms of a sequence, find the pattern by deciding what number was added, subtracted, multiplied, or divided from each term to create the sequence.
This number is called a **constant**.

Sequence of multiples of 7: 7, 14, 21, 28, 35, . . . — Each term is a multiple of 7.

Sequence in which each term increases
by 7 but is *not* a multiple of 7: 5, 12, 19, 26, . . . — 7 is added to each term.
No term is a multiple of 7.

Find the next three terms in each sequence.*

1. 4, 8, 12, 16, . . .
2. 0, 3, 6, 9, . . .
3. 100, 92, 84, 76, . . .
4. 76, 74, 72, 70, . . .
5. 45, 41, 37, 33, . . .
6. 16, 18, 20, 22, . . .
7. 52, 59, 66, 73, . . .
8. 40, 43, 46, 49, . . .
9. 7.1, 7.4, 7.7, 8.0, . . .
10. 0.01, 0.011, 0.012, 0.013, . . .
11. $1\frac{1}{3}, 2\frac{1}{3}, 3\frac{1}{3}, 4\frac{1}{3}, \ldots$
12. $\frac{1}{2}, 1, \frac{3}{2}, 2, \ldots$

Find the pattern for each sequence. (Hint: More than one constant was used.)

Example: 1, 5, 4, 8, 7, . . .

1,   5,   4,   8,   7, . . .
  +4   −1   +4   −1   Pattern: + 4, − 1

13. 38, 32, 31, 25, 24, . . .
14. 5, 7, 10, 12, 15, . . .
15. 6, 4, 8, 6, 12, . . .
16. 2, 3, 5, 8, 12, . . .
17. 15, 20, 26, 33, . . .
18. 1, 1, 2, 3, 5, 8, . . .

Find the next three terms. [Hint: The constant can be the square ($3^2 = 9$) or the cube ($3^3 = 27$) of a number.] Use your calculator.

19. 4, 16, 64, . . .

4,   16,   64,   ? , . . .
  $\times 2^2$ $\times 2^2$ $\times 2^2$ Pattern: $\times 2^2$

20. 7, 56, 448, . . .
21. 1, 27, 729, . . .
22. 2, 32, 512, . . .
23. 3, 9, 27, . . .
24. 3, 24, 192, . . .
25. 5, 25, 125, . . .

CRITICAL  THINKING

26. Use the formula $2n - 1$ to name the next three terms. ⁻1, 1, 3, __?__, __?__, __?__

27. Write the formula that was used to create each sequence.

   a. 0, ⁻2, ⁻4, ⁻6, . . .
   b. ⁻1, 2, 5, 8, 11, . . .
   c. $0, \frac{-1}{2}, -1, \frac{-3}{2}, -2, \ldots$

5-7 Introduction to Truth Tables

Logic: the study of reasoning.

Symbols such as **p, q,** and **r** are used to represent
simple, closed statements.

Every statement has *two* possible truth values:
A statement can be true *or* a statement can be false.
A statement cannot be both true *and* false at the same time.

Negation: the opposite of any statement "**p**."
The symbol "**~p**" is used to show negation.
Read "**~p**" as "**not p**."

Truth table: shows all possible truth values
for a statement and its opposite.

Let **p** represent the statement "Money grows on trees." Then ~**p**
represents the statement, "It is not true that money grows on trees."

To construct a truth table:

- In the first column list the two possible
truth values for the original statement **p**.

- In the second column list the two possible
truth values for the negation of **p**.

If **p** is true, then ~**p** must be false.
If **p** is false, then ~**p** must be true.

p	
T	
F	

p	~p
T	F
F	T

Write the negation of each statement.

1. The sky is blue.
2. 44% of all junk mail is never opened.
3. Apples are round.
4. 7 is an even number.
5. Michigan is a city.
6. Earth is the fifth planet from the sun.

Use p, q, and r to write a statement for each symbol in exercises 7–12, and write its truth value where:*

p represents "Broccoli is good for you."
q represents "Lemons are sweet."
r represents "Potatoes have eyes."

7. ~p
8. q
9. r
10. p
11. ~q
12. ~r

Construct a truth table for each.

13. p ~ p
14. q ~ q
15. r ~ r

5-8 Connectives

Connective: a compound statement formed by combining two or more simple statements.

Four kinds of connectives are given in this chart.

Let p represent "I save money," and q represent "I buy a car."

Connective	Connecting Words	Symbol	Example
Conjunction	and	$p \wedge q$	I save money and I buy a car.
Disjunction	or	$p \vee q$	I save money or I buy a car.
Conditional	if...then...	$p \rightarrow q$	If I save money, then I buy a car.
Biconditional	p if and only if q	$p \leftrightarrow q$	I save money if and only if I buy a car.

These statements show the negation of a connective.

"I do *not* save money and I do not buy a car." $\longrightarrow$ $\sim p \wedge \sim q$

"It is *not true* that I save money and I buy a car." $\longrightarrow$ $\sim(p \wedge q)$

Use p, q, and r to write each connective in symbols where:

p: I close the door. q: You open the window. r: Gil turns on the radio.

1. I close the door and you open the window.
2. I close the door or you open the window.
3. If you open the window, then Gil turns on the radio.
4. You open the window if and only if I close the door.
5. I do *not* close the door and Gil does *not* turn on the radio.
6. I close the door and you do *not* open the window.
7. If Gil turns on the radio, then I close the door and you open the window.
8. If you open the window, then I close the door and Gil turns on the radio.
9. It is *not true* that I close the door and you open the window.
10. It is *not true* that if you open the window, then Gil turns on the radio.

Use r, s, and t to write a statement for each connective in exercises 11–22 where:

r: Silence is golden. s: Knowledge is power. t: Time flies.

11. $r \wedge s$ 12. $s \wedge t$ 13. $r \vee \sim t$ 14. $t \vee r$

15. $\sim(r \vee t)$ 16. $\sim(s \vee t)$ 17. $s \rightarrow t$ 18. $r \rightarrow s$

19. $r \rightarrow t$ 20. $s \leftrightarrow t$ 21. $\sim(r \wedge s) \rightarrow t$ 22. $r \rightarrow (s \wedge t)$

Truth Tables for Connectives

These truth tables show the truth values of these connectives for any statements *p* and *q*.

Conjunction

p	*q*	*p*∧*q*
T	T	T
T	F	F
F	T	F
F	F	F

True only when *both p* and *q* are *true*.

Disjunction

p	*q*	*p*∨*q*
T	T	T
T	F	T
F	T	T
F	F	F

False only when *both p* and *q* are *false*.

Conditional

p	*q*	*p*→*q*
T	T	T
T	F	F
F	T	T
F	F	T

False only when *p* is *true* and *q* is *false*.

Biconditional

p	*q*	*p*↔*q*
T	T	T
T	F	F
F	T	F
F	F	T

True only when *p* and *q* have the *same* truth value.

This truth table shows the truth values for the conjunction *p* ∧ ~*q*.

p	*q*	~*q*	*p*∧~*q*
T	T	F	F
T	F	T	T
F	T	F	F
F	F	T	F

Since ~*q* is a part of the conjunction, there must be a column showing ~*q* in the truth table.

Copy and complete.*

23.

p	*q*	~*q*	*p*∧~*q*
T	T		
T	F		
F	T		
F	F		

24.

p	*q*	~*p*	~*p* → *q*
T	T		
T	F		
F	T		
F	F		

25.

p	*q*	~*p*	~*p* ↔ *q*

Construct a truth table for each.

26. *p* → ~*q*

27. ~*p* ∧ ~*q*

28. ~(*p* ∧ *q*)

29. ~(*p* → *q*)

30. ~(*p* ↔ *q*)

31. **Complete a truth table for the conditional** (*p* ∨ *q*) → (*p* ∧ *q*).

p	*q*	*p* ∨ *q*	*p* ∧ *q*	(*p* ∨ *q*) → (*p* ∧ *q*)
T	T	T	T	T
T	F	T	F	?
F	T	T	F	?
F	F	F	F	?

*See pages 488-492 for more work on connectives, conjunctions, and conditionals.   141

5-9 Converse, Inverse, and Contrapositive

For any conditional ($p \rightarrow q$) there are three related conditionals that can be formed from the original.

Symbol	Connective	Truth Value
Original $p \rightarrow q$	If Fluffy is a poodle, then it is a dog.	True. (Given.)
Converse $q \rightarrow p$	If Fluffy is a dog, then it is a poodle.	False. (Fluffy could be a collie.)
Inverse $\sim p \rightarrow \sim q$	If Fluffy is not a poodle, then it is not a dog.	False. (Same as for the converse.)
Contrapositive $\sim q \rightarrow \sim p$	If Fluffy is not a dog, then it is not a poodle.	True. (Always equivalent to the original.)

This is a truth table for a conditional and its related conditionals.

				Original	Converse	Inverse	Contrapositive
p	q	$\sim p$	$\sim q$	$p \rightarrow q$	$q \rightarrow p$	$\sim p \rightarrow \sim q$	$\sim q \rightarrow \sim p$
T	T	F	F	T	T	T	T
T	F	F	T	F	T	T	F
F	T	T	F	T	F	F	T
F	F	T	T	T	T	T	T

Write the converse, inverse, and contrapositive for each conditional.
Discuss the truth value of each.

1. If it is July, then it is summer.
2. If we score one basket, then we win the game.
3. If a number is divisible by 9, then it is divisible by 3.
4. If it is raining, then the road gets wet.
5. If it does not rain, then I go to the park.

Using symbols, write the contrapositive of each.

6. $s \rightarrow r$ 7. $q \rightarrow w$ 8. $t \rightarrow p$ 9. $\sim p \rightarrow q$ 10. $\sim r \rightarrow w$

11. $r \rightarrow \sim t$ 12. $s \rightarrow \sim p$ 13. $\sim p \rightarrow \sim q$ 14. $\sim t \rightarrow \sim w$

Write the converse of each statement.

15. If a polygon has exactly three sides, then it is a triangle.
16. If it is snowing, then it is cold.
17. If you studied and did your homework, then you passed the test.

18. **Write the inverse of each statement in exercises 15–17.**

Choose the correct answer.

19. A conditional is false if:
  a. p is true and q is false. **b.** both p and q are true.
  c. p is false and q is true. **d.** both p and q are false.

20. Which is the contrapositive of the statement "If it is Saturday, then I sleep late"?
  a. If I sleep late, then it is Saturday.
  b. If it is *not* Saturday, then I do *not* sleep late.
  c. If I do *not* sleep late, then it is *not* Saturday.
  d. If I sleep late, then it is *not* Saturday.

21. What is the converse of $\sim p \rightarrow q$?
  a. $p \rightarrow q$ **b.** $p \rightarrow \sim q$ **c.** $\sim q \rightarrow p$ **d.** $q \rightarrow \sim p$

22. If p represents "It is cold" and q represents "I will go skating," which represents "If it is cold, then I will not go skating"?
  a. $\sim p \rightarrow q$ **b.** $p \rightarrow \sim q$ **c.** $q \rightarrow p$ **d.** $\sim q \rightarrow p$

23. What is the inverse of $\sim p \rightarrow q$?
  a. $p \rightarrow \sim q$ **b.** $q \rightarrow \sim p$ **c.** $\sim p \rightarrow \sim q$ **d.** $\sim q \rightarrow \sim p$

Copy and complete each truth table.

24.

p	q	$(p \rightarrow q)$ Conditional: false only if p is true and q is false.	$\sim p$ Opposite of p	$\sim q$ Opposite of q	$(\sim p \rightarrow \sim q)$ Conditional: false only if $\sim p$ is true and $\sim q$ is false.	$(p \rightarrow q) \rightarrow (\sim p \rightarrow \sim q)$ Conditional: false only if $(p \rightarrow q)$ is true and $(\sim p \rightarrow \sim q)$ is false.
T	T					
T	F					
F	T					
F	F					

25.

p	q	$(p \rightarrow q)$	$(q \rightarrow p)$	$(p \rightarrow q) \rightarrow (q \rightarrow p)$
T	T			
T	F			
F	T			
F	F			

26.

p	q	$(p \rightarrow q)$	$\sim q$	$\sim p$	$(\sim q \rightarrow \sim p)$	$(p \rightarrow q) \rightarrow (\sim q \rightarrow \sim p)$
T	T					
T	F					
F	T					
F	F					

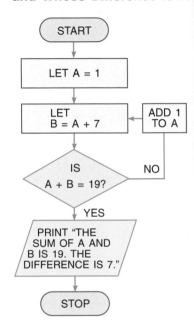

Technology

Flowcharting

A **flowchart** is a diagram of the step-by-step procedure for reaching a goal.
Look at the steps in each of these flowcharts.

Flowchart to Order Pizza

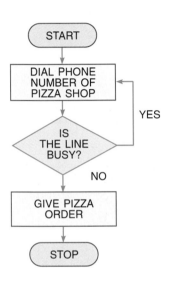

Each flowchart symbol has a special meaning.

START OR STOP

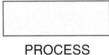

PROCESS

DECISION MAKING

INPUT OR OUTPUT

Flowchart to Find Two Numbers Whose Sum is 19. and Whose Difference is 7.

Give the output of each flowchart.

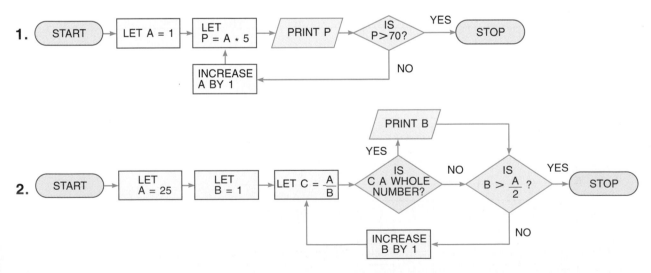

3. Construct a flowchart that gives the steps for changing a percent to a decimal.
4. Construct a flowchart that shows how to test for divisibility by 5, by 6.

Flowcharts and Computer Programs

This program was written to follow the steps outlined in the flowchart at the left.

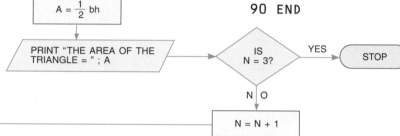

```
10 FOR N = 1 TO 3
20 PRINT "WHAT IS THE LENGTH OF THE BASE
   OF A TRIANGLE?"
30 INPUT B
40 PRINT "WHAT IS THE HEIGHT OF THE
   TRIANGLE?"
50 INPUT H
60 A = 1/2 * B * H
70 PRINT "THE AREA OF THE TRIANGLE = "; A
80 NEXT N
90 END
```

Write a program to follow these flowcharts.

5.

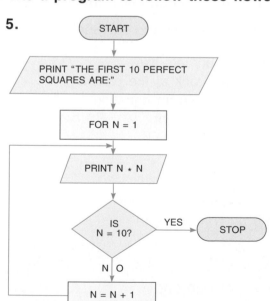

6.

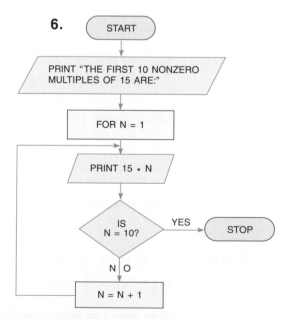

Construct a flowchart and its corresponding program to do the following:

7. Find the perimeters of four rectangles.

8. List the first 20 multiples of 13.

9. Test for divisibility by 9.

10. Raise a number to any power.

145

Problem: A space probe measured the average distance from the Sun to the inner planets. The average distance of Mercury is 3.6×10^7 miles. The average distance of Mars is 105,000,000 miles farther than that of Mercury. What is the average distance of Mars from the Sun?

1 IMAGINE

You are an astronomer measuring planetary distances from the Sun. Draw a picture showing the distances.

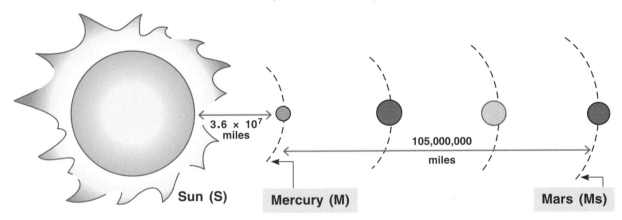

2 NAME

Facts: M to S $\approx 3.6 \times 10^7$ miles

Ms to S $\approx (3.6 \times 10^7$ miles$) + 105,000,000$ miles more

Question: What is the average distance from Mars to the Sun?

3 THINK

Reread this problem, substituting simpler numbers like 6 and 2 to help you figure out what to do. Look at the picture to see what is happening. Then write and solve an equation using these simpler numbers to see if you are right.

Mercury to Sun (M) = 6 miles
   Mars to Sun (Ms) = 6 miles + 2 miles more
                 Ms = 6 + 2 = 8

Now rewrite the equation using the given numbers.
                 Ms = $(3.6 \times 10^7) + 105,000,000$

4 COMPUTE

Ms = $(3.6 \times 10^7) + 105,000,000$

Ms = 36,000,000 + 105,000,000 = 141,000,000

The average distance from Mars to the Sun is 141,000,000 miles.

5 CHECK

Use a calculator to check your computation.

Solve by using simpler numbers.

1. The average distance of the orbit of Saturn from the Sun is 900 million miles. The average distance of the orbit of Jupiter from the Sun is 4.6×10^8 miles. How much farther from the Sun is Saturn's orbit than Jupiter's orbit?

   1 IMAGINE Draw and label a picture. ⟶ **2 NAME** ⟶ Facts
   ⟶ Question

   3 THINK To find the difference between the distances, subtract: $900,000,000 - 4.6 \times 10^8 = $?

   Remember to change 4.6×10^8 to a standard number first.

   Exercise 1

   4 COMPUTE ⟶ **5 CHECK**

2. The orbit of Earth is about 9.29×10^7 miles from the Sun. The average distance between the orbits of Earth and Mars is 48,732,000 miles. The average distance between the orbits of Mars and Saturn is about 745,395,000 miles. About how far is Saturn from the Sun?

3. Triton and Nereid are two of the satellites of Neptune. The average distance of Triton to Neptune is 2.207×10^5 miles. The average distance of Nereid to Neptune is 3,456,000 miles. How much closer to Neptune is Triton than Nereid?

4. Jupiter has 17 or more satellites. The average distance of one of its satellites, Adrastea, from Jupiter is about 1.32×10^7 miles. Another satellite, Poseidon, is an average of 14,594,300 miles from Jupiter. What is the average distance between these two satellites?

5. The diameter of Earth is 7926 miles. The diameter of Mercury is 0.38 of the diameter of Earth. What is the diameter of Mercury?

6. The diameter of Venus is 7550 miles. The diameter of Neptune is about 2.8×10^4 miles. How many times larger is Neptune's diameter? (Round the answer to the nearest hundredth.)

7. The speed of light is 1.86×10^5 miles per second. If Earth is 92,900,000 miles from the Sun, about how long does it take light energy to travel from the Sun to Earth?

8. A light year is used to measure distances in space. Light travels about 5.87×10^{12} miles in one year. At this rate, what is the distance in light years from our planet to the nearest star, Alpha Centauri, which is 27,000,600,000,000 miles from Earth?

5-12 | Problem Solving: Applications

Solve.

1. What is the least three-digit number divisible by 9 and 4?

2. What is the greatest five-digit number divisible by 8 and 6?

3. What is the least number that when divided by either 3, 4, 5, or 6 has a remainder of 2?

4. What is the least number that when divided by either 3, 4, 6, or 9 has a remainder of 2?

FEBRUARY

Sunday	Monday	Tuesday	Wednesday	Thursday	Friday	Saturday
1	2	3	4	5	6	7
8	9	10	11	12	13	14
15	16	17	18	19	20	21
22	23	24	25	26	27	28

Exercise 5

5. Starting on the first day in February, Elena takes a vitamin C tablet every third day and a vitamin B tablet every fourth day. On which dates in February will Elena take both vitamin tablets?

6. Beginning with the first car off the assembly line, Robot X12-0 checks every fifth car for fuel efficiency, and Robot Y34-0 checks every fourth car for braking power. Of the first 100 cars to come off the line, how many will both robots check?

7. A piece of paper is 0.0008 mm thick. How high is a stack of 1000 sheets of paper? A dozen reams? (A ream is 500 sheets.)

8. If the bureau of printing and engraving produces 125,000 twenty-dollar bills, 200,000 ten-dollar bills, and 10^6 one-dollar bills, how much money has the bureau produced?

9. A laser-light printer prints one character in 2.5×10^{-5} sec. A certain document takes 10 minutes to print. How many characters are contained in the document?

10. A satellite travels about 36 000 km each day. How many kilometers will it travel in a year?

11. A certain computer can perform about 16,800,000 additions in a minute. How many additions can it perform in a second? How long will it take to perform one addition?

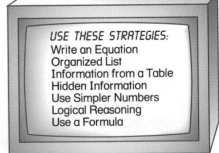

USE THESE STRATEGIES:
Write an Equation
Organized List
Information from a Table
Hidden Information
Use Simpler Numbers
Logical Reasoning
Use a Formula

12. The first electronic computer, built in 1946, weighed 6.0×10^4 lb. How many tons did it weigh?

13. The first computer contained 1.8×10^3 vacuum tubes. Express this as a standard numeral.

14. In 10 seconds an electric current travels 984 ft. How far will a current travel in 10 minutes?

15. A radio signal traveled 1.62×10^{10} m in 1.5 hours. How far did it travel in one second?

16. In the electromagnetic spectrum each color has a particular wavelength. The wavelength of violet is 4×10^{-5} cm and the wavelength of red is 7×10^{-5} cm. Which color has the longer wavelength and by how much?

17. A space tracking station is 4.2×10^4 m by 6.5×10^3 m. What is the area of the tracking station?

18. The speed of a jet plane is about 0.1 times the speed of a space shuttle. The plane travels 3.2×10^6 meters per hour. Express the speed of the shuttle as a standard numeral.

19. An island has a population of 540,000 people and an area of 1.5×10^4 km^2. What is the population density?

20. Hadrons are the largest subatomic particles. The length of a hadron is 1.7×10^{-15} m. Express this as a standard numeral.

21. The radioactive half-life of radium is 1600 years. The half-life of uranium 238 is 4.52×10^9 years. How many times longer is the half-life of uranium than that of radium?

22. The DNA molecule has a diameter of 0.0000025 mm. Express the length of its radius in scientific notation.

23. The human brain has on the average 35 billion nerve cells and an average mass of 1400 g. Express the mass of a single nerve cell in scientific notation.

The chart shows the temperature of the different parts of the Sun. Use the chart to complete exercises 24–26.

24. How much cooler are the sunspots than the photosphere?

25. How much hotter than the photosphere is the core?

26. How many times hotter is the core than the sunspots?

Part of Sun	Temperature in °F
core	2.7×10^7
photosphere	11,000
sunspots	9000

Let p represent "6 is divisible by 2."
Let q represent "6 is divisible by 3."
Write the sentence represented by each symbol.

27. p **28.** $\sim q$ **29.** $\sim p$ **30.** $p \lor q$

Construct a truth table for each.

31. $p \land q$ **32.** $\sim p \lor q$ **33.** $p \rightarrow (p \land q)$

More Practice

Find the product or quotient.

1. 0.0452×10^2 **2.** $5656 \div 1000$ **3.** $10^5 \div 10^3$ **4.** 7000×100

Write in expanded form using positive and negative exponents.

5. 6.5 **6.** 0.00004 **7.** $3,590.0303$ **8.** 117.017

Write in scientific notation.

9. 740 **10.** $225,000$ **11.** 0.00009 **12.** 2000.2

Write the standard numeral.

13. 6.18×10^3 **14.** 2.45×10^{-4} **15.** 5.671×10^{10} **16.** 4.404×10^{-6}

Which is greater?

17. 3.04×10^4 or 2.6×10^5 **18.** 4.8×10^{-3} or 4.4×10^{-2}

Compute using scientific notation.

19. $17,000 \times 392,000,000$ **20.** $4,200,000 \div 70,000$

21. 0.75×0.007 **22.** $0.625 \div 0.005$

Is the first number divisible by the second number?
Write yes or no.

23. $345; 5$ **24.** $4188; 8$ **25.** $1242; 3$ **26.** $644; 4$

27. $23,190; 10$ **28.** $971,326; 2$ **29.** $171,171; 9$ **30.** $111,111; 3$

By inspection, name the divisors (2, 3, 4, 5, 8, 9, 10) for each number.

31. 652 **32.** 8425 **33.** 7260 **34.** 6336

Find the pattern for each sequence. Then find the next three terms.

35. $21, 24, 27, 30, \ldots$ **36.** $10, 13, 12, 15, 14, \ldots$

37. $2\frac{1}{4}, 4\frac{1}{4}, 6\frac{1}{4}, 8\frac{1}{4}, \ldots$ **38.** $3, 3, 6, 9, 15, \ldots$

Solve using scientific notation.

39. The population of a city is 9,500,000 and its area is 25 square miles. What is the city's population density?

40. Light travels at a speed of 300,000 km per second. How far does light travel in 25.5 seconds?

Math Probe

SEQUENCE SUMS

Find the sum of the whole numbers 9 through 16.

There is an easy way to find the sum of the terms in a sequence.

Step 1: Match the terms in pairs beginning on each end.

Step 2: Add the pairs. The sums are the same. (25)

Step 3: Multiply by the number of pairs. (4)
$4 \times 25 = 100$

9 10 11 12   13 14 15 16
12 + 13
11 + 14
10 + 15
9 + 16

Check: $9 + 10 + 11 + 12 + 13 + 14 + 15 + 16 = 100$

There is a formula for finding the sum of the terms in a sequence.

Let Σ = sum, f = first term, ℓ = last term, n = number of terms

Then:
$$\Sigma = \frac{n}{2}(f + \ell)$$

Half the number of terms is the number of pairs.

The sum of each pair is the same, so you can use the sum of the simplest pair.

$$\Sigma = \frac{8}{2}(9 + 16)$$
$$= 4(25)$$
$$\Sigma = 100$$

Use the formula to find these sums.

1. the first ten nonzero whole numbers

2. the first twenty nonzero whole numbers

3. the first fifty nonzero whole numbers

4. the first twenty-five even numbers

5. the first twelve multiples of 3

6. the first eight multiples of 5

Use your calculator and the formula to find the sums of these terms.

7. from 100 through 500

8. from 47 through 126

9. from 9 through 99

10. from 3 through 300

Check Your Mastery

Find the product or quotient.   See pp. 128–129

1. 0.0637×10^3 **2.** $4798 \div 100$ **3.** $10^4 \div 10^2$ **4.** 9000×1000

Write in expanded form using positive and negative exponents.   See pp. 130–131

5. 3.8 **6.** 0.00005 **7.** 7008.4004 **8.** 222.022

Write in scientific notation.   See pp. 132–133

9. 960 **10.** $177{,}000$ **11.** 0.00002 **12.** 1000.1

Write the standard numeral.

13. 7.08×10^3 **14.** 6.09×10^{-8} **15.** 7.315×10^{10} **16.** 1.111×10^{-3}

Which is greater?

17. 2.75×10^6 or 3.8×10^4 **18.** 3.7×10^{-2} or 5.5×10^{-3}

Compute using scientific notation.   See pp. 134–135

19. $4{,}800{,}000{,}000 \div 6000$ **20.** 0.82×0.00005

21. $7{,}200{,}000{,}000 \times 90{,}000$ **22.** $0.225 \div 0.000015$

Is the first number divisible by the second number?   See pp. 136–137
Write yes or no.

23. 1408; 5   **24.** 8235; 9   **25.** 744; 4   **26.** 4932; 6

27. 10,170; 10   **28.** 555,374; 2   **29.** 536; 3   **30.** 1592; 8

By inspection, name the divisors (2, 3, 4, 5, 8, 9, 10)
for each number.

31. 460   **32.** 3279   **33.** 6445   **34.** 7342

Find the pattern for each sequence. Then find the next three terms.   See p. 138

35. 43, 46, 49, 52, . . .   **36.** 12, 16, 14, 18, 16, . . .

37. $5\frac{1}{2}$, $7\frac{1}{2}$, $9\frac{1}{2}$, $11\frac{1}{2}$, . . .   **38.** 2, 5, 11, 23, 47, . . .

Solve using scientific notation.

39. The population of a city is 14,000,000 and its area is 20 square miles. What is the city's population density?

40. An apple orchard is 5.7×10^5 m by 4.3×10^5 m. Express the area in scientific notation.

6 Ratio and Proportion

In this chapter you will:

- Identify ratios and rates
- Read, write, and solve proportions
- Use proportion in a variety of ways
- Use scale drawings
- Identify and work with inverse proportion
- Identify and work with partitive proportion
- Identify similar triangles
- Use trigonometric ratios
- Solve problems: draw a picture

Do you remember?

Equivalent fractions can be found by multiplying or dividing the numerator and denominator by the same number:

$$\frac{2}{5} = \frac{4}{10} = \frac{6}{15} = \frac{8}{20} = \frac{10}{25}$$

$$\frac{2 \times 1}{5 \times 1} = \frac{2 \times 2}{5 \times 2} = \frac{2 \times 3}{5 \times 3} = \frac{2 \times 4}{5 \times 4} = \frac{2 \times 5}{5 \times 5}$$

$$\frac{15}{20} = \frac{12}{16} = \frac{9}{12} = \frac{6}{8} = \frac{3}{4}$$

$$\frac{15 \div 5}{20 \div 5} = \frac{12 \div 4}{16 \div 4} = \frac{9 \div 3}{12 \div 3} = \frac{6 \div 2}{8 \div 2} = \frac{3 \div 1}{4 \div 1}$$

6-1 Ratios and Rates

Ratio: a comparison of two numbers by division.

Ratios are used to compare two quantities or to express rates.

▶ **Comparison of two quantities**

The ratio, or comparison, of the calories burned while sleeping (65 Cal) to those burned while lying awake (100 Cal) is:

$$65 \text{ Cal to } 100 \text{ Cal} \qquad \text{OR} \qquad 65 \text{ Cal} : 100 \text{ Cal} \qquad \text{OR} \qquad \frac{65 \text{ Cal}}{100 \text{ Cal}}$$

To simplify a ratio, express it as an equivalent fraction in lowest terms.

$$65 : 100 = \frac{65}{100} = \frac{13}{20}$$

> $\frac{13}{20}$ is the value of the ratio.

The ratio or comparison of 4 days to 2 weeks is: 4 days to 2 weeks.
To express a ratio of two measures, the *units of measure* must be the same.

$$4 \text{ days} : \underline{2 \text{ weeks}} \qquad 4 \text{ days} : \underline{14 \text{ days}} = \frac{4}{14} = \frac{2}{7}$$

2 weeks = 14 days

▶ **Rate: Comparison of *unlike* quantities**

The rate of calories used per minute of severe exercise if 480 calories are used per hour is:

> Rates compare unlike units.

$$480 \text{ Cal to } 60 \text{ minutes} = 480 \text{ Cal} : 60 \text{ min}$$

$$\frac{480 \text{ Cal}}{60 \text{ min}} = \frac{8 \text{ Cal}}{1 \text{ min}} = 8 \text{ calories used per minute}$$

To find *equal* or *equivalent ratios* or *rates*, find equivalent fractions.

Each set of equivaient fractions contains equal ratios. $\left\{\frac{3}{8}, \frac{6}{16}, \frac{9}{24}\right\}$ and $\left\{\frac{18}{24}, \frac{9}{12}, \frac{6}{8}\right\}$

To find equal ratios or the value of a ratio when one or more parts of the ratio are fractions or decimals:

Write the ratio as a fraction. Then divide the numerator of the ratio by the denominator of the ratio.

Value of Ratio

$$1\frac{7}{8} \div 3\frac{3}{4} = \frac{1\frac{7}{8}}{3\frac{3}{4}} = \frac{\frac{15}{8}}{\frac{15}{4}} = \frac{15}{8} \div \frac{15}{4} = \frac{\overset{1}{\cancel{15}}}{\underset{2}{\cancel{8}}} \times \frac{\overset{1}{\cancel{4}}}{\underset{1}{\cancel{15}}} = \frac{1}{2} \times \frac{1}{1} = \frac{1}{2}$$

$$1.8 \div 0.5 = \frac{1.8}{0.5} = 0.5\overline{)1.80} \text{ or } 1.8 : 0.5 = \underline{3.6 : 1} = 3.6$$

> To find if two ratios are equal, express each as a fraction in lowest terms and compare.
>
> Equal Ratios
>
> $$9 : 12 \overset{?}{=} 27 : 36 \longrightarrow \frac{9}{12} = \frac{3}{4} \text{ and } \frac{27}{36} = \frac{3}{4} \longrightarrow 9 : 12 = 27 : 36$$

Write a ratio. Express it as a fraction in lowest terms. Change to like units where necessary.

1. 6 rainy days out of 15 rainy days
2. 12 years to 36 years
3. 1 day to one week
4. days in March to days in June
5. 1 quarter to 2 nickels
6. 6 out of 8 correct
7. the number of odd digits to the number of even digits in 1,362,578
8. the number of even digits to the total number of digits in 2589
9. the number of consonants to the number of vowels in your first name
10. the number of vowels to the number of consonants in this exercise

Write a rate in simplest form.

11. $15 for 2 umbrellas
12. 100 meters run in 10 seconds
13. 180 km traveled in 2 hours
14. 510 words read in 3 minutes
15. 3 books for $2.10
16. $4.80 per dozen flowers
17. $4.20 for 3 gallons
18. 105 wheel revolutions in 3 minutes

19. Now write exercises 11–18 as rates *per unit*. Exercise 11 is done:

$$\$15 : 2 \text{ umbrellas} \longrightarrow 15 : 2 = \frac{15}{2} = \frac{\$7.50}{1}, \text{ or } \$7.50 \text{ per umbrella}$$

Write three equal ratios for each.

20. $\frac{3}{5}$
21. $\frac{3}{4}$
22. $\frac{9}{2}$
23. $\frac{0.2}{0.3}$
24. $\frac{0.1}{0.7}$
25. $\frac{0.2}{0.5}$

Find the value of each ratio.

26. $16 : 40$
27. $14 : 42$
28. $28 : 7$
29. $81 : 18$
30. $\frac{3}{5} : \frac{7}{10}$
31. $\frac{1}{4} : \frac{1}{2}$
32. $\frac{1}{8} : \frac{1}{6}$
33. $\frac{2}{15} : \frac{1}{10}$
34. $20 : 50$
35. $4\frac{1}{2} : 9$
36. $1\frac{3}{8} : \frac{4}{9}$
37. $6\frac{2}{5} : 1\frac{1}{7}$
38. $1.5 : 4.5$
39. $4.4 : 8.8$
40. $2.2 : 1.1$
41. $3 : 0.5$

Write a ratio and solve.

42. What is the ratio of the length of Box A to the length of Box B?

43. What is the ratio of the width of Box B to the width of Box A?

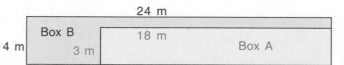

44. What is the ratio of the perimeter of Box A to that of Box B? What is the ratio of their areas?

155

Proportions

Proportion: an equation stating that two ratios or rates are equal.

Compare trees. $\dfrac{30}{300} = \dfrac{1}{10}$

Compare metric tons. $\dfrac{2.5}{25} = \dfrac{25}{250} = \dfrac{1}{10}$

Our Town's Recycling Center

30 trees saved for every 2.5 metric tons of paper collected.

Trees Saved: 300
Paper Collected: 25 metric tons

$\dfrac{30}{300}$ and $\dfrac{2.5}{25}$ are equal ratios. Both equal $\dfrac{1}{10}$.

Write this proportion as:

$$\dfrac{30}{300} = \dfrac{2.5}{25} \text{ or } 30 : 300 = 2.5 : 25$$

Read this proportion as:

30 is to 300 as 2.5 is to 25

means

extremes

Each number in a proportion is called a *term.* The first and fourth terms are called the *extremes.* The second and third terms are called the *means.*

Cross-Products Rule

The product of the extremes equals the product of the means in any proportion.

$$\dfrac{30}{300} \diagdown \dfrac{2.5}{25} \longrightarrow 30 \times 25 = 300 \times 2.5 \longrightarrow 750 = 750$$

extremes   means

If the cross products are *not* equal, the two ratios do *not* form a proportion.

$$\dfrac{2}{5} \overset{?}{=} \dfrac{4}{9} \longrightarrow \dfrac{2}{5} \diagdown \dfrac{4}{9} \longrightarrow 2 \times 9 \overset{?}{=} 5 \times 4 \longrightarrow 18 \neq 20$$

$$\boxed{\dfrac{2}{5} = \dfrac{4}{9} \text{ is } not \text{ a proportion.}}$$

To find any "missing term" in a proportion, use the cross-products rule:

Solve for *n*: $\dfrac{n}{4} = \dfrac{9}{12} \longrightarrow \dfrac{n}{4} \diagdown \dfrac{9}{12} \longrightarrow 12n = 36 \longrightarrow n = \dfrac{36}{12} \longrightarrow n = 3$

Check: Substitute 3 for *n*. $\dfrac{n}{4} = \dfrac{9}{12} \longrightarrow \dfrac{3}{4} \diagdown \dfrac{9}{12} \longrightarrow 3 \times 12 = 4 \times 9 \longrightarrow 36 = 36$

Solve for *a*: $\dfrac{\frac{1}{2}}{5} \diagdown \dfrac{a}{4} \longrightarrow \dfrac{1}{2} \times 4 = 5a \longrightarrow 2 = 5a \longrightarrow 5a = 2 \longrightarrow a = \dfrac{2}{5}$

Check: Substitute $\dfrac{2}{5}$ for *a*. $\dfrac{\frac{1}{2}}{5} \diagdown \dfrac{\frac{2}{5}}{4} \longrightarrow \dfrac{1}{\overset{}{\underset{1}{2}}} \times \overset{2}{\cancel{4}} = \overset{1}{\cancel{5}} \times \dfrac{2}{\underset{1}{\cancel{5}}} \longrightarrow 2 = 2$

Copy and complete.

1. $\dfrac{b}{32} = \dfrac{4}{8}$

    $8b = 32 \times 4$

    $b = \underline{\ ?\ }$

2. $\dfrac{6}{21} = \dfrac{2}{n}$

    $6n = \underline{\ ?\ }$

    $n = \underline{\ ?\ }$

3. $\dfrac{18}{30} = \dfrac{r}{5}$

    $\underline{\ ?\ } = 90$

    $r = \underline{\ ?\ }$

4. $\dfrac{7}{a} = \dfrac{35}{60}$

    $35a = \underline{\ ?\ }$

    $a = \underline{\ ?\ }$

Solve.

5. $\dfrac{3}{18} = \dfrac{10}{n}$

6. $\dfrac{9}{15} = \dfrac{m}{30}$

7. $\dfrac{9}{t} = \dfrac{36}{8}$

8. $\dfrac{x}{36} = \dfrac{24}{48}$

Write = or ≠.

9. $\dfrac{6}{12} \overset{?}{=} \dfrac{10}{18}$

10. $\dfrac{18}{27} \overset{?}{=} \dfrac{14}{21}$

11. $\dfrac{20}{25} \overset{?}{=} \dfrac{5}{7}$

12. $\dfrac{64}{32} \overset{?}{=} \dfrac{12}{3}$

13. $\dfrac{6}{36} \overset{?}{=} \dfrac{6}{1}$

14. $\dfrac{35}{42} \overset{?}{=} \dfrac{10}{12}$

15. $\dfrac{3}{4} : \dfrac{7}{10} \overset{?}{=} \dfrac{5}{8} : \dfrac{7}{12}$

16. $5\dfrac{1}{4} : 1\dfrac{3}{4} \overset{?}{=} \dfrac{1}{9} : \dfrac{1}{3}$

17. $4\dfrac{1}{2} : 9 \overset{?}{=} \dfrac{4}{5} : \dfrac{2}{5}$

Using each set of numbers, write a proportion and check it. (The first one is set up.)

18. $35, 70, 50, 25 \longrightarrow 35 : 70 = 25 : 50$

19. $50, 22.5, 100, 45$

20. $0.04, 0.08, 5, 10$

21. $2.7, 10, 0.3, 90$

22. $5, 1.5, 6, 1.8$

23. $96, 17, 3, 544$

24. $0.04, 6, 7.5, 0.05$

25. $10, 100, 3, 30$

Find the missing term. Label the answer where names occur.

26. $\dfrac{6}{12} = \dfrac{2}{n}$

27. $\dfrac{18}{30} = \dfrac{r}{5}$

28. $\dfrac{7}{s} = \dfrac{35}{60}$

29. $\dfrac{9}{t} = \dfrac{36}{8}$

30. $\dfrac{n}{3\frac{1}{4}} = \dfrac{28}{39}$

31. $\dfrac{\frac{2}{3}}{x} = \dfrac{\frac{1}{5}}{\frac{1}{7}}$

32. $\dfrac{1.2}{0.6} = \dfrac{3.6}{n}$

33. $\dfrac{0.04}{0.06} = \dfrac{a}{0.24}$

34. $\dfrac{b}{5.6} = \dfrac{0.8}{6.4}$

35. $\dfrac{x}{\$36} = \dfrac{24 \text{ tons}}{48 \text{ tons}}$

36. $\dfrac{n}{81 \text{ min}} = \dfrac{15 \text{ days}}{45 \text{ days}}$

37. $\dfrac{\$7}{\$14} = \dfrac{n}{8 \text{ kg}}$

38. $\dfrac{1.5 \text{ hr}}{a} = \dfrac{480 \text{ words}}{120 \text{ words}}$

39. $\dfrac{0.8 \text{ cm}}{1.4 \text{ cm}} = \dfrac{16 \text{ km}}{x}$

40. $\dfrac{6 \text{ books}}{r} = \dfrac{\$10}{\$25}$

Solve for x.

41. $75x = 2250$

42. $13x = 286$

43. $0.9x = 1.26$

44. $0.32x = 4.8$

45. $\dfrac{3}{5}x = 27$

46. $1\dfrac{2}{5}x = 2\dfrac{1}{10}$

6-3 | Direct Proportions

Direct proportion: as one quantity *increases,* the second quantity *increases,* OR
as one quantity *decreases,* the second quantity *decreases.*

The ocean has different temperature layers. Below a certain depth,
the ocean temperature decreases 4° Celsius for every 100 meters.
What would the temperature drop be for a 300-meter increase in depth?

This problem compares two quantities: a drop in
temperature and an increase in depth. It can be
solved by means of proportion, using these steps:

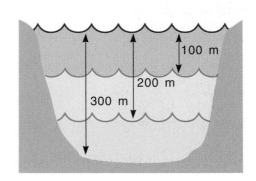

- Write the two comparisons in words.

$$\frac{\text{temperature drop}}{\text{meter increase}} = \frac{\text{temperature drop}}{\text{meter increase}}$$

- Substitute numbers for the words. Choose a
  variable to represent the unknown number.

Place variable as first
term of proportion. $\longrightarrow$ $\dfrac{t}{300 \text{ m}} = \dfrac{4°C}{100 \text{ m}} \longrightarrow \dfrac{t}{300} = \dfrac{4}{100}$

- Use the cross-products rule to solve the proportion.

$$\frac{t}{300} \diagdown \frac{4}{100} \qquad 100t = 300 \times 4 \qquad 100t = 1200$$

$$t = \frac{1200}{100} \qquad t = 12°C \text{ drop}$$

- Check: Substitute 12 for *t.*

$$\frac{12}{300} \diagdown \frac{4}{100} \qquad 12 \times 100 = 300 \times 4 \qquad 1200 = 1200$$

Another way of writing the proportion is to compare like units to like units. Be sure to
arrange both ratios in the same order, that is, larger to smaller or smaller to larger.

$$\frac{\text{temperature drop}}{\text{temperature drop}} = \frac{\text{meter increase}}{\text{meter increase}}$$

$$\frac{\text{(larger)}}{\text{(smaller)}} \frac{t}{4} = \frac{300}{100} \frac{\text{(larger)}}{\text{(smaller)}}$$

$$100t = 4 \times 300 \qquad t = \frac{1200}{100} \qquad t = 12°C \text{ drop}$$

Write a proportion for each in two ways.

1. 6 hours to travel 360 miles is the same as 2 hours to travel 120 miles.

2. 3 books for $5.85 is the same as 12 books for $23.40.

3. 45 miles in 25 minutes is the same as 18 miles in 10 minutes.

True or false? Correct any false statements.

4. $\frac{t\,s}{1500\,m} = \frac{1.8\,s}{2000\,m}$ is the same as $\frac{t\,s}{1.8\,s} = \frac{1500\,m}{2000\,m}$

5. $\frac{t\,min}{300\,words} = \frac{4\,min}{120\,words}$ is the same as $\frac{t\,min}{4\,min} = \frac{300\,words}{120\,words}$

6. $\frac{d\,cost}{18\,roses} = \frac{\$15.00\,cost}{12\,roses}$ is the same as $\frac{d\,cost}{\$15.00\,cost} = \frac{12\,roses}{18\,roses}$

Solve by proportion.

7. If it costs $50.40 to make 9 gallons of ice cream, how much will it cost to make 15 gallons?

8. If 15 tickets for the ball game cost $97.50, how many can be bought for $71.50?

9. A large team and a smaller team go on a camping trip and agree to pay the expenses in the ratio 9 to 7. If the smaller team pays $107.45, what will the larger team pay?

10. If Wanda reads 180 pages of her book in $2\frac{3}{4}$ hours, how many pages can she read in $1\frac{3}{8}$ hours?

11. The Grant family's vacation cost $1540.15 for $2\frac{1}{2}$ weeks. How much would a $5\frac{1}{2}$-week vacation have cost?

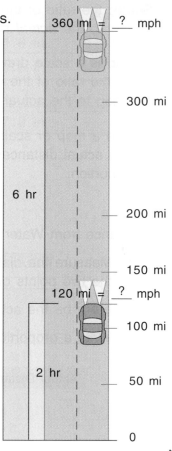

Exercise 1

400 mi

360 mi = __?__ mph

300 mi

200 mi

6 hr

150 mi

120 mi = __?__ mph

100 mi

2 hr

50 mi

0

Rate is the ratio of *distance* to *time*.
This formula expresses the ratio used
with problems involving distance, rate, and time.

$$\frac{r}{1} = \frac{d}{t}$$
$$r = \frac{d}{t}$$

---

12. In 6 hours a plane can travel 5000 km. How far will it travel in $1\frac{1}{2}$ hours?

13. A jet plane traveled 1800 km in 2.5 hr. At this rate, how long would it take to travel 2000 km?

14. Kevin rides his bicycle 3 miles in a half hour. How long will it take him to ride $5\frac{1}{2}$ miles?

15. A track star runs 100 yards in 12.6 sec. How far can the star run in 1 min?

16. A car travels 85 km in $1\frac{1}{6}$ hours. How far will it travel in $4\frac{1}{5}$ hours?

17. It takes 24 minutes for Lou to walk $1\frac{1}{3}$ miles home from school. How far could he walk in a half hour?

18. A garden is 14 m long and 8 m wide. The width of another garden of equal area is 12 m. Find its length.

19. At a sale, 4 bars of soap are sold for $1.12. What would you pay for 2 dozen bars?

6-5   Inverse Proportion

Inverse proportion: as one quantity *increases,* the second quantity *decreases,* OR
as one quantity *decreases,* the second quantity increases.

To compare quantities or rates that are in inverse proportion, use
the same procedure as used in direct proportion.

> At the Flower Power Shop, 10 florists make 15 wreaths in 12 hours.
> If 6 extra florists are hired, how much time is needed to do the same work?

▶ **To solve:**

- Write the two comparisons in words.

    10 florists work 12 hours = 16 florists work h hours

    > Both groups make 15 wreaths.

    The 16 workers will take fewer than 12 hours. This is an inverse proportion
    because *more* workers take *fewer* hours to do the same job.

- Let h equal the fewer number of hours the 16 florists worked.
    Write the two ratios comparing the smaller to the greater quantity in both.

    $$\frac{\text{fewer hours}}{\text{more hours}} = \frac{\text{fewer florists}}{\text{more florists}}$$

    > **Compare**
    > hours : hours
    > and
    > florists : florists

- Substitute numbers in the ratios.

    $$\frac{h}{12} = \frac{10}{16} \longrightarrow \frac{h}{12} \times \frac{10}{16} \longrightarrow 16h = 12 \times 10$$

    $$h = \frac{120}{16} \longrightarrow h = 7.5 \text{ hours for 16 workers to do the job}$$

- Check: Substitute 7.5 for h.

    $$\frac{7.5}{12} \times \frac{10}{16} \longrightarrow 7.5 \times 16 = 12 \times 10 \longrightarrow 120 = 120$$

    > Does it make sense that 16 florists need 7.5 hours to do a job
    > that takes 10 florists 12 hours? Yes, the answer is reasonable.

Write a proportion. Solve.

1. 9 designers do a project in 6 days.
   12 designers do it in __?__ days.

2. 4 technicians do a job in 8 days.
   __?__ technicians do it in 16 days.

3. 5 editors do a project in $3\frac{1}{2}$ weeks.
   __?__ editors do it in $1\frac{1}{6}$ weeks.

4. 5 painters work on a house $3\frac{1}{2}$ weeks.
   7 painters take __?__ weeks.

Solve. Check to see if each answer is reasonable.

5. If 6 workers can put a prefabricated home together in $1\frac{2}{3}$ days, how long will it take 9 workers to do the same work?

6. At a cruising speed of 240 km/h, an airplane has sufficient fuel to last for 7 hours. If it increases its speed to 560 km/h, how long will the fuel last?

7. A group of 900 people have provisions to last 8 weeks. How long will the provisions last if 100 extra people join the group?

8. It took $2\frac{1}{2}$ hours for 12 students to decorate the cafeteria for a party. How many hours would it have taken if 16 students worked at the same rate?

9. In two hours 15 farmers can set 450 tomato plants. If 5 more farmers are hired, how long will it take to set the plants?

10. Eight students catalogued some books for the school library in $1\frac{3}{4}$ hours. How many students would it take to catalogue the same number of books in 2 hours?

11. It took 4 hours for 12 students to shovel snow from the school property. How long would it have taken if only 6 students had done the work?

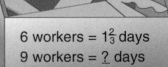

6 workers = $1\frac{2}{3}$ days
9 workers = ? days

12. When Mrs. Gosnell drives her car at a speed of 60 mph, she only gets 18 miles/gallon. If she reduces her speed to use less fuel, how many miles/gallon will she use traveling 45 mph?

13. In 9 days 8 census-takers visited all the homes in a district. If 18 people had worked in that district, how long would the job have taken?

14. In art class 6 students completed a mural in 15 days. How long would it have taken if 9 students had worked on the project?

15. Three members of the Green Lawn Corporation can mow a lawn in 45 minutes. How long will it take 9 members working at the same rate?

16. Nine workers can plant 50 rows of corn in an 8-hour workday. If three more workers are hired, how long will it take to plant the same number of rows of corn?

17. If 4 scouts set up a tent in 3 hours, how long will it take if 2 more scouts help them construct another?

18. Two workers build a canoe in 9 days. Two others help them to build another canoe. In how many days will the second boat be finished?

6-6 Partitive Proportion

Partitive proportion, or proportion by parts: used to solve problems describing a total amount being distributed into unequal parts.

A nursery divided 360 acres of land into three sections to grow evergreen, flowering, and fruit trees in the ratio of 1 : 4 : 5. How many acres were used for each type?

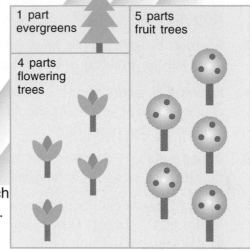

1 part evergreens

4 parts flowering trees

5 parts fruit trees

To solve using partitive proportion:

- Multiply each part by the same number, m, such that the sum of the three parts equals the total.

- To find the multiplier, m, form an equation.

(1 part evergreen $\times$ m) + (4 parts flower $\times$ m) + (5 parts fruit $\times$ m) = 360 acres

$$(1 \times m) + (4 \times m) + (5 \times m) = 360$$
$$(1 + 4 + 5)\, m = 360$$
$$10m = 360$$
$$m = \frac{360}{10} = 36$$

- To find the value of each part, multiply by the value of m.

$1m$ = evergreen = 1×36 =   36   acres of evergreen trees

$4m$ =   flower = 4×36 = 144   acres of flowering trees

$5m$ =   fruit = 5×36 = <u>180</u>   acres of fruit trees

Total = 360   acres of trees

Solve, using partitive proportion.

1. Divide 300 into two parts with a ratio of 2 to 3.

2. Divide 600 into two parts with a ratio of 11 to 13.

3. Divide 180 into three parts with a ratio of 2 : 3 : 4.

4. Divide 450 into three parts proportional to 4 : 5 : 6.

5. Divide 7200 into parts proportional to 2 : 3 : 4.

6. Divide 7500 into parts proportional to 4 : 5 : 6.

Solve, using partitive proportion. (Check answers with a calculator.)

7. In an orchard of 1800 trees, there are peach, apple, and pear trees planted in the ratio of 7 : 3 : 2. How many trees of each kind are there?

8. A certain alloy is made of tin and copper in the ratio of 4 parts tin to 8 parts copper. How many kilograms of each are there in 156 kilograms of the alloy?

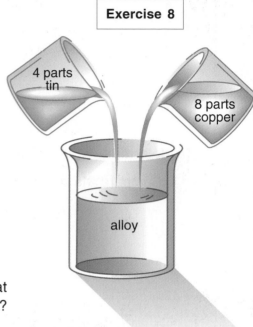

Exercise 8

4 parts tin

8 parts copper

alloy

9. In a recent election for class president, Tara received 5 votes for every 3 that Justin received. How many votes did each receive if 240 votes were cast?

10. A man left his estate of $81,000 to his wife and son. For every $5.00 he gave his wife, he gave $4.00 to his son. What was each person's share?

11. Maria mixed cream and milk in a ratio of 2 parts cream to 3 parts milk. How many liters of each did she need to make 20 liters of the mixture?

12. Juana, Linette, and Erica entered a partnership and invested $6000, $9000, and $10,000 respectively. What will each woman's share be if the overall gain is $8400?

13. Oats and barley were ground together in the ratio of 3 bushels of oats to 2 bushels of barley. How many bushels of each were in 120 pounds of the mixture?

14. Divide the contents of a private library of 1250 books among three schools so that their shares will be in the ratio of 2 to 3 to 5. How many books will be given to each school?

15. Mr. Lon invests $15,000; Ms. Smythe, $20,000; and Mr. Ford, $30,000. Find each person's share if the profits of the company amount to $31,200.

CHALLENGE

16. A fertilizer is made up of 1 part potash to 3 parts phosphate. If the entire mixture weighs 3 metric tons, how much of each element is needed?

17. Chris, Suzi, and Tony sent a package that cost $124.20 in freight charges. If Chris's part of the shipment weighed 5.8 kg, Suzi's 3.4 kg, and Tony's 12.6 kg, how much should each pay?

18. A substance contained 12.5 parts sulphur, 50 parts potassium nitrate, and 37.5 parts charcoal. How many pounds of each are in 250 pounds of the substance?

Similar triangles have the same shape but are different in size. Their *corresponding angles* are *congruent* and the *ratios* of their *corresponding sides* are *equal*.

Congruent ($\cong$):
same size
same shape
Similar ($\sim$):
different size
same shape

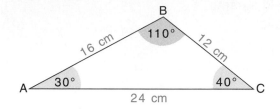

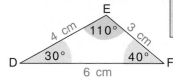

To determine whether two triangles are similar:

- Compare the angles.

$$\angle A \cong \angle D \qquad \angle C \cong \angle F \qquad \angle B \cong \angle E$$

AND

- Compare the ratios of the corresponding sides.

$$\frac{\overline{AB}}{\overline{DE}} = \frac{16}{4} = \frac{4}{1} \qquad \frac{\overline{AC}}{\overline{DF}} = \frac{24}{6} = \frac{4}{1} \qquad \frac{\overline{BC}}{\overline{EF}} = \frac{12}{3} = \frac{4}{1}$$

Sides have equal ratio, $\frac{4}{1}$, so sides are in proportion.

Since their corresponding angles are equal and the ratios of their corresponding sides are in proportion, triangles *ABC* and *DEF* are similar ($\triangle ABC \sim \triangle DEF$).

Which pairs of figures are similar?
Show by naming congruent corresponding parts.

1.

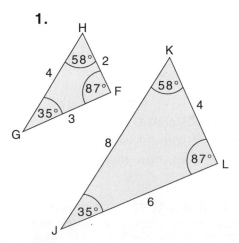

2.

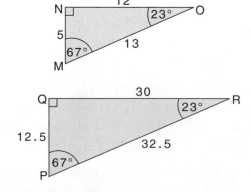

3.

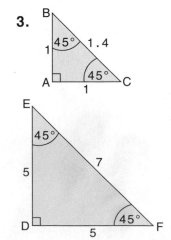

Use similar triangles *EFG* and *HJK* to complete exercises 4–7.
(Hint: The sum of the 3 angles of a triangle equals 180°.)

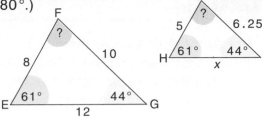

4. $\dfrac{\overline{FG}}{\overline{JK}} = \dfrac{\overline{EG}}{?}$

5. $\dfrac{\overline{HJ}}{\overline{EF}} = \dfrac{?}{\overline{EG}}$

6. $\angle F \cong \angle J = \underline{\ ?\ }$

7. $\dfrac{x}{12} = \dfrac{6.25}{10}$

The figures below are similar. Write and solve proportions to find each of the indicated sides.

8.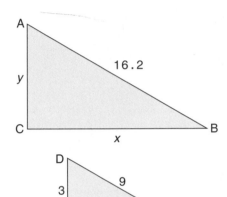

9.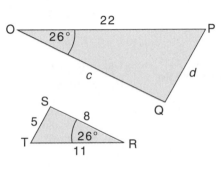

Solve. (The triangles are similar.)

10. A tree casts a shadow 10 ft long. At the same time, a 4.5-ft-tall truck casts a shadow 3 feet long. How tall is the tree?

11. A 50.2-ft-high clock tower casts a shadow. At the same time, the 125.5-ft-high building next to it casts a 50-ft-long shadow. How long is the shadow cast by the clock tower?

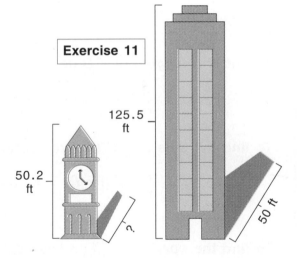

Exercise 11

CRITICAL THINKING

True or false? Explain.

12. All triangles are similar.

13. All right triangles are similar.

14. All equilateral triangles are similar.

15. All isosceles triangles are similar.

16. All rectangles are similar.

17. All squares are similar.

18. All circles are similar.

19. All parallelograms are similar.

20. Can you draw two acute triangles that are not similar?

Trigonometric Ratios

For every *right triangle* there are three ratios involving the relationship between the measures of the angles and the lengths of the sides.

The side opposite the right angle is the **hypotenuse**.

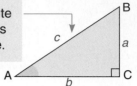

Side *a* is **opposite** $\angle A$.

Side *b* is **adjacent** to $\angle A$.

tangent of angle = $\dfrac{\text{side opposite}}{\text{side adjacent}}$ ⟶ $\tan A = \dfrac{a}{b}$

$\tan B = \dfrac{b}{a}$

sine of angle = $\dfrac{\text{side opposite}}{\text{hypotenuse}}$ ⟶ $\sin A = \dfrac{a}{c}$

$\sin B = \dfrac{b}{c}$

cosine of angle = $\dfrac{\text{side adjacent}}{\text{hypotenuse}}$ ⟶ $\cos A = \dfrac{b}{c}$

$\cos B = \dfrac{a}{c}$

To find the *tangent* of $\angle D$ (to three decimal places):

$$\tan D = \frac{4}{10} = 0.400$$

To find the *sine* of $\angle G$ (to three decimal places):

$$\sin G = \frac{11}{16} \approx 0.688$$ ⟶ $\dfrac{11}{16}$ is equal to 0.6875, which is *approximately equal to* ($\approx$) 0.688.

To find the *cosine* of $\angle J$ (to three decimal places):

$$\cos J = \frac{11}{16} \approx 0.688$$

Why does $\sin G = \cos J$?

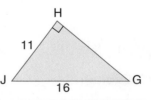

Find the values. Use triangle *MNQ*.

1. $\sin M$
2. $\cos M$
3. $\tan M$
4. $\sin N$
5. $\cos N$
6. $\tan N$

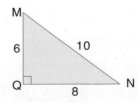

Using A Trigonometric Table

A *table of trigonometric ratios* (for tangents, sines, and cosines) can be used to find:
- the measure of an angle when the lengths of the sides are known.
- the length of a side when the measure of one of the acute angles is known.

Copy and complete each chart. Use the values in the table on p. 552. (The first is done.)

	Angle	Sin	Cos	Tan
7.	30°	0.500	0.866	0.577
8.	41°			
9.	15°			
10.	36°			

	Angle	Sin	Cos	Tan
11.	83°			
12.	77°			
13.	4°			
14.	89°			

Use the table of trigonometric ratios for exercises 15–20.
Find each angle measure. (The first is done.)

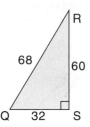

In the "Tan" column of the table 0.533 is closest to 0.532, for which the angle measure is 28°. So, $\angle R$ measures 28°.

15. $\tan R = \dfrac{32}{60} = 0.533$ **16.** $\sin Q$ **17.** $\cos R$

18. $\sin R$ **19.** $\cos Q$ **20.** $\tan Q$

Solve, using a scientific calculator.

21. Find the length of side *t*.

$\cos 25° = \dfrac{t}{30}$

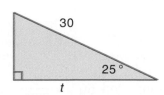

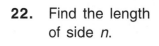

22. Find the length of side *n*.

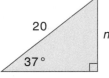

23. Find the length of side *x*.

24. Find the distance (*d*) between the cat and its rescuer.

169

STRATEGY
Problem Solving: Drawing a Picture

The terms **angle of elevation** and **angle of depression** are used in problems about right angles.

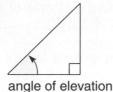

angle of elevation

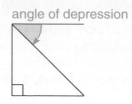

angle of depression

Problem:

To find the depth of a canyon, a surveyor first measured the length of a bridge that spanned it. The bridge measured 350 m.
Then, using a clinometer, she found the angle of depression to be 50°.
How deep was the canyon?

1 IMAGINE

Draw a picture, imagining that you are looking down into the canyon from the bridge.

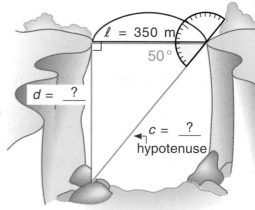

2 NAME

Facts: 350 m — ℓ, length of footbridge
50° — angle of depression

Question: ? m — d, depth of canyon

3 THINK

To solve this problem, relate the facts to the parts of a right triangle.
The sides that are being considered are the opposite and adjacent sides.

Use the tangent ratio:

$$\text{tangent of } 50° \text{ angle} = \frac{\text{opposite}}{\text{adjacent}}$$

Let d = depth. Write an equation: $\tan 50° = \dfrac{d}{350}$

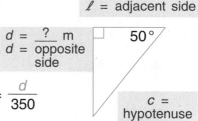

$\ell = 350$ m
$\ell = $ adjacent side

$d = \underline{\ ?\ }$ m
$d = $ opposite side

$c = $ hypotenuse

4 COMPUTE

Solve the equation. Use the table on page 552 to find tan 50°.

$\tan 50° = 1.19$

$1.19 = \dfrac{d}{350} \longrightarrow 1.19 \times 350 = d \longrightarrow 416.5 = d$

The depth of the canyon is 416.5 m.

5 CHECK

Use a calculator and the cross-products rule to check your computation.

$1.19 = \dfrac{d}{350} \longrightarrow \dfrac{119}{100} \overset{?}{=} \dfrac{416.5}{350}$

$$41{,}650 = 41{,}650$$

Solve these problems. Draw a picture for each.

1. A flagpole casts a shadow 6 ft long. At the same time Max, who is $5\frac{1}{2}$ ft tall, casts a shadow $1\frac{1}{3}$ ft long. How tall is the flagpole?

| **1 IMAGINE** | Draw and label a picture $\longrightarrow$ of a flagpole and its shadow. | **2 NAME** | $\longrightarrow$ *Facts*
 $\longrightarrow$ *Question* |

3 THINK Draw a diagram showing the pole and its shadow as one triangle similar to the other triangle, which shows Max and his shadow. Let x = the height of the flagpole. Write and solve a proportion:

$$\frac{\text{height}}{\text{shadow}} \longrightarrow \frac{x}{6} = \frac{5\frac{1}{2}}{1\frac{1}{3}}$$

4 COMPUTE $\longrightarrow$ **5 CHECK**

2. A tree casts a shadow 25.2 m long. Nearby, Daria holds a meter stick perpendicular to the ground. The shadow cast by the stick is 1.2 m long. How tall is the tree?

3. A pilot is flying above Town A. At an angle of depression of 15°, he sights Town B, which he knows is 8 miles from Town A. At what altitude is he flying?

4. A camper sees a mountain in the distance. She knows the mountain is 1020 m high. The angle of elevation from where she stands to the top of the mountain is 30°. How far is she from the top of the mountain?

5. A 40-ft ladder is placed against a building. The ladder forms a 75° angle with the ground. How high up the building does the ladder reach?

6. Stephen wants to make a scale model of a triangular traffic sign to use with his train set. The actual sign measures 3 ft by 3 ft by 5 ft. The largest side of his model sign will be 2.5 inches. What is the length of the other sides?

7. A window washer on a high-rise building knows that he is 250 ft from the ground. The angle of depression from his position to the base of the high-rise across the street is 80°. How many feet separate the two high-rise buildings?

8. Jon's cat has been treed by a neighbor's dog. If Jon is sitting six meters from the base of the tree and the angle of elevation to his cat is 35°, how far up the tree will he have to climb to rescue his pet?

9. An artist planned a fabric design composed of similar triangles. The largest triangle in the pattern is a right triangle with legs measuring 15 cm and 25 cm. The shortest leg of the smallest triangle measures 3 cm. What is the measure of the other leg of the smallest triangle?

177

6-10 Problem Solving: Applications

Choose the correct type of proportion for exercises 1–15. Then solve.

   a. direct   **b. inverse**   **c. partitive**

1. May and her brother cleaned the yard in $2\frac{3}{4}$ hours. How long would it have taken if a friend had helped them?

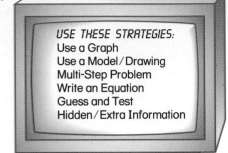

USE THESE STRATEGIES:
Use a Graph
Use a Model/Drawing
Multi-Step Problem
Write an Equation
Guess and Test
Hidden/Extra Information

2. Tomas earned $24 in 3 weeks. At this rate, how much would he earn in 5 weeks?

3. Divide 120 into two parts having a ratio of 3 to 2.

4. A jet plane traveled 2040 km in 3 hours. At this rate, how far would it travel in 6.5 hours?

5. Divide 540 into three parts having a ratio of 5 : 6 : 7.

6. It usually takes 6 waiters 20 minutes to serve 200 guests. If two waiters call in sick, how long will it take the remaining 4 to serve the 200?

7. If 2 kg of meatloaf will serve 12 people, how much meatloaf will be needed to serve 16 people?

8. Three stamp collectors divided 90 stamps in a ratio of 4 : 5 : 6. How many stamps did each collector receive?

9. One day Elena sold 252 cones at the *Cool and Creamy Snack Bar*. If Elena sold 5 soft ice cream cones for every 4 yogurt cones, how many of each kind did she sell?

10. The four workers at *Pretty Pets* grooming center can groom 6 dogs in $1\frac{1}{2}$ hours. If the boss wants the same job done in only 1 hour, how many more workers must she hire?

11. The ratio of the smaller to the larger of two supplementary angles, which have a sum of 180°, is 2 : 7. What is the measure of each angle?

12. A giant redwood casts a shadow 432 feet long. At the same time Cecile, who is 5 feet 3 inches tall, casts a 7-foot shadow. How tall is the giant redwood?

13. In a certain solution the ratio of salt to water is 1 to 5. How many mL of salt and water each were used if there were 3 liters of the solution?

14. Mr. Brent divided $360 among his three children in a ratio of 3 : 4 : 5. How much money did each receive?

15. It took Lee $2\frac{1}{2}$ hours to complete a project. How long would it have taken if her 2 sisters had joined her in the work?

Use the graph to complete exercises 16–19.
Write a ratio in lowest terms for the number of decibels:

16. of a whisper to the number of decibels at a live rock concert.

17. of an alarm clock to the number of decibels of a power lawn mower.

18. of a rock concert to the number of decibels of a jet taking off.

19. of a whisper to the number of decibels of a jet taking off.

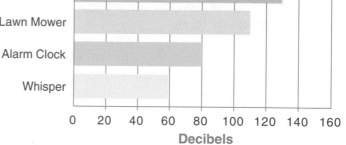

Decibels of Sound

Jet Take off
Live Rock Concert
Power Lawn Mower
Alarm Clock
Whisper

0 20 40 60 80 100 120 140 160
Decibels

20. The Johnson family decided to spend the day at the *Are You Ready for Adventure Park*. If they can buy 15 ride tickets for $10.50, how many can be purchased for $25.20?

21. The ratio of the cost of an adult ticket to the cost of a child's ticket is 5 to 3. If Mr. and Mrs. Johnson spent $32 on admission tickets for themselves and their children, how much was spent on tickets for the children, and how many of each ticket did they purchase?

22. The Johnsons spent $15.66 for fuel to reach the park. If the fuel cost $1.16 a gallon, how many gallons did they use?

23. A snapshot taken of the children at the park is to be enlarged to make a print that is 15 cm wide. If the snapshot is 10 cm long and 6 cm wide, how long will the enlarged print be?

The *Future Frontier* brochure displays a map of the park. Use the scale to find the actual distances between each location in exercises 24–27.

24. Vitron Videorama to Robotic Restaurant = 2 cm

25. 25th Century Towers to Oceanosphere = 1.8 cm

26. Space Shuttle Souvenirs to Vitron Videorama = 2.2 cm

27. Robotic Restaurant to Oceanosphere = 2.4 cm

28. Look at the diagram and use a proportion to find the approximate height of the tree.

SCALE
1 cm = 0.25 km

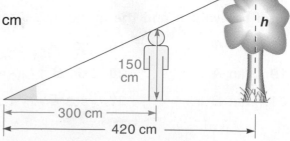

150 cm

300 cm

420 cm

h

More Practice

Find the value of each ratio.

1. $8 : 32$
2. $14 : 63$
3. $\dfrac{1}{8} : \dfrac{1}{2}$
4. $2.5 : 7.5$

Find the missing term.

5. $\dfrac{3}{8} = \dfrac{18}{a}$
6. $\dfrac{42}{6} = \dfrac{b}{12}$
7. $\dfrac{n}{1.8} = \dfrac{2}{1.2}$
8. $\dfrac{\frac{1}{2}}{x} = \dfrac{2}{6}$

Solve by proportion.

9. If 3 cans of orange juice cost $2.15, what will 9 cans cost?

10. If $6\frac{1}{4}$ yd of fabric cost $25.50, what will $2\frac{1}{2}$ yd cost?

Solve.

11. The scale of a map is 2.5 cm = 10 km. What is the actual distance if the scale distance is 10.25 cm?

12. The scale of a map is 1 in. = 25 mi. The actual distance between two cities is 105 mi. What is the distance between these two cities on the map?

Solve. Check to see if each answer is reasonable.

13. It took 8 workers $4\frac{1}{2}$ hours to clean up the park after a concert. How many hours would it have taken if 20 people worked at cleaning up?

Solve using partitive proportion.

14. There is $3600 in a bank account. Divide this money among three people in the ratio of $2 : 3 : 4$.

The figures below are similar.

15. Find the measure of $\angle BAC$.

16. Find the measure of side d.

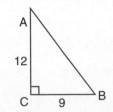

Find the values and the angle measures. Use the table on p. 552.

17. sin A
18. cos A
19. tan A
20. sin B
21. tan B
22. cos B

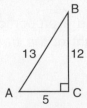

*See *Still More Practice*, pp. 503–504.

Math Probe

GENERATING SPIROLATERALS

A fascinating part of mathematics involves sequences and patterns of numbers. One exciting way of visualizing these patterns and sequences is with a *spirolateral*.

On square dot paper, follow the pattern that is created by starting at point Q and turning at a 90 degree angle in a counterclockwise direction.

Sequence: 1, 2, 3, 4, 5, 6

This is a *closed* spirolateral. ⟶

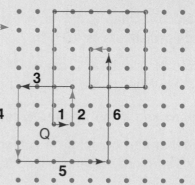

Try your own spirolateral with the sequence 1, 2, 3, 4.

What can you tell about your pattern? What is the difference between a closed and an *open* spirolateral?

Why do you think some spirolaterals are symmetrical while others are not?

For something completely different, try to create several spirolaterals on triangular dot paper. Remember that the angles of turning will *not* be 90°. Try 60° or 120°. Do not forget that counterclockwise direction!

Challenge: Discover what types of graphics you can create with the computer language LOGO in your spirolateral investigation.

Check Your Mastery

Find the value of each ratio.

See pp. 154–155

1. $15 : 48$

2. $45 : 10$

3. $4\frac{1}{2} : 27$

4. $5 : 2.5$

Find the missing term.

See pp. 156–157

5. $\dfrac{5}{6} = \dfrac{30}{y}$

6. $\dfrac{1}{8} = \dfrac{b}{40}$

7. $\dfrac{c}{0.4} = \dfrac{1.2}{1.6}$

8. $\dfrac{\frac{1}{4}}{x} = \dfrac{1\frac{1}{2}}{3}$

Solve by proportion.

See pp. 158–159

9. If 4 boxes of stationery cost $24.40, what will 6 boxes cost?

10. If 2.5 m of fabric cost $15.60, what will 2.25 m cost?

Solve.

See pp. 160–161

11. The scale of a map is $1\frac{1}{2}$ in. = 50 mi. What is the actual distance if the scale distance is $10\frac{1}{2}$ in.?

12. The scale of a map is 1 cm = 15 km. The actual distance between two cities is 127.5 km. What is the distance between these two cities on the map?

Solve. Check to see if the answer is reasonable.

See pp. 162–163

13. Six students can complete a science project in $8\frac{1}{2}$ hours. How long would it take if two more students joined them?

Solve using partitive proportion.

See pp. 164–165

14. In a recent fund raising raffle event, Carmen sold 5 tickets for every 3 tickets that Lynn sold. How many tickets did they each sell if they sold 240 tickets?

The figures below are similar.

See pp. 166–167

15. Find the measure of $\angle EFD$.

16. Find the measure of side a.

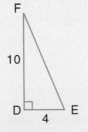

Find the values and the angle measures. Use the table on p. 552.

See pp. 168–169

17. $\sin X$

18. $\cos X$

19. $\tan X$

20. $\sin Y$

21. $\tan Y$

22. $\cos Y$

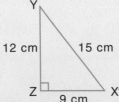

Cumulative Review

Choose the correct answer.

1. The product of 10^4 and 10^{-4} is how much less than 10^2?

   a. 10   **b.** 99

   c. 100   **d.** 90

2. 2×10^5 is 4 times which number?

   a. 2×10^4 **b.** 2×10^3

   c. 8×10^4 **d.** 5×10^4

3. The sum of 2.5×10^3 and 2.05×10^4 is:

   a. 2.25×10^3 **b.** 2.3×10^3

   c. 2.255×10^2 **d.** 2.3×10^4

4. 3360 divided by 0.056 can be expressed as:

   a. 6×10^4 **b.** 6×10^6

   c. 6×10^5 **c.** 6×10^3

5. The next number in the sequence 4, 3, 6, 5, 10, 9 is:

   a. 11
   b. 8
   c. 15
   d. 18

6. If $165.00 is divided among 3 clubs in the ratio of 2 : 3 : 6, what is the difference between the least and the greatest amounts received?

   a. $30.00   **b.** $60.00

   c. $45.00   **d.** $90.00

7. Which triangles are similar?
   a. *A* and *B*
   b. *B* and *C*
   c. *A* and *C*
   d. None

8. What is the ratio of figure *A* to figure *B*?

   a. 0.5
   b. 0.3
   c. 0.8
   d. 0.6

9. The length and width of a rectangle have a ratio of 8 : 6. The perimeter is 42 cm. What is the length of the rectangle?

   a. 9 cm   **b.** 12 cm

   c. 18 cm   **d.** 24 cm

10. If 9 children work on costumes for 6 days, how long will it take 12 children to do the same work?

    a. 5 days   **b.** $4\frac{1}{2}$ days

    c. 8 days   **d.** 6 days

11. What is the ratio of the area of triangle *A* to that of triangle *B* given these dimensions:

    $\triangle A$ $b = 4$ cm, $h = 12$ cm
    $\triangle B$ $b = 6$ cm, $h = 18$ cm

         a. 4 : 9   **b.** 4 : 12

         c. 9 : 4   **d.** 9 : 12

12. The product of
    $0.000000000000089 \times 234{,}050{,}000{,}000$ is:

    a. 20.83045×10^2
    b. 2.083045×10^{-12}
    c. 2.083045×10^{-2}
    d. 2.083045×10^{12}

13. Divide the sum of 3.5×10^3 and 2.9×10^4 by 2.5×10^{-3}.

    a. 1.3×10^7 **b.** 2.56×10^6

    c. 1.3×10^5 **d.** 2.56×10^7

14. Which formula is used to complete the sequence 6, 3, 2, $1\frac{2}{3}$, ...?

    a. $n + 1$ **b.** $\frac{1}{3}n - 1$

    c. $\frac{n}{3} + 1$ **c.** $\frac{1}{3} + n$

Find the product.

15. 2.4×10^3 **16.** 0.07×10^{-4} **17.** 0.16×10^6 **18.** 6.8×10^{-5}

Express each as a fraction.

19. 10^{-4} **20.** 6^{-3} **21.** 10^{-6} **22.** 5^{-5}

Write in scientific notation:

23. $2,456,000$ **24.** 0.0000631 **25.** $31,240,000$ **26.** 0.000000249

Multiply.

27. $10^4 \times 10^5$ **28.** $10^8 \times 10^{-2}$ **29.** $10^{-6} \times 10^0$ **30.** $10^{-8} \times 10^2$

Divide.

31. $\dfrac{10^6}{10^5}$ **32.** $\dfrac{10^8}{10^{-4}}$ **33.** $\dfrac{10^3}{10^0}$ **34.** $\dfrac{10^2}{10^7}$

Compute. Express the answer in scientific notation.

35. $(2.6 \times 10^4) \times (3.2 \times 10^2)$ **36.** $(3.2 \times 10^{-2}) \times (1.4 \times 10^{-8})$

37. $\dfrac{2.4 \times 10^8}{0.8 \times 10^3}$ **38.** $\dfrac{2.1 \times 10^{-5}}{7 \times 10^{-4}}$ **39.** $\dfrac{7.13 \times 10^8}{2.3 \times 10^3}$ **40.** $\dfrac{37.17 \times 10^1}{6.3 \times 10^7}$

Find the value of each ratio.

41. $\dfrac{1}{8} : \dfrac{1}{3}$ **42.** $0.5 : 0.06$ **43.** $2\dfrac{2}{9} : 11\dfrac{2}{3}$ **44.** $2.01 : 12$

Find the missing term.

45. $48 : 24 = 36 : t$ **46.** $0.5 : 0.25 = 0.15 : r$

Solve.

47. If a plane travels 900 miles in 75 min, how far will it travel in 2 hr?

48. Stan drove 90 miles in $1\dfrac{1}{2}$ hours. How long will it take him to drive 300 miles?

49. If 20 tickets for a baseball game cost $250, what is the cost of 35 tickets?

50. Leon used 40 skeins of yarn to hook a rug. If 8 skeins were brown, what percent of the rug was brown?

51. A club has 120 students signed up for volunteer work. If this number is 96% of the total number of club members, how many members are there in all?

52. If a winning candidate received 8 votes for every 3 received by the loser, how many votes did each receive if the total number of votes was 5390?

```
+10 BONUS
```

53. Use proportion to plan some penny-saving. If on your next birthday you begin to save 5 pennies each and every day, how many pennies will you have saved on your birthday one year later?

7 Percent

In this chapter you will:

- Rename fractions, mixed numbers, and decimals as percents and vice versa
- Find: parts or percentages; percents; and original numbers
- Estimate with percent
- Find the percent of increase or decrease
- Solve problems: using percent formulas
- Use technology: binary and hexadecimal numbers

Do you remember?

Change percents to fractions and decimals in this way:

$$20\% \longrightarrow \frac{20}{100} \left(\text{or } \frac{1}{5}\right) \longrightarrow 0.20$$

$$2\% \longrightarrow \frac{2}{100} \left(\text{or } \frac{1}{50}\right) \longrightarrow 0.02$$

$$2\frac{1}{2}\% \longrightarrow \frac{25}{1000} \left(\text{or } \frac{1}{40}\right) \longrightarrow 0.025$$

RESEARCHING TOGETHER

A Percent Fiesta!

Percents are everywhere! Study newspapers, television, and magazines to see how percent is used in: various professions, sports, home life, etc. Challenge your friends to come up with the most unique, the most useful, and the most common uses of percent that you can find.

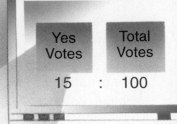

Yes Votes	Total Votes
15	:	100

Percent: the ratio of a number to 100.

15 out of 100 people polled liked the new TV show.
The ratio of *yes* votes to total votes is 15 : 100.
The ratio can be written as a fraction, a decimal, or a percent.

Fraction	Decimal	Percent	
$\frac{15}{100}$	0.15	15%	Percent Symbol

To change a fraction to a percent:

- If the denominator is 100, the numerator is the percent.

    Example: $\frac{7}{100} = 7\%$

- If the denominator is *not* 100, write and solve a proportion.

$\frac{3}{5} = \underline{\ ?\ }\%$ ⟶ $\frac{3}{5} \diagup\!\!\!\diagdown \frac{x}{100}$ | $\frac{7}{8} = \underline{\ ?\ }\%$ ⟶ $\frac{7}{8} \diagup\!\!\!\diagdown \frac{x}{100}$

$3 \times 100 = 5x$ | $7 \times 100 = 8x$

$300 = 5x$ | $700 = 8x$

$60 = x$ | $87\frac{1}{2} = x$

$\frac{3}{5} = 60\%$ | $\frac{7}{8} = 87\frac{1}{2}\%$

To change a decimal to a percent:

- Write the decimal as a fraction.
- Change the fraction to a percent.

    Example: $0.19 = \frac{19}{100} = 19\%$

Example: $0.123 = \frac{123}{1000}$

$\frac{123}{1000} \diagup\!\!\!\diagdown \frac{x}{100}$

$12{,}300 = 1000x$

$1000x = 12{,}300$

$x = 12.3 \longrightarrow 12.3\%$

Shortcut:

Move the decimal point 2 places to the right.

$0.19. = 19\%$ ← Write % symbol.

$0.12.3 = 12.3\%$ ←

Change each fraction or decimal to a percent.

1. $\frac{62}{100}$ 2. $\frac{47}{100}$ 3. $\frac{302}{100}$ 4. $\frac{161}{100}$ 5. $\frac{3}{10}$ 6. $\frac{8}{10}$

7. $\frac{1}{8}$ 8. $\frac{1}{20}$ 9. $\frac{1}{6}$ 10. $\frac{2}{3}$ 11. $\frac{1}{16}$ 12. $\frac{5}{8}$

13. 0.03   14. 0.23   15. 1.75   16. 1.03   17. 3.1   18. 2.4

19. 0.001   20. 0.005   21. 0.012   22. 0.146   23. 5.02   24. 3.1

Change each fraction to a percent.

25. $\frac{23}{100}$ **26.** $\frac{68}{100}$ **27.** $\frac{125}{100}$ **28.** $\frac{250}{100}$ **29.** $\frac{6}{25}$ **30.** $\frac{3}{20}$

31. $\frac{17}{20}$ **32.** $\frac{7}{10}$ **33.** $\frac{1}{9}$ **34.** $\frac{3}{7}$ **35.** $\frac{7}{12}$ **36.** $\frac{8}{15}$

37. $1\frac{1}{10}$ **38.** $1\frac{2}{5}$ **39.** 3   **40.** 6   **41.** $2\frac{3}{25}$ **42.** $5\frac{1}{4}$

Change each decimal to a percent.

43. 0.34   **44.** 0.76   **45.** 0.24   **46.** 0.36   **47.** 0.79   **48.** 0.31

49. 0.07   **50.** 0.02   **51.** 0.016   **52.** 0.423   **53.** 2.63   **54.** 1.47

55. 5.17   **56.** 1.09   **57.** 0.103   **58.** 0.911   **59.** 3.4   **60.** 1.2

True or false? If false, rewrite the percent to make a true statement.

61. 0.05 = 50%   **62.** 0.67 = 67%   **63.** 0.23 = 23%

64. 0.19 = 190%   **65.** 1.83 = 183%   **66.** 2.04 = 204%

67. 0.256 = 25.6%   **68.** 0.375 = 375%   **69.** 0.3 = 3%

70. 0.8 = 80%   **71.** 0.007 = 7%   **72.** 0.025 = 2.5%

73. Rewrite this report by changing each circled part to a percent.

Nineteen out of 20 students in Ryan School are involved in a recycling project. They spend $\frac{3}{4}$ of the time collecting items to recycle. Of the items collected, five eighths are plastic or aluminum. One out of 12 plastic items are clear plastic and 0.8 of the aluminum items are cans.

CALCULATOR ACTIVITY

Change each fraction to a percent. For a fraction equivalent to a repeating decimal, round to the nearest tenth of a percent. (The first one is done.)

74. $\frac{10}{12}$ ⟶   ÷ % = ⟶ 83.3%

75. $\frac{3}{75}$ **76.** $\frac{39}{55}$ **77.** $\frac{55}{111}$ **78.** $\frac{87}{190}$ **79.** $\frac{63}{95}$ **80.** $\frac{77}{299}$

7-2 Percents to Fractions and Decimals

To change a percent to a fraction:

- Write the number with a denominator of 100.
- Simplify the fraction.

Examples: $37\frac{1}{2}\% = \dfrac{37\frac{1}{2}}{100}$

$= 37\frac{1}{2} \div 100$

$= \dfrac{\overset{3}{\cancel{75}}}{2} \times \dfrac{1}{\underset{4}{\cancel{100}}}$

$37\frac{1}{2}\% = \dfrac{3}{8}$

$140\% = \dfrac{140}{100}$

$= \dfrac{7}{5}$

$140\% = 1\frac{2}{5}$

To change a percent to a decimal:

- Write the number with a denominator of 100.
- Divide the numerator by the denominator.

Examples: $4\% = \dfrac{4}{100}$

$= 100\overline{)4.00}^{\;0.04}$

$4\% = 0.04$

$64.7\% = \dfrac{64.7}{100}$

$= 100\overline{)64.700}^{\;0.647}$

$64.7\% = 0.647$

Shortcut:

Move the decimal point two places to the left.
Drop the percent sign.

$4\% \longrightarrow 0.04. = 0.04 \qquad 64.7\% \longrightarrow 0.64.7 = 0.647$

Change each percent to a fraction in lowest terms.

1. 20%	**2.** 50%	**3.** 35%	**4.** 45%	**5.** 150%	**6.** 110%
7. 72%	**8.** 89%	**9.** 375%	**10.** 225%	**11.** $62\frac{1}{2}\%$	**12.** $33\frac{1}{3}\%$
13. 87.5%	**14.** 10.1%	**15.** 3.8%	**16.** 2.2%	**17.** 0.2%	**18.** 0.7%

Change each percent to a decimal.

19. 6%	**20.** 1%	**21.** 61%	**22.** 56%	**23.** 5%	**24.** 4%
25. 21%	**26.** 27%	**27.** 13%	**28.** 92%	**29.** 143%	**30.** 103%
31. 8%	**32.** 2%	**33.** 4.9%	**34.** 9.2%	**35.** 152.9%	**36.** 192.5%

Copy and complete the chart.

	Fraction	Decimal	Percent
37.	$\frac{3}{8}$		
38.	$\frac{2}{5}$		
39.			4%
40.			9%
41.		0.3125	
42.		0.875	
43.	$\frac{9}{10}$		
44.	$\frac{3}{20}$		

	Fraction	Decimal	Percent
45.	$4\frac{2}{3}$		
46.	$1\frac{1}{5}$		
47.			500%
48.			800%
49.		0.004	
50.		0.007	
51.	$\frac{4}{9}$		
52.	$\frac{5}{6}$		

Change each percent to a decimal. (The first one is done.)

53. $\frac{1}{5}\% \longrightarrow \dfrac{\frac{1}{5}}{100} \longrightarrow \dfrac{0.2}{100} \longrightarrow 100\overline{)0.200}^{\,0.002} \longrightarrow \frac{1}{5}\% = 0.002$

54. $\frac{1}{4}\%$ 55. $\frac{2}{5}\%$ 56. $\frac{1}{2}\%$ 57. $\frac{1}{8}\%$ 58. $\frac{3}{4}\%$ 59. $\frac{5}{8}\%$ 60. $\frac{3}{5}\%$

Solve.

61. Sixty-eight percent of the books sold yesterday at the book fair were fiction books. Write this percent as a fraction in lowest terms.

62. Attendance at the PTA meetings increased by 175% last year. Write this percent as a decimal.

63. The bank pays $5\frac{1}{4}\%$ interest per year. Write this percent as a decimal.

64. Eighty-three percent of the class is going on a field trip. Write this percent as a fraction in simplest form.

65. Profits of the Gummy Glue Company increased 275% last year. Write this percent as a decimal.

66. A store is offering $\frac{1}{9}$ off all merchandise. Another store is reducing prices by $12\frac{1}{2}\%$. Which store is offering the larger reduction?

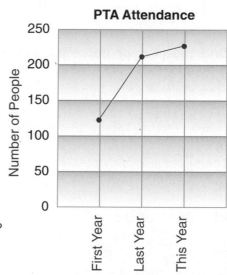

PTA Attendance

Exercise 62

183

7-3 Finding a Part or a Percentage of a Number

A school poll showed that 15% of the 180 students who responded wanted a career in the communications field. How many students was that?

To find a part or percentage **(P)** of a number **(B)**, use *one* of these two ways:

First Way

Use the percent formula:

$P = B \times R$ where:

P = part or percentage of base

R = rate or percent

B = base or original number or whole

$P = B \times R$

$P = 180 \times 15\%$

$P = 180 \times \dfrac{3}{20}$ OR 180×0.15

$P = \overset{9}{\cancel{180}} \times \dfrac{3}{\underset{1}{\cancel{20}}}$ OR $\begin{array}{r} 1\,8\,0 \\ \times 0.1\,5 \\ \hline 2\,7.0\,0. \end{array}$

$P = 27$

Second Way

Write a proportion.
Solve it.
Check by substitution.

part $\longrightarrow \dfrac{P}{B} = \dfrac{R}{100}$ $\leftarrow$ percent of the part
whole $\longrightarrow$ ← total percent

$\dfrac{\text{part} \longrightarrow P}{\text{whole} \longrightarrow B} = \dfrac{R}{100}$ $\leftarrow$ percent of the part ← total percent

$\dfrac{P}{180} \diagup\hspace{-0.9em}\diagdown \dfrac{15}{100}$

$100P = 2700$

$P = 27$

Check: $\dfrac{27}{180} \diagup\hspace{-0.9em}\diagdown \dfrac{15}{100} \longrightarrow 2700 = 2700$

Both ways show that 27 students want a career in communications.

Find the part or percentage of the number.

1. 30% of 60	**2.** 70% of 90	**3.** 8% of 50
4. 5% of 60	**5.** 50% of 140	**6.** 75% of 100
7. 30% of 300	**8.** 40% of 400	**9.** 52% of 150
10. 98% of 200	**11.** 16% of 135	**12.** 44% of 160
13. 85% of 15	**14.** 90% of 18	**15.** $33\frac{1}{3}$% of 36
16. $37\frac{1}{2}$% of 84	**17.** 120% of 400	**18.** 250% of 300
19. $\frac{1}{4}$% of 40	**20.** $\frac{1}{2}$% of 32	**21.** 2.125% of 400
22. 1.875% of 100	**23.** 140% of 150	**24.** 160% of 600

Solve.

There were 360 items on sale at a giant clearance sale.
Tell how many items were on sale at each discount:

25. $16\frac{2}{3}$% of the items were on sale for $\frac{1}{2}$ off.

26. 25% of the items were on sale for $\frac{1}{3}$ off.

27. 15% of the items were on sale for $\frac{1}{4}$ off.

28. Lauren's team scored 500 points during the basketball season. If Lauren scored 6% of the points, how many points did she score?

29. Last year the school raised $1280 selling plants. The eighth graders raised 40% of the money. How much money did the eighth graders raise?

30. At the beginning of the school year there were 600 students at the Hayden School. During the year $5\frac{1}{2}$% of the students moved. How many students moved?

31. There are 4800 students attending a local college. Fifty-eight percent of the students are females. How many female students attend the college?

32. The Winston family traveled 2464 miles on their vacation. They traveled $87\frac{1}{2}$% of the distance by plane and the remaining miles by car. How many miles did they travel by car?

Exercise 32

$87\frac{1}{2}$ % $12\frac{1}{2}$ %

2464 miles

33. Mr. Sanchez earned $28,250 last year. This year he earned 25% more. How much did he earn this year?

34. A town near the ocean had a population of 18,600 people. 35% of them worked on the fishing fleet. How many of them fished for a living?

Compute mentally.

35. 48% of 39 is 18.72.   What is 24% of 39?

36. $87\frac{1}{2}$% of 64 is 56.   What is $87\frac{1}{2}$% of 32?

37. 75% of 372 is 279.   What is 75% of 744?

SKILLS TO REMEMBER   Simplify each fraction.

38. $\frac{6}{30}$ **39.** $\frac{24}{36}$ **40.** $\frac{8}{80}$ **41.** $\frac{70}{420}$ **42.** $\frac{90}{45}$ **43.** $\frac{264}{12}$

7-4 Finding Percent

A state legislator sent out 500 questionnaires to determine her constituents' environmental concerns. 400 questionnaires were answered and returned. What percent is that?

To find what percent (**R**) one number (**P**) is of another (**B**), use *one* of these two ways:

First Way

Use the percent formula:

$$P = B \times R$$

Substitute known values.

$$400 = 500 \times R$$

$$400 = 500R$$

$$500R = 400$$

$$R = \frac{400}{500}$$

$R = \frac{4}{5}$ or 80% of questionnaires returned

Finding the Percent Rule

If $P = B \times R$, then

$$R = \frac{P}{B}$$

Second Way

Write a proportion.

Solve it.

Check it by substitution.

part $\longrightarrow$ $\dfrac{P}{B} = \dfrac{R}{100}$ $\longleftarrow$ percent of part
whole $\longrightarrow$ $\phantom{\dfrac{P}{B}}$ $\longleftarrow$ total percent

$$\frac{400}{500} \diagdown\!\!\!\!\diagup \frac{R}{100}$$

$$500R = 40,000$$

$$R = 80\% \text{ of questionnaires returned}$$

Check: $\dfrac{400}{500} \diagdown\!\!\!\!\diagup \dfrac{80}{100} \longrightarrow 40,000 = 40,000$

Find the percent. Round to the nearest tenth, if necessary.

1. 6 is what percent of 30?

2. 4 is what percent of 40?

3. What percent of 45 is 3?

4. What percent of 64 is 8?

5. What percent of 40 is 60?

6. What percent of 10 is 60?

7. 7 is what percent of 21?

8. 6 is what percent of 72?

9. 135 is what percent of 75?

10. 180 is what percent of 90?

11. What percent of an hour is 20 minutes?

12. What percent of a day is 36 hours?

13. What percent of a dollar is 45¢?

14. What percent of a gallon is 1 quart?

Copy and complete the chart.

a = part or percentage; c = original number or base

	15.	16.	17.	18.	19.	20.	21.	22.
a	8	9	16	24	75	30	28	90
c	200	90	40	30	100	150	140	180
% a is of c	?	?	?	?	?	?	?	?
% c is of a	?	?	?	?	?	?	?	?

Solve.

23. Erik had $54. He spent $18 at an amusement park. What percent did he spend?

24. If 3 out of every 20 people go on a roller coaster, what percent is this?

25. Of 1080 pennies in Jamal's coin collection 270 are Canadian pennies. What percent of the collection are the Canadian pennies?

26. Michele had $250 in her savings account. She withdrew $60 to buy new clothes for school. What percent is still in her savings account?

27. At the Strang Middle School 30% of the 60 teachers tutor students after school. If six more teachers become tutors, what percent of the teachers tutor now?

28. Lauren earned $310 last summer. She saved $70. What percent of her earnings did she spend?

29. Two neighboring towns are considering a plan for renovating a bridge between them. In one town 110 of the 240 people polled liked the plan. In the other town 250 of the 420 people polled liked the plan. Find the percent that liked the plan for each town. Then find the percent of all those polled who liked the plan.

30. 40% of 80 employees enrolled in a special dental plan. Eight more employees have just joined the plan. What percent are now enrolled in the plan?

31. The mayors of Katonah and Somers propose to build a playground to be shared by both towns. In Somers 293 of the 500 citizens want the new playground. In Katonah 285 of the 480 citizens favor the playground. Find the percent of citizens in each town who favor the shared playground. Then find the percent of citizens of both towns who favor the playground project.

Translate each sentence into an equation and solve. (The first one is done.)

32. e% of 70 is 10. $\rightarrow \frac{e}{100} \times 70 = 10 \rightarrow \frac{7}{10}e = 10 \rightarrow e = \frac{100}{7} \rightarrow e = 14\frac{2}{7}$%

33. h% of 16 is 6.　　34. c% of 21 is 9.　　35. d% of 80 is 35.

36. f% of 560 is 28.　　37. a% of 9 is 40.　　38. e% of 720 is 120.

7-5 Finding the Original Number

30% of the junior high schools participated in Marin County's Earth Day Festival. If 6 schools participated, what is the total number of junior high schools in the county?

To find the original number **(B)** when the percent **(R)** of it is given, use *one* of these two ways:

First Way

Use the percent formula:

$$P = B \times R$$

Substitute known values.

$$6 = B \times 30\%$$

$$6 = 0.30\,B \text{ (or } 6 = \tfrac{3}{10}B)$$

$$0.30B = 6 \longrightarrow B = 6 \div 0.30$$

$$B = 20 \text{ Junior High Schools}$$

Finding the Original Number Rule

If $P = B \times R$, then

$$B = P \div R$$

Second Way

Write a proportion. Solve and check it.

$$\text{part} \longrightarrow \frac{P}{B} = \frac{R}{100} \longleftarrow \text{percent of part}$$
$$\text{whole} \qquad\qquad\qquad\qquad \longleftarrow \text{total percent}$$

$$\frac{6}{B} \diagdown \frac{30}{100}$$

$$30B = 600$$

$$B = 600 \div 30$$

$$B = 20 \text{ Junior High Schools}$$

Check: $\dfrac{6}{20} \diagdown \dfrac{30}{100} \longrightarrow 600 = 600$

There are 20 junior high schools in Marin County.

Find the original number.

1. 10% of $n = 10$
2. 10% of $n = 11$
3. 25% of $n = 40$

4. 50% of $n = 60$
5. 20% of $n = 24$
6. 60% of $n = 27$

7. 40% of $n = 30$
8. 80% of $n = 72$
9. 75% of $n = 27$

10. 45% of $n = 27$
11. 15% of $n = 0.48$
12. 80% of $n = 5.5$

13. 1.5% of $n = 3$
14. 0.5% of $n = 7$
15. $12\frac{1}{2}$% of $n = 64$

16. $2\frac{1}{2}$% of $n = 18$
17. $33\frac{1}{3}$% of $n = 54$
18. $66\frac{2}{3}$% of $n = 66$

Copy and complete the table. *a* = rate; *b* = percentage; *c* = original number or base

	a	b	c
19.	15%	25	?
20.	20%	21	?
21.	7%	?	100
22.	9%	?	200
23.	?	60	400
24.	?	84	700
25.	$12\frac{1}{2}$%	160	?
26.	$62\frac{1}{2}$%	625	?

	a	b	c
27.	5%	?	25
28.	2%	?	16
29.	?	88	2000
30.	?	36	2400
31.	28%	210	?
32.	36%	300	?
33.	?	12	108
34.	?	3	99

Solve.

35. Alicia put aside \$150, or $12\frac{1}{2}$ %, of her monthly salary for a special vacation trip. What is her monthly salary?

36. There are 63 boys in a rural school. If this is 45% of the entire enrollment, how many pupils attend the school?

37. A team lost 41, or 20%, of the total number of games played. How many games were played?

38. 140 students signed up for the field-day activities. If this number is $83\frac{1}{3}$ % of the total number of students, how many students are there in all?

39. 6.25% of the people who signed a petition lived in Newton. If 100 signers were from Newton, how many people signed the petition?

40. A solution must contain 2% acetic acid. If 24 ounces of acid are available, how much solution can be made?

Yearly Budget

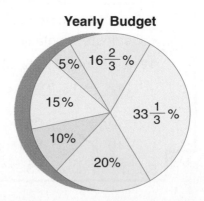

◁ MAKE UP YOUR OWN ▷

41. Imagine you have your own company. Determine what categories would be in your yearly budget. Label the graph. Let $33\frac{1}{3}$ % equal \$60,000. Find the amount budgeted for each category. Then find the total yearly budget.

Estimating with Percents

73.4% of 358 eighth graders want to attend college. About how many want to attend college?

Table of Common Percents		

To estimate the percentage (P):

- Round the percent to a common percent.
- Round the base to a compatible number.
- Compute mentally.

$$73.4\% \text{ of } 358 = \underline{\ ?\ }$$
$$75\% \text{ of } 360 = \underline{\ ?\ }$$
$$\frac{3}{4} \times \overset{90}{\cancel{360}} = 270$$
$$\underset{1}{}$$

About 270 students want to attend college.

To estimate the percent or rate (R):

- Write the given numbers as a ratio.
- Round both numbers to compatible numbers.
- Write the ratio in lowest terms and use the table of common percents to find the rate.

About what percent of 358 is 92?

$$\frac{92}{358} \longrightarrow \frac{90}{360} \longrightarrow \frac{1}{4} = 25\%$$

So, 92 is about 25% of 358.

To estimate the original number or base (B):

- Round the percent to a common percent.
- Round the percentage to a compatible number.
- Compute mentally.

42 is about 13.7% of what number?

$$42 = 13.7\% \times \underline{\ ?\ }$$
$$40 = 14\tfrac{2}{7}\% \times \underline{\ ?\ }$$
$$40 = \frac{1}{7}n \longrightarrow 280 = n$$

So, 42 is about 13.7% of 280.

Table of Common Percents

$$25\% = \frac{1}{4}$$
$$50\% = \frac{2}{4} = \frac{1}{2}$$
$$75\% = \frac{3}{4}$$

$$10\% = \frac{1}{10}$$
$$30\% = \frac{3}{10}$$
$$70\% = \frac{7}{10}$$
$$90\% = \frac{9}{10}$$

$$20\% = \frac{1}{5}$$
$$40\% = \frac{2}{5}$$
$$60\% = \frac{3}{5}$$
$$80\% = \frac{4}{5}$$

$$16\tfrac{2}{3}\% = \frac{1}{6}$$
$$33\tfrac{1}{3}\% = \frac{2}{6} = \frac{1}{3}$$
$$66\tfrac{2}{3}\% = \frac{4}{6} = \frac{2}{3}$$
$$83\tfrac{1}{3}\% = \frac{5}{6}$$

$$12\tfrac{1}{2}\% = \frac{1}{8}$$
$$37\tfrac{1}{2}\% = \frac{3}{8}$$
$$62\tfrac{1}{2}\% = \frac{5}{8}$$
$$87\tfrac{1}{2}\% = \frac{7}{8}$$

$$14\tfrac{2}{7}\% = \frac{1}{7}$$
$$11\tfrac{1}{9}\% = \frac{1}{9}$$
$$8\tfrac{1}{3}\% = \frac{1}{12}$$

Use the Table of Common Percents to estimate each percent.

1. 34%   2. 71.2%   3. 9%   4. 65.5%   5. 29%   6. $10\frac{3}{4}$%

7. 62%   8. 27%   9. 14%   10. 88.9%   11. 17%   12. 38%

Estimate the percentage.

13. 8% of 61   14. 67% of 22   15. 51% of 63.8   16. 86% of 23.5

17. 69% of 49   18. 13% of 31.5   19. 91% of 28   20. 61% of 41

21. $9\frac{3}{4}$% of 12   22. 38% of 17   23. 42% of 14   24. 13.8% of 78

Choose the best ratio and then estimate each percent.

25. __?__% of 19 is 3.   a. $\frac{5}{20}$ b. $\frac{3}{18}$ c. $\frac{20}{3}$

26. __?__% of 22 is 7.   a. $\frac{6}{24}$ b. $\frac{8}{20}$ c. $\frac{7}{21}$

27. __?__% of 31 is 9.   a. $\frac{9}{30}$ b. $\frac{8}{32}$ c. $\frac{32}{8}$

28. __?__% of 29 is 6.4.   a. $\frac{6}{30}$ b. $\frac{28}{7}$ c. $\frac{7}{28}$

29. __?__% of 194 is 95.   a. $\frac{90}{200}$ b. $\frac{200}{90}$ c. $\frac{100}{200}$

30. __?__% of 13 is 9.2.   a. $\frac{9}{12}$ b. $\frac{10}{12}$ c. $\frac{9}{15}$

Estimate the original number. (The first one is done.)

31. 82% of __?__ is 17. ⟶ 80% of __?__ is 16. ⟶ $\frac{4}{5}n = 16$ ⟶ $n = 20$

32. 29% of __?__ is 26.5.   33. 76% of __?__ is 14.6.

34. $48\frac{1}{2}$% of __?__ is 16.   35. $69\frac{1}{3}$% of __?__ is 29.

36. 52 is 26% of __?__.   37. 46 is 91% of __?__.

38. 15.7 is 66% of __?__.   39. 17.8 is $58\frac{3}{4}$% of __?__.

Solve.

40. Of 242 colleges $23\frac{4}{5}$% offer degrees in theater. About how many colleges offer degrees in this field?

41. Fifty-eight out of 418 students belong to the honor society. About what percent of the student body belongs to the honor society?

42. About 13% of the enrollment, or 78 students, play in the Sussex School Band. About how many students are enrolled in Sussex School?

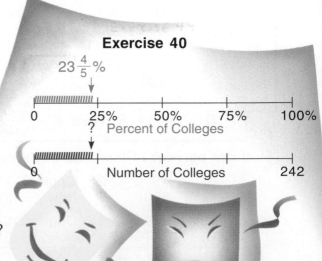

Exercise 40

$23\frac{4}{5}$%

0   25%   50%   75%   100%
? Percent of Colleges

0   Number of Colleges   242

191

7-7 | Percent of Increase or Decrease

A seashore town's population increased from 7500 to 8154 during the summer. What was the percent of increase?

▶ **To find the percent or rate of increase:**

- Find the amount of increase.
  8154 (New Amount) − 7500 (Original Amount) = 654 (Increase)
- Use *one* of these two ways to solve:

First Way	**Second Way**
Use the percent formula: $P = B \times R$	Write and solve a proportion.
Or: Increase (I) = Original Amount (OA) $\times$ R	$\dfrac{\text{Amount of Increase}}{\text{Original Amount}} = \dfrac{\text{Rate of Increase}}{\text{Total Percent}}$
Substitute known values in $I = OA \times R$	
$654 = 7500 \times R$	$\dfrac{654}{7500} \diagdown \dfrac{R}{100}$
$R = \dfrac{654}{7500} = 8.72\%$ (rounds to 9%)	$654 \times 100 = 7500\,R$
	$R = \dfrac{65400}{7500}$
If $I = OA \times R$, then $R = \dfrac{I}{OA}$.	$R = 8.72\%$ (rounds to 9%)

There was a decline in visitors to the Marine Museum from 320 in August to 284 in September. What was the percent of decrease?

▶ **To find the percent or rate of decrease:**

- Find the amount of decrease.
  320 (Original Total) − 284 (New Total) = 36 (Decrease)
- Proceed as for percent or rate of increase.

First Way	**Second Way**
Decrease (D) = Original Amount (OA) $\times$ R	$\dfrac{\text{Amount of Decrease}}{\text{Original Amount}} = \dfrac{\text{Rate of Decrease}}{\text{Total Percent}}$
Substitute known values in $D = OA \times R$	
$36 = 320 \times R$	$\dfrac{36}{320} \diagdown \dfrac{R}{100}$
$R = \dfrac{36}{320} = 11.25\%$ (rounds to 11.3%)	$320\,R = 3600$
	$R = \dfrac{3600}{320}$
If $D = OA \times R$, then $R = \dfrac{D}{OA}$.	$R = 11.25\%$ (rounds to 11.3%)

Find the percent of increase or decrease. Round to the nearest tenth of a percent.

1. Original: 4500
   New: 6000

2. Original: 720
   New: 630

3. Original: $3500
   New: $2100

4. Original: $960
   New: $440

5. Original: 245
   New: 1470

6. Original: $420
   New: $180

7. Original: 6750
   New: 8250

8. Original: $810
   New: $720

This report shows the amount of money the Kessler Corporation spent on expenses.

Copy and complete. Round answers to the nearest tenth of a percent.

	Expense	Budget		Increase		Decrease	
		Last year	This year	Amount	%	Amount	%
9.	Rent/Mortgage	$27,600	$31,200				
10.	Gas/Electric	$5850	$5550				
11.	Telephone/FAX	$6400	$9000				
12.	Medical/Dental	$28,250	$15,250				
13.	Insurance	$7500	$9600				
14.	Transportation	$3475	$5375				
15.	Expense Account	$9500	$6200				
16.	Office Supplies	$3950	$2700				

Solve.

17. Amanda earned $12.50 babysitting last week and $9.75 babysitting this week. What percent of change is that?

18. The Alert Agency spent $140,000 on advertising last year. This year they spent $145,250 on advertising. What is the percent of change?

19. Last year there were 144 students in eighth grade. This year there are 120. What is the percent of decrease?

20. One baby monkey weighed 5.4 kg. Another weighed 5.1 kg. What is the percent of their weight difference?

21. A delivery person earned $9.00 in tips one morning and $7.60 the following morning. What percent of change is that?

22. Last year there were 45 members in the science club. This year 51 more students joined. What is the percent of increase?

23. Calendar sales decreased one month from 345 to 299. What was the percent of decrease?

24. A recent census showed that the population of a large city rose from 6,243,915 to 6,260,565. What is the percent of change? (Check your answer on a calculator.)

25. Stock shares fell in one day from $56,498.27 to $54,621.80. What was the percent of decrease in price? (Check your answer on a calculator.)

Exercise 20

193

Binary and Hexadecimal Numbers

In a computer, numbers and letters are expressed as **binary** or **base-two numerals.** A base-two numeral consists of a combination of the digits 0 and 1.

The value of the numeral is determined by the places the 0's and 1's occupy. The chart shows the corresponding values of base-two and base-ten numerals.

Base-Two Values

128	64	32	16	8	4	2	1
0	0	1	0	0	1	1	0
0	0	0	0	1	1	1	1
0	0	1	0	1	0	0	1
0	1	0	0	0	0	1	1

Base-Ten Values

32 + 4 + 2 = 38
8 + 4 + 2 + 1 = 15
32 + 8 + 1 = 41
64 + 2 + 1 = 67

Binary digits or *bits* are used in computers because the 0's and 1's can be controlled electrically as *open circuits* (0) or as *closed circuits* (1).
Each byte consists of 8 bits or circuits which are either opened or closed.

Write a decimal numeral for each binary numeral.

1. 0001011
2. 0111000
3. 0110011
4. 0110111
5. 0101010
6. 0011011
7. 0101110
8. 0010010
9. 0111111

10. **Write a seven-digit binary numeral for each base-ten numeral.** (The first is done.)

Base-Two Values

	64	32	16	8	4	2	1
45	0	1	0	1	1	0	1
12							
7							
50							
31							

Base-Two Values

	64	32	16	8	4	2	1
63							
5							
25							
15							
20							

Write a decimal numeral for each binary numeral.

11. 01010010
12. 10001000
13. 01100110
14. 10011001
15. 01111000
16. 11000011

CHALLENGE

Make a flowchart to show the process used to change a binary numeral into a base-ten numeral.

Hexadecimal Numbers

Hexadecimal or base 16 number system uses the 16 symbols:
0 through 9 and the letters A, B, C, D, E, F.

This chart shows the corresponding values of base 16 and base 10 numerals.

Base-Sixteen Values

16	1
2	3
1	D

Base-Ten Values

$2(16)$	$+$	$3(1)$	$=$	35
$1(16)$	$+$	$13(1)$	$=$	29

Many computer systems use hexadecimal notation to simplify binary notation.
Using the chart, notice how each set of four binary digits converts directly to hexadecimal notation.

Look at this chart. —————————→

▶ To convert binary ——→ hexadecimal:

$$158_{10} = 1001\,1110_2$$
$$9 \quad E \longrightarrow 9E_{16}$$

▶ To convert hexadecimal ——→ binary:

$$124_{10} = 7C_{16}$$
$$01111100 \longrightarrow 01111100_2$$

Decimal	Hexadecimal	Binary			
(10)	(16)	8s	4s	2s	1s
0	0	0	0	0	0
1	1	0	0	0	1
2	2	0	0	1	0
3	3	0	0	1	1
4	4	0	1	0	0
5	5	0	1	0	1
6	6	0	1	1	0
7	7	0	1	1	1
8	8	1	0	0	0
9	9	1	0	0	1
10	A	1	0	1	0
11	B	1	0	1	1
12	C	1	1	0	0
13	D	1	1	0	1
14	E	1	1	1	0
15	F	1	1	1	1

Change each binary number to a hexadecimal number.
17. 01110010 **18.** 10001100 **19.** 01001111 **20.** 01111010
21. 00001100 **22.** 00111100 **23.** 01101011 **24.** 01011010

Change each hexadecimal number to a binary number:
25. 7F **26.** 2B **27.** 8A **28.** 3D
29. 4D **30.** 5C **31.** 6E **32.** 9B

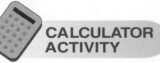
CALCULATOR ACTIVITY A fraction calculator is useful in expressing a base-ten number in hexadecimal (base 16) notation. Use the ⟨INT ÷⟩ key.

$$217_{10} = \,?_{16} \longrightarrow \boxed{217}\ \boxed{INT \div}\ \boxed{16}\ \boxed{=}\ \boxed{13 \quad 9}$$

$$13 = D$$
$$9 = 9$$
$$\longrightarrow D9_{16}$$

33. Change to base 16: **a.** 302 **b.** 198 **c.** 255

195

Remember the percent formulas:
To find a part or percentage *(P)*: $P = B \times R$
To find a percent or rate *(R)*: $R = \frac{P}{B}$
To find the original number *(B)*: $B = P \div R$

Problem: Of the land in the park $37\frac{1}{2}$% is forested. If 4.5 acres of the land are not forested, how large is the park?

1 IMAGINE Draw and label the parts of the park that are *not* forested.

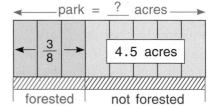

2 NAME *Facts:* $37\frac{1}{2}$% — forested land
4.5 acres — unforested land

Question: ? acres — total parkland

3 THINK To find the whole or original size of the parkland, you need to determine the percent of the land that is *not* forested and solve using the following formula:

$$B = P \div R$$

$37\frac{1}{2}$%, or $\frac{3}{8}$, is forested, so subtract to find the part that is not forested:

$$100\% - 37\frac{1}{2}\% \longrightarrow \frac{8}{8} - \frac{3}{8} = \frac{5}{8} \text{ (Not forested)}$$

$$B = 4.5 \div \frac{5}{8} \longleftarrow$$

4 COMPUTE Use fractions or decimals to solve: $B = 4.5 \div \frac{5}{8}$

$B = 4.5 \div 0.625$ OR $B = \frac{45}{10} \div \frac{5}{8}$

$B = 0.625\overline{)4.5000}$ $B = \frac{\overset{9}{\cancel{45}}}{\cancel{10}} \times \frac{\overset{4}{\cancel{8}}}{\cancel{5}}$
 $\; 5 \quad\quad 1$

$B = 7.2$ $B = \frac{36}{5} \longrightarrow 7.2$

The parkland covers 7.2 acres.

5 CHECK Use cross products to check your computations.

$$\frac{P}{B} = \frac{R}{100} \longrightarrow \frac{4.5 \text{ acres}}{7.2 \text{ total acres}} \overset{\text{unforested}}{\underset{}{\times}} \frac{62.5 \text{ unforested}}{100 \text{ total percent}} \longrightarrow 450 = 450$$

Solve by using the correct percentage formula.

1. Twenty items in the math contest were multiple-choice questions, 25 were computation questions, and the remaining 25% were word problems. What percent of the contest were multiple-choice questions?

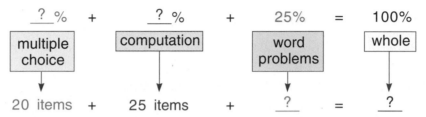

| 1 IMAGINE | Draw and label a picture → 2 NAME |
of the contest questions.

→ *Facts*

→ *Question*

3 THINK   In this problem the whole (100%) is composed of three parts:

$$\underline{\ ?\ }\% \ + \ \underline{\ ?\ }\% \ + \ 25\% \ = \ 100\%$$

| multiple choice | computation | word problems | whole |

$$20 \text{ items} \ + \ 25 \text{ items} \ + \ \underline{\ ?\ } \ = \ \underline{\ ?\ }$$

To find the percent of the questions that were multiple choice, first find the total number of questions. If 25% of the items were word problems, then 75% of the items were multiple-choice or computation questions.

$$B = (20 + 25) \div 75\%$$

Use the total number of items to find the rate.

4 COMPUTE ⟶ 5 CHECK

2. There were 75 questions on the history test. Jill got only 3 wrong. What percent did she answer correctly?

3. 40% of the school's freshmen elected to take Spanish. Of these students, 16 are also taking art. If there are 400 freshmen, what percent of the Spanish class is also taking art?

4. Twelve percent, or 30, of the students who take French joined the French Club. How many students take French?

5. Of the students in one class, 20% expressed an interest in a career in politics. If there were 40 students in the class, how many were interested in politics?

6. On the first day of a textbook sale, 25% of the books were sold. If 18 textbooks were sold, how many were on sale?

7. Professor Tsing meets five classes each day. One has 26 students, another has 30, another has 33, and a fourth has 28 students. If this represents 78% of the students in her classes, what is the total number of students she teaches?

7-10 Problem Solving: Applications

Choose the correct equation (a–f). Then solve.

1. 75% of what number is 24?
2. What number is 24% of 75?
3. What percent of 25 is 24?
4. 25% of 24 is what percent of 6?
5. 75 is what percent of 25?
6. 24% of 75 is 6% of what number?

a. $n\% \times 25 = 24$

b. $75 = n\% \times 25$

c. $75\% \, n = 24$

d. $24\% \times 75 = 6\% \, n$

e. $n = 24\%$ of 75

f. $25\% \times 24 = n\% \times 6$

Express each percent as a fraction and a decimal.

7. More than 70% of the earth is covered with water.

8. About 97% of the world's water is salt water.

9. About 20% of the world's electricity is generated by water.

10. When it rains, the relative humidity can equal 100%.

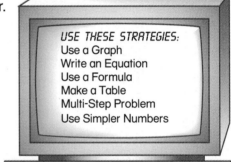

USE THESE STRATEGIES:
Use a Graph
Write an Equation
Use a Formula
Make a Table
Multi-Step Problem
Use Simpler Numbers

Solve.

11. Of the 189 trees in the neighborhood, 105 have lost all their leaves. What percent of the trees have lost their leaves?

12. The junior ranger organization has reserved 120 of the 2700 seats in the bleacher section of the stadium. What percent of the bleacher section is not reserved for the organization?

13. Eighty-five percent of the items recycled by Caretown are glass, plastic, and metals. The rest is paper. If Caretown recycled 1760 lb of materials in one month, how many pounds of paper were recycled?

14. A magazine surveyed 24,000 subscribers to find out if the majority preferred crossword puzzles or word searches. If $33\frac{1}{3}\%$ preferred word searches, how many subscribers preferred crossword puzzles?

15. An editor paid a doctor bill of $100, or 8% of her savings. What were her savings?

16. Subscribers to a monthly magazine received a special renewal offer of 10 issues for $21. If the newsstand price is $2.25 per issue, what percent can be saved by taking advantage of the special offer?

17. Subscribers to a music magazine range in age from 15 to 50. How many subscribers fall into each category if $33\frac{1}{3}\%$ are between the ages of 15 and 25; 12,000 are between 26 and 35; and $22\frac{2}{9}\%$ are between 36 and 50?

18. A newspaper editor received a 12% increase in salary. If the new salary was $31,920, what was the original pay?

19. Last month a writer received checks for 4 published articles. The checks were in the amounts of $240, $500, $520, and $420. If these payments represented 70% of the writer's earnings for the month, how much more money did the writer earn last month?

20. 60% of the cost of printing a political newsletter was paid by donations. The rest, $430, was paid for by the politician.
   a. What was the total printing cost?
   b. How much money was donated to pay for printing?

21. If 24 of the 30 magazines sold at a newsstand are published once a month, what percent of the magazines are published at some other rate?

22. Monthly sales of a specialty magazine fell by $16\frac{2}{3}\%$ after the price was raised. If there were 4325 sales in the month after the price increase, how many sales were there before?

23. A newspaper vender estimates that she must increase her sales by 4%, to 6032 copies per day, in order to make a profit. How many newspapers per day is she currently selling?

24. If the circulation of Winston's Weekly this year is 3200 and increases 5% per year, what will its circulation be in two years?

The graph shows the results of a survey of subscribers to the Daily Byline News. Use the graph to answer exercises 25–27.

25. $\frac{1}{8}$ of the subscribers read for 1 hour. What percent is that?

26. If 3240 read for a half hour, how many subscribers were surveyed?

27. How many more subscribers read for 20 minutes than for 40 minutes?

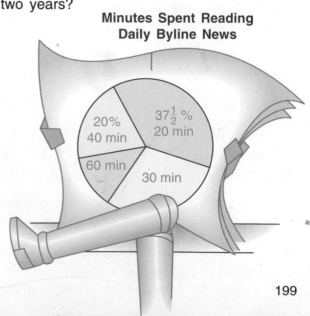

Minutes Spent Reading Daily Byline News

20% 40 min
$37\frac{1}{2}\%$ 20 min
60 min
30 min

More Practice

Change each fraction or decimal to a percent.

1. $\frac{48}{100}$ **2.** $\frac{61}{1000}$ **3.** $\frac{3}{5}$ **4.** $\frac{9}{25}$ **5.** $\frac{1}{6}$ **6.** $2\frac{1}{4}$

7. 0.57   **8.** 0.09   **9.** 0.045   **10.** 0.001   **11.** 5.47   **12.** 2.3

Change to a fraction in lowest terms.

13. 55%   **14.** 38%   **15.** 175%   **16.** $66\frac{2}{3}$%   **17.** 20.5%   **18.** 0.4%

Change to a decimal.

19. 7%   **20.** 29%   **21.** 106%   **22.** 7.8%   **23.** 155.4%   **24.** $\frac{4}{5}$%

Find the part or percentage of the number.

25. 40% of 80   **26.** 6% of 100   **27.** 125% of 200

28. $66\frac{2}{3}$% of 75   **29.** 6.375% of 800   **30.** $\frac{1}{2}$% of 50

Find the percent. Round to the nearest tenth, if necessary.

31. 5 is what percent of 40?   **32.** What percent of 12 is 3?

33. 244 is what percent of 400?   **34.** What percent of 12 is 18?

Find the original number.

35. 20% of $n = 3$ **36.** 25% of $n = 55$ **37.** 80% of $n = 80$

38. 15% of $n = 0.96$ **39.** 0.5% of $n = 21$ **40.** $7\frac{1}{2}$% of $n = 9$

Estimate the percentage.

41. 19% of 50   **42.** 14.9% of 35   **43.** $10\frac{3}{4}$% of 78

Find the percent of increase or decrease. (Round answers to the nearest tenth of a percent.)

44. Original: 3200
New: 5000

45. Original: $1400
New: $925

46. Original: $420
New: $600

47. Original: 7.5
New: 6.3

48. Original: 5895
New: 7578

49. Original: $80
New: $68

Solve.

50. A nursery sold $67\frac{1}{2}$% of their 120 plants last week. How many plants did they have left?

51. In 1980, Mr. Carson purchased a house for $55,000. Ten years later he sold the house for $126,500. What was the percent of increase in the value of his house?

52. A lawyer paid medical bills of $8200 or $6\frac{2}{3}$ % of her annual income. What is her annual income?

200   *See Still More Practice, pp. 504–505.*

Math Probe

TRICKY TESSELLATIONS

Have some mathematical fun with tessellations.

A *tessellation* is a pattern formed by covering a plane with a set of congruent polygons such that no parts overlap and there are no gaps between the polygons. Here are some tessellations for two regular polygons.

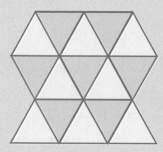

Tessellation of Equilateral Triangle

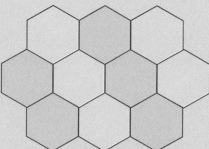

Tessellation of Regular Hexagon

1. Try using this regular pentagon to form a tessellation. Can it be done?

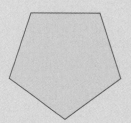

2. Draw and cut out any polygon that is not regular. Will it tessellate?

3. Try to form tessellations by using a combination of these regular polygons.

Square

Equilateral Triangle

Regular Hexagon

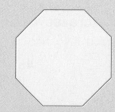

Regular Octagon

4. Artists and designers frequently create tessellating patterns in their work. See if you can discover any around your home. THINK: "Tessellation" comes from a Latin word meaning "tile."

5. Create your initials as a tessellated pattern.

Check Your Mastery

Change each fraction or decimal to a percent. See pp. 180–181

1. $\frac{31}{100}$ **2.** $\frac{85}{1000}$ **3.** $\frac{5}{8}$ **4.** $\frac{13}{25}$ **5.** $\frac{1}{6}$ **6.** $1\frac{3}{4}$

7. 0.03 **8.** 0.51 **9.** 0.097 **10.** 0.006 **11.** 4.09 **12.** 3.8

Change to a fraction in lowest terms. See pp. 182–183

13. 58% **14.** 65% **15.** 225% **16.** $12\frac{1}{2}$% **17.** 16.8% **18.** 0.6%

Change to a decimal.

19. 5% **20.** 72% **21.** 130% **22.** 4.7% **23.** 109.5% **24.** $\frac{1}{4}$%

Find the part or percentage of the number. See pp. 184–185

25. 30% of 100 **26.** 4% of 65 **27.** 150% of 90

28. $33\frac{1}{3}$% of 120 **29.** 7.25% of 400 **30.** $\frac{1}{4}$% of 40

Find the percent. Round to the nearest tenth, if necessary. See pp. 186–187

31. 9 is what percent of 72? **32.** What percent of 25 is 10?

33. 360 is what percent of 600? **34.** What percent of 60 is 75?

Find the original number. See pp. 188–189

35. 30% of n = 12 **36.** 15% of n = 15 **37.** 32% of n = 48

38. 0.75% of n = 0.75 **39.** 83% of n = 166 **40.** $16\frac{2}{3}$% of n = 282

Estimate the percentage. See pp. 190–191

41. 28% of 82 **42.** 76.6% of 125 **43.** $8\frac{1}{4}$% of 158

Find the percent of increase or decrease. (Round answers to the nearest tenth of a percent.) See pp. 192–193

44. Original: 1800 **45.** Original: $2650 **46.** Original: $635
   New: 750   New: $3500   New: $1070

47. Original: 8.6 **48.** Original: 3290 **49.** Original: $65
   New: 6.5   New: 4575   New: $90

Solve.

50. A bookstore sold 62% of their 250 paperback books last week. How many paperback books did they sell?

51. In 1988, Ms Wayne bought a car for $12,750. Three years later she sold the car for $7968.75. What was the percent of decrease in the value of the car?

8 ▾ Consumer Mathematics

In this chapter you will:

- Compute profit and loss
- Find discount, sale price, rate of discount, and list price
- Find sales tax
- Find commission, rate of commission, and total sales
- Find simple interest
- Find compound interest
- Find the cost of buying on credit
- Find paycheck deductions
- Compute income tax
- Solve problems: multi-step

Do you remember?

To compute with percents, change percents to fractions or decimals:

$$10\% \longrightarrow 0.10 \longrightarrow \frac{1}{10}$$

$$20\% \longrightarrow 0.20 \longrightarrow \frac{20}{100} \longrightarrow \frac{1}{5}$$

RESEARCHING TOGETHER

A Penny Saved . . .

Congratulations! You have just won the teen tournament on the TV show *Opportunity*. The cash prize is $25,000. Wisely, you decide to put 85% of this into a savings account at $8\frac{1}{2}\%$ interest. What will you have in the bank at the end of 1 year? If you leave the money untouched for 6 years, how much will you have? In 10 years, how much?

8-1 Profit and Loss

Profit (P), or gain: the money realized when an item is sold *above* the cost.

Loss (L): the money lost when an item is sold *below* the cost.

Cost (C): the *original* amount spent for an item.

A microwave oven that originally cost $200 was sold at a gain of 15%. What profit was realized?

To find profit (P), use *one* of these two ways:

First Way	Second Way
Write and solve a formula.	Write and solve a proportion.

First Way

$P =\ C \times R$

$P = \$200 \times 15\%$

$P = \$200 \times 0.15$

$P = \$30.00$

P = Percentage
C = Base
R = Rate

The profit is $30.

Second Way

$$\frac{\text{Profit}}{\text{Cost}} = \frac{\text{Rate of Profit}}{\text{Rate of Cost}}$$

$$\frac{P}{\$200} \times \frac{15}{100}$$

$100P = \$3000$

$P = \$30\ \text{Profit}$

A lamp costs $25.50 and is sold at a loss of 20%. What is the loss?

To find loss (L), use *one* of these two ways:

First Way

Write and solve a formula.

$L =\ C\ \times R$

$L = \$25.50 \times 20\%$

$L = \$25.50 \times 0.20$

$L = \$5.10$

L = Percentage
C = Base
R = Rate

The loss is $5.10.

Second Way

Write and solve a proportion.

$$\frac{\text{Loss}}{\text{Cost}} = \frac{\text{Rate of Loss}}{\text{Rate of Cost}}$$

$$\frac{L}{\$25.50} = \frac{20}{100}$$

$100L = \$510$

$L = \$5.10\ \text{Loss}$

Find the profit or loss to the nearest cent.

1. Cost: $75
   Rate of Profit: $33\frac{1}{3}\%$

2. Cost: $48.60
   Rate of Profit: 25%

3. Cost: $132
   Rate of Loss: $12\frac{1}{2}\%$

4. Cost: $124
   Rate of Loss: $6\frac{1}{4}\%$

5. Cost: $8420
   Rate of Profit: $8\frac{1}{3}\%$

6. Cost: $385.20
   Rate of Loss: 3.5%

7. Cost: $36.40
   Rate of Loss: 4.5%

8. Cost: $92.50
   Rate of Profit: 9.2%

9. Cost: $79.25
   Rate of Loss: 3.4%

Finding Selling Price

The **selling price (SP)** is the amount for which an item is sold.

When an item is sold at a gain, or profit, the selling price is *more than* the cost.

　To find this selling price (SP), add:　$SP = C + P$

When an item is sold at a loss, the selling price is *less than* the cost.

　To find this selling price (SP), subtract:　$SP = C - L$

Find the selling price. (The first two are done.)

10. Cost: $200　$SP = \$200 + \$30$
　　Gain: $ 30　$SP = \$230$

11. Cost: $25.50　$SP = \$25.50 - \$5.10$
　　　Loss: $ 5.10　$SP = \$20.40$

12. Cost:　$79.20
　　Profit: $ 9.90

13. Cost:　$165
　　　Profit: $　8.25

14. Cost:　$21.80
　　　Loss: $ 3.27

15. Cost:　$175.50
　　Loss: $ 28.08

16. Cost:　$154.02
　　　Gain: $ 25.67

17. Cost:　$306
　　　Gain: $ 25.50

Solve.

18. A bookstore sold a shipment of books originally costing $1089 at a gain of $33\frac{1}{3}$ %. How much money did the bookstore gain from the sale of the shipment?

19. The Silvesi family sold their camper, which cost them $21,000, at a loss of 30%. How much money did they lose?

20. A farmer made a profit of 18% on a crop that cost $1500 to grow. What was the selling price of the crop?

21. A greenhouse realized a gain of 17% on trees originally costing $495. What was the selling price of the trees?

SUPPOSE 　 THAT...

22. Since $P = C \times R$, what formula can you use to find the rate of profit?

23. Since $L = C \times R$, what formula can you use to find the rate of loss?

24. Use appropriate formulas and a calculator to find the rates of profit or loss in exercises 10–17.

8-2 Discount and Sale Price

Discount (D): a reduction on the **list price (LP)** (the original, or regular, price) of an item.

Rate of discount (R): the percent taken off the price.

Sale price (SP): the difference between the list price **(LP)** and the discount **(D)**.

How much will a microwave oven cost if it is listed at $210 and discounted at 25%?

To find the discount (D), use *one* of these two ways:

First Way
Write and solve a formula.

$D = LP \times R$

$D = \$210 \times 25\%$

$D = \$210 \times 0.25$

$D = \$52.50$ Discount

D = Percentage
R = Rate
LP = Base

Second Way
Write and solve a proportion.

$$\frac{\text{Discount}}{\text{List Price}} = \frac{\text{Rate of Discount}}{\text{Rate of List Price}}$$

$$\frac{D}{\$210} \times \frac{25}{100}$$

$100D = \$5250$

$$D = \frac{\$5250}{100}$$

$D = \$52.50$ Discount

To find the sale price (SP), subtract:

$SP = LP - D$
$SP = \$210 - \$52.50$
$SP = \$157.50$ Sale Price

The microwave oven will cost $157.50.

Find the discount and the sale price to the nearest cent.

1. Bookcase—Regular price: $60; discount: 15%

2. Desk—Original price: $80; discount: $33\frac{1}{3}\%$

3. Clock—List price: $36; discount: 7%

4. Poster—Original price: $12.75; discount: $12\frac{1}{2}\%$

5. Area rug—Regular price: $25.25; discount: 3%

6. Solar calculator—List price: $15.39; discount: $33\frac{1}{3}\%$

7. Skin cream—List price: $6.75; discount: $16\frac{2}{3}\%$

Which is the better buy, "a" or "b"?

8. a clock radio   **a.** $45 at 10% discount   **b.** $50 at 12% discount

9. a typewriter   **a.** $198 at 15% discount   **b.** $209 at 17% discount

10. a sewing machine   **a.** $119 at $\frac{1}{7}$ off   **b.** $129 at 22% discount

11. a bicycle   **a.** $122 at $\frac{1}{5}$ off   **b.** $135 at $\frac{1}{4}$ off

---

Using Rate of Sale Price

You can use a calculator and the **rate of sale price** to find the sale price.

Two concert tickets originally listed at $75 are discounted 20%.
What is the sale price?

Since the rate of discount is 20%, subtract to find the rate of sale price.

100%   −   20% ◄——— =   ———► 80%
                    Rate of   Rate of
                    Discount   Sale Price

To find the sale price,
use this key sequence:

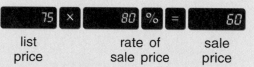

                                      list   rate of   sale
                                     price   sale price   price

The sale price of the concert tickets is $60.

Complete the chart to find the rate of sale price and sale price.

	Item	Regular Price	% Discount	% Sale Price	Sale Price
12.	jewelry	$40.00	16%	?	?
13.	cosmetic kit	$25.00	15%	?	?
14.	wristwatch	$38.00	$12\frac{1}{2}$%	?	?
15.	sunglasses	$18.90	10%	?	?

Solve. (Hint: Use a calculator to find the discount:  .)

16. Find the amount saved by buying a team jacket marked
$63.49 at a reduction of 25%.

17. Tennis rackets originally marked $49.75 each were sold at a discount
of 35%. What was the selling price of a dozen rackets?

CHALLENGE

18. An exercise bike originally listed at $280 was reduced 20%.
The following week the price was discounted another 10%. Finally,
another 25% reduction was made. What was the final price of the bike?

Rate of Discount and List Price

A camera store sold a 35-mm camera originally priced at $139 for $122.32.
Find the rate of discount.

To find the rate of discount:
- Find the amount of discount.

    $139 List Price − $122.32 Sale Price = $16.68 Discount

- Then use *one* of these two ways to find the rate:

First Way	**Second Way**
Write and solve a formula.	Write and solve a proportion.

First Way

$D = LP \times R$
$16.68 = \$139 \times R$
$R = \$16.68 \div \$139$
$R = 12\%$

The rate of discount is 12%.

Second Way

$$\frac{D}{LP} = \frac{R \text{ of } D}{R \text{ of } LP}$$

$$\frac{\$16.68}{\$139} \diagup\!\!\!\diagdown \frac{R}{100}$$

$139 \times R = \$1668$
$R = \$1668 \div \$139$
$R = 12\%$ Rate of Discount

Binoculars were sold at 15% off the regular price.
This was a discount of $6.27. What was the list, or regular, price?

To find the list price, use *one* of two ways:

First Way	**Second Way**
Write and solve a formula.	Write and solve a proportion.

First Way

$D = LP \times R$
$6.27 = LP \times 15\%$
$LP = \$6.27 \div 0.15$
$LP = \$41.80$

The list price was $41.80.

Second Way

$$\frac{D}{LP} = \frac{R \text{ of } D}{R \text{ of } LP}$$

$$\frac{\$6.27}{LP} \diagup\!\!\!\diagdown \frac{15}{100}$$

$15 \times LP = \$627$
$LP = \$627 \div 15$
$LP = \$41.80$ List Price

Find the rate of discount.

1. List price: $12; discount: $1.20

2. Original price: $75; discount: $9

3. Regular price: $180; sale price: $151.20

4. List price: $30.99; sale price: $20.66

Find the original price.

5. Discount: $75; rate of discount: 25%

6. Discount: $8.24; rate of discount: 4%

Copy and complete the table.

	List Price	Rate of Discount	Discount
7.	$35	?	$5
8.	$20	?	$3
9.	$18	?	$ .72
10.	$98	?	$7.84
11.	?	10%	$5.20

	List Price	Rate of Discount	Discount
12.	?	$33\frac{1}{3}\%$	$180
13.	?	6%	$ 3.90
14.	?	25%	$ 50
15.	$200	$5\frac{1}{2}\%$	?
16.	$ 14	$12\frac{1}{2}\%$	?

Solve.

Exercise 22

17. Ten cartons of copy machine paper originally marked $250 were reduced $75 for a sale. What was the rate of discount?

18. The sale price of a desk lamp is $30.40. The discount is $4.56. What is the rate of discount?

19. The discount for a microcomputer is $88.99. At a rate of 5%, what was the original price?

20. Office chairs were marked down from $98 to $84.77. What was the rate of discount?

21. If 15% off a listed price is $28, what is the listed price? What is the sale price?

22. What would you spend for 3 books on sale, all the same price, if you received a 9%, or $2.25, discount on each one?

CRITICAL THINKING

23. Explain how you can use the discount formula to determine the correct calculator key sequence for finding:
    a. the rate of discount.　　　　**b.** the list price.

24. Check exercises 17–22, using a calculator.

25. Boomerang Toy Store is having a 15% sale on all items. Fun For You Shoppe is offering $4 off on the same items. At which store would you save more on these?

puzzle .... $ 6.80	building blocks ... $ 7.20	doll house $140
craft kit $14.20	model train $90	toddler gym set ...$ 45

SKILLS TO REMEMBER　　　**Round to the nearest cent.**

26. $3.477　　　27. $41.244　　　28. $.863　　　29. $.095

8-4 Sales Tax

Sales tax (T): the amount added to the **marked price (MP)** of an item and collected by the local and state governments that levied the tax.

Rate of sales tax (R): the percent of the marked price **(MP)** levied as a tax.

Total cost (TC): the sum of the marked price **(MP)** and the tax **(T)**.

A student bought art supplies costing $45. She lives in a state that charges $7\frac{1}{2}$% sales tax. What was the amount of sales tax on the supplies? What was the total cost?

To find the sales tax (T), use *one* of these ways:

First Way

Write and solve a formula.

$T = MP \times R$

$T = \$45 \times 7\frac{1}{2}\%$

$T = \$45 \times 0.075$

$T = \$3.375$

Round to the nearest cent.
$T = \$3.38$

T = Percentage
R = Rate
MP = Base

Second Way

Write and solve a proportion.

$$\frac{T}{MP} = \frac{R \text{ of } T}{R \text{ of } MP}$$

$$\frac{T}{\$45} \times \frac{7\frac{1}{2}}{100}$$

$100 \times T = 7\frac{1}{2}\% \times \$45$

$100T = \$337\frac{1}{2}$

$T = \$3.37\frac{1}{2}$

Round to nearest cent.
$T = \$3.38$

To find the total cost (TC), add:

$TC = MP + T$
$TC = \$45 + \$3.38 = \$48.38$ Total Cost of Art Supplies

Tax "X"

Total Cost "X"

Find the sales tax and the total cost.

1. Price: $9.60
   Tax: 5%

2. Price: $10.50
   Tax: 4%

3. Price: $90
   Tax: $5\frac{1}{4}$%

4. Price: $149.80
   Tax: $5\frac{1}{2}$%

5. Price: $86.75
   Tax: $6\frac{1}{2}$%

6. Price: $9.75
   Tax: $4\frac{1}{2}$%

7. Price: $42.90
   Tax: $4\frac{3}{4}$%

8. Price: $210
   Tax: $6\frac{1}{4}$%

9. Price: $392.10
   Tax: $6\frac{1}{3}$%

Here is part of an $8\frac{1}{4}$% sales tax table.

Sale	Tax	Sale	Tax	Sale	Tax
$ .01 to $ .10	None	$5.04 to $5.15	$.42	$ 8.79 to $8.90	$.73
.11 to .17	$.01	5.16 to 5.27	.43	8.91 to 9.03	.74
.18 to .29	.02	5.28 to 5.39	.44	9.04 to 9.15	.75
.30 to .42	.03	5.40 to 5.51	.45	9.16 to 9.27	.76
.43 to .54	.04	5.52 to 5.63	.46	9.28 to 9.39	.77
.55 to .66	.05	5.64 to 5.75	.47	9.40 to 9.51	.78
.67 to .78	.06	5.76 to 5.87	.48	9.52 to 9.63	.79
.79 to .90	.07	5.88 to 5.99	.49	9.64 to 9.75	.80
.91 to $1.03	.08	6.00 to 6.12	.50	9.76 to 9.87	.81
1.04 to 1.15	.09	6.13 to 6.24	.51	9.88 to 9.99	.82
1.16 to 1.27	.10	6.25 to 6.36	.52	10.00 and over — multiply by 0.0825	

Use the table above to find the sales tax and the total cost of:

10. a shirt that costs $11.95.

11. a notebook marked $.95 and a pen priced at $1.02.

12. three pairs of socks at $2.50 a pair and a set of handkerchiefs for $1.75.

13. a book that regularly sells for $10 but is now selling at a 5% discount.

14. a pound of coffee priced at $6.75 a pound selling at a discount of 15%.

Solve. Round to the nearest cent.

15. A sofa bed is marked $795 plus tax. If the sales tax is $5\frac{1}{4}$%, what is the total cost?

16. Which is the better buy for a gallon of paint?
a. Reg. $15.75, $33\frac{1}{3}$% off, 4% tax   **b.** Reg. $16.20, 25% off, 2% tax

17. Kim bought a pair of $65 boots on sale at a 15% discount. If the sales tax is $7\frac{1}{2}$%, what did Kim pay for the boots?

18. In one state food does not have a sales tax but cleaning materials have a 6% sales tax. What is the total cost of these purchases: milk, $1.19; meat, $9.50; floor wax, $4.19; furniture polish, $1.89; and soup, $2.35?

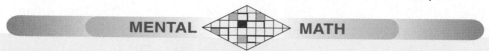
MENTAL ◁▷ MATH

Use estimation to find a 5% sales tax on each. (The first one is done.)

19. $15.70

  10% tax on $15.70 ⟶ 1.570 = $1.57, or about $1.60

  5% = $\frac{1}{2}$ of 10% ⟶ $\frac{1}{2}$ × $1.60 = $.80   So, 5% tax is about $.80.

20. $14.20   **21.** $153.50   **22.** $17.98   **23.** $289.40   **24.** $86.30

8-5 | Commission

Commission (C): the amount of money earned for selling goods or services.

Rate of commission (R): the percent of the total amount of goods or services sold that is earned by the seller.

Total sales (TS): the total amount of goods or services sold.

Sadlier Book C

Ms. Liz sells textbooks. Her commission is 7% of the sales she makes for her company each week. How much commission does Ms. Liz earn if her sales are $2985 for one week?

To find the commission (C), use *one* of these two ways:

First Way	**Second Way**
Write and solve a formula.	Write and solve a proportion.

First Way

$C = TS \times R$ ←

$C = \$2985 \times 7\%$

$C = \$2985 \times 0.07$

$C = \$208.95$ Commission

C = Percentage
R = Rate
TS = Base

Second Way

$\dfrac{C}{TS} = \dfrac{R \text{ of } C}{R \text{ of } TS}$

$\dfrac{C}{\$2985} \diagdown \dfrac{7}{100}$

$100 \times C = \$2985 \times 7$

$100C = \$20,895$

$C = \dfrac{\$20,895}{100}$

$C = \$208.95$ Commission

Ms. Liz makes a commission of $208.95.

Find the commission.

1. Total sales: $4800
   Rate: 2.5%

2. Total sales: $2400
   Rate: 2%

3. Total sales: $356
   Rate: 15%

4. Total sales: $508
   Rate: 12%

5. Total sales: $986
   Rate: 30%

6. Total sales: $6000
   Rate: 1.5%

7. Total sales: $85.18
   Rate: 50%

8. Total sales: $4593.50
   Rate: 6%

9. Total sales: $6475
   Rate: 4.2%

10. Total sales: $8730
    Rate: 3%

11. Total sales: $8276.50
    Rate: 5%

12. Total sales: $548
    Rate: 32%

Solve. Check, using a calculator:  `TS` `×` `R` `%` `=`

13. An agent's fee for collecting rents is $4\frac{1}{2}$%. If he collects $3400, how much commission does he earn?

14. Rosa sold $140 worth of cosmetics at $3\frac{1}{2}$% commission. How much did she earn?

15. A sailboat was sold for $4200. The seller received a commission of 5%. What was the amount of the commission?

16. A salesperson received a $4\frac{1}{4}$% commission on a sale of two sets of encyclopedias selling for $950 each. What was the commission?

17. A salesperson receives a 4% commission on every computer sold. If the salesperson sells a $2450 computer, find the net proceeds. (Hint: Net proceeds is the money returned to the company by a salesperson.)

18. Dr. Penny hires a collection agency to collect the balance due of $2000 on a medical bill. If the agency deducts a $3\frac{1}{2}$% fee, how much money does Dr. Penny receive?

19. Mr. Walez is a book salesperson. He receives a salary of $420 per week plus 4% of his sales. One week his sales total was $1760. How much did he earn in all that week?

20. Ms. Ortega is paid $350 a week and a commission of 6% on all sales over $1200. What were her earnings for a week in which she sold $1500 worth of goods?

21. Ms. Roberts sold materials to a new sewing store. She sold them 10 sewing machines at $179 each. She sold 350 yards of fabric at $2.50 per yard. She gets a 10% commission on sewing machine sales and a 15% commission on fabric sales. What were her total earnings?

22. Mr. Randolph gets paid a salary of $400 per week. He also gets a commission on sales according to this schedule: sales up to $1000 — 2%; sales from $1001 to $5000 — 3%. What are his total earnings for a week in which his total sales were $2500?

CHALLENGE

23. Ms. Wilson wants to make a profit of $154,000 on the sale of her home. If the real-estate agent makes a 10% commission, what must the total cost of the house be?

24. Find the real cost of $25,000 worth of wheat purchased through an agent who is paid 4% commission.

Tami sells oven ware on a commission basis. She sold $200 worth of dishes and sent $158 to the company. What rate of commission did she receive?

To find the rate of commission:
- Find the amount of the commission.
  $200 sales − $158 to company = $42 commission
- Use *one* of these two ways to find the rate:

First Way

Write and solve a formula.

$$C = TS \times R$$
$$\$42 = \$200 \times R$$
$$R = \$42 \div \$200$$
$$R = 0.21 = 21\%$$

Second Way

Write and solve a proportion.

$$\frac{C}{TS} = \frac{R \text{ of } C}{R \text{ of } TS}$$
$$\frac{\$42}{\$200} \times \frac{R}{100}$$
$$42 \times 100 = R \times 200$$
$$R \times 200 = 4200$$
$$R = 4200 \div 200$$
$$R = 21\%$$

Ben has a summer job selling craft kits.
He gets a commission of 5%.
How much must he sell to earn $122?

To find the total sales, use *one* of two ways:

First Way

Write and solve a formula.

$$C = TS \times R$$
$$\$122 = TS \times 5\%$$
$$TS = \$122 \div 5\%$$
$$TS = \$122 \div 0.05$$
$$TS = \$2440$$

Second Way

Write and solve a proportion.

$$\frac{C}{TS} = \frac{R \text{ of } C}{R \text{ of } TS}$$
$$\frac{\$122}{TS} \times \frac{5}{100}$$
$$\$122 \times 100 = 5 \times TS$$
$$5 \times TS = \$12,200$$
$$TS = \$12,200 \div 5 = \$2440$$

Find the rate of commission or the total sales.

1. Commission: $800
   Total sales: $6400

2. Commission: $24
   Total sales: $800

3. Commission: $120
   Total sales: $4800

4. Commission: $180
   Total sales: $9000

5. Commission: $380
   Rate: 5%

6. Commission: $800
   Rate: 10%

7. Commission: $36.25
   Rate: $2\frac{1}{2}\%$

8. Commission: $150
   Rate: $7\frac{1}{2}\%$

9. Commission: $270
   Total sales: $9000

Copy and complete the table.

	Total Sales	Rate of Commission	Commission
10.	$ 610	30%	?
11.	?	6%	$396
12.	?	4%	$36.80
13.	$7000	?	$525
14.	$ 50	?	$ 6.25

	Total Sales	Rate of Commission	Commission
15.	$ 450	30%	?
16.	?	2%	$ 19
17.	?	$1\frac{1}{2}$%	$190
18.	$ 200	?	$ 10
19.	$36,000	?	$ 1260

Solve.

20. Ms. Fox received $40 for selling goods at a commission of 2%. What was the amount of her sales?

Exercise 22

21. An agent was instructed to sell a house and to keep for her commission all above $70,000. She sold the house for $75,000. What was her rate of commission?

22. A real estate agent sold 2 townhouses for one owner: one for $85,000 and the other for $71,000.
He sent the owner $143,000.
What percent commission did he charge?

Total Sales: $156,000
Commission: $13,000
Rate of
  Commission: ?

23. Mr. Collins received $1560 to buy merchandise. He deducted $65 for his commission. What was the rate of commission?

24. What rate of commission does Ms. Wong receive if she sold 5 television sets at $275 each and received $27.50 as commission?

25. Ms. Bianchi sold 5 pianos at $1450 each. If she received a commission of 6%, what did the piano company receive from the sale?

CRITICAL THINKING **Use a calculator and the commission formula to solve.**

26. A buyer received $25 commission for purchasing some fabric at $5 a yard. He receives a commission of 5%. How many yards of fabric did he buy?

27. Ms. Fredricks sold 9 lawn tractors and received a commission of $793.80. Her commission rate is 7%. What was the cost of each tractor?

28. Mark wants to earn $1200 this summer by selling pet supplies. He will work for 6 weeks at $80 per week and receive a commission of 20% on all sales over $1000. What must his total sales for the summer be?

8-7 Simple Interest

The terms *principal, interest, rate of interest,* and *time* can refer to money deposited in a savings account or to money borrowed from a bank.

Principal (*p*): the amount of money deposited in a bank (or the amount of money borrowed from the bank).

Simple Interest (*I*): the amount paid by the bank to the depositor on the principal alone for a stated period of time (or the amount to be paid by the borrower on the principal for a stated period of time).

Rate of Interest (*r*): the percent of interest to be taken on the principal.

Time (*t*): represents how long the principal is left on deposit, (or for how long the money is borrowed).

> **Interest = principal × rate × time (in years)**
>
> $I = prt$

Ms. Suarez read an ad for a bank offering $6\frac{1}{2}$ % interest, paid yearly on savings accounts. What would a deposit of $550 earn in one year?

$I = prt$

$I = \$550 \times 0.065 \times 1$

$I = \$35.75$

Mr. Lester borrowed $700 for 9 months at $10\frac{1}{2}$ % per year. What interest did he pay?

$I = prt$

$I = \$700 \times 0.105 \times 0.75 \leftarrow$ $\qquad \dfrac{9 \text{ mo}}{12 \text{ mo}} = \dfrac{3}{4} = 0.75$ of a year

$I = \$55.13$ (rounded to nearest cent)

Find the interest.

1. Principal: $850
   Rate: $9\frac{1}{2}$ %
   Time: 1 yr

2. Principal: $1150
   Rate: $12\frac{1}{2}$ %
   Time: 2 yr

3. Principal: $41,975
   Rate: 9 %
   Time: 1 yr

4. Principal: $149
   Rate: 7 %
   Time: 1 yr

5. Principal: $877
   Rate: $8\frac{1}{4}$ %
   Time: 6 mo

6. Principal: $2196
   Rate: $6\frac{1}{2}$ %
   Time: 6 mo

Find the amount in the savings account after the given time.

7. Principal: $1800
    Rate: 12%
    Time: 6 mo

8. Principal: $178
    Rate: $9\frac{1}{2}$%
    Time: 6 mo

9. Principal: $9200
    Rate: $8\frac{1}{2}$%
    Time: 2 mo

10. Principal: $1530
    Rate: 6%
    Time: 4 mo

11. Principal: $5170
    Rate: 9%
    Time: 3 mo

12. Principal: $8640
    Rate: $11\frac{1}{2}$%
    Time: 3 yr

Find the total amount due to the bank after the given time.

13. Principal: $3400
    Rate: 9.5%
    Time: 6 mo

14. Principal: $10,000
    Rate: 14%
    Time: 5 yr

15. Principal: $75,000
    Rate: $10\frac{1}{2}$%
    Time: 9 mo

16. Principal: $40,000
    Rate: 11%
    Time: 20 yr

17. Principal: $1200
    Rate: 18%
    Time: 4 mo

18. Principal: $600
    Rate: $15\frac{1}{4}$%
    Time: 1 mo

Solve.

You can use a calculator to find the interest and the total amount.

Interest: Total Amount: $P + I =$

19. Find the interest on $850 for 3 years at $4\frac{1}{2}$%.

20. What will be the amount due on a loan of $1200 at the rate of $14\frac{1}{2}$% after a year?

21. Mr. Prinz deposited $3750 in an account for $2\frac{1}{2}$ years at 9.08%. How much will he have in all at the end of the period?

22. Ms. Timco borrowed $500 at $10\frac{1}{2}$% for 4 months. How much will she have to pay back?

23. You save $1000 for 1 year at $5\frac{1}{2}$%. How much will you have in the bank at the end of the year?

24. You leave the principal plus interest in the bank for another year at the same rate. (See exercise 23.) How much will you have after the second year?

25. Ms. Stark has two savings certificates. One is for $500 at $7\frac{1}{2}$% for 270 days. The other is for $750 at 8% for 180 days. Which certificate will earn more interest? (Hint: Use 360 days = 1 year.)

Exercise 25

$500
$7\frac{1}{2}$%
270 days

$750
8%
180 days

8-8 Compound Interest

Compound interest: interest paid on the principal deposited in the
bank plus any previously earned interest.

$900 is deposited in an account that pays 6% interest, compounded annually.
How much will be in the account after 3 years?

To find the **total amount** in the account:

- Find the interest earned after the first year.   ($I = prt$)
- Add the interest to the principal when computing interest for the next year.

$900	Principal
×0.06	Rate of interest
$ 54.00	Interest for first year
+ 900.00	
$ 954.00	New principal after 1 year
× 0.06	
$ 57.24	Interest for second year
+ 954.00	
$1011.24	New principal after 2 years
× 0.06	
$ 60.67	Interest for third year, rounded to nearest cent
+1011.24	
$1071.91	Principal after 3 years (total amount)

$900
6% interest

After
3 years
?

---

1. Copy and complete the chart to find the total amount in an
    account of $200 at 5%, compounded semiannually for $2\frac{1}{2}$ years.
    Then find the total interest earned.

Principal: $200
Interest at 6 months: $I = p \times r \times t$
$I = \$200 \times 0.05 \times \frac{1}{2}$ (compounded semiannually, or every half-year)
$I = \$5.00$

New principal: $205.00

Interest at 1 year = __?__
New principal = __?__
Interest at $1\frac{1}{2}$ years = __?__
New principal = __?__

Interest at 2 years = __?__
New principal = __?__
Interest at $2\frac{1}{2}$ years = __?__
Total amount = __?__

Interest Earned = Total Amount − Original Principal
__?__ = __?__ − $200

Find the total amount and the compound interest earned. (Use a calculator.)

2. Principal \$100; rate $7\frac{1}{2}$ %, compounded annually; time 2 years

p   *r*

$\boxed{100}$ $\boxed{+}$ $\boxed{7.5}$ $\boxed{\%}$ $\boxed{=}$ ⟶ new principal

3. Principal \$250; rate 5%, compounded semiannually;
   time 1 year

p   *r*

$\boxed{250}$ $\boxed{+}$ $\boxed{2.5}$ $\boxed{\%}$ $\boxed{=}$ ⟶ new principal
(at 6 months)

4. Principal \$200; rate 6%, compounded annually; time 4 years

5. Principal \$1000; rate 6%, compounded semiannually; time 2 years

6. Principal \$500; rate 5%, compounded annually; time 3 years

7. Principal \$400; rate 10%, compounded quarterly; time 1 year

*8. Principal \$5000; rate $4\frac{1}{2}$ %, compounded quarterly; time 10 years

*9. Principal \$7500; rate $7\frac{1}{2}$ %, compounded annually; time 20 years

*10. Principal \$12,300; rate 8%, compounded semiannually; time 30 years

Solve.

11. When Jane was 16 years old, her father put \$600 into a bank account that paid 6% interest. If the interest was compounded semiannually, how much was in the account on Jane's eighteenth birthday?

12. What will be the interest earned after one year on \$6000 deposited in a savings account that pays 8%, compounded semiannually?

13. What will be the interest on \$850 compounded semiannually at 5% for 2 years?

14. Dave has \$500 to deposit. One bank offers a simple interest rate of 9%. Another bank offers 8%, compounded quarterly. Which bank would pay more interest after 2 years?

15. To the nearest cent, what is the difference earned on:
    a. \$2000 at 5% simple interest for 2 years?
    b. \$2000 at 5% interest, compounded semiannually for 2 years?

Exercise 14

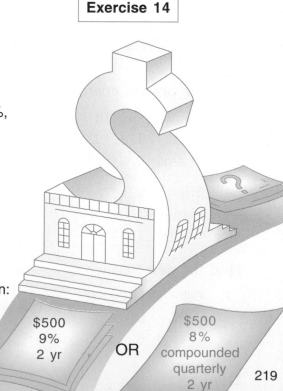

\$500
9%
2 yr

OR

\$500
8%
compounded
quarterly
2 yr

219

8-9 Buying on Credit

Using **credit** means purchasing goods or obtaining services immediately without paying the entire cost at once. The company issuing credit adds a **finance charge** to your bill.

If you use a credit card, the credit company pays the bill. You pay the credit company back monthly. After the first month's payment, you pay a **finance charge** on the unpaid balance.

Lisa charged $250 worth of camping equipment on her bank credit card. She paid $50 during the first month and paid the balance the second month. The credit agreement is to pay a $1\frac{1}{4}$ % finance charge per month after the first month. How much did Lisa pay in all?

Compute her bill for each month.

```
1st month:        $250  Bill
                 –  50  Paid
                  $200  Unpaid balance
```

```
2nd month:        $200  Unpaid balance
               ×0.0125  Finance charge of 1¼%
                 $2.50  Finance charge
              +200.00
               $202.50  Balance due 2nd month
```

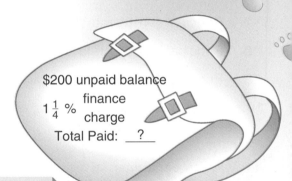

$200 unpaid balance

$1\frac{1}{4}$ % finance charge

Total Paid: ___?___

Lisa paid $50 + $202.50, or $252.50 in all.

Find the finance charge for one month on the unpaid balance.

1. Bill: $52.16
   Paid: $22.16
   Charge: 2%

2. Bill: $500
   Paid: $125
   Charge: 1%

3. Bill: $273.10
   Paid: $ 50
   Charge: $2\frac{1}{2}$ %

4. Bill: $25.75
   Paid: $10
   Charge: $1\frac{1}{2}$ %

5. Bill: $165.26
   Paid: $ 40
   Charge: $1\frac{3}{4}$ %

6. Bill: $178.20
   Paid: $100
   Charge: $1\frac{1}{4}$ %

Find the new balance.

7. Bill: $329
   Paid: $160
   Charge: $ 3.38

8. Bill: $495.50
   Paid: $225
   Charge: $ 4.85

9. Bill: $210.90
   Paid: $ 90
   Charge: $ 2.18

Solve.

10. Keri bought a $215 stereo on credit. She paid $15 each month for two months and paid the balance in the third month. If there was a 2% per month finance charge after the first month, how much did Keri actually pay for the stereo?

Complete this solution:

1st month:

```
  $215   bill
 –   15   paid
  $200   unpaid balance
 +    0   finance charge
  $200   unpaid balance
```

2nd month:

```
  $   2 00
  ×   0.02   finance charge of 2%
  $   4.00   finance charge
  +200.00
  $204.00   bill for 2nd month
 –  15.00   paid
  $189.00   unpaid balance
```

Exercise 12

Total Purchase: $520
Paid: $200
Unpaid Balance: $320
Finance Charge: 1.5%
Total Paid: ?

3rd month:

```
  $   1 89
  ×   0.02   finance charge of 2%
  $   3.78   finance charge
  + 189.00
  ?        bill for 3rd month
```

Total cost of stereo:

$215 + __?__ + __?__ = __?__
          finance charge

11. Mr. Ruiz used his credit card in March to purchase $175 worth of goods. He paid $50 on his bill the first month and the balance at the end of the second month. If there was a 1% finance charge after the first month, how much did he pay?

12. Ms. Constantine made purchases totaling $520 in May. She used her credit card, paying $200 the first month and the remainder the second month. If the finance charge is 1.5% on the unpaid balance after the first month, what did she pay in all? How much could she have saved if she had paid cash?

13. Bart paid for his college textbooks with his credit card. The total bill was $142.35. He paid $50 the first month and $75 the second month. He paid the balance, including the finance charge, the third month. What did he pay the third month if the finance charge is $1\frac{1}{2}$% per month on the unpaid balance?

14. Mr. Jackson purchased a suit for $210, using his credit card. He was able to pay $100 the first month and $25 each month for the next 3 months. He paid the balance at the end of the 5th month. If there was a 2% finance charge after the first month, how much did he pay in all?

CHALLENGE **15.** A company wants to purchase new equipment. The equipment costs $11,500. Company X will sell the equipment for a $1500 deposit and ten monthly payments of $1000 plus a $1\frac{1}{2}$% finance charge each month. Company Y will sell the equipment for a $500 deposit and 10 monthly payments of $1100 plus a 1% finance charge. Which company offers the lower total price?

8-10 | Checking Accounts

Checking account: one type of bank account.

Check: tells the bank to take the stated amount of money from a person's account and deposit it into the account of the person or company named on the check **(payee)**. The amount in the account after any deposit or withdrawal is called the **balance.**

Ms. Jacobs paid by check for house paint at Wilson Supplies.

```
Susan R. Jacobs                                  398
1422 South Pine St.
Bakerstown, Florida          March 20    19 93

PAY TO THE
ORDER OF    Wilson Supplies               $  73.29
Seventy-three and 29/100 _____ DOLLARS

        A   Anytown Bank
            Bakerstown, Florida

MEMO  house paint              Susan R. Jacobs
   ⑉0⑤⑤⑤00⑤06⑉: 00  097  00⑤ 8⑉  0398
```

Notice that Ms. Jacobs:

- Filled in the date and the name of the payee.
- Wrote the amount of the check twice—once using numerals and once in words, with cents written as a fraction of a dollar.
- Signed the check.
- Wrote what the check paid for.
- Recorded the check number and information in her record book. (See page 223.)

Write each amount in proper word form for a check.

1. $19.35   2. $42.12   3. $439.90   4. $326.50

5. $1012   6. $2109   7. $3075.57   8. $5109.31

Write out a check for each of the following. Sign your own name.

9. To Forest Pharmacy for $25.98 for a prescription

10. To J. Miller for $75.30 for garden supplies

11. To Handy Supermarket for $121.99 for food

12. To Dr. Ross for $75 for an office visit

13. Copy and complete this record of Ms. Jacobs' checking account. Replace the question marks with the correct answers.

		PLEASE BE SURE TO DEDUCT CHARGES THAT AFFECT YOUR ACCOUNT						BALANCE FORWARD	
NO.	DATE	ISSUED TO DESCRIPTION OF DEPOSIT	PAYMENT (-)			DEPOSIT (+)		660	50
398	3-20-93	TO Wilson Supplies	73	29				− 73	29
		FOR paint supplies						BAL 587	21
399	4-3-93	TO Books Plus	18	89				− 18	89
		FOR paperback books						BAL ?	
	4-12-93	TO Deposit				50	75	?	
		FOR refund check						BAL ?	
400	4-18-93	TO Handy Supermarket	75	40				?	
		FOR groceries						BAL ?	
401	4-20-93	TO Dr. Leopold	48	00				?	
		FOR dental work						BAL ?	
402	4-27-93	TO AMCO Telephone Co.	29	95				?	
		FOR telephone bill						BAL ?	
	4-28-93	TO Deposit				150	50	?	
		FOR part-time salary						BAL ?	

Answer these questions about Ms. Jacobs' account record.

14. What was the balance in the account after the deposit made on April 12?

15. For what amount was check number 400 written?

16. What was the balance in the account after the deposit made on April 28?

On May 14 Ms. Jacobs deposited a check for $45.52 and the following coins: 10 half-dollars, 25 quarters, 50 dimes, and 37 pennies.

17. Copy and complete her deposit slip.

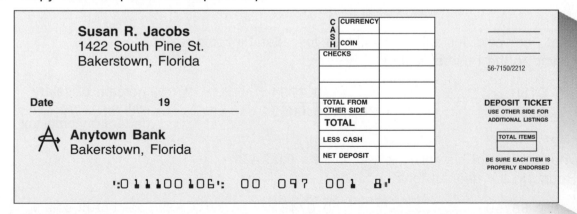

SUPPOSE THAT... **18.** You have $1000 in your checking account. Make up 4 checks and 2 deposits. Write an account record for these transactions.

8-11 | Paychecks: Deductions

When people receive their first paychecks, they may be surprised by the amount they receive. The federal government, acting through their employer, withholds part of their salary each week for income tax payments. The federal government also withholds part of their earnings for Social Security.

Study this paycheck stub.

Pay Period 6/1–6/7	Employer Winston Robotics		Check Number 413816
Employee Moon, David	Social Security No. 012-36-9661		Employee No. 76142
① Gross Pay $784.00	② Fed. Inc. Tax $136.00	③ F.I.C.A. $58.50	State Tax City Tax
④ Net Pay $589.50			

① **Gross Pay** — total wages (before deductions) paid to David Moon by Winston Robotics during the pay period 6/1–6/7.

② **Fed. Inc. Tax** — federal income tax withheld during the pay period 6/1–6/7.

③ **F.I.C.A.** — Social Security tax withheld from David Moon's wages during the pay period 6/1–6/7.

④ **Net Pay** — the amount of David Moon's paycheck after deductions are made.

▶ David Moon works 40 hours per week. How much does he earn per hour?

$$\$784 \div 40 \text{ hours} \longrightarrow 40\overline{)\$784.00} \quad \$19.60 \longrightarrow \$19.60 \text{ pay per hour}$$

▶ What percent of his salary is withheld for federal income tax? (Round to the nearest tenth.)

$$\frac{\$136}{\$784} \longrightarrow 784\overline{)136.0000} \quad 0.1734 \longrightarrow 17.3\% \text{ percent of salary withheld for federal income tax}$$

▶ What percent of his salary is withheld for F.I.C.A.? (Round to the nearest tenth.)

$$\frac{\$58.50}{\$784.00} \longrightarrow 784\overline{)58.5000} \quad 0.0746 \longrightarrow 7.5\% \text{ percent of salary withheld for F.I.C.A.}$$

Solve, using this information.

Pay Period 3/15–3/21	Employer Sports Therapy, Inc.			Check Number 15987
Employee Michaels, Lauren	Social Security No. 130-45-6641			Employee No. 4286
① Gross Pay $568.75	② Fed. Inc. Tax $80.30	③ F.I.C.A. $42.43	State Tax	City Tax
④ Net Pay ?				

1. Lauren Michaels works 37.5 hours per week. How much does she earn per hour? (Round to the nearest cent.)

2. What percent of her gross pay is withheld for federal income tax? (Round to the nearest tenth.)

3. What percent of her gross pay is withheld for F.I.C.A.? (Round to the nearest tenth.)

4. What is her net pay?

5. Use this information to complete Jon Hutko's paycheck stub.
   a. Jon works 35 hours per week. He earns $20 per hour.
   b. 19.5% of his gross pay is withheld for federal income tax.
   c. 7.5% of his gross pay is withheld for F.I.C.A.

Pay Period 10/1–10/7	Employer United Telephone			Check Number 68848
Employee Jon Hutko	Social Security No. 105-72-0801			Employee No. 12064
① Gross Pay ?	② Fed. Inc. Tax ?	③ F.I.C.A. ?	State Tax	City Tax
④ Net Pay ?				

6. Use this information to complete Donna Montano's paycheck stub. She gets paid every two weeks.
   a. Donna works 35 hours per week. She earns $19.50 per hour.
   b. 17.8% of her gross pay is withheld for federal income tax.
   c. 7.5% of her gross pay is withheld for F.I.C.A.

Pay Period 4/1–4/14	Employer Calco Computers, Inc.			Check Number 282901
Employee Montano, Donna	Social Security No. 088-18-1368			Employee No. 2606
① Gross Pay ?	② Fed. Inc. Tax ?	③ F.I.C.A. ?	State Tax	City Tax
④ Net Pay ?				

8-12 | Income Tax

Income tax: a tax paid on taxable income. The federal government and many state and city governments collect income taxes.

Gross income: the money received from earnings and from other sources.

Taxable income: gross income minus *exemptions* and *deductions*.

Exemption: amount a person is allowed to subtract for himself or herself and for each dependent. For example, someone with 2 dependents would have $4500 in exemptions ($1500 each).

Deduction: amount a person is allowed to subtract for medical, charitable, and certain other expenses.

The federal income tax schedule changes every year. Suppose that last year the schedule was the following:

If the amount of taxable income is:	**Tax Rate Schedule for Head of Household**			
	Over—	**But not over—**	**Enter tax of**	**of the amount over**
	$24,850	$ 64,200	$ 3,727.50 + 28%	$24,850

Suppose you earned $31,000. Besides yourself, you had 2 dependents, and you can deduct $1200 in medical expenses. What was your federal income tax?

- Determine your gross income. $31,000

- Find the amount for exemptions and deductions.

  Number of Dependents × Amount for Each = Exemptions

        3   × $1500   = $4500

  Exemption Amount + Deduction Amount = Total Deduction

      $4500   + $1200   = $5700

- Determine your taxable income.

  Gross Income – Total Deduction = Taxable Income

    $31,000 – $5700   = $25,300

- Compute your federal income tax.

  $25,300 (taxable income) $3727.50

  – 24,850   + 126.00 (tax on amount over $24,850)

  $ 450 (amount over $24,850) $3853.50

$3853.50 is your federal income tax for the year.

Use the table for exercises 1–16.

If the amount of taxable income is:	Tax Rate Schedule for Head of Household			
	Over—	But not over—	Enter tax of	of the amount over
	$0	$ 24,850	- - - - - - - - - 15%	$0
	$24,850	$ 64,200	$ 3,727.50 + 28%	$24,850
	$64,200	$128,810	$14,745.50 + 33%	$64,200

What is the income tax to the nearest dollar for each of these taxable incomes?

1. $9,000

2. $11,050

3. $16,700

4. $21,000

5. $22,500

6. $24,400

7. $27,300

8. $31,500

9. $38,000

10. $45,000

11. $54,000

12. $81,000

Solve.

13. Mario's gross earnings are $27,000.
His exemptions and deductions total $5400.
What is his income tax?

14. Teri's gross earnings are $35,000.
She has 3 dependents, plus $1100 in deductions.
What is her federal income tax?

15. Eric has a taxable income of $33,000.
A total of $4500 of federal tax was deducted from
his weekly paychecks during the year. How much
does Eric still owe the federal government?

16. A family's federal income tax for this year was $7840
and its income was $36,800. What percent of the
family's income was spent on federal income taxes?

Taxable
  Income: $36,800
Federal Tax: $ 7840
Tax Rate:

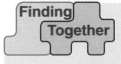

17. Use an almanac to look up the state income-tax rate schedule
for your state. Then use this schedule to compute the
state income tax for exercises 1–12.

18. Use your social studies textbook or an encyclopedia to prepare
a report about the history of federal and state income taxes.

Problem: A word processor listed at $1250 is on sale at a computer store for $\frac{1}{5}$ off. Store employees also receive a 10% discount off the sale price. If an employee decides to buy the word processor, what total rate of discount would he or she receive?

1 IMAGINE Draw and label the word processor sale.

Sale: _?_ %
$1250

2 NAME
Facts: $1250 — list price
$\frac{1}{5}$ — rate of sale discount
10% — rate of employee discount
Question: _?_ % — total rate of discount

3 THINK To find the total rate of discount,
first find the sale discount, using the formula:
$$D = LP \times R$$
Then find the discount for an employee on the sale:
$$D = SP \times R$$
Lastly, find the rate of total discount for an employee:
$$R = D \div LP$$

Employee discount, 10%
+
Sale discount, $\frac{1}{5}$ off =
Total discount = _?_

4 COMPUTE Sale discount of $\frac{1}{5}$ off: $D = LP \times R$

$$D = \$\cancel{1250}^{250} \times \frac{1}{\cancel{5}_1}$$

$$D = \$250$$

10% employee discount: $D = SP \times R$

$$D = \$1000 \times 0.1$$

$$D = \$100$$

Total discount to employees = $250 + $100 = $350

Rate of discount for employees: $R = D \div LP$

$$R = \$350 \div \$1250$$

$$R = 28\%$$

An employee would receive a 28% rate of discount.

5 CHECK Use a calculator to check your computations.
Does 28% of $1250 equal $350?

$$0.28 \times \$1250 \overset{?}{=} \$350$$
$$\$350 = \$350$$

Solve by using more than one step.

1. A family budgets 45% of its weekly income for food and clothing, 5% for savings, 20% for rent, and the remaining $216 for miscellaneous expenses. How much money is budgeted for food and clothing?

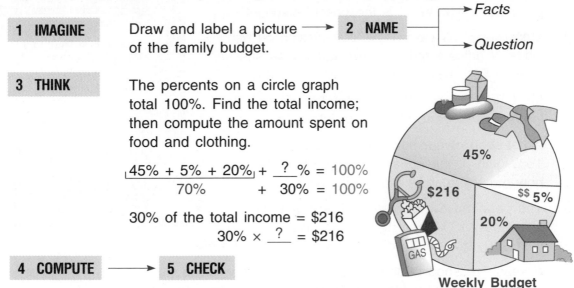

| **1 IMAGINE** | Draw and label a picture ⟶ **2 NAME** ⟶ Facts ⟶ Question |

of the family budget.

3 THINK

The percents on a circle graph total 100%. Find the total income; then compute the amount spent on food and clothing.

$45\% + 5\% + 20\% + \underline{\ ?\ }\% = 100\%$
$\qquad 70\% \qquad\quad + \ 30\% = 100\%$

30% of the total income $= \$216$
$30\% \times \underline{\ ?\ } = \$216$

4 COMPUTE ⟶ **5 CHECK**

Weekly Budget

2. The following supplies were ordered for office use:
   - 20 reams of paper at $5.60 per ream
   - 12 tape dispensers at $3.50 each
   - 25 boxes of pens at $14.50 per box
   - 12 desk blotters at $2.75 each

   A 1% discount is allowed if the bill is paid within 10 days of receipt of merchandise. What will the total bill be if there is a 5% sales tax and the amount is paid within the discount period?

3. Ms. Lorenz just got a job with a toy manufacturer. She will receive a weekly salary of $475 and a commission of 20% on all sales that she makes. Her supervisor estimates that her sales will be about $2000 per month for the first six months and about $5000 per month after that. How much can Ms. Lorenz expect to earn in her first year?

4. Last year the total sales of a small business amounted to $240,000. If the goods cost the owner $180,000 and expenses were $28,000, what rate of gain did the owner realize?

5. Mr. Ayers is a car salesman. He is paid $8.80 per hour and receives a 6% commission on sales. Last week he worked 40 hours and sold a car for $12,700. What was his take-home pay if 20% of his total earnings are withheld for federal income tax and $14.48 is deducted for medical insurance?

6. Ms. Green and Ms. Brown each bought a bicycle that cost $119. Ms. Green bought hers on an installment plan. She put down $20 and paid $23 per month for 5 months. To purchase her bike Ms. Brown used a credit card that added a monthly finance charge of $1\frac{1}{2}\%$ to unpaid balances. She paid $20 each month for five months and the remaining balance in the sixth month. Which one paid more for her bike? How much more?

8-14 Problem Solving: Applications

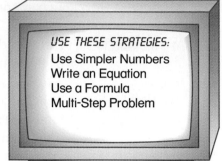

USE THESE STRATEGIES:
Use Simpler Numbers
Write an Equation
Use a Formula
Multi-Step Problem

1. A jogging suit is on sale for $29.50. The original price was $40. What is the rate of discount?

2. Mrs. Diego will earn a 4% commission on her sales of office furniture. How much must she sell to earn $2000?

3. Mr. O'Toole took out a loan for $1500 at 12% interest for 1 year. How much interest will he pay?

4. A pet-shop owner sold a deluxe aquarium at a 15% gain. If the aquarium originally cost $295, how much profit did the owner make?

5. The pet-shop owner also sold an aquarium stand at a 15% loss. If the stand originally cost $69, how much did the owner lose on the sale?

6. A seashore shop offered a 45% end-of-season discount on every purchase. How much did Ms. Singh save on a sandcastle sculpture listed at $24 and on a landscape painting listed at $75?

7. What percent did Lee save when he paid $65.19 for a remote-control boat regularly priced at $79.50?

8. A carpenter spent $450 making a dollhouse. If he sold it at a gain of 8%, what was the selling price?

9. Which is a better buy for a barbeque grill?
   a. regular price $24.95, 20% discount, 6% sales tax
   b. regular price $23.49, 15% discount, 8% sales tax

10. Last week, Camping Trails advertised a $654 canoe for a 7.5% discount. This week they have advertised the same canoe for $625.
    a. During which week would a customer have saved more?
    b. How much more would a customer have saved?

11. Mr. Vocheck, a salesperson at Camping Trails, sold 4 tents for $129.50 each. If he received a 4.5% commission, what did he earn in commission?

12. Green Bank pays $8\frac{1}{3}$% interest on a $1240 deposit for 5 years 3 months. What interest does the bank pay?

13. Alexa ordered a dozen computer programs listed at $20.80 each. If the bill included a $2.50 shipping charge and $7\frac{1}{2}$% sales tax, what was her bill?

14. When Ms. Peliz used her credit card, she was charged $3\frac{1}{3}$% interest. If her monthly expenses totaled $602.10, what was she charged for interest?

15. Juan saved 30%, or $2.55, when he bought guitar strings. What was the list price of the strings?

16. Pine Hill School received an 8% student discount on the admission fee to the Environmental Center. If this saved the school $21.84, what was the original total admission cost? If 42 students visited the center, what would the per-student admission charge have been without the discount?

17. After 1 year Mr. Yanni's certificate of deposit earned $127.50. If this equaled an 8.5% rate of interest, what was the value of his certificate?

18. A car salesperson received $986.25, or $6\frac{1}{4}$% commission, for selling a car. What was the car's selling price?

19. A silk flower arrangement cost $24.75 to make but was sold for $30. What rate of gain was realized?

20. The cash receipts for 1 day totaled $2709. If this included a 7.5% sales tax, what were the receipts before sales tax?

21. Arlo's grandparents deposited $1200 in a savings account that earned 6.5% annually. If the earned interest remained in the account, how much money was in the savings account after 3 years? How much interest was earned?

22. What percent did a builder lose if it cost him $72,000 to complete a job he had contracted to do for $63,000?

23. The Howe family bought a new bedroom set that cost $1750. They paid a 25% down payment and monthly payments of $75 for $1\frac{1}{2}$ years. How much more did it cost the Howes to buy the set on installment rather than pay for it outright?

24. The Centuras bought a dishwasher listed at $434. They paid 20% down and agreed to pay the rest in 8 equal payments. How much was each payment?

25. Ms. Lee earned a $2800 commission in one month. If she had sold an additional $5000 worth of goods, her commission would have been $3000. What was her rate of commission?

26. If Mr. Zoli had earned 1.5% more in annual interest last year, he would have earned $60 more in interest. How much had he invested at the beginning of last year?

27. By selling a painting valued at $120 for $165, an art museum realized what rate of gain?

$30

More Practice

Find the profit or loss to the nearest cent.

1. Cost: $65
   Rate of profit: 25%

2. Cost: $79.50
   Rate of profit: $37\frac{1}{2}$%

3. Cost: $245.75
   Rate of loss: 6.8%

Find the discount and the sale price to the nearest cent.

4. Coat rack: Regular price: $75 Discount: 20%

5. Desk lamp: Original price: $32.50 Discount: $12\frac{1}{2}$%

Find the missing information. Round to the nearest cent.

6. List price: $24
   Discount: $2.40
   Rate of discount: _?_

7. Original price: $250
   Discount: $50
   Rate of discount: _?_

8. Discount: $50
   Rate of discount: 6%
   Original price: _?_

9. Price: $12.50
   Rate: 5%
   Sales tax: _?_
   Total cost: _?_

10. Price: $169.75
    Rate: 12%
    Sales tax: _?_
    Total cost: _?_

11. Price: $250
    Rate: $6\frac{3}{4}$%
    Sales tax: _?_
    Total cost: _?_

12. Commission: _?_
    Rate: 3.5%
    Total sales: $2500

13. Commission: $5850.50
    Rate: 12%
    Total sales: _?_

14. Commission: $630
    Rate of commission: _?_
    Total sales: $10,500

Find the interest. Round to the nearest cent.

15. Principal: $270
    Rate: 5%
    Time: 1 yr

16. Principal: $1050
    Rate: $6\frac{1}{2}$%
    Time: 2 yr

17. Principal: $12,675
    Rate: $12\frac{1}{2}$%
    Time: 6 mo

Find the total amount and the compound interest earned.

18. Principal: $300
    Rate: 6%, compounded annually
    Time: 3 yr

19. Principal: $750
    Rate: 5%, compounded semi-annually
    Time: 2 yr

Find the finance charge for one month on the unpaid balance.

20. Bill: $83.50
    Paid: $25
    Charge: $1\frac{1}{2}$%

21. Bill: $1000
    Paid: $350
    Charge: 2%

22. Bill: $350.75
    Paid: $50
    Charge: $1\frac{3}{4}$%

Solve.

23. Joel works 35 hours a week. He earns $15.25 per hour. The following amounts are withheld from his gross pay: 15.4% for Fed. Inc. Tax and 7.7% for F.I.C.A. What is his gross pay? What is his net pay?

Math Probe

PROFIT AND LOSS: BUYING STOCKS

Frieda Financier wants to start a new business called Frieda's Fancy Fries, Inc. (FFF). She needs other people to invest their money to help her start the company. So Frieda sells shares of stock in FFF.

People who buy stocks in FFF will become *stockholders* and will share in the FFF's profits and losses. If FFF makes a profit, all the stockholders will divide the profits depending on the number of shares they bought. These divided profits are called *dividends*. These dividends will vary each year.

As a smart business person, you believe that FFF will do well. So you go to your stock *broker,* who buys and sells stocks to others. The broker tells you that stock prices are recorded in whole dollars and in eighths of a dollar. But added to this, your broker will charge you a 1.5% commission on the total amount of money you spend buying stocks.

Imagine that you buy stock in FFF for four years. Follow the first example in the chart below. Then complete the chart.

Years	Price per Share	No. of Shares Purchased	Total Cost
1. First	$102\frac{1}{8}$	100	$10,365.69 $\longrightarrow$ $102\frac{1}{8} \times 100$ $102.125 \times 100 = \$10,212.50$
2. Second	$100\frac{1}{2}$	30	$10,212.50 $\times$ 0.015
3. Third	$101\frac{1}{2}$	200	$153.1875 Commission
4. Fourth	$106\frac{1}{4}$	90	$10,212.50 + 153.19 $10,365.69 Total Cost

5. Look at the stock-market page in the newspaper. Choose a company in which you would like to invest. Keep a daily chart of the closing price of the stock for four weeks. Create a line or bar graph, tracking the stock. Then answer the following questions: What was the overall trend of the company? What was the four-week high? Low? Would you consider buying stock in this company? Why or why not?

Check Your Mastery

Find the profit or loss to the nearest cent. See pp. 204–205

1. Cost: $92
   Rate of profit: 15%

2. Cost: $57.25
   Rate of profit: $33\frac{1}{3}$%

3. Cost: $350
   Rate of loss: $12\frac{1}{2}$%

Which is a better buy, "a" or "b"? See pp. 206–207

4. Calculator **a.** $52 at 10% discount **b.** $48 at 9% discount

5. Computer **a.** $1529 at $\frac{1}{8}$ off **b.** $1550 at 15% discount

Find the missing information. See pp. 208–215

6. List price: $114
   Discount: $17.50
   Rate of discount: __?__

7. Original price: $95
   Discount: $20
   Rate of discount: __?__

8. Discount: $45
   Rate of discount: 15%
   Original price: __?__

9. Price: $38.75
   Rate: $5\frac{1}{4}$%
   Sales tax: __?__
   Total cost: __?__

10. Price: $205.25
    Rate: 8%
    Sales tax: __?__
    Total cost: __?__

11. Price: $1260
    Rate: $3\frac{3}{4}$%
    Sales tax: __?__
    Total cost: __?__

12. Commission: __?__
    Rate: 5%
    Total sales: $5750

13. Commission: $8500
    Rate: 9%
    Total sales: __?__

14. Commission: $570.50
    Rate of commission: __?__
    Total sales: $15,250

Find the interest. See pp. 216–217

15. Principal: $650
    Rate: 6%
    Time: 2 yr

16. Principal: $2300
    Rate: $8\frac{1}{2}$%
    Time: 1 yr

17. Principal: $31,525
    Rate: $10\frac{1}{2}$%
    Time: 6 mo

Find the total amount and the compound interest earned. See pp. 218–219

18. Principal: $625
    Rate: 4%, compounded annually
    Time: 2 yr

19. Principal: $1900
    Rate: 6%, compounded semi-annually
    Time: 3 yr

Find the finance charge for one month on the unpaid balance. See pp. 220–221

20. Bill: $829.50
    Paid: $64
    Charge: $3\frac{1}{4}$%

21. Bill: $3500
    Paid: $575
    Charge: $2\frac{1}{2}$%

22. Bill: $705.30
    Paid: $70
    Charge: $1\frac{3}{4}$%

Solve. See pp. 222–227

23. Alice works $37\frac{1}{2}$ hours a week. She earns $9.70 per hour. The following amounts are withheld from her gross pay: 11.4% for Fed. Inc. Tax and 6.8% for F.I.C.A. What is her gross pay? What is her net pay?

Cumulative Review

Choose the correct answer.

1. Which of the following is 15% of $120?
   a. $100
   b. $115
   c. $18
   d. $102

2. If 9 out of 24 students failed the test, what percent passed?
   a. 50%
   b. 62.5%
   c. 37.5%
   d. 46.7%

3. 500 runners reported for the marathon. 38% finished. How many did not?
   a. 190
   b. 390
   c. 380
   d. 310

4. How many times greater than $\frac{1}{8}$% is 12.5%?
   a. 10
   b. 100
   c. 1000
   d. 10000

5. 37.5% is 5 times what number?
   a. 0.75
   b. 0.075
   c. 0.037
   d. 0.375

6. 0.025 is how much less than 100%?
   a. 95%
   b. 25%
   c. 97.5%
   d. 99.975%

7. $3\frac{1}{4}$% expressed as a fraction in lowest terms is how much less than one?
   a. $\frac{13}{400}$
   b. $\frac{13}{4}$
   c. $\frac{387}{400}$
   d. $97\frac{1}{2}$

8. Which of the following is the reciprocal of 0.45 in lowest terms?
   a. $\frac{9}{20}$
   b. 2.2
   c. $\frac{100}{45}$
   d. $\frac{20}{9}$

9. 20% of what number is 3 times 2^3?
   a. 144
   b. 24
   c. 240
   d. 120

10. What percent of 32 is 14?
    a. 50%
    b. 2.28%
    c. 22.8%
    d. 43.75%

11. If 57 is 30% of a number, what is 12.5% of the same number?
    a. 190
    b. 171
    c. 2375
    d. 23.75

12. A baseball team won 12 games and lost 8. What was their percent of victory?
    a. 25%
    b. 60%
    c. 40%
    d. 30%

13. A bike listed at $96 was sold for $84. What was the rate of discount?
    a. 15%
    b. 12.5%
    c. 20%
    d. 87.5%

14. Margaret bought a new $30 tire for her bike. With a 30% discount and a sales tax of 7%, what did she pay?
    a. $27.93
    b. $26.10
    c. $35.70
    d. $22.47

235

Change each fraction to a decimal.

15. $\frac{5}{8}$ 16. $\frac{2}{15}$ 17. $\frac{2}{20}$ 18. $\frac{4}{9}$ 19. $\frac{15}{3}$ 20. $\frac{7}{12}$

Change each fraction to a percent.

21. $\frac{5}{16}$ 22. $\frac{3}{7}$ 23. $\frac{7}{8}$ 24. $\frac{2}{9}$ 25. $\frac{7}{5}$ 26. $\frac{41}{12}$

Change each decimal to a percent.

27. 0.006   28. 4.01   29. 0.018   30. 3.002   31. 0.165   32. 2.013

Find the percent of increase or decrease. (Round to the nearest tenth of a percent.)

33. Original: 720   34. Original: 840   35. Original: 5500   36. Original: 6000
     New: 810   New: 960   New: 6000   New: 2500

Find the discount and the sale price to the nearest cent.

37. Original price: $120; discount: 25%

38. Original price: $360; discount: $11\frac{1}{9}$%

Find the sales tax and the total cost.

39. Price: $240   40. Price: $1040

     Tax: 7%   Tax: $6\frac{1}{4}$%

Find the rate of commission or the total sales.

41. Commission: $48   42. Commission: $400   43. Commission: $190
     Total Sales: $1600   Total Sales: $3200   Rate: 5%

Solve.

44. The fabric store marked a particular fabric at $4.50 per yard, less 20% discount. If the store then made a profit of 25%, what was the cost of the material per yard?

45. A compact disc player, originally marked at $249, was sold for $212. What was the approximate rate of discount?

46. Tracy bought a cassette tape for $6.95. The sales tax was 7%. What did she pay for the tape?

47. Betsy bought a new car for $16,490. If the salesperson received a $2\frac{1}{2}$% commission, how much did he earn?

48. Linda put $3500 in the bank. If the annual rate of interest is 8.5%, how much money will she have in 2 years?

49. Ms. Engard purchased 150 acres of land at $2500 an acre. She resold it at a gain of $12\frac{1}{2}$%. What was the resale price?

+10 BONUS

50. You manage a sporting goods store. Make up a bill for three items originally listing for $500 or more and three originally listing at less than $500. What would the total bill be if you sell all six items at a 30% discount?

Cumulative Test I

Choose the correct answer.

1. Round 581,734,429,506 to the greatest place-value position.
   a. 581,700,000,000 **b.** 580,000,000,000 **c.** 600,000,000,000 **d.** none of these

2. 16.070629, rounded to the nearest hundred thousandth is:
   a. 16.0606 **b.** 16.07063 **c.** 16.07062 **d.** none of these

3. If $r + 24 = 37$, then $r = \underline{\ ?\ }$
   a. 61 **b.** 13 **c.** 12 **d.** 1.69

4. If $4n + 3 = 23$, then $n = \underline{\ ?\ }$
   a. $3\frac{2}{23}$ **b.** $5\frac{4}{23}$ **c.** 5 **d.** 4

5. If $\frac{s}{8} + 4 = 6$, then $s = \underline{\ ?\ }$
   a. $\frac{1}{2}$ **b.** 16 **c.** 20 **d.** 4

6. Which equation would you solve by dividing both sides by 4?
   a. $n + 4 = 9$ **b.** $4n = 20$ **c.** $\frac{n}{4} = 5$ **d.** $n - 4 = 3$

7. 5×10^6 is:
   a. 500,000 **b.** 5,000,000 **c.** 50,000 **d.** 50,000,000

8. $17.72 \div 10^5$ is:
   a. 0.001772 **b.** 0.177200 **c.** 0.0001772 **d.** 0.1772

9. Express 26,345,000 in scientific notation.
   a. 2.6345×10^7 **b.** 2.6345×10^8 **c.** $26,345 \times 10^3$ **d.** none of these

10. An example of a prime number is:
    a. 15 **b.** 27 **c.** 31 **d.** 99

11. The prime factorization of 240 is:
    a. 24×10 **b.** $2^4 \times 3 \times 5$ **c.** $2^3 \times 3 \times 5$ **d.** $2^2 \times 5^2$

12. The ratio of 21 to 27 is equivalent to the ratio of 7 to $\underline{\ ?\ }$
    a. 8 **b.** 9 **c.** 48 **d.** 3

13. The GCF of 16 and 48 is:
    a. 8 **b.** 4 **c.** 16 **d.** 24

14. The LCM of 4, 6, and 8 is:
    a. 46 **b.** 32 **c.** 24 **d.** 48

15. The decimal equivalent of 204% is:
    a. 2.04 **b.** 2.40 **c.** 0.204 **d.** 2.20

16. If $16\frac{2}{3}$ % of $72 = n$, then $n = \underline{\ ?\ }$
    a. 12 **b.** 10 **c.** 7.2 **d.** 9

17. If 6.4% of $n = 1.28$, then $n = \underline{\ ?\ }$
    a. 64 **b.** 48 **c.** 96 **d.** none of these

Compute.

18. 25,864,397 + 41,763,528

19. 6,000,000 − 439,871

20. 43.096 + 312.7 + 2.8031

21. 29.3 + 31.684 + 8.0091

22. 52.06 − 34.8

23. 87.4 − 9.8635

24. 9.9 − 0.804

25. 3524 × 6.09

26. 2538 × 6.94

27. 8.73 × 13.94

28. $84\overline{)50{,}820}$

29. $63\overline{)6287.4}$

30. $0.2\overline{)54.83}$

31. 4859.36 ÷ 7.04

32. 24.63 ÷ 3

33. $5500 ÷ 62.5

34. 3500 × 70

35. $|^-2.5| + |^+2.5|$

36. $|^+7| - |^-2.5|$

37. $\frac{3}{4} + \frac{7}{8}$

38. $2\frac{5}{6} + 20\frac{5}{9}$

39. $\frac{2}{3} - \frac{1}{5}$

40. $(\frac{1}{2} - \frac{1}{4}) + \frac{5}{6}$

41. $24\frac{7}{8} - 15\frac{5}{6}$

42. $30 - 16\frac{7}{8}$

43. $\frac{3}{8} \times \frac{2}{3}$

44. $\frac{1}{6} \times 25$

45. $2\frac{1}{8} \times 3\frac{1}{5}$

46. $\frac{2}{3} \times \frac{3}{4} \times \frac{4}{5}$

47. $\frac{7}{12} \div \frac{3}{4}$

48. $6\frac{1}{2} \div 2\frac{3}{5}$

49. $^+7 + {}^-4$

50. $^-9 - {}^-6$

51. $^-96 \div {}^+4$

52. $^+16 \times {}^-8$

53. $^-5 + {}^+4 - {}^-7$

54. $^+8 + {}^-9 - {}^+2$

55. $^-1.5 + {}^+4.2$

56. $^+3.7 - (^-6\frac{1}{2} + {}^+7)$

57. $^-8.1 \div (^-2.1 + {}^-6.9)$

58. $^-\frac{2}{3}(^+1\frac{2}{5} + {}^-3\frac{1}{2})$

59. $(^+1\frac{2}{3} + {}^+4\frac{1}{6}) \div {}^-2\frac{2}{3}$

60. $^-3\frac{1}{4} + {}^+2\frac{1}{7} - {}^-3\frac{1}{4}$

Complete.

61. 1.8 = __?__ %

62. $\frac{1}{2}$ % of 10 = __?__

63. 18 is __?__ % of 40

64. $3\frac{1}{2} : 6 = 7 : $ __?__

65. A sales tax of $6\frac{1}{2}$ % on $28.60 is __?__

66. One trillion written in scientific notation is __?__

67. The next number in a series 1, 4, 7, ... is __?__

68. The number 12 has exactly __?__ factors.

69. A number may be classified as prime or __?__

70. The opposite of $^-20$ is __?__

71. With a scale of 1 cm = 20 km, 2.5 cm represents a measure of __?__ km.

72. Divide $6000 in a ratio of 3 : 4 : 5.

Solve.

73. How long will it take the librarian to mend 30 books today, if he mended 12 books in 1 hour and 30 minutes yesterday?

74. Complete this truth table.

p	q	$\sim q$	$p \longrightarrow \sim q$
T	T		
T	F		
F	T		
F	F		

75. Ms. Kara receives a 9% commission on all property sales. What were her earnings on two pieces of land that sold for $68,500 and $84,900?

76. Six club members worked together to complete a volunteer job in 10 hours and 30 minutes. How many members could have finished the job in 7 hours?

9 Probability and Statistics

In this chapter you will:

- Determine the probability of single and compound events
- Use permutations
- Conduct and analyze random samples
- Read and interpret data on frequency tables and pictographs, single and double bar and line graphs, and circle graphs
- Construct and use frequency tables, scattergrams, and box-and-whisker plots to interpret data
- Solve problems: using Venn diagrams
- Use technology: graphing software

Do you remember?

Spinning this dial involves *equally likely* events.

Spinning this dial involves events that are *not equally likely.*

Game, Set, Match

Fe, Fi, Fo, and Fum had a tennis tournament.
Fi never defeated Fum. Fe lost every match.
Fum never beat Fo. Fi had to drop out of match 3.
Fe did not become a champ. Can you show what
happened, using 3 tournament brackets like these?

Fe
Fi
Fum
Fo   Winners

Fe
Fo
Fi   Winners
Fum

Fe
Fum
Fi   Winners
Fo

Probability of a Single Event

Probability (P): the number representing the chance that a given event **E** will occur.

This dial is divided into equal parts. So in spinning the dial, it is equally likely that the dial will stop on 2, 3, 5, or 7.

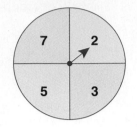

To find the probability of an event **P(E)** in which each outcome is *equally likely* to occur, use this formula:

$$P(E) = \frac{\text{Number of favorable outcomes}}{\text{Total number of possible outcomes}}$$

$P(2)$: Probability that the dial will stop on 2.

$P(2) = \frac{1}{4}$ — number of favorable outcomes
           — total number of possible outcomes

$P(\text{odd}) = \frac{3}{4}$ — There are three odd outcomes.

$P(1) = \frac{0}{4} = 0$ It is impossible for spinner to stop on 1.

Zero is the probability of an *impossible* event.

$P(\text{number less than 8}) = \frac{4}{4} = 1$

One is the probability of a *certain* event.

To find the probability of an event $P(E)$ in which each outcome is *not equally likely*:

- Make events equally likely.
- Use the $P(E)$ formula.

Look at this marker. The marker could land on a blue region, a yellow region, or a red region. These outcomes are *not* equally likely.

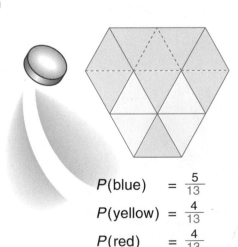

To find the probabilities, first divide the board into 13 equal regions. Now there are 13 equally likely outcomes.

$P(\text{blue}) = \frac{5}{13}$

$P(\text{yellow}) = \frac{4}{13}$

$P(\text{red}) = \frac{4}{13}$

Find the probability of each event when tossing a number cube whose faces are marked 3, 6, 9, 12, 15, 18.

Experiment A

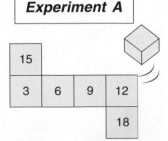

1. $P(3)$
2. $P(\text{even})$
3. $P(\text{multiple of 3})$
4. $P(\text{multiple of 6})$
5. $P(21)$
6. $P(\text{less than 4})$
7. $P(\text{greater than 9})$
8. $P(\text{odd})$
9. $P(\text{multiple of 9})$

Find the probability.

Experiment B: Each letter of the alphabet is written on a card.
Choose a card without looking.

10. $P(X)$ **11.** $P(A, B, \text{ or } C)$ **12.** $P(\text{a letter before M})$

13. $P(3)$ **14.** $P(\text{letter in the word "wish"})$ **15.** $P(\text{letter in the word "attic"})$

Experiment C: Without looking, choose a marble from a bag that
contains 5 red marbles, 4 blue marbles, 2 yellow marbles,
6 green marbles, and 3 black marbles.

16. $P(\text{blue})$ **17.** $P(\text{black})$ **18.** $P(\text{white})$

19. $P(\text{blue or green})$ **20.** $P(\text{not red})$ **21.** $P(\text{red, yellow, or black})$

Experiment D: Spin the dial.

22. $P(4)$ **23.** $P(\text{even})$ **24.** $P(2)$

25. $P(\text{odd})$ **26.** $P(\text{greater than 6})$ **27.** $P(\text{prime number})$

28. $P(\text{less than 12})$ **29.** $P(\text{fraction})$ **30.** $P(\text{rational number})$

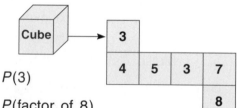

Experiment E: Toss this number cube.
(Hint: Is every event equally likely?)

31. $P(\text{even})$ **32.** $P(5)$ **33.** $P(3)$

34. $P(2)$ **35.** $P(\text{factor of 6})$ **36.** $P(\text{factor of 8})$

37. $P(\text{prime})$ **38.** $P(\text{multiple of 3})$ **39.** $P(\text{factor of 4})$ **40.** $P(\text{integer})$

41. $P(\text{greater than 8})$ **42.** $P(\text{less than 8})$ **43.** $P(\text{between 4 and 7})$

Experiment F: Without looking, choose a game marker from a bag
that contains 2 white markers, 4 orange markers,
3 red markers, and 3 black markers.

44. $P(\text{red})$ **45.** $P(\text{black})$ **46.** $P(\text{not black})$ **47.** $P(\text{not white})$

48. $P(\text{not orange or white})$ **49.** $P(\text{red or black})$ **50.** $P(\text{not yellow or not red})$

MAKE UP YOUR OWN...

51. Create an event so that $P = 0$, using this dial.

52. Create an event so that $P = 1$, using this dial.

9-2 Compound Events: Independent/Dependent

Compound events: One event follows the other.

Choose the A block, then the B block. **P(A and B)** = __?__

▶ **Independent events:** First event does *not* affect second event.

Choose the A block. $P(A) = \frac{1}{4}$

Return the A block.

Then choose the B block. $P(B) = \frac{1}{4}$

So, $P(A \text{ and } B) = \frac{1}{4} \times \frac{1}{4} = \frac{1}{16}$

P(A and B) = __?__

▶ **Dependent events:** First event *does* affect second event.

Choose the A block. $P(A) = \frac{1}{4}$

Keep the A block.

Then choose the B block. $P(B) = \frac{1}{3}$ ◀ When the A block is chosen, there are only 3 blocks left.

So, $P(A \text{ and } B) = \frac{1}{4} \times \frac{1}{3} = \frac{1}{12}$

To find the probability of a compound event:
- Find P(first event).
- Decide if the next event(s) are *independent* or *dependent*.
- Find the probability of each succeeding event.
- Multiply all the probabilities.

Three blocks, A, B, and C, are chosen. Each is returned after it is picked.

$$P(A, B, C) = P(A) \times P(B) \times P(C) = \frac{1}{4} \times \frac{1}{4} \times \frac{1}{4} = \frac{1}{64}$$

If each of the blocks is *not* returned, then:

$$P(A, B, C) = P(A) \times P(B) \times P(C)$$

But, P(B) and P(C) are *dependent* events.

So, $P(A, B, C) = \frac{1}{4} \times \frac{1}{3} \times \frac{1}{2} = \frac{1}{24}$

↑ 3 blocks left   ↑ 2 blocks left

Find the probability. Use the blocks above.

For independent events:

1. P(B, C)   2. P(C, D)   3. P(B, C, D)   4. P(A, B, C, D)

For dependent events:

5. P(B, C)   6. P(C, D)   7. P(B, C, D)   8. P(A, B, C, D)

Find the probability.

Experiment A: An envelope contains 10 cards numbered from 1 to 10.
Choose a card and put it back. Then choose another card.

9. *P*(7, even)
10. *P*(odd, even)
11. *P*(multiple of 3, 7)
12. *P*(prime, integer)
13. *P*(rational number, 10)
14. *P*(1, 2, 3, 4, 5)

Experiment B: Choose a card from Experiment A. Do *not* put it back.
Then choose another card.

15. *P*(5, 9)
16. *P*(4, 6, 8)
17. *P*(2, odd)
18. *P*(prime, integer)
19. *P*(5, multiple of 4)
20. *P*(6, 7, 8, 9, 10)

Experiment C: Toss a coin and spin the dial.

21. Copy and complete the **tree diagram** for these two independent events.
(H = heads; T = tails)

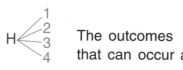

The outcomes
that can occur are:

(H, 1) (H, 2) (H, 3) (_?_, _?_)

(T, 1) (_?_, _?_) (_?_, _?_) (_?_, _?_)

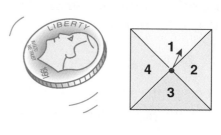

22. What is the probability that any two of these independent outcomes will occur?

Experiment D: Toss a coin and roll a number cube.

23. Make a tree diagram. List all possible outcomes.
24. Find *P*(H, even).
25. Find *P*(T, odd).
26. For tossing a coin, what is *P*(H)?
27. For rolling a number cube, what is *P*(even)?
28. Multiply *P*(H) × *P*(even).
Compare with your answers for exercises 26 and 27.
29. Find and multiply *P*(T) × *P*(odd).
Compare with your answer for exercise 25.

H
or
T

Sides:
7 or 8 or 9
or 10 or 11
or 12

Experiment E: An envelope contains 10 cards. Four cards are blue,
3 cards are green, 2 cards are red, and 1 card is yellow.
Choose a card and do *not* replace it.

30. *P*(red, red)
31. *P*(blue, red)
32. *P*(green, not red)
33. *P*(yellow, not blue)
34. *P*(not red, not yellow)
35. *P*(not blue, not green)

36. You have a box that holds 48 containers of yogurt. There are
4 flavors, 12 containers of each. What is the probability of
choosing the same flavor 3 times in a row? (You eat each one!)

9-3 Permutations

Permutation (P): an arrangement of items in a *particular* order.

Here 3 cars are parked in three spaces in 6 different ways.

This permutation can be written 3!, where "!" is called "factorial."

$$n! = n \times (n - 1) \times (n - 2) \times \ldots \times 1$$
$$3! = 3 \times 2 \times 1 = 6$$

To find the permutations, or arrangements, of items in groups of *more than one at a time*, use this formula:

$$_nP_r = \frac{n!}{(n - r)!}$$

where n = number of items
r = number taken at a time

Way 1	Way 4
Way 2	Way 5
Way 3	Way 6

Look at the word T A B L E.
How many permutations of the letters in T A B L E are there if the letters are taken *two* at a time?

$n = 5$ because 5 letters in T A B L E
$r = 2$ because letters are taken *two* at a time

$$_nP_r = {_5P_2} = \frac{5!}{(5 - 2)!} = \frac{5!}{3!} = \frac{5 \cdot 4 \cdot \cancel{3} \cdot \cancel{2} \cdot \cancel{1}}{\cancel{3} \cdot \cancel{2} \cdot \cancel{1}} = 20 \text{ permutations}$$

To find the number of *different* permutations among groups with *like* or *identical* items, use this formula:

$$P = \frac{n!}{q!}$$

where n = number of items
q = number of repeated items

Look at the numerals in 911. How many different permutations can be formed using the numerals in 911?

9̱11 has 3 items, but two of them are the same.

| 911 | 191 | 119 |
| 911 | 191 | 119 |

same

$$P = \frac{n!}{q!}$$

$n = 3$ and $q = 2$

$$P = \frac{3!}{2!} = \frac{3 \cdot \cancel{2} \cdot \cancel{1}}{\cancel{2} \cdot \cancel{1}} = 3 \text{ different permutations}$$

Find the value of each factorial expression.

1. 5!

2. 2!

3. 4!

4. 8!

5. 3! · 4!

6. (2 · 3)!

7. 4! + 6!

8. 3! · 2!

9. 6! – 3!

10. 8! – 6!

11. $\dfrac{7!}{(7 - 3)!}$

12. $\dfrac{9!}{(9 - 5)!}$

How many different permutations can be made using the letters in each word?

13. LINE

14. DECIMAL

15. SUBSET

16. ALGEBRA

17. COMPUTER

18. SQUARE

19. METER

20. FACTORIAL

Evaluate. (The first one is done.)

21. $_4P_2 \longrightarrow \dfrac{4!}{(4-2)!} = 12$

22. $_6P_1$

23. $_7P_6$

24. $_8P_6$

25. $_7P_5$

26. $_{12}P_3$

27. $_5P_4$

28. $_{18}P_4$

29. $_{15}P_5$

30. $_{14}P_7$

31. $_{21}P_3$

Solve.

32. How many 3-letter permutations can be formed using the letters in the word HISTORY?

33. How many different permutations can be formed using the letters in the word SCHOOL?

34. There are nine players on a baseball team. How many different batting lineups are possible?

35. Evaluate an arrangement of 12 different precious stones arranged on a bracelet in clusters of 4.

36. A typical freshman's high school roster includes English, Social Studies, Foreign Language, Mathematics, Related Arts, Gym, and Lunch. How many different rosters are possible?

Combinations

A **combination** is an arrangement in which order does *not* matter.

How many committees of 3 can be formed using 8 people?

Let the letters A – C represent 3 of the 8 people.

Group ABC is the same as   ACB, CBA, CAB, BAC, and BCA.

1 arrangement

$_8C_3$ means the combination of 8 people taken 3 at a time.

A combination is a special permutation.

Compute $_8C_3$ using $_nC_r = \dfrac{_nP_r}{r!}$ ← Permutation of $_8P_3$ divided by 3!

So $_8C_3 = \dfrac{8 \times 7 \times 6 \times \cancel{5} \times \cancel{4} \times \cancel{3} \times \cancel{2} \times \cancel{1}}{\cancel{5} \times \cancel{4} \times \cancel{3} \times \cancel{2} \times \cancel{1}} \div 3!$ OR $\dfrac{8 \times 7 \times \overset{1}{\cancel{6}}}{\underset{1}{\cancel{3}} \times \underset{1}{\cancel{2}} \times 1} = 56$

There are 56 possible combinations.

Evaluate.

37. $_6C_4$

38. $_7C_5$

39. $_8C_4$

40. $_5C_2$

41. $_9C_3$

9-4 Random Samples

Sample: a part of a whole group. If the sample, or subgroup, is taken according to definite rules, conclusions can be statistically inferred about the whole group.

$$S = \frac{P}{T}$$

Random sample (S): a subgroup, or part (**P**), of the total (**T**) group, *each* member of which has an *equally likely* chance of being chosen.

A supermarket wants to sponsor "Cooking and Eating Wisely" classes. It needs to know about what percent of its customers would be interested in these classes. The marketing team decided to ask 300 out of one week's 900 customers about their interest.

To select a *random sample* of 300, the team polled every *third* customer.

A random-sample survey must be large enough and must be unbiased.

$$\frac{1}{3} \text{ of } 900 = \frac{1}{3} \times 900 = 300 \text{ polled.}$$

Of the 300 customers asked, 180 expressed interest. To estimate the percent of interest:

$$\frac{180 \text{ customers}}{300 \text{ polled}} \times \frac{n}{100} \quad \begin{array}{l} \text{percent who were interested} \\ \text{total percent polled} \end{array}$$

$$300 \, n = 18,000$$

$$n = \frac{18,000}{300} = 60\% \text{ of those polled interested in classes}$$

Since 60% of the *random sample* of customers were interested, the marketing team could estimate or predict that about 60% of all the 900 customers would probably be interested in the classes.

Solve.

1. A random sample of 75 students leaving Redbank Junior High School one afternoon were asked if they walk at least one mile a week. Fifteen students said they do. What percent of this sample walk at least one mile a week?

2. At a shopping mall 200 people were asked if they exercise at least once a week. 64 said yes. What percent of the sample exercise once a week? What percent of all the people visiting the mall could be expected to exercise? Do you think the percent is great enough to make opening a gymnasium worthwhile?

Selecting a Random Sample

Select a random sample of 25% of all the eighth-grade students in your school. (Round to the nearest whole student.)
List their names. Here is one way to select your random sample.

Since $25\% = \frac{1}{4}$, choose 1 out of every *four* students.

Suppose there are 300 students.
To find how many names this will be:

$$\frac{1}{4} \text{ of } 300 = \frac{1}{4} \times 300 = 75$$

Then, write a fraction in lowest terms:

$$\frac{\text{needed in sample}}{\text{total number}} \longrightarrow \frac{75}{300} = \frac{1}{4}$$

To choose every fourth student, use one of these methods:

- Make an alphabetical list and choose every *fourth* name.

- Visit each eighth-grade homeroom and choose the student sitting in every *fourth* seat.

3. Select a random sample of $33\frac{1}{3}$% of all the eighth-grade students in your school. Compute, using the steps above.

4. Describe other ways that you can select a random sample for every "n^{th}" student.

5. *Question:* Do you own a CD player?

Asked of: 50 people who were selected each week for a 4-week period

Answers: 1st week — 15 said Yes
2nd week — 30 said Yes
3rd week — 26 said Yes
4th week — 18 said Yes

For each week what percent of the people asked owned a CD player? For the 4-week period, what is the average percent of people who own a CD player? If 15,758 people were surveyed, how many would probably answer that they own a CD player?

SKILLS TO REMEMBER

Order from least to greatest.

6. 2017, 987, 2071, 2000

7. 3.27, 3.2, 3.7, 3.07

8. $1.61, $.61, $6, $1

9. ⁻12, ⁺3, ⁻15, ⁺10, ⁻14

10. 72, 67, 83, 70, 78

11. $13\frac{1}{5}$, $13\frac{2}{3}$, $12\frac{1}{10}$, $13\frac{1}{4}$

9-5 Pictographs

Pictograph: a graph that uses a symbol to represent a number.

The number of pennants sold by different stands at a baseball stadium are illustrated in this pictograph.

Key

= 100 pennants

= 75 pennants
(three fourths of the symbol)

= 50 pennants
(one half of the symbol)

= 25 pennants
(one fourth of the symbol)

Stand	Number of Pennants Sold
Stand A	
Stand B	
Stand C	
Stand D	
Stand E	
Stand F	

Stand C has $5\frac{3}{4}$ symbols:

$$(5 \times 100) + (\tfrac{3}{4} \times 100) = 500 + 75 = 575 \text{ pennants sold}$$

Answer these questions about the pictograph above.

1. What is the number of pennants sold at Stand A?

2. What is the number of pennants sold at Stand E?

3. How many more pennants were sold at Stand D than at Stand F?

4. How many fewer pennants were sold at Stand B than at Stand E?

Read the key below; then answer the questions about the pictograph at the right.

Key

= 10,000 seats
= 7500 seats
= 5000 seats
= 2500 seats

Date	Seats Occupied
April 10	
May 10	
June 10	
July 10	
August 10	
September 10	
October 10	

5. On which date were the most number of seats occupied?

6. What is the difference between the number of seats occupied on April 10 and those occupied on October 10?

9-6 Bar Graphs

Frequency table: a record that shows how often a given event occurred.

A sports magazine polled 90 people to find their favorite spectator sport.

To make a frequency table:

- Make a stroke for each choice.
- Group the tallies in fives.
- Count the tallies.

Favorite Spectator Sports		
Name	Tally	Number
Baseball	JHT JHT JHT JHT JHT	25
Football	JHT JHT IIII	14
Basketball	JHT JHT JHT JHT I	21
Hockey	JHT JHT II	12
Bowling	JHT	5
Soccer	JHT JHT III	13

Bar graph: a graph used to organize frequency-table information visually.

To make a bar graph:

- Choose a title.
- Draw and label the horizontal and vertical axes.
- Choose a convenient unit for the scale. (Start the scale at 0.)
- Draw the bars on the graph.

This bar graph is *vertical.*

If the scale was placed along the bottom and the names were placed along the side, it would be a *horizontal* graph.

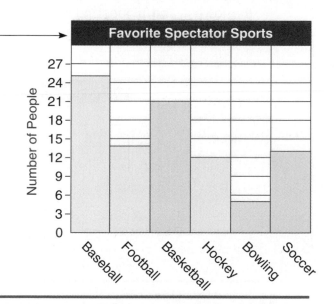

1. Construct a horizontal bar graph to represent the data above. Choose a unit of 5 for a scale from 0 to 30.

2. Construct a frequency table to represent five places your classmates visit most frequently; for example, zoo, art museum, planetarium, amusement park, historical landmark.

3. Construct a bar graph to represent the data gathered in exercise 2.

4. Poll 30 people on their favorite flavor of yogurt. Construct a frequency table from the data. Then construct a bar graph.

*See page 507 for more practice.

Histograms

Histogram: a type of bar graph that shows the *number* of results that occur within an interval.

The chart shows the number of telephone calls made by fifteen teenagers last week. The telephone company made a histogram to show these numbers.

Teenagers' Telephone Calls April 7 – April 13					
Demi:	36	Frank:	30	Pablo:	28
Megan:	32	Shari:	38	Kelly:	31
Carol:	34	Areem:	50	Daryl:	43
Dave:	40	Iris:	26	Lynn:	25
Lisa:	22	Don:	42	Elise:	37

To make a histogram:

- Look at the lowest and highest numbers (22, 50).

- Construct a frequency table using *equal* intervals that include the lowest and highest numbers of calls.

- Construct a bar graph showing the results.

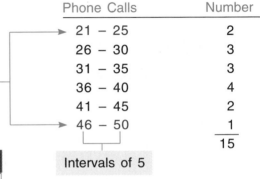

Phone Calls	Number
21 – 25	2
26 – 30	3
31 – 35	3
36 – 40	4
41 – 45	2
46 – 50	1
	15

Intervals of 5

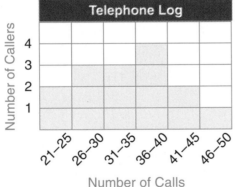

A histogram presents information visually.

---

1. Make a histogram to show the height of seedlings.

Height in cm	45	20	52	60	57	46	70	62	35	40	55	52	65	32	42

2. Make a histogram to show distances covered in a Bike-a-Thon.

Rider	1	2	3	4	5	6	7	8	9	10
Kilometers	80	88	78	82	91	75	87	95	72	83

3. Look up the yearly tuition of at least 12 schools, camps, day-care centers, or colleges. Construct a histogram to summarize your findings.

4. Use an almanac or other reference material to find the average annual rainfall in at least one country in each of the earth's continents. Make a histogram of the results.

9-8 Line Graphs

Line graph: a graph that displays data to show a pattern or trend.

This graph shows sales during a 6-month period.

The scale starts at 0 and uses convenient units of $50.

Notice that you can easily see that the greatest sales were $350 in September. The lowest sales were $50 in January.

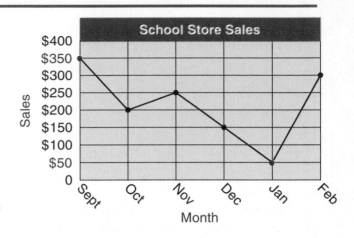

Sometimes a line graph allows you to read results that are not plotted on the graph.

This graph shows the change in the depth of water in a reservoir every 4 hours for a certain 24-hour period.

But the data a graph presents can be misused. It would be invalid to assume that at 10 P.M. on Thursday the depth of the reservoir was 7 feet.

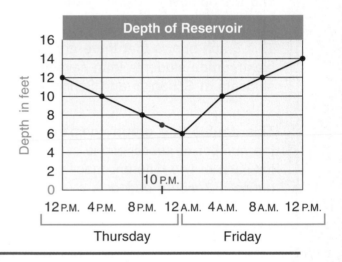

Answer these questions about the graphs above.

1. What amount of sales was recorded in October?

2. Which month had the greatest increase over the month before?

3. What was the depth of the reservoir at 8 P.M. on Thursday?

4. On Friday, how much deeper was the reservoir at 12 P.M. than at 4 A.M.?

Make a line graph for each set of data.

5. Shrub Oak Recycling collected the following numbers of newspaper bundles last year: Jan, 75; Feb, 125; Mar, 150; Apr, 100; May, 125; June, 200; July, 250; Aug, 225; Sept, 175; Oct, 150; Nov, 175; Dec, 75.

6. On 7 consecutive days the high temperatures in Shrub Oak were: 30°F, 28°F, 24°F, 15°F, 21°F, 25°F, 22°F.

9-9 Double Bar and Double Line Graphs

To make a **double bar graph** or a **double line graph:**

- Make a frequency table for each set of data.

- Draw each graph.

- Use a different color, design, or type of line to identify each.

- Put this information in the key.

This is a **double bar graph** comparing the number of seventh-grade students and the number of eighth-grade students for three different schools.

This graph shows that there are more eighth-grade students than seventh-grade students at School 1 and School 3.

This **double line graph** compares the number of subscriptions sold for each of two different magazines during a 3-month period.

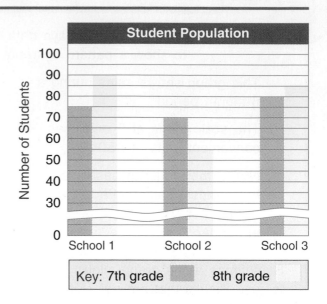

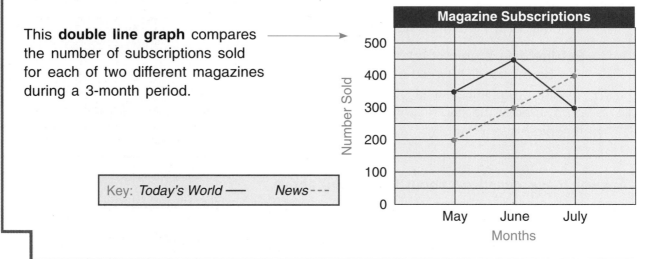

Key: *Today's World* ——— *News* - - -

Use the graphs above to answer the following questions.

1. How many eighth-grade students are in School 2?

2. Compare the number of seventh-grade students in the three schools.

3. Which of the two magazines sold more subscriptions in June? in July?

4. Which magazine had a decrease in the number of subscriptions sold from June to July?

5. In the 3-month period how many more subscriptions were sold for *Today's World* compared to *News*?

Make a double bar graph for each table.

6.

Number of Videos Rented at Viewer Videos		
	Last Month	This Month
New Arrivals	320	525
Adventure	426	375
Mystery	105	150
Comedy	250	260
Exercise	125	95
Music	225	162

7.

Number of Pizzas Sold		
	Large	Small
Extra Cheese	18	21
Mushroom	12	15
Meat	6	10
Regular	33	27
4-Topping Special	22	31
Green Vegetable	6	4

Make a double line graph for each table.

8.

Number of Tents Sold at Two Camping Stores		
	Store A	Store B
Jan	6	8
Feb	8	10
Mar	10	10
Apr	20	15
May	15	20
June	10	25
July	10	30
Aug	8	5
Sept	4	6
Oct	2	2
Nov	3	8
Dec	5	10

9.

Number of Resort Visitors		
	Echo Lake	Miller Lake
Jan 1	50	75
Feb 1	60	90
Mar 1	55	95
Apr 1	80	120
May 1	100	150
June 1	125	175
July 1	120	175
Aug 1	200	250
Sept 1	175	250
Oct 1	150	200
Nov 1	80	85
Dec 1	70	80

10. Draw either a double bar or a double line graph.

Temperature Readings for Two Resorts on Jan 1												
	7 A.M.	9 A.M.	11 A.M.	1 P.M.	3 P.M.	5 P.M.	7 P.M.	9 P.M.	11 P.M.	1 A.M.	3 A.M.	5 A.M.
Echo Lake	$^-2°C$	$^-2°C$	$^-1°C$	0°C	3°C	3°C	0°C	0°C	0°C	$^-2°C$	$^-3°C$	$^-4°C$
Miller Lake	$^-5°C$	0°C	3°C	6°C	6°C	4°C	2°C	2°C	1°C	0°C	$^-1°C$	$^-1°C$

Finding Together

11. Use the circulation record from your library to find the number of fiction and nonfiction books signed out each day for a 5-day period. Draw a double line graph for your data.

9-10 | Circle Graphs

Circle graph: another type of graph used to display information. It compares percentages or parts of a whole. In a circle graph the whole represents *100%* or *360°*.

To construct a circle graph:

- Find the percent, (P), of the total that each item represents.

$$\frac{\text{Vowel A}}{\text{Total Number}} \longrightarrow \frac{144}{720} \diagup\kern-1.2em\diagdown \frac{P}{100}$$

$$720P = 14{,}400$$

$$P = 20\%$$

- Find the number of degrees, (d), of a circle that the percent, 20%, represents.

20% of 360° = ?

$$\frac{20}{100} \diagup\kern-1.2em\diagdown \frac{d}{360} \longrightarrow \begin{array}{l} 100d = 7200 \\ d = 72° \end{array}$$

OR $d = \dfrac{1}{5} \times 360° = 72°$

- On a circle, measure the degrees for each item. Use a protractor to draw the correct central angle for each item.

Results of Word Game Survey *Frequency of Vowels*	
Vowel	Number
A	144
E	240
I	160
O	120
U	56
Total	720

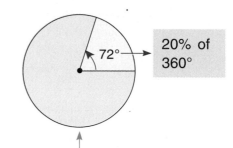

20% of 360°

Copy and complete the chart. (Make sure the sum of the numbers equals the total given.)

	Vowel	Number	Percent	Degrees
	A	144	20%	72°
1.	E	240	?	120°
2.	I	160	$22\frac{2}{9}\%$	?
3.	O	120	?	?
4.	U	56	?	?
	Totals	720	100%	360°

5. Construct a circle graph with the information from the chart above.

Construct a circle graph for each.

6. A car dealer has a total of 200 vehicles on the lot. The four different types and the number of each type are posted on a display board: full-size cars, 80; compact cars, 40; vans, 50; trucks, 30.

7. The parkland in South Salem is divided for use in the following way: picnic area, 75 acres; playgrounds, 30 acres; parking, 25 acres; lake, 50 acres; ball fields, 70 acres; woods (undeveloped), 150 acres.

8. Joe had 3 hours of homework last weekend. He spent the following amount of time on each subject: math, 30 min; science, 60 min; spelling, 15 min; social studies, 45 min; English, 30 min.

9. The art club asked 250 people, "What is your favorite shade of blue?" These were the results: turquoise, 100; pale blue, 60; navy blue, 40; royal blue, 50.

10. The Haidri family recorded these expenses on their recent vacation: inns, $350; food, $275; entertainment, $500; gasoline, $75; miscellaneous, $50.

11. A gift shop owner recorded the number of different types of cards out of 500 sold. The different types of cards sold were: birthday, 320; thank-you, 40; hello, 20; special holiday, 60; get-well, 40; anniversary, 20.

12. This circle graph shows the percent of each different kind of apple tree grown in an apple orchard. Find how many of each kind of apple tree are in the orchard if there are a total of 480 trees.
(The first is done.)
MacIntosh apples: 20% of 480 trees

$$\frac{20}{100} = \frac{n}{480}$$

$100n = 9600$

$n = 96$ MacIntosh   **OR** $\frac{1}{5}$ of 480 = 96 MacIntosh

Kinds of Apple Trees

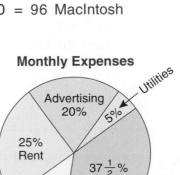

13. This circle graph shows the monthly expenses of a small business. The graph shows what percent of the monthly budget is spent on each item. The total monthly budget is $2400. Find the actual amount spent on each item.

Monthly Expenses

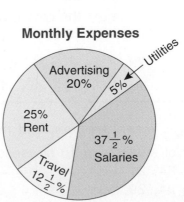

9-11 | Central Tendency

A set of data can be analyzed numerically in several ways.

Range: the difference between the highest and lowest scores of a set of scores.

Mean: the average score. Add the scores and divide by the number of scores.

Median: the middle score. Arrange the scores in order. For an odd number of scores the median is the middle score. For an even number it is the average of the two middle scores.

Mode: the score that occurs most frequently.

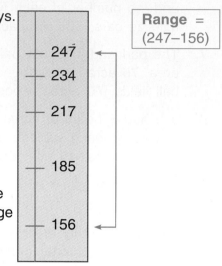

Range = (247–156)

247
234
217
185
156

Mean, median, and mode are measures of **central tendency**.

Justin kept a record of the distance he traveled each day on his 6-day vacation. The record is as follows: 234 mi, 185 mi, 217 mi, 185 mi, 247 mi, 156 mi.

Range: 247 (Highest) – 156 (Lowest) = 91 mi $\longrightarrow$ 91 mi is the range.

Mean: 234 + 185 + 217 + 185 + 247 + 156 = 1224
1224 ÷ 6 = 204 mi $\longrightarrow$ 204 mi is the mean, or average.

Median: Arrange the distances from least to greatest.

156   185   ⌞185   217⌟   234   247

middle distances

Divide the sum of the two middle distances by two to find the median.

$$\begin{array}{r} 185 \\ +217 \\ \hline 402 \end{array}$$

402 ÷ 2 = 201
Median = 201

Mode: 185 mi is the distance that is repeated most often, so 185 mi is the mode. Sometimes a set of data has NO mode. Sometimes a set of data has *more than one* mode.

129, 116, 205, 113, 129, 210, 113, 236 $\longrightarrow$ 129 and 113 are both used twice.

Here both 129 and 113 are modes.

Find the range, mean, median, and mode for each set of data.

1. Number of students in 10 classes:
   23, 27, 34, 21, 22,
   29, 31, 24, 29, 30

2. Test scores of 10 students:
   81, 82, 76, 95, 88
   81, 85, 86, 83, 93

256

3. Savings for the past 8 months:
$65, $00, $45, $06,
$85, $45, $50, $38

4. Heights of 9 students:
145 cm, 120 cm, 152 cm,
145 cm, 160 cm, 162 cm,
135 cm, 155 cm, 152 cm

5. Ken took eight math quizzes. He scored: 70, 65, 71, 86, 78, 82, 87, 85. Make a bar graph to show this information. Then compute the average quiz score, the range, and the median.

6. 8 classes in the eighth grade have the following numbers of students: 24, 35, 27, 25, 30, 26, 28, 29. Make a bar graph to show this information. Then find the average number of students, the range, and the median.

Use this graph for exercises 7–10.

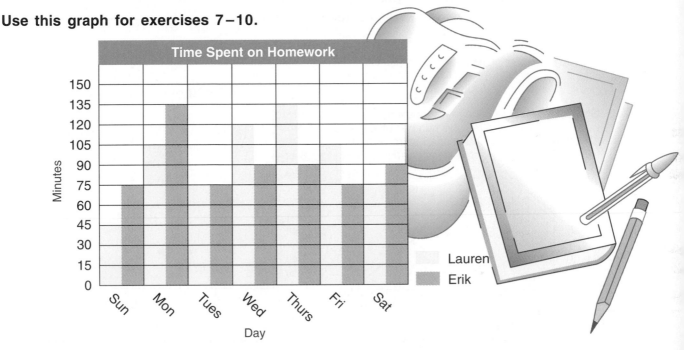

7. Which student spent more time doing homework this week? What is the mean for each student?

8. What is the range of all the times spent doing homework? What is the range for Lauren? For Erik?

9. Name the modes:
a. for Lauren. b. for Erik.

10. Find the median time:
a. for Lauren. b. for Erik.

Use this chart for exercises 11–12.

11. Find the mean time.

12. Which runners had speeds better than average?

200-Yard-Dash Times	
Runner	Time
Larry	22.8 sec
Alex	25.9 sec
Joseph	28.6 sec
Kris	24.3 sec
Douglas	22.1 sec

9-12 | Scattergrams

Scattergram: a graph that can be used to find whether there is a relationship between two sets of data.

This scattergram shows the relationship between speed and stopping distance.

In a **positive** relationship (correlation), *both* values increase or *both* decrease.

In a **negative** relationship (correlation), as one value *increases*, the other *decreases*.

Study the relationship in each of these scattergrams, A, B, and C.

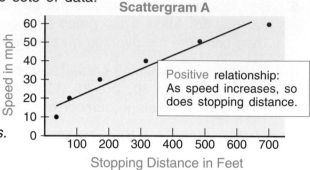

Positive relationship: As speed increases, so does stopping distance.

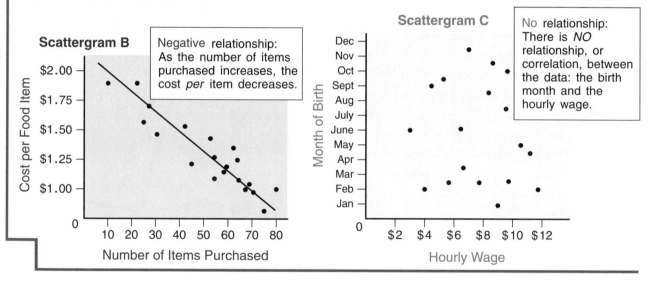

Negative relationship: As the number of items purchased increases, the cost *per* item decreases.

No relationship: There is *NO* relationship, or correlation, between the data: the birth month and the hourly wage.

Decide whether a *positive,* a *negative,* or *no* correlation may exist between:

1. outside temperature and fuel use

2. height and spelling score

3. hand size and foot size

4. salary and date of birth

5. amount of snow and elevation

6. rainfall and time of day

7. hourly wage and number of years employed

8. number of years employed and length of vacation time

9. distance from center of earth and weight

10. use of fluoride toothpaste and number of cavities

Making a Scattergram

To make a scattergram:

- Draw and label each axis.
- Graph the collected data.
- Draw a straight line close to the points that seem to be related.
- Decide whether relationship is positive, negative, or no relationship.

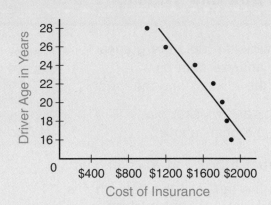

Age	16	18	20	22	24	26	28
Insurance Cost	$1900	$1850	$1800	$1700	$1500	$1200	$1000

Make a scattergram for each set of data.

11.

Years employed	1 – 5	6 – 10	11 – 20	21 and up
Days of vacation	10	15	20	25

12.

Calcium in diet (in mg)	1200	1000	800	600	500	400	300
Number of fractures	10	12	15	24	28	34	40

13. What relationship (correlation) is present in exercises 11 and 12? Explain.

 SUPPOSE THAT...

This scattergram displays the results of a survey on the age when students wear braces on their teeth.

Notice that the points seem to *cluster* around 13 years.

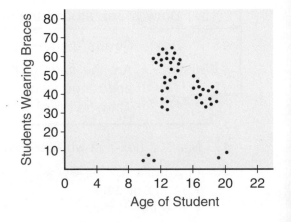

14. The number wearing braces also seems to cluster around:
   a. 8 years   **b.** 20 years   **c.** 18 years

Sometimes data displayed in scattergrams leads to false conclusions. Label the statements true or false.

15. Most people wear braces in their teenage years.

16. No one needs braces after age 24.

17. No one needs braces before age 10.

18. Write a true statement, using this scattergram.

19. Write a false statement, using this scattergram.

Box-and-Whisker Plots

"Flavor-Full" Crackers	Cartons	■	●	★	▲
From each of 5 cartons of different-shaped crackers, 100 are chosen *at random* and the *number* of each type of cracker is counted.	1	41	20	2	37
	2	36	14	12	38
	3	43	13	13	31
	4	27	16	16	41
	5	38	14	14	34

Box-and-whisker plots are graphs used to analyze data by plotting the median and the range.

Draw a box-and-whisker plot for "■" in the chart above.

To construct a box-and-whisker plot:

1. Find the range of the data, that is, the least value (27) and the greatest value (43). Arrange all the given values in order between these.

2. Find the median of the data.

3. Using the median, separate the data into an "upper half" and a "lower half."

4. Find the median of the upper half data. (41 and 43)

5. Find the median of the lower half data. (27 and 36)

6. Draw a number line using intervals appropriate to the data.

7. Label the points found in steps **1, 2, 4,** and **5.** Connect these points with a line. Draw a dotted line through the median of all the data. (38)

8. Draw a **box** around the medians.

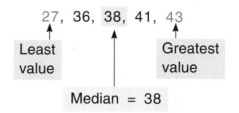

27, 36, **38**, 41, 43

Least value — Greatest value

Median = 38

lower half   upper half

27, 36, **38**, 41, 43

Median of 41 and 43 $\dfrac{41 + 43}{2} = 42$

Median of 27 and 36 $\dfrac{27 + 36}{2} = 31.5$

Intervals of 4 going from 0 through 44

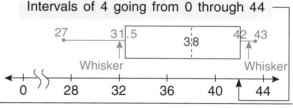

Box: Covers the *median* values of the data.

Whiskers: Are the parts of the line, drawn to connect the median and range values, that extend outside the median box. They trail like "whiskers" from the box.

1. Make a box-and-whisker plot for ●, ★, and ▲.

2. In a table list for ●, ★, and ▲:
   - range of data
   - median of data
   - upper half median
   - lower half median

3. Compare ● and ▲.
   - Which has a wider range?
   - Which occurs in greater numbers?

4. Which cracker shape is the most common? Explain.

5. If ● and ★ are cheese-flavored, make up a reason for fewer cheese crackers.

Line Plot.
To construct a **line plot**, draw a line, divide it into equal intervals, and use an "X" to represent each item in the data.

Line Plot

for ■ and ▲ crackers

Stem-and-Leaf plots

Stem – The tens digit in all 2-digit numbers in the data.
A 1-digit number has a stem of zero.

Leaves – The ones digits of every number in the data written in ascending order.

Stem Plot.
To make a **stem-and-leaf plot** for ■ and ▲ crackers:

- Draw 3 columns as shown.

- Look at the tens digits for the data in both ■ and ▲. Write them in order. (Smallest number in both sets of data is 27 and the largest is 43. So stems are 2, 3, and 4)

- Write the leaves or ones digits of each number in the ▲ data in the right column in ascending order. (There are no "twenties" so column is blank after Stem 2. But there are 4 "thirties" with ones digits of 1, 4, 7 and 8.)

- Do the same in the left "leaves" column for the ■ data.

Leaves ■	Stem	Leaves ▲
7	2	
8 6	3	1, 4, 7, 8
3 1	4	1

Ones digits for ■ data

Ones digits for ▲ data

Tens digits for ■ and ▲

By looking at the leaves and stem columns for ■ we see a 7 and a 2. But a leaf is a ones digit, so the data reads "27" not 72. Can you read all the others?

Identify the range, median, and extremes for each. Then draw the plot indicated.

6. Some of the PBA records for annual bowling averages from 1962 are: 213, 210, 211, 212, 209, 212, 212, 213, 215, 214, 215, 219, 216, 218, 222, 219, 216, 220, 219, 219 (line plot)

7. Twenty 14-year-olds from Kingsley School recorded their weights in kg: 53, 72, 51, 38, 43, 49, 64, 49, 60, 62, 48, 40, 58, 47, 48, 56, 68, 45, 51, 60 (stem-and-leaf plot)

8. Brad looked up the record speeds of the first 15 years of the Indy 500: 120, 121, 124, 126, 129, 128, 131, 128, 129, 136, 134, 136, 139, 139, 140 (box-and-whisker plot)

9. The speed of a human is listed at about 29 mph. Rita found the speeds of the 20 fastest animals to be: 30, 32, 70, 61, 30, 43, 32, 50, 45, 42, 50, 47, 35, 39.4, 40, 50, 45, 35, 40, 35 (box-and-whisker plot)

MAKE UP YOUR OWN...

10. Poll your classmates on a popular topic of the day. Then use one of the plots to display your data.

TECHNOLOGY

Go Graphic

A picture can be worth a thousand words. That is why we use graphs. It is important, however, to choose the best kind of graph to convey the information you want to share.

The supervisor of Chichester School District used graphing software to create a bar graph and a line graph to illustrate the results of a joint school fund-raising drive. The following results were used.

Amount	$467	$421	$395	$208	$553	$512	$267	$449	$764
Grade	K	1	2	3	4	5	6	7	8

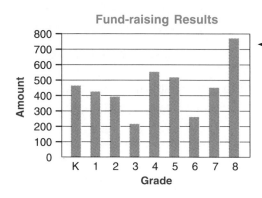

Bar graphs present information so that comparisons of two or more given subjects can be made.

Each school's principal put a copy of the **bar graph** on the bulletin board. The students could see how well their grade did.

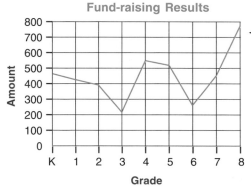

Line graphs present information on one subject so that trends can be identified and comparisons made.

The supervisor decided not to use the line graph since it did not display a trend.

Identify the type of graph you would create with graphing software.
Describe how you would set it up on the screen.

1. The number of visitors to an aquarium each month for one year.
2. The cost for each month to maintain all the aquarium's tanks.
3. The water-level variation of each tank for one week.
4. The monthly profit made on goods sold in the souvenir shop.

Technology Graphing

A video store owner used graphing software to create a circle graph to show his operating budget plan for one month.

Operating Expenses

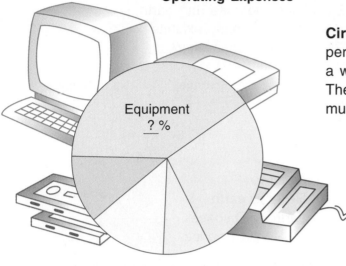

Equipment
? %

Circle graphs present information as percents or percentages, and show how a whole is divided into fractional parts. The sum of the data in the circle graph must total 100%.

Use the following information to explain how each section should be labeled for categories and percents.

Money amount	$7500	$1000	$600	$3000	$850	$2050
Category	Total	New Tapes	Util.	Equipment	Advs.	Misc.

Create a set of data for each situation below. Identify the type of graph that will best illustrate the data. Then use graphing software to create each graph.

5. The trend in music listening by your class during the school year

6. The food budget of your family for one month

7. The age categories of visitors to an amusement park during one month

8. The number of each type of fruit tree planted in an orchard

9. The most popular TV show of your classmates

10. Your family's vacation budget planning

CALCULATOR ACTIVITY Use a calculator to find the number of degrees of a circle that each percent represents.

11. 30% 12. 55% 13. $10\frac{1}{2}$% 14. 60% 15. $6\frac{1}{4}$%

Problem: A science center has 22 special exhibits: 12 on life science; 11 on space science; and 9 on earth science. One deals with all 3; 6 deal *only* with life science; 2 deal with *both* life and earth; and 3 deal with *both* earth and space. How many exhibits deal with earth science *only*? with space science *only*?

1 IMAGINE Draw and label three overlapping circles, or Venn diagrams, to represent the three types of exhibits.

Life Science (LS) = 12   **Earth Science (ES) = 9**

6   2
1
3

Space Science (SS) = 11

2 NAME *Facts:*

12 – life science	1 – all three
11 – space science	2 – life AND earth
9 – earth science	3 – earth AND space
	6 – ONLY life science

Questions: __?__ earth science ONLY   __?__ space science ONLY

3 THINK How can 12 + 11 + 9 = 22?

Some exhibits display 2 or 3 science topics. Fill in the overlapping areas. Subtract these from each total. Think:

$$[LS – \text{parts given in diagram}] = \underline{\ ?\ }$$

Then, from the *total* number of space science exhibits subtract to find the number that deal *only* with space.

Lastly, from the *total* number of earth science exhibits subtract the overlapping exhibits to find the number that deal only with earth science.

4 COMPUTE

LS 12   **ES 9**

$LS – (6 + 2 + 1) = \underline{\ ?\ }$ life and space
$12 – (6 + 2 + 1) = 3$ life and space ⎯⎯

6   2   3
1
3   3

$SS – (3 + 1 + 3) = \underline{\ ?\ }$ space science only
$11 – (3 + 1 + 3) = 4$ space science only ⎯⎯

4

SS 11

$ES – (2 + 1 + 3) = \underline{\ ?\ }$ earth only
$9 – (2 + 1 + 3) = 3$ earth only ⎯⎯

5 CHECK Do the numbers within all the areas of the Venn diagram add up to the total number of exhibitions?   Yes:

$$6 + 2 + 3 + 4 + 3 + 3 + 1 = 22$$

Do the numbers corresponding to each circle check? ⎯⎯→

12 (Life)	= 6 + 2 + 3 + 1
11 (Space)	= 3 + 1 + 3 + 4
9 (Earth)	= 3 + 3 + 1 + 2

All Check.

Solve by using diagrams.

1. Spin a dial once and then toss a coin twice.
   What is the probability that the result
   will be either heads or tails and 2 or 3?
   (Use a tree diagram to display the outcomes.)

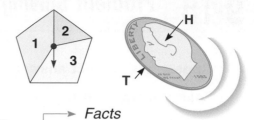

| **1 IMAGINE** | Draw a tree diagram. ⟶ | **2 NAME** | ⟶ Facts |
| | | | ⟶ Question |

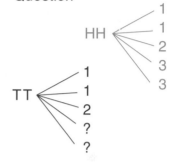

| **3 THINK** | Is spinning a 3 an *equally likely* outcome?
No, the dial must be divided
into 5 equal sections. Is tossing heads
an *equally likely* outcome? Yes, a coin
has 2 equal sides.

Use these and other tree diagrams
to find P [(H or T), (2 or 3)]. |

| **4 COMPUTE** ⟶ | **5 CHECK** |

2. Joel spent 20% of his monthly allowance on clothing, 50% on
   food, and the rest, $10.20, he saved. What did he spend on
   clothing? (Use a circle graph to solve.)

3. What is the probability of getting a product of 12 on a single
   toss of a pair of cubes numbered 1 through 6? (Use a tree diagram.)

4. Of 56 ecologists surveyed, 24 work on both air- and water-
   pollution problems, 32 work on water-pollution problems, and
   38 work on air-pollution problems. Of the ecologists surveyed, how
   many work on neither problem, but on endangered species instead?

5. There were 3 different courses offered by the art department of
   the local community college. How many students were enrolled
   in the art program if no students took all 3 courses, 15 took
   calligraphy, 15 took pottery, and 15 took painting? (Of the students
   in the art program, 6 took only painting, 7 took only calligraphy,
   and 4 took both pottery and painting.)

6. Use this frequency table to make a
   histogram displaying students' scores.
   What was the range, mean, median, and
   mode of the scores? What percent of
   these students scored 85 or more?

Test Scores of Students		
100 – IIII	88 – JHH I	76 – JHH
97 – III	85 – JHH JHH	73 – III
94 – JHH I	82 – II	71 – I
91 – IIII	79 – JHH III	70 – III

Choose the correct answer.

Toss a marker on this board.

1	3		5	6	8
2		4		7	

USE THESE STRATEGIES:
Use a Graph
Use a Model/Drawing
Write an Equation
Use a Diagram
Information From a Table
Multi-Step Problem

1. The outcomes of this event are: **a.** equally likely **b.** not equally likely **c.** can not tell

2. The probability of tossing an odd number is:
   a. $\frac{4}{8}$ **b.** $\frac{8}{16}$ **c.** $\frac{8}{12}$

3. The probability of tossing an integer is:
   a. 0   **b.** 1   **c.** $\frac{1}{16}$

4. P(a number greater than 8) is:
   a. 0   **b.** 1   **c.** $\frac{1}{12}$

Given 10 cards, 4 labeled "A," 3 labeled "B," and 3 labeled "C."

5. If a card is drawn, returned, and another is drawn, what is P(A, A)?
   a. $\frac{4}{25}$ **b.** $\frac{4}{10}$ **c.** $\frac{8}{20}$

6. If a card is drawn, not returned, and another is drawn, what is P(A, A)?
   a. $\frac{8}{20}$ **b.** $\frac{16}{100}$ **c.** $\frac{12}{90}$

7. If a card is drawn, not returned, and another is drawn, what is P(A, not B)?
   a. $\frac{28}{100}$ **b.** $\frac{24}{90}$ **c.** $\frac{11}{20}$

Solve.

8. There are 6 commuter rail lines leading into a city and 4 commuter rail lines leaving the city. What is the total number of different ways a commuter can go into and out of the city?

9. If two coins are tossed, what is the probability of getting a head and a tail?

10. The ages of 5 workers are 41, 27, 38, 40, 41. What is their median age?

11. An invitation can be made from 4 different colors of paper and 5 styles of printing. How many different invitations can be made?

12. In how many different ways can a secretary schedule the CEO to meet with 4 different committees on a given workday?

13. The probability of a hurricane striking a city is 0.6. What is the probability of this storm not striking the city?

14. The mean of 4 test scores is 89.5. What is the sum of the scores? If a fifth test score makes the mean 90, what was the score of the fifth test?

15. What is your prediction of the percent of any group of teenagers that could program a microcomputer?

Question:	Can you program a microcomputer?
Asked of:	345 teenagers
Answers:	Yes—115 No—230

16. A poll of 8th graders on their favorite pastime was recorded on this frequency table. Use the table to complete **a–d**.

   a. Construct a bar graph of the data.
   b. How many were polled?
   c. How many more enjoyed reading than games?
   d. How many fewer enjoyed dancing than sports?

Favorite Pastime	
Reading	ⅢⅠ ⅢⅠ I
Sports	ⅢⅠ ⅢⅠ ⅢⅠ II
Arts/Music	ⅢⅠ III
Dancing	IIII
Games	ⅢⅠ

17. Students were polled as to the type of literature they read most frequently. Use the circle graph to complete **a–c**.

   a. How many students were polled in all?
   b. What 2 types represent $\frac{1}{2}$ of the students polled?
   c. How many more students read biographies than classics?

Literature Types

Mystery $8\frac{1}{3}$%   35% Biography

40 Students

Science Fiction $8\frac{1}{3}$% Autobiography

15% Classics

18. Use the data and given intervals to complete the table. Then construct a histogram and complete exercises **a–d**.

   a. What is the range of the bowler's scores?
   b. What is the mode of the scores?
   c. What is the median of the scores?
   d. Within what interval do most of the scores lie?

Bowling Scores				
119	121	98	132	140
115	108	100	120	130
138	125	120	128	141
96	135	131	120	118

Interval	90–100	101–110	111–120	121–130	131–140	141–150
Frequency	3					

19. Students were asked to rate two books on a scale of 1 to 100. Use the box-and-whisker plots to complete exercises **a–c**.

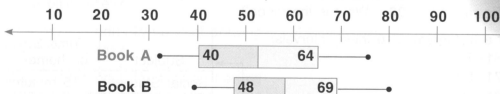

   a. Which book received the higher rating?
   b. The interquartile range for book A was 24. What is the interquartile range for book B?
   c. For which book was the median lower?

Check Your Mastery

A bag contains 6 marbles. One is blue, one red, one green, one yellow, one black, and one brown. Answer these questions.

See pp. 240–243

One card is chosen without looking. Find the probability.

1. $P(\text{red})$
2. $P(\text{not green})$
3. $P(\text{blue or black})$
4. $P(\text{white})$

One marble is chosen and replaced. Another marble is chosen. Find the probability.

5. $P(\text{yellow, green})$
6. $P(\text{black, black})$
7. $P(\text{pink, brown})$

One marble is chosen and *not* replaced. Another marble is chosen. Find the probability.

8. $P(\text{red, black})$
9. $P(\text{not blue, yellow})$
10. $P(\text{brown, green})$

Find the value of each factorial expression.

See pp. 244–245

11. $7! - 4!$
12. $(5 \cdot 2)!$
13. $9! + 2!$
14. $\dfrac{6!}{(6 - 4)!}$

Evaluate.

15. $_9P_5$
16. $_6P_2$
17. $_8C_3$
18. $_5C_2$

19. In a random sampling of 75 people, 60 said they drive to work. If the total number of 1275 employees were asked the same question, about how many would say they drive to work?

See pp. 246–247

20. Look at the circle graph. Complete the chart.

See pp. 254–255

Sales Report

Number of Items Sold

Items	Number	Percent	Degrees in Circle
shirts	3240	45%	?
socks	?	25%	90°
shoes	1440	20%	?
pants	720	?	36°
Totals	7200	100%	360°

See pp. 256–257

8 members of the track team ran in the town's festival 6-kilometer footrace.

21. Find the mean speed of the track team.

22. Find the median speed.

23. What is the mode?

24. Between whose times was the greatest difference?

Festival Footrace

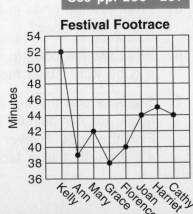

270

10 Geometry and Measurement

In this chapter you will:

- Work with basic geometric concepts
- Construct congruent angles and bisect an angle
- Determine congruency of triangles
- Work with customary and metric measures
- Work with precise measures and significant digits
- Work with parallel and perpendicular lines
- Solve problems: interpreting the remainder

Do you remember?

Right angle facts:

ray

right angle

Symbol means 90°

ray

right triangle

congruent right triangles

Time After Time

Who ever thought of clocks? See how far back you can trace the different ways people have determined time. How did the Egyptians do it? the Greeks? The Dutch had a unique way, so did the Japanese. Explain and illustrate your findings. Fascinate your friends by creating a *new* way to tell time.

10-4 Parallel and Intersecting Lines

Plane: a flat surface that extends indefinitely in all directions.

Parallel lines: lie in the same plane and *never* intersect.

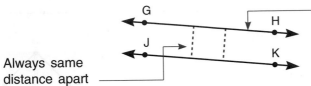

Line *GH* is parallel to line *JK*.
$$\overleftrightarrow{GH} \parallel \overleftrightarrow{JK}$$

Always same distance apart

Transversal: a line that intersects a pair of lines forming interior and exterior angles.

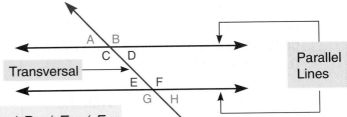

Transversal

Parallel Lines

Find these in this diagram:

interior angles:	$\angle C$, $\angle D$, $\angle E$, $\angle F$
exterior angles:	$\angle A$, $\angle B$, $\angle G$, $\angle H$
alternate interior angles:	$\angle D$ and $\angle E$
	$\angle C$ and $\angle F$
alternate exterior angles:	$\angle B$ and $\angle G$
	$\angle A$ and $\angle H$
corresponding angles:	$\angle A$ and $\angle E$, $\angle B$ and $\angle F$,
	$\angle C$ and $\angle G$, $\angle D$ and $\angle H$

Use this figure to name all the pairs of:

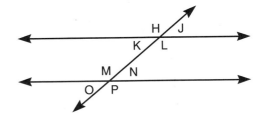

1. alternate interior angles.

2. alternate exterior angles.

3. corresponding angles.

Identify each pair of angles as alternate interior, alternate exterior, or corresponding angles.

4.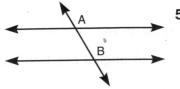

5.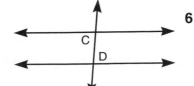

6.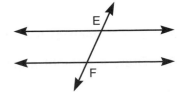

Vertical Angles and Adjacent Angles

Two kinds of angles are formed by the intersection of two lines: **vertical angles** and **adjacent angles**.

Vertical angles: have a common vertex but no common side; have the same measure and are congruent.

Adjacent angles: have *both* the vertex and one side in common.

∠2 and ∠4 are vertical angles. Name another pair.

∠1 and ∠2 are adjacent angles. Name 3 more pairs.

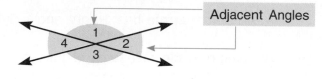

Intersecting lines that form right angles at their point of intersection are **perpendicular** to each other.

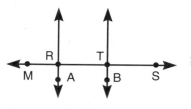

$$\overleftrightarrow{GH} \perp \overleftrightarrow{FJ}$$

For this figure where $\overleftrightarrow{RA} \perp \overleftrightarrow{MS}$ and $\overleftrightarrow{TB} \perp \overleftrightarrow{MS}$:

7. Name the transversal.   8. Which lines are parallel?

9. What kinds of angles are ∠MRA and ∠RTB?

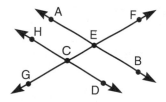

For this figure where $\overleftrightarrow{AB} \parallel \overleftrightarrow{HD}$:

10. Name the transversal.   11. Name two pairs of vertical angles.

12. Name four pairs of adjacent angles.

13. Name alternate interior angles.

14. Name alternate exterior angles.

15. Name corresponding angles.

 A NEW LOOK SUPPOSE THAT...

∠*HCE* measures 120°. What is the measure of:

16. ∠*CEB*?   17. ∠*HCG*?   18. ∠*AEF*?   19. ∠*FEB*?

 CHALLENGE

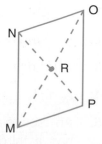

20. In parallelogram *MNOP* how many congruent angles can you name? Prove that they are congruent, using what you have learned about parallel lines, intersecting lines, and transversals.

10-5 Classifying Triangles

Triangles may be classified:

- According to the measures of their angles.

  An **acute triangle** has 3 acute angles.

  An **obtuse triangle** has 1 obtuse angle.

  A **right triangle** has 1 right angle (90°).

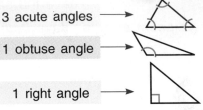

3 acute angles →

1 obtuse angle →

1 right angle →

- According to the measures of their sides.

  An **equilateral triangle** has 3 congruent sides and 3 congruent angles.

  An **isosceles triangle** has 2 congruent sides and 2 congruent angles.

  A **scalene triangle** has no congruent sides and *no* congruent angles.

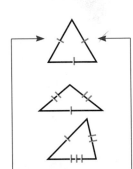

The marks indicate which sides are congruent.

The sum of the measures of the angles of a triangle is equal to 180°. To show that the sum is 180°:

- Draw a triangle and color each angle differently.

- Cut out the angles and arrange them along a straight angle.

- Since the measure of a straight angle is 180°, the sum of the measures of the angles is also 180°.

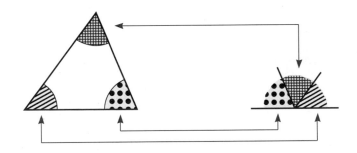

True or false? Explain.

1. A right triangle cannot be equilateral.

2. A triangle with an angle of 110° is acute.

3. A triangle with sides that measure 6 in., 7 in., and 8 in. is scalene.

4. A right triangle is always scalene.

5. An isosceles triangle with two angles that each has a measure of 40° has a third angle that has a measure of 90°.

Copy and complete the missing measures for each triangle.
Classify the triangle.

	Type of Triangle	∠a	∠b	∠c
6.	?	30°	65°	?
7.	right	40°	?	?
8.	?	5°	?	13°
9.	?	17°	40°	?
10.	?	89°	1°	?

	Type of Triangle	∠a	∠b	∠c
11.	?	60°	60°	?
12.	?	105°	13°	?
13.	right	30°	?	?
14.	?	11°	100°	?
15.	?	32°	140°	?

16. Use a protractor and straightedge to draw each of the triangles in exercises 6–15. Then classify each triangle according to the measures of its sides.

In this diagram two parallel lines are crossed by two transversals. Use the diagram to complete exercises 17–31.

17. ∠8 is congruent to __?__ because they are vertical angles.

18. ∠8 is congruent to __?__ because they are alternate interior angles.

19. The sum of the measures of ∠8, ∠5, and ∠11 is __?__ because __?__ .

20. The sum of the measures of ∠6, ∠5, and ∠4 is __?__ because __?__ .

21. The sum of the measures of ∠1, ∠2, ∠3, ∠4, ∠5 and ∠6 is __?__ .

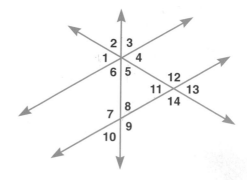

22. ∠3 and ∠__?__ are vertical angles.

23. m ∠1 + m ∠2 + m ∠3 = __?__

24. ∠3 and ∠__?__ are adjacent angles.

25. m ∠7 + m ∠8 = __?__

26. ∠4 and ∠__?__ are alternate interior angles.

27. m ∠7 + m ∠6 = __?__

28. ∠1 and ∠__?__ are alternate exterior angles.

29. m ∠1 + m ∠12 = __?__

30. ∠11 and ∠__?__ are corresponding angles.

31. m ∠1 + m ∠5 + m ∠3 = __?__

CRITICAL **THINKING**

32. The measure of ∠A is twice the measure of ∠B. If the measure of ∠C = 80°, what are the measures of ∠A and ∠B?

281

10-6 Congruent Triangles

Congruent triangles have exactly the same size and shape.
Their *corresponding angles* and *sides* are congruent.

The marks indicate which sides of each triangle correspond
to the sides of the other, and which angles of each triangle
correspond to the angles of the other.

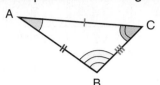
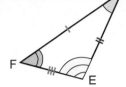

$\angle A \cong \angle D$ $\overline{CA} \cong \overline{FD}$
$\angle C \cong \angle F$ and $\overline{AB} \cong \overline{DE}$
$\angle B \cong \angle E$ $\overline{BC} \cong \overline{EF}$

So, $\triangle ABC \cong \triangle DEF$

Triangles can be shown to be congruent when less
information about corresponding sides and angles is available.

Follow these three rules:

Side-Side-Side (SSS)	Side-Angle-Side (SAS)	Angle-Side-Angle (ASA)
If all 3 corresponding sides of both triangles are congruent, the triangles are congruent.	If 2 corresponding sides and the included angle of both triangles are congruent, the triangles are congruent.	If 2 corresponding angles and the included side of both triangles are congruent, the triangles are congruent.
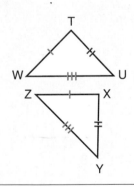	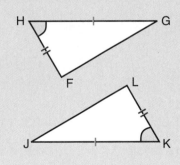	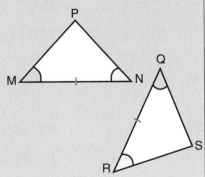

Complete for these congruent triangles.

1. $\overline{BC} \cong$ ___?___   4. $\angle D \cong$ ___?___

2. ___?___ $\cong \overline{EF}$ 5. $\angle B \cong$ ___?___

3. ___?___ $\cong \overline{DF}$ 6. $\angle F \cong$ ___?___

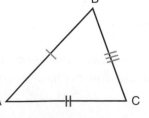
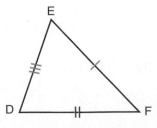

For exercises 7–10, use the triangles on page 282 and the congruent triangle rules.

7. Measure the angles opposite the congruent sides
   of triangles *TUW* and *XYZ*.

   Is $\angle T \cong \angle X$?   Is $\angle U \cong \angle Y$?   Is $\angle W \cong \angle Z$?

8. Try to draw a triangle that has sides of the same length as the sides
   of triangles *TUW* and *XYZ*, but is *not* congruent to these triangles.

9. Look at triangles *GHF* and *JKL*.
   Construct a line segment congruent to $\overline{HG}$ and $\overline{JK}$.

   Construct an angle congruent to $\angle H$ and $\angle K$ at either end
   of the line segment. Then mark off the length of $\overline{HF}$ and $\overline{KL}$
   as the second side of the triangle. Draw the third side.
   Is this triangle congruent to triangles *GHF* and *JKL*?

10. Look at triangles *MNP* and *QRS*.
    Construct a line segment congruent to $\overline{MN}$ and $\overline{RQ}$.

    Construct an angle congruent to $\angle M$ and $\angle Q$ on one end,
    and an angle congruent to $\angle N$ and $\angle R$ on the other end.
    Is the triangle congruent to triangles *MNP* and *QRS*?

Tell which rule, *SSS* or *ASA* or *SAS*, states why the pairs of triangles are congruent.

11.

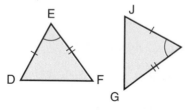

12.

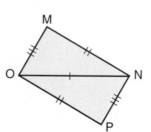

13.

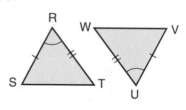

14.

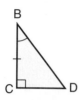

15.

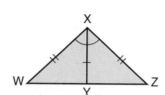

16.

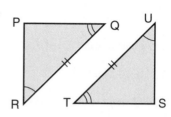

SKILLS TO REMEMBER

Write the standard numeral.

17. 3.5×10^{-3}

18. 410×10^{-2}

19. 0.6×10^{-4}

20. $1.8 \div 10^3$

21. $200 \div 10^4$

22. $0.31 \div 10^2$

It is often necessary to convert from one unit of measure to another.

The chart shows some of the relationships between customary units.

Length	Weight
1 foot (ft) = 12 inches (in.)	1 pound (lb) = 16 ounces (oz)
1 yard (yd) = 3 ft or 36 in.	1 ton (T) = 2000 lb
1 mile (mi) = 1760 yd or 5280 ft	

Capacity

1 cup (c) = 8 fluid ounces (fl oz)

1 pint (pt) = 2 c = 16 fl oz

1 quart (qt) = 2 pt = 4 c = 32 fl oz

1 gallon (gal) = 4 qt = 8 pt = 16 c

The office is $4\frac{2}{3}$ yd long.

How many feet long is the office?

$$4\frac{2}{3} \text{ yd} = \underline{\ ?\ } \text{ ft}$$

1 yd = 3 ft, so *multiply* by 3.

$$4\frac{2}{3} \text{ yd} \times 3 \text{ ft} = 14 \text{ ft}$$

The desk is 75 in. long.

How many feet long is the desk?

$$75 \text{ in.} = \underline{\ ?\ } \text{ ft} \underline{\ ?\ } \text{ in.}$$

12 in. = 1 ft, so *divide* by 12.

$$75 \text{ in.} \div 12 \text{ in.} = 6 \text{ ft } 3 \text{ in.} = 6\frac{1}{4} \text{ ft}$$

Remember: ′ means feet **and** ″ means inches.

Copy and complete.

1. 2 yd = $\underline{\ ?\ }$ ft

2. 3 lb = $\underline{\ ?\ }$ oz

3. 10 qt = $\underline{\ ?\ }$ c

4. 2 mi = $\underline{\ ?\ }$ yd

5. $2\frac{1}{2}$ gal = $\underline{\ ?\ }$ pt

6. $3\frac{1}{4}$ ft = $\underline{\ ?\ }$ in.

7. 60 in. = $\underline{\ ?\ }$ ft

8. 128 fl oz = $\underline{\ ?\ }$ qt

9. 5 ft = $\underline{\ ?\ }$ yd

10. 40 oz = $\underline{\ ?\ }$ lb

11. 1 mi = $\underline{\ ?\ }$ in.

12. 880 yd = $\underline{\ ?\ }$ mi

13. 2 yd 2 ft = $\underline{\ ?\ }$ in.

14. 2 gal 3 qt = $\underline{\ ?\ }$ pt

15. 6′1″ = $\underline{\ ?\ }$ in.

16. 4′11″ = $\underline{\ ?\ }$ in.

17. 3 qt 3 pt 1 c = $\underline{\ ?\ }$ fl oz

18. 1 yd 8 ft 5 in. $\underline{\ ?\ }$ in.

19. 1.5 mi = $\underline{\ ?\ }$ yd

20. 2.5 T = $\underline{\ ?\ }$ lb

21. 112 oz = $\underline{\ ?\ }$ lb

Computing and Regrouping Measures

To *add or subtract* customary units:

- Add or subtract *like* units.
- Regroup to change from one unit to another.

$$
\begin{array}{r}
7 \text{ gal } 3 \text{ qt} \\
+ 2 \text{ gal } 6 \text{ qt} \\
\hline
9 \text{ gal } 9 \text{ qt} = 2 \text{ gal } 1 \text{ qt}
\end{array}
$$

↑ Regroup ↑

9 gal + 2 gal 1 qt
= 11 gal 1 qt

$$
\begin{array}{r}
\overset{4}{5} \text{ yd } \overset{12+5}{\cancel{5}} \text{ ft } \overset{17}{\cancel{5}} \text{ in.} \\
- 2 \text{ yd } 3 \text{ ft } 8 \text{ in.} \\
\hline
3 \text{ yd } 1 \text{ ft } 9 \text{ in.}
\end{array}
$$

= 3 yd 1 ft 9 in.

Regroup 5 ft 5 in. to 4 ft 17 in.

To *multiply* with customary units:

- Multiply *each* unit.
- Regroup to change from one unit to another.

$$
\begin{array}{r}
6 \text{ lb } 12 \text{ oz} \\
\times \quad 3 \\
\hline
18 \text{ lb } 36 \text{ oz}
\end{array}
$$

18 lb + 2 lb 4 oz
= 20 lb 4 oz

Divide 324 oz by 16 for regrouping.

OR

- Change all units to *like* units.
- Multiply; then regroup.

OR

6 lb 12 oz is same as 96 oz + 12 oz = 108 oz
× 3   × 3   × 3

324 oz = 20 lb 4 oz

To *divide* with customary units:

- Change all units to *like* units.
- Divide.
- Then regroup.

Regroup each to inches.

1 yd   1 ft   8 in. ÷ 4

36 in. + 12 in. + 8 in. ÷ 4

Regroup to ft and in.

= 56 in. ÷ 4 = 14 in. = 1 ft 2 in.

Regroup.

22. 65 in. = ___?___ ft ___?___ in.   **23.** 28 ft = ___?___ yd ___?___ in.   **24.** 9 fl oz = ___?___ c ___?___ fl oz

25. 1 mi 240 yd = ___?___ yd   **26.** 5 ft 4 in. = ___?___ in.   **27.** 2 T 50 lb = ___?___ lb

Compute.

28.
$$
\begin{array}{r}
3 \text{ yd } 2 \text{ ft} \\
+ 1 \text{ yd } 2 \text{ ft} \\
\hline
\end{array}
$$

29.
$$
\begin{array}{r}
6 \text{ ft } 9 \text{ in.} \\
+ 2 \text{ ft } 3 \text{ in.} \\
\hline
\end{array}
$$

30.
$$
\begin{array}{r}
4 \text{ gal } 3 \text{ qt} \\
+ 3 \text{ gal } 6 \text{ qt} \\
\hline
\end{array}
$$

31.
$$
\begin{array}{r}
3 \text{ qt } 1 \text{ c} \\
- \quad 6 \text{ c} \\
\hline
\end{array}
$$

32.
$$
\begin{array}{r}
8 \text{ lb } 7 \text{ oz} \\
- 2 \text{ lb } 9 \text{ oz} \\
\hline
\end{array}
$$

33.
$$
\begin{array}{r}
3 \text{ c } 6 \text{ fl oz} \\
- \quad 10 \text{ fl oz} \\
\hline
\end{array}
$$

34.
$$
\begin{array}{r}
1 \text{ mi } 200 \text{ ft} \\
- \quad 780 \text{ ft} \\
\hline
\end{array}
$$

35.
$$
\begin{array}{r}
12 \text{ ft } 2 \text{ in.} \\
- 9 \text{ ft } 9 \text{ in.} \\
\hline
\end{array}
$$

36. 5(3 ft 10 in.)   **37.** 4(1 gal 3 qt)   **38.** 8(1 T 600 lb)

39. (2 gal 3 c) ÷ 5   **40.** (4 mi 60 yd) ÷ 50   **41.** (20 lb 8 oz) ÷ 8

10-8 | Metric Units of Length

Meter: the basic unit of length used in the metric system. All other units are related to the meter by powers of 10.

On the metric place-value chart, each unit is 10 times the unit directly to its right.

thousands	hundreds	tens	ones	tenths	hundredths	thousandths
kilometer (km)	hectometer (hm)	dekameter (dam)	**meter (m)**	decimeter (dm)	centimeter (cm)	millimeter (mm)
1000 m	100 m	10 m	1 m	0.1 m	0.01 m	0.001 m

Kilometer, meter, centimeter, and millimeter are the units most commonly used.

Use a metric ruler to find the measure of $\overline{AB}$ to the nearest centimeter and the nearest millimeter.

The length of $\overline{AB}$ to the nearest centimeter is 2 cm.

The length of $\overline{AB}$ to the nearest millimeter is 22 mm.

Choose the most reasonable measurement.

		a.	**b.**	**c.**
1.	length of a pencil	14 cm	1.4 cm	140 cm
2.	width of a pinpoint	1 mm	10 mm	0.01 m
3.	height of a mountain	8.8 mm	8.8 cm	8.8 km
4.	length of a toothbrush	15 mm	15 cm	15 m
5.	thickness of 10 sheets of paper	1 mm	10 mm	10 cm
6.	length of a baseball bat	11 m	0.1 m	1.1 m
7.	width of a dollar bill	6.5 m	6.5 mm	6.5 cm
8.	distance from home to school	1 m	1 km	1 cm
9.	height of a soup can	10 cm	10 m	10 mm
10.	height of an adult	165 m	165 mm	165 cm

Draw a line segment showing each of the measures below.

11. 25 mm   **12.** 91 mm   **13.** 56 mm

14. 77 mm   **15.** 8 cm   **16.** 20 cm

17. 2.5 cm   **18.** 9.1 cm   **19.** 0.5 cm

Measure each line segment. Give its length to the nearest centimeter.

20. ●————————●   **21.** ●————————●

22. ●————————●   **23.** ●——●

Express the length of each line segment to the nearest millimeter.

24. ●————————————●   **25.** ●———————●

26. ●————————————●   **27.** ●———————●

Choose the most reasonable unit of measure.

    a. km   **b.** m   **c.** cm   **d.** mm

28. Which unit would you use to measure the distance between Dallas and San Francisco?

29. Which unit would you use to measure the length of a key?

30. Which unit would you use to measure the height of a three-story building?

31. Which unit would you use to measure the thickness of a piece of cardboard?

32. Which unit would you use to measure the depth of an ocean?

33. Which unit would you use to measure the width of a leather belt?

 **Finding Together**   Look up these prefixes used in the metric system. Write the meaning of each.

34. tera–   **35.** giga–   **36.** mega–

37. micro–   **38.** nano–   **39.** pico–

10-9 Changing Metric Units

Changing one unit of length to another unit of length always involves multiplying or dividing by a multiple of ten.

kilometer	hectometer	dekameter	meter	decimeter	centimeter	millimeter
(km)	(hm)	(dam)	(m)	(dm)	(cm)	(mm)
1000 m	100 m	10 m	1m	0.1 m	0.01 m	0.001 m

To change one metric unit to another, multiply.

$$7.4 \text{ m} = \underline{\ ?\ } \text{ dm}$$
$$1 \text{ m} = 10 \text{ dm}$$
$$\text{So } 7.4 \text{ m} = (7.4 \times 10) \text{ dm}$$
$$7.4 \text{ m} = 74 \text{ dm}$$

Here are some other examples.

$22 \text{ km} = \underline{\ ?\ } \text{ m}$	$3.5 \text{ cm} = \underline{\ ?\ } \text{ m}$	$6 \text{ mm} = \underline{\ ?\ } \text{ cm}$
$1 \text{ km} = 1000 \text{ m}$	$1 \text{ cm} = 0.01 \text{ m}$	$1 \text{ mm} = 0.1 \text{ cm}$
$22 \text{ km} = (22 \times 1000) \text{ m}$	$3.5 \text{ cm} = (3.5 \times 0.01) \text{ m}$	$6 \text{ mm} = (6 \times 0.1) \text{ cm}$
$22 \text{ km} = 22\ 000 \text{ m}$	$3.5 \text{ cm} = 0.035 \text{ m}$	$6 \text{ mm} = 0.6 \text{ cm}$

To change smaller units to larger ones, *divide* by 10 for every place moved to the *left.*

To change larger units to smaller ones, *multiply* by 10 for every place moved to the *right.*

Copy and complete the chart so that each row shows equivalent measurements.

	kilometer	hectometer	dekameter	meter	decimeter	centimeter	millimeter
1.	0.008	?	?	8	?	800	?
2.	?	0.41	?	41	?	?	41 000
3.	?	?	?	?	?	207	?
4.	?	?	?	0.33	?	?	?
5.	?	49	?	?	?	?	?
6.	?	?	?	?	88.1	?	?
7.	?	?	0.5	?	?	?	?

Shortcut for Converting Metric Units

Use the metric place-value chart to change units with this shortcut.

kilometer	hectometer	dekameter	meter	decimeter	centimeter	millimeter

19 km = __?__ m
Move the decimal point
3 places to the right.

19.000 km = 19 000 m

6.3 cm = __?__ m
Move the decimal point
2 places to the left.

06.3 cm = 0.063 m

Copy and complete.

8. 18 m = __?__ cm

9. 5 km = __?__ m

10. 0.6 m = __?__ cm

11. 0.03 cm = __?__ mm

12. 127 mm = __?__ cm

13. 42 m = __?__ km

14. 6000 cm = __?__ m

15. 50 mm = __?__ m

16. 12 dm = __?__ m

17. 12 dam = __?__ m

18. 150 km = __?__ m

19. 20 m = __?__ mm

20. 400 m = __?__ cm

21. 5.3 m = __?__ km

22. 2.7 km = __?__ dam

23. 2.7 km = __?__ dm

24. 3 mm = __?__ km

25. 42 hm = __?__ m

26. 36 cm = __?__ hm

27. 4016 cm = __?__ km

28. 290 mm = __?__ m

In each row which measure is not equivalent?

29. 5.1 m   **a.** 0.051 km   **b.** 510 cm   **c.** 5100 mm

30. 2000 mm   **a.** 200 cm   **b.** 20 m   **c.** 0.002 km

31. 52.9 cm   **a.** 5.29 mm   **b.** 0.529 m   **c.** 0.0529 dam

32. 45 000 m   **a.** 45 km   **b.** 4500 dam   **c.** 450 000 cm

33. 325 dm   **a.** 32.5 m   **b.** 0.325 hm   **c.** 3250 dam

34. 6.4 km   **a.** 0.64 dam   **b.** 6400 m   **c.** 64 hm

Express each measure as a single unit in two different ways.
(The first one is done.)

35. 5 m 6 cm 7 mm ⟶ 5.067 m or 5067 mm

36. 3 dm 8 cm

37. 7 km 4 m

38. 6 m 15 dm 12 cm

39. 12 m 15 cm 27 mm

40. 2 dm 5 cm 9 mm

41. 4 cm 21 mm

42. 9 dam 8 m 3 dm

43. 5 km 8 m 3 cm

44. 4 km 30 hm 36 m

Compare. Write <, =, or >.

45. 3.2 m __?__ 32 cm

46. 180.4 mm __?__ 1.804 dam

47. 0.16 km __?__ 16 m

48. 0.2 hm __?__ 20 cm

49. 45.1 dm __?__ 4510 dam

50. 180 cm __?__ 18 dm

Precision in Measurement

All measurements are approximations and can only be as precise as the measuring instrument that is used.

Celia and Stanley both kept a record of the growth of the same lima bean plant for a science assignment. Five days after germination, they recorded their results. Compare them.

Celia: 4 cm

Stanley: 44 mm

Both measurements are correct, but Stanley used the smaller unit.

The smaller the unit of measure, the more precise the measurement.

Greatest possible error (GPE) of any measurement: one half of the unit of measure.

Range, or **interval, of measure:** the given measure plus or minus (±) the greatest possible error.

Celia's measurement is correct to within one half of a centimeter. This is written as 4 ± 0.5 cm.

Stanley's measurement is correct to within one half of a millimeter. This is written as 44 ± 0.5 mm.

Name the more precise measurement.

1. 9.2 m or 92.1 cm

2. 2 yd or 6 ft

3. 2 m or 199 cm

4. 5000 ft or 1 mi

5. 10 km or 11 000 m

6. $6\frac{1}{2}$ c or $1\frac{1}{2}$ qt

Arrange in order from least precise to most precise.

7. foot
mile
inch
yard

8. centigram
milligram
kilogram
gram

9. week
day
month
minute
second

10. cup
quart
ounce
pint
gallon

11. 0.1 m 1 m 0.01 m 0.001 m	**12.** $\frac{1}{2}$ in. 1 in. $\frac{1}{4}$ in.	**13.** 1 km 0.1 km 1 m 0.01 km	**14.** 0.001 kg 1 kg 0.1 kg 0.01 kg

Copy and complete this chart.

	Measure	Unit	GPE	Range of Measure
15.	36 cm	1 cm	?	36 ± 0.5 cm
16.	6 in.	1 in.	$\frac{1}{2}$ in.	6 ± ? in.
17.	4.6 cm	0.1 cm	0.05 cm	4.6 ± ? cm
18.	28 mi	1 mi	?	?
19.	7 m	?	?	?
20.	14.3 cm	?	?	?
21.	0.6 mm	?	?	?

Lisa and Frank measured a seedling's growth for one week in April.

Lisa
Monday   3 cm
Tuesday   0 cm
Wednesday 1 cm
Thursday   2 cm
Friday   2 cm
Saturday   0 cm
Sunday   0 cm

Frank
Monday   31 mm
Tuesday   0 mm
Wednesday   6 mm
Thursday   17 mm
Friday   21 mm
Saturday   3 mm
Sunday   0 mm

22. Whose measurements are more precise, Lisa's or Frank's?

23. What is the greatest possible error of Lisa's measurements?

24. What is the greatest possible error of Frank's measurements?

25. What is the interval of measure for Lisa's Thursday reading?

26. What is the interval of measure for Frank's Wednesday reading?

Name the more precise measurement.

27. 0.3 cm or 0.32 cm	**28.** 0.7 m or 0.75 m	**29.** 15 m or 14.8 m
30. 66.7 km or 55.73 km	**31.** 59 m or 59.02 m	**32.** 85 km or 84.92 km
33. 42.7 cm or 427 mm	**34.** 15 m or 148 dm	**35.** 33 mm or 3 cm
36. 7.2 m or 721 cm	**37.** 3 km or 3150 m	**38.** 52 cm or 600 mm

CHALLENGE

How old are you:

39. in years?   **40.** in months?   **41.** in days?   **42.** in hours?

Temperature

Compare the Celsius and Fahrenheit temperature scales.

▶ **How they are alike:**

- They are both based on the same reference points.

  The boiling point of water: (100°C)   (212°F)
  The freezing point of water: (0°C)   (32°F)

▶ **How they are different:**

- The Celsius scale divides the difference between reference points into 100 units, called degrees Celsius (°C).

- The Fahrenheit scale divides the difference into 180 units, called degrees Fahrenheit (°F).

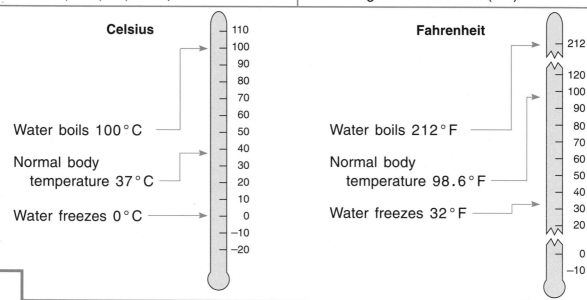

Celsius

Water boils 100°C

Normal body temperature 37°C

Water freezes 0°C

Fahrenheit

Water boils 212°F

Normal body temperature 98.6°F

Water freezes 32°F

Which is the most reasonable temperature?

1. hot oven
   a. 100°C   **b.** 90°C   **c.** 200°C   **d.** 1000°C

2. hot radiator
   a. 40°F   **b.** 90°F   **c.** 200°F   **d.** 1000°F

3. inside a freezer
   a. 50°C   **b.** ⁻5°C   **c.** 32°C   **d.** 15°C

4. sled-riding weather
   a. 100°F   **b.** 80°F   **c.** 50°F   **d.** 10°F

5. high body temperature
   a. 35°C   **b.** 39°C   **c.** 98°C   **d.** 100°C

Converting Temperatures From One Scale to Another

To convert from Fahrenheit to Celsius, use this formula:

$$C = \frac{5}{9}(F - 32)$$

Express 68°F in degrees Celsius.

$$C = \frac{5}{9}(F - 32)$$

$$C = \frac{5}{9}(68 - 32)$$

$$C = \frac{5}{9}(36) \longrightarrow 20°C$$

So, 68°F = 20°C

To convert from Celsius to Fahrenheit, use this formula:

$$F = \frac{9}{5}C + 32$$

Express 45°C in degrees Fahrenheit.

$$F = \frac{9}{5}C + 32$$

$$F = \left(\frac{9}{5} \times 45\right) + 32$$

$$F = 81 + 32 \longrightarrow 113°F$$

So, 45°C = 113°F

Convert these Fahrenheit temperatures to Celsius temperatures.

6. 32°F   **7.** 77°F   **8.** 131°F   **9.** ⁻4°F   **10.** 86°F

11. 65°F   **12.** 98°F   **13.** 50°F   **14.** ⁻10°F   **15.** 26°F

Convert these Celsius temperatures to Fahrenheit temperatures.

16. 10°C   **17.** 25°C   **18.** 100°C   **19.** ⁻10°C   **20.** ⁻5°C

21. 37°C   **22.** 24°C   **23.** 0°C   **24.** 90°C   **25.** ⁻4°C

Finding Together

26. Keep a record of the temperature in your classroom for one month. Use degrees Celsius. If your thermometer is marked in degrees Fahrenheit, use the formula to change to degrees Celsius.

27. Keep a record of the temperature outdoors for one month. Always measure at the same time and at the same site. Use degrees Celsius. If your thermometer measures degrees Fahrenheit, use the formula to change to degrees Celsius.

28. Use your data from exercise 27 to make a graph. Put the temperature on the vertical axis and the dates on the horizontal axis.

STRATEGY

Problem Solving: Interpreting the Remainder

Problem: Paul's Pizzeria makes pizzas that are cut into 9 slices. Nora is having a party for her soccer teammates and knows that each person will eat 4 slices. If there are 21 on the team, how many of Paul's pizzas must Nora order?

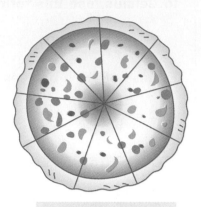

1 IMAGINE Draw and label a picture of this problem.

2 NAME
Facts: 1 pizza — 9 slices
1 person — 4 slices
21 people — team

Question: How many pizzas must Nora order?

> 1 pie = 9 slices
> 1 person = 4 slices
> 21 people = team

3 THINK
How many slices of pizza will be needed for 21 persons to eat 4 slices each?

number of slices needed	÷	9 slices in each pizza	=	number of pizzas
(21 × 4)	÷	9	=	?

But you know that (21 × 4) cannot be exactly divided by 9!
[Hint: (21 × 4) = 3 × 7 × 2 × 2, and none of these factors can be divided by 9.]

4 COMPUTE $(21 \times 4) \div 9 = 84 \div 9 = 9.3333\ldots.$ or $9.\overline{3}$ or $9\frac{1}{3}$.

Think: Can Nora order $\frac{1}{3}$ of a pizza? No!

In problems of this type, take time to interpret the remainder. If Nora rounds the quotient to 9 and orders that many pizzas, will there be enough? No, Nora must round *up* and order 10 pizzas!

5 CHECK 10 pizzas × 9 slices = 90 slices

Since there are 84 or (21 × 4) slices needed, there will be enough food if Nora orders 10 pizzas.

$$
\begin{array}{r}
4 \ R6 \\
\text{or } 21\overline{)\ 90} \text{ slices} \\
-84 \\
\hline
6
\end{array}
$$

→ 4 slices each and 6 extra slices

Solve by interpreting the remainder.

1. The athletic director needs to hire buses to transport 260 students to the championship football game. If the bus company has available buses that each seat 49 passengers, how many buses should be hired?

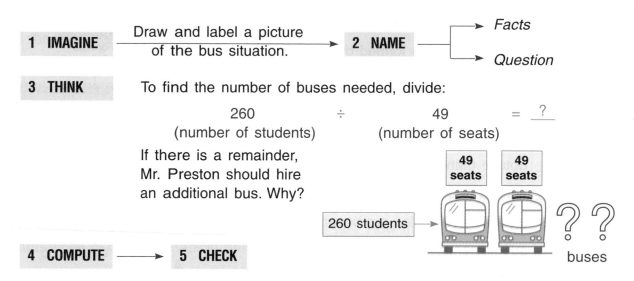

1 IMAGINE — Draw and label a picture of the bus situation. → **2 NAME** — Facts / Question

3 THINK — To find the number of buses needed, divide:

260   ÷   49   = <u>?</u>
(number of students)   (number of seats)

If there is a remainder, Mr. Preston should hire an additional bus. Why?

49 seats   49 seats

260 students

buses

4 COMPUTE ⟶ **5 CHECK**

2. The color guard needs new flags. Each flag uses 2 square yards of blue material and 1 square yard of white material. After buying 16 square yards of blue material and 10 square yards of white material, 9 square yards of blue material and 3 square yards of white material were found in the store room. How many new flags can be made? How much of each color is left?

3. Mr. Snell is planning the awards banquet. He knows that 14 guests will sit at the head table and that at each round table 8 guests may be seated. How many tables should he set up if 185 people have said they will attend? If four more persons send in their acceptances late, will he still have enough seats?

4. A coach orders letters to be given out at the awards banquet. Six track stars, 15 football players, 7 cheerleaders, and 3 basketball players are to be presented with letters. If a half-dozen letters are in each box, how many boxes should the coach order? If each box costs $13.50, what is the total cost?

5. The students sold cookies to raise funds for new cheerleading outfits. The students received $4.25 for each full carton they sold, but only $.15 for each pack of cookies when a full carton was not sold. There were 24 packs in each carton. How much money did the students earn if they sold 395 packs of cookies?

6. Tony decided to make pennants and sell them to his classmates. The dowel sticks cost $18.29, the fabric cost $21.45, and the glue cost $2.19. If he was able to make 27 pennants with these materials, what should he charge his classmates to completely cover the cost of the materials?

11-4 | Area of Trapezoids and Mixed Polygons

To find the **area of a trapezoid,**
think about two congruent trapezoids
placed as shown to make a parallelogram.
The height is the same as that of the trapezoid.
The base of the parallelogram is the
sum of the 2 bases of the trapezoid ($b_1 + b_2$).

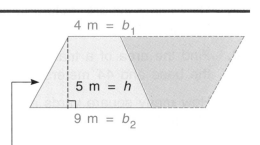

The area of the trapezoid is one half ——→
of the area of this parallelogram.

Formula: $A = \frac{1}{2}(b_1 + b_2)h$

$A = \frac{1}{2}(b_1 + b_2)h$

$A = \frac{1}{2}(4 + 9)5$

$A = \frac{1}{2} \times 13 \times 5$

$A = 32.5 \text{ m}^2$

Find the area of each trapezoid. Write the area in the unit of measure indicated.

1. bases: 5 cm, 7 cm
   height: 3 cm
   Area: __?__ cm^2

2. bases: 11 m, 17 m
   height: 7 m
   Area: __?__ m^2

3. bases: 10 dm, 6 dm
   height: 9.4 dm
   Area: __?__ dm^2

4. bases: 18.6 cm, 11.4 cm
   height: 8 cm
   Area: __?__ cm^2

5. bases: 1.4 m, 2.2 m
   height: 640 cm
   Area: __?__ cm^2

6. bases: 32 mm, 40 mm
   height: 16 cm
   Area: __?__ cm^2

7.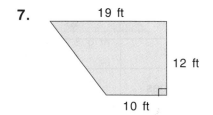

8.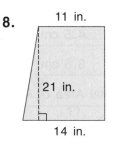

9.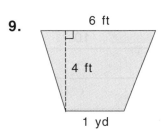

Solve.

10. The end of a barn roof is shaped like a trapezoid. What is its area
    if the sum of the bases is 18 meters and the altitude is 3 meters?

11. A signboard shaped like a trapezoid has an upper base of 290 cm,
    a lower base of 310 cm, and a height of 250 cm. Find the area
    in square meters.

Use the correct formula to find the area.

12.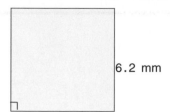
6.2 mm

13.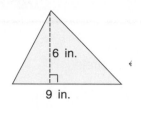
6 in.
9 in.

14.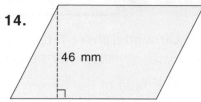
72 mm
46 mm

15.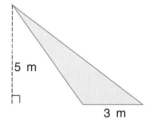
5 m
3 m

16.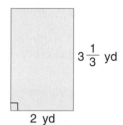
$3\frac{1}{3}$ yd
2 yd

17.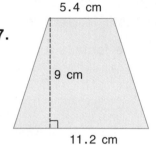
5.4 cm
9 cm
11.2 cm

Solve.

18. How many square meters of floor space are there in a room 9.6 meters on each side?

19. A playground is in the shape of a trapezoid. If the lower base is 38 yd, the upper base 70 yd, and the height $65\frac{1}{2}$ yd, what is the area of the playground?

20. A carpenter had a piece of plywood in the shape of a parallelogram, with a base of 30 in. and a height of $24\frac{1}{2}$ in. How many square inches is that?

21. What is the difference in the area of a triangle with a base of 16 cm and a height of 18 cm and the area of a parallelogram with a base of 12 cm and a height of 10 cm?

22. How many square yards of plastic will be needed to cover the top of a table that is shaped like a trapezoid, with an upper base of 6 feet, a lower base of 7 feet, and a height of 4 feet?

23. A triangular plot of land has a base of 400 m and a height of 550 m. Find the cost of buying this land at $15,000 per hectare.

24. What will it cost to paint the floor of a room 25 feet by 14 feet at $10.50 per gallon? (Allow 1 gallon of paint to 500 square feet.)

25. The sides of the foundation of a monument are in the shape of four trapezoids. In each trapezoid the bases are 5 m and 4 m and the height is 204 cm. Find the total area of the trapezoids.

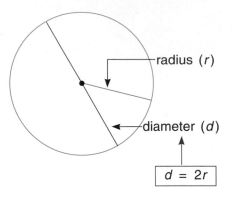

11-5 Circumference

Circumference: the distance around, or perimeter of, a circle.

The *ratio* of the circumference to the diameter of any circle is a constant value, π. (This is a Greek letter called "pi.")

$d = 2r$

The formula for the circumference of a circle is:

$$C = \pi d \text{ or } C = 2\pi r$$

diameter   radius

The approximate value of π is expressed as the decimal 3.14 or as the fraction $\frac{22}{7}$.

$$\pi \approx 3.14 \text{ or } \pi \approx \frac{22}{7}$$

If the diameter is 6 cm:

$C = \pi d$

$C = \pi 6$

$C \approx 3.14 \times 6$

$C \approx 18.84$ cm

If the radius is 21 m:

$C = 2\pi r$

$C = 2\pi 21$

$C \approx 2 \times \frac{22}{7} \times 21$

$C \approx 132$ m

Find the circumference.

1. $d = 22$ cm
2. $d = 8$ m
3. $d = 2.8$ m
4. $d = 4.2$ km

5. $r = 7$ cm
6. $r = 6$ m
7. $r = 3.5$ cm
8. $r = 1.4$ dm

9. $r = 11$ in.
10. $r = 27$ yd
11. $d = 2.03$ m
12. $d = 17.5$ cm

13. $d = 6.307$ cm
14. $d = 8.47$ m
15. $r = 4\frac{1}{12}$ in.
16. $r = 17\frac{1}{2}$ ft

Measure the radius or diameter to the nearest millimeter. Then find the circumference.

17.
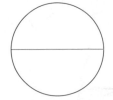

18.

19.

Solve.

20. How many yards of fencing are needed to enclose a circular playground 49 yd in diameter?

21. A metal pipe has an outside diameter of 40 cm. If the metal is 6 cm thick, find the circumference of the pipe.

22. A race track has a diameter of 430 m. Find the circumference in kilometers.

23. How many meters of metal edging are needed for the top of a round table 0.7 meter in diameter?

24. How much steel is used for the outside rim of a bicycle wheel if one spoke measures $10\frac{1}{2}$ inches?

25. Find the distance around this swimming pool. (Each end is a semicircle.)

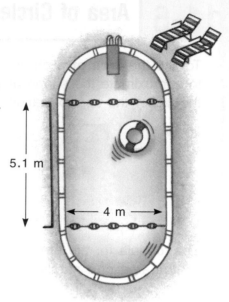

Exercise 25

26. Which circle would have a circumference *not* equal to the others?
    a. $r = 1.5$ m   **b.** $r = 1500$ mm   **c.** $d = 3$ dm   **d.** $d = 300$ cm

27. Which circle has a circumference of approximately 0.03 m?
    a. $d = 10$ m   **b.** $d = 1.1$ m   **c.** $d = 0.01$ m   **d.** $d = 100$ m

28. Which circle has a circumference of approximately 11.6 km?
    a. $r = 18.5$ km   **b.** $r = 185$ km   **c.** $r = 1.85$ km   **d.** $r = 0.185$ km

 **CALCULATOR ACTIVITY**

Find the circumference of each circle in terms of π. Then use the π key on a calculator to compute each circumference. (The first one is done.)

29. $d = 18$ m $\longrightarrow C = \pi \times 18 \longrightarrow C = 18\pi$ m $\longrightarrow C \approx$

30. $d = 35$ yd   31. $r = 8.3$ cm   32. $r = 2.5$ ft   33. $d = 3.2$ in.

 **Finding Together**

34. Complete these steps.

    a. Using a measuring tape marked in millimeters or a string and metric ruler, measure and record the circumference and diameter of five circular objects.

    b. Compute the ratio $\dfrac{C}{d}$ for each object. Use a calculator.

    c. Find the average of the five ratios. Round your answers to the nearest hundredth.

Sometimes, more than one area formula is needed to find the area of an irregular figure.

▶ **To find the area of this figure:**

- Draw a dotted line to separate the figure into a triangle and a square.

- Find the area of the triangle and the area of the square.

- Add the two areas to find the total area of the irregular figure.

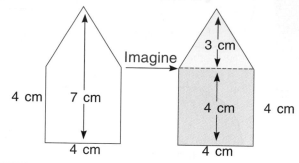

Imagine

Irregular Figure

▶ **Total area = Area of triangle + Area of square**

$$A = (\tfrac{1}{2}\,bh) + s^2$$

$$A = \tfrac{1}{2}(4 \times 3) + (4)^2$$

$$A = 6 + 16$$

$$A = 22 \text{ cm}^2$$

Find the area.

1.

3 cm

2 cm

2.

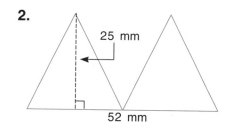

25 mm

52 mm

3.

12 mm

15 mm

28 mm

34 mm

12 mm

20 mm

4.

15 cm

30 cm

20 cm

5.

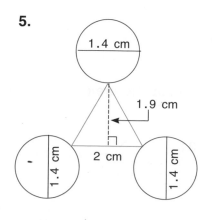

1.4 cm

1.9 cm

1.4 cm

2 cm

1.4 cm

6.

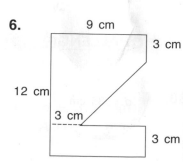

9 cm

3 cm

12 cm

3 cm

3 cm

Find the area of each shaded region. (The first one is done.)

7. To find the area of the shaded region, subtract the area of the circle from the area of the square.

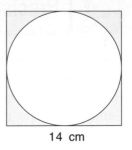

14 cm

$$\boxed{\text{Area of square} - \text{Area of circle}}$$

$$14 \times 14 - \pi (7)^2$$
$$196 - (49 \times 3.14)$$
$$196 - 153.86 \approx 42.14 \text{ cm}^2$$

8.

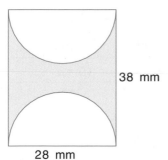

38 mm

28 mm

9.

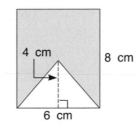

4 cm

8 cm

6 cm

10.

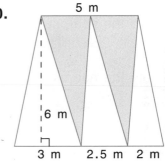

5 m

6 m

3 m   2.5 m   2 m

11.

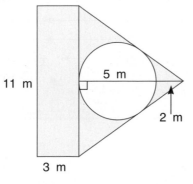

11 m

5 m

2 m

3 m

12.

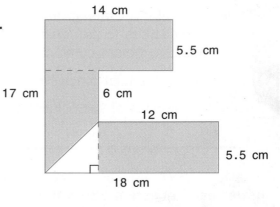

14 cm

5.5 cm

17 cm

6 cm

12 cm

5.5 cm

18 cm

13.

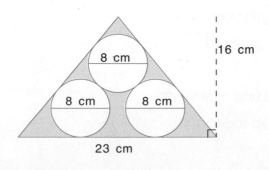

8 cm

8 cm   8 cm

16 cm

23 cm

14.

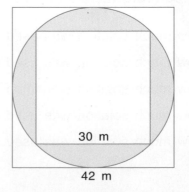

30 m

42 m

11-8 | Precision and Computation

The Science Club kept a record of the amount of solution used by various club members to grow different crystals. Some members reported their information in these different units of precision.
(Remember: The smaller the unit used, the more precise the measure.)

Precision

to the nearest 0.1 milliliter

to the nearest 10 milliliters — (Least precise)

to the nearest 0.01 milliliter — (Most precise)

to the nearest whole milliliter

Name	Salt	Salol	Sugar
Rhea	5.5 mL	18.7 mL	12.3 mL
Tony	10 mL	10 mL	20 mL
Anton	15 mL	12 mL	17 mL
Hannah	14.25 mL	16.31 mL	8.22 mL
Ivo	5 mL	12 mL	7 mL
Lucia	18 mL	15 mL	7 mL

What is the total amount of salt solution?

To add or subtract measures,
round all measures to the *least precise* unit of measure before computing.

For this data the least precise measure is 10 mL.

About 80 milliliters of salt solution were used.

5.5 mL	⟶	10 mL
10 mL	⟶	10 mL
15 mL	⟶	20 mL
14.25 mL	⟶	10 mL
5 mL	⟶	10 mL
+18 mL	⟶	+20 mL
		80 mL

**Answer each question about the Science Club record above.
Use the correct precision of measurement for each.**

1. How much solution was used to grow salol crystals?

2. How much solution was used to grow sugar crystals?

3. How much solution did Anton use in all?

4. How much solution was used by Rhea and Lucia together?

5. How much solution was used by Tony and Ivo together?

Significant Digits

The number of *significant digits* tells how accurate the measure is.

Look at this chart. Notice that zeros at the beginning or end are *not* considered significant.

When multiplying or dividing measures, round the answer to the *same* number of significant digits as in the measure with the *least number* of significant digits.

Measurement	Number of Significant Digits	Significant Digits
45 m	2	4, 5
36.1 m	3	3, 6, 1
5.301 km	4	5, 3, 0, 1
1700 cm	2	1, 7
0.009 km	1	9

Give the number of significant digits for each measure.

6. 40 m   **7.** 12.06 cm   **8.** 231 m   **9.** 0.052 mm   **10.** 1.002 km

11. 1500 m   **12.** 1501 m   **13.** 13 026 m   **14.** 25.002 cm   **15.** 0.006 m

Find each area. Round to the correct number of digits. (The first one is done.)

16. 0.45 m × 0.361 m

    $A = \ell w$
    $A = 0.45 \times 0.361$
    $A = 0.16245 \text{ m}^2$
    0.45 m ⟶ 2 significant digits
    0.361 m ⟶ 3 significant digits
    Round answer to 2 significant digits.
    $A = 0.16 \text{ m}^2$

17. 1 km × 4 km

18. 2.7 km × 5.301 km

19. 1700 m × 500 m

20. 0.009 km × 1.1 km

21. 8.86 m × 50.11 m

Solve for the missing dimension in these rectangles.
Round to the correct number of significant digits.

	22.	23.	24.	25.	26.	27.
Area	?	?	5.3 m²	?	?	42 cm²
Length	7.2 cm	5.1 km	2.5 m	0.7 km	11.9 cm	12 cm
Width	6.1 cm	1.4 km	?	0.3 km	0.2 cm	?

Solve. Use the correct technique for obtaining the most precise answer.

28. Find the area of a triangle with a base of 20 mm and a height of 14.1 mm.

29. Find the length of a rectangle that has an area of 600 m² and a width of 15 m.

Solving for Missing Dimensions

To find the missing dimension of a figure, given its area,
use the area formula, substitute, and solve.

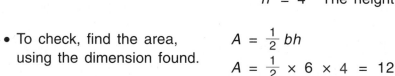

A triangle has an area of 12 yd^2 and a base of 6 yd.
Find the altitude, or height, of the triangle.

- Write the formula. $\longrightarrow$ $A = \frac{1}{2}bh$
- Substitute. $\longrightarrow$ $12 = \frac{1}{2} \times 6 \times h$
- Solve. $\longrightarrow$ $12 = 3h$

$$\frac{12}{3} = \frac{3h}{3}$$

$$h = 4 \quad \text{The height is 4 yd.}$$

$A = 12 \text{ yd}^2$
$b = 6 \text{ yd}$
$h = \underline{\ ?\ } \text{ yd}$

- To check, find the area, $\qquad A = \frac{1}{2}bh$
  using the dimension found. $\quad A = \frac{1}{2} \times 6 \times 4 = 12$

To find the missing dimension of a figure, given its perimeter,
use the perimeter formula, substitute, and solve.

A rectangle has a perimeter of 34 m and a width of 5 m.
Find the length of the rectangle.

- Write the formula. $\longrightarrow$ $P = 2\ell + 2w$
- Substitute. $\longrightarrow$ $34 = 2\ell + 2(5)$
- Solve. $\longrightarrow$ $34 = 2\ell + 10$

$$34 - 10 = 2\ell + 10 - 10$$

$$\frac{24}{2} = \frac{2\ell}{2}$$

$$\ell = 12 \quad \text{The length is 12 m.}$$

- To check, find the perimeter, $\quad P = 2\ell + 2w$
  using the dimension found. $\qquad P = 2(12) + 2(5)$
  $\qquad\qquad\qquad\qquad\qquad\quad P = 24 + 10$
  $\qquad\qquad\qquad\qquad\qquad\quad P = 34$

Find the missing dimension.

1. Square, $A = 49 \text{ m}^2$
   side: $\underline{\ ?\ }$

2. Rectangle, $A = 54 \text{ cm}^2$
   length: 9 cm; width: $\underline{\ ?\ }$

3. Triangle, $A = 14 \text{ m}^2$
   height: 2.8 m; base: $\underline{\ ?\ }$

4. Square, $P = 84 \text{ yd}$
   side: $\underline{\ ?\ }$

5. Rectangle, $P = 45 \text{ ft}$
   length: $\underline{\ ?\ }$; width: 8 ft

6. Parallelogram, $A = 40 \text{ yd}^2$
   base: $5\frac{1}{3}$ yd; height: $\underline{\ ?\ }$

Solve.

7. A club banner that covers 91 square meters has a length of 13 meters. What is its width?

8. Find the height of a triangle if its area is 64.8 cm^2 and its base is 18 cm.

9. A parking lot has the shape of a parallelogram. It has an area of 960 square meters. If cars parked side by side across the length of the lot occupy 120 meters, how wide is the lot?

10. A garage covers 725 square meters and is 29 meters wide. How long is it?

11. A radio station broadcasts to a circular area of 1256 square kilometers. How far in each direction from the station does the broadcast reach?

12. What is the height of a triangular poster with a base of 24 inches and an area of 216 square inches?

13. It takes 28.4 meters of fencing to enclose a rectangular plot that is 6 meters wide. What area does the fence enclose?

14. Find the area of a square that has a perimeter of 22 cm.

15. A rectangle has a perimeter of 50 feet. If the length is 14 feet, what is the area?

16. A square has an area of 100 square feet. Find the perimeter of a rectangle having an area equal to that of the square and a width of 4 feet.

17. A circle has a circumference of 9.42 m. Find its area.

18. Mrs. Roberts has $120 to spend on carpeting. The kind she wants is 12 feet wide and costs $7.50 a square yard. How long a piece of carpet can she buy?

19. A square contains 324 m^2. It is divided into four equal squares. Find the side of one of the small squares.

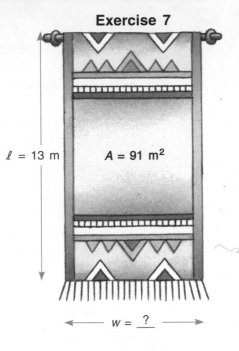
$\ell = 13$ m $A = 91$ m^2

$w = \underline{?}$

$\dfrac{A}{4}$

◀ SKILLS TO REMEMBER ▶

State whether each is a true or false statement when $r = 10$.

20. $r - 6 < 8$

21. $4r + 3 = 34$

22. $7r - 2 > 68$

23. $0.2r = 2$

24. $10 - r \neq 0$

25. $\frac{1}{2}r - 1 \geq 4$

26. $r \div 0.1 \leq 0$

27. $r^2 \neq 20$

Spreadsheet Geometry

An **electronic spreadsheet** is a useful tool for displaying and evaluating data.

The *columns* (A, B, C,...) and *rows* (1, 2, 3,...) accept text, formula, and values.

The cell is the place where a particular row and column meet. Each cell can hold a:
- **label** — title or words
- **value** — number
- **formula** — steps for calculations

FILENAME: GEOMETRY			
	A	B	C	D
1				
2				
3				
4				
5				

cell A1

Electronic spreadsheets are widely used in business; however, they can be used to solve problems in geometry too!

Problem: A 9′ × 8′ kitchen is to be tiled.
There are three sizes of tiles on sale.

$$12'' \times 12'' \text{ costs } \$1.29 \text{ each}$$
$$9'' \times 9'' \text{ costs } \$.89 \text{ each}$$
$$8'' \times 8'' \text{ costs } \$.69 \text{ each}$$

What is the most economical way to tile the floor?

A spreadsheet program can be used to solve the problem.

FILENAME: FLOOR COVERING						
	A	B	C	D	E	F	G
1	ROOM	LENGTH	WIDTH	AREA	TILE	TILE	NUMBER
2					SIZE	AREA	OF TILES
3	Kitchen	9	8	(+B3*C3)	12	(+E3*E3/144)	(+D3/F3)
4		9	8	(+B4*C4)	9	(+E4*E4/144)	(+D4/F4)
5		9	8	(+B5*C5)	8	(+E5*E5/144)	(+D5/F5)
6							

1. What does the formula (+B3*C3) represent?

2. What does the formula (+E3*E3/144) represent?

3. Why is the area in column F divided by 144?

4. In which cells are there labels?

5. In which cells are there values?

```
FILENAME: FLOOR COVERING
```

	H	I	J	K	L	M
1	COST	COST OF	TAX	TOTAL		
2	PER TILE	FLOORING		COST		
3	1.29	(+G3*H3)	(+0.06*I3)	(+I3+J3)		
4	0.89	(+G4*H4)	(+0.06*I4)	(+I4+J4)		
5	0.69	(+G5*H5)	(+0.06*I5)	(+I5+J5)		

6. Use a spreadsheet program or a calculator to complete the data in these spreadsheets.

7. How would you change your spreadsheet if the sales tax was 7%?

8. How much was saved by buying the tiles measuring 12″ × 12″?

9. Suppose that the different size tiles were on sale. The 12″ × 12″ was 10% off, the 9″ × 9″ was 15% off, and the 8″ × 8″ was 20% off. Write the formulas for computing the discount and the sale price for each tile size. Then solve.

LOGO and Symmetry

The **REPEAT** command in LOGO tells the *turtle* (cursor) to execute a procedure a specific number of times.

```
To SQUARE
REPEAT 4(FD 80 RT 90)
```

```
To PENTAGON
REPEAT 5(FD 70 RT 72)
```

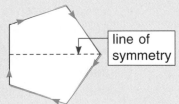
line of symmetry

A *line of symmetry* divides a polygon into two congruent parts. You can use the turtle to draw all the lines of symmetry in the figures shown on the screen.

10. How many lines of symmetry does each of the regular polygons drawn above have?

11. How would the procedure for drawing a regular polygon be changed so that the turtle would draw a regular octagon?

12. Write a procedure to draw a regular decagon.
Check your procedure using a LOGO program.

13. How many lines of symmetry are there in a regular octagon? a regular decagon?

Problem: Sixty meters of fencing is donated to the Environmental Center to enclose an area for growing endangered plants. One side of the center has a door that will open out into the area. What are the dimensions of the largest rectangular area that the new fence can enclose?

1 IMAGINE Visualize, draw, and label a picture of the enclosed area.

60 m of fencing = 3 sides to be enclosed

2 NAME *Facts:* 60 m — length of fencing

3 — sides in need of fencing

w   w

Questions: __?__ m = length   __?__ m = width

ℓ

3 THINK This problem involves several strategies.

The first is the diagram you have just visualized and drawn.

The diagram shows that the perimeter for 3 sides of the fence is known:

$P = 2w + 1\ell$ ⟶ Substitute. ⟶ $60 = 2w + 1\ell$

Since both dimensions are unknown, we need to use a second strategy, "guess and test."

Try: $w = 20$ m ⎱ $P = 2w + 1\ell$ ⟶ $2(20) + 1(20) = 60$ m
$\quad\ \ell = 20$ m ⎰   and $A = 20 \times 20 = 400$ m^2

Keep "guessing and testing" to find the largest rectangular area that the 60 m of fence could enclose.

A third strategy is to make a table to organize and analyze the guesses.

w	20	18	16	14	12
ℓ	20	24	28	32	36
$A = \ell w$	400	432	448	448	432

+ 32↑ + 16↑ + 0↑ − 16↑

Notice that the area increases to $w = 16$, $\ell = 28$. The area decreases for $w = 12$, $\ell = 36$. So try a width between 16 m and 14 m. ($w = 15$ m)

4 COMPUTE $P = 2w + 1\ell$ ⟶ $60 = 2(15) + \ell$ ⟶ $60 = 30 + \ell$ ⟶ 30 m $= \ell$

$A = \ell w$ ⟶ $A = (30)(15)$ ⟶ $A = 450$ m^2

5 CHECK Make a model with a strip of paper 60 mm long. Does the rectangle having maximum area have a width of 15 m and a length of 30 m? Notice the pattern on the chart. When the increase equals 0, the averaged length and width are the solutions.

Solve by combining several strategies.

1. A tinsmith cuts the largest circle possible from a square sheet of metal 441 in.^{2} in area. What is the circumference of the tin circle?

$s = \underline{\ ?\ }$

1 IMAGINE	Draw and label ⟶	2 NAME	⟶ Facts
	a picture.		⟶ Question

3 THINK   By drawing a picture you can see that the diameter (d) of the largest circle is equal to the sides (s) of the square. Use the area formula ($A = s^2$) to find the missing side of the square. Then use the formula for circumference ($C = \pi\, d$).

$d = \underline{\ ?\ }$

4 COMPUTE ⟶ **5 CHECK**

$A = 441$ in.^{2}

2. A hooked rug in the shape of a regular hexagon has a border of 3.6 m. How many cm long is each side?

3. What does the side of a square measure if it has the same perimeter as a rectangle 9 m × 4 m?

4. The side of a square having a perimeter of 48 ft is equal to the width of a rectangle. If the perimeter of the rectangle is twice that of the square, how long is the rectangle?

5. Carter made a fabric design consisting of an equilateral triangle with each side serving as the diameter of a semicircle. If the triangle's perimeter is 21 in., how much trim is needed to outline the design?

6. What is the area of the largest possible triangular swimming pool that could be built on a square plot of land measuring 81 m^2?

7. A circular pool has a circumference of 88 m. How many meters does a person cover if he/she swims the diameter of the pool four times?

Exercise 8

8. Rebecah made a "stoplight" by drawing three congruent circles within a rectangle. If the length of the rectangle is 30 in., what is its perimeter? What is the circumference of each circle?

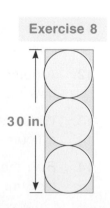

30 in.

9. A square plot of ground has an area of 49 m^2. What is the area of the largest possible circular fountain that could be constructed on the plot?

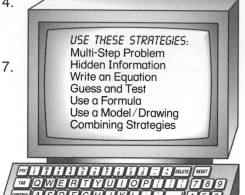

USE THESE STRATEGIES:
Multi-Step Problem
Hidden Information
Write an Equation
Guess and Test
Use a Formula
Use a Model / Drawing
Combining Strategies

1. The ratio of length to width of a rectangle is 5 : 4. If the perimeter is 45 in., what is the length of the rectangle?

2. The ratio of width to length of a rectangle is 3 : 7. If the rectangle's perimeter is 400 cm, what is its width?

3. The ratio of the three sides of a triangle is 3 : 4 : 5. If the longest side is 1.5 m, what is the triangle's perimeter?

4. The height of a rhombus is equal to the side of a square having a perimeter of 23 in. If the base of the rhombus is 6 in., what is its area?

5. A heavy trunk is being moved by rolling it on logs that are each 1 m in diameter. How far does the trunk move for each rotation of the logs?

6. How many tiles 8 in. on each side will be needed to cover a floor measuring 12 ft by 9 ft?

7. The length of a rectangular garden is twice its width. If its area is 98 square feet, how long is the garden?

8. The length of a rectangular playground is twice its width. If its area is 72 sq ft, what is its perimeter?

9. How many yards of edging are needed to trim the edge of a square cover that covers $7\frac{1}{9}$ square yards? (Hint: What number times itself equals $\frac{64}{9}$?)

10. A square sheet of paper 36 sq in. in area is divided into 4 equal squares. What is the perimeter of each square?

11. Find the side of a square that is equal in area to a triangle having a 27-in. base and a 6-in. height.

12. A horse is tied by a rope to a stake. If the rope is 21 feet long, how many square feet of grazing area does the horse have?

13. Which is larger and by how much: a figure 5 feet square or a figure containing 5 square feet?

14. Find the ratio of the area of a rectangle measuring 4 in. by 3 in. to the area of a rectangle measuring 12 in. by 3 in.

15. The perimeter of a regular hexagon is three times longer than the perimeter of a square. If the square is $1\frac{1}{2}$ ft on each side, how long is each side of the hexagon?

16. The face of a house gable is shaped like a trapezoid. What is the area of the gable face if its parallel sides are 9.2 m and 6.4 m long and the height is 3.5 m?

17. A triangular field with an area of 141.12 hectares has a height of 12.6 hectometers. What is the base of the field?

18. A park shaped like a triangle covers an area of 12 hectares. If its base is 640 meters, what is its height?

19. A square has an area of 100 square feet. Find the perimeter of a rectangle having an area equal to that of the square and a width of 4 feet.

20. The circumference of an archer's target is 91.06 cm. What is the distance from the center to the edge of the target?

21. The outside rim of a cylinder can measures 25.12 cm. What is the radius of the lid of the can?

22. What is the diameter of a circle whose area is 25π square units?

23. What is the radius of a circle whose circumference is 18.2π cm?

24. The diameter of a circular jigsaw puzzle is 30.5 cm. After it is assembled, what area does it cover?

25. If the radius of circle Y is 7 cm and the measure of central angle XYZ is 120°, what is the area of the shaded region?

26. A trapezoid has an area of 32.4 m². How high is the trapezoid if its parallel sides measure 7.5 m and 8.7 m?

27. The ratio of the sides of a quadrilateral is 3 : 4 : 5 : 6. If its smallest side measures 2.1 cm, what is its perimeter?

28. The diameter of circle P is 16 cm and $m\angle OPR = 90°$. Find the area of the shaded region.

Exercise 25

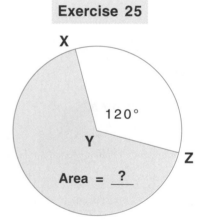

Exercise 28

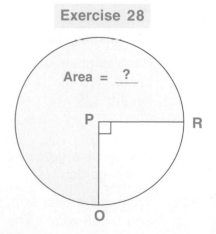

327

More Practice

Find the perimeter.

1. Square
   side: 4.7 m

2. Rhombus
   side: $4\frac{1}{2}$ ft

3. Parallelogram
   length: 48 cm
   width: 18 cm

4. Rectangle
   length: 6 yd
   width: $2\frac{1}{4}$ yd

Find the area.

5.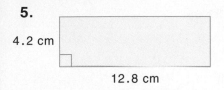
4.2 cm
12.8 cm

6.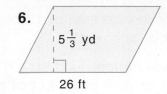
$5\frac{1}{3}$ yd
26 ft

7.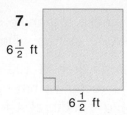
$6\frac{1}{2}$ ft
$6\frac{1}{2}$ ft

8.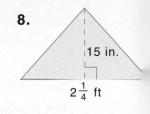
15 in.
$2\frac{1}{4}$ ft

Find the area of each trapezoid.

9.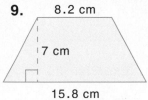
8.2 cm
7 cm
15.8 cm

10.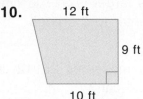
12 ft
9 ft
10 ft

11.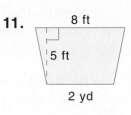
8 ft
5 ft
2 yd

Find the circumference and area of each circle.

12. $d = 7$ m

13. $r = 2.4$ cm

14. $d = 15$ yd

15. $r = 6\frac{1}{4}$ ft

Find the area.

16.
5 cm
8 cm
16 cm

17.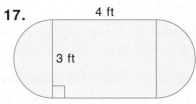
4 ft
3 ft

Give the number of significant digits for each measure.

18. 30 m

19. 24.15 cm

20. 3600 m

21. 0.038 mm

22. 3.001 m

Find the missing dimension.

23. Parallelogram, $A = 16.2$ m²
    base: 4.5 m
    height: _?_

24. Triangle, $A = 7$ ft²
    height: $5\frac{3}{5}$ ft
    base: _?_

Solve.

25. A vegetable garden is 22 m long and has an area of 330 m². What is the perimeter of the garden?

26. What will it cost to put wall-to-wall carpeting on the floor of a room that is 12 ft long and $9\frac{1}{2}$ ft wide? The carpeting costs $14.99 per square ft.

Math Probe

PREDICTING PERIMETER

1. What is the perimeter of a *unit triangle*? If two unit triangles are placed side by side, what is their perimeter? What is the perimeter of three such triangles?

| 1 unit on each side → P = 3 |

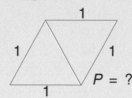
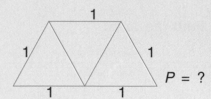

Copy and complete the chart.

Number of △'s	1	2	3	4	5	10	24	31
Perimeter								

2. Write a rule or formula to find the perimeter of *any* number (*n*) of unit triangles placed side by side.

3. What is the perimeter of a *unit square*? What is the perimeter of two unit squares?

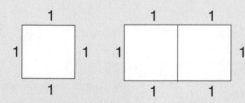

Copy and complete the chart.

Number of □'s	1	2	3	4	5	15	28	36
Perimeter								

4. Write a formula for the perimeter of *any* number (*n*) of unit squares placed side by side.

5. Explain the relationship between increasing numbers of unit hexagons and their perimeters. Write a formula for *any* number (*n*) of unit hexagons placed side by side.

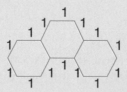

Look at your formula. What is the relationship between the number of sides of the polygon and the formula?

Check Your Mastery

Find the perimeter.

See pp. 304–305

1. Square
   side: 36 cm

2. Quadrilateral
   side 1: 6 in.; side 2: $4\frac{1}{2}$ in.
   side 3: 8 in.; side 4: $3\frac{1}{4}$ in.

3. Equilateral triangle
   side: $5\frac{2}{3}$ yd

Find the area.

See pp. 306–311

4.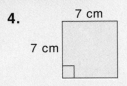
   7 cm
   7 cm

5. 7 ft
   15 ft

6. 15.5 m
   9 m
   8.5 m

7.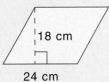
   18 cm
   24 cm

8.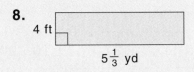
   4 ft
   $5\frac{1}{3}$ yd

9. 20 m
   10 m
   16 m

Find the circumference and area of each circle.

See pp. 312–315

10. $d = 14.2$ cm
11. $r = 3\frac{1}{2}$ ft
12. $d = 25$ in.
13. $r = 7$ m

Find the area.

See pp. 316–317

14.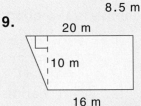
    6 cm   9 cm   6 cm
    24 cm

15. 4 ft   1 ft
    2 ft   2 ft
    4 ft   8 ft   4 ft
    13 ft

Give the number of significant digits for each measure.

See pp. 318–319

16. 25 cm
17. 32.1 m
18. 2046 m
19. 0.007 mm
20. 1.0 m

Find the missing dimension.

See pp. 320–321

21. Rectangle, $P = 22$ ft
    length: __?__
    width: 3 ft

22. Triangle, $A = 16$ m^2
    height: 8 m
    base: __?__

Solve.

23. A park is shaped like a regular pentagon. The length of one side
    of the park is 65.5 m. What is the perimeter of the park?

24. How many meters of wooden edging are needed for the top of a round table
    that has a diameter of 0.9 m?

25. A shed covers 186 square feet and is 12 feet wide. How long is it?

12 Real Numbers

In this chapter you will:

- Express rational numbers in fractional form
- Find squares and square roots
- Identify rational and irrational numbers
- Recognize some properties of the real number system
- Use the Pythagorean Theorem
- Solve problems: making a list or table

Do you remember?

To change a decimal to a fraction:

$$0.35 = \frac{35}{100} = \frac{7}{20}$$

To evaluate expressions with exponents:

exponent

$$5^2 = \underline{5 \times 5} = 25$$

base

Base used as a factor twice.

$$10^{-3} = \frac{1}{\underline{10 \times 10 \times 10}} = \frac{1}{1000}$$

Base used as a factor three times in the denominator.

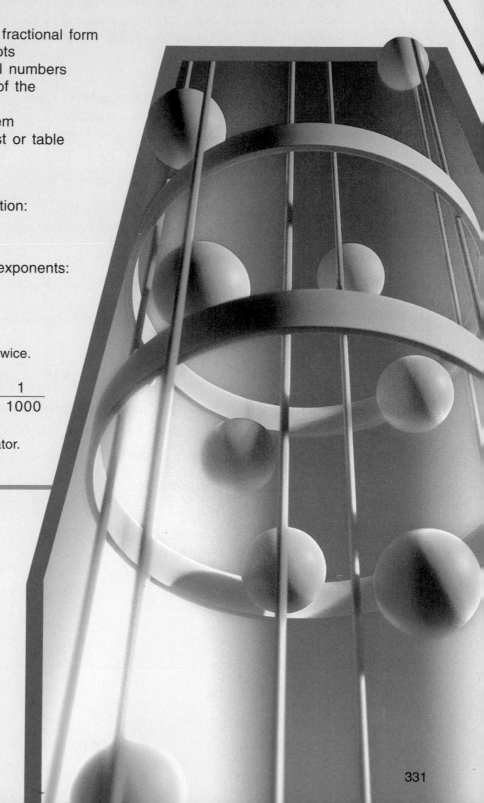

RESEARCHING TOGETHER

Mystical Numbers

Since time began, numbers in our universe have fascinated many. Pythagoras, a Greek philosopher and mathematician, lived in Italy around 525 B.C. Discover what you can about these ideas of Pythagoras:

- What did he discover about $\sqrt{2}$?

- What did he discover about $a^2 + b^2 = c^2$?

Repeating Decimals as Fractions

Rational numbers: numbers that can be expressed in the fractional form $\dfrac{a}{b}$ where a and b are integers and $b \neq 0$. The rational numbers include whole numbers, integers, fractions, and some decimals. Each of these can be written in fractional form:

Whole Number $\quad 4 = \dfrac{4}{1}$ Negative Integer $\quad ^-8 = \dfrac{^-8}{1}$ Decimal $\quad 0.2 = \dfrac{2}{10}$ or $\dfrac{1}{5}$

Terminating decimals are decimals with a definite number of places. Any terminating decimal can be written in the fractional form of a rational number:

$$0.4 = \dfrac{4}{10} \qquad 0.525 = \dfrac{525}{1000} \qquad 0.00009 = \dfrac{9}{100,000}$$

Nonterminating repeating decimals are decimals like:

$$0.333 \ldots, \text{ or } 0.\overline{3} \qquad\qquad 0.353535 \ldots, \text{ or } 0.\overline{35}$$

These decimals have digits *that begin* to repeat at the decimal point.

To change these decimals to fractions:

- Let x = decimal.

- When two digits repeat, multiply each side by 100.

- Subtract $x = 0.\overline{35}$.

$$\text{Let } x = 0.\overline{35}$$

$$100x = 35.\overline{35}$$

$$\begin{array}{r} -\quad x = -0.\overline{35} \\ \hline 99x = 35.00 \end{array} \longrightarrow x = \dfrac{35}{99}$$

Other **nonterminating repeating decimals** are decimals like:

$$0.1636363 \ldots, \text{ or } 0.1\overline{63} \qquad\qquad 0.02444 \ldots, \text{ or } 0.02\overline{4}$$

These decimals have digits that *do not begin* to repeat at the decimal point.

To change these decimals to fractions:

- Let x = decimal.

- Multiply by 100 so only repeating digits are to the right of the decimal point.

- Since only one digit repeats, multiply each side by 10.

- Subtract $100x = 2.\overline{4}$.

$$\text{Let } x = 0.02\overline{4}$$

$$100x = 2.\overline{4}$$

$$1000x = 24.\overline{4}$$

$$\begin{array}{r} -\ 100x = -2.\overline{4} \\ \hline 900x = 22.0 \end{array} \longrightarrow x = \dfrac{22}{900} = \dfrac{11}{450}$$

Change to the fractional form.

1. $^-16$ 2. $^+8$ 3. 0.25 4. 0.8 5. $1\frac{2}{7}$

6. $^-3\frac{1}{4}$ 7. 0 8. 0.006 9. 1.45 10. $^-0.36$

Change to the fractional form. Complete exercise 11.

11. $0.\overline{6}$ $\longrightarrow$

Let $x = 0.\overline{6}$

$10x = 6.\overline{6}$ $\longleftarrow$ Multiply by 10 since 1 digit repeats.

$-\quad x = 0.\overline{6}$

$\underline{?\ x\ =\ ?}$

$x = \dfrac{?}{?}$

12. $0.\overline{7}$ 13. $0.\overline{9}$ 14. $0.\overline{2}$ 15. $0.\overline{94}$ 16. $0.\overline{65}$

17. $0.\overline{03}$ 18. $0.\overline{08}$ 19. $0.\overline{182}$ 20. $0.\overline{261}$ 21. $0.\overline{006}$

22. $0.\overline{004}$ 23. $0.\overline{1426}$ 24. $0.\overline{5107}$ 25. $0.\overline{0032}$ 26. $0.\overline{0075}$

Change to the fractional form. Complete exercise 27.

27. $0.03\overline{2}$

Let $x = 0.03\overline{2}$

$100x = 3.\overline{2}$ $\longleftarrow$ Multiply by 100 so that only repeating digits are to the right of the decimal point.

$1000x = 32.\overline{2}$ $\longleftarrow$

$-\ \underline{\ 100x = 3.\overline{2}\ }$ Multiply by 10 since one digit repeats.

$\underline{?\ x = 29.0}$ $\longrightarrow$ $x = \dfrac{?}{?}$

28. $0.04\overline{8}$ 29. $0.6\overline{3}$ 30. $0.2\overline{6}$ 31. $0.08\overline{2}$ 32. $0.05\overline{1}$

33. $0.3\overline{32}$ 34. $0.7\overline{21}$ 35. $3.0\overline{26}$ 36. $8.6\overline{34}$ 37. $2.1\overline{45}$

38. $5.3\overline{74}$ 39. $2.0\overline{256}$ 40. $3.1\overline{457}$ 41. $6.2\overline{575}$ 42. $4.0\overline{141}$

SKILLS TO REMEMBER

Write each rational number as a terminating or repeating decimal.
Check your answers with a calculator.

43. $^-14$ 44. $^+23$ 45. $\dfrac{1}{16}$ 46. $\dfrac{2}{32}$ 47. $\dfrac{7}{30}$

48. $\dfrac{2}{5}$ 49. $^+\dfrac{1}{15}$ 50. $^-\dfrac{6}{11}$ 51. $^-1\dfrac{1}{9}$ 52. $^-3\dfrac{1}{12}$

CHALLENGE   **Solve.** (Hint: First change to the fractional form.)

53. $7.1\overline{6} + 3.\overline{5}$ 54. $8.\overline{2} - 6.1\overline{5}$ 55. $7.\overline{09} \times 2.\overline{83}$

56. Explain how to solve these on a calculator.

12-2 Squares, Square Roots, and Irrational Numbers

To square a number, multiply the number by itself.

$$9^2 = 9 \times 9 = 81 \qquad (^-9)^2 = ^-9 \times ^-9 = 81 \qquad \left(\frac{7}{4}\right)^2 = \frac{7}{4} \times \frac{7}{4} = \frac{49}{16}$$

The inverse operation of squaring a number is finding its **square root.**

To find the square root of 49, find the number that when squared equals 49.

$$7 \times 7 = 49$$
$$^-7 \times ^-7 = 49$$
7 and $^-7$ are square roots of 49.

The symbol $\sqrt{}$ usually represents the positive square root.

$$\sqrt{1.44} = 1.2 \quad 1.2 \times 1.2 = 1.44 \qquad\qquad \sqrt{\frac{81}{25}} = \frac{9}{5} \quad \frac{9}{5} \times \frac{9}{5} = \frac{81}{25}$$

▶ **Irrational numbers:** numbers that cannot be expressed as rational numbers. When expressed as decimals, they are *nonterminating, nonrepeating decimals.*

$$\sqrt{14} \approx \underline{\ ?\ }$$

- Estimate. $3^2 = 9$ and $4^2 = 16$, so $\sqrt{14}$ is between 3 and 4.

- Try 3.8 as a possible square root.

$$\begin{array}{r} 3.68 \\ 3.8.\overline{)14.000} \end{array}$$

Compute to two places.

- Since $3.8 \times 3.68 \approx 14.00$, find their average.

$$\frac{3.8 + 3.68}{2} = 3.74$$

- Try 3.74 as a possible square root.

$$\begin{array}{r} 3.743 \\ 3.74.\overline{)14.00000} \end{array}$$

Compute to three places.

- Since $3.74 \times 3.743 \approx 14.00$, find their average.

$$\frac{3.74 + 3.743}{2} = 3.7415$$

Use a calculator to repeat this process again and again. Each time the estimate is closer to $\sqrt{14}$. But the repetition will always result in a decimal that will *not* terminate and will *not* repeat because $\sqrt{14}$ is an irrational number.

Use a calculator to show that these are irrational numbers: $\sqrt{2}$, $\sqrt{3}$, $\sqrt{5}$, π.

Find the square.

1. 0.4
2. 0.5
3. 1.3
4. 1.7
5. 0.06
6. 0.08
7. $^-9$
8. $^-4$
9. $\frac{3}{5}$
10. $\frac{7}{9}$

Number	1	2	3	4	5	6	7	8	9	10	11	12	13	14	15	16	17	18	19	20
Square	1	4	9	16	25	36	49	64	81	100	121	144	169	196	225	256	289	324	361	400

A Square Table

Use this table to find the square roots.

11. $\sqrt{25}$ **12.** $\sqrt{49}$ **13.** $\sqrt{121}$ **14.** $\sqrt{324}$ **15.** $\sqrt{\frac{9}{16}}$

16. $\sqrt{\frac{25}{49}}$ **17.** $\sqrt{\frac{100}{225}}$ **18.** $\sqrt{\frac{144}{400}}$ **19.** $\sqrt{2.89}$ **20.** $\sqrt{1.96}$

Between which two whole numbers would the square root be? Use the table above.
(The first one is done.)

21. $\sqrt{8}$: $\sqrt{4} < \sqrt{8} < \sqrt{9}$ or $2 < \sqrt{8} < 3$ So, $\sqrt{8}$ is between 2 and 3.

22. $\sqrt{32}$ **23.** $\sqrt{175}$ **24.** $\sqrt{6}$ **25.** $\sqrt{71}$ **26.** $\sqrt{85}$

27. $\sqrt{152}$ **28.** $\sqrt{245}$ **29.** $\sqrt{170}$ **30.** $\sqrt{300}$ **31.** $\sqrt{382}$

Find a decimal approximation correct to the nearest thousandth.
Use a calculator to check answers.

32. $\sqrt{41}$ **33.** $\sqrt{72}$ **34.** $\sqrt{85}$ **35.** $\sqrt{39}$ **36.** $\sqrt{132}$

37. $\sqrt{150}$ **38.** $\sqrt{297}$ **39.** $\sqrt{376}$ **40.** $\sqrt{518}$ **41.** $\sqrt{620}$

**Make a table of square roots from 1–20. Use a calculator.
Round to the nearest thousandth.**

42.

Number	1	2	3	4	5	6	• • •	20
Root	1	1.414	1.732	?	?	?	• • •	?

CRITICAL THINKING   **Complete each sum or difference by naming two perfect squares.**

43. $10 = \underline{\ ?\ } + \underline{\ ?\ }$ **44.** $53 = \underline{\ ?\ } + \underline{\ ?\ }$ **45.** $106 = \underline{\ ?\ } + \underline{\ ?\ }$

46. $24 = \underline{\ ?\ } - \underline{\ ?\ }$ **47.** $20 = \underline{\ ?\ } - \underline{\ ?\ }$ **48.** $140 = \underline{\ ?\ } - \underline{\ ?\ }$

49. $73 = \underline{\ ?\ } + \underline{\ ?\ }$ **50.** $96 = \underline{\ ?\ } - \underline{\ ?\ }$ **51.** $130 = \underline{\ ?\ } + \underline{\ ?\ }$

52. What two perfect squares when subtracted equal another perfect square?

12-3 | Square-Root Algorithm

To find the square root of a number: $\sqrt{5329} = \underline{\ ?\ }$

- Estimate the answer, using numbers close to 5329 that have known square roots.

$$70 \times 70 = 4900 \qquad \sqrt{4900} < \sqrt{5329} < \sqrt{6400} \qquad 80 \times 80 = 6400$$

$$70 < \sqrt{5329} < 80$$

- Follow these steps.

Step 1:	Mark the number off in *periods of 2 digits*, going left from the decimal point. (53′29)	
Step 2:	Name the square root closest to, but less than, the square root of the first period. (7)	
Step 3:	Try this number as the first digit of the square root. Subtract the *square* of this number from the first period. (53 − 49 = 4)	
Step 4:	*Bring down* the next period. (29)	
Step 5:	Estimate the next digit by doubling the first digit of the square root. (7) Use this as a *trial divisor.* (42 ÷ 14 = 3)	
Step 6:	Use the quotient obtained in step 5 (3) as the next digit of the square root.	
Step 7:	Write the quotient to the right of the doubled first digit. Multiply this number, (143), by the second digit of the square root, (3). Subtract the product, (429). If this product is greater than the minuend, choose a smaller second digit for the square root. If the remainder is zero, the number obtained is the square root.	
Step 8:	For still larger numbers, double the digits of the square root and repeat steps 4–7.	

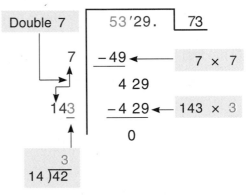

Double 7

$$
\begin{array}{r|l}
53'29. & \underline{73} \\
-49 \quad\leftarrow & 7 \times 7 \\
\hline
4\ 29 & \\
-4\ 29 \quad\leftarrow & 143 \times 3 \\
\hline
0 &
\end{array}
$$

$$14\overline{)42} \quad \frac{3}{}$$

Check: $70 < \sqrt{5329} < 80 \longrightarrow 70 < 73 < 80$

Copy and complete.

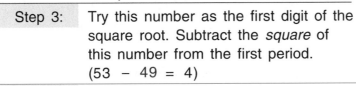

1.
$$
\begin{array}{r|l}
5'76. & \underline{2\ ?} \\
2 \mid -4 & \\
\hline
1\ 76 & \\
4\ \underline{?} \mid -1\ 76 & \\
\hline
0 &
\end{array}
$$

Only the left-hand period can be one digit.

2.
$$
\begin{array}{r|l}
9'61. & \underline{3\ ?} \\
3 \mid -9 & \\
\hline
61 & \\
6\ \underline{?} \mid -\ ? & \\
\hline
? &
\end{array}
$$

3.

```
        1'56'25. |125
    1  | -1
          56
   22  | -44
          12 25
   24 ?  | -    ?
```

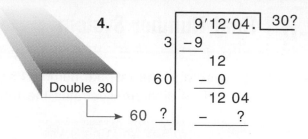

Double 30
→ 60 ?

4.

```
        9'12'04. |30?
    3  | -9
          12
   60  | - 0
          12 04
   60 ?  | -    ?
```

Find the square root.

5. $\sqrt{841}$	**6.** $\sqrt{484}$	**7.** $\sqrt{576}$	**8.** $\sqrt{961}$
9. $\sqrt{1369}$	**10.** $\sqrt{1764}$	**11.** $\sqrt{2916}$	**12.** $\sqrt{6724}$
13. $\sqrt{9409}$	**14.** $\sqrt{7744}$	**15.** $\sqrt{14,641}$	**16.** $\sqrt{17,689}$
17. $\sqrt{67,081}$	**18.** $\sqrt{54,289}$	**19.** $\sqrt{40,401}$	**20.** $\sqrt{92,416}$

Find the square root of these decimals. (The first two are done.)

21.

```
       4'49'44' |21.2
    2 | -4
         49
   41 | -41
          8 44
  422 | -8 44
```

Mark off periods of two digits right and left of the decimal point.

22.

```
       31'36' |5.6
    5 | -25
         6 36
  106 | -6 36
```

23. $\sqrt{10.24}$	**24.** $\sqrt{40.96}$	**25.** $\sqrt{67.24}$	**26.** $\sqrt{47.61}$
27. $\sqrt{630.01}$	**28.** $\sqrt{806.56}$	**29.** $\sqrt{660.49}$	**30.** $\sqrt{718.24}$
31. $\sqrt{0.0961}$	**32.** $\sqrt{0.5625}$	**33.** $\sqrt{0.2025}$	**34.** $\sqrt{0.8649}$
35. $\sqrt{1.5129}$	**36.** $\sqrt{6.8121}$	**37.** $\sqrt{9.0601}$	**38.** $\sqrt{4.2849}$

Solve.

39. The square of a number is 1.69. Find the number.

40. The square root of a number is 29. Find the number.

41. Three times the square root of a number is 15. Find the number.

42. A number is squared, then doubled. The result is 72. Find the number.

43. The square of a number is 0.36. Find the number.

44. Find the perimeter of a square circus stage having a floor area of 1936 square feet.

45. A square pool has an area of 7056 square feet. Find its perimeter in yards.

Exercise 44

A = 1936 sq ft
P = ?

Real number system: the rational numbers and the irrational numbers.
This diagram illustrates the real number system.

Real Numbers

Rational Numbers:

numbers that can be expressed as $\frac{a}{b}$ where a and b are integers and $b \neq 0$.

Irrational Numbers:

numbers that are nonterminating, nonrepeating decimals.

Every real number is either rational or irrational.

Another illustration of the real number system is a number line. Every point on the line can be associated with a real number.

True or false? Explain.

1. Zero is a real number.

2. All whole numbers are real numbers.

3. Some integers are irrational numbers.

4. The square root of any whole number is a rational number.

5. The square root of any whole number is a real number.

6. Terminating decimals are sometimes irrational numbers.

7. Every real number can be expressed as a decimal.

8. Every real number can be expressed as $\frac{a}{b}$ where a and b are integers and $b \neq 0$.

9. Some square roots are not rational numbers.

10. Nonterminating repeating decimals are irrational numbers.

∞ = **Infinity**

Classify each real number as rational or irrational.

11. 8   **12.** 13   **13.** $\sqrt{5}$

14. $\sqrt{10}$ **15.** $^-14$ **16.** $^-28$

17. $0.\overline{4}$ **18.** 0.6   **19.** $^-0.429$

20. $^-0.4\overline{07}$ **21.** 0.1234...   **22.** 0.01001...

23. $3\frac{2}{5}$ **24.** $(^+8.7)^2$ **25.** $(^-0.9)^2$

Draw the number line between $^-6$ and 6. Show approximately where each of the following real numbers would go.

26. 2.7   **27.** 5.4   **28.** $\frac{4}{3}$ **29.** $\frac{1}{3}$ **30.** $\sqrt{35}$

31. $\sqrt{23}$ **32.** $\sqrt{19}$ **33.** $\sqrt{30}$ **34.** $^-3.\overline{8}$ **35.** $^-2.\overline{2}$

Solve. (The first is done.)

36. If $b^2 = 25$, then $b = \underline{\ ?\ } \longrightarrow b = \pm 5$ because $\left\{\begin{array}{c} ^+5 \times {}^+5 \\ ^-5 \times {}^-5 \end{array}\right\} = 25$

37. If $a^2 = 36$, then $a = \underline{\ ?\ }$ **38.** If $c^2 = 144$, then $c = \underline{\ ?\ }$

39. If $b^2 = 81$, then $b = \underline{\ ?\ }$ **40.** If $c^2 = 225$, then $c = \underline{\ ?\ }$

Finding the Midpoint

Finding the **midpoint** between two numbers on a number line is the same as finding the **average** of the numbers.

What number is halfway between $^-1.7$ and $^-1.8$?

$$\frac{^-1.7 + {}^-1.8}{2} = \frac{^-3.5}{2} = {}^-1.75$$

$^-1.75$ is the midpoint (average) of $^-1.7$ and $^-1.8$.

Find the midpoint between each pair of numbers. Then check, using a calculator.

41. 0.5 and 0.6   **42.** 2.3 and 2.41   **43.** $\frac{2}{5}$ and $\frac{3}{5}$

44. $\frac{3}{7}$ and $\frac{4}{7}$ **45.** $11\frac{1}{2}$ and $11\frac{2}{3}$ **46.** $^-0.45$ and $^-0.46$

47. 0.006 and 0.007   **48.** $^-0.02$ and $^-0.002$ **49.** 7.089 and 7.09

50. How many numbers are there between any two real numbers?

MENTAL MATH

Name two irrational numbers between each pair. (The first one is done.)

51. 3 and 4 $\longrightarrow \sqrt{10}, \sqrt{11}, \ldots, \sqrt{15}$ **52.** 4 and 5   **53.** 11 and 12

54. 9 and 10   **55.** 6 and 7   **56.** 14 and 15   **57.** 18 and 19

12-5 Real Number Solutions for Inequalities

▶ **Adding or subtracting** the same positive or negative real number to or from *both* sides of an inequality leaves the inequality relationship the *same*.

$6 > 3$ Add 1 to both sides. ⟶ $(6 + 1) > (3 + 1)$ ⟶ $7 > 4$

$6 > 3$ Add $^-3$ to both sides. ⟶ $(6 + {}^-3) > (3 + {}^-3)$ ⟶ $3 > 0$

$6 > 3$ Subtract 2.5 from both sides. ⟶ $(6 - 2.5) > (3 - 2.5)$ ⟶ $3.5 > 0.5$

▶ **Multiplying or dividing** *both* sides of an inequality by the same positive real number leaves the inequality relationship the *same*.

$4 < 12$ Multiply both sides by $\frac{1}{2}$. ⟶ $(4 \times \frac{1}{2}) < (12 \times \frac{1}{2})$ ⟶ $2 < 6$

$4 < 12$ Divide both sides by 4. ⟶ $(4 \div 4) < (12 \div 4)$ ⟶ $1 < 3$

▶ **To find real number solutions for an inequality**, use the method for solving equations.

Let r be any real number, find the solution set for:

$r + 7 > 10.5$ *Think of the related equation:* $r + 7 = 10.5$

$r + 7 - 7 > 10.5 - 7$

$r > 3.5$ The solution set is all real numbers (r) *greater than* 3.5.

The solution set can be written: $\{r : r > 3.5\}$

This is read: "The set of all real numbers, r, such that r is greater than 3.5."

▶ **To check the solution of a given inequality:**

- Choose a real number greater than 3.5.   ⟶

> **Choose 5.**
> $r + 7 > 10.5$
> $5 + 7 > 10.5$
> $12 > 10.5$

- Substitute and solve.

- Check the truth of the solution. ⟶ 12 *is greater than* 10.5.

Write the solution set for each inequality.

1. $r + 4 > 11$

2. $5r < 35$

3. $r - 9 < 21$

4. $\dfrac{r}{2} > 12$

5. $r + {}^-6 < 10$

6. $r - {}^-8 > 2$

7. $5r + {}^-3 > {}^-13$

8. $2r - 6 < 12$

9. $4r - {}^-2 > 10$

Write the solution set for each inequality. (The first one is done.)

10. $\dfrac{a}{3} - 2 \leq 6 \longrightarrow \dfrac{a}{3} - 2 + 2 \leq 6 + 2$

$\dfrac{a}{3} \leq 8 \longrightarrow a \leq 24 \longrightarrow \{a : a \leq 24\}$

11. $3n + 10 < 25$

12. $9r + 7 \geq 34$

13. $4t - 2 < 14$

14. $7s - 5 > 23$

15. $\dfrac{t}{5} - 3 \geq 1$

16. $\dfrac{r}{2} + 5 \leq 8$

17. $\dfrac{x}{4} - 3 > 2$

18. $\dfrac{a}{6} + 2 \leq 3$

19. $\dfrac{r}{3} + 7 \geq 9$

20. $2c + {}^{-}11 \geq 15$

21. $3b - {}^{-}8 \leq {}^{-}10$

22. $2n - 3 \leq 7$

23. $\dfrac{x}{2} + {}^{-}1 \leq 11$

24. $\dfrac{t}{5} - {}^{-}3 \geq 5$

25. $\dfrac{s}{3} + {}^{-}6 \geq 24$

Multiplying or Dividing by Negative Numbers

When an inequality is multiplied or divided by a *negative* real number, the relation symbol must be *reversed* to form a true statement.

Multiplying by a Negative

$$3 \;<\; 15$$
$$3 \times {}^{-}2 \;\underline{\;?\;}\; 15 \times {}^{-}2$$
$${}^{-}6 \;>\; {}^{-}30$$

Relationship is reversed from "<" to ">"

Dividing by a Negative

$$8 \;\geq\; {}^{-}4$$
$$8 \div {}^{-}4 \;\underline{\;?\;}\; {}^{-}4 \div 4$$
$${}^{-}2 \;\leq\; {}^{-}1$$

Relationship is reversed from "≥" to "≤"

Write the solution set for each inequality. (The first one is done.)

26. ${}^{-}7r - 2 < 12 \longrightarrow {}^{-}7r - 2 + 2 < 12 + 2$

${}^{-}7r < 14 \longrightarrow r > {}^{-}2 \longrightarrow \{r : r > {}^{-}2\}$

27. ${}^{-}5m - 10 \geq 5$

28. ${}^{-}3r - 1 < 20$

29. ${}^{-}4n + 3 > 19$

30. ${}^{-}6c - 3 \leq 21$

31. ${}^{-}3t + 4 \geq 16$

32. ${}^{-}2r - 6 \leq 10$

33. $\dfrac{d}{-3} + 1 \geq 5$

34. $\dfrac{m}{-4} - 2 < 3$

35. $\dfrac{a}{-2} + 10 > 15$

36. $\dfrac{n}{-3} - 2 \leq 6$

37. $\dfrac{t}{-5} - 2 < {}^{-}1$

38. $\dfrac{d}{-2} + {}^{-}3 \geq 1$

39. $\dfrac{y}{-4} + 1 \leq 2.5$

40. $\dfrac{m}{-6} + 3 \geq 1.5$

41. $\dfrac{c}{-2} + 2 \leq 2.5$

12-6 | Pythagorean Theorem

In ancient Greece a special relationship among the three sides of a right triangle was known. It is called the **Pythagorean Theorem**. It states:

> The sum of the squares of the legs of a right triangle equals the square of the hypotenuse.

$$a^2 + b^2 = c^2$$

The **hypotenuse, c,** is always the longest side of a right triangle, and it is opposite the right angle.

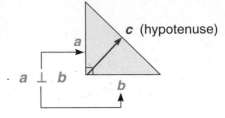

The **Pythagorean Theorem** can be used to determine if a triangle is a right triangle.

Given: △ABC has sides with lengths
 of 6 cm, 8 cm, 10 cm
Let a = 6 cm, b = 8 cm, c = 10 cm

$$a^2 + b^2 \overset{?}{=} c^2$$
$$6^2 + 8^2 \overset{?}{=} 10^2$$
$$36 + 64 \overset{?}{=} 100$$
$$100 = 100$$

△ABC is a right triangle.

Given: △DEF has sides with lengths
 of 5 cm, 5 cm, 8 cm
Let a = 5 cm, b = 5 cm, c = 8 cm

$$a^2 + b^2 \overset{?}{=} c^2$$
$$5^2 + 5^2 \overset{?}{=} 8^2$$
$$25 + 25 \overset{?}{=} 64$$
$$50 \neq 64$$

△DEF is *not* a right triangle.

The **Pythagorean Theorem** can be used to find the missing length of a side of a right triangle.

Given: △MNP as illustrated
Let a = 8 m, b = __?__ m, c = 17 m

$$a^2 + b^2 = c^2$$
$$8^2 + b^2 = 17^2 \longrightarrow 64 + b^2 = 289$$
$$b^2 = 289 - 64 \longrightarrow b^2 = 225$$
$$b = \sqrt{225} \longrightarrow b = 15$$

M
c = 17 m
a = 8 m
N b = __?__ P

△MNP is a right triangle.

Check: $8^2 + 15^2 \overset{?}{=} 17^2 \longrightarrow 64 + 225 = 289 \longrightarrow 289 = 289$

Which sets of measures form right triangles?

1. 3 m, 4 m, 5 m   **2.** 9 cm, 12 cm, 16 cm   **3.** 1 mm, 1 mm, 2 mm

4. 4 mm, 5 mm, 7 mm   **5.** 7 cm, 24 cm, 25 cm   **6.** 15 cm, 20 cm, 25 cm

7. 5 cm, 5 cm, 9 cm   **8.** 6 m, 7 m, 8 m   **9.** 2 m, 2 m, 4 m

10. 14 mm, 48 mm, 50 mm   **11.** 1.6 m, 3 m, 3.4 m   **12.** 0.8 cm, 1.2 cm, 1.7 cm

Copy and complete. Find the missing dimension in these right triangles.

	13.	14.	15.	16.	17.	18.	19.	20.
Leg	7 m	?	27 km	80 cm	1.5 m	0.3 cm	0.6 cm	?
Leg	?	48 cm	?	60 cm	?	0.4 cm	?	2.1 mm
Hypotenuse	25 m	60 cm	45 km	?	2.5 m	?	1 cm	7.5 mm

Draw a picture and solve. (The first one is done.)

21. An automobile traveled 21 miles directly north from the airport. It turned directly west and traveled 28 miles. How far is the automobile from the airport?

The missing dimension is the hypotenuse:

$$a^2 + b^2 = c^2$$
$$21^2 + 28^2 = c^2$$
$$441 + 784 = c^2$$
$$1225 = c^2$$
$$\sqrt{1225} = c$$
$$35 = c \longrightarrow \text{The car is 35 mi from its starting point.}$$

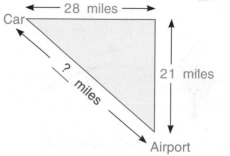

22. What is the longest straight line that can be drawn on a piece of paper 9 cm by 12 cm?

23. A play area is 20 m long and 21 m wide. How long is the walk that extends diagonally across the play area?

24. The diagonal of a rectangle is 15 mm. If the length of the rectangle is 12 mm, what is the width?

Right Triangles and Irrational Numbers

Each leg of a right triangle measures 1 unit. What is the length of the hypotenuse?

- Write the Pythagorean Theorem. $\longrightarrow a^2 + b^2 = c^2$
- Substitute. $\longrightarrow 1^2 + 1^2 = c^2$
- Solve. $\longrightarrow 1 + 1 = c^2$

$$\sqrt{2} = c \text{ Length of hypotenuse}$$

Use a calculator to find an approximation for $\sqrt{2}$. $\longrightarrow$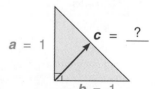

What is the hypotenuse if each leg measures:

25. 3 cm   26. 5 cm   27. 2 in.   28. 9 ft   29. 7 m

12-7 Problem Solving: Make an Organized List/Table

Problem: A social studies class played a game. Each "contestant" was asked to name the nation to which the teacher pointed on an unlabeled map, and identify its capital. For each nation identified correctly, 3 points were awarded; for each capital, 6 points. A 1-point bonus was awarded if both nation and capital were correctly identified. In how many ways could the winner have scored 22 points?

1 IMAGINE Draw and label a picture, visualizing how the winning 22 points were won.

Name	Contestant 1	Contestant 2	Etc.
Nations	3 points each	?	
Capitals	6 points each	?	
Both	1 point	?	
Total	Winner–22 pts.	?	

2 NAME *Facts:* 3 points — Each nation named
6 points — Each capital named
1 point — Naming both nation and capital

Question: In how many ways could 22 points have been scored?

3 THINK Expand the table above in order to list and organize all possibilities.

Start with 7 "nations." 8 would be too many because 8 × 3 = 24, and 24 > 22, the winning score.

4 COMPUTE Complete your table and find the different ways 22 points may be scored.

Nations	7	6	5	4	3	2	2	1	0	0
Capitals	–	1	1	2	2	2	2	3	3	4
Both	–	–	1	–	1	1	2	1	–	–
Total	21	24	22	24	22	19	20	22	18	24

Not every guess needs to be listed on the table. Some combinations fall too far above or below the 22 points.

The only possibilities are: 5 nations, 1 capital, 1 bonus point
3 nations, 2 capitals, 1 bonus point
1 nation, 3 capitals, 1 bonus point

5 CHECK Redo the table, starting at a different point. For example, begin with 4 "capitals" and work down.

Solve. (Make a list or table.)

1. It costs 29¢ to mail a letter and 19¢ to mail a postcard.
   A pen pal wrote to 15 friends and spent $3.35 on postage.
   How many letters and how many postcards did the pen pal send?

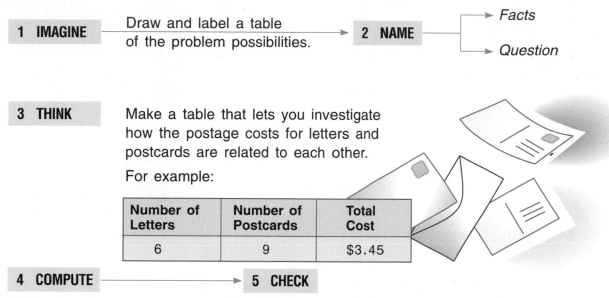

Number of Letters	Number of Postcards	Total Cost
6	9	$3.45

2. Adrian has $11.86 in change. He has 3 times as many dimes as nickels, 4 more nickels than pennies, and 4 fewer quarters than twice the number of nickels. What coins does he have?

3. The florist had 4 roses, 3 daisies, and 8 carnations. The florist put them in 3 vases so that no more than 4 carnations were in any one vase and at least one flower of each kind was in each vase. In how many different ways might the florist have arranged the flowers so that all were used?

4. Granger bought a box of shapes at a garage sale. The box contained a large red triangle, a small blue circle, a small blue square, a large and a small red circle, a large yellow circle, and a small yellow square. If he wants to have every possible combination of sizes (big and small) and colors (red, yellow, blue) for each shape (triangle, square, circle), what pieces must he add to the box?

5. Cynthia has 12 coins in her pocket. Only one is a quarter. If the coins add up to $.75, what combinations of coins might be in her pocket?

6. A football team won a game with a score of 28 to 0. A field goal scores 3 points, a touchdown scores 6 points, and the extra point can be scored only after a touchdown. Points were not scored in any other way. In how many ways might the winners have scored 28 points?

7. Rates for overseas calls are as follows: $1.50 for the first three minutes and $.25 for each additional minute. There is also an $.85 charge for overseas directory assistance. If a telephone bill records $4.85 for a call to Switzerland, how long was the conversation? Was directory assistance needed?

Choose the correct answer.

1. What is the side of a square having an area of 144 ft^2?
   - **a.** 36 ft
   - **b.** 12 ft
   - **c.** 72 ft

2. Find a number whose square is 361.
   - **a.** 130,321
   - **b.** 19
   - **c.** 29

3. What value makes the equation $n^2 = \sqrt{n}$ true?
   - **a.** 2
   - **b.** 1
   - **c.** $^-1$

4. Which of these is a rational number?
   - **a.** $\sqrt{14}$
   - **b.** $^-2$
   - **c.** $\sqrt{35}$

5. Which of these is an irrational number?
   - **a.** $\sqrt{8}$
   - **b.** $-\frac{1}{9}$
   - **c.** $^+3.14$

6. The square root of a number is 26. Find the number.
   - **a.** 52
   - **b.** $\sqrt{26}$
   - **c.** 676

7. Three times the square root of a number is 27. Find the number.
   - **a.** 81
   - **b.** $^-2$
   - **c.** 35

8. A number is squared, then doubled. The result is 32. Find the number.
   - **a.** 4
   - **b.** 8
   - **c.** 88

9. The square of a number is 0.09. What is the number?
   - **a.** 0.03
   - **b.** 0.3
   - **c.** 0.0081

10. One half of a number squared is 98. Find the number.
    - **a.** 16
    - **b.** 14
    - **c.** 7

11. What is the solution set for the inequality $3n + 4 \leq 10$?
    - **a.** $\{n : n < 2\}$
    - **b.** $\{n : n \geq 2\}$
    - **c.** $\{n : n \leq 2\}$

12. Which relation symbol makes the inequality true? $^-2x \geq 16$ so $x \underline{\ ?\ } ^-8$.
    - **a.** $>$
    - **b.** $\geq$
    - **c.** $\leq$

13. Which measures form a right triangle?
    - **a.** 0.9 cm, 1.2 cm, 1.5 cm
    - **b.** 4', 4', 4'
    - **c.** 7 m, 8 m, 9 m

14. The diagonal of a square measuring 3 in. on each side is:
    - **a.** 9 in.
    - **b.** $3\sqrt{2}$ in.
    - **c.** 6 in.

USE THESE STRATEGIES:
Use a Model/Drawing
Use a Formula
Write an Equation
Multi-Step Problem
Combining Strategies

Solve.

15. If ornament railing sells for $20 per foot, how much would it cost to purchase enough to enclose a square site that has an area of 100 square feet?

Exercise 19

16. Find the side of a square circus stage having a floor area of 1024 square feet.

17. During a bus trip a driver drove 42 km directly south and 56 km directly east. How far was the bus from its starting point?

18. Two boats leave a pier at the same time. One travels north at a rate of 28 km per hour. The other travels east at a rate of 21 km per hour. How far apart are they in 4 hours?

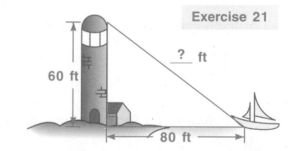

13 ft   ? ft

5 ft

19. A ladder 13 ft long extends 5 feet from a building. How high up the building does the ladder reach?

20. The diagonal of a television picture screen is 2.5 ft. The screen is 1.5 ft long. How wide is the screen?

21. A boat is anchored 80 ft from the foot of the lighthouse. The lighthouse is 60 ft tall. What is the distance from the top of the lighthouse to the boat?

Exercise 21

? ft

60 ft

80 ft

22. Beth rode her bicycle 6 miles south. She then rode 3 miles west. How many miles, to the nearest tenth, is she from her starting point?

23. A tree in the park is 36 ft high. A wire 45 ft long extends from the top of the tree to a staple in the ground. What is the distance from the staple to the base of the tree?

Exercise 24

24. The distance from the base of a ramp to the base of a platform is 15 m. The platform is 5 m high. To the nearest tenth, how many meters long is the ramp?

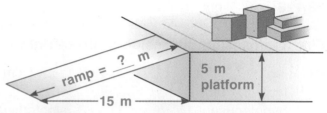

ramp = ? m

5 m platform

15 m

25. A baseball "diamond" is a square 90 ft on a side. What is the straight-line distance from home plate to second base? (Answer to the nearest tenth.)

More Practice

Change to the fractional form.

1. $^-11$ 2. 0.45 3. $2\frac{3}{4}$ 4. $0.\overline{5}$ 5. $4.0\overline{3}$

Find the square.

6. 25 7. 14 8. 0.03 9. $^-1.8$ 10. 0.005

Between which two whole numbers would the square root be?

11. 7 12. 72 13. 348 14. 118 15. 157

Find the square root.

16. $\sqrt{961}$ 17. $\sqrt{529}$ 18. $\sqrt{3136}$ 19. $\sqrt{1849}$

20. $\sqrt{28.09}$ 21. $\sqrt{47.61}$ 22. $\sqrt{0.4489}$ 23. $\sqrt{0.1521}$

Classify each real number as rational or irrational.

24. 6 25. $^-1.4$ 26. $0.4567...$ 27. $^-(3)^2$

28. $9\frac{2}{5}$ 29. $3.0\overline{8}$ 30. $\sqrt{12}$ 31. $^-6\frac{3}{8}$

Write the solution set for each inequality.

32. $4n + 13 > 45$ 33. $7t - 2 \leq 12$ 34. $6s - 5 < 31$

35. $\frac{r}{4} + 6 \geq 10$ 36. $\frac{x}{3} - 2 \leq 4$ 37. $\frac{a}{6} + 4 > 9$

Which sets of measures form right triangles?

38. 3 cm, 5 cm, 5 cm 39. 9 m, 25 m, 16 m 40. 1.4 mm, 4.8 mm, 5 mm

Find the missing dimension in these right triangles.

41. leg: __?__ 42. leg: 7 cm 43. leg: 28 mm
    leg: 12 m   leg: __?__   leg: 21 mm
    hypotenuse: 15 m hypotenuse: 25 cm hypotenuse: __?__

Solve.

44. A number is squared, then tripled. The result is 192. Find the number.

45. What is the longest straight line that can be drawn on a piece of wood 3 in. by 4 in.?

Math Probe

This is a statue of Pericles. He was the most famous leader of the ancient Greeks. "The Golden Age" is also called "The Age of Pericles."

GOLDEN SECTION

A line segment is said to be divided by a **golden section** if the ratio of the whole segment to the longer part equals the ratio of the longer part to the shorter part.

A ———————— B ———————— C

Point B divides $\overline{AC}$ in *golden section* when $\dfrac{AC}{AB} = \dfrac{AB}{BC}$.

This ratio, considered pleasing to the eye, was used as early as the fifth century by the Greeks. Examples of this ratio can be found in architecture, art, and nature.

The golden ratio equals the number $\dfrac{(1 + \sqrt{5})}{2}$.

Is this number a rational or an irrational number?

Use your scientific calculator to find an estimate.

To construct a golden section:

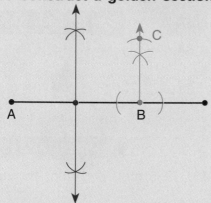

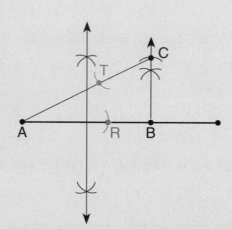

Draw $\overline{AB}$. Find the midpoint. Then construct a perpendicular to $\overline{AB}$ at B that is congruent to half of $\overline{AB}$. Call it $\overline{BC}$.

Connect $\overline{AC}$. Construct $\overline{CT}$ congruent to $\overline{BC}$. Construct $\overline{AR}$ congruent to $\overline{AT}$. Point R divides $\overline{AB}$ in golden section.

Use a ruler and a compass to make a 4-inch square. Construct a golden section on one side. Copy the length onto the other sides. Connect the points. Continue this process, using the golden section to create squares within squares. Color one section of each square to show a spiral.

Challenge: Can you discover how the ancient Greeks applied the golden section to their sculptures? Give an example.

349

Check Your Mastery

Change to the fractional form. See pp. 332–333

1. $^-15$
2. 0.38
3. $4\frac{1}{2}$
4. $0.\overline{7}$
5. $3.00\overline{4}$

Find the square. See pp. 334–335

6. 8
7. 13
8. $^-0.06$
9. 1.9
10. 0.004

Between which two whole numbers would the square root be?

11. 6
12. 56
13. 181
14. 115
15. 379

Find the square root. See pp. 336–337

16. $\sqrt{361}$
17. $\sqrt{576}$
18. $\sqrt{2209}$
19. $\sqrt{6561}$

20. $\sqrt{46.24}$
21. $\sqrt{75.69}$
22. $\sqrt{0.2304}$
23. $\sqrt{82.81}$

Classify each real number as rational or irrational. See pp. 338–339

24. 8
25. $^-3.8$
26. $0.5678\ldots$
27. $^-(7)^2$

28. $5\frac{1}{4}$
29. $4.0\overline{9}$
30. $\sqrt{29}$
31. $^-5\frac{3}{10}$

Write the solution set for each inequality. See pp. 340–341

32. $3n + 6 < 27$
33. $4t + 3 \geq 15$
34. $5s - 1 \leq 14$

35. $\frac{r}{4} + 3 > 12$
36. $\frac{x}{2} - 5 \leq 9$
37. $\frac{a}{3} - 3 < 1$

Which sets of measures form right triangles? See pp. 342–343

38. 8 m, 13 m, 15 m
39. 0.7 km, 2.4 km, 2.5 km
40. 3.5 mm, 4.5 mm, 5 mm

Find the missing dimension in these right triangles.

41. leg: ?
    leg: 30 cm
    hypotenuse: 50 cm

42. leg: 12 m
    leg: ?
    hypotenuse: 12.5 m

43. leg: 0.03 m
    leg: 0.04 m
    hypotenuse: ?

Solve.

44. A number is squared, then doubled. The result is 242. Find the number.

45. Mr. Hoch's square flower garden has an area of 196 square feet. Find its perimeter.

Cumulative Review

Choose the correct answer.

1. Which formula would give the area of this figure?

   a. ab

   b. $\frac{1}{2} ab$

   c. $2ab$

   d. $\frac{1}{2} a - 2b$

   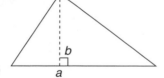

2. The square root of 1225 is 5 times larger than the square root of what number?

   a. 35   **b.** 49

   c. 7   **d.** 15.6

3. What is the ratio of $0.\overline{3}$ to $\frac{5}{9}$?

   a. $\frac{5}{27}$ **b.** $\frac{27}{5}$

   c. $\frac{5}{3}$ **d.** $\frac{3}{5}$

4. What is the height of a trapezoid with an area of 18 ft^2 and bases of 5 ft and 7 ft?

   a. 3 ft   **b.** 10 ft

   c. 9 ft   **d.** 6 ft

5. What is the length of the diagonal of a rectangle 9 cm wide and 12 cm long?

   a. 21 cm   **b.** 15 cm

   c. 10 cm   **d.** 24 cm

6. What is the area of the shaded region? Use $\frac{22}{7}$ for π.

   14 in.

   a. 154 in.^{2}
   b. 42 in.^{2}
   c. 196 in.^{2}
   d. 152 in.^{2}

7. Twenty-four circles each 2 cm in diameter are cut from a 12 cm × 9 cm paper. How many square centimeters are wasted?

   a. 150.72 cm^2 **b.** 75.36 cm^2

   c. 32.64 cm^2 **d.** 108 cm^2

8. How much greater than 2.4 is $2.\overline{4}$?

   a. $\frac{4}{100}$ **b.** $\frac{4}{90}$

   c. $\frac{4}{99}$ **d.** $\frac{4}{1000}$

9. What is the length of a rectangle whose perimeter is 32 cm if the length is 3 times the width?

   a. 4 cm   **b.** 8 cm

   c. 12 cm   **d.** 6 cm

10. 3 times the square root of 81 is n^3. What number is n?

    a. 4   **b.** 9

    c. 27   **d.** 3

11. Find the side of a square whose area is the same as that of a rectangle 8 inches wide and 32 inches long.

    a. 16 in.   **b.** 8 in.

    c. 32 in.   **d.** 64 in.

12. It takes 201.64 yd^2 of carpet to completely cover the floor of a square room. Find the length of one side of the room in feet.

    a. 14.2 ft   **b.** 42.6 ft

    c. 136.3 ft   **d.** 64.2 ft

13. The midpoint between 0.03 and 0.003 is what number?

    a. 0.027
    b. 0.017
    c. 0.150
    d. 0.0165

14. For which inequality is $\{s : s < {}^-9\}$ the solution set?

    a. $2s + 5 > 13$
    b. $^-2s + 5 < 23$
    c. $^-2s - 5 > 13$
    d. $^-2s - 5 > 18$

Find the area of each figure.

15.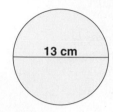

13 cm

16.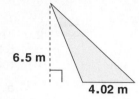

6.5 m

4.02 m

17.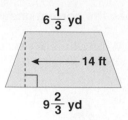

$6\frac{1}{3}$ yd

14 ft

$9\frac{2}{3}$ yd

18. Find the circumference of a circle with a diameter of 15 m.

19. Find the circumference of a circle with a diameter of 11.06 cm.

Find the missing dimension.

20. Rectangle: $A = 40$ yd^2
    width: $5\frac{1}{3}$ yd; length: ___?___

21. Triangle: $A = 71.4$ cm^2
    base: 10.2 cm; height: ___?___

Change to fractional form.

22. $0.02\overline{3}$ 23. $0.05\overline{64}$ 24. $0.\overline{12}$ 25. $4.01\overline{7}$ 26. $3.\overline{02}$ 27. $6.0\overline{102}$

Find a decimal approximation correct to the nearest thousandth.

28. $\sqrt{52}$ 29. $\sqrt{67}$ 30. $\sqrt{28}$ 31. $\sqrt{171}$

Find the square root of these decimals.

32. $\sqrt{0.3364}$ 33. $\sqrt{0.425104}$ 34. $\sqrt{1.4641}$ 35. $\sqrt{0.106929}$

Classify each real number as rational or irrational.

36. $\sqrt{7}$ 37. $0.121121112\ldots$ 38. $\sqrt{13}$
39. $^{-}(3.4)^2$ 40. $\sqrt{289}$ 41. 0.0347222

Solve. Round to the nearest tenth when necessary.

42. A circular park has an area of 15,400 sq ft. Find the length of a path from the center of the park to the outside rim.

43. A tree in the center of a circular platform is 14 ft from the edge. How many feet of lights are needed to encircle the edge of the platform?

44. If a bicycle wheel has a diameter of 28 in., how many revolutions will it make in 6 miles?

45. Fifty feet of fencing encloses a rectangular garden that is 14 feet long. What is the area of the garden?

46. A triangular piece of land is 320 ft deep and 140 ft wide. If a house is to be 30 ft by 50 ft, how much of the land will not be covered?

47. A circular swimming pool has a tile trim 1.5 ft from the edge. The pool is 12 ft in diameter. How many square feet of tile are there?

+10 BONUS

48. Design a picture frame that is not square or rectangular in shape. Label the dimensions. Find the perimeter of the frame and the area of the picture part.

13 Surface Area and Volume

In this chapter you will:

- Compute the surface area of prisms, pyramids, and curved solid figures
- Compute the volume of prisms, pyramids, cylinders, and cones
- Work with metric units of liquid volume and mass
- Solve problems: volume formulas
- Use technology: BASIC programming

Do you remember?

Polyhedrons are solid figures whose faces are polygons.

Polyhedrons have faces, bases, edges, and vertices.

face: any of the polygons that make up the figure
base: the face on which the figure rests
edge: a line segment common to two faces
vertex: a point of intersection of three or more faces

RESEARCHING TOGETHER

Model Mania

Create a model mania in the wonderful world of *polyhedrons*. Using straws, pipe cleaners, and so on, design polyhedrons such as, an octahedron, tetrahedron, dodecahedron, hexahedron, and icosahedron. Display your models. Then talk about the beginnings of polyhedrons and your models.

Surface Area of Prisms

Prism: a polyhedron with two parallel and congruent bases.
The shape of the base names the prism.

pentagonal prism

hexagonal prism

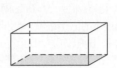
rectangular prism

triangular prism

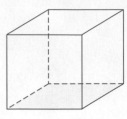
square prism (cube)

The **surface area of a prism** is the *sum* of the areas of all the faces.

▶ The formula for the *surface area of a rectangular prism* is: $S = 2[(\ell w) + (\ell h) + (wh)]$

$\ell = 30$ in.
$w = 16$ in.
$h = 7$ in.
$S = \underline{?}$

$S = 2[(\ell w) + (\ell h) + (wh)]$
$S = 2[(30 \times 16) + (30 \times 7) + (16 \times 7)]$
$S = 2[(480) + (210) + (112)]$
$S = 2(802) = 1604$ in.^{2}

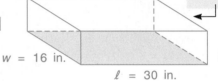

$w = 16$ in. $h = 7$ in. $\ell = 30$ in.

▶ The formula for the *surface area of a triangular prism* is: $S = 2(\frac{1}{2}bh) + (\ell_1 w) + (\ell_2 w) + (\ell_3 w)$

$b = 6$ m
$h = 1$ m
$\ell_1 = 4$ m
$\ell_2 = 5$ m
$\ell_3 = 6$ m
$w = 9$ m
$S = \underline{?}$

$S = 2(\frac{1}{2}bh) + (\ell_1 w) + (\ell_2 w) + (\ell_3 w)$
$S = 2(\frac{1}{2} \times 6 \times 1) + (4 \times 9) + (5 \times 9) + (6 \times 9)$
$S = 2(3) + (36) + (45) + (54)$
$S = 6 + 36 + 45 + 54 = 141$ m^2

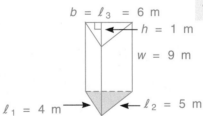

$b = \ell_3 = 6$ m
$h = 1$ m
$w = 9$ m
$\ell_1 = 4$ m $\ell_2 = 5$ m

Find the surface area.

1.

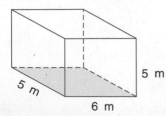

5 m   5 m   6 m

2.

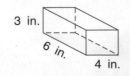

3 in.   6 in.   4 in.

3.

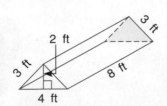

2 ft   3 ft   3 ft   8 ft   4 ft

4.

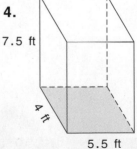

7.5 ft   4 ft   5.5 ft

5.

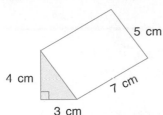

5 cm

4 cm

7 cm

3 cm

6.

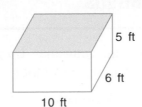

5 ft

6 ft

10 ft

7.

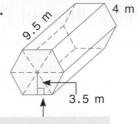

9.5 m

4 m

3.5 m

The bases are regular hexagons.

8.

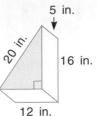

5 in.

20 in.

16 in.

12 in.

Surface Area of a Cube

What is the surface area of a cube 1.5 m on an edge?

The formula for the *surface area of a cube* is: $S = 6e^2$

$S = 6e^2$

$S = 6(1.5)^2$ ⟵ Square the edge.

$S = 6(2.25)$ ⟵ Then multiply.

$S = 13.5 \text{ m}^2$

$S = \underline{\ ?\ }$

$e = 1.5 \text{ m}$

Find the surface area of a cube with an edge of:

9. 31 in. **10.** 17 in. **11.** 0.6 yd **12.** 6.75 ft **13.** $6\frac{1}{2}$ ft **14.** $2\frac{1}{4}$ in.

Find the surface area of each rectangular prism.

15. $\ell = 24$ ft
$w = 15$ ft
$h = 6$ ft

16. $\ell = 36$ in.
$w = 7$ in.
$h = 3$ in.

17. $\ell = 7.6$ cm
$w = 3.4$ cm
$h = 2.5$ cm

18. $\ell = 3.5$ m
$w = 2.1$ m
$h = 10$ m

Solve.

19. Find the surface area of a school library this size.

20. What is the surface area of this triangular glass prism?

21. Find the surface area of both the inside and outside of this trough.

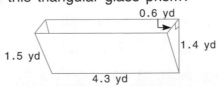

0.6 yd

1.4 yd

1.5 yd

4.3 yd

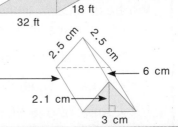

12 ft

32 ft

18 ft

2.5 cm 2.5 cm

6 cm

2.1 cm

3 cm

22. If one gallon of paint covers 150 square feet of surface, how many gallons are needed to paint the outside of this barn?

23. The surface area of a cube is 37.5 in.². What is the length of each edge of the cube?

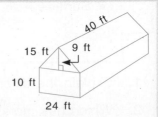

40 ft

15 ft

9 ft

10 ft

24 ft

13-2 Surface Area of Pyramids

Pyramid: a polyhedron with one base. The base may be a rectangle, a square, a triangle, or a pentagon. The pyramid's other faces are triangles.

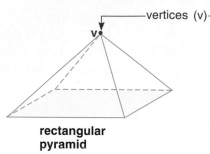 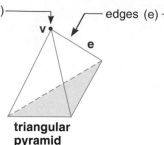 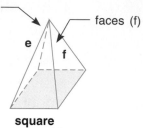 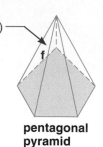

| rectangular pyramid | triangular pyramid | square pyramid | pentagonal pyramid |

The **surface area of a pyramid** is the *sum* of the areas of all the surfaces.

Find the surface area of this rectangular pyramid:

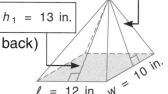

- Area of base: $\ell w = 12 \times 10 = 120$ in.^{2}

- Area of triangle:

$$\tfrac{1}{2}\,bh = \tfrac{1}{2}(12 \times 13) = 78 \text{ in.}^2 \text{ (front and back)}$$

- Area of triangle:

$$\tfrac{1}{2}\,bh = \tfrac{1}{2}(10 \times 15) = 75 \text{ in.}^2 \text{ (2 sides)}$$

$h_2 = 15$ in.
$h_1 = 13$ in.
$\ell = 12$ in. $w = 10$ in.

ℓ	= 12 in.
w	= 10 in.
h_1	= 13 in.
h_2	= 15 in.
S	= ?

- Surface Area (S):

$$\underline{120 + 78 + 78 + 75 + 75} = 426 \text{ in.}^2$$

Sum of the 5 surfaces

A **regular pyramid** has a base that is a regular polygon and has congruent isosceles triangles for its other faces.

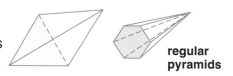

regular pyramids

In a regular pyramid the surface area is the area of the base plus *m* times the area of one triangular face, where *m* is the number of faces.

Find the surface area of this regular pyramid:

$h = 7$ cm

$b = 4$ cm

$s = 4$ cm

b	= 4 cm
h	= 7 cm
s	= 4 cm
S	= ?

- Area of square base: $s^2 = 4^2 = 16 \text{ cm}^2$

- Area of one triangular face: $\tfrac{1}{2}\,bh = \tfrac{1}{2}(4 \times 7) = \tfrac{1}{2}(28) = 14 \text{ cm}^2$

- Surface Area (S): $16 + 4(14) = 16 + 56 = 72 \text{ cm}^2$

↑ Number of triangular faces

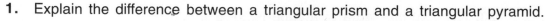

1. Explain the difference between a triangular prism and a triangular pyramid.

2. Which has more faces, a prism or a pyramid with the same-shaped base?

Find the surface area.

3.

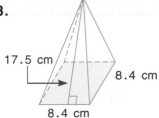

17.5 cm

8.4 cm

8.4 cm

4.

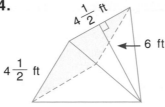

$4\frac{1}{2}$ ft

$4\frac{1}{2}$ ft

6 ft

5. The faces are congruent equilateral triangles.

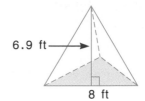

6.9 ft

8 ft

6. The base is an equilateral triangle.

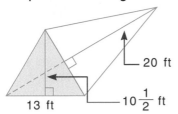

20 ft

13 ft

$10\frac{1}{2}$ ft

7.

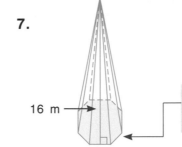

16 m

1 m

The base is a regular octagon with an area of 15.5 m².

Solve.

8. Which has the greater surface area, a square pyramid with a base edge of 8 in. and a triangle height of 4 in., *or* a square prism with an edge of 5 in.?

9. Karl made a rectangular pyramid. How much cardboard did he use if the base was 20 in. long and 24 in. wide and the height of each triangular face was 20 in.?

10. Find the surface area of the outside of this warehouse. The building is cubical in shape and each edge is 20 ft long.

Exercise 10

6.5 ft

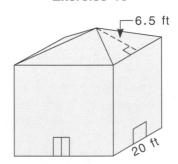

20 ft

SKILLS TO REMEMBER   **Copy and complete.**

		Prism			Pyramid		
			Number of:			Number of:	
		Faces	Edges	Vertices	Faces	Edges	Vertices
11.	Triangular	?	?	6	?	?	4
12.	Rectangular	6	?	8	?	8	?
13.	Pentagonal	?	15	?	6	?	?
14.	Hexagonal	8	?	?	?	?	7

CRITICAL **THINKING**

15. Let *n* represent the number of edges along the base of a prism. Write a formula for finding the number of faces, edges, and vertices of any prism. Repeat for a pyramid.

13-3 Surface Area of Curved Solid Figures

These solid figures have
curved surfaces.

cylinder   **cone**   **sphere**

Surface area of a cylinder: equals the sum of the area of its two congruent
circular bases and its rectangular surface.

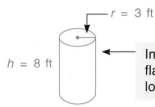

$r = 3$ ft

$h = 8$ ft

Imagine the cylinder
flattened. It would
look like this. ⟶ $h = 8$ ft

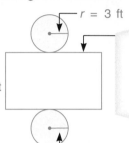

$r = 3$ ft

The length of the
rectangle equals
the circumference
of the circular
base, or $2\pi r$

$r = 3$ ft

▶ The formula for the *surface area of a cylinder* is:
$$S = (2 \times \pi r^2) + (2\pi r \times h)$$

$S = (2 \times \pi r^2) + (2\pi r \times h)$
$S \approx (2 \times 3.14 \times 3 \times 3) + (2 \times 3.14 \times 3 \times 8)$
$S \approx 56.52 + 150.72$
$S \approx 207.24$ ft^2

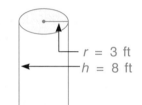

$r = 3$ ft
$h = 8$ ft

▶ The formula for the *surface area of a cone*
(where "ℓ" is the "slant height") is:
$$S = \pi r^2 + \pi r\ell \quad \text{or} \quad S = \pi r(r + \ell)$$

$S = \pi r^2 + \pi r\ell$
$S \approx (3.14 \times 8 \times 8) + (3.14 \times 8 \times 15)$
$S \approx (200.96) + (376.8)$
$S \approx 577.76$ in.^{2}

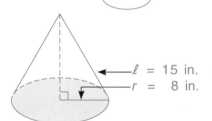

$\ell = 15$ in.
$r = 8$ in.

▶ The formula for the *surface area of a sphere* is:
$$S = 4\pi r^2$$

$S = 4\pi r^2$
$S \approx 4(3.14 \times 6 \times 6)$
$S \approx 4(113.04)$
$S \approx 452.16$ cm^2

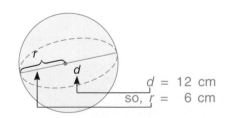

r
d

$d = 12$ cm
so, $r = 6$ cm

Find the surface area. (Use 3.14 for π.)

1.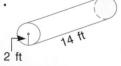

14 ft

2 ft

2.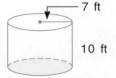

7 ft

10 ft

3.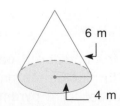

6 m

4 m

4.

3 in.

10 in.

358

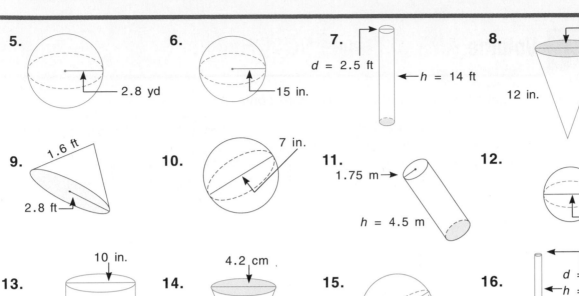

5. 2.8 yd

6. 15 in.

7. $d = 2.5$ ft, $h = 14$ ft

8. 8 in., 12 in.

9. 1.6 ft, 2.8 ft

10. 7 in.

11. 1.75 m, $h = 4.5$ m

12. 1.4 yd

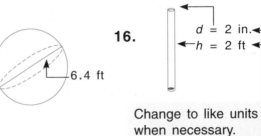

13. 10 in., $10\frac{1}{2}$ in.

14. 4.2 cm, 12.5 cm

15. 6.4 ft

16. $d = 2$ in., $h = 2$ ft

Change to like units when necessary.

Solve. Express the surface area in terms of π.
Then use the [π] key on a calculator to find the
approximate surface area. (The first one is done.)

17. What is the surface area of a 20-yard-high tank with a 2.5-yard diameter?

$$S = 2\pi\left(\frac{2.5}{2}\right)^2 + 2\pi\left(\frac{2.5}{2} \times 20\right) = 53.125\pi \text{ yd}^2 \longrightarrow S = 53.125 \times \pi$$
$$S \approx 166.89711 \text{ yd}^2$$

18. How many square feet of plastic are needed to line 5 dozen
waste baskets, each 26 inches in diameter and 30 inches high?
(Round to the nearest whole number.)

19. A cone-shaped drinking cup has a radius (r) of 1.5 in. and a
slant height (ℓ) of 4 in. How many square inches of paper are
needed to make 50 drinking cups?

20. A beach ball has a radius of 3.8 in. What is its surface area?

21. How much insulation is needed to cover the outside of a
steam pipe 16 inches in diameter and 60 inches high?

SUPPOSE THAT...

22. Lea made 3 cone-shaped ornaments each 3 inches in diameter
and 6 inches long (ℓ) from a rectangular sheet of silver
measuring 20 inches by 7 inches. If the ornaments were
open at the base, how much silver did she have left?

13-4 Volume

Volume: the number of cubic units a solid figure contains.

If a cube is 1 unit on a side, how many cubes will fit into a box 6 units long, 4 units wide, and 2 units high?

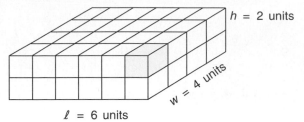

▶ **To find the volume,**

Think: $6 \times 4 = 24$ cubes in one layer
2 layers $= 2 \times 24 = 48$ cubes

The box has a volume of 48 cubic units.

The formula for the *volume of a cube* with edge *e* is:
$$V = e \times e \times e \quad \text{or} \quad V = e^3$$

▶ **To find the cube of a number,** use the number as a factor three times:

$$4^3 = 4 \times 4 \times 4 = 64$$
$$5^3 = 5 \times 5 \times 5 = 125$$

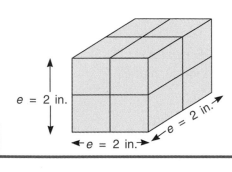

$V = e^3$

$V = 2^3$ ◀——— 2 to the third power is called "2 cubed."

$V = 2 \times 2 \times 2$

$V = 8 \text{ in.}^3$ ◀——— Read: "8 cubic inches."

Express the volume of each solid figure in cubic units.

1.

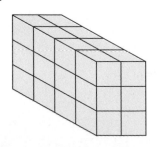

2.

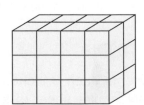

3.

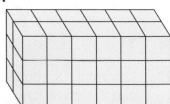

360

Express the volume of each solid figure in cubic units.

4.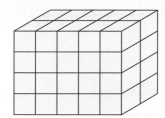

5.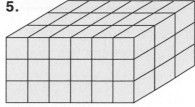

6.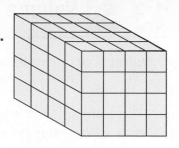

7. Write a formula that can be used to find the volume in exercises 1–6.

Copy and complete this table of cubes.
Use the y^x key on your calculator to check computations.

	Factor	Computation	Cube
8.	1	$1^3 = 1 \times 1 \times 1$	?
9.	2	$2^3 = 2 \times 2 \times 2$	?
10.	3	?	27
11.	4	?	?
12.	5	?	?
13.	6	?	?
14.	7	?	?

	Factor	Computation	Cube
15.	8	?	?
16.	9	?	?
17.	10	?	?
18.	15	?	?
19.	20	?	?
20.	25	?	?
21.	40	?	?

Find the volume of each cube.

22. $e = 5$ in.   **23.** $e = 4.8$ cm   **24.** $e = 7.5$ cm   **25.** $e = 12$ in.

26. $e = 14$ cm   **27.** $e = 6$ in.   **28.** $e = 10$ in.   **29.** $e = 20.3$ cm

Solve.

30. What is the volume of a storage box that measures 4 ft on each edge?

31. How many cubes 6 in. on an edge will fit into a bin that is 24 in. on an edge?

A NEW LOOK **SUPPOSE THAT...**

32. $2^3 = 8$ and $20^3 = 8000$, so $200^3 = $ __?__

33. $3^3 = 27$ and $(0.3)^3 = 0.027$, so $(0.03)^3 = $ __?__

Find the cube of each number. (Use the pattern in exercises 32 and 33.)

34. 30^3 **35.** 50^3 **36.** 70^3 **37.** $(0.1)^3$

38. $(0.2)^3$ **39.** $(0.5)^3$ **40.** $(0.4)^3$ **41.** $(0.06)^3$

42. $(0.004)^3$ **43.** $(0.008)^3$ **44.** $(0.07)^3$ **45.** $(0.09)^3$

Volume of a prism: equals the area of the base (**B**) multiplied by the height (**h**).

The formula for the *volume of a rectangular prism* is:
$$V = Bh$$

$V = Bh$ Area of Base = B

$V = (\ell w)h$

$V = (8 \times 7) \times 20$

$V = 1120 \text{ cm}^3$

$h = 20 \text{ cm}$

$\ell = 8 \text{ cm}$

$w = 7 \text{ cm}$

The formula for the *volume of a triangular prism* is:
$$V = Bh \text{ where } B = \text{Area of the base } (\tfrac{1}{2} bh)$$

$V = \quad B \ h$ where $B = (\tfrac{1}{2} bh)$

$V = \quad (\tfrac{1}{2} bh) \quad h$

$V = \quad [\tfrac{1}{2} (3 \times 2)] \times 9$

$V = \quad [\tfrac{1}{2} \times 6] \times 9 = 27 \text{ ft}^3$

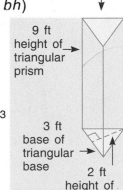

9 ft height of triangular prism

3 ft base of triangular base

2 ft height of triangular base

Volume of a pyramid: equals one third the volume of a prism having the same base and height.

The formula for the *volume of a pyramid* is: $V = \tfrac{1}{3} Bh$

Rectangular Pyramid

$V = \tfrac{1}{3} Bh$

$V = \tfrac{1}{3} (\ell w)h$

$V = \tfrac{1}{3} (11 \times 5) \times 6$

$V = 110 \text{ cm}^3$

$h = 6 \text{ cm}$

$\ell = 11 \text{ cm}$

$w = 5 \text{ cm}$

Triangular Pyramid

$V = \tfrac{1}{3} Bh$

$V = \tfrac{1}{3} (\tfrac{1}{2} bh)h$

$V = \tfrac{1}{3} (\tfrac{1}{2} \times 8 \times 3) \times 10$

$V = 40 \text{ ft}^3$

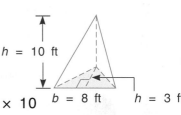

$h = 10 \text{ ft}$

$b = 8 \text{ ft}$ $h = 3 \text{ ft}$

Name the figure. Then find the volume.

1.

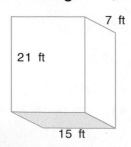

7 ft

21 ft

15 ft

2.

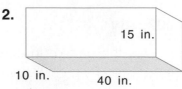

15 in.

10 in.   40 in.

3.

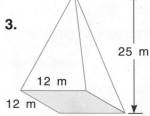

25 m

12 m

12 m

4.

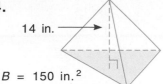

14 in. →

$B = 150$ in.^{2}

5.

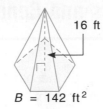

16 ft

$B = 142$ ft^2

6.

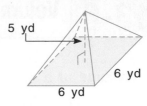

5 yd

6 yd

6 yd

Find the volume of each.

7. a rectangular prism

$\ell = 6\frac{1}{2}$ in.

$w = 4$ in.

$h = 12$ in.

8. a rectangular pyramid

$\ell = 2.7$ m

$w = 1.3$ m

$h = 2.4$ m

9. a pentagonal prism

$B = 3168$ ft^2

$h = 70$ ft

10. a square prism

$e = 7$ in.

$h = 5$ in.

11. a square pyramid

$e = 5.2$ m

$h = 5.2$ m

12. a square prism

$e = 15.2$ m

$h = 8.7$ m

13. a triangular prism

base of triangle $= 4\frac{1}{2}$ yd

height of triangle $= 4$ yd

height of prism $= 2\frac{2}{3}$ yd

14. a triangular pyramid

height of triangular base $= 3$ cm

base of triangle $= 2.7$ cm

height of pyramid $= 5.4$ cm

Solve.

15. Mike and Bob pitched a pyramid-shaped tent that covered an area of 11 square yards. If the tent was 1.5 yards high, what was its capacity (volume)?

16. Find the volume of a box 78 in. long, 2 ft wide, and 56 in. tall.

17. A room is 16 ft high. Its floor has an area of 648 square feet. How many people can meet in the room if each person should have 300 cubic feet of air to breathe?

18. How many cubic feet of marble are there in a statue base that is 10 ft long, 9 ft wide, and 6.5 ft high?

19. Which of these pyramids has the greater volume?

a.

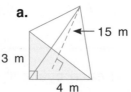

15 m

3 m

4 m

b.

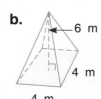

6 m

4 m

4 m

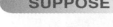

SUPPOSE

THAT...

20. A cube 5 cm on an edge is cut out of a rectangular prism 8 cm long, 9 cm wide, and 10 cm high. What is the volume of the solid figure that is left?

13-6 | Volume of Cylinders and Cones

Volume of a cylinder: equals the area of the base multiplied by the height.

> The formula for the *volume of a cylinder* is:
> $$V = \pi r^2 h$$

What is the volume of a cylindrical mold 5 meters in diameter and 50 meters high?

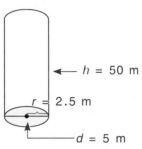

$$V = \quad \pi \qquad r^2 \qquad h$$
$$V = \quad \pi \times (2.5)^2 \times (50)$$
$$V \approx 3.14 \times 312.5$$
$$V \approx 981.25 \text{ m}^3$$
$$V \approx 981 \text{ m}^3 \text{ (rounded to the nearest whole number)}$$

$h = 50$ m
$r = 2.5$ m
$d = 5$ m
so, $r = 2.5$ m

Volume of a cone: equals one third the volume of a cylinder having the same base and height.

> The formula for the *volume of a cone* is:
> $$V = \frac{1}{3} \pi r^2 h$$

What is the volume of a conical (cone-shaped) mold if the diameter of its base is 16 in. and its height is 20 in.?

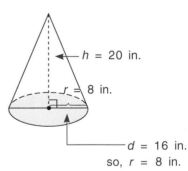

$$V = \frac{1}{3} \quad \pi \qquad r^2 \qquad h$$
$$V = \frac{1}{3} \quad \pi \times (8)^2 \times (20)$$
$$V \approx \frac{1}{3}(3.14) \times (64) \times (20)$$
$$V \approx 1339.733 \text{ in.}^3 \approx 1339.7 \text{ in.}^3 \text{ (rounded to the nearest tenth)}$$

$h = 20$ in.
$r = 8$ in.
$d = 16$ in.
so, $r = 8$ in.

Find the volume of each cylinder to the nearest tenth. (Use 3.14 for π.)

1. $r = 7$ ft
   $h = 5$ ft

2. $r = 3$ m
   $h = 15$ m

3. $r = 43$ in.
   $h = 90$ in.

4. $r = 6$ ft
   $h = 9$ ft

5. $r = 20$ yd
   $h = 75$ yd

6. $r = 18$ cm
   $h = 4$ cm

7. $d = 16$ ft
   $h = 6$ ft

8. $d = 11$ cm
   $h = 0.8$ cm

Find the volume of each cone to the nearest tenth. (Use 3.14 for π.)

9. $r = 9$ in.
   $h = 10$ in.

10. $r = 2$ yd
    $h = 6$ yd

11. $d = 20$ dm
    $h = 42$ dm

12. $r = 18$ ft
    $h = 14$ ft

13. $d = 22$ yd
    $h = 30$ yd

14. $d = 50$ ft
    $h = 25$ ft

15. $r = 8.1$ cm
    $h = 7$ cm

16. $r = 1.5$ mm
    $h = 3.6$ mm

Choose the best estimate. Then find the volume to the nearest tenth.

17. An underground storage tank is in the form of a cylinder with a diameter of 7 ft and a height of 4 ft. What is the capacity (volume)?

   a. 150 ft^3
   b. 50 ft^3
   c. 300 ft^3
   d. 88 ft^3

18. What is the capacity of a conical cup with a diameter of 5 in. and a height of 8 in.?

   a. 125 in.^{3}
   b. 21 in.^{3}
   c. 200 in.^{3}
   d. 50 in.^{3}

Solve. Express the volume in terms of π. Then use the $\boxed{\pi}$ key on a calculator to find the approximate volume. (The first one is done.)

19. Sula made a centerpiece in the shape of a cone. It measured 18 inches in diameter and 27 inches in height. What is the volume of the centerpiece?

   $$V = \frac{1}{3}\pi \times (9)^2 \times 27 = 729\pi \text{ in.}^3 \longrightarrow V = 729 \times \pi \approx 2290.221 \text{ in.}^3$$

20. A noisemaker was made by placing two cones rim to rim and inserting plastic chips to make the noise. What is the volume of the noisemaker if the cones are identical and measure 5 inches in diameter and 12 inches in height?

21. Raoul made a conical pedestal 32 inches high from a tree trunk 6 inches in diameter. How many cubic inches of wood did he use? (Round to the nearest tenth.)

22. What is the capacity of a circular swimming pool that is 16 ft in diameter and 9 ft deep?

23. The water tank for Desert City is 49 m tall and has a diameter of 12.5 m. What is its capacity?

24. If the tank in exercise 23 is half filled with water, how many cubic meters of water are there in the tank?

Exercise 22

$d = 16$ ft

$h = 9$ ft

13-7 Metric Units: Liquid Volume

Liter (L): the basic unit for measuring liquid volume, or capacity, in the metric system. All other units are related to the liter by powers of 10. The meaning of the metric prefixes will help in remembering how to change from one metric unit to another.

kiloliter	hectoliter	dekaliter	liter	deciliter	centiliter	milliliter
kL	hL	daL	L	dL	cL	mL
1000 L	100 L	10 L	1 L	0.1 L	0.01 L	0.001 L

The **kiloliter** is used to measure very large quantities.

The **liter** is used to measure average-size quantities.

The **milliliter** is used to measure very small quantities.

There is a special relationship between cubic units of volume and liquid capacity.

$$1 \text{ cm}^3 = 1 \text{ mL}$$
$$1 \text{ dm}^3 = 1 \text{ L}$$
$$1 \text{ m}^3 = 1 \text{ kL}$$

This cube holds 1 mL.

How many liters will this container hold?
Change to decimeters.

40 cm = 4 dm   18 cm = 1.8 dm   1 dm = 1 dm

$V = \ell w h$

$V = 4 \times 1.8 \times 1$

$V = 7.2 \text{ dm}^3$ or 7.2 L

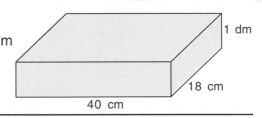

Change to milliliters.

6.7 L = __?__ mL

Use 1 L = 1000 mL

6.7 L = 6.7 × 1 L

6.7 L = 6.7 × 1000 mL

6.7 L = 6700 mL

Change to liters.

158 cL = __?__ L

Use 1 cL = 0.01 L

158 cL = 158 × 1 cL

158 cL = 158 × 0.01 L

158 cL = 1.58 L

Which unit of capacity (liter, kiloliter, or milliliter) would you use to measure the amount of:

1. water in a bucket?
2. water in a lake?
3. swimming-pool water?
4. soup on a spoon?
5. oil in a car?
6. water in a watering can?
7. juice in a pitcher?
8. milk in a cup?
9. liquid in an eyedropper?

Complete.

10. 4 mL = _?_ L
11. 425 mL = _?_ L
12. 6 L = _?_ mL
13. 2400 kL = _?_ L
14. 52 kL = _?_ L
15. 257 mL = _?_ dL
16. 74 kL = _?_ hL
17. 23 cL = _?_ mL
18. 2.16 mL = _?_ L
19. 2.91 dL = _?_ L
20. 1255 L = _?_ kL
21. 0.0076 L = _?_ mL
22. 0.2 L = _?_ mL
23. 46 cL = _?_ mL
24. 0.05 dL = _?_ L
25. 0.0007 dL = _?_ mL
26. 81.6 L = _?_ mL
27. 3150 kL = _?_ L

kilo	=	1000
hecto	=	100
deka	=	10
deci	=	$\frac{1}{10}$ = 0.1
centi	=	$\frac{1}{100}$ = 0.01
milli	=	$\frac{1}{1000}$ = 0.001

Change the cubic unit of volume to a unit of liquid capacity.

28. 34 cm^3
29. 7 m^3
30. 4.7 dm^3
31. 14 m^3
32. 2.5 dm^3
33. 2.6 m^3
34. 600 cm^3
35. 0.2 dm^3
36. 97 cm^3
37. 1.1 dm^3
38. 6.4 m^3
39. 3 dm^3

Solve. (Use 3.14 for π.)

40. How many milliliters of liquid will this container hold?

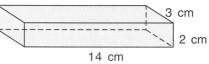

3 cm
2 cm
14 cm

41. Mr. James bought a new water heater 50 cm in diameter and 120 cm high. How many liters of water does it hold when filled to a depth of 100 cm?

42. How many liters of liquid are needed to fill this cylinder? (Round to the nearest liter.)

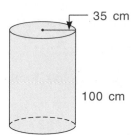

35 cm
100 cm

43. An oil tank is 4 m in diameter and 6.8 m deep. How many kiloliters of oil does it hold when it is 0.8 full? (Round to the nearest kiloliter.)

Finding Together

Imagine that a leaky faucet loses 2.5 mL of water a minute.

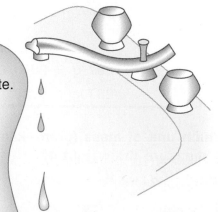

44. How much water would be lost in an hour?

45. Compute how much water is wasted in a day, in a month, and in a year.

46. Compute how much water is lost in a year if each one in your class has one leaky faucet at home.

47. Use a reference book to discover how this lost water could have been used by your community.

13-8 | Metric Units: Mass

Gram (g): the basic unit of mass (weight) in the metric system.
The meaning of the metric prefixes will help in remembering
how to change from one metric unit to another.

kilogram kg 1000 g	hectogram hg 100 g	dekagram dag 10 g	gram g 1 g	decigram dg 0.1 g	centigram cg 0.01 g	milligram mg 0.001 g

Milligrams and **grams** are used to report small weights.

A 1-carat gem weighs 200 mg.

A tennis ball weighs about 56 g.

Kilograms and **metric tons** are used to
report greater weights.

A thirteen-year-old weighs about 39 kg.

An elephant weighs about 3 t.

1 metric ton (t) = 1000 kg

There is a special relationship between cubic units
and metric measures of capacity and mass.

1 dm^3 holds 1 L of water and has a mass of 1 kg.

1 cm^3 holds 1 mL of water and has a mass of 1 g.

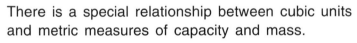

287 g = _?_ kg

Use 1 g = 0.001 kg

287 g = 287 × 1 g

287 g = 287 × 0.001 kg

287 g = 0.287 kg

580 mg = _?_ g

Use 1 mg = 0.001 g

580 mg = 580 × 1 mg

580 mg = 580 × 0.001 g

580 mg = 0.58 g

**Which unit of mass (gram, kilogram, metric ton, or milligram) would you use
to measure the weight of:**

1. a dog?
2. a motorcycle?
3. an adult?

4. a penny?
5. a truck?
6. a sand grain?

7. a pencil?
8. a postage stamp?
9. a baseball?

Complete.

10. 3 g = _?_ mg   **11.** 7 kg = _?_ g   **12.** 700 cg = _?_ g

13. 35 cg = _?_ kg   **14.** 4.1 t = _?_ kg   **15.** 16.5 t = _?_ kg

16. 0.008 cg = _?_ g   **17.** 360 cg = _?_ g   **18.** 0.5 t = _?_ kg

19. 4.73 g = _?_ mg   **20.** 1.7 g = _?_ mg   **21.** 0.56 kg = _?_ g

22. 34 000 g = _?_ kg   **23.** 6.5 t = _?_ kg   **24.** 0.035 mg = _?_ g

25. 5600 kg = _?_ t   **26.** 2.8 kg = _?_ g   **27.** 19 g = _?_ cg

28. 740 000 mg = _?_ g = _?_ kg = _?_ t

Copy and complete each chart.

	Capacity	Cubic Volume	Mass
29.	1 L	1 dm^3	?
30.	1 mL	?	1g
31.	?	5 cm^3	?
32.	?	?	6.2 g

	Capacity	Cubic Volume	Mass
33.	5.7 L	?	?
34.	?	2.7 dm^3	?
35.	8 L	?	?
36.	?	?	2.7 g

Solve.

37. Jesse bought a sports car that weighs 830 kg. How many grams is that?

38. Keri weighs 38 kg. Steven weighs 41.6 kg. How much more than Keri does Steven weigh?

39. The smallest type of whale weighs 45 kg. The largest type of whale weighs 136 t. What is the difference in their weights?

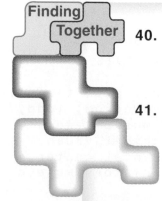

Finding Together

40. Use a reference book to find how each unit of measure is used.

     a. angstrom   **b.** microgram
     c. micron   **d.** megaton

41. Copy and complete the following.

     a. 1 angstrom = _?_ mm = _?_ cm = _?_ m

     b. 1 microgram = _?_ mg = _?_ cg = _?_ g

     c. 1 micron = _?_ mm = _?_ cm = _?_ m

     d. 1 megaton = _?_ t = _?_ kg

Programming: READ-DATA and GOTO Statements

A **READ statement** directs the computer to find a list of **DATA** and to use this data in the program the programmer wants to execute.

The data may consist of numbers, characters, and/or both. If characters are used, the variable name in the READ statement must include the character symbol, $.

READ
STATEMENT →

```
10   PRINT "NAME", "AGE"  ──────→  OUTPUT
20   READ N$, A
30   PRINT N$, A                    NAME   AGE
40   GOTO 20                        JOE    12
100  DATA JOE, 12, KELLY, 15,       KELLY  15
     NANCY, 13, TIM, 14             NANCY  13
                                    TIM    14
```

A **GOTO statement** is a statement that changes the normal flow of the program.

If the programmer wants to break the sequence of statements, a GOTO statement is used. This causes the program to continue processing on the line number indicated. This is called **branching** to that line number.

GOTO
STATEMENT →

```
10   PRINT "LENGTH", "WIDTH", ──────→  OUTPUT
     "PERIMETER"
20   READ L, W                    LENGTH  WIDTH  PERIMETER
30   LET P = 2*(L + W)              2       5       14
40   PRINT L, W, P                  9       8       34
50   GOTO 20                        4.2     6.9     22.2
100  DATA 2, 5, 9, 8, 4.2, 6.9
```

Give the output for each program.

1.
```
10   READ A, B, C
20   LET D = (A+B+C)/3
30   PRINT D; "IS THE AVERAGE
     OF"; A, B, C
40   GOTO 10
100  DATA 5, 8, 20, 7, 8, 9,
     20, 50, 20, 11,
     14, 20
```

2.
```
10   READ A$, B$
20   PRINT A$; "VISITED"; B$
30   GOTO 30
100  DATA Earl, planetarium,
     Karen, aquarium, Todd,
     science museum, Roy,
     space exhibit, Juan,
     environmental center,
     Rhonda, history museum
```

Powers, Square Roots, and Integer Functions

▶ **Powers of numbers** are indicated in two ways.

First Way
(↑) up arrow

```
           OUTPUT
PRINT  6↑2    36
```

Second Way
(^) circumflex

```
           OUTPUT
PRINT  6^2    36
```

▶ **Square roots** are found using the function **SQR**.

```
                OUTPUT
PRINT  SQR(36)     6
PRINT  SQR(81)     9
```

▶ **The integer function** is often used with IF-THEN statements to test for whole numbers.

```
                                   OUTPUT
10    LET X = 15
20    LET Y = 3            3 IS A FACTOR OF 15
30    LET Z = X/Y
40    IF Z = INT (X/Y) THEN PRINT Y; " IS A FACTOR
      OF "; X: GOTO 60
50    PRINT Y; " IS NOT A FACTOR OF "; X
60    END
```

Give the output for each statement.

3. PRINT 2↑5
4. PRINT INT (15.6)
5. PRINT SQR (49)
6. PRINT SQR (25)
7. PRINT INT (18/7)
8. PRINT INT (SQR(20))

9. Give the output for each program.

a.
```
10 PRINT "NUMBER", "SQUARE"
20 FOR N = 1 TO 12
30 LET M = N↑2
40 PRINT N, M

50 NEXT N
```

b.
```
10 FOR N = 1 TO 10
20 LET A = SQR (N)
30 IF A = INT (A)
   THEN PRINT N;"IS A
   PERFECT SQUARE"
40 NEXT N
```

10. Write a program that will print out a table of cubes for any number.

11. Write a program which asks the user for a number less than 500 and which will test for divisibility by 11. Then print out the message that the number *is* or *is not* divisible by 11.

CALCULATOR CHALLENGE

12. If someone in your class had $1 billion and gave away $500 to a charity every hour, how long would it take to give away all of the money?

Problem: A carpenter is cutting as large a pyramid as possible from a wooden cube 4.5 cm on an edge. What is the volume of the leftover wood?

e = 4.5 cm

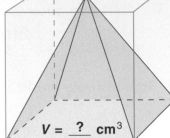

1 IMAGINE Visualize the largest possible pyramid within a cube of wood. Draw and label your visualization.

2 NAME

Fact: 4.5 cm — edge of cube

$V = $ _?_ cm³

Question: _?_ cm³ — volume of leftover wood

V of cube – V of pyramid = _?_

3 THINK This problem involves more than one volume question. Look at your picture and see:

First you find the volume of the entire cube:

$V = e^3 \longrightarrow V = 4.5^3$

Then you find the volume of the pyramid.

$V = \frac{1}{3} Bh \longrightarrow B = (4.5 \times 4.5)$ and $h = 4.5$

Finally, the difference between these volumes will give you the volume of the leftover wood.

V (cube) – V (pyramid) = V (leftover wood)

4 COMPUTE

Volume of Cube	Volume of Pyramid
$V = e^3$	$V = \frac{1}{3} Bh$
$V = (4.5)^3$	$V = \frac{1}{3} (4.5 \times 4.5 \times 4.5)$
$V = 91.125$ cm³	$V = 30.375$ cm³

Leftover Wood Volume:

$$\underbrace{91.125 \text{ cm}^3}_{V \text{ (cube)}} - \underbrace{30.375 \text{ cm}^3}_{V \text{ (pyramid)}} = \underbrace{60.75 \text{ cm}^3}_{V \text{ (leftover wood)}}$$

The volume of the wood *not* used is 60.75 cm³.

5 CHECK $\frac{1}{3}$ of the wood is used for the pyramid (30.375 cm³).

$\frac{2}{3}$ of the wood is *not* used (60.75 cm³).

30.375 cm³ + 60.75 cm³ = 91.125 cm³   Total Volume of Cube

Solve by using a formula.

1. A water trough shaped like a triangular prism is 2 yards long, 2 feet wide, and $1\frac{2}{3}$ feet deep is $\frac{3}{4}$ full of water. What is the volume of the water in the trough?

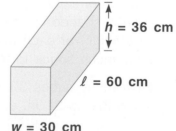

1 IMAGINE	Draw and label a picture of the water trough. →	2 NAME	┌→ *Facts*
			└→ *Question*

3 THINK

Be sure all units of measure are like.
(Change 2 yards to feet.)
Find the volume of the triangular prism
in cubic feet. Use the formula:

$$V = Bh$$
$$V = \boxed{\frac{1}{2}\,bh} \times \boxed{h} \quad 1\frac{2}{3}\text{ ft}$$

Area of Base   Depth of Prism

Now, multiply the volume by $\frac{3}{4}$.

4 COMPUTE ──→ **5 CHECK**

2. A rectangular container for popcorn is $\frac{2}{3}$ full. If the container measures 21 in. by $1\frac{1}{2}$ ft by 16 in., how much space does the popcorn fill?

3. Jeff wants to fill a flower bed with gravel. The flower bed measures 9 m by 6 m and will be filled to a depth of 0.02 m. How much will it cost him to fill the flower bed if gravel costs $25 a cubic meter?

4. A coffee urn 10 inches in diameter and 18 inches high is packed in a box that is 12 inches long, 12 inches wide, and 20 inches high. What is the volume of the box that is not occupied by the urn?

5. How many liters of juice are there in 6 cans, each of which has a diameter of 4 cm and a height of 10.5 cm?

6. Gratia prepared her new aquarium for her fish. The aquarium is 60 cm long, 30 cm wide, and 36 cm high. She spread 2 cm of gravel along the bottom, and filled the aquarium with water to a level 1.5 cm from the top. About how many mL of water did she put into the aquarium?

   $h = 36$ cm
   $\ell = 60$ cm
   $w = 30$ cm

7. A cone 20 cm in diameter and 14 cm high was used to fill a cubical planter, 25 cm on each side, with soil. About how many cones-ful of soil were needed to fill the planter?

13-11 Problem Solving: Applications

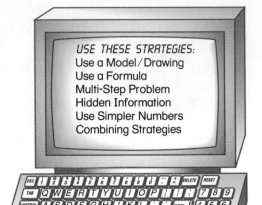

USE THESE STRATEGIES:
Use a Model/Drawing
Use a Formula
Multi-Step Problem
Hidden Information
Use Simpler Numbers
Combining Strategies

1. How many different sets of two parallel edges are there in a cube?

2. How many different sets of two parallel faces are there in a rectangular prism?

3. How many different sets of two parallel faces are there in a hexagonal prism?

4. How many different sets of two parallel edges are there in a triangular prism?

5. About how many square centimeters of plastic are used to make a dozen beach balls each having a diameter of 35 cm?

6. Trudy's roll of wrapping paper will cover 400 sq in. How many square inches of paper will she have left if she covers the curved surface of 4 coffee cans each 7 in. tall and 4 in. in diameter?
   (Hint: Lateral surface = perimeter of base × height.)

7. How many cubic inches of soil will fill 2 cone-shaped planters each 8 in. deep and 5 in. in diameter?

8. How many square inches of paper would be needed to cover the 6 sides of a box 18 inches long, 12 inches wide, and 9 inches high?

9. Cheerleaders cover the outsides of three megaphones with foil paper. If the megaphones have a 20-cm diameter and slant height of 64 cm, how much foil paper will they use?
   (Hint: Use $\pi r \ell$.)

Exercise 9

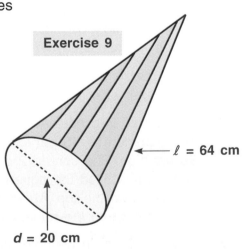

$\ell = 64$ cm

$d = 20$ cm

10. The cheerleaders pack the three megaphones into a cube-shaped carton 64 cm on each edge. The height of each megaphone is 63 cm. How much space in the carton will be left over?

11. How many cubes 3 in. on an edge will fit into a bin that is 21 in. on an edge?

12. How many liters of yogurt will a container hold if it has a diameter of 63 cm and a depth of 30 cm?

13. Mia bought 4 drinking glasses. If each glass has a diameter of $3\frac{1}{4}$ inches and a depth of $5\frac{1}{2}$ inches, what is their total volume (to the nearest cubic inch)?

14. Directions on a frozen-juice can 5.1 cm in diameter and 10.5 cm deep recommend adding 3 cans of water to the concentrate. To the nearest milliliter, what will the total volume be when this is done?

15. At $1 per square foot, what is the cost of painting the entire inside of a closed tank that is 20 yards high and has a 7-foot diameter?

16. What is the surface area of 6 spherical candles each having a diameter of $4\frac{1}{2}$ inches?

17. Plastic is shaped into a cone to make a funnel. If the cone has a diameter of 7 in. and a slant height (ℓ) of 15 in., how much plastic is used to make the cone?

18. What is the difference in surface area between a sphere with a 20-in. diameter and a cube with a 20-in. edge?

19. What is the capacity of a prism-shaped clothes hamper that is 2 ft 3 in. deep and has a base measuring 2 ft by 1 ft 4 in.?

20. How many cubic feet smaller is the volume of a pentagonal pyramid 12 ft high whose base has an area of 296 ft² than the volume of a square pyramid 15 ft high whose base is 18 ft on each edge?

21. A candle maker forms a half-dozen cone-shaped candles from wax. The candles all have a diameter of 40 cm and are 21 cm high.

   a. What is the volume of one candle?

   b. How many cubic centimeters of wax are needed to make the half-dozen candles?

   c. Wax chips are sold in 100 cm³ blocks each costing $2.09. How much will it cost for the wax to make the candles?

   d. Wick costs 39¢ per 10 cm. If the candle maker allows 1 cm of extra wick at the top and at the bottom of the candles, how many cm must be bought? How much will the wick cost?

   e. How many liters of wax are used to make the candle?

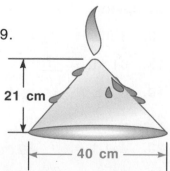

21 cm

40 cm

More Practice

Find the surface area.

1.
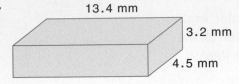
13.4 mm
3.2 mm
4.5 mm

2.
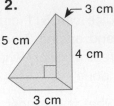
3 cm
5 cm
4 cm
3 cm

3.
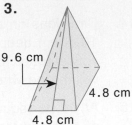
9.6 cm
4.8 cm
4.8 cm

4.
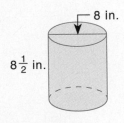
8 in.
$8\frac{1}{2}$ in.

5.
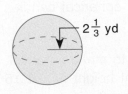
$2\frac{1}{3}$ yd

6.
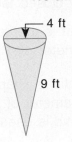
4 ft
9 ft

Find the volume.

7.
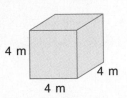
4 m
4 m
4 m

8.
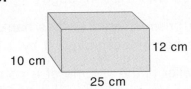
12 cm
10 cm
25 cm

9.
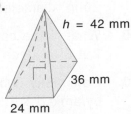
h = 42 mm
36 mm
24 mm

10.
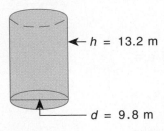
h = 13.2 m
d = 9.8 m

11.
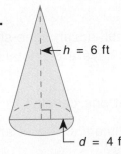
h = 6 ft
d = 4 ft

12.
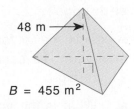
48 m
B = 455 m²

Complete.

13. 3 mL = __?__ L

14. 5 L = __?__ mL

15. 1700 kL = __?__ L

16. 61 kL = __?__ L

17. 15 cL = __?__ mL

18. 0.5 L = __?__ mL

19. 3.76 dL = __?__ L

20. 1513 L = __?__ kL

21. 2150 kL = __?__ L

22. 5 g = __?__ mg

23. 6 kg = __?__ g

24. 600 cg = __?__ g

25. 4.1 t = __?__ kg

26. 3.7 kg = __?__ g

27. 0.045 mg = __?__ g

28. 21 g = __?__ cg

29. 36 000 g = __?__ kg

30. 2400 kg = __?__ t

Math Probe

SOLIDS – HOW IRREGULAR!

This irregular figure has the general characteristics of a prism, so its volume should be equal to the product of the *area of its base* and its *height*.

$$V = Bh$$

5 cm

To approximate the area of the base, trace the base onto centimeter graph paper.

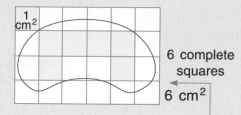

6 complete squares

6 cm²

Count the number of *complete* squares within the base.

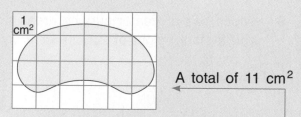

A total of 11 cm²

Count the number of square units needed to cover the base completely.

$$6 \text{ cm}^2 < B < 11 \text{ cm}^2$$

Find the average of the two areas to give an estimate for B.

$$B \approx \frac{6 + 11}{2} \longrightarrow B \approx 8.5 \text{ cm}^2$$

Then use the formula $V = Bh$. $\longrightarrow$ $V \approx 8.5 \text{ cm}^2 \times 5 \text{ cm}$ $\longrightarrow$ $V \approx 42.5 \text{ cm}^3$

Trace these figures on cm graph paper. Then for each, compute the volume if it were the base of a solid figure having a height of 4 cm.

1.

2.

3.

4. Draw some irregular figures on graph paper. Challenge a friend to estimate their volume if each were the base of a solid figure.

Check Your Mastery

Find the surface area.

See pp. 354–359

1.

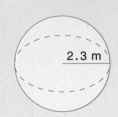

2.3 m

2.

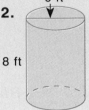

6 ft

8 ft

3.

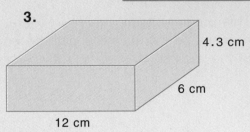

4.3 cm

6 cm

12 cm

4. A ball has a diameter of 36.4 cm. What is its surface area?

5. A cubical box measures 3.4 ft on a side. What is its surface area?

6. Which has a greater surface area, a square pyramid with a base edge of 5 in. and a slant height of 2.5 in. or a square prism with an edge of 6 in.?

Find the volume.

See pp. 360–365

7.

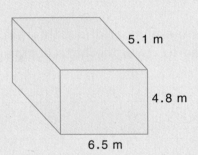

5.1 m

4.8 m

6.5 m

8.

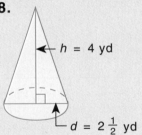

$h = 4$ yd

$d = 2\frac{1}{2}$ yd

9.

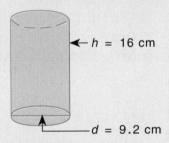

$h = 16$ cm

$d = 9.2$ cm

10. a rectangular prism
$\ell = 9$ m
$w = 4$ m
$h = 10$ m

11. a cylinder
$r = 5\frac{1}{2}$ ft
$h = 14$ ft

12. a cone
$r = 25$ cm
$h = 40$ cm

Complete.

See pp. 366–369

13. 7 mL = _?_ L

14. 2 L = _?_ mL

15. 2500 kL = _?_ L

16. 38 kL = _?_ L

17. 18 cL = _?_ mL

18. 0.7 L = _?_ mL

19. 2.91 dL = _?_ L

20. 1314 L = _?_ kL

21. 3225 kL = _?_ L

22. 8 g = _?_ mg

23. 3 kg = _?_ g

24. 400 cg = _?_ g

25. 3.5 t = _?_ kg

26. 4.2 kg = _?_ g

27. 0.065 mg = _?_ g

28. 35 g = _?_ cg

29. 43 000 g = _?_ kg

30. 2800 kg = _?_ t

14 | Coordinate Geometry

In this chapter you will:

- Graph points on the real number line
- Graph points on all four quadrants of the coordinate plane
- Solve equations with two variables
- Graph equations and inequalities
- Graph and solve systems of equations and inequalities
- Graph curves on the coordinate plane
- Solve problems: solving systems of equations

Do you remember?

Equations with one variable have one solution.

$$x + 5 = 9 \longrightarrow x = 9 - 5 \longrightarrow x = 4$$
$$x + 18 = 11 \longrightarrow x = 11 - 18 \longrightarrow$$
$$x = 11 + {}^-18 \longrightarrow x = {}^-7$$

Inequalities can have more than one solution.

$$x + 4 > 3 \longrightarrow x > 3 - 4 \longrightarrow x > {}^-1$$

The solution set of $x > {}^-1$, if the replacement set is the real numbers, is all numbers, rational and irrational, greater than ${}^-1$.

Some of these solutions are:
${}^-0.9, \ldots, {}^-0.8, \ldots, 0, \ldots.$
$0.8, \ldots, 0.9, \ldots, 1, \ldots.$

Creating a Treasure Map

The grizzled old prospector, Arroyo Al, buried his new-found gold nuggets in the desert 75 paces from the largest cactus. Then he went off to the Tumbleweed Hotel. When he returned some days later, he carefully paced off the distances and dug... and dug... and dug. The gold was not there! Can you draw a map and help Arroyo Al find it?

14-1 Graphing on the Real Number Line

Every point on a number line can be named by a real number.
Coordinates are numbers matched with points on a number line.

Point A is marked by the coordinate $^-5$.
The coordinate of point B is $^+2$.
What are the coordinates of points C, D, and E?

The solution of an *equation* can be graphed on a number line.

$x - 2 = 3$

$x - 2 + 2 = 3 + 2$

$x = 5$

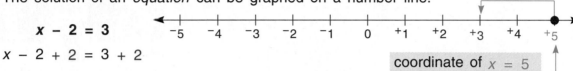

coordinate of $x = 5$

The solution of an *inequality* can also be graphed on a number line.

$x + 5 > 3$

$x + 5 - 5 > 3 - 5$

$x > {}^-2$

S: $\{x: x > {}^-2\}$

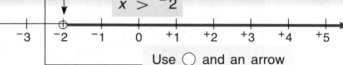

Use ◯ and an arrow
to graph $<$ or $>$.

$x - 6 \le {}^-4$

$x - 6 + 6 \le {}^-4 + 6$

$x \le 2$

S: $\{x: x \le 2\}$

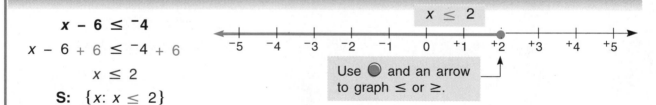

Use ● and an arrow
to graph $\le$ or $\ge$.

$^-2x > {}^-8$

$\dfrac{^-2x}{^-2} < \dfrac{^-8}{^-2}$

$x < {}^+4$

S: $\{x: x < {}^+4\}$

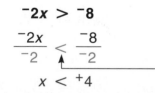

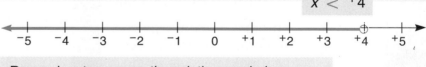

Remember to reverse the relation symbol
when multiplying or dividing by a negative number.

Give the coordinate for each point on the line.

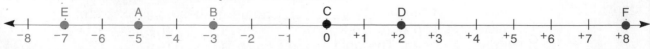

1. A 2. B 3. C 4. D 5. E 6. F

Find the solution. Graph it on a real number line.

7. $x + 3 = 9$ 8. $x - 4 = 9$ 9. $5x = {}^-10$ 10. $x \div 4 = 2$

11. $x + 5 < 8$ 12. $x + 7 < 11$ 13. $x - 4 \geq 2$ 14. $x - 3 > 2$

15. $6x > 24$ 16. $3x > 15$ 17. $5x \leq {}^-20$ 18. $6x \leq {}^-18$

19. ${}^-x > {}^-3$ 20. ${}^-x > {}^-1$ 21. ${}^-2x \leq 4$ 22. ${}^-3x \geq 21$

23. $2x + 1 \geq 7$ 24. $3x + 1 \leq 10$ 25. $5x - 1 < 14$ 26. $7x - 2 > 26$

27. $\dfrac{x}{4} < 1$ 28. $\dfrac{x}{2} > 3$ 29. $\dfrac{x}{-5} \leq 1$ 30. $\dfrac{x}{-3} > {}^-2$

Graphing Compound Inequalities

Graph this compound inequality: $\{x: {}^-2 < x < {}^+1.5\}$

To graph the real numbers (x) between ${}^-2$ and ${}^+1.5$: $x > {}^-2$ and $x < {}^+1.5$

- Place ○ on the boundary points ${}^-2$ and ${}^+1.5$.
- Shade the number line between these boundary points.

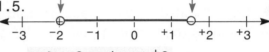

Graph: $\{x: {}^-3 \leq x < {}^+2\}$

$x \geq {}^-3$ and $x < {}^+2$
boundary points

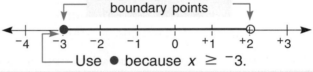

Use ● because $x \geq {}^-3$.

Graph each compound inequality.

31. $\{x: {}^-3 < x \leq {}^+1\}$ 32. $\{x: 0 \leq x \leq 5\}$ 33. $\{x: {}^-2.5 \leq x \leq 2\}$

Which equations or inequalities have their solution shown on these graphs?

34.
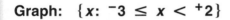

a. $\dfrac{x}{6} = 0$ b. $x - 4 = {}^-4$ c. $x + 2 = {}^-2$ d. $\dfrac{x}{2} = {}^-4$

35.

a. $x \geq {}^-1$ b. $x \leq {}^-1$ c. $x > 1$ d. $x \geq 1$

36.

a. $x + 4 = 7$ b. $x - 2 = {}^-5$ c. $x^2 = 9$ d. $x^3 = 27$

37.

a. ${}^-2 \leq x \leq 4$ b. ${}^-2 < x < 4$ c. ${}^-2 \leq x < 4$ d. $4 > x > {}^-2$

Coordinate axes: a horizontal and a vertical line can be placed together to form a grid.

X-axis: the horizontal line of the axes.
Y-axis: the vertical line of the axes.

Point of origin: the point where the horizontal and vertical axes meet.

Use ordered pairs of numbers (*x*, *y*) to locate points on the **coordinate grid.**

Set of coordinates: each ordered pair of numbers represents a point on the grid.

The first number in the ordered pair gives the *x-value.* The second number in the ordered pair gives the *y-value.*

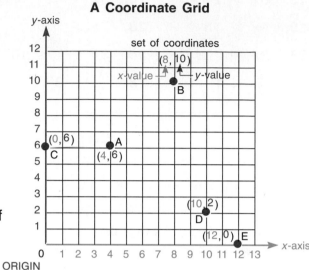

A Coordinate Grid

The *x-* and *y-values* are called the coordinates of the point. The coordinates of the **point of origin** are (0, 0).

Point *A* with coordinates (4, 6) can be described as being:

4 units to the right of the origin.

6 units up from the origin.

4 is the horizontal or *x*-coordinate.

6 is the vertical or *y*-coordinate.

Name the coordinates or ordered pairs for each point.

1. *A*
2. *B*
3. *C*
4. *D*
5. *E*
6. *F*
7. *G*
8. *H*
9. *K*

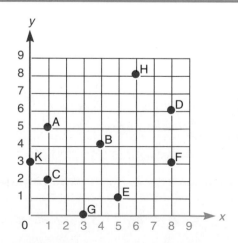

**Match each ordered pair
with the letter of its graph.**

10. (8, 2) **11.** (5, 7)

12. (2, 6) **13.** (4, 0)

14. (10, 9) **15.** (6, 4)

16. (12, 12) **17.** (11, 7)

18. (7, 10) **19.** (0, 8)

20. (1, 4) **21.** (10, 1)

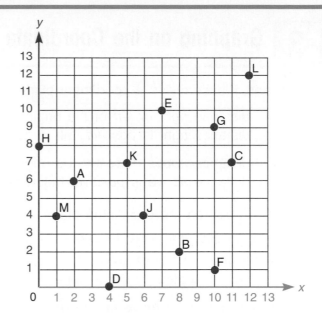

**On a piece of graph paper draw a set of coordinate axes.
Then graph the point for each ordered pair.**

22. A(7, 3) **23.** B(4, 1) **24.** C(2, 2) **25.** D(6, 0)

26. E(5, 6) **27.** F(0, 5) **28.** G(3, 7) **29.** H(1, 4)

30. M(0, 0) **31.** J(5, 5) **32.** K(7, 0) **33.** L(12, 3)

**For each exercise draw a set of coordinate axes. Graph each set of points.
Then connect the points in the order listed. Name the figure that results.**

34. (3, 1); (5, 6); (2, 6); (2, 8); (7, 8); $(4\frac{1}{2}, 1)$; (3, 1)

35. (4, 3); (4, 7); $(5\frac{1}{2}, 7)$; (7, 9); (2, 9); (2, 1); (7, 1); $(5\frac{1}{2}, 3)$; (4, 3)

36. (5, 6); (5, 4); (7, 4); (7, 6); (9, 6); (9, 8); (7, 8);

(7, 10); (5, 10); (5, 8); (3, 8); (3, 6); (5, 6)

37. Draw a set of coordinate axes on a piece of graph paper.
Then draw a quadrilateral and label its coordinates.

38. Use formulas to find the perimeter and area of your quadrilateral.

Graphing on the Coordinate Plane: Four Quadrants

The *x*- and *y*-axes divide a coordinate plane into **four quadrants** named: **I, II, III, IV**.

x-value: distance *right or left* of the origin.
distance right is *positive*; left is *negative*.

y-value: distance *above or below* the origin.
distance above is *positive*; below is *negative*.

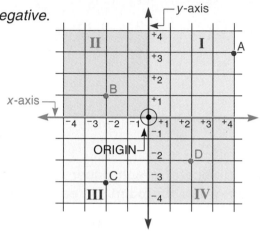

To graph a point on the coordinate plane:

- Find the *x*-value. Then begin at the origin and move the number of units left or right of the origin indicated by the *x*-value.

- Then from that point move the given number of units above or below the *x*-axis indicated by the given *y*-value.

The graphs of the following points are given.

($^-$2, 1) = coordinates of point *B*.
   B is 2 units to the left of and 1 unit above the origin.

($^-$2, $^-$3) = coordinates of point *C*.
   C is 2 units to the left of and 3 units below the origin.

(4, 3) = coordinates of point *A*.
   A is 4 units to the right of and 3 units above the origin.

(2, $^-$2) = coordinates of point *D*.
   D is 2 units to the right of and 2 units below the origin.

This graph shows the signs in each quadrant.

Within each quadrant every *x*-coordinate and every *y*-coordinate has the sign indicated on this graph.

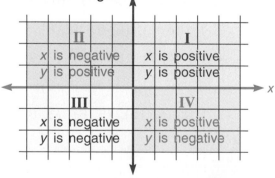

Name the coordinates of each point.

1. *A*   2. *B*   3. *C*

4. *D*   5. *E*   6. *F*

7. *G*   8. *H*   9. *K*

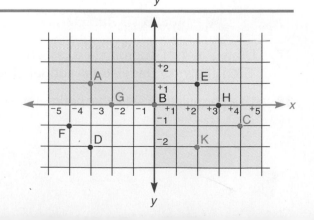

Match each ordered pair with the letter of its graph.

10. $(^+4, ^+5)$ **11.** $(^+2, ^+2)$ **12.** $(^-3, 0)$

13. $(^-4, ^-2)$ **14.** $(0, ^-4)$ **15.** $(0, ^+3)$

16. $(^+5, 0)$ **17.** $(^-3, ^+2)$ **18.** $(^-1, ^+4)$

19. $(0, 0)$ **20.** $(^+3, ^-2)$ **21.** $(^+2, ^-4)$

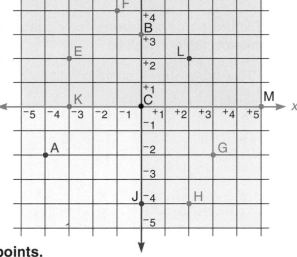

22. Which points are in Quadrant I?

23. Which points are in Quadrant II?

24. Which points are in Quadrant III?

25. Which points are in Quadrant IV?

26. Which points lie on the *x*-axis?

Draw a pair of coordinate axes. Graph these points.

27. $A(^+6, ^+1)$ **28.** $B(^+2, ^+5)$ **29.** $C(^+3, ^+7)$ **30.** $D(^+5, 0)$

31. $E(^+1, 0)$ **32.** $F(^+4, ^-2)$ **33.** $G(^+7, ^-4)$ **34.** $H(^-6, ^+1)$

35. $R(^-8, ^+3)$ **36.** $J(^-2, ^-5)$ **37.** $K(^-5, ^+2\frac{1}{2})$ **38.** $L(^+3\frac{1}{2}, ^-6\frac{1}{2})$

39. $M(^-2\frac{1}{2}, ^+4\frac{1}{2})$ **40.** $N(^+4.5, ^+1)$ **41.** $O(^-4.5, ^-1)$ **42.** $P(^-6.5, ^+2.5)$

Complete each statement.

43. The point $(0, 0)$ is called the ___?___ .

44. Another name for the vertical axis is the ___?___ .

45. All points with both *x*- and *y*-coordinates negative lie in Quadrant ___?___ .

Draw a pair of coordinate axes. Graph and connect each set of points.

46. $(^-5, 4)$; $(^-3, 4)$; $(^-1, 4)$ **47.** $(2, ^-1)$; $(2, ^-4)$; $(2, ^-6)$

48. $(1, 1)$; $(2, 2)$; $(3, 3)$ **49.** $(^-1, 1)$; $(^-2, 2)$; $(^-3, 3)$

50. Which line segments in exercises 46 – 49 are:
    a. horizontal?   **b.** vertical?   **c.** diagonal?

CRITICAL THINKING

51. Explain the relationship between a vertical line and its coordinates. (Hint: Use exercises 46 – 50.)

52. Explain the relationship between a horizontal line and its coordinates.

53. Predict coordinates that would form a diagonal line segment in Quadrant III. Graph your coordinates to check your prediction.

14-4 | Equations with Two Variables

To find some solutions for equations with two variables, make a table of values.

This table shows some solutions of: **$y = 2x + 3$**

x	$^-3$	$^-2$	$^-1$	0	1	2	3
y	$^-3$	$^-1$	1	3	5	7	9

When values are assigned to x, find the corresponding values for y.

$y = \quad 2x + 3$
$y = 2(^-3) + 3$
$y = \quad ^-6 + 3$
$y = ^-3$

$y = \quad 2x + 3$
$y = 2(^-1) + 3$
$y = \quad ^-2 + 3$
$y = 1$

$y = \quad 2x + 3$
$y = 2(2) + 3$
$y = \quad 4 + 3$
$y = 7$

The x- and y-values in the table above can be written as ordered pairs:

$(^-3, \ ^-3)$; $(^-2, \ ^-1)$; $(^-1, \ 1)$; $(0, \ 3)$; $(1, \ 5)$; $(2, \ 7)$; $(3, \ 9)$

A **solution** of an equation with two variables is an ordered pair of numbers that forms a true number sentence.

To find a solution of an equation with two variables
such as $\boxed{y = 2x - 5}$, give x a value and find the y-value that, when paired with x, results in a true number sentence.

$y = 2x - 5 \longrightarrow$ Let $x = 2$
$y = 2(2) - 5 \longrightarrow y = 4 - 5 \longrightarrow y = ^-1$
One solution: $(2, \ ^-1)$

When a given equation has both x and y on the same side of the equation, change it to an equivalent equation of this form: $y = \underline{\ ?\ }$

$y - 3x = 7 \xrightarrow{\text{Add } 3x} y = 7 + 3x$

$5x + 2y = 9 \xrightarrow{\text{Subtract } 5x} 2y = 9 - 5x \xrightarrow{\text{Divide by 2}} y = \dfrac{9 - 5x}{2}$

Use the equation $y = 4x - 8$ to find the y-value that makes each ordered pair a solution.

1. $(4, \ \underline{\ ?\ })$
2. $(3, \ \underline{\ ?\ })$
3. $(^-4, \ \underline{\ ?\ })$
4. $(^-3, \ \underline{\ ?\ })$

5. $(0, \ \underline{\ ?\ })$
6. $(1, \ \underline{\ ?\ })$
7. $(^-2, \ \underline{\ ?\ })$
8. $(^-1, \ \underline{\ ?\ })$

Change each to an equivalent equation in this form: $y = \underline{\ ?\ }$.

9. $y + 3x = 9$ **10.** $y + 2x = 13$ **11.** $4x + y = 12$

12. $5x + y = 16$ **13.** $6x + 3y = 15$ **14.** $15x + 5y = 35$

Complete each table of values.

15. $y = 4x + 3$

x	⁻2	⁻1	0	1	2	3	4	5
y								

16. $y = 3x - 2$

x	⁻3	⁻2	⁻1	0	1	2	3	4
y								

17. $y - 3x = 8$ (Change to equivalent equation: $y = \underline{\ ?\ }$)

x	⁻3	⁻1	0	1	3	5	7	9
y								

For each given equation find the *y*-value that completes the ordered pair.

18. $y = x - 3$
(⁻3, _?_); (0, _?_); (1, _?_); (2, _?_)

19. $y + x = 12$
(⁻2, _?_); (⁻1, _?_); (2, _?_); (3, _?_)

20. $y + 3x = 15$
(⁻1, _?_); (0, _?_); (2, _?_); (5, _?_)

21. $2x + y = 10$
(⁻2, _?_); (0, _?_); (2, _?_); (4, _?_)

22. $y - 3x = 7$
(⁻3, _?_); (⁻2, _?_); (0, _?_); (3, _?_)

23. $y - 5x = 8$
(⁻2, _?_); (⁻1, _?_); (0, _?_); (1, _?_)

24. $x + 2y = 16$
(⁻2, _?_); (0, _?_); (2, _?_); (6, _?_)

25. $x + 3y = 10$
(⁻2, _?_); (1, _?_); (4, _?_); (7, _?_)

CHALLENGE

Complete the table for $3x + y = 15$. Connect the points. Then construct a line parallel to $3x + y = 15$ that passes through $P = (3, 0)$.

26.

x	⁻1	0	2	4	5	6	8	9
y								

Graphing Equations

Relation: a set of ordered number pairs.

Function: a special relation of ordered pairs such that the first component (x) in the relation is paired with, or corresponds to, only *one* second component (y).

A function may be expressed in many ways, such as equations, function tables, or graphs.

The function $y = x + 1$ is expressed as an equation. Below is the same function expressed in a function table which is used to show it as a graph on the coordinate grid.

To graph equations or functions on a coordinate grid:

- Substitute some values for x in this equation: $y = x + 1$
  Let $x = {}^-2, {}^-1, 0, 1, 2, 3$
- Solve for x to find the corresponding values for y. Use a function table like the one below which shows the value of y for each given value of x.

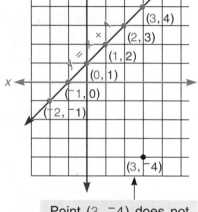

Graph of:
$y = x + 1$

Point $(3, {}^-4)$ does not lie on line $y = x + 1$

Function Table →

x	⁻2	⁻1	0	1	2	3
y	⁻1	0	1	2	3	4

- From the function table write ordered pairs for the x- and y-values:
  $({}^-2, {}^-1), ({}^-1, 0), (0, 1), (1, 2), (2, 3), (3, 4)$
- Graph each ordered pair.
- Connect the points.

Note that the Point $(3, {}^-4)$ does NOT lie on the line $y = x + 1$ graphed above.

If an ordered pair does not satisfy the equation, the point does *not* lie on the line.

Substitute $(3, {}^-4)$ into the equation:

$$y = x + 1 \longrightarrow {}^-4 = 3 + 1 \text{ but } {}^-4 \neq 3 + 1$$

So, $(3, {}^-4)$ does *not* lie on the line $y = x + 1$.

Copy and complete.

1.

x	x − 5 =	y	Ordered Pair
⁻2	⁻2 − 5	⁻7	(⁻2, ⁻7)
⁻1	?	?	(⁻1, ⁻6)
0	?	?	?
1	?	?	?
2	?	?	?

2.

x	3x =	y	Ordered Pair
⁻2	3(⁻2)	⁻6	(⁻2, ⁻6)
⁻1	?	?	?
0	?	?	?
$\frac{1}{3}$	?	?	?
2	?	?	?

3.

x	$2x + 3 =$	y	Ordered Pair
$^-3$	$^-6 + 3$	?	$(^-3, ^-3)$
0	?	?	?
1	?	?	?
3	?	?	?
5	?	?	?

4.

x	$1 - x =$	y	Ordered Pair
4	?	?	$(4, ^-3)$
2	?	?	?
$-\frac{1}{2}$	?	?	?
0	?	?	?
$\frac{1}{2}$	?	?	?

Without graphing, tell which ordered pairs satisfy each equation.

5. $y = x + 2$ **a.** $(4, 8)$ **b.** $(3, 5)$ **c.** $(2, 4)$ **d.** all of these

6. $y = x + 5$ **a.** $(3, 8)$ **b.** $(6, 1)$ **c.** $(0, ^-5)$ **d.** all of these

7. $y = 2x - 3$ **a.** $(^-1, ^-5)$ **b.** $(2, 1)$ **c.** $(0, ^-3)$ **d.** all of these

8. $y = 3x - 1$ **a.** $(^-1, 4)$ **b.** $(0, ^-1)$ **c.** $(2, 6)$ **d.** all of these

9. $y = 6 - 2x$ **a.** $(3, 0)$ **b.** $(^-1, 8)$ **c.** $(^-2, 2)$ **d.** all of these

10. $y = 7 - 3x$ **a.** $(1, 4)$ **b.** $(^-2, 13)$ **c.** $(3, ^-2)$ **d.** all of these

Complete each table. Graph the equation.

11. $y = 3x - 2$

x	y
$^-4$	$^-14$
$^-2$	
0	
2	
4	

12. $y = 4x - 1$

x	y
$^-2$	$^-9$
$^-1$	
0	
1	
2	

13. $y = 2 + 2x$

x	y
$^-3$	$^-4$
$^-1$	
0	
1	
3	

14. $y = \dfrac{x}{2} + 3$

x	y
$^-8$	$^-1$
$^-6$	
2	
0	
4	

Graph each equation, using five points.

15. $y = x + 5$ **16.** $y = ^-3x$ **17.** $y = \frac{1}{2}x$ **18.** $y = \frac{1}{3}x$

SUPPOSE **THAT...**

Construct a table of values for each equation, and then graph the results.

19. $x + y = 4$ and $x + y = ^-4$

20. $x + y = 3$ and $x + y = ^-3$

21. Describe the relationship between the graphs and the equations for exercises 19 and 20.

Solving Systems of Equations

Two or more equations can form a **system of equations.**

$$y = x - 1 \text{ and } y = 3 - x \longrightarrow \text{system of equations}$$

One way to solve a system of equations:

- Graph each of the equations on the same coordinate grid.

- Look at the graph to find the point of intersection. (x, y) is called the **common solution** of the system of equations because it satisfies both equations.

Choose zero and two positive and two negative values for x.

$y = x - 1$ **AND** $y = 3 - x$

x	y
$^-4$	$^-5$
$^-2$	$^-3$
0	$^-1$
2	1
4	3

Function Tables

x	y
$^-3$	6
$^-1$	4
0	3
1	2
3	0

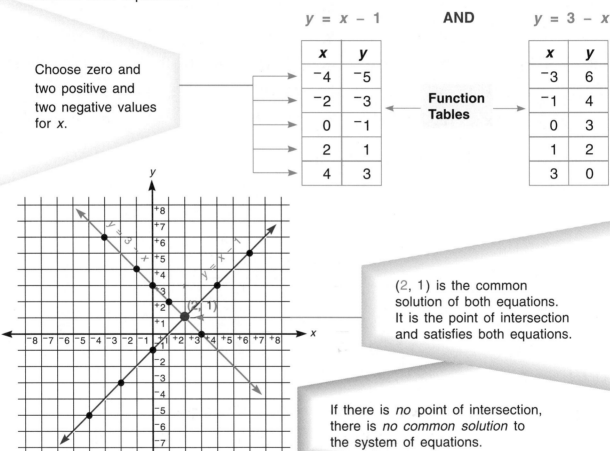

$(2, 1)$ is the common solution of both equations. It is the point of intersection and satisfies both equations.

If there is *no* point of intersection, there is *no common solution* to the system of equations.

To check that $(2, 1)$ satisfies both equations, substitute the values $x = 2$ and $y = 1$ in each equation.

$$y = x - 1 \longrightarrow 1 = 2 - 1 \longrightarrow 1 = 1$$
$$y = 3 - x \longrightarrow 1 = 3 - 2 \longrightarrow 1 = 1$$

Copy and complete each function table. Graph all three equations on the same coordinate grid. Which equations intersect? What is the *common solution* of these equations?

1. $y = x + 5$

x	y
⁻2	
⁻1	
0	
1	
2	

2. $y = 2x + 2$

x	y
⁻2	
⁻1	
0	
1	
2	

3. $y = 3x - 2$

x	y
⁻2	
⁻1	
0	
1	
2	

Copy and complete each function table. Which pairs of equations intersect when graphed?

4. $y = 5x - 4$

x	y
⁻2	
⁻1	
0	
1	
2	

5. $x + y = 8$

x	y
⁻2	
⁻1	
0	
1	
2	

6. $y + 2x = 4$

x	y
⁻2	
⁻1	
0	
1	
2	

7. $y = 6 - 3x$

x	⁻2	⁻1	0	1	2
y					

8. $y = 10 - 2x$

x	⁻2	⁻1	0	1	2
y					

9. $y = 2 - \frac{1}{2}x$

x	⁻2	⁻1	0	1	2
y					

Without graphing, tell which ordered pairs satisfy the equation.

10. $y = x - 4$ **a.** (⁻5, ⁻9)   **b.** (⁻4, 0)   **c.** (0, 4)   **d.** all of these

11. $y = \frac{1}{3}x$ **a.** (3, 1)   **b.** (12, 4)   **c.** (9, 3)   **d.** all of these

12. $y = x$ **a.** (2, ⁻2)   **b.** (0, 0)   **c.** (⁻6, ⁻6)   **d.** all of these

Graph the equations. Where do they intersect?

13. $y = 2x - 5$ and $x = y + 1$

14. $y - x = 0$ and $y + x = 6$

15. $y = 3x$ and $y = 2x + 2$

16. $3y = 3 - x$ and $2y + x = 4$

17. $y = 4 - 6x$ and $y = ⁻6x + 9$

18. $2y = x + 2$ and $y = 7x + 14$

391

14-7 | Simultaneous Equations

> **Simultaneous Equations:** a system of equations that can be solved by **substitution** or by **addition and subtraction**. These methods are usually quicker than graphing to find solutions.

Find the common solution for: $y = 2x + 2$ and $y - x = 3$

Substitution Method:

- If necessary, rewrite one of the equations as y in terms of x (or x in terms of y).

  $y = 2x + 2$ is already written as y in terms of x.
  $y - x = 3$ is the same as $y = x + 3$.
  Both equations are now written as y in terms of x.

- Substitute the expression $(x + 3)$ for y in the first equation.

  $$y = 2x + 2$$
  $$x + 3 = 2x + 2$$

- Now solve for x by collecting x terms on one side of the equation and constant terms on the other. Here this means subtracting an x and a 2 from both sides of the equation.

  $$x + 3 = 2x + 2$$
  $$\cancel{x} + 3 - \cancel{x} - 2 = 2x + \cancel{2} - x - \cancel{2}$$
  $$3 - 2 = 2x - x$$
  $$1 = x$$

- Now substitute the value found for x into the second equation and solve to find the value of y.

  $$y - x = 3$$
  $$y - (+1) = 3 \longrightarrow y = 4 \longrightarrow \text{Solution} = (1, 4)$$

- Check that the solution $(1, 4)$ makes *both* original equations true.

$y = 2x + 2$	AND	$y - x = 3$
$(4) = 2(1) + 2$		$(4) - (1) = 3$
$4 = 2 + 2$		$3 = 3$
$4 = 4$		

Write y in terms of x.

1. $x + y = 5$ **2.** $x - y = 2$ **3.** $2x + 2y = 4$

4. $2x + 2y = 6$ **5.** $x - y = 5$ **6.** $3x - 3y = 6$

7. $2x - 2y = 10$ **8.** $y + x = {}^-5$ **9.** $y - x = {}^-3$

Solve these equations by substitution. Then find the common solution.

10. $y = 2x$
    $y = x - 4$

11. $y = x + 6$
    $y = 3x$

12. $y = {}^-x$
    $y = 3x - 8$

13. $y = {}^-3x$
    $y = x - 4$

14. $y = \frac{x}{2}$
    $y = x - 4$

15. $y = x + 1$
    $y = 2x + 2$

16. $y = 2x + 1$
    $y = 3x - 1$

17. $y = \frac{x}{3}$
    $y = x + 4$

Solving Equations by Addition and by Subtraction

Find the common solution for: $2x - y = 5$ and $2x + y = 11$

Change signs of subtrahend.

By Addition

$$2x - \cancel{y} = 5$$
$$+\ 2x + \cancel{y} = 11$$
$$\overline{4x \quad\quad = 16}$$

$$\frac{\cancel{4}x}{\cancel{4}} = \frac{16}{4}$$

$$x = 4$$

$$2(4) - y = 5$$
$$8 - y = 5$$
$$y = 3$$

Common Solution: $(4, 3)$

- Eliminate one variable by adding or subtracting the two equations.

- Solve the remaining equation.

- Substitute the solution into the original equation and solve the equation for the other variable.

- Check that the ordered pair (4, 3) works in both equations.

By Subtraction

$$2x - y = 5$$
$$\mp 2x \mp y = \mp 11$$
$$\overline{\ -2y = -6}$$

$$\frac{-2y}{-2} = \frac{-6}{-2}$$

$$y = 3$$

$$2x - 3 = 5$$
$$2x = 8$$
$$x = 4$$

Common Solution: $(4, 3)$

Check: $2x - y = 5 \longrightarrow 2(4) - 3 = 5 \longrightarrow 8 - 3 = 5 \longrightarrow 5 = 5$
         $2x + y = 11 \longrightarrow 2(4) + 3 = 11 \longrightarrow 8 + 3 = 11 \longrightarrow 5 = 5$

So $(4, 3)$ is the common solution. We can say that the coordinates $(4, 3)$ are the point of intersection.

Add these equations. Then find the common solution.

18. $x + y = 10$
    $x - y = 8$

19. $x - y = 9$
    $x + y = {}^-3$

20. $x + 2y = 5$
    $x - 2y = 7$

21. $3x + 2y = 7$
    $^-3x + 2y = 1$

22. $5x - 2y = 11$
    $4x + 2y = {}^-2$

23. $x + 4y = 3$
    $^-x + y = 7$

Subtract these equations. Then find the common solution.

24. $x + y = 7$
    $x + 2y = 5$

25. $x - y = 4$
    $2x - y = 2$

26. $3x - y = 5$
    $2x - y = 3$

27. $9x + 2y = 10$
    $7x + 2y = 6$

28. $x - y = 8$
    $x + y = 2$

29. $5x - 2y = 25$
    $4x - 2y = 24$

CHALLENGE

Use one of the two methods to solve these systems of equations. Then graph the systems.

30. $y = x - 5$
    $y = x + 5$

31. $y = x - 2$
    $y = 2x - 4$

32. $y = 2x - 1$
    $y = 2x + 1$

33. Describe your results.

Mapping Expansions and Contractions

Expansions (Dilations) transform a figure in a plane to a *similar* figure by enlarging the figure. The shape does *not* change.

To graph an expansion:

- Multiply the coordinates of each vertex by the same number. This number is called the *scale factor.*

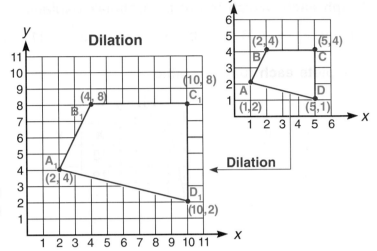

Scale factor = 2

$A(1, 2) \times 2 \longrightarrow A_1(2, 4)$
$B(2, 4) \times 2 \longrightarrow B_1(4, 8)$
$C(5, 4) \times 2 \longrightarrow C_1(10, 8)$
$D(5, 1) \times 2 \longrightarrow D_1(10, 2)$

- On the coordinate grid, graph the enlarged similar figure.

Contractions transform a figure in a plane to a *similar* figure by reducing the figure. The shape does *not* change.

To graph a contraction:

- Divide the coordinates of each vertex by the same number.

$A_1(2, 4) \div 4 \longrightarrow A_2(\frac{1}{2}, 1)$
$B_1(4, 8) \div 4 \longrightarrow B_2(1, 2)$
$C_1(10, 8) \div 4 \longrightarrow C_2(2\frac{1}{2}, 2)$
$D_1(10, 2) \div 4 \longrightarrow D_2(2\frac{1}{2}, \frac{1}{2})$

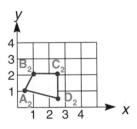

Contraction

- On the coordinate grid, graph the reduced similar figure.

Given a scale factor of 3, complete the coordinates for each point in an enlarged figure.

1. $N(^-3, 2)$; $N_1(\underline{\ ?\ }, \underline{\ ?\ })$ 2. $P(4, ^-1)$; $P_1(\underline{\ ?\ }, \underline{\ ?\ })$ 3. $M(0, ^-2)$; $M_1(\underline{\ ?\ }, \underline{\ ?\ })$
4. $E(5, 0)$; $E_1(\underline{\ ?\ }, \underline{\ ?\ })$ 5. $R(\frac{1}{2}, 1)$; $R_1(\underline{\ ?\ }, \underline{\ ?\ })$ 6. $F(3, ^-6)$; $F_1(\underline{\ ?\ }, \underline{\ ?\ })$

Given a scale factor of 4, name the coordinates for each point in a reduced figure.

7. $S(0, 8)$; $S_1(\underline{\ ?\ }, \underline{\ ?\ })$ 8. $R(4, ^-4)$; $R_1(\underline{\ ?\ }, \underline{\ ?\ })$ 9. $A(^-6, 12)$; $A_1(\underline{\ ?\ }, \underline{\ ?\ })$
10. $J(^-2, ^-8)$; $J_1(\underline{\ ?\ }, \underline{\ ?\ })$ 11. $F(^-20, 0)$; $F_1(\underline{\ ?\ }, \underline{\ ?\ })$ 12. $M(^-10, 2)$; $M_1(\underline{\ ?\ }, \underline{\ ?\ })$

Graph enlarged figures similar to the ones given below.

13. Scale factor = 2

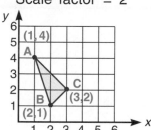

14. Scale factor = 3

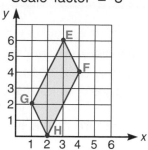

15. Scale factor = 4

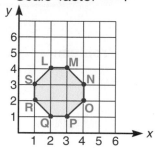

16. Multiply the coordinates of each figure by the opposite of the given scale factor in exercises 13–15.

17. Using the coordinates from exercise 16, graph each figure.

18. Name the corresponding parts of each similar figure from exercise 17.

Graph figures similar to the ones given below.

19. Scale factor = $\frac{1}{2}$

20. Scale factor = $\frac{1}{4}$

21. Scale factor = $\frac{1}{3}$

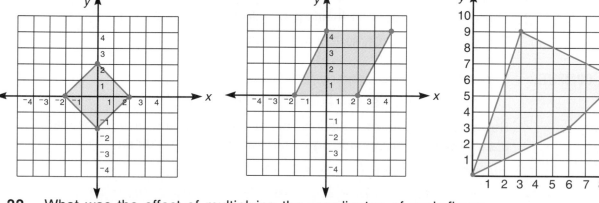

22. What was the effect of multiplying the coordinates of each figure by a unit fraction ($\frac{1}{2}$, $\frac{1}{4}$, $\frac{1}{3}$)? Explain.

Name the scale factor that was used to transform the coordinates given below.

23. $P(^-8, 24)$; $P_1(^-4, 12)$ **24.** $T(^-6, 0)$; $T_1(^-1, 0)$ **25.** $A(5, ^-3)$; $A_1(2.5, ^-1.5)$

26. $H(^-10, ^-4)$; $H_1(2.5, 1)$ **27.** $V(^-\frac{1}{2}, 2)$; $V_1(3, ^-12)$ **28.** $B(4, 3.5)$; $B_1(^-12, ^-10.5)$

29. Which coordinates in exercises 23–28 are dilations? Explain.

Choose the scale factor that matches each description.

30. Which scale factor transforms the figure by dilation?
  a. $\frac{1}{4}$ **b.** 4 **c.** $-\frac{1}{2}$

31. Which scale factor transforms the figure by contraction?
  a. $^-3$ **b.** $\frac{1}{2}$ **c.** 5

32. Graph this figure: $W(1, 3)$; $X(^-2, 3)$; $Y(^-2, ^-5)$; $Z(1, ^-5)$. Find its perimeter. Then graph $W_1X_1Y_1Z_1$ (scale factor = 3). Find its perimeter. What is the ratio of the perimeter of $WXYZ$ to $W_1X_1Y_1Z_1$?

Problem: "Twice the sum of my two brothers' ages is 18. If the difference between their ages is three years, can you guess their ages?" asked Becky.

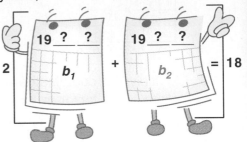

1st brother   **2nd brother**

1 IMAGINE   Draw and label a picture of the two ages.

2 NAME   *Facts:*   The sum of their ages when multiplied by two equals 18.

Question: _?_ ages of Becky's brothers

3 THINK   Look at the picture. There are two unknowns.
(Let b_1 = one brother's age. Let b_2 = the other's.)

Twice the sum of their ages equals 18: $2(b_1 + b_2) = 18$

The difference between their ages is three: $b_1 - b_2 = 3$

The common solution of the two equations is their ages.

4 COMPUTE   Use the distributive property first.

$$2(b_1 + b_2) = 18 \longrightarrow 2b_1 + 2b_2 = 18$$

Solve the systems of equations either by: graphing on a coordinate plane, substitution, or adding or subtracting the equations.

Substitution: Since $b_1 - b_2 = 3$, then $b_1 = 3 + b_2$

- Substitute. $2b_1 + 2b_2 = 18 \longrightarrow 2(3 + b_2) + 2b_2 = 18$
- Simplify. $2(3 + b_2) = 18 \longrightarrow 6 + 2b_2 + 2b_2 = 18$
$$6 + 4b_2 = 18$$
- Solve for b_2. $6 + 4b_2 = 18 \longrightarrow 4b_2 = 12 \longrightarrow b_2 = 3$
- Substitute $b_2 = 3$. $b_1 - b_2 = 3 \longrightarrow b_1 - 3 = 3$
$$b_1 = 6$$

The ordered pair (6, 3) is the solution: Therefore, Becky's brothers' ages are 6 and 3.

5 CHECK   To prove that their ages are 6 and 3, substitute these values into each equation.

$$2(b_1 + b_2) = 18 \longrightarrow 2(6 + 3) \stackrel{?}{=} 18 \longrightarrow 2 \times 9 = 18$$
$$b_1 - b_2 = 3 \longrightarrow 6 - 3 \stackrel{?}{=} 3 \longrightarrow 3 = 3$$

When the system of equations is graphed on the coordinate plane, the point of intersection should be (6, 3).

Solve by using one of these methods: graphing, substitution, or addition/subtraction.

1. Together Leroy and Rusty have 4 pets. If the number of pets Leroy has is subtracted from three times the number of pets Rusty has, the difference is 8. How many pets does each boy have?

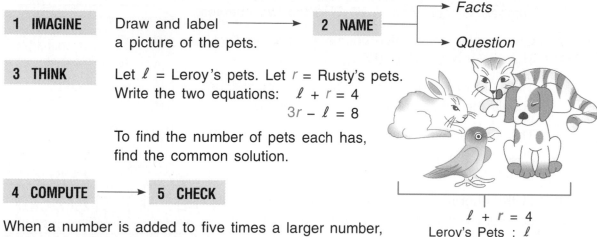

| 1 IMAGINE | Draw and label → a picture of the pets. | 2 NAME |

Facts

Question

| 3 THINK | Let ℓ = Leroy's pets. Let r = Rusty's pets. Write the two equations: $\ell + r = 4$ |
| | $3r - \ell = 8$ |

To find the number of pets each has, find the common solution.

| 4 COMPUTE | → | 5 CHECK |

$\ell + r = 4$
Leroy's Pets : ℓ
Rusty's Pets : r

2. When a number is added to five times a larger number, the sum is 165. The smaller number is half the other. Find both numbers.

3. Leigh has three times as much money as her brother. If the difference in the money each has is eight dollars, how much money does each one have?

4. Roseanne is one third her sister's age. If Roseanne's age is doubled and added to her sister's age, the sum is 35 years. How old are both girls?

5. Half the sum of the books read by Rita and Renee equals six books. The difference of the number of books they read equals 2. How many books did each one read if Rita read the most?

6. If a number is subtracted from twice a larger number, the difference is 12. If twice the smaller number is added to the larger number, the sum is 21. Find both numbers.

7. Mr. Finelli is three years older than his wife. The sum of their ages is 73. How old are Mr. and Mrs. Finelli?

8. When one number is divided by another, the quotient is three. The sum of the numbers is 16. Find both numbers.

9. When the number represented by the tens digit is added to three times the number represented by the ones digit, the sum is 29. If the digits are added, the sum is 5. What is the original 2-digit number?

10. My father is half my grandfather's age. The sum of the ages of my father, grandfather, and myself equals 115. If I am thirteen years old, how old are my father and grandfather?

1. The first number, x, plus three is equal to the second number, y. Their sum is 27. Find the two numbers.

2. One number minus five equals another number. Their sum is 27. Find the two numbers.

3. The sum of two numbers is six. Half one number equals the other number. Find the numbers.

4. The sum of two numbers is 20. Triple one number plus four equals the other number. Find the numbers.

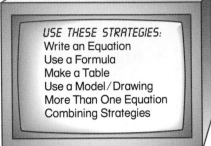

USE THESE STRATEGIES:
Write an Equation
Use a Formula
Make a Table
Use a Model/Drawing
More Than One Equation
Combining Strategies

5. In the coordinate plane find the midpoint of the segment whose endpoints are ($^-3$, $^-5$) and ($^-3$, $^+7$).

6. In the coordinate plane find the coordinates of the point halfway between ($^-6$, $^-9$) and ($^+3$, $^-9$).

7. Find the perimeter of the rectangle whose coordinates are (3, 1); (7, 1); (7, $^-1$); (3, $^-1$).

8. Find the area of the rectangle in exercise 7.

9. Find the area of the triangle whose coordinates are ($^-1$, 4); (3, 1); ($^-1$, 1).

10. Find the perimeter of a square whose coordinates are ($^-2$, 0); (2, 0); (2, $^-4$); ($^-2$, $^-4$).

11. Find the area of the square in exercise 10.

12. The coordinates of the vertices of trapezoid ($^-1$, 1); (3, 1); (7, $^-3$); ($^-3$, $^-3$) lie on the coordinate plane. What is its area?

13. How many integers are common to the solution sets of both inequalities? $x + 3 > 5$ and $x - 2 < 7$

14. How many integers are common to the solution sets of both inequalities? $7x > 14$ and $2x + 1 < 11$

15. The maximum daily temperature was 32° less than twice the minimum. The difference in these temperatures was 23°. Find both temperatures. (Hint: x = maximum and y = minimum.)

16. The minimum daily temperature was 7° less than one third the maximum. The maximum temperature was 17° more than the minimum. Find both temperatures.

Age Problems

Mindy is 2 years older than her sister. In 5 years the sum of their ages will be 40. How old is Mindy?

Person	Age Now	Age in 5 Years
Mindy	x	$x + 5$
sister	y	$y + 5$

Solve the equations by addition.

$$x = y + 2 \longrightarrow x - y = 2 \longrightarrow$$

$$\begin{aligned} x + y + 10 &= 40 \\ x - y \quad\quad &= 2 \end{aligned}$$

$$2x + 10 = 42$$
$$2x = 32 \longrightarrow x = 16$$
$$x - y = 2$$
$$16 - y = 2 \longrightarrow y = 14$$

Check:
$$x + y + 10 = 40$$
$$16 + 14 + 10 \stackrel{?}{=} 40$$
$$40 = 40$$

17. The sum of Pablo's age and his father's age is 60 years. Pablo is one third his father's age. How old is Pablo? (Let x = Pablo's age and y = his father's age.)

18. Becky is three years younger than Carly. Three years ago the sum of their ages was 27. Find their ages.

19. The difference in Milo's and Mike's ages is 6 years. In 8 years the sum of their ages will be 50. What are their ages now?

Coin Problems

Raisa has 1 more nickel than dimes. The sum of their value is $1.85. How many of each coin has she?

Coin	Number	Value
nickel	x	$0.05x$
dime	y	$0.10y$

Equations:
$$x = y + 1$$
$$0.05x + 0.10y = 1.85$$
$$5x + 10y = 185$$

Substitute, $x = y + 1$, in:
$$5x + 10y = 185$$
$$5(y + 1) + 10y = 185$$
$$5y + 5 + 10y = 185$$
$$15y + 5 = 185$$
$$15y = 180$$
$$y = 12$$
$$x = y + 1 = 13$$

Check: There are 12 dimes (y) and 13 nickels (x).

$$\begin{aligned} &\$1.20 \\ &\underline{\$\ .65} \\ \text{Sum of value} \longrightarrow &\$1.85 \end{aligned}$$

20. There are twice as many dimes as quarters in my piggy bank. The difference in the value of these coins is 45¢. How many quarters are in my bank?

21. My change purse has 3 less quarters than pennies. If I have $1.85 in pennies and quarters, how many pennies are in my change purse?

More Practice

Write an inequality for each graph.

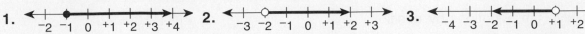

1. 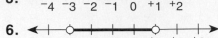 2. 3.

4. 5. 6.

Find the solution and graph it on a real number line.

7. $x + 5 < {}^-3$ 8. $x - 2 > {}^-1$ 9. ${}^-x > {}^-2$ 10. ${}^-5x < {}^-5$

11. ${}^-3x \geq 9$ 12. $4x + 1 > {}^-3$ 13. $6x - 3 < {}^-7$ 14. $2x - 1 \geq {}^-5$

15. $\dfrac{x}{3} < 2$ 16. $\dfrac{x}{{}^-2} < {}^-3$

Graph each compound inequality.

17. $\{x : {}^-4 < x \leq 0\}$ 18. $\{x : {}^-8 < x \leq {}^-2\}$ 19. $\{x : 0 \leq x \leq 4\}$

Match each ordered pair with the letter of its graph.

20. $({}^-4, 0)$ 21. $({}^-4, {}^-2)$ 22. $(0, 0)$ 23. $(0, {}^-1)$
24. $(3, {}^-2)$ 25. $({}^-2, 1)$ 26. $({}^-4, 4)$ 27. $(3, 1)$

Complete each table of values. Graph the results.

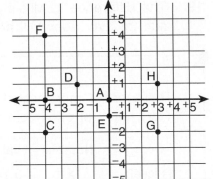

28. $y = 2x - 2$

x	${}^-3$	${}^-2$	${}^-1$	0	1	2	3
y							

29. $y - 2x = {}^-3$ (change to equivalent equation: $y = ?$)

x	${}^-3$	${}^-2$	${}^-1$	0	1	2	3
y							

Write y in terms of x.

30. $y - x = 8$ 31. $x + y = 7$ 32. $5x - 5y = 10$ 33. $2y + 2x = 9$

34. $y + 2x = 7$ 35. $4x - y = 11$ 36. $4y - 2x = 12$ 37. $6x - 3y = 15$

Add or subtract these equations. Then find the common solution.

38. $2x - y = 3$
    $4x + y = 9$

39. $2x + y = 10$
    $3x - y = 5$

40. $9x + 2y = 13$
    $7x + 2y = 5$

Solve these equations by substitution. Then find the common solution.

41. $y = 3x$
    $y = x + 8$

42. $y = {}^-x$
    $y = 6x - 14$

43. $y = {}^-2x$
    $y = x - 9$

44. $y = x + 1$
    $y = 3x - 1$

Write y in terms of x. Describe each boundary line.

45. $x + y > 3$ **46.** $y - 4x \leq 0$ **47.** $3x - y \leq 5$ **48.** $\frac{y}{3} + 9x \geq 1$

49. $y - 4 \leq x$ **50.** $2y - 3x \geq 8$ **51.** $4y - 5 \leq x$ **52.** $x + 3y < 6$

Graph the solution set for each system of inequalities.

53. $x \geq 0$ **54.** $y \geq 2x - 3$ **55.** $y < {}^{-}x + 5$ **56.** $y \geq 2x - 3$
      $y \leq 7$ $y < 3 - x$ $y \geq x + 3$ $y \leq 3 - 2x$

Complete each function table.

57. $y = x^2 - 7$

x	0		$^{+}3$	$^{-}3$	
y		$^{-}6$			9

58. $y = {}^{-}x^2 + 4$

x	$^{+}1$	$^{-}1$			$^{+}3$
y			0	0	

59. $y = 2x^2 - 1$

x			$^{+}2$	$^{-}2$	$^{-}3$
y	1	1			

Graph each equation.

60. $y = x^2 - 6$ **61.** $y = x^2 + 7$ **62.** $y = x^2 - 1$ **63.** $y = 2x^2 + 1$

64. $y = x^2 - 8$ **65.** $y = 2x^2 + 2$ **66.** $y = 2x^2 - 3$ **67.** $y = {}^{-}3x^2$

Solve. (The first one is done.)

68. The sum of two consecutive odd integers is less than 24. Find the greatest possible values for the integers.

     $x + (x + 2) < 24$ Solve $\longrightarrow$ $2x + 2 < 24$ $\longrightarrow$ $x < 11$

     $x < 11$ So, $x = 9$ AND $x + 2 = 11$.
     9 and 11 are the greatest values.   Check: $9 + 11 < 24$ $\longrightarrow$ $20 < 24$
                                                $11 + 13 \not< 24$ $\longrightarrow$ $24 \not< 24$

69. The sum of two consecutive even numbers is greater than 25. Find the least possible values for the numbers.

70. The perimeter of a rectangle is 58 cm. The length is 7 cm longer than the width. Find the length.

71. The sum of the ages of April and her mother is 63. The difference in their ages is 33. How old is April?

72. The sum of the digits in a 2-digit number is 14. The units digit is 4 less than the tens digit. Find the number.

73. One hamster weighed 300 g less than half the weight of a second. If their combined weights were 1950 g, how much did each hamster weigh?

More Practice

Equations with two variables

Solve. (The first one is done.)

74. Three adult tickets and 4 children's tickets cost $32.50. Two adult tickets and 1 child's ticket cost $16.25. Find the cost of each kind of ticket.

Let a = adult ticket price and c = child's ticket price

First Equation: $3a + 4c = 32.50$
Second Equation: $2a + 1c = 16.25$

Solve by substitution: $2a + 1c = 16.25 \longrightarrow 1c = 16.25 - 2a$

$$
\begin{aligned}
3a + \quad\quad 4c \quad\quad\quad &= 32.50 \\
3a + 4(16.25 - 2a) &= 32.50 \\
3a + \quad 65 \quad - 8a &= 32.50 \\
65 \quad - 5a &= 32.50 \\
- 5a &= 32.50 - 65 \\
a &= 6.5
\end{aligned}
$$

One adult ticket costs $6.50 and one child's ticket costs $3.25.

75. At a book fair one student bought 1 hardback and 3 paperbacks for $45.50. Another bought one of each type and paid $33. How much did each type of book cost?

76. The total value of the coins in a piggy bank is $7.60. There are twice as many dimes as quarters and 8 less nickels than quarters. How many coins of each type are there?

77. The perimeter of a rectangle is 32 m. The width is 6 m less than the length. What is the width of the rectangle? What is the area of the figure?

78. A video store rented or sold 20 videos in one hour. The rental fee is $3.50 and the selling price is $25. If the sales for the hour totaled $242, how many of the videos were sold?

79. The sum of two numbers is 120. The larger number is 8 more than the smaller number. Find both of the numbers.

80. $\angle XYZ$ and $\angle ABC$ are complementary angles. $\angle XYZ$ is 6° less than half of $\angle ABC$. Find the measure of both of the angles.

81. Student council members washed or waxed a total of 45 cars and raised a total of $178.50. The cost of a car wash was $3.50 and waxing cost an additional $1.50. How many cars did they both wash and wax?

82. A parallelogram has a perimeter of 29 cm. The shorter sides are 0.5 cm less than the longer sides. Find its dimensions.

83. The robot EZ2DO and its pet together weigh 205 kg. Four times the weight of the pet is 5 kg less than the weight of EZ2DO. How much does EZ2DO weigh?

Math Probe

MAPPING ROTATIONS

Rotations: transform a figure in a plane by turning (rotating) it around a *fixed* point.

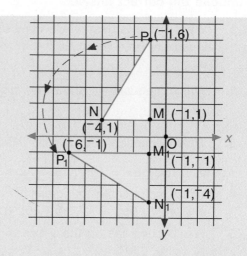

$\triangle NPM$ is rotated 90° about the origin (0,0) in a *counterclockwise* direction.

$\triangle N_1 P_1 M_1$ is called the *image* of $\triangle NPM$. The origin (0,0) is the *fixed point.*

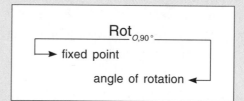

The symbol $\triangle NPM \xrightarrow{\text{Rot}_{O,90°}} \triangle N_1 P_1 M_1$.

Use graph paper. Find the image of each point for Rot$_{O,-90°}$.

1. $(^-2,3)$ 2. $(^-1,3)$ 3. $(2,^-4)$ 4. $(0,^-4)$

Graph the figures in exercises 5–6. Rotate each figure 180° around the origin.

5. $X(^-6,1);\ Y(^-3,4);\ Z(0,0)$ 6. $A(^-6,2);\ B(^-4,6);\ C(^-2,6);\ D(^-4,^-2)$

What is the least number of degrees of rotation through which this figure must be turned to look the same if:

7. this design is colored with one color?

8. this design is colored with two alternating colors?

9. this design is colored with three alternating colors?

This regular hexagon has rotational symmetry.

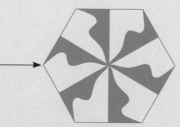

Draw circles of varying sizes. Use them to create designs having:

10. 90° rotational symmetry   11. 45° rotational symmetry

12. 30° rotational symmetry   13. 180° rotational symmetry

Pre-Advanced Placement Practice

Choose the correct answer.

1. What is the largest whole number that is a solution for the inequality $5n - 8 < 20$?
   a. 6   **b.** 5   **c.** 3   **d.** 2

2. Which inequality is shown on this graph?
   a. $^-3 \leq x < {}^+1$ **b.** $^-3 < x \leq {}^+1$ **c.** $^-3 < x < {}^+1$ **d.** $^-3 > x > {}^+1$

3. Which equation is shown on this graph?
   a. $13 - 2x = 21$ **b.** $2x > {}^-8$ **c.** $13 + 2x = 21$ **d.** $x - 4 = 0$

4. Which point lies in quadrant IV?
   a. $A(^-3, 0)$ **b.** $B(^+6, {}^-2)$ **c.** $C(^-6, {}^+2)$ **d.** $A(3, 0)$

5. Which point lies on the y-axis?
   a. $X(0, {}^-8)$ **b.** $Y(\frac{1}{2}, 0)$ **c.** $Z(^-2, {}^-2)$ **d.** none of these

6. The inequality $2n + 4 > 3n$ is equivalent to:
   a. $n > 4$ **b.** $n > {}^-4$ **c.** $n < {}^-4$ **d.** $n < 4$

7. The graph at the right is the solution of which inequality:

   a. $x < 2$ **b.** $x \leq 2$ **c.** $x \geq 2$ **d.** $x > 2$

8. Which graph represents the solution of the inequality $2d - 3 \leq {}^-7$?

   a.   **b.**

   c.   **d.**

9. The graph of the solution set for $n^2 = 1$ is:

   a.   **b.**

   c.   **d.**

10. Which equation is the graph of a straight line?
    a. $x^2 - 2y = 3$ **b.** $x^2 + y^2 = 1$ **c.** $x - y^2 = 3$ **d.** $x + y = 1$

11. Solve the inequality $^-6 < 2n < 0$ for n if the replacement set is the set of integers.
    a. $n = 1, 2, 3$ **b.** $n = {}^-1, {}^-2, {}^-3$ **c.** $n = {}^-1, {}^-2$ **d.** $n = {}^-2, {}^-3$

12. If point $R(2, m)$ lies on the graph of the equation $2x - y = 1$, what is the value of m?
    a. $m = 0$ **b.** $m = {}^-2$ **c.** $m = 3$ **d.** $m = {}^-3$

13. Write y in terms of x for the equation $2x + y = 5$
    a. $2x + 5 = y$ **b.** $y = 5 - 2x$ **c.** $y = 2x + {}^-5$ **d.** $y = {}^-5 - 2x$

14. Point $(r, {}^-6)$ lies in the solution half-plane of $^-2y \leq x + 9$. What is the value of r?
    a. 1   **b.** $^-1$ **c.** 3   **d.** $^-3$

15. In the coordinate plane which point does not lie on the same line as $A(^-2, 0)$ and $B(^-4, {}^-1)$?
    a. $(0, 1)$ **b.** $(3, 2)$ **c.** $(4, 3)$ **d.** $(2, 2)$

Pre-Advanced Placement Practice

16. In the coordinate plane what are the coordinates of the midpoint of $E(^-3, 5)$ and $F(^-3, ^-1)$?
    a. $(^-2, 2)$ b. $(2, ^-3)$ c. $(^-2, 3)$ d. $(^-3, 2)$

17. If x varies directly as y and $x = 7$ when $y = 42$, find x when $y = 24$.
    a. 4   b. 6   c. 21   d. 7

18. Solve for y: $y - x = 3$ and $y + x = ^-5$
    a. $^-2$ b. 1   c. 2   d. $^-1$

19. Which integers are in the common solution set of both inequalities $y - x > ^-3$ and $x + y \le 4$?
    a. $(0, 0)$ b. $(5, 7)$ c. $(0, ^-6)$ d. $(0, 5)$

20. Which point lies on the graph of $y = x^2 - 1$?
    a. $(0, 0)$ b. $(1, ^-1)$ c. $(^-1, 0)$ d. $(3, 2)$

Solve.

21. What is the common solution of the equations $x = 7$ and $x + y = ^-2$

22. Write y in terms of x for the equation $3y - 6 = 2x$.

23. Solve the equations $y = 2x + 1$ and $5y = 25$ by substitution.

24. On a number line graph the solution set of $2x + 1 < 9$ and $5 - x \le 5$.

25. On a coordinate plane graph the common solution of $x - y = 7$ and $2x + y = 20$.

26. What is the graph of the common solution of $x + 2y \le 8$ and $x - y > 2$?

27. Graph the equation $^-2x^2 + 1 = y$.

28. What are the coordinates of the point where $y = x^2 + 5$ crosses the y-axis?

29. What is the area of a square whose vertices are: $M(^-2, 4)$; $N(^-2, ^-2)$; $O(4, ^-2)$; $P(4, 4)$?

30. What is the perimeter of the rectangle whose vertices are: $C(^-3, 8)$; $D(4, 8)$; $E(4, 1)$ and $F(^-3, 1)$?

31. What is the area of a parallelogram whose vertices are: $W(^-1, 1)$; $X(2, 1)$; $Y(^-2, ^-3)$ and $Z(^-5, ^-3)$?

32. The sum of 2 consecutive integers is $^-95$. Find the numbers.

33. Given $RSTU$ is a parallelogram:
    a. Find x.
    b. What is $m\angle STU$?
    c. What is $m\angle RST$?

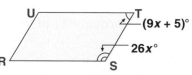

34. The sum of the digits of a 2-digit number equals 11. The digit in the tens place is 5 more than the digit in the ones place. Find the original number.

35. A collector has 12 stamps in her collection. 3 less than twice the number of 40-cent foreign stamps are U.S. stamps. The U.S. stamps are 25-cent stamps. How many of each type does the collector have?

36. Write a truth table for each.
    a. $p \rightarrow q$ b. $p \leftrightarrow q$ c. $p \wedge \sim q$ d. $[p \wedge (p \rightarrow q)] \rightarrow q$

411

Cumulative Test II

Choose the correct answer.

1. In a small cup there were 3 red, 1 black, 4 green, and 6 white jelly beans. The probability of picking a green one at random is:

   a. $\dfrac{3}{10}$ **b.** $\dfrac{4}{10}$ **c.** $\dfrac{2}{7}$ **d.** $\dfrac{10}{14}$

2. For the set of scores 8, 4, 7, 10, 9, 3, 6, 7, the mean score is:

   a. 6.75   **b.** 7   **c.** 8   **d.** 3

3. Two angles are complementary if the sum of their measures is:

   a. 60°   **b.** 90°   **c.** 180°   **d.** 120°

4. In a right triangle the side opposite the right angle is called the:

   a. base   **b.** altitude   **c.** hypotenuse   **d.** length

5. The supplement of an angle of 65° is:

   a. 75°   **b.** 35°   **c.** 115°   **d.** 125°

6. The perimeter of a regular pentagon is 2.5 meters. Each side measures:

   a. 21 cm   **b.** 50 cm   **c.** 1.4 m   **d.** 0.3 m

7. If 1 mm represents 100 km on a map, then 380 km will be represented by:

   a. 38 mm   **b.** 3.8 mm   **c.** 0.38 mm   **d.** none of these

8. To express area in hectares when the other dimensions are given in meters, divide the area by:

   a. 10,000   **b.** 10   **c.** 100   **d.** 1000

9. The number of significant digits in the number 95,000 is:

   a. 4   **b.** 3   **c.** 2   **d.** 5

10. 2.689 m × 6.4 m = _?_ m². Rounded to the number of significant digits or the measure with the smallest number of significant digits, the answer is:

    a. 17.2 m²   **b.** 17.209 m²   **c.** 17 m²   **d.** none of these

11. Which measure is the least precise?

    a. 7.0 m²   **b.** 40 m²   **c.** 7.5 m²   **d.** 0.71 m²

12. A rectangular desk top 1.4 m long has an area of 0.868 m². How many centimeters wide is it?

    a. 62 cm   **b.** 60 cm   **c.** 64.4 cm   **d.** none of these

With one spin of this spinner, what is the probability of getting:

13. an even number

14. a number divisible by 3

15. a number more than 2

16. a number less than 7

17. the number 7

From cards labeled APPLE choose a card, do not replace it and choose again. Find:

18. $P(P, P)$ 19. $P(\text{vowel, vowel})$ 20. $P(E, \text{consonant})$

Compute.

21. 18 in. × 14 in. = __?__ ft²

22. 15 ft × $8\frac{1}{2}$ ft = __?__ yd²

23. 98 cm × 75 cm = __?__ m²

24. 322 m × 104 m = __?__ ha

25. $9\frac{1}{2}$ in. × $6\frac{2}{3}$ in. × 6 in. = __?__ in.³

26. 64.8 cm × 9.5 cm × 4 cm = __?__ cm³

27. $\frac{1}{2}$ (18 ft × 12 ft) × $9\frac{1}{4}$ ft = __?__ ft³

28. $\frac{1}{3}$ (8 m × 4.6 m) × 7.2 m = __?__ m³

29. $\sqrt{441}$

30. $\sqrt{2.56}$

31. $\sqrt{1156}$

32. $\sqrt{50}$ (to the nearest hundredth)

Find the surface area.

Find the volume.

33.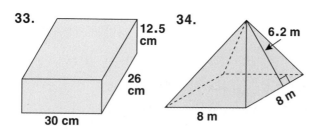

34.

35.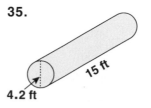

36.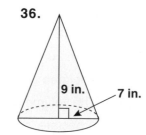

In exercises 37–40 write the letter of the graph that is the solution of the sentence.

37. __?__ $\frac{x}{3} = {}^-2$

a.

38. __?__ $x + 2 \leq 4$

b.

39. __?__ $3x < {}^-6$

c.

40. __?__ $x - 5 > {}^-3$

d.

Solve.

41. How many yards of fencing are needed to enclose a triangular flower bed measuring 28 ft, 30 ft, and 32 ft 9 in. on its sides?

Exercise 43

42. A building casts a 160-m shadow at the same time that a 1.2-m-high bush nearby casts a 4-m shadow. How high is the building?

43. Alfred wants to know the height of this radio tower. From a point 8 m from the base he sights the top of it at an angle of 60°. How high is the tower? (Use the table on page 552 to find the tangent ratio.)

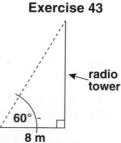

44. Complete this table of values for the equation $y = 2x - 3$.

x	⁻2	⁻1	0
y			

45. What is the common solution of $2x - 3y = {}^-1$ and $x + 3y = 10$?

Name each figure.

46. A rectangular prism with 6 congruent faces

47. A prism with 6 rectangular faces

48. A prism with 2 parallel faces that are 6-sided polygons

49. A solid figure with a curved surface all of whose points are equidistant from the center

50. A polyhedron with a square base and all other faces triangles

51. A quadrilateral with 2 pairs of parallel sides

52. A quadrilateral with all sides congruent and opposite angles congruent

53. A polygon with 3 sides and 3 angles, one of which is a right angle

Complete.

54. 4 m 12 cm 15 mm = __?__ m

55. 2 km 20 hm 12 dam = __?__ km

56. The area of a parallelogram is the same as the area of a __?__ with like dimensions.

57. The volume of a cone is $\frac{1}{3}$ the volume of a __?__ having the same base and height.

58. A hectare is equivalent to __?__ m^2.

59. The inverse operation of squaring a number is finding the __?__ of the number.

60. The number of significant digits in 1720 cm is __?__

61. Construct a truth table for each.
    a. $\sim (p \longleftrightarrow q)$ **b.** $(p \longrightarrow q) \longrightarrow (q \longrightarrow p)$

Look at the graph of 2y = 2 − x.

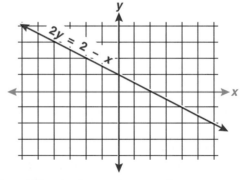

62. Name two points on the line.

63. Graph $x + y = 4$.

64. Where do these lines intersect?

Solve.

65. Which has a larger area and by how much? A square 7 cm on a side or a circle with a 7 cm diameter?

66. What is the perimeter of a regular hexagon with sides of 28 cm?

67. How many tons of ice are needed to fill a skating rink 20 yards by 10 yards if the ice is to be 1 ft. thick? (Hint: 1 ton occupies 35 cubic feet. 1 cu ft of ice weighs 57.51 lb.)

68. Find the area of a semicircle that has a diameter of 8 in. Report your answer in pi units.

+10 BONUS

69. Write any five names. How many different ways can they be arranged vertically on a poster?

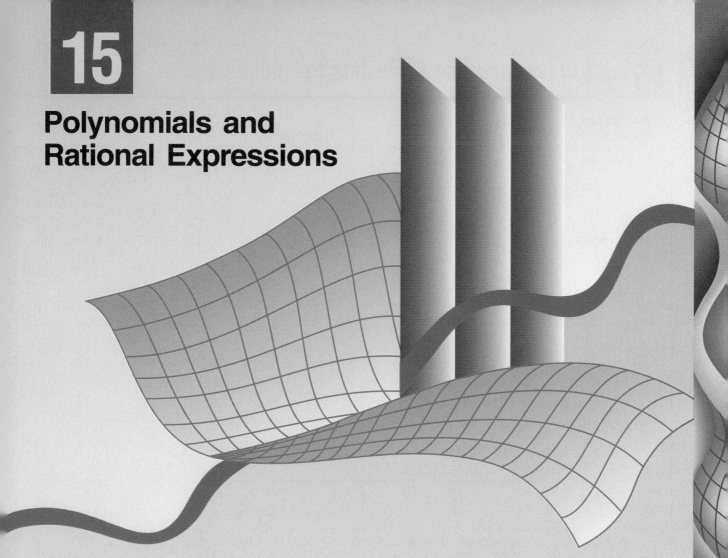

15

Polynomials and Rational Expressions

In this chapter you will:

- Classify and evaluate polynomials
- Add and subtract polynomials
- Multiply polynomials
- Factor polynomials
- Divide polynomials
- Compute with rational expressions
- Solve problems: finding a pattern

Do you remember?

$10^3 \times 10^5 = 10^8$

$10^6 \div 10^4 = 10^2$

GCF of 12 and 42 is 6.

LCM of 12 and 8 is 24.

$n^2 = n \times n \longrightarrow 3^2 = 3 \times 3 = 9$

RESEARCHING TOGETHER

Chances Are . . .

Bulletin from the planet Shazbat! A mathematician, Logo by name, was recently condemned to death for adding in her head. The REDAEL (Leader) offered to spare her life if she could solve this problem.

Two planet terrain vehicles left the planetport at the same time and traveled in opposite directions. One traveled 96 km/h; the other 89 km/h. In how many hours were they 1864 km apart?

Logo won her freedom. What about you? Would you be dead or alive?

For Mathletes

Algebraic Expression	Definition	Examples
Monomial	A numeral (constant), a variable, or a product of a numeral and one or more variables	9, t^2, $-3a$, $25a^2b$
Polynomial	A monomial or the sum or difference of two or more monomials	$(9 + s)$, $(-3a + 6b)$, $(2x^2 + 8x - 16)$
Binomial	A polynomial that is the sum or difference of *two* monomials	$(3x + 7)$, $(2a^2 - 6b^2)$, $(x^3 - 9x^2y^2)$
Trinomial	A polynomial that is the sum or difference of *three* monomials	$(2x^2 + 8x + 3)$, $(-5xy - 4x + 17)$

Exponent: tells how many times a base is used as a factor.

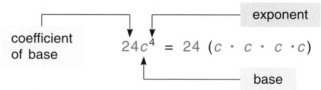

$$24c^4 = 24\,(c \cdot c \cdot c \cdot c)$$

coefficient of base   exponent   base

If no exponent is expressed, *one* is understood: $6c = 6(c) = 6c^1$

The **degree** of a monomial is the sum of the exponents of the variables in the monomial. A monomial that is a nonzero constant and has no variables has zero degree.

$7x^2 \longrightarrow$ Degree 2 $3m^3n = 3m^3n^1 \longrightarrow$ Degree 4

$-\frac{1}{4}ab = -\frac{1}{4}a^1b^1 \longrightarrow$ Degree 2   27 has *no* variable. It is a nonzero constant. $\longrightarrow$ Degree 0

The degree of a polynomial is the *greatest* of the degrees of its *monomials*.

Polynomial	Degrees of its Monomials	Degree of Polynomial
$5y^2 + 16y$	2, 1	2
$3m^2n^3 + 2mn - n^4$	5, 2, 4	5
$19 - 3x$	0, 1	1

Classify each polynomial as a monomial, binomial, or trinomial. Give its degree.

1. $a^2 - 16$ 2. 15 3. $3x + y$ 4. $15a^2 + b$

5. $x^2 + 2x + 1$ 6. s^3 7. $9 - r$ 8. $4x^2 + 6xy + 1$

9. -1 10. $r^2s^2 + 8rs$ 11. $2z^3 + 4z^2 - z$ 12. $-2x^2y^2z - 3x^3$

Evaluating Polynomials

Order of Operations
1. ( ) before [ ]
2. Exponents
3. "x" or "÷" left to right
4. "+" or "–" left to right

To find the value of an algebraic expression:
- Substitute the assigned value for each variable.
- Perform the computation following the order of operations.

Evaluate: $x^2 + 7x - 9$ for $x = 3$	Evaluate: $y^2z - 8z$ for $y = 2$ and $z = \frac{1}{4}$
$x^2 + 7x - 9 = \underline{\ ?\ }$ $(3)^2 + 7(3) - 9 = \underline{\ ?\ }$ $9 + 21 - 9 = 21$	$y^2z - 8z = \underline{\ ?\ }$ $(2)^2(\frac{1}{4}) - 8(\frac{1}{4}) = \underline{\ ?\ }$ $(4)(\frac{1}{4}) - 2 = \underline{\ ?\ }$ $1 - 2 = -1$

Evaluate each expression for $x = 5$ and $y = -2$.

13. $(xy)^2$ **14.** xy^2 **15.** $x^2 + y^2$ **16.** $-x^2$

17. $(-x)^2$ **18.** $5x - 9y$ **19.** $9y - 5x$ **20.** $-6y + 1$

21. $x^2 + 4xy - 5y^2$ **22.** $6y^2 + 10y + 18$ **23.** $y^2 + 2y + 1$ **24.** $2x - \frac{1}{2}y$

Evaluate each expression below for $r = \frac{1}{2}$, $s = \frac{3}{4}$, and $t = \frac{1}{8}$.

25. rt **26.** s^2 **27.** $r + s^2$ **28.** rt^2

Choose the values of x and y that will make each equation true.
(There may be more than one correct answer.)

29. $x^2 - xy = -4$

  a. $x = 2; y = 0$ **b.** $x = 4; y = 5$ **c.** $x = 2; y = 4$ **d.** $x = 1; y = 3$

30. $2x - 3y = 0$

  a. $x = 2; y = 1$ **b.** $x = 0; y = -1$ **c.** $x = 3; y = 2$ **d.** $x = -3; y = -2$

31. $-x + y = 17$

  a. $x = -8; y = 9$ **b.** $x = 18; y = 1$ **c.** $x = -17; y = 0$ **d.** $x = 7; y = -10$

32. $x + 2y + 1 = 1$

  a. $x = -1; y = 1$ **b.** $x = 6; y = -3$ **c.** $x = 4; y = -1$ **d.** $x = -1; y = \frac{1}{2}$

33. $x^2 - 2xy + 4 = 8$

  a. $x = 2; y = 0$ **b.** $x = 0; y = -4$ **c.** $x = -2; y = 0$ **d.** $x = 1; y = -2$

34. $x^2 + xy - 1 = 7$

  a. $x = 0; y = 8$ **b.** $x = 1; y = 8$ **c.** $x = 2; y = 2$ **d.** $x = -2; y = -2$

CHALLENGE

35. Find at least one more set of values for x and y that will make each of the equations in exercises 29 through 34 true.

15-2 Addition and Subtraction of Polynomials

A polynomial is in simplest form when all like terms have been combined.

To simplify a polynomial, if necessary, rewrite it such that like terms are grouped together.

$2x^2 + 3x - x^2 - 5x = \underline{\ ?\ }$
$2x^2 - x^2 + 3x - 5x$
$= (2 - 1)x^2 + (3 - 5)x$
$= 1x^2 + {}^-2x$
$= x^2 - 2x$

Polynomials often have unlike terms which cannot be simplified.
DO NOT FORGET to put these terms back in the original polynomial after it has been simplified.

$3mn - 2 + 6m^2 - 2m^2 + 4mn = \underline{\ ?\ }$
$3mn + 4mn + 6m^2 - 2m^2 - 2$
$= (3 + 4)mn + (6 - 2)m^2 - 2$
$= 7mn + 4m^2 - 2$ Do not forget the 2.

To add polynomials:

- Rewrite each polynomial with like terms grouped together.

- Simplify by adding the coefficients of the like terms and any constants.

$(2x^2 + 11x + 9) + (3x^2 - 6x) = \underline{\ ?\ }$
$2x^2 + 11x + 9 + 3x^2 - 6x$
$= (2x^2 + 3x^2) + (11x - 6x) + 9$
$\qquad$ Like terms $\qquad$ Like terms
$= (2 + 3)x^2 + (11 - 6)x + 9$
$= 5x^2 + 5x + 9$

Adding is sometimes easier if the like terms in each polynomial are arranged in a column.

$(4x^2 + 3xy - 9y^2) + (6x^2 - 7y^2) = \underline{\ ?\ }$
$$4x^2 + 3xy - 9y^2$$
$$\underline{+\ 6x^2 \qquad\quad -\ 7y^2}$$
$$10x^2 + 3xy - 16y^2$$

To subtract polynomials:

Add the opposite of the polynomial to be subtracted.
$(6m^2 + 9) - (4m^2 + 3) = \underline{\ ?\ }$
$(6m^2 + 9) - (4m^2 + 3)$
$= (6m^2 + 9) + (-4m^2 - 3)$ ← Adding the opposite of $(4m^2 + 3)$ is $+(-4m^2 - 3)$
$= (6m^2 + {}^-4m^2) + (9 - 3)$
$= (6 + {}^-4)m^2 + 6 = 2m^2 + 6$

Arranging the like terms of the polynomials in columns sometimes makes subtraction easier.
$(4x^2 + 3xy - 9y^2) - (5xy - 4y^2) = \underline{\ ?\ }$
$$4x^2 + 3xy - 9y^2$$
$$\underline{\mp\ 5xy \pm 4y^2}$$ ← Change the signs in the subtrahend and add.
$$4x^2 - 2xy - 5y^2$$

418

Add or subtract. (The first two are done.)

1. $12m^2n + 7m^2n \longrightarrow (12 + 7)m^2n = 19m^2n$ 2. $3xy - 6xy \longrightarrow (3 - 6)xy = -3xy$

3. $14a^2b^2 + 9a^2b^2$

4. $11c^2d^3 - 9c^2d^3$

5. $(6x + 9y) + (-8x + 15y)$

6. $(-4a^2 + 7) + (12a^2 - 9)$

7. $(11r - 16s) + (2r + 19s)$

8. $(4t^2 + 9t) - (12t^2 + 11t)$

9. $(2b^2 + 11c) - (8b^2 + 17c)$

10. $(5k + 26) + (-9k + 13)$

11. $(x^2 + 16) - (3x^2 + 22)$

12. $(13c - 25d) - (16c - 15d)$

13. $(14xy - 2y) + (18xy - 5y)$

14. $(0.74t - 0.09) + (0.29t - 0.17)$

15. $(5k^2 - 20) - (3k^2 - 15)$

16. $(3.8a + 0.18b) - (5.1a + 0.25b)$

17. $(a^2 - 12a - 15) + (3a^2 + 22)$ 18. $(-3c^2 + 8d^2) + (10c^2 + 14cd - 20d^2)$

19. $(x^2 + 5xy - 14y^2) - (4x^2 - 19y^2)$ 20. $(-0.5p^2 + 1.2q^2) + (9.9q^2 - 2.1p^2)$

Add.

21. $45x^3 + 19x - 22$
    $17x^3 - 24x + 19$

22. $-4t^2 - 8t + 96$
    $30t^2 \quad\quad - 102$

23. $61x^2 \quad\quad - 128$
    $\quad\quad 44x + 17$

Subtract.

24. $23s^2 - 18t^2$
    $16s^2 - 13t^2$

25. $42x^2 - 36x + 64$
    $28x^2 + 11x$

26. $27p - 19q$
    $18p + 22q - 15$

Ascending and Descending Order of Polynomials

A polynomial with one variable is written in **ascending order** when the degree of each term is **less than** the degree of the term that follows it.

$7 - 2y + 8y^2 = 7 - 2y^1 + 8y^2 \longleftarrow$ | $0 < 1 < 2$
Ascending order

A polynomial with one variable is in **descending order** when the degree of each term is **greater than** the degree of the term that follows it.

$5c^3 + 3c^2 - c + 1 = 5c^3 + 3c^2 - c^1 + 1 \longleftarrow$ | $3 > 2 > 1 > 0$
Descending order

A polynomial with more than one variable can be written in either ascending order or descending order for any *one* of its variables.

$x^3y^2 + 2x^2y - 3x = x^3y^2 + 2x^2y^1 - 3x^1 \longleftarrow$ | Descending order of x
$9m^2 + 4mn - n^2 = 9m^2 + 4m^1n^1 - n^2 \longleftarrow$ | Ascending order of n

---

Arrange in ascending powers of x.

27. $2x^3 + 8 - 9x^2$

28. $6x + 17 + 11x^2$

29. $x^2y + xy^2 + x^3$

Arrange in descending powers of t.

30. $t + 9t^2 - 15$

31. $6t^3 - 20t + t^2$

32. $9 - t^4 + 18t$

15-3 | Exponents

Law of Exponents for Products

$$a^m \cdot a^n = a^{m+n}$$

$$a^3 \cdot a^2 = a^{3+2} = a^5$$

$$x^2 \cdot x = x^2 \cdot x^1 = x^{2+1} = x^3$$

Remember: $10^3 \cdot 10^2$

$$(10 \cdot 10 \cdot 10)(10 \cdot 10) = 10^5$$

OR, $\quad 10^3 \cdot 10^2 = 10^{3+2} = 10^5$

Law of Exponents for Quotients

If $m > n$, $\dfrac{a^m}{a^n} = a^{m-n}$

$$\frac{a^6}{a^4} = \frac{\cancel{a} \cdot \cancel{a} \cdot \cancel{a} \cdot \cancel{a} \cdot a \cdot a}{\cancel{a} \cdot \cancel{a} \cdot \cancel{a} \cdot \cancel{a}} = a^2$$

OR $\quad \dfrac{a^6}{a^4} = a^{6-4} = a^2$

If $m < n$, $\dfrac{a^m}{a^n} = \dfrac{1}{a^{n-m}}$

NOTE: Powers are reversed.

Remember:
$$\frac{10^4}{10^5} = \frac{\cancel{10} \cdot \cancel{10} \cdot \cancel{10} \cdot \cancel{10}}{\cancel{10} \cdot \cancel{10} \cdot \cancel{10} \cdot \cancel{10} \cdot 10} = \frac{1}{10^1}$$

$$\frac{a^4}{a^5} = \frac{\cancel{a} \cdot \cancel{a} \cdot \cancel{a} \cdot \cancel{a}}{\cancel{a} \cdot \cancel{a} \cdot \cancel{a} \cdot \cancel{a} \cdot a} = \frac{1}{a^1}$$

OR $\quad \dfrac{a^4}{a^5} = \dfrac{1}{a^{5-4}} = \dfrac{1}{a^1}$

If $m = n$, $\dfrac{a^m}{a^n} = a^{m-n} = a^0 = 1$

$$\frac{a^5}{a^5} = \frac{\cancel{a} \cdot \cancel{a} \cdot \cancel{a} \cdot \cancel{a} \cdot \cancel{a}}{\cancel{a} \cdot \cancel{a} \cdot \cancel{a} \cdot \cancel{a} \cdot \cancel{a}} = 1$$

OR $\quad \dfrac{a^5}{a^5} = a^{5-5} = a^0 = 1$

Remember:
Any variable raised to the *zero* power equals 1.

Law of Exponents for Powers

$$(a^m)^n = a^{mn}$$

$$(a^3)^2 = (a^3)(a^3)$$
$$= (a \cdot a \cdot a)(a \cdot a \cdot a) = a^6$$

OR $(a^3)^2 = a^{3 \times 2} = a^6$

Remember:
$$(10^3)^2 = (10^3)(10^3)$$
$$= (10 \cdot 10 \cdot 10)(10 \cdot 10 \cdot 10)$$
$$= 10^6$$

Simplify by using the correct Law of Exponents.*

1. $t^2 \cdot t^5$
2. $x^4 \cdot x$
3. $r^3 \cdot r^4$
4. $s^2 \cdot s^3$
5. $m^8 \cdot m^5$
6. $\dfrac{k^9}{k^7}$
7. $\dfrac{y^{10}}{y^4}$
8. $\dfrac{y^2}{y^5}$
9. $\dfrac{x^6}{x^6}$
10. $\dfrac{t^3}{t^5}$
11. $(a^2)^4$
12. $(s^4)^3$
13. $(y^2)^7$
14. $(r^3)^3$
15. $(x^6)^2$
16. $(t^4)^4$
17. $(ab)^2$
18. $(rt)^4$
19. $(4a^2)^3$
20. $(y^3z)^2$

Multiplying Monomials

To multiply two or more monomials:

- Multiply the coefficients. (Remember: 1 is the coefficient of any variable that does not have another expressed coefficient.)
- Multiply the variables using the appropriate Law of Exponents.

$(-3x^2)(8x^5) = \underline{\ ?\ }$

$= (-3)(8)(x^2)(x^5) = -24x^{(2+5)} = -24x^7$

$(5xy)(11x^2) = \underline{\ ?\ }$

$= (5)(11)(x)(x^2)(y) = 55x^{(1+2)}y$

$= 55x^3y$

$(4x)(-5x^2y)(y^2) = \underline{\ ?\ }$

$= (4)(-5)(x)(x^2)(y)(y^2) = -20x^{(1+2)}y^{(1+2)}$

$= -20x^3y^3$

Find the fourth power of z^2.

$(z^2)^4 = z^{2\cdot4} = z^8$

Find the cube of mn.

$(mn)^3 = (m^1n^1)^3 = m^{1\cdot3}n^{1\cdot3} = m^3n^3$

To multiply a polynomial by a monomial:

- Distribute the monomial across the polynomial.
- Proceed as above.

$2y(3y^2 + 9) = \underline{\ ?\ }$

$(2y \cdot 3y^2) + (2y \cdot 9) = 6y^{1+2} + 18y$

$= 6y^3 + 18y$

$-5k(k^2 - 3k + 2) = \underline{\ ?\ }$

$(-5k)(k^2) - (-5k)(3k) + (-5k)(2)$

$= -5k^{1+2} - (-15k^{1+1}) + (-10k)$

$= -5k^3 + 15k^2 - 10k$

Multiply.*

1. $8y^3 \cdot -9y^4$
2. $10x^4 \cdot 17x^9$
3. $7cd \cdot -4cd$
4. $(11x^2y)(3xy^3)$
5. $(6r)(-2s)(5r^2s)$
6. $(-7k^5)(-12k^3)$
7. $2c^2d \cdot 24c^2$
8. $(-9x^4)(-6x^4y^2)$
9. $(-4m)^2$
10. $(-2cd)^3$
11. $3x(2x^2 + 8x + 9)$
12. $5y(y^2 - 8y + 6)$
13. $-4t^2(9t^2 - 7t - 10)$
14. $r^2s(2r^3 - 3rs + 2s^3)$
15. $6t(5r^2 - 8rt)$
16. $-2k(k^2 - 16)$
17. $(-4a^2)(-3ab + 2b^2)$
18. $-3a^2(a^2 - 4a + 7)$
19. $6b(-7b^2 + b^3)$
20. $r^2s(2s^2 - 4r^2)$
21. $-9k^2(8k + 17)$
22. $(5s^2t^2)^2$
23. $(d^2ef^4)^4$
24. $(6m^4n^5)^2$

Fill in the missing factor.

25. $8r^3y^2 \cdot \underline{\ ?\ } = -24r^6y^4$
26. $(-3y^2)(\underline{\ ?\ }) = 9y^4$
27. $k^2(2k + \underline{\ ?\ }) = 2k^3 + 18k^2$
28. $10st \cdot \underline{\ ?\ } = 180s^2t$
29. $4k^4m \cdot \underline{\ ?\ } = -28k^6m^5$
30. $-10s(\underline{\ ?\ } + 13s^2) = 240s - 130s^3$

To multiply two binomials:

$$(x + 4)(x + 6) = \underline{\ ?\ }$$

- Distribute the first term of the first binomial across both terms of the second binomial.

$$(x + 4) \quad \bullet \quad (x + 6) = \underline{\ ?\ }$$

1st binomial   2nd binomial

$$= x(x + 6) \quad \text{and} \quad 4(x + 6)$$

- Do the same with the second term.

$$= x^2 + 6x \quad + \quad 4x + 24$$

- Combine any similar terms and simplify.

$$= x^2 + 6x \quad + \quad 4x + 24$$

similar terms

$$= x^2 \quad + \quad 10x \quad + \quad 24$$

The first step of distributing the first binomial may be done mentally, following these 4 steps.

$$(x + 4)(x + 6) =$$

① $x \cdot x = x^2$

② $x \cdot 6 = 6x$

③ $4 \cdot x = 4x$

④ $4 \cdot 6 = 24$

$$x^2 + (6x + 4x) + 24$$

$$x^2 + 10x + 24 = x^2 + 10x + 24$$

Study these. (Examine how carefully coefficients and signs must be kept track of.)

$$(x - 7)(x + 8) = \underline{\ ?\ }$$

$$= (x \cdot x) + (x \cdot 8) + (-7)(x) + (-7)(8)$$

$$= x^2 \quad + 8x \quad - 7x \quad - 56$$

$$= x^2 + 1x - 56$$

$$= x^2 + x - 56$$

$$(3x - 2)(4x - 5) = \underline{\ ?\ }$$

$$= (3x)(4x) + (3x)(-5) + (-2)(4x) + (-2)(-5)$$

$$= (12x \cdot x) + (-15x) + (-8x) + (10)$$

$$= 12x^2 - 15x - 8x + 10$$

$$= 12x^2 - 23x + 10$$

Multiply.

1. $(x + 7)(x + 9)$
2. $(y + 2)(y + 5)$
3. $(y + 7)(y + 4)$
4. $(a - 3)(a - 5)$
5. $(x - 6)(x - 8)$
6. $(y - 9)(y - 11)$
7. $(x + 4)(x - 6)$
8. $(m - 10)(m + 3)$
9. $(m - 4)(m + 2)$
10. $(y - 8)(y + 9)$
11. $(x + 6)(x + 3)$
12. $(b - 8)(b + 12)$
13. $(d + 10)(d - 5)$
14. $(d + 10)(d + 5)$
15. $(d - 10)(d - 5)$
16. $(n + 2)(n - 6)$
17. $(p + 7)(p - 2)$
18. $(r + 3)(r + 3)$

Multiply.

19. $(2x + 3)(x + 4)$ **20.** $(3y - 2)(2y - 4)$ **21.** $(m - 7)(3m - 4)$

22. $(x - 9)(x - 10)$ **23.** $(2c - 5)(3c + 7)$ **24.** $(5d - 2)(6d + 5)$

25. $(4a - 5)(3a + 2)$ **26.** $(a + 15)(a + 6)$ **27.** $(z - 7)(3z - 6)$

28. $(2x + 1)(4x - 1)$ **29.** $(3x - 11)(2x + 12)$ **30.** $(m - 8)(m + 8)$

31. $(7d + 4)(7d - 4)$ **32.** $(b + 15)^2$ **33.** $(6n + 1)^2$

Choose the correct product from among these answers: a, b, c, or d.

a. $6x^2 + 13x + 6$ **b.** $6x^2 - 13x + 6$ **c.** $6x^2 - 5x - 6$ **d.** $6x^2 + 5x - 6$

34. $(2x + 3)(3x - 2)$ **35.** $(2x - 3)(3x - 2)$

36. $(2x + 3)(3x + 2)$ **37.** $(2x - 3)(3x + 2)$

Special Cases in Multiplying Polynomials

When TWO variables are used:

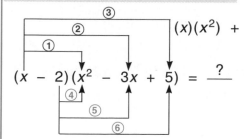

$$(x)(3x) + (x)(-4y) + (2y)(3x) + (2y)(-4y)$$
$$(x + 2y)(3x - 4y) = \underline{\ ?\ }$$
$$= 3x^2 - 4xy + 6yx + (-8)y^2$$
$$= 3x^2 \underline{-4xy + 6xy} - 8y^2$$
$$= 3x^2 + 2xy - 8y^2$$

When trinomials are involved:

$$(x)(x^2) + (x)(-3x) + (x)(5) + (-2)(x^2) + (-2)(-3x) + (-2)(5)$$
$$(x - 2)(x^2 - 3x + 5) = \underline{\ ?\ } = x^3 - 3x^2 + \overbrace{5x - 2x^2}^{\text{combine}} + \underbrace{6x}_{\text{combine}} - 10$$
$$= x^3 - 5x^2 + 11x - 10$$

Multiply.

38. $(3x + 5y)(2x + 7y)$ **39.** $(2x - 3y)(5x - 6y)$ **40.** $(a + 2b)(3a - b)$

41. $(c - 4d)(2c + 11d)$ **42.** $(4m + n)(4m + n)$ **43.** $(7a - 3b)(a + 5b)$

44. $(a + 1)(a^2 + 2a + 1)$ **45.** $(x + 3)(x^2 + 2x + 5)$ **46.** $(n - 1)(7 - 2n - n^2)$

47. $(y - 3)(2y^2 - 2y - 1)$ **48.** $(x + 3)(x^2 - 2x - 3)$ **49.** $(2 - m)(m^2 - 3m + 4)$

15-6 Monomial Factors of Polynomials

To factor a number: rewrite it as a product of two or more numbers. (See page 38.)

Prime Factors $\begin{cases} 12 = 2 \cdot 2 \cdot 3 \\ 30 = 2 \cdot 3 \cdot 5 \end{cases}$ ⟶ Common Factors = 2 and 3
of 12 and 30

Greatest Common Factor (GCF) = $2 \cdot 3 = 6$

To factor a polynomial: rewrite it as a product of two or more polynomials by finding the greatest common monomial factor (GCF).

- To get the GCF of a polynomial like $6x^2y + 45x^3y^2$, find the:

  Prime Factors
  of each term

  $\begin{cases} 6x^2y = 2 \cdot 3 \cdot x \cdot x \cdot y \\ 45x^3y^2 = 3 \cdot 3 \cdot 5 \cdot x \cdot x \cdot x \cdot y \cdot y \end{cases}$

  Then the common factors are: 3 and $x \cdot x$ and y
  So, the GCF is: $3 \cdot x^2 \cdot y = 3x^2y$

- To factor out the GCF from the polynomial, express each term as a product of the GCF and another polynomial.

  GCF is: $3x^2y$

  $6x^2y + 45x^3y^2$

  Factor out the GCF, $3x^2y$.

  $= (2 \cdot 3)(x^2y) + (3 \cdot 15)(x)(x^2y)y$

  $= 2(3x^2y) + (3x^2y)(15xy)$

  $= (3x^2y)(2) + (3x^2y)(15xy)$

- Now rewrite the polynomial as a product of this monomial and another polynomial. ⟶

  $= 3x^2y(2 + 15xy)$

  $6x^2y + 45x^3y^2 = 3x^2y(2 + 15xy)$

Study these.

Factor: $12x^3 + 24x^2y = \underline{\quad?\quad}$

Find the common factors of each term to get the **GCF:**

$12x^3 = (2 \cdot 2 \cdot 3) \cdot (x \cdot x \cdot x)$

$24x^2y = (2 \cdot 2 \cdot 2 \cdot 3) \cdot (x \cdot x) \cdot y$

GCF $= 2 \cdot 2 \cdot 3 \cdot x \cdot x = 12x^2$

Now factor out $12x^2$ from:

$12x^3 + 24x^2y$

$= 12x \cdot x \cdot x + (12 \cdot 2)(x \cdot x) \cdot y$

$= (12x^2)(x) + (12x^2)(2)(y)$

$= 12x^2(x + 2y)$

Factor: $8x^5y^2 - 16x^4y^3 + 12x^3y^3 = \underline{\quad?\quad}$

$8x^5y^2 = (2 \cdot 2 \cdot 2) \cdot (x \cdot x \cdot x \cdot x \cdot x) \cdot (y \cdot y)$

$-16x^4y^3 = (2 \cdot 2 \cdot 2 \cdot 2)(x \cdot x \cdot x \cdot x) \cdot (y \cdot y \cdot y)$

$+12x^3y^3 = (2 \cdot 2 \cdot 3)(x \cdot x \cdot x)(y \cdot y \cdot y)$

GCF $= 2 \cdot 2 \cdot x \cdot x \cdot x \cdot y \cdot y = 4x^3y^2$

Now factor out $4x^3y^2$ from:

$8x^5y^2 - 16x^4y^3 + 12x^3y^3$

$= (2)(4)(x^3)(x^2)(y^2) - (4)(4)(x^3)(x^1)(y^2)(y^1) + (4)(3)(x^3)(y^2)(y^1)$

$= 4x^3y^2(2x^2) - 4x^3y^2(4xy) + 4x^3y^2(3y)$

$= 4x^3y^2(2x^2 - 4xy + 3y)$

Identify the GCF.

1. $3x \cdot x + 3 \cdot 5 \cdot x$ 2. $2 \cdot 2 \cdot x + 2 \cdot 3 \cdot x \cdot x$ 3. $5 \cdot 7 \cdot x \cdot x \cdot x + 2 \cdot 5 \cdot 7 \cdot x \cdot x$

4. $8x^3 + 8x^2$ 5. $6x^2y + 7x^3y$ 6. $9a^3 + 6b^3$

7. $10a^2b + 30a^4$ 8. $9m^4n^3 + 27m^5$ 9. $4y^3z + 8y^5z^6 + 4y^2z$

10. $8x^2 + 24x = \underline{\ ?\ }(x + 3)$ 11. $20y^3 + 10y^5 = \underline{\ ?\ }(2 + y^2)$

A Shortcut in Factoring

Factor: $6x^2y + 45x^3y^2 = \underline{\ ?\ }$

Find GCF (see page 424): $3x^2y$

Divide each term by GCF: $\dfrac{6x^2y}{3x^2y} = 2$ $\dfrac{+45x^3y^2}{3x^2y} = 15xy$

Express polynomial as product of GCF and other factors: $6x^2y + 45x^3y^2 = 3x^2y(2 + 15xy)$

Factor: $8x^5y^2 - 16x^4y^3 + 12x^3y^3 = \underline{\ ?\ }$

Find GCF: $4x^3y^2$

Divide each term by GCF: $\dfrac{8x^5y^2}{4x^3y^2} = 2x^2$ $\dfrac{-16x^4y^3}{4x^3y^2} = -4x^1y^1$ $\dfrac{+12x^3y^3}{4x^3y^2} = 3y^1$

Express polynomial as product of GCF and other factors: $8x^5y^2 - 16x^4y^3 + 12x^3y^3$
$= 4x^3y^2(2x^2 - 4xy + 3y)$

Factor.

12. $8x^2 + 24x$ 13. $20y^3 + 10y^5$ 14. $6ab + 12a$

15. $9a^4 + 12a^5$ 16. $18x^4y - 27y^5$ 17. $a^4b^3 + a^2b^4$

18. $7x^4 + 28y^5$ 19. $3m^7n - 9m^4n^6$ 20. $25 - 15x^4$

21. $x^2 - 3x^3$ 22. $6y^3z + 8y^4z^2$ 23. $c^2d^2 - cd$

24. $20x^2 + 15x^3 + 25x^4$ 25. $18m^4 + 27m^6 + 45m^8$

26. $4a^3b - 8a^4b^2 + 12a^5b^3$ 27. $6xy - 12x^2y^2 + 18x^3y^3$

28. $7x^4y - 9x^3y + 3x^2y^5$ 29. $16a^4 - 24a^6 + 18a^8$

30. $25x^4 + 50x^5 - 75x^6$ 31. $16n^3 - 18n^2 - 20n$

32. $21a^4 + 18a^3b + 15b^4$ 33. $2x^2 + 18x - 24$

34. $m^{10} + m^6 + m^2$ 35. $r^2s^3 + r^3s^4 + r^4s^5$

36. $24a^3b^2c^4 - 18a^4b^3c^2$ 37. $49xyz - 56x^2z^3$

38. $6axy - 8bxy + 10cxy$ 39. $32a^5b^5 + 48a^3b^9 - 16a^3b^5$

Factoring Trinomials

Some trinomials are of this form: $x^2 + bx + c.$

$$x^2 \qquad + \qquad bx \qquad + \qquad c$$

| 2nd-power term with only 1 as the coefficient | 1st-power term with any coefficient | 3rd term is a constant |

▶ **To factor such trinomials:**

$$x^2 + \overset{b}{7}x + \overset{c}{10} = \underline{\ ?\ }$$

- List the factors of the constant, **c.**

  $c = 10$: $\{1, 2, 5, 10\}$ Factors

- Examine the **bx** term to see which factors of the constant, **c,** sum to the coefficient, **b.**

  $b = {}^{+}7$. Factors of 10 that sum to ${}^{+}7$ are: 2, 5.

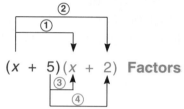

- Use these to create two factors whose product is $x^2 + bx + c.$

  $(x + 5)(x + 2)$ **Factors**

- Check to see if the product of these factors gives back the original trinomial.

  Check: $(x + 5)(x + 2) \overset{?}{=} x^2 + 7x + 10$
  $$= x^2 + 2x + 5x + 10$$
  $$(x + 5)(x + 2) = x^2 + 7x + 10$$

Study this. (Watch out for the sign of **b**!)

Factor: $x^2 - x - 6 = \underline{\ ?\ }$

$$b = -1 \qquad c = -6$$

$c = -6$: $\{1, 2, 3, 6\}$ Factors

$b = -1$. Factors of -6 that sum to $b = -1$ are: 2, -3.

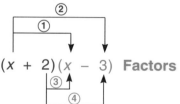

$(x + 2)(x - 3)$ **Factors**

Check: $(x + 2)(x - 3) \overset{?}{=} x^2 - x - 6$
$$= x^2 - 3x + 2x - 6$$
$$(x + 2)(x - 3) = x^2 - x - 6$$

Complete the factors. Check by multiplication.

1. $x^2 + 8x + 12 = (x + 6)(x + \underline{\ ?\ })$
2. $x^2 - 3x - 10 = (x - 5)(x + \underline{\ ?\ })$
3. $x^2 - 12x + 35 = (x - 7)(x - \underline{\ ?\ })$
4. $x^2 - 10x + 16 = (x - \underline{\ ?\ })(x - \underline{\ ?\ })$
5. $x^2 + 2x - 3 = (x + \underline{\ ?\ })(x - \underline{\ ?\ })$
6. $x^2 - 4x + 4 = (x - \underline{\ ?\ })(x - \underline{\ ?\ })$

Choose the correct factorization.

7. $x^2 + 7x + 12$
   a. $(x + 12)(x + 1)$ b. $(x + 6)(x + 2)$ c. $(x + 4)(x + 3)$

8. $x^2 - 3x - 4$
   a. $(x - 4)(x + 1)$ b. $(x + 4)(x - 1)$ c. $(x + 2)(x - 2)$

9. $x^2 + 2x - 48$
   a. $(x + 8)(x + 6)$ b. $(x - 8)(x + 6)$ c. $(x + 8)(x - 6)$

10. $x^2 - 11x + 30$
   a. $(x + 2)(x - 15)$ b. $(x - 5)(x - 6)$ c. $(x - 6)(x + 5)$

Factor. Check by multiplication.

11. $x^2 + 8x + 12$ 12. $y^2 - 6y + 8$ 13. $z^2 - 10z + 21$

14. $y^2 + 12y + 27$ 15. $a^2 + 8a - 33$ 16. $z^2 + 8z - 20$

17. $m^2 - 13m + 30$ 18. $x^2 - 8x + 7$ 19. $a^2 - 2a - 63$

20. $z^2 - z - 20$ 21. $m^2 + 9m + 20$ 22. $x^2 - x - 2$

23. $b^2 + 6b + 5$ 24. $z^2 + 15z + 50$ 25. $m^2 + 9m - 10$

26. $s^2 + 10s + 9$ 27. $n^2 + 3n - 18$ 28. $s^2 - 4s - 21$

29. $n^2 - 4n - 12$ 30. $s^2 - 13s + 40$ 31. $x^2 + 5x - 14$

32. $b^2 - 10b + 25$ 33. $y^2 - 6y - 16$ 34. $n^2 + 14n + 33$

35. $x^2 + 8x + 16$ 36. $a^2 - 6a + 9$ 37. $b^2 - 8b - 33$

38. $y^2 + 5y - 24$ 39. $s^2 + 2s - 35$ 40. $m^2 - 7m - 60$

41. $n^2 - 13n + 42$ 42. $b^2 + 11b - 12$ 43. $n^2 - 10n + 16$

Factor. Check by multiplication. (The first one is done.)

44. $x^2 + 4xy + 3y^2 = (x + 3y)(x + y)$ 45. $x^2 + xy - 2y^2$

$$3xy$$
$$1xy$$

46. $a^2 + 5ab + 6b^2$ 47. $x^4 - 3x^2y^2 - 10y^4$ 48. $m^4 + 3m^2n^2 + 2n^4$

15-8 Factoring More Polynomials

Some trinomials are of this form: $ax^2 + bx + c$ when $a \neq \pm 1$.

$$\overset{a}{\downarrow}\;\;\overset{b}{\downarrow}\;\;\overset{c}{\downarrow}$$
$$2x^2 + 7x + 6 = \underline{\;?\;}$$

To factor such trinomials:

- List the factors of the coefficient, **a**.

  2: $\{1, 2\}$

- List the factors of the constant, **c**.

  6: $\{1, 2, 3, 6\}$

- Use the factors of **a** to find two first terms whose product will be **ax²**. Here, $ax^2 = 2x^2$.

  Need $2x^2$:
  $$\underline{\;?\;} \cdot \underline{\;?\;} = 2x^2$$
  $$(2x)(x) = 2x^2$$

  Keep these as the *first* term of each factor: $(2x + \underline{\;?\;})(x + \underline{\;?\;})$

- Use the factors of the constant, **c**, to find two second terms whose product will equal **c** and will give back a second term of **bx**.

  Look at factors of 6: $\{1, 2, 3, 6\}$. Now create combinations that will give you $c = +6 \longrightarrow (2, 3)$ or $(1, 6)$. Try out each to find the combination that sums to $+7$.

- Work out possible combinations such that:

  $$(2x + \underline{\;?\;})(x + \underline{\;?\;}) \longrightarrow bx = +7$$
  $$\text{and } c = +6$$

  $(2x + 6)(x + 1) \longrightarrow bx = 8x$
  and $c = 6$ NO!

  $(2x + 1)(x + 6) \longrightarrow bx = 13x$
  and $c = 6$ NO!

  $(2x + 2)(x + 3) \longrightarrow bx = 8x$
  and $c = 6$ NO!

  $(2x + 3)(x + 2) \longrightarrow bx = 7x$
  and $c = 6$ WORKS!

- Check by multiplying the factors to see if the product is $ax^2 + bx + c$.

  $(2x + 3)(x + 2) = \underline{\;?\;}$ Checks!
  $2x^2 + 4x + 3x + 6 = 2x^2 + 7x + 6$ ◄

Study this. (Watch out for signs!)

Factor: $10x^2 + 3x - 7 = \underline{\;?\;}$
$a = 10 \quad b = +3 \quad c = -7$

Factors of $a = 10$: $\{1, 2, 5, 10\}$
Coefficients of two first terms must $= a = 10$: (1 and 10) **or** (2 and 5)
Factors of $c = -7$: $\{1, 7\}$

Coefficients of two second terms must $= c = -7$: Combinations with ± 1 and ± 7.
(Remember: Choose a combination that will yield $c = -7$ **and** $bx = 3x$.)

Try: $(x + 1)(10x - 7)$ WORKS! $(2x + 1)(5x - 7)$ NO!
  $(x - 1)(10x + 7)$ NO! $(2x - 1)(5x + 7)$ NO!
  $(x + 7)(10x - 1)$ NO! $(2x + 7)(5x - 1)$ NO!
  $(x - 7)(10x + 1)$ NO! $(2x - 7)(5x + 1)$ NO!

Complete the factors. Check by multiplication.

1. $12x^2 + 11x + 2 = (3x + 2)(\underline{\ ?\ } + 1)$ 2. $10x^2 - 29x + 21 = (\underline{\ ?\ } - 7)(2x - 3)$

3. $12x^2 + 8x - 15 = (\underline{\ ?\ } - 5)(\underline{\ ?\ } + 3)$ 4. $16x^2 + 2x - 5 = (\underline{\ ?\ } + 5)(\underline{\ ?\ } - 1)$

5. $9x^2 - 6x - 8 = (3x - \underline{\ ?\ })(3x + \underline{\ ?\ })$ 6. $14y^2 + 29y + 12 = (7y + \underline{\ ?\ })(2y + \underline{\ ?\ })$

7. $15y^2 - 2y - 8 = (\underline{\ ?\ } + 2)(5y - \underline{\ ?\ })$ 8. $6y^2 - 13y + 2 = (6y - \underline{\ ?\ })(\underline{\ ?\ } - 2)$

9. $16x^2 + 8x + 1 = (\underline{\ ?\ } + 1)(\underline{\ ?\ } + 1)$ 10. $4a^2 - 4a - 15 = (2a + \underline{\ ?\ })(\underline{\ ?\ } - 5)$

Factor. Check by multiplication.

11. $2x^2 + 3x + 1$

12. $5x^2 + 9x + 4$

13. $3y^2 - 10y + 3$

14. $5y^2 - 12y + 4$

15. $3x^2 + 11x + 6$

16. $2b^2 + 3b - 14$

17. $5x^2 + 11x + 2$

18. $3y^2 - 7y - 6$

19. $7y^2 + 15y + 2$

20. $4x^2 - 8x - 5$

21. $7a^2 - 11a + 4$

22. $7c^2 + c - 6$

23. $11a^2 + 16a + 5$

24. $6z^2 - 5z + 1$

25. $7x^2 + 23x + 6$

26. $8c^2 - 6c + 1$

27. $6m^2 - 11m - 10$

28. $12c^2 - c - 6$

29. $35x^2 - 18x - 8$

30. $12a^2 - 8a + 1$

31. $22m^2 - 17m + 3$

32. $20x^2 + 23x + 6$

33. $18n^2 + 9n - 5$

34. $49x^2 + 28x + 4$

35. $2x^4 + 7x^2 + 3$

36. $4y^4 + 14y^2 + 12$

37. $3c^6 + 7c^3 + 2$

38. $2a^2 + 5ab + 2b^2$

39. $6c^2 + 11cd + 3d^2$

40. $8m^2 + 18mn - 5n^2$

41. $14a^2 + 24a - 8$

42. $10r^2 - 9r - 7$

43. $10c^2 + 11c - 6$

44. $18x^2 - 5x - 2$

45. $3b^2 - 19b + 28$

46. $15y^2 + 14y - 8$

47. $4s^2 - 11st + 6t^2$

48. $15n^2 - mn - 2m^2$

49. $12x^2 - 8xy - 15y^2$

50. $6m^2 - 23m + 10$

51. $16r^2 + 34r - 15$

52. $12t^2 + 11t - 15$

53. $30d^2 + de - 14e^2$

54. $8c^2 + 14c - 15$

55. $20b^2 + 9bc - 20c^2$

56. $2s^2 + 19st - 33t^2$

57. $2a^4 + 5a^2 - 63$

58. $2z^4 - z^2 - 21$

59. $6a^2 - 5ab - 6b^2$

60. $2m^6 - 7m^3n + 6n^2$

61. $15c^4 - c^2d^4 - 28d^8$

62. $6 + 25x^4 + 4x^8$

63. $5e^6 - 21e^3f + 4f^2$

64. $35p^6 - 33p^3r^3 - 8r^6$

65. $7 - 26m^2 + 15m^4$

66. $6 - 7d^3 - 20d^6$

67. $8 - 6h^2 - 35h^4$

15-9 Perfect Square Trinomials

Perfect Square Trinomial: the product of two like binomials.

To square a binomial:

Factor: $(x + 3)^2 = (x + 3)(x + 3)$

like binomials

$(x + 3)^2 = (x + 3)(x + 3)$

$= x^2 + 6x + 9$

Shortcut: Square mentally $(x + 3)^2$

Square 1st term, x: x^2

Square 2nd term, 3: 9

To find the middle term:
Double the product of the two terms of the binomial:

$2(x \cdot 3) = (2)(3)(x) = 6x$

So, $(x + 3)^2 = x^2 + 6x + 9$

To factor a perfect square trinomial:

Factor: $4x^2 - 20x + 25$

Of form $ax^2 + bx + c$

1st term, $4x^2$, is a perfect square.

3rd term, 25, is a perfect square.

Middle term, $20x$, has coefficient, b, of 20.

$20 = 2 \times (\sqrt{4} \cdot \sqrt{25}) = 2(2 \cdot 5)$

Whenever a trinomial of the form $ax^2 + bx + c$ has a and c as perfect squares, and b is twice the product of their square roots $[b = 2(\sqrt{a}\sqrt{c})]$, then it is a perfect square trinomial.

So, $4x^2 - 20x + 25$ factored equals:

$(2x - 5)(2x - 5) = (2x - 5)^2$

Simplify.*

1. $(x - 3)^2$
2. $(y + 4)^2$
3. $(z + 5)^2$
4. $(x + 2)^2$
5. $(y - 4)^2$
6. $(z - 5)^2$
7. $(2x + 1)^2$
8. $(5y + 2)^2$
9. $(3a - 2)^2$
10. $(3y - 5)^2$
11. $(6x + 1)^2$
12. $(x - 10)^2$
13. $(2a + b)^2$
14. $(3x + 2y)^2$
15. $(5y - 2z)^2$

Determine if the polynomial is a perfect square trinomial. If it is, factor.*

16. $x^2 + 2x + 1$
17. $x^2 + 5x + 6$
18. $x^2 + 4x + 4$
19. $y^2 - 12y + 36$
20. $y^2 - 7y + 10$
21. $z^2 - 14z + 49$
22. $x^2 + 16x + 64$
23. $9x^2 + 6x + 1$
24. $16a^2 - 8a + 1$
25. $81a^2 + 36a + 4$
26. $4x^2 + 12x + 9$
27. $9c^2 - 12c + 4$
28. $a^2 + 2ab + b^2$
29. $m^2 - 2mn + n^2$
30. $9a^2 + 30ab + 25b^2$
31. $16 - 24y + 9y^2$
32. $9 - 12b - 4b^2$
33. $100 + 60m + 9m^2$
34. $25 + 60s + 36s^2$
35. $x^2 - 6xy + 9y^2$
36. $36c^2 - 12cd + d^2$
37. $49r^2 - 14rs + s^2$
38. $4b^2 + 32bc + 64c^2$
39. $9m^2n^2 - 24mn + 16$
40. $\frac{1}{4}a^2 + 2a + 4$
41. $\frac{1}{9}b^2 - 4b + 36$
42. $25x^2 + 5xy + \frac{1}{4}y^2$

Difference of two squares, $(x^2 - c^2)$:

Every equation of the form
$(x + c)(x - c) = x^2 - c^2$ ⟶ $(x + c)(x - c) =$ ___?___

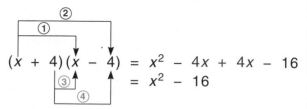

$$= x^2 - cx + cx - c^2 = x^2 - c^2$$

Multiply: $(x + 4)(x - 4) =$ ___?___

$$(x + 4)(x - 4) = x^2 - 4x + 4x - 16$$
$$= x^2 - 16$$

Shortcut for finding the difference of two squares: $(x + 4)(x - 4)$

Square 1st term, x: x^2
Subtract square of last term, 4: 16
So, $(x + 4)(x - 4) = x^2 - 16$

Factor: $4x^2 - 25 =$ ___?___

1st term is square root of $4x^2$: $2x$

2nd terms are
$\pm$ square root of 25: $+5$ and -5

So, $4x^2 - 25 = (2x + 5)(2x - 5)$

Check:

$$(2x + 5)(2x - 5)$$

$$= 4x^2 - 10x + 10x - 25$$
$$= 4x^2 - 25$$

Multiply.*

1. $(x + 3)(x - 3)$
2. $(x - 7)(x + 7)$
3. $(x - 11)(x + 11)$
4. $(y - 1)(y + 1)$
5. $(2x + 3)(2x - 3)$
6. $(5y + 4)(5y - 4)$
7. $(3y + 4)(3y - 4)$
8. $(6a + 1)(6a - 1)$
9. $(2m - 7)(2m + 7)$
10. $(9k + 4)(9k - 4)$
11. $(4t - 5s)(4t + 5s)$
12. $(a - b)(a + b)$
13. $(7x + 2y)(7x - 2y)$
14. $(12a + 5b)(12a - 5b)$
15. $(x^2 - 1)(x^2 + 1)$

Factor. Check.*

16. $x^2 - 49$
17. $y^2 - 25$
18. $z^2 - 9$
19. $4a^2 - b^2$
20. $49x^2 - 64y^2$
21. $9m^2 - 1$
22. $x^2 - 121$
23. $y^2 - 100$
24. $z^2 - 1$
25. $4m^2 - 9$
26. $25x^2 - 9$
27. $x^2 - 400$
28. $a^2 - c^2$
29. $49 - t^2$
30. $1 - 64a^2$
31. $225 - 16x^2$

Challenge

32. Factor in 2 different ways: $(3x + 4)^2 - (2x - 1)^2$

15-11   Complete Factorization

To factor a polynomial completely:

$2x^3 + 4x^2 - 6x = \underline{\ ?\ }$

- Factor out any GCF.

   GCF: $2x$ because $2x$ is a factor of each term.

- Factor out or divide each term by the GCF.

$$\frac{2x^3}{2x} + \frac{4x^2}{2x} - \frac{6x}{2x}$$

- Now factor, if possible, the new polynomial.

$$= x^2 + 2x - 3$$
$$= (x + 3)(x - 1)$$

- Rewrite the original polynomial as a product of GCF and these factors.

$$2x^3 + 4x^2 - 6x$$
$$= 2x(x + 3)(x - 1)$$

Complete Factorization

Factor: $4x^2 + 8x = \underline{\ ?\ }$

GCF: $4x$

$$\frac{4x^2}{4x} + \frac{8x}{4x} = (x + 2)$$

So, $4x^2 + 8x = 4x(x + 2)$

Factor: $9m^2 - 81 = \underline{\ ?\ }$

GCF: 9

$$\frac{9m^2}{9} - \frac{81}{9} = (m^2 - 9)$$

Difference of 2 squares

$$m^2 - 9 = (m - 3)(m + 3)$$

So, $9m^2 - 81 = 9(m - 3)(m + 3)$

Factor out the GCF.

1. $6x + 14$

2. $10c^2 - 4c$

3. $3y^2 + 6y + 6$

4. $12b - 27$

5. $3x^2 + 2x$

6. $9m^2 + 9m$

Factor out the GCF, if there is one. Factor the remaining polynomial.

(Hint for exercises 7–12:   Look for $x^2 + bx + c$.)

7. $2x^2 - 6x - 56$

8. $3x^2 + 9x + 6$

9. $a^2 - 14a + 45$

10. $n^2 + 4n - 12$

11. $2m^2 + 20m + 48$

12. $b^2 - 7b + 6$

(Hint for exercises 13–18:   Look for $ax^2 + bx + c$.)

13. $2x^2 - 7x - 15$

14. $7a^3 - 30a^2 + 8a$

15. $10a^2 + 7a - 12$

16. $10a^4 + 9a^3 + 2a^2$

17. $6y^2 - 13y + 2$

18. $20x^2 + 30x + 10$

(Hint for exercises 19–27:   Look for perfect square trinomials.)

19. $2x^2 + 16x + 32$

20. $4a^3 + 28a^2 + 49a$

21. $3x^2 - 30x + 75$

22. $4y^2 - 4y + 1$

23. $x^3 + 2x^2 + x$

24. $9x^2 - 6x + 1$

25. $25a^2 - 20ab + 4b^2$

26. $4a^2 - 12ab + 9b^2$

27. $8x^2 - 24xy + 16y^2$

(Hint for exercises 28–33:   Look for the difference of 2 squares.)

28. $2m^2 - 288$

29. $12n^2 - 3$

30. $2x^2 - 72$

31. $am^5 - 36am^3$

32. $5b^2 - 45$

33. $8de^2 - 50df^2$

Factor completely.

34. $6xy + 21$

35. $4x^2 - 8x + 4$

36. $9y^2 - 100$

37. $4x^2 + 4x - 8$

38. $2n^2 - 13n + 20$

39. $2x^2 + 28x + 98$

40. $3x^2 + 9x + 6$

41. $b^2 + 4b - 60$

42. $a^2 - 36$

43. $y^2 - 22y + 121$

44. $16 - 49x^2$

45. $3x^2 - 48$

46. $m^2 - 16m + 63$

47. $6xy - 8x$

48. $9x^2 + 24x + 16$

49. $6y^2 - 4y - 2$

50. $c^2 + 2cd + d^2$

51. $100 - 81d^2$

52. $3a^2 - 26a + 16$

53. $z^2 - 81$

54. $c^2 + 15c + 44$

55. $28y^2 + y - 2$

56. $m^2 - 2mn + n^2$

57. $4x^2 - 25$

58. $5x^2 - 45$

59. $y^2 + 18y + 81$

60. $81 + 18y + y^2$

61. $8m^2 - 32$

62. $m^4 + 2m^3 + m^2$

63. $3x^2 - 10xy - 8y^2$

64. $16x^2y^2 - 36y^2z^2$

65. $3a^2 - 12ab^2$

66. $2d^2 + 4d + 12$

67. $3y^2 - 6y + 3$

68. $c^2d^2 - 15cd^2 + 54d^2$

69. $r^2 - 3r - 28$

70. $6b^3 + 10b^2 + 4b$

71. $3 + 6n - 24n^2$

72. $5 - 5a^2$

Factor after rearranging the terms.

73. $y - 2 + 15y^2$

74. $6m^2 - 12 - m$

75. $6 + 7r^2 - 23r$

76. $4x^2 - 49$

77. $3x + 6y - 9z$

78. $6w^2 - 19wx^2 + 3x^4$

79. $5x^2 - 20$

80. $a^2 - 24 - 25$

81. $-64d^2 + e^4$

82. $x^4 - 16$

83. $5n^7 + 125n$

84. $4x^2 - 36y^2$

85. $am^3 - 36am^7$

86. $25a^2 - 100b^2$

87. $2e^4 - 10e^2 - 72$

Factor each polynomial. If a polynomial cannot be factored, label it _prime_.

88. $5d^2 + 8e^2 \rightarrow$ No factors. $5d^2 + 8e^2$ is prime.

89. $8x^2 + 6x$

90. $x + 8x + 6$

91. $b^2 - 6b + 5$

92. $9a^2 + 30a + 25$

93. $6x^2 - 7x + 3$

94. $x^8 - y^8$

95. $16 + 47d^4 - 3$

96. $81r^8 - s^4$

97. $14x^3 - 56x$

98. $10v^4 - 32v^2 + 6$

99. $a^4 - 5a^2 - 36$

100. $g^2 + 2gh + h^2$

101. $9x^2 - 24xy + 16y^2$

102. $12e^4 - 7e + 1$

103. $49s^6 - 324$

104. $4(a + b)^2 + 17(a + b) - 15$

105. $x^5 + y^6$

106. $7a^2 - 7b^2$

107. $9c^2d^2 + 4 - 12cd$

108. $256r^4 - 1$

109. $9d^2 - 18e^2$

110. $10(x + y)^2 - 11(x + y) - 6$

111. $16c^4 - 81$

112. $24a^3 + 30a^2 + 9a$

113. $18m^2 + 15mn - 18n^2$

114. $2n^4 - 26n^2 + 72$

115. $x^2 - 30 - 7x$

116. $(r + s)^2 + 6(r + s) + 9$

117. $7t^2 + 14 + 21t$

118. $8n^2 + s^2 + 2ns$

119. $(a + b)^2 - (c + d)^2$

15-12 Division of Polynomials

> **To divide a polynomial by a monomial:**
>
> - Divide each term of the polynomial by the monomial.
> - Divide the coefficients.
> - Divide the variables, using the **Law of Exponents** for quotients. (See page 420.)

Polynomial division may be expressed in 3 ways:

$$a^7 \div a^5 = \underline{\;?\;} \qquad \text{OR} \qquad \frac{a^7}{a^5} = \underline{\;?\;} \qquad \text{OR} \qquad a^5\overline{)a^7}$$

In each case, $a^7 \div a^5 = a^{7-5} = a^2$

Check: $\quad \underset{\text{Quotient}}{a^2} \cdot \underset{\text{Divisor}}{a^5} = a^{2+5} = \underset{\text{Dividend}}{a^7}$

$$(8a^4 + 6a^3 - 10a^2) \div 2a^2 = \underline{\;?\;}$$

$$\frac{8a^4 + 6a^3 - 10a^2}{2a^2} = \underline{\;?\;} \qquad \text{OR} \qquad 2a^2\overline{)8a^4 + 6a^3 - 10a^2}^{\;?}$$

$$= \frac{8a^4}{2a^2} + \frac{6a^3}{2a^2} - \frac{10a^2}{2a^2}$$

$$= 4a^2 + 3a - 5 \qquad\qquad\qquad 2a^2\overline{)8a^4 + 6a^3 - 10a^2}^{\;4a^2 + 3a - 5}$$

Check: $\underset{\text{Quotient}}{(4a^2 + 3a - 5)} \; \underset{\text{Divisor}}{2a^2} = \underset{\text{Dividend}}{8a^4 + 6a^3 - 10a^2}$

Divide.

1. $\dfrac{m^{10}}{m^4}$

2. $\dfrac{s^{12}}{s^4}$

3. $\dfrac{20x^7}{5x}$

4. $\dfrac{36x^4 + 12x^3 + 24x^2}{4x^2}$

5. $\dfrac{x^8}{x}$

6. $\dfrac{-24y^6}{6y^5}$

7. $\dfrac{8x^4 - 4x^7}{2x^2}$

8. $\dfrac{25a^3 + 10a^2 + 35a}{5}$

9. $\dfrac{-9a^4b^2}{-3ab}$

10. $\dfrac{10a^7 + 20a^9}{10a^4}$

11. $\dfrac{16m^4 - 8m}{4m}$

12. $\dfrac{49t^6 - 7t^4 - 56t^2}{7t^2}$

13. $\dfrac{-b^6}{-b}$

14. $\dfrac{-d^{12}}{-d^{11}}$

15. $\dfrac{12c - 24d}{6}$

16. $\dfrac{14k^6 - 42k^4 + 56k^2}{-14k^2}$

17. $\dfrac{c^9}{-c^4}$

18. $\dfrac{-18q^7r^3}{8q^7r}$

19. $\dfrac{16a^2b - 40a^3}{2a + 6a}$

20. $\dfrac{14r^6\ell^8 - 42r^4\ell^9 + 56r^2\ell^4}{7r^2\ell^3}$

Division of a Polynomial by a Binomial

To divide a polynomial by a binomial:

Recall the procedure for division. ⟶
(Use usual long division rules.)

$$(x^2 - x - 20) \div (x + 4) = \underline{\ ?\ }$$

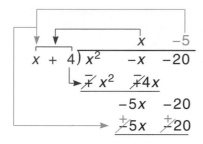

- **Estimate** the partial quotient by dividing x^2 by x. ($x^2 \div x = x$)
- **Try "x"** in the quotient.
- **Multiply** $(x + 4)$ by x: $x^2 + 4x$. Write this product under $(x^2 - x)$.
- **Subtract** $x^2 + 4x$ from $x^2 - x$. Remember: **add** the opposite of $(x^2 + 4x)$, which is $-x^2 - 4x$. Write the difference, $-5x$.
- **Bring down** the next term, -20.

REPEAT PROCEDURE

- **Estimate** the partial quotient by dividing $-5x$ by x. ($-5x \div x = -5$)
- **Try "-5"** in the quotient.
- **Multiply** $(x + 4)$ by -5: $(-5x - 20)$. Write this product under $-5x - 20$.
- **Subtract** $(-5x - 20)$ from $(-5x - 20)$. Remember: **add** the opposite of $(-5x - 20)$, which is $5x + 20$.

Check: $\underbrace{(x - 5)}\underbrace{(x + 4)} \overset{?}{=} \underbrace{x^2 - x - 20}$

Quotient Divisor   Dividend

$(x - 5)(x + 4) = x^2 - 5x + 4x - 20$

$(x - 5)(x + 4) = x^2 - x - 20$ *Checks.*

$$(6x^2 + 7x + 1) \div (3x - 1) = \underline{\ ?\ }$$

$6x^2 \div 3x = 2x$
Try $2x$.

$9x \div 3x = +3$
Try $+3$.

$$
\begin{array}{r}
2x + 3 \\
3x - 1 \overline{)\, 6x^2 + 7x + 1} \\
\mp 6x^2 \not{\mp}\, 2x \\
\hline
9x + 1 \\
\mp 9x \not{\mp}\, 3 \\
\hline
+ 4 \ \text{Remainder}
\end{array}
$$

Check:

$\underbrace{(2x + 3)}\underbrace{(3x - 1)} + 4 \overset{?}{=} \underbrace{(6x^2 + 7x + 1)}$

Quotient Divisor + Remainder Dividend

$(2x + 3)(3x - 1) + 4 \overset{?}{=} (6x^2 + 7x + 1)$
$= (6x^2 - 2x + 9x - 3) + 4$
$= 6x^2 + 7x + 1$ *Checks.*

$$(6x^2 + 7x + 1) \div (3x - 1) = 2x + 3 + \frac{4}{3x - 1}$$

Express remainder as fraction with divisor as denominator.

Divide and check.

21. $(x^2 + 7x + 12) \div (x + 4)$

22. $(x^2 - 11x + 30) \div (x - 5)$

23. $(4x^2 - 12x + 5) \div (2x - 1)$

24. $(3x^2 - 17x - 28) \div (3x + 4)$

25. $(4a^2 + 4a + 1) \div (2a + 1)$

26. $(15t^2 - 11t + 1) \div (3t - 1)$

Multiplication and Division of Rational Expressions

Rational expressions: have the form $\dfrac{a}{b}$ where a and b are polynomials and $b \neq 0$.

Examples: $\quad \dfrac{1}{2x} \quad$ **AND** $\quad \dfrac{2x - 1}{8x - 3} \quad$ **AND** $\quad \dfrac{x - 7}{x^2 - 4}$

Here $x \neq 0$ because $2 \cdot 0 = 0$. But denominator cannot $= 0$. A denominator of zero makes a fraction or rational expression **undefined.**

Rational expressions $\left(\dfrac{a}{b}, b \neq 0\right)$ are in **simplest form** when the numerator, **a,** and the denominator, **b,** have *no* common factors other than 1.

▶ **To simplify a rational expression:**

• Completely factor the numerator and denominator.

• Divide out any common factors.

$$\frac{5x^2}{20x^3} = \frac{?}{}$$

$$\frac{5x^2}{20x^3} = \frac{(5)(x)(x)}{(4)(5)(x)(x)(x)} = \frac{1}{4x} \text{ Product}$$

▶ **To multiply rational expressions:**

• Completely factor all numerators and denominators.

• Divide out any common factors.

• Multiply the numerators.

• Multiply the denominators.

• Simplify the product, if necessary.

$$\frac{5}{2x - 12} \cdot \frac{x - 6}{x^2 - 10} = \frac{?}{}$$

$$= \frac{5}{2(x - 6)} \cdot \frac{(x - 6)}{(x^2 - 10)} = \frac{5}{2(x^2 - 10)}$$

$$= \frac{5}{2x^2 - 20} \text{ Product}$$

Study this. $\dfrac{x - 3}{x - 2} \cdot \dfrac{x^2 - 4}{x^2 - 5x + 6} = \dfrac{?}{}$

$x^2 - 4$ is the difference of two squares.

$$\frac{x - 3}{x - 2} \cdot \frac{(x - 2)(x + 2)}{(x - 3)(x - 2)} = \frac{x + 2}{x - 2} \quad \text{Product}$$

Give the values of the variable for which each expression is undefined.

1. $\dfrac{3}{x}$ 2. $\dfrac{x}{x - 1}$ 3. $\dfrac{7k}{k + 2}$ 4. $\dfrac{m^2}{m^2 - 25}$ 5. $\dfrac{3x}{5x - 2}$

Simplify each rational expression.

6. $\dfrac{3k}{12k}$ 7. $\dfrac{2k + 1}{6k + 3}$ 8. $\dfrac{x + 5}{x^2 - 25}$ 9. $\dfrac{9s - 18}{3s - 6}$

10. $\dfrac{t^2 - 16}{t^2 - 8t + 16}$ 11. $\dfrac{5x - 10}{x^2 - 7x + 10}$ 12. $\dfrac{4s^2t}{20s^5t^3}$ 13. $\dfrac{x - y}{x^2 - y^2}$

Multiply.

14. $\dfrac{6}{m} \cdot \dfrac{m + 1}{6m - 18}$

15. $\dfrac{4x + 12}{7} \cdot \dfrac{14}{5x + 15}$

16. $\dfrac{8k^2}{k^2 - 1} \cdot \dfrac{k - 1}{2k^3}$

17. $\dfrac{t - 1}{t^2 - 2t - 15} \cdot \dfrac{t + 3}{t^2 - 2t + 1}$

18. $\dfrac{k + 1}{k^2} \cdot \dfrac{k^5}{k^2 + 8k + 7}$

19. $\dfrac{r^2 + 7r + 10}{r + 1} \cdot \dfrac{r^2 - 1}{r^2 + 2r - 15}$

20. $\dfrac{3s + 18}{s^2 + 25} \cdot \dfrac{s + 5}{7s + 42}$

21. $\dfrac{3k^2 + 14k + 8}{k} \cdot \dfrac{6k^2}{k^2 - 16}$

22. $\dfrac{3a^2 + 12a + 6}{a + 2} \cdot \dfrac{a^2 + 6a + 8}{9a + 36}$

23. $\dfrac{2a + 3}{2a^2 + 9a + 4} \cdot \dfrac{a^2 + 8a + 16}{10a + 15}$

Dividing Rational Expressions

To divide rational expressions: $\quad \dfrac{5x}{8} \div \dfrac{6x}{x + 2} = \underline{\ ?\ }$ $\qquad$ Divisor is: $\dfrac{6x}{x + 2}$

- Multiply by the reciprocal of the divisor. $\longrightarrow$ Reciprocal of $\dfrac{6x}{x + 2}$ is: $\dfrac{x + 2}{6x}$.
- Proceed as in multiplication.

$$\dfrac{5x}{8} \times \dfrac{x + 2}{6x} = \dfrac{5 \cdot \cancel{x}}{8} \cdot \dfrac{(x + 2)}{6 \cdot \cancel{x}} = \dfrac{5(x + 2)}{8 \cdot 6} = \dfrac{5x + 10}{48} \quad \textbf{Quotient}$$

$$\dfrac{2x - 16}{x + 4} \div \dfrac{x^2 - 16x + 64}{x^2 - 16} = \underline{\ ?\ } \longrightarrow \dfrac{(2x - 16)}{x + 4} \times \dfrac{x^2 - 16}{x^2 - 16x + 64} \quad \boxed{\textbf{Reciprocal}}$$

$$= \dfrac{2(\cancel{x - 8})}{(\cancel{x + 4})} \times \dfrac{(x - 4)\cancel{(x + 4)}}{\cancel{(x - 8)}(x - 8)} = \dfrac{2(x - 4)}{(x - 8)} = \dfrac{2x - 8}{x - 8} \quad \textbf{Quotient}$$

Divide.

24. $\dfrac{5t}{9} \div \dfrac{t}{3}$

25. $\dfrac{x + 2}{x^2} \div \dfrac{3x + 6}{x^5}$

26. $\dfrac{5}{r^2 + 8r} \div \dfrac{r^4}{r + 8}$

27. $\dfrac{2x - 1}{x^2 - 25} \div \dfrac{6x - 3}{x + 5}$

28. $\dfrac{y^2 + 7}{y - 4} \div \dfrac{3y^2 + 21}{2y^2 - 9y + 4}$

29. $\dfrac{s^2 + 13s + 36}{3s} \div \dfrac{4s + 36}{15}$

30. $\dfrac{t^2 + 5t - 24}{t + 5} \div \dfrac{t^2 - 10t + 16}{3t + 15}$

31. $\dfrac{t^2 + 6t + 9}{t + 6} \div \dfrac{t + 3}{5t + 30}$

32. $\dfrac{x^2 - 2x - 8}{3x + 3} \div \dfrac{x - 4}{x^2 + 2x + 1}$

33. $\dfrac{y + 5}{y^2 - 2y} \div \dfrac{y^2 + 10y + 25}{y}$

To add or subtract rational expressions with *like denominators:*

Add: $\dfrac{2x + 7}{x^2 - 9} + \dfrac{x - 2}{x^2 - 9} = \underline{\ ?\ }$

This expression has like denominators $(x^2 - 9)$.

- Add or subtract the numerators.

$(2x + 7) + (x + 2) = (2x + x) + (7 + 2)$
$= 3x + 9$

- Write the sum or difference over the like, or common, denominator.

$\dfrac{3x + 9}{x^2 - 9} = \dfrac{3(x + 3)}{(x + 3)(x - 3)} = \dfrac{3}{x - 3}$

Difference of two squares

Sum in simplest form

- Express the sum or difference in simplest form.

Subtract: $\dfrac{3}{y^2} - \dfrac{8}{y^2} = \underline{\ ?\ }$

$\dfrac{3}{y^2} - \dfrac{8}{y^2} = \dfrac{3}{y^2} + \dfrac{-8}{y^2}$ ← Opposite of subtrahend

$= \dfrac{3 + -8}{y^2} = \dfrac{-5}{y^2}$ ← **Difference**

Subtract: $\dfrac{y + 1}{2y + 7} - \dfrac{3y - 8}{2y + 7} = \underline{\ ?\ }$

$\dfrac{(y + 1) + ^-(3y - 8)}{(2y + 7)}$ ← Opposite of subtrahend

$= \dfrac{y + 1 - 3y + 8}{2y + 7} = \dfrac{-2y + 9}{2y + 7}$ ← **Difference**

Add or subtract. Simplify answers where possible.*

1. $\dfrac{3}{2y} + \dfrac{8}{2y}$

2. $\dfrac{5}{k + 1} + \dfrac{2k}{k + 1}$

3. $\dfrac{3x}{x - y} - \dfrac{y}{x - y}$

4. $\dfrac{2s + 1}{s + 1} + \dfrac{1}{s + 1}$

5. $\dfrac{x}{x^2 - 4} + \dfrac{2}{x^2 - 4}$

6. $\dfrac{-5m}{m^2} - \dfrac{7m + 1}{m^2}$

7. $\dfrac{9}{k} + \dfrac{7}{k} - \dfrac{11}{k}$

8. $\dfrac{4s}{2s + 3} + \dfrac{6}{2s + 3}$

9. $\dfrac{2x + 9}{3x + 2} - \dfrac{7x - 8}{3x + 2}$

10. $\dfrac{5}{2p} - \dfrac{8}{2p} + \dfrac{13}{2p}$

11. $\dfrac{s}{s^2 - 16} + \dfrac{4}{s^2 - 16}$

12. $\dfrac{3t - 9}{6t} - \dfrac{t - 6}{6t}$

13. $\dfrac{5a - 4}{a^3} + \dfrac{a^2 + 1}{a^3}$

14. $\dfrac{2y + 1}{1 + 3y} + \dfrac{y}{1 + 3y}$

15. $\dfrac{7b^2 + 12b}{4b^2 + 3b} - \dfrac{-5b^2 + 3b}{4b^2 + 3b}$

16. $\dfrac{2y^2 + 3}{2y + 3} + \dfrac{7y + 3}{2y + 3}$

17. $\dfrac{3x^2 - 2y^2}{x^2 + y^2} - \dfrac{2x^2 - 3y^2}{x^2 + y^2}$

18. $\dfrac{16t + 8}{4t + 5} + \dfrac{4t + 17}{4t + 5}$

19. $\dfrac{5a^2 - 18}{a^2 - 9} - \dfrac{4a^2 - 3a}{a^2 - 9}$

20. $\dfrac{-6k}{4k + 8} + \dfrac{18k}{4k + 8}$

21. $\dfrac{5x - 2}{3x - 4} - \dfrac{16x - 26}{3x - 4}$

22. $\dfrac{3x - 2}{2x^2 + 5x - 3} + \dfrac{7x - 3}{2x^2 + 5x - 3}$

23. $\dfrac{3s + 1}{s^2 - 7s + 12} + \dfrac{s - 17}{s^2 - 7s + 12}$

24. $\dfrac{7c - 2d}{5x + 3} - \dfrac{4c - 3d}{5x + 3}$

25. $\dfrac{3a - 2b}{4a + 3b} - \dfrac{2a - 5b}{4a + 3b}$

Least Common Denominator of Rational Expressions

To find the Least Common Denominator (LCD) of two or more rational expressions:

- Completely factor each denominator.

- Express every prime factor with the greatest exponent it has in any denominator.

- Multiply these prime factors with their greatest exponents. This product is the LCD of the given rational expressions.

LCD of $\dfrac{3}{4x^3}$ and $\dfrac{5}{6x^2y}$ = $\underline{\ ?\ }$

- Factors: $4x^3$: $2^2,\ x^3$
              $6x^2y$: $2^1 \cdot 3^1 \cdot x^2 \cdot y$
- Common Factors: $2^2,\ 2^1,\ x^2,\ x^3$
- Choose *greatest* exponent for each common factor: $2^2,\ x^3$
- Include noncommon factors: $3,\ y$
- Multiply: $2^2 \cdot 3 \cdot x^3 \cdot y$
            $= 4 \cdot 3 \cdot x^3 \cdot y = 12x^3y$ LCD

Find the LCD of: $\dfrac{2}{3x + 3}$ and $\dfrac{9}{x^2 - 1}$

$3x + 3 = 3(x + 1)$ Factors: $3,\ (x + 1),\ (x - 1)$
$x^2 - 1 = (x - 1)(x + 1)$ Multiply: $3(x + 1)(x - 1) = 3(x^2 - 1) = 3x^2 - 3$ LCD

To change a rational expression to an equivalent expression with a different denominator:

$\dfrac{3}{4x^3} = \dfrac{?}{12x^3y}$

- Find what new factors the new denominator has that the original denominator does not have.

- Multiply both the numerator and the denominator by these new factors. (Only the numerator need be multiplied, since the new denominator is already given.)

Original Denominator: $4x^3 = 4 \cdot x^3$

New Denominator: $12x^3y = 3 \cdot 4 \cdot x^3 \cdot y$

$\dfrac{3}{4x^3} \cdot \dfrac{3y}{3y} = \dfrac{9y}{12x^3y}$

Same as multiplying by 1

3 and y are *not* in original denominator.

$\dfrac{2}{3x + 3} = \dfrac{?}{3x^2 - 3} \longrightarrow \dfrac{2}{3x + 3} \cdot \dfrac{(x - 1)}{(x - 1)} = \dfrac{2(x - 1)}{(3x + 3)(x - 1)} = \dfrac{2x - 2}{3x^2 - 3}$

$3x + 3\ = 3(x + 1)$ New factor
$3x^2 - 3 = 3(x^2 - 1) = 3(x + 1)(x - 1)$

So, $\dfrac{2}{3x + 3} = \dfrac{2x - 2}{3x^2 - 3}$

Find the LCD and complete.*

1. $\dfrac{5}{x + 1} = \dfrac{?}{8x + 8}$

2. $\dfrac{7}{t^2} = \dfrac{?}{s^2t^3}$

3. $\dfrac{k}{2k + 2} = \dfrac{?}{6k^2 - 6}$

4. $\dfrac{8}{3x^2y} = \dfrac{?}{15x^2y^2}$

5. $\dfrac{9a}{a + 6} = \dfrac{?}{a^2 + 6a}$

6. $\dfrac{-2y}{y + 4} = \dfrac{?}{y^2 + 3y - 4}$

7. $\dfrac{4}{ab} = \dfrac{?}{a^2b}$

8. $\dfrac{k}{6k + 3} = \dfrac{?}{12k^2 + 6k}$

9. $\dfrac{y}{y - 3} = \dfrac{?}{y^2 - 9}$

*See page 514 for more practice.   439

To add and subtract rational expressions with unlike denominators:

$$\frac{-6}{a^2b} + \frac{4}{3b} = \underline{\;?\;}$$

Unlike denominators

• Find the LCD.

Factors of a^2b and $3b$: $a^2b = a^2,\ b$

$$3b = 3,\ b$$

$$LCD = 3 \cdot a^2 \cdot b = 3a^2b$$

• Change each rational expression to an equivalent fraction with the LCD as denominator.

$$\frac{-6}{a^2b} = \frac{?}{3a^2b} \longrightarrow \frac{(-6)\,(3)}{3a^2b} = \frac{-18}{3a^2b}$$

$$\frac{4}{3b} = \frac{?}{3a^2b} \longrightarrow \frac{4(a^2)}{3a^2b} = \frac{4a^2}{3a^2b}$$

• Add or subtract.

$$\text{Add:}\ \frac{-18}{3a^2b} + \frac{4a^2}{3a^2b} = \frac{-18 + 4a^2}{3a^2b}$$

• Simplify, if necessary.

$$= \frac{4a^2 - 18}{3a^2b} = \frac{2(2a^2-9)}{3a^2b}\ \text{Sum}$$

$$\frac{d}{2d-2} + \frac{d-2}{d^2-1} = \underline{\;?\;}$$

$$2d - 2 = 2(d-1)$$
$$d^2 - 1 = (d-1)(d+1)$$
$$LCD = 2(d-1)(d+1)$$

$$\frac{d}{2d-2} = \frac{?}{2(d-1)(d+1)} \quad \text{AND} \quad \frac{d-2}{d^2-1} = \frac{?}{2(d-1)(d+1)}$$

$$= \frac{d}{2(d-1)} \cdot \frac{(d+1)}{(d+1)} = \frac{d(d+1)}{2(d-1)(d+1)} \quad \text{AND} \quad \frac{d-2}{(d-1)(d+1)} \cdot \frac{2}{2} = \frac{2(d-2)}{2(d-1)(d+1)}$$

Add two fractions above that now have like denominators:

$$\frac{d(d+1)}{2(d-1)(d+1)} + \frac{2(d-2)}{2(d-1)(d+1)} = \frac{d^2+d+2d-4}{2(d-1)(d+1)}$$

$$= \frac{d^2+3d-4}{2(d-1)(d+1)} = \frac{(d+4)(d-1)}{2(d-1)(d+1)} = \frac{d+4}{2d+2}\ \text{Sum}$$

Add or subtract. (The first one is done.)

1. $\dfrac{4}{x} - \dfrac{3}{y} = \underline{\;?\;} \longrightarrow$ LCD: xy $\dfrac{4}{x} \cdot \dfrac{y}{y} = \dfrac{4y}{xy}$ AND $\dfrac{3}{y} \cdot \dfrac{x}{x} = \dfrac{3x}{xy}$

$$\frac{4y}{xy} - \frac{3x}{xy} = \frac{4y - 3x}{xy}\ \text{Difference}$$

2. $\dfrac{9}{y^2} - \dfrac{11}{y}$

3. $\dfrac{7}{4x} + \dfrac{-12}{5x}$

4. $\dfrac{1}{2} + \dfrac{9}{d}$

5. $\dfrac{a}{a-5} + \dfrac{6}{3a-18}$

6. $\dfrac{-6}{cd} + \dfrac{11}{d^2}$

7. $\dfrac{10}{3k} - \dfrac{9}{k^2}$

8. $\dfrac{20}{r^2s} - \dfrac{5}{s^3}$

9. $\dfrac{2a}{2a+1} - \dfrac{5a}{4a+2}$

Study this.

$$\frac{8k}{k^2 - 36} - \frac{3}{k - 6} = \frac{?}{}$$

Factors of $k^2 - 36$ are: $(k - 6)(k + 6)$, and of $k - 6$ is: $(k - 6)$
So, LCD is: $(k - 6)(k + 6)$

$$\frac{8k}{\boxed{k^2 - 36}} = \frac{?}{(k - 6)(k + 6)} \quad \text{AND} \quad \frac{3}{k - 6} = \frac{?}{(k - 6)(k + 6)}$$

$$\frac{8k}{(k - 6)(k + 6)} \cdot \frac{1}{1} = \frac{8k}{(k - 6)(k + 6)} \quad \text{AND} \quad \frac{3}{(k - 6)} \cdot \frac{(k + 6)}{(k + 6)} = \frac{3(k + 6)}{(k - 6)(k + 6)}$$

Subtract: $\quad \dfrac{8k}{(k - 6)(k + 6)} - \dfrac{3(k + 6)}{(k - 6)(k + 6)} = \dfrac{8k - 3(k + 6)}{(k - 6)(k + 6)} = \dfrac{8k - 3k - 18}{(k - 6)(k + 6)}$

Numerator is completely factored, so it cannot be simplified further.

$$= \frac{5k - 18}{(k - 6)(k + 6)} = \frac{5k - 8}{k^2 - 36} \quad \textbf{Difference}$$

Add or subtract.

10. $\dfrac{-4}{y^2 - 9} + \dfrac{2}{y - 3}$

11. $\dfrac{4}{x + 7} + \dfrac{x}{x - 7}$

12. $\dfrac{2b}{b^2 - 3b} + \dfrac{7}{b^2 - 2b - 3}$

13. $\dfrac{5}{x^2 y} + \dfrac{20}{xy}$

14. $\dfrac{5d}{d^2 - 16} - \dfrac{3}{d + 4}$

15. $\dfrac{21b}{9b - 54} - \dfrac{6b}{b - 6}$

16. $\dfrac{5x}{x^2 - y^2} - \dfrac{3y}{x - y}$

17. $\dfrac{9t}{2t - 1} - \dfrac{5t}{12t - 6}$

18. $\dfrac{x - 2}{x^2 - 11x + 24} - \dfrac{x + 7}{x - 8}$

Add or subtract.

19. $\dfrac{17}{3x} + \dfrac{21}{5x}$

20. $\dfrac{16}{xy} - \dfrac{3}{x^2}$

21. $\dfrac{x^2 + 9}{x^2 - 25} + \dfrac{11}{x + 5}$

22. $\dfrac{-t}{2t - 14} - \dfrac{5t}{t - 7}$

23. $\dfrac{3x + 1}{2x - 20} - \dfrac{9x}{2}$

24. $\dfrac{s - 6}{4s - 1} + \dfrac{s - 3}{12s - 3}$

25. $\dfrac{4p}{p^2 + 1} - \dfrac{9p}{2p^2 + 2}$

26. $\dfrac{-5y}{36 - y^2} - \dfrac{-3y}{6 + y}$

27. $\dfrac{m + 6}{9m} + \dfrac{2m - 7}{81m^2}$

28. $\dfrac{9s^2}{s^2 - 100} + \dfrac{5s}{s - 10}$

29. $\dfrac{11}{r + 4} - \dfrac{15}{r - 4}$

30. $\dfrac{3c + d}{15c^2 d} - \dfrac{c + 2d}{5cd}$

Compute. (The first one is done.)

31. $\dfrac{3}{x - y} + \dfrac{5}{y - x} = \dfrac{?}{}$

$$\frac{3}{x - y} + \frac{5}{-x + y} = \frac{3}{x - y} + \frac{5}{-(x - y)} = \frac{3}{x - y} + \frac{-5}{x - y} = \frac{-2}{x - y}$$

32. $\dfrac{2}{a - b} + \dfrac{7}{b - a}$

33. $\dfrac{16}{5 - a} + \dfrac{9}{a - 5}$

34. $\dfrac{2d}{7 - d} - \dfrac{3d}{d - 7}$

35. $\dfrac{4n}{m - 8} - \dfrac{2n}{8 - m}$

36. $\dfrac{8}{r - 6} - \dfrac{2s}{6 - r}$

37. $\dfrac{6}{10 - 2b} + \dfrac{8}{2b - 10}$

38. $\dfrac{2ab}{ab - 4b} + \dfrac{3b}{4b - ab}$

39. $\dfrac{mn}{2m - 6n} + \dfrac{5mn}{6n - 2m}$

40. $\dfrac{3r}{1 - 2r} - \dfrac{6r^2}{2r - 1}$

41. $\dfrac{m^2}{m - n} - \dfrac{n^2}{n - m}$

42. $\dfrac{a}{a - 4b} + \dfrac{4b}{4b - a}$

43. $\dfrac{c - d}{2c - 8d} - \dfrac{c - d}{8d - 2c}$

Problem: A certain radioactive isotope has a half-life of 6 months. How much of the mass of a 5000-g sample of this isotope will still be radioactive after 5 years?

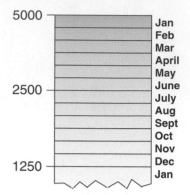

1 IMAGINE

Visualize, draw, and label the amount of the isotope that is radioactive and continually decreasing at a nonsteady rate.

2 NAME

Facts: 5000 g — mass of isotope

6 months — time after which $\frac{1}{2}$ of mass is no longer radioactive

Question: __?__ grams — mass still radioactive after 5 years
(How many 6-month periods is this?)

3 THINK

Make a chart to study what happens during the first four 6-month periods. Look for a pattern:

Elapsed Time	No. of 6-month Periods	Mass
0 mo	0	5000 g
6	1	2500 g
12	2	1250 g
18	3	625 g
.	.	.
.	.	.
.	.	.
.	.	.
60	10	__?__

$2500 = 5000 \left(\frac{1}{2}\right)$

$1250 = 5000 \left(\frac{1}{2}\right) \left(\frac{1}{2}\right)$ or $5000 \left(\frac{1}{2}\right)^2$

$625 = 5000 \left(\frac{1}{2}\right) \left(\frac{1}{2}\right) \left(\frac{1}{2}\right)$ or $5000 \left(\frac{1}{2}\right)^3$

$\underline{\quad?\quad} = 5000 \left(\frac{1}{2}\right)^n$ $n =$ number of 6-month periods

4 COMPUTE

$5000 \cdot \left(\frac{1}{2}\right)^{10} \approx 4.88$ grams

5 CHECK

Use a calculator to check computations:

4997.12 is close to 5000, the starting mass of the isotope.

Solve.

1. A certain protozoan that reproduces itself every $\frac{1}{2}$ hour is isolated in a petrie dish. How many protozoa will the dish contain after 4 hours?

$\frac{1}{2}$ hour   4 hours

1 IMAGINE	Draw and label ⟶	**2 NAME**	⟶ Facts
	a picture.		⟶ Question

3 THINK Make a chart and look for a pattern as you divide.

Number	1	2	4	8	. . .
Time	0	$\frac{1}{2}$	1	$1\frac{1}{2}$	. . .

4 COMPUTE ⟶ **5 CHECK**

2. The first day of the year is Tuesday. On what day of the week will February 14 fall?

3. The chart to the right shows the relationship between the number of sides a regular polygon has and the sum of its interior angles. Use this information to calculate the sum of the interior angles of a duodecagon, a polygon having 12 sides.

Polygon	Sum of Interior Angles
triangle	180°
quadrilateral	360°
pentagon	540°
hexagon	720°

4. Find the pattern. Complete the others without computing.

9 × 1 = 9	9 × 12 = 108	9 × 123 = 1107	9 × 1234 = 11106

So, 9 × 12345 = __?__   and 9 × 123456 = __?__ . . .

5. Sam has a temporary job for the month of June. He asks his employer to pay him 1 cent on June 1, and each day after that to pay him twice the amount he was paid the day before. At this rate, how much will he be paid on June 30 (assuming he works every day)?

6. Find the 53rd term in this sequence: 5, 9, 13, 17, . . .

Term	1	2	3	4	. . .
Value	5	9	13	17	. . .

7. Attendance at the first baseball game of the season was 1250. Attendance is expected to increase by 125 people for each game of the season. What is the expected attendance for the 10th game?

8. 4, 12, 36, 108, . . .   What is the 12th term in this sequence?

9. a. Find the volume of a rectangular prism with a length of 3, a width of 4, and a height of 5 units.
   b. Find the volume of a rectangular prism with dimensions that are twice those of the prism in part **a**.
   c. Use the results of part **b** to predict the volume of a prism with dimensions triple those in part **a**.
   d. Compute the volume of the prism described in part **c**; compare the predicted answer with your calculation.

Motion Problems

Solve. (The first one is done.)

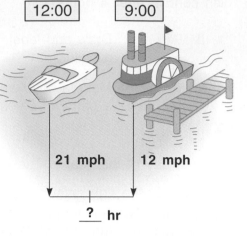

1. A paddle boat left the dock traveling 12 miles per hour. Three hours later, a speedboat left the same dock, following the same path as the paddle boat but traveling at 21 miles per hour. How long did it take the speedboat to reach the paddle boat?

   Let b = the time of the speedboat and
   $b + 3$ = the time of the paddle boat

   • Use the distance formula ($d = rt$)
   to express the distance covered.

   $21b$ = speedboat's distance
   $12(b + 3)$ = paddle boat's distance

   • Write and solve an equation.

   $$21b = 12(b + 3)$$
   $$21b = 12b + 36$$
   $$21b - 12b = 36$$
   $$9b = 36$$
   $$b = 4$$

   The speedboat reached the paddle boat in 4 hours.

2. A cyclist covered a distance in 6 hours. If the cyclist bicycled at a speed of 12 miles per hour and jogged back over the same route at 4 miles per hour, for how many hours did the cyclist jog?

3. Two cyclists started from the same point at the same time but went in opposite directions. After 6 hours, they were 126 miles apart. The rate of the second cyclist was 4 mph faster than the first. How fast was each one traveling?

4. Two boats started at the same time and traveled in opposite directions from the same port. One traveled at 17 mph and the other at 22 mph. When were they 429 miles apart?

5. A mountain climber has 10.5 hr to complete her climb and return to her base camp. For how many hours can she climb at 2 mph if her return rate is 5 mph?

6. How far can a helicopter fly out to sea at 120 mph and return at 80 mph if it has fuel for a 12-hour trip?

7. Two cyclists started toward each other at the same time from cities 156 mi apart. One traveled at 5 mph and the other at 8 mph. In how many hours did they meet?

8. Two trains started from town, traveling west. The faster train traveled 20 mph less than 3 times the rate of the slower train. If they were 176 miles apart in 4 hours, what was the rate of each?

Work Problems

One farmer plows a field in 6 hours; another completes the same job in 4 hours. If they work together on the same field, how long will it take both farmers to plow it?

Let x = number of hours needed working together. It is helpful to use a chart.

	1st farmer	2nd farmer	Together
Hours needed:	6	4	x
Part done in 1 hour:	$\dfrac{1}{6}$	$\dfrac{1}{4}$	$\dfrac{1}{x}$

USE THESE STRATEGIES:
Write an Equation
Make a Table
Use a Formula
Draw a Picture
Hidden Information
Combining Strategies

- Write an equation. $\longrightarrow$ $\dfrac{1}{6} + \dfrac{1}{4} = \dfrac{1}{x}$

- Solve the equation.
(Multiply by LCM $\longrightarrow$ $12x\left[\dfrac{1}{6} + \dfrac{1}{4} = \dfrac{1}{x}\right]$
of 6, 4, and x
which is $12x$.)

$$2x + 3x = 12$$
$$5x = 12$$
$$x = 2\frac{2}{5} \text{ hours}$$

- Check: $\dfrac{1}{6} + \dfrac{1}{4} \overset{?}{=} \dfrac{1}{2\frac{2}{5}} \longrightarrow \dfrac{2}{12} + \dfrac{3}{12} \overset{?}{=} 1 \div \dfrac{12}{5} \longrightarrow \dfrac{5}{12} = \dfrac{5}{12}$

Solve.

1. One hose can empty a pool in 3 hours. A wider hose can empty the same pool in 2 hours. How long will it take the 2 hoses working together to empty the pool?

2. A carpenter can install cabinets in 8 hours. Another carpenter can do the same job in 6 hours. If the carpenters work together, how long will it take them to install the cabinets?

3. A group of 3 scientists planned to work together on an experiment. Prof. Oz knew he could do it alone in 9 hours. Prof. Whiz knew he could do it alone in 6, while Prof. Zip knew he could do it in just 2 hours. How long should the experiment take them when they work together?

4. Working together, two robots assembled a bicycle in 12 minutes. One robot working

alone would have taken $\dfrac{1}{2}$ hour. How long would it have taken the other robot to assemble the bicycle alone?

5. One machine working alone can complete a job in 12 hours. Working with another machine, the job would take $6\frac{2}{3}$ hours. How long would it take the other machine to finish the job working alone?

(Hint: Use $\dfrac{1}{12} + \dfrac{1}{x} = \dfrac{1}{6\frac{2}{3}}$.)

6. One computer solved a problem in 40 seconds. Another solved the same problem in 60 seconds. Working together with a third computer, the problem was solved in only $13\frac{1}{3}$ seconds. How long would it take the third computer to solve it working alone?

445

More Practice

Classify each polynomial. Then give its degree.

1. $m^2 + n^3$ 2. $2m$ 3. $^-8.5$ 4. $^-4m^2n^3 + 5$

5. $5a^4 - 2ab^2$ 6. $3abc$ 7. $c^2 - 2a$ 8. $a^2b^2c + 1$

9. Evaluate the polynomials in exercises 5−8.
   Let $m = 3$, $n = ^-2$, $a = ^-1$, $b = 4$, $c = 0$

Compute.

10. $(m^3 - 2) + (12 + m - 3m^3)$ 11. $(^-4a + 4) + (2 - 6a)$

12. $(b^3 + 3b) - (3b + 1)$ 13. $(m^2n + 3mn) - (4m^2n^2 - mn)$

14. $2st^2 - (3s^2 - 5st^2 - 6s^2)$ 15. $(3c - 2d) - (4d + 1)$

16. $4y \cdot 3y^2$ 17. $(2ab)(7b)(^-2a)$ 18. $(2m^2n)^3$

19. $(^-3r^3s^2)^4$ 20. $\dfrac{x^3y^5}{xy^3}$ 21. $\dfrac{4d^2e^4}{^-2de}$

22. $\dfrac{27a^2 \cdot 3a}{3a}$ 23. $^-2b^3(^-3b + 9)$ 24. $\frac{1}{2}r^2(6 - 2rs)$

25. $\dfrac{a^2b^3 - 2ab^4}{ab}$ 26. $(x + 6)(x - 2)$ 27. $(m - 1)(m + 4)$

28. $(r - 4)(r - 3)$ 29. $(y + 6)^2$ 30. $(xy - 4)^2$

31. $(a + 3)(4a - 2)$ 32. $(2 - 3m)^2$ 33. $(3m + 3n)(5m + 2n)$

34. $(a + 1)(a - 1)$ 35. $(7 - t)(7 + t)$ 36. $(5 + c^2d)(5 - c^2d)$

37. $(a - 3)(4a^3 - a + 3)$ 38. $(k + 5)(3 - km - 6m^2)$ 39. $(t - 1)(t^2 - 2t - 4)$

40. $(7r + 2r^2 + 3) \div (r + 3)$ 41. $(e^2 - 6e - 16) \div (e - 8)$

42. $(30b^2 - 61b + 30) \div (6b - 5)$ 43. $(n^2 + 18n + 50) \div (n + 3)$

44. $\dfrac{^-7t + 2t^2 + 3}{t - 3}$ 45. $\dfrac{6 - 32h + 10h^2}{5h - 1}$ 46. $\dfrac{21x^2 - 6y^2 + 5xy}{3x + 2y}$

Factor. (Label any polynomial *prime* that cannot be factored.)

47. $4x^2 - 8x$ 48. $3a^2b - 2cd^2$ 49. $m^2 - 6m + 5$

50. $y^2 + y - 6$ 51. $3 - 9a^2$ 52. $b^2 + 49$

53. $2a^2 - ab - b^2$ 54. $a^2 + ab + 2b^2$ 55. $9 - 36x^2$

56. $x^2y^2 - 64$ 57. $3x^2 - 2y^2 + 5xy$ 58. $9s^2 - 24st + 16t^2$

59. $5x^2 - 5$ 60. $7w^2 - 63s^2$ 61. $9a^2b^2 - 12ab + 4$

62. $2h^2 - 32k^2$ 63. $15s^2 + 29st - 14t^2$ 64. $3s^2 + 12s - 36$

65. $18y^2z^2 + 24yz + 8$ 66. $64e^4f^4 - 49$ 67. $s^2 + 4n^2$

Name the values of the variable that make the expression undefined.

68. $\dfrac{a + 4}{d - 1}$ **69.** $\dfrac{4a - 2c}{5 + c}$ **70.** $\dfrac{6y - 5}{25 - y^2}$ **71.** $\dfrac{x + 3}{x^2 - 16}$

Name the GCF. Simplify.

72. $\dfrac{a^2 b}{ab^2}$ **73.** $\dfrac{a(b + c)}{3(b + c)}$ **74.** $\dfrac{56x^3 y^5}{20xy^2}$ **75.** $\dfrac{12a^2 - 48}{3(2a - 4)^2}$

Compute.

76. $\dfrac{x^2 - 9}{2} \cdot \dfrac{6}{x}$ **77.** $\dfrac{m + n}{2x^2} \cdot \dfrac{5x}{3(m + n)}$ **78.** $\dfrac{x^2 + 10x + 25}{8y} \cdot \dfrac{4y - 8}{x + 5}$

79. $\dfrac{3d^2 - 3}{2} \div \dfrac{d^2 - 1}{6}$ **80.** $\dfrac{x^2 - y^2}{4x^2} \div \dfrac{(x + y)^2}{6x^3}$ **81.** $\dfrac{5r^2 - 20}{6} \div \dfrac{r^2 - 4r + 4}{3}$

82. $\dfrac{5r^2 - 20}{10} \div \dfrac{r^2 - 4rt}{2r}$ **83.** $\dfrac{n^2 - m^2}{5} \div \dfrac{n + m}{15}$ **84.** $\dfrac{(x + 5)(x - 5)}{2a} \div \dfrac{x - 5}{4a^3}$

Name the LCD of each. Then compute.

85. $\dfrac{5}{c^2} - \dfrac{2}{d}$ **86.** $\dfrac{2a - 3}{a} + \dfrac{8 - a}{4a^2}$ **87.** $\dfrac{2d}{5e} - \dfrac{3c}{10e} + \dfrac{cd}{f}$

88. $\dfrac{12b}{a + b} - 8$ **89.** $3c - \dfrac{2c^2}{c + d}$ **90.** $\dfrac{8}{5x} - 2 + \dfrac{3}{4x}$

91. $\dfrac{2}{(3m + 6n)} + \dfrac{2}{(m + 2n)}$ **92.** $\dfrac{r + 5}{9r - 45} + \dfrac{3}{3r + 15}$ **93.** $\dfrac{5d + 2}{3 + e} + \dfrac{7 - 2d}{e + 3}$

94. $\dfrac{4x + 3}{x^2 y} - \dfrac{x - 2y}{x^2 y} + \dfrac{8}{x^2 y}$ **95.** $\dfrac{3n - m}{2m^2} - \dfrac{2m - 3n}{2m^2} + \dfrac{m}{2m^2}$

96. $1 + \dfrac{3}{x} + \dfrac{2x}{4}$ **97.** $\dfrac{2r - 3}{5} + 3r$ **98.** $\dfrac{9}{x} - \dfrac{3}{2x} + \dfrac{1}{6}$

99. $\dfrac{5}{n + 2} + \dfrac{4}{n - 2}$ **100.** $\dfrac{4}{2m - 6} - \dfrac{3}{4m - 8}$ **101.** $\dfrac{x}{x^2 - 1} + \dfrac{1}{(x^2 + 3x + 2)}$

102. $\dfrac{3}{y^2 - 9} - \dfrac{y}{3 + y}$ **103.** $\dfrac{m}{n - 3} - \dfrac{2m}{3 - n}$ **104.** $\dfrac{4d}{(c + d)(c - d)} - \dfrac{c}{c + d}$

Solve.

105. The sum of the reciprocals of 2 consecutive numbers is $\dfrac{9}{20}$. Find the numbers.

106. The difference between the reciprocals of two numbers is $\dfrac{2}{15}$. If one number is 1 less than twice the other, find the numbers.

107. Four added to twice the product of two consecutive numbers is equal to twice the square of the larger number decreased by 8. Find the numbers.

447

More Practice

Solve. (The first one is done.)

108. *ABCD* and *EFGH* are parallelograms having equal areas. Find the base and height of *EFGH*.

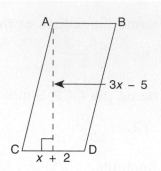

Let x = height of *EFGH* and $3x$ = base of *EFGH*.

Let $3x - 5$ = height of *ABCD* and $x + 2$ = base of *ABCD*.

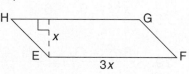

$$\text{Area } (ABCD) = \text{Area}_2 \, (EFGH)$$

- Write the formula. ⟶ $b_1 \times h_1 = b_2 \times h_2$
- Substitute. ⟶ $(x + 2)(3x - 5) = (3x)(x)$
- Solve. ⟶ $3x^2 + x - 10 = 3x^2$

$$3x^2 - 3x^2 + x - 10 = 3x^2 - 3x^2$$
$$x - 10 = 0$$
$$x = 10$$

Check:
$$(10 + 2)(30 - 5) \stackrel{?}{=} (30)(10)$$
$$(12)(25) = 300 \longrightarrow 300 = 300$$

So, height $(x) = 10$ and base $(3x) = 30$.

109. The side of one square is 3 cm longer than the side of a second square. The area of the larger square is 21 cm² more than the area of the smaller. Find the length of the side of each square. (Hint: $A_1 = A_2 + 21 \text{ cm}^2$)

110. The length of a rectangle is 3 cm longer than the side of a square. The width of the rectangle is 2 cm shorter than the side of the square. If the area of the square is 1 cm² larger than the area of the rectangle, what are the dimensions of the rectangle? (Hint: Draw and label each figure.)

111. The side of one square is 1 cm longer than twice the length of the side of a smaller square. The area of the larger square is 13 cm² larger than 4 times the area of the smaller square. Find the side of each square. What is the perimeter of each?

112. These rectangles are equal in area.
   a. Find a.
   b. Find the dimensions of each rectangle.
   c. Find the area of the rectangles.

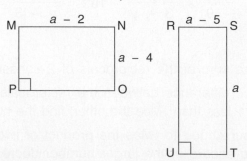

Math Probe

DIRECT VARIATION — Directly to the Point!

Day	Worked	Earnings
Monday	10 hr	$40
Tuesday	6.5 hr	$26
Wednesday	8 hr	$32

The chart at the left shows the number of hours Brian worked and his earnings for the first three days of the week.

Note that for each day the ratio of earnings to hours is the same.

$$\frac{40}{10} = \frac{26}{6.5} = \frac{32}{8} = \frac{4}{1} \text{ (lowest terms)} \qquad \frac{y}{x} = 4 \quad \begin{array}{l}\text{(let } y = \text{earnings)}\\ \text{(let } x = \text{hours)}\end{array}$$

Also, for each day, the earnings equal 4 times the hours worked: $y = 4x$.
This relationship is called a *DIRECT VARIATION*.

A *direct variation* is a *function* in which for each ordered pair (x, y), $y = kx$, $k \neq 0$. k is called the *constant of variation* or the *constant of proportion*.

The graph of a direct variation will always be a straight line through the origin. ⟶

Problems involving direct variation can be solved by proportion.

How many hours will Brian have to work to earn $150?

$$\begin{array}{l}\text{salary} \rightarrow \\ \text{hours}\end{array} \quad \frac{4}{1} \diagdown \frac{150}{x}$$

$$4x = 150$$

$$x = 37.5 \text{ hours to earn } \$150$$

How much will he earn in 18 hours?

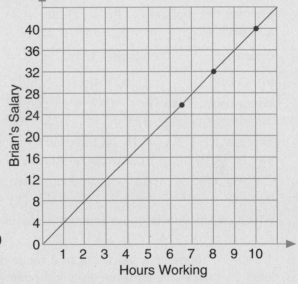

Identify the direct variations and their constants of variation.

1. $y = {}^-2x$ 2. $x + y = 3$ 3. $xy = {}^-4$ 4. $2y = 6x$

Now try graphing these variations.

5. The distance Carl travels in a day varies directly as the number of hours he drives. If he travels 270 miles in 6 hours, how far will he travel in 15 hours? How long will it take him to travel 180 miles?

6. A recipe for 4 cups of taco dip requires $\frac{2}{3}$ cup of mayonnaise. How much mayonnaise is needed to make 6 cups of the dip? If Joan used $\frac{1}{2}$ cup of mayonnaise, how much taco dip did she prepare?

Advanced Placement Practice

Choose the correct answer.

1. Find the sum of $13w^2 - 9w + 8$ and $w^2 - 9$.
   a. $13w^2 - 18w + 8$
   b. $14w^2 - 9w - 17$
   c. $14w^2 + 8$
   d. $14w^2 - 9w - 1$

2. From $7t + 8s$ take $2t + 11s$.
   a. $9t + 19s$
   b. $5t - 3s$
   c. $^-9t + 3s$
   d. $^-5t + 3s$

3. Add $8y(y + 1)$ to $6(y - 1)$.
   a. $8y^2 + 14y - 6$
   b. $14y^2 + 2xy$
   c. $8y^2 + 14y - 1$
   d. $2xy + 8y^2$

4. What is $2x^3y^4$ squared?
   a. $4x^9y^{16}$
   b. $2x^6y^8$
   c. $4x^6y^8$
   d. none of these

5. What is the product of $7mn^3$ and $9mn^5$?
   a. $63mn^8$
   b. $63m^8n^2$
   c. $63m^2n^8$
   d. $63mn^{15}$

6. When $2a^2b^3$ is multiplied by $^-3ab^2$, the product is:
   a. $^-6a^2b^5$
   b. $6a^2b^5$
   c. $6a^5b^3$
   d. $^-6a^3b^5$

7. Take $3(m - 2)$ from $4m(m + 3)$.
   a. $4m^2 + 9m + 6$
   b. $4m^2 + 15m - 6$
   c. $4m^2 + 9m - 6$
   d. $^-4m^2 - 9m - 2$

8. What is $23 - x$ decreased by $5x^2 - 2x - 1$?
   a. $^-5x^2 + x + 24$
   b. $^-5x^2 + x + 22$
   c. $5x^2 - x - 24$
   d. $5x^2 - 3x + 22$

9. Express the product of $(2n - 1)(3n + 4)$ as a trinomial.
   a. $6n^2 + 7x - 4$
   b. $6n^2 + 5n - 4$
   c. $6n^2 + 12n - 4$
   d. $6n^2 - 5n + 4$

10. Express $\dfrac{24m^2n}{^-6mn}$ in simplest form.
    a. ^-4mn
    b. $4m$
    c. $4mn$
    d. ^-4m

11. When $6xy^2 + 8x^2y - 10x^3$ is divided by ^-2x the quotient is:
    a. $^-3y^2 - 4xy - 5x^2$
    b. $5x^2 - 4xy - 3y^2$
    c. $3y^2 + 4xy - 5x^2$
    d. $3y^2 + 4xy + 5x^2$

12. Express $x^2 + 5x - 14$ as the product of two binomials.
    a. $(x + 2)(x - 7)$
    b. $(x - 2)(x + 7)$
    c. $(x + 7)(x + 2)$
    d. $(x - 7)(x - 2)$

13. Express $x^2y^2 - 16$ as the product of two binomials.
    a. $(xy - 4)^2$
    b. $(xy + 4)^2$
    c. $(xy - 4)(xy + 4)$
    d. $(x^2 - 4)(y^2 + 4)$

14. Which expression is prime (cannot be factored)?
    a. $3x^2 + x - 4$
    b. $x^2 + 25$
    c. $4m^2 - 49$
    d. none of these

15. If $3a - b$ represents the width of a rectangle and $4a$ represents the length, which binomial represents the perimeter?
    a. $12a^2 - 4ab$
    b. $7a - b$
    c. $14a - b$
    d. $14a - 2b$

16. If $3m - 2$ represents the radius of a circle, which binomial represents the circumference?
    a. $(6m - 4)\pi$
    b. $6m - 4\pi$
    c. $6\pi m - 4$
    d. $(6m - 4)\pi d$

17. Express as a fraction in simplest form $\dfrac{b}{4} + \dfrac{5b}{6}$.
    a. $\dfrac{13b}{24}$
    b. $\dfrac{13b}{12}$
    c. $\dfrac{13b}{18}$
    d. $\dfrac{6b}{10}$

18. Take $\dfrac{6}{ab}$ from $\dfrac{2}{a}$.
    a. $\dfrac{2b - 6}{ab}$
    b. $\dfrac{8}{ab + a}$
    c. $\dfrac{6 - 2b}{ab}$
    d. $\dfrac{8}{ab}$

Advanced Placement Practice

19. If $(3a + 4)(a - k)$ is $3a^2 - 2a - 8$, find k.
    a. $^-2$ **b.** 2 **c.** 4 **d.** $^-4$

20. If $\dfrac{n}{n - 3} = \dfrac{3mn}{k}$, find k.
    a. $3m - 9$ **b.** $3mn^2 - 9mn$ **c.** $3mn - 9m$ **d.** $3m - 9mn$

21. One factor of $84n^4 - 3n^2 - 45$ is $12n^2 - 9$. Find the other factor.
    a. $7n + 5$ **b.** $7n - 5$ **c.** $7n^2 + 5$ **d.** $7n^2 - 5$

22. What is $^-3a^2$ raised to the third power?
    a. $27a^5$ **b.** $^-27a^6$ **c.** $9a^5$ **d.** $^-9a^6$

23. Express $16a^2b^2 - 25$ as a product of two binomials.   **a.** $(4ab + 5)(4ab - 5)$
    b. $(8ab - 5)(2ab - 5)$ **c.** $(4a^2 - 5)(4b^2 + 5)$ **d.** $(4ab - 5)^2$

24. The expression $4m^2 + 20m + 25$ is the square of:
    a. $2m + 5$ **b.** $2m^2 + 5$ **c.** $2m - 5$ **d.** $2m^2 - 5$

25. Which equation is used to solve this sentence: "If the sum of the squares of 2 consecutive numbers is 145, what are the numbers?"
    a. $a(a + 1) = 145$ **b.** $(a + 1) = 145$
    c. $a^2 + (a + 1)^2 = 145$ **d.** $(a + a + 1)^2 = 145$

Evaluate each expression if $x = {}^-2$ and $y = {}^+3$.

26. $x^2 - xy + y^2$ **27.** $2x - \dfrac{1}{3}y$ **28.** $4x^2 + xy - 2y^2$

Compute.

29. $(a^2 - 8) + (16 - a + 2a^2)$ **30.** $(^-2m + 1) - (4 - 5m)$

31. $(3a^2b + 2ab) + (2a^2b^2 - 4ab)$ **32.** $(m^2 + 2m) - (5m + 3)$

33. $6r \cdot 2r^2$ **34.** $(7m^3n)^2$

35. $\dfrac{a^2b^4}{ab^3}$ **36.** $\dfrac{8a^3x^2}{2ax^2}$ **37.** $3d^2 \cdot {}^-2cd$

38. $^-8a^2(^-2a + 6)$ **39.** $(n + 3)(n - 5)$ **40.** $(s - 2)(s + 6)$

41. $(d - 8)(d - 2)$ **42.** $(ab + 2)^2$ **43.** $(3x + 2)(2x - 7)$

44. $(3r - 1)^2$ **45.** $(5x + 2y)(3x - 4y)$ **46.** $(x - 2y)(2x^2 - 4x + 5)$

Factor. (Label any expression prime that cannot be factored.)

47. $m^2 - n^2$ **48.** $36 - a^2b^2$ **49.** $1 - 100c^2$

50. $6y^2 - 18y$ **51.** $3m^2n + 15mn^2$ **52.** $a^2b^4 + a^3b^5 + a^4b^6$

53. $32cd - 40c^2de^2$ **54.** $a^2 + 10a + 21$ **55.** $r^2 - 8r + 12$

56. $n^2 - 5n - 14$ **57.** $x^2 + 6x - 27$ **58.** $2x^2 + 13x + 15$

59. $3y^2 - 3y - 4$ **60.** $6x^2 - 5x + 1$ **61.** $9b^2 - 30b + 25$

62. $s^2 - 2st + t^2$ **63.** $1 - 25b^2$ **64.** $m^2n^2 - 144$

65. $9x^3 - x$ **66.** $8c^2 - 4c$ **67.** $2x^2 - 14x - 16$

68. $2n^2 + 16n + 12$ **69.** $3m^2 - 12$ **70.** $a^2b^2 + 4a^2c^2$

71. For p and q write its: **a.** disjunction   **b.** biconditional

72. For $\sim p$ and $\sim q$ write its: **a.** conjunction   **b.** conditional

Advanced Placement Practice

Solve.

73. $(x^2 + 6x - 30) \div (x - 3)$ **74.** $(x^2 + x - 18) \div (x + 5)$

75. $(6x^2 + 13x - 1) \div (2x + 5)$ **76.** $\dfrac{12}{4x - 2}$ **77.** $\dfrac{6n^2}{n + 1} \cdot \dfrac{n^2 - 1}{3n}$

78. $\dfrac{a^3 - 5a^2 + 6a}{5ab} \cdot \dfrac{10b}{2a - 6}$ **79.** $\dfrac{4t^2 + 8}{7t} \div \dfrac{t^2 + 2}{7}$

80. $\dfrac{y^2 - y - 30}{y + 6} \div \dfrac{y^2 - 36}{y + 6}$ **81.** $\dfrac{3r - 12}{r^5} \div \dfrac{5r - 2}{r^2}$

82. $\dfrac{3}{5r} + \dfrac{2}{5r}$ **83.** $\dfrac{x}{x^2 - 4x + 3} - \dfrac{3}{x^2 - 4x + 3}$

84. $\dfrac{3x - 2}{2x^2 + 5x - 3} + \dfrac{7x - 3}{2x^2 + 5x - 3}$ **85.** $\dfrac{3b}{b + 1} = \dfrac{?}{b^2 + 2b + 1}$

86. $\dfrac{^-3}{a + b} = \dfrac{?}{a^2 - b^2}$ **87.** $\dfrac{4}{ab} + \dfrac{6}{a^2b}$ **88.** $\dfrac{13}{20x} - \dfrac{4}{5x}$

89. $\dfrac{12}{4r} - \dfrac{8}{r^2}$ **90.** $\dfrac{x}{4} + \dfrac{x}{7}$ **91.** $\dfrac{3n^3 + 12n^2 + 12n}{n^2 - 4} - \dfrac{2 - n}{n + 2}$

Solve for x.

92. $\dfrac{12}{x} + \dfrac{8}{x} = 5$ **93.** $\dfrac{3}{x} - \dfrac{1}{2x} + \dfrac{1}{3x} = 6$ **94.** $\dfrac{6}{x - 7} + 2 = 5$

95. The side of one square is 1 cm shorter than that of another. The difference in their areas is 27 cm². Find the side of each square.

96. A rectangular field has an area of $m^2 - 15m + 56$ square units. If $m - 8$ represents its length, what expression represents its width?

97. The ratio of blue chips to green chips is $x:(x + 3)$ or $(x + 16):(x + 25)$. How many blue chips are there? How many green chips are there?

98. If the fraction $\dfrac{1}{4}$ is added to a certain fraction whose denominator is 2 more than its numerator, the sum is $\dfrac{17}{20}$. What is the fraction?

99. The sum of the reciprocal of a number and $\dfrac{2}{5}$ is $\dfrac{11}{15}$. Find the number. (Hint: Let $\dfrac{1}{m}$ = the reciprocal of the number, m.)

100. The difference between a positive number and its reciprocal is $\dfrac{7}{12}$. What is the number?

101. Dr. Suong is 4 years less than 4 times her daughter's age. Her daughter is ten years less than half her mother's age. Find their ages.

102. The difference of the reciprocals of two numbers is $\dfrac{2}{3}$. One number is 3 times the other. Find the numbers. (Hint: one number = x, reciprocal, $\dfrac{1}{x}$.)

103. Complete the truth table.

p	q	$\sim p$	$(p \rightarrow q)$	$(\sim p \vee q)$	$(p \rightarrow q) \leftrightarrow (\sim p \vee q)$

Advanced Placement-Type Test I

Choose the correct answer.

1. Which of the following equations would have these ordered pairs:
   $(^-6, ^-7)$; $(^-4, ^-5)$; $(^-2, ^-3)$; $(0, ^-1)$; $(2, 1)$; $(4, 3)$?
   a. $y = 2x - 1$ **b.** $y = 2x + 1$ **c.** $y = x + 1$ **d.** $y = x - 1$

2. If $(2, M)$ is a point on the line $2x - y = 1$, what is the value of M?
   a. $\dfrac{1}{4}$ **b.** 3   **c.** $^-3$ **d.** none of these

3. What point lies on the graph of the equation $2y - x = 9$?
   a. $(0, ^-9)$ **b.** $(4, ^-1)$ **c.** $(0, 9)$ **d.** $(^-1, 4)$

4. Which point lies on the graph of $y = x^2 - 1$?
   a. $(0, 0)$ **b.** $(2, ^-3)$ **c.** $(^-2, ^-3)$ **d.** $(^-2, 3)$

5. What is the point of intersection for these two equations?
   $2x - y = ^-3$ and $x + 2y = 6$
   a. $(0, 3)$ **b.** $(0, 2)$ **c.** $(1, ^-2)$ **d.** $(^-1, 2)$

6. Select the missing head for this table.

p	q	?
T	T	T
T	F	F
F	T	T
F	F	T

   a. $p \wedge \sim q$
   b. $p \rightarrow q$
   c. $p \vee q$
   d. $p \leftrightarrow q$

7. Find the difference between $8c^2 - 2c + 4$ and $4(c^2 + 1)$.
   a. $4c^2 + 2c$ **b.** $4c^2 - 2c + 3$ **c.** $4c^2 + 2c + 3$ **d.** $4c^2 - 2c$

8. Find the sum of $9y^3 - 13y + 2$ and $y^3 - 1$.
   a. $8y^3 - 13y + 1$ **b.** $8y^3 - 14y + 2$ **c.** $8y^3 - 13y$ **d.** $10y^3 - 13y + 1$

9. Add $14m(m + 2)$ to $7(m - 2)$.   **a.** $14m^2 + 35m - 14$
   b. $21m^2 + 28m - 4$ **c.** $14m^2 + 21m - 4$ **d.** $21m^2 + 21m - 4$

10. From $6b + 4s$ take $2b + 7s$.
    a. $^-4b + 3s$ **b.** $4b - 3s$ **c.** $4b + 3s$ **d.** $8b + 11s$

11. What is $5a^2n^3$ squared?
    a. $25a^4n^6$ **b.** $10a^4b^5$ **c.** $10a^4b^6$ **d.** $25a^4n^4$

12. What is the product of $4ab^4$ and $5ab^7$?
    a. $20ab^{28}$ **b.** $1.25b^3$ **c.** $1.25b^4$ **d.** $20a^2b^{11}$

13. When $8(y - 4)$ is subtracted from $6y(y + 2)$ the result is:
    a. $6y^2 + 4y + 32$ **b.** $6y^2 - 8y - 30$ **c.** $6y^2 + 20y - 32$ **d.** $12y^2 - 4 + 2$

14. Express the product of $(3n - 7)(2 + n)$ as a trinomial.
    a. $3n^2 - 4n - 14$ **b.** $3n^2 - n - 14$ **c.** $n - 14 + 3n^2$ **d.** $3n^2 + 4n - 14$

15. Express $\dfrac{32x^2n}{^-8xn}$ in simplest form.
    a. ^-4xn **b.** ^-4x **c.** $4xn$ **d.** $4x$

16. If $(4x + 5)(x - y)$ is $4x^2 - 7x - 15$, find y.
    a. $^-3$ **b.** 3   **c.** $^-20$ **d.** 20

17. If $\dfrac{a}{a - 5} = \dfrac{4ab}{x}$, find x.
    a. $4ab - 20b$ **b.** $4a^2b - 20ab$ **c.** ^-20ab **d.** none of these

18. Evaluate $3c^2d - 2cd + 4d^2$ when $c = {}^-1$ and $d = 2$.
  a. 14   **b.** 24   **c.** 18   **d.** 26

19. When $12cd^3 + 9c^2d^2 - 3d$ is divided by $3d$, the quotient is: **a.** $4cd^2 + 3c^2d^2 - d$
  b. $4cd^2 + 3c^2d - 1$ **c.** $4cd + 9c^2 - 1$ **d.** $4cd + 3c^2 - d$

20. Express $n^2 + 5n - 6$ as the product of 2 binomials.   **a.** $(n + 6)(n - 1)$
  b. $(n + 3)(n + 2)$ **c.** $(n - 6)(n - 1)$ **d.** $(n - 3)(n - 2)$

21. Which expression is prime (cannot be factored)?
  a. $a^2 - b^2$ **b.** $y^2 - z^2$ **c.** $y^2 + 36$ **d.** $6y^2 + 27z^2$

22. Choose the simplest form of: $\dfrac{x}{3} + \dfrac{7x}{4}$.   **a.** $\dfrac{8x}{12}$ **b.** $\dfrac{7x}{12}$ **c.** $\dfrac{25x}{12}$ **d.** $\dfrac{8x}{7}$

23. Take $\dfrac{8}{mn}$ from $\dfrac{3}{m}$.   **a.** $\dfrac{3mn - 8}{m^2n}$ **b.** $\dfrac{3n - 8}{mn}$ **c.** $\dfrac{3m^2n - 8}{mn}$ **d.** $\dfrac{3n - m}{m^2n}$

24. If $(x - D)(3x + 4)$ is $3x^2 - 11x - 20$, find D.   **a.** 5   **b.** 2   **c.** $^-5$ **d.** $^-2$

25. Factor $x^2 - 13x - 48$.
  a. $(x - 6)(x - 8)$ **b.** $(x + 3)(x - 16)$ **c.** $(x - 12)(x + 4)$ **d.** $(x - 8)(x + 4)$

26. If $(3x - 5)(2x - 6)$ is $6x^2 + Rx + 30$, find R.   **a.** 28   **b.** $^-21$ **c.** $^-28$ **d.** $^-19$

27. What is the *LCM* of $6x + 2$ and $2y$?
  a. $2y(3x + 1)$ **b.** $12xy + 4y$ **c.** $4y(3x + 1)$ **d.** none of these

Solve.

28. Find three consecutive numbers such that half the smallest increased by $\frac{1}{5}$ of the largest equals 6.

29. Graph the solution of the inequalities $2x \geq {}^-8$ and $x - 2y < 8$.

30. The sum of two numbers is 37. One number is 5 less than the other. Find both numbers. (Solve algebraically.)

31. Complete the truth table for: $(p \rightarrow q) \leftrightarrow \sim(\sim p \wedge q)$

p	q	$p \rightarrow q$	$\sim p$	$\sim p \wedge q$	$\sim(\sim p \wedge q)$	$(p \rightarrow q) \leftrightarrow \sim(\sim p \wedge q)$
T	T					
T	F					
F	T					
F	F					

32. $\triangle ABC$ and $\triangle XYZ$ have equal areas.
  a. Find the value of a.
  b. What is the base and height of $\triangle XYZ$?
  c. What is the area of each?

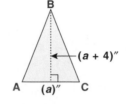
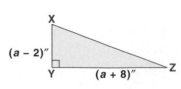

33. The area of trapezoid *PQRS* is $16\,\text{in.}^2$ less than the area of square *WXYZ*.
  a. Find the value of m.
  b. Find the area of each figure.

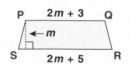

Linear and Quadratic Relations

A Pisa Not Pizza Problem

According to legend the people of Pisa thought this mathematician was really crazy when they saw him dropping objects from the top of the Leaning Tower.

What he was doing was studying the relationship between velocity and weight. This creative and brilliant mathematician was also a gifted artist and musician.

Who was this genius? Find out his life story. Then, with others, create and act out a TV math panel among Euler, Archimedes, and himself around his "Pisa Problem."

For Mathletes

Linear Equations: equations of the form $ax + by + c = 0$ where a, b, and c are real numbers.

The graph of a *linear* equation is a *straight line.**

A. $2x - 3y = {}^-3$ $a = 2$
$b = {}^-3$
$c = 3$

x	⁻3	0	3
y	⁻1	1	3

B. $\frac{1}{3}x + y = 0$ $a = \frac{1}{3}$
$b = 1$
$c = 0$

x	⁻3	0	3
y	1	0	⁻1

C. $y = 3$ $a = 0$
$b = 1$
$c = {}^-3$

x	⁻1	0	2
y	3	3	3

Slope of a nonvertical line between any two given points, P_1 and P_2, is the ratio of the vertical change to the horizontal change given that the horizontal change is *not* zero.

For every 3 ft it moves vertically, the boulder moves 5 ft horizontally.

Slope, or steepness: 3 ft to 5 ft $= \dfrac{3'}{5'}$ $\dfrac{\text{vertical change}}{\text{horizontal change}}$

Slope $m = \dfrac{(y_2 - y_1)}{(x_2 - x_1)}$ if $(x_2 - x_1) \neq 0$

To find the **slope** of a line represented by a linear equation like **A:** $2x - 3y = {}^-3$

- Choose any 2 points, P_1 and P_2, on the line. Name their coordinates, $P_1(x_1, y_1)$ and $P_2(x_2, y_2)$.

- Substitute the values of these coordinates in the slope formula:
$$m = \dfrac{(y_2 - y_1)}{(x_2 - x_1)}$$

To graph **A:** $2x - 3y = {}^-3$, choose 2 points:

$P_1 = ({}^-3, {}^-1)$ and $P_2 = (0, 1)$

$x_1 = {}^-3$ $y_1 = {}^-1$
$x_2 = 0$ $y_2 = 1$

So, $m = \dfrac{(1 - {}^-1)}{(0 - {}^-3)} = \dfrac{1 + 1}{0 + 3} = \dfrac{2}{3}$ **Slope**

Positive Slope (Graph A)*	**Negative Slope (Graph B)***	**Zero Slope (Graph C)***
Line *rises* from left to right.	Line *falls* from left to right.	This is a *horizontal, or nonvertical* line.

A: $2x - 3y = {}^-3$

Let $P_1 = ({}^-3, {}^-1)$
$P_2 = (0, 1)$
$m = \dfrac{2}{3}$

B: $\frac{1}{3}x + y = 0$

Let $P_1 = ({}^-3, 1)$
$P_2 = (3, {}^-1)$
$m = \dfrac{{}^-1 - {}^+1}{{}^+3 - {}^-3} = \dfrac{{}^-2}{6} = \dfrac{{}^-1}{3}$

C: $y = 3$

Let $P_1 = ({}^-1, 3)$
$P_2 = (2, 3)$
$m = \dfrac{3 - 3}{2 - {}^-1} = \dfrac{0}{3} = 0$

Graph A	Graph B	Graph C	Graph D

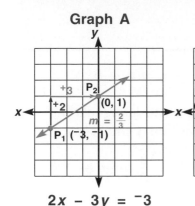

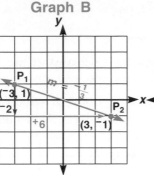

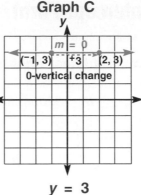

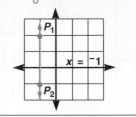

Slope is undefined for vertical lines such as $x = {}^-1$ because: $m = \frac{n}{0}$ is undefined.

$2x - 3y = {}^-3$ $\qquad$ $\frac{1}{3}x + y = 0$ $\qquad$ $y = 3$

Find the slope of each line.

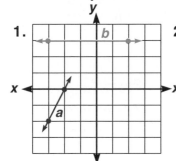

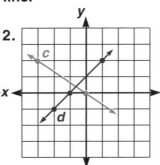

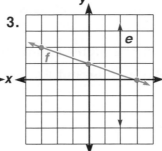

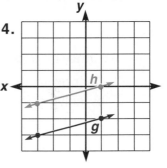

1. $\qquad$ 2. $\qquad$ 3. $\qquad$ 4.

Find the slope of the line that connects each pair of points.

5. $({}^-3, 1)\ (5, 2)$ $\qquad$ 6. $(0, 0)\ ({}^-1, 6)$ $\qquad$ 7. $(2, {}^-4)\ (3, 2)$ $\qquad$ 8. $(3, {}^-2)\ ({}^-2, 6)$

9. $({}^-3, 7)\ (5, 7)$ $\qquad$ 10. $(0, {}^-2)\ ({}^-1, 5)$ $\qquad$ 11. $(1, {}^-2)\ (3, {}^-4)$ $\qquad$ 12. $({}^-8, {}^-2)\ ({}^-6, {}^-4)$

Find the slope of each line.

13. $3x - y = 9$ $\qquad$ 14. $x + 4y = {}^-16$ $\qquad$ 15. $3y = 12$ $\qquad$ 16. ${}^-2x + y = {}^-10$

17. $x - 5y = 17$ $\qquad$ 18. $2x - y = 0$ $\qquad$ 19. $x = {}^-4$ $\qquad$ 20. $x + y = 6$

Tell whether the slope is positive, negative, zero, or undefined.

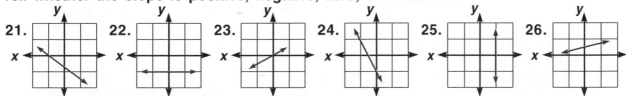

21. $\qquad$ 22. $\qquad$ 23. $\qquad$ 24. $\qquad$ 25. $\qquad$ 26.

***A* through *F* name different slopes. For each exercise below, select the correct slope. A given slope may be the answer to more than one linear equation.**

A. $\frac{1}{4}$ $\qquad$ B. ${}^-\frac{1}{4}$ $\qquad$ C. 4 $\qquad$ D. ${}^-4$ $\qquad$ E. 0 $\qquad$ F. undefined

27. $y = \frac{1}{4}$ $\qquad$ 28. $x = {}^-4$ $\qquad$ 29. $x + 4y = 7$ $\qquad$ 30. $4x + y = 0$

31. $x + \frac{y}{4} = 1$ $\qquad$ 32. $\frac{y}{4} - x = 3$ $\qquad$ 33. ${}^-2x + 8y = 9$ $\qquad$ 34. $4x - y = {}^-4$

16-2 | Slope-Intercept Form

Slope-Intercept Form of a linear equation is represented by: $y = mx + b$

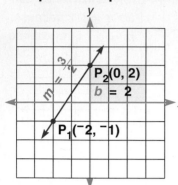

m = slope and b = point at which the line intersects the y-axis. It is called the **y-intercept.**

In this graph: $m = \dfrac{(^-1 - 2)}{(^-2 - 0)} = \dfrac{^-3}{^-2} = \dfrac{3}{2}$ and $b = 2$

Slope-Intercept Form: $y = \dfrac{3}{2}x + 2$

Equation of Line: $2y = 3x + 4$ or $3x - 2y = {^-4}$

▶ **To find m and b in the linear equation $3x - 2y = {^-4}$:**

Change to the **Slope-Intercept Form** by solving for y:

$$3x - 2y = {^-4}$$
$$(^-3x) + 3x - 2y = {^-4} - 3x$$

Divide each term by $^-2$. $\quad \dfrac{^-2y}{^-2} = \dfrac{^-3x}{^-2} - \dfrac{4}{^-2}$

$y = \dfrac{3}{2}x + 2 \longrightarrow m = \dfrac{3}{2}$ and $b = 2$

▶ **Given: $2x + y = 3$.** Find the slope (m) and the y-intercept (b).

Change to the **Slope-Intercept Form** by solving for y:

$\quad (^-2x) + 2x + y = (^-2x) + 3$

Add ^-2x to both sides.

$y = {^-2x} + 3 \longrightarrow m = {^-2}$ and $b = 3$

▶ **To graph this equation given b, the y-intercept:**

- Plot the y-intercept.

  If $b = 3$, then coordinates of y-intercept are $(0, 3)$.

- From this point, use the slope to find a second point on the line.

  If $m = {^-2} = \dfrac{^-2}{1}$, then move down 2 and move right 1.

- Connect the two points.

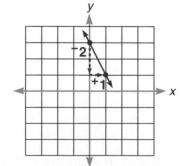

▶ **To write the equation of a line, given the slope, m, and the y-intercept, b:**

Substitute the values of m and b in the **Slope-Intercept Form,** $y = mx + b$.

$m = \dfrac{4}{3}, \qquad b = {^-1}$

$y = \dfrac{4}{3}x + {^-1} \longrightarrow y = \dfrac{4}{3}x - 1$

or $\quad 4x - 3y - 3 = 0$

Find the slope and *y*-intercept.

1. $3x - y = 7$

2. $^-2x + y = 11$

3. $x + 3y = ^-6$

4. $2x - 4y = 12$

5. $8y = 6x - 15$

6. $^-7x + y = ^-2$

7. $3x - y = ^-9$

8. $x - 10y = 25$

9. $5x - 10y = ^-40$

10. $\frac{x}{2} + 3y = 4$

11. $\frac{x}{3} - 2y = ^-3$

12. $3y - \frac{1}{2}x = ^-10$

Use the slope and *y*-intercept to graph the following lines.

13. $y = ^-2x + 1$

14. $y = \frac{1}{3}x - 2$

15. $y = \frac{^-2}{5}x - 1$

16. $y = \frac{3}{4}x + 1$

17. $y = x + 3$

18. $y = \frac{3}{2}x$

Write the equation for the lines that have the given slopes and intercepts.

19. $m = \frac{1}{2}$; $b = ^-2$

20. $m = 3$; $b = 1$

21. $m = \frac{^-2}{5}$; $b = ^-4$

22. $m = ^-1$; $b = 0$

23. $m = 0$; $b = ^-4$

24. $m = \frac{^-3}{4}$; $b = \frac{1}{2}$

25. $m = \frac{2}{7}$; $b = 0$

26. $m = ^-2$; $b = 3$

27. $m = \frac{1}{4}$; $b = ^-5$

28. $m = \frac{2}{3}$; $b = 8$

29. $m = \frac{^-1}{4}$; $b = \frac{3}{4}$

30. $m = 3$; $b = 0$

31. $m = \frac{^-1}{2}$; $b = ^-1$

32. $m = \frac{^-1}{5}$; $b = ^-2$

33. $m = \frac{^-1}{3}$; $b = \frac{1}{2}$

34. $m = ^-5$; $b = 0$

Special Cases

Two lines that are ***parallel*** will have the **same** slope, but **different** *y*-intercepts.

$y = \frac{1}{3}x + 2$
$\uparrow\uparrow$
mb

$y = \frac{1}{3}x - 1$
$\uparrow\uparrow$
mb

These lines are parallel.

Two lines that are *perpendicular* will have slopes that are the **negative reciprocals** of each other.

$y = 2x - 1$
$y = \frac{^-1}{2}x + 2$

The slopes, $^+2$ and $\frac{^-1}{2}$, are negative reciprocals.

These lines are perpendicular.

Tell whether each pair of lines is parallel, perpendicular, or neither.

35. $3y = 2x - 6$
    $y = \frac{2}{3}x + 10$

36. $y = \frac{3}{4}x - 6$
    $y = \frac{^-3}{4}x + 2$

37. $2x + y = 5$
    $x - 2y = ^-3$

16-3 Finding the Equation of a Line

To find the equation of a line, given the slope, _m_, and one point, _P_:

$$m = 2 \qquad P = (^-1, 1)$$

$$x = {}^-1; \ y = {}^+1$$

- Find the *y*-intercept, *b*, by substituting the values for the slope, *m*, and the coordinates of point (x, y) into the Slope-Intercept Form, $y = mx + b$.

$$y = mx + b$$
$$y = 2x + b$$
$$(1) = 2(^-1) + b$$
$$1 = {}^-2 + b$$
$$3 = b, \text{ the } y\text{-intercept}$$

- Now write the equation of the line, substituting the values of *m* and *b* into the Slope-Intercept Form.

$$y = mx + b$$
$$y = 2x + 3 \longrightarrow \text{Equation of line}$$

Given a slope of $\frac{1}{4}$ and point P ($^-8$, 1), find the equation of the line through point _P_.

$$y = mx + b$$
$$1 = \frac{1}{4}(^-8) + b \leftarrow \begin{array}{l}\text{Substitute} \\ \text{values for} \\ \textbf{\textit{m}} \text{ and } \textbf{\textit{x}} \text{ and } \textbf{\textit{y}}.\end{array}$$
$$1 = {}^-2 + b$$
$$3 = b$$

Now, substitute values for *m* and *b*. $\quad y = mx + b \longrightarrow y = \frac{1}{4}x + 3$

OR $\quad x - 4y = {}^-12 \longrightarrow$ Equation of line

Find the *y*-intercept of each line that has slope 3 and goes through the given point below.

1. (2, 5)
2. ($^-1$, 2)
3. (2, 2)
4. (0, $^-2$)
5. (1, 3)

Find the equation of each line that has slope $^-\frac{3}{2}$ and goes through the given point below.

6. (2, $^-1$)
7. ($^-2$, 2)
8. (0, 0)
9. $\left(1, \frac{9}{2}\right)$
10. (3, $^-4$)

Find the equation of each line that goes through the origin and has the slope given below.

11. 1
12. $^-2$
13. 4
14. $^-\frac{1}{3}$
15. $\frac{1}{5}$
16. $^-\frac{2}{3}$
17. 3
18. $^-\frac{1}{2}$

Find the equation of each line given below.

19. $P = (3, 1)$
    $m = {}^-1$
20. $P = (^-2, {}^-2)$
    $m = {}^-2$
21. $P = (^+4, 0)$
    $m = \frac{1}{2}$
22. $P = (^-3, 4)$
    $m = {}^-\frac{2}{3}$

Writing Equations Given Two Points on the Line

Given: $P_1(2, {}^-3)$ and $P_2(6, {}^-1)$

Find the slope, m: $\quad m = \dfrac{(y_2 - y_1)}{(x_2 - x_1)} = \dfrac{({}^-1 - {}^-3)}{(6 - 2)} = \dfrac{2}{4} = \dfrac{1}{2}$

Find the y-intercept, b: Substitute the value of m and the coordinates of *either* point in the Slope-Intercept Form.

$$y = mx + b \quad \text{where} \quad m = \tfrac{1}{2} \quad \text{and} \quad P_1 = (2, {}^-3)$$

$${}^-3 = \tfrac{1}{2}(2) + b \longrightarrow {}^-3 = 1 + b \longrightarrow {}^-3 - 1 = b \longrightarrow b = {}^-4$$

Substitute values of m and b in the Slope-Intercept Form:
$$y = mx + b$$
$$y = \tfrac{1}{2}x - 4 \text{ or } x - 2y = 8 \longrightarrow \text{Equation of line}$$

Find the equation of the line that passes through each pair of points.

23. $(3, {}^-5); ({}^-6, 2)$ **24.** $({}^-1, 4); (1, {}^-6)$ **25.** $(4, 5); (8, 4)$ **26.** $(0, 0); ({}^-3, {}^-2)$

27. $(3, 0); ({}^-4, 1)$ **28.** $({}^-2, {}^-2); ({}^-6, {}^-6)$ **29.** $(3, 4); (2, {}^-1)$ **30.** $({}^-3, 1); (3, {}^-1)$

Write the equation of the line that:

31. has slope 3 and passes through the point $({}^-2, {}^-3)$.

32. passes through the points $(4, {}^-1)$ and $(8, 0)$.

33. is parallel to the line $y = \tfrac{2}{3}x + 1$ and has y-intercept ${}^-6$.

34. has slope 0 and passes through the point $(4, 3)$.

35. passes through the origin and has slope ${}^-1$.

36. is perpendicular to the line $y = 3x - 1$ and has the same y-intercept.

37. passes through the origin and point $({}^-3, {}^-2)$.

38. passes through the origin and is parallel to $y = \dfrac{x}{2} - 1$.

Find the equation of each line.

39. 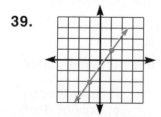 **40.** 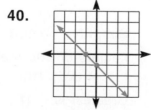 **41.** 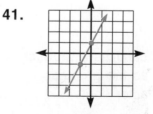 **42.**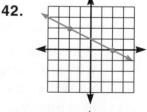

43. 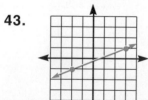 **44.** 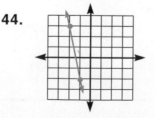 **45.** 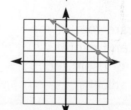 **46.**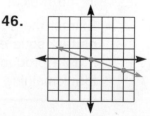

461

16-4 Simplifying Radical Expressions

Radicand: the number or expression under a radical sign ($\sqrt{}$).

Radical:	$\sqrt{6x}$
Radicand:	$6x$

In general:

$\sqrt{a}$ is a **rational number** if "a" is a perfect square.

$\sqrt{16}$ is rational because 16 is the square of 4.

$\sqrt{a}$ is an **irrational number** if "a" is NOT a perfect square.

$\sqrt{17}$ is irrational because 17 is NOT a perfect square.

x^n is a **perfect square** if "n" is an even number. Its square root is $x^{\frac{n}{2}}$.

$$\sqrt{x^6} = x^{\frac{6}{2}} = x^3$$

$$\sqrt{x^5} = x^{\frac{5}{2}} \neq \text{a perfect square}$$

The exponent, 5, is odd; not exactly divisible by 2.

Product Property of Square Roots: $\sqrt{ab} = \sqrt{a} \cdot \sqrt{b}$ AND $\sqrt{a} \cdot \sqrt{b} = \sqrt{ab}$

$\sqrt{72} = \sqrt{36 \cdot 2} = \sqrt{36} \cdot \sqrt{2} = 6\sqrt{2}$	$\sqrt{y^5} = \sqrt{y^4 y^1} = \sqrt{y^4} \cdot \sqrt{y} = y^2 \sqrt{y}$
$\sqrt{3}\,\sqrt{12} = \sqrt{3 \cdot 12} = \sqrt{36} = 6$	$\sqrt{x^3} \cdot \sqrt{x} = \sqrt{x^3 x^1} = \sqrt{x^4} = x^2$

Quotient Property of Square Roots: $\sqrt{\dfrac{a}{b}} = \dfrac{\sqrt{a}}{\sqrt{b}}$ AND $\dfrac{\sqrt{a}}{\sqrt{b}} = \sqrt{\dfrac{a}{b}}$

$\sqrt{\dfrac{3}{4}} = \dfrac{\sqrt{3}}{\sqrt{4}} = \dfrac{\sqrt{3}}{2}$	$\sqrt{\dfrac{9}{x^2}} = \dfrac{\sqrt{9}}{\sqrt{x^2}} = \dfrac{3}{x}$
$\dfrac{\sqrt{12}}{\sqrt{3}} = \sqrt{\dfrac{12}{3}} = \sqrt{4} = 2$	$\dfrac{\sqrt{32x^2}}{\sqrt{2x}} = \sqrt{\dfrac{32x^2}{2x}} = \sqrt{16x} = \sqrt{16} \cdot \sqrt{x} = 4\sqrt{x}$

Square Root Radical is in *simplest form* when:
- the radicand has *no* factors, other than 1, that are *perfect squares*.
- *no fraction* exists under the radical sign.
- *no radical* is in the denominator.

To simplify a radical:

- Rewrite the radicand as a product with one factor as the greatest perfect square factor contained in the radicand.

- Extract the square root of the perfect square and express it as a product of itself and the remaining radical.

Simplify: $\sqrt{500}$

Factors of 500 that are perfect squares:
$$4, 25, 100$$

Greatest is: 100.

Product Property of Square Roots

Rewrite: $\sqrt{500} = \sqrt{100 \cdot 5}$

$$\sqrt{100} \cdot \sqrt{5} = 10\sqrt{5}$$

Identify each expression as a rational or irrational number.

1. $\sqrt{36}$ 2. $\sqrt{200}$ 3. $\sqrt{144}$ 4. $\sqrt{50}$ 5. $\sqrt{10}$ 6. $\sqrt{49}$

Simplify. (The first one is done.)

7. $\sqrt{75x^2} = \sqrt{75}\sqrt{x^2} = \sqrt{25 \cdot 3}\sqrt{x^2} = \sqrt{25}\sqrt{3}\sqrt{x^2} = 5\sqrt{3x^2} = 5x\sqrt{3}$

8. $\sqrt{20}$ 9. $\sqrt{108}$ 10. $\sqrt{121x^2}$ 11. $\sqrt{500}$

12. $\sqrt{112}$ 13. $\sqrt{99y^2}$ 14. $\sqrt{2000}$ 15. $\sqrt{y^5}$

16. $\sqrt{288}$ 17. $\sqrt{54}$ 18. $\sqrt{80x^4}$ 19. $\sqrt{98a^3b^2}$

Simplifying Quotients/Rationalizing Denominators

- Use the **Quotient Property of Square Roots.**
- **Rationalize the denominator,** if necessary; that is, multiply the numerator and denominator by the radical expression in the denominator.

Simplify: $\dfrac{5}{\sqrt{2}}$

$$\dfrac{5}{\sqrt{2}} \cdot \dfrac{\sqrt{2}}{\sqrt{2}} = \dfrac{5\sqrt{2}}{\sqrt{4}} = \dfrac{5\sqrt{2}}{2}$$

Simplify: $\dfrac{3x}{\sqrt{8x}}$

$$\dfrac{3x}{\sqrt{8x}} \cdot \dfrac{\sqrt{8x}}{\sqrt{8x}} = \dfrac{3x\sqrt{8x}}{8x} = \dfrac{3\sqrt{8x}}{8}$$

$$= \dfrac{3\sqrt{4} \cdot \sqrt{2x}}{8} = \dfrac{3 \cdot 2\sqrt{2x}}{8} = \dfrac{3\sqrt{2x}}{4}$$

Simplify: $\sqrt{\dfrac{11x^2}{16}}$

$$\sqrt{\dfrac{11x^2}{16}} = \dfrac{\sqrt{11x^2}}{\sqrt{16}} = \dfrac{\sqrt{11x^2}}{4}$$

$$= \dfrac{\sqrt{11} \cdot \sqrt{x^2}}{4} = \dfrac{\sqrt{11}\, x}{4} = \dfrac{x\sqrt{11}}{4}$$

Simplify.

20. $\dfrac{6}{\sqrt{5}}$ 21. $\dfrac{10}{\sqrt{2}}$ 22. $\dfrac{9}{\sqrt{3a}}$ 23. $\dfrac{30x}{\sqrt{2}}$ 24. $\dfrac{6\sqrt{8}}{\sqrt{2}}$

25. $\dfrac{56}{\sqrt{11}}$ 26. $\dfrac{y^2}{\sqrt{y}}$ 27. $\dfrac{22a}{\sqrt{6}}$ 28. $\dfrac{16}{\sqrt{14}}$ 29. $\dfrac{5\sqrt{20}}{\sqrt{5}}$

30. $\sqrt{\dfrac{3}{5}}$ 31. $\sqrt{\dfrac{1}{16}}$ 32. $\sqrt{\dfrac{6}{25}}$ 33. $\sqrt{\dfrac{100}{3}}$ 34. $\dfrac{\sqrt{50m^5}}{\sqrt{2m^3}}$

35. $\sqrt{\dfrac{4x^2}{9}}$ 36. $\sqrt{\dfrac{20x^2}{49}}$ 37. $\sqrt{\dfrac{y^6}{16}}$ 38. $\sqrt{\dfrac{81}{100a^4}}$ 39. $\sqrt{\dfrac{15x^3}{64x}}$

40. $\sqrt{3} \cdot \sqrt{\dfrac{3}{5}}$ 41. $\sqrt{6} \cdot \sqrt{\dfrac{6}{5}}$ 42. $ab\sqrt{\dfrac{a}{3b}}$ 43. $2n\sqrt{\dfrac{n}{2}}$ 44. $xy\dfrac{\sqrt{x^3}}{\sqrt{3x}}$

45. $5\sqrt{\dfrac{6n^5}{5n^3}}$ 46. $3\sqrt{\dfrac{24c^7}{18c}}$ 47. $2\sqrt{\dfrac{75n}{2n^3}}$ 48. $y\sqrt{\dfrac{5y}{15y^2}}$ 49. $4\sqrt{\dfrac{2d^5}{6d}}$

50. $\sqrt{\dfrac{a^3b^4}{b^3c^5}}$ 51. $\sqrt{\dfrac{9m^3}{32n^3}}$ 52. $\sqrt{\dfrac{18x^3y^3}{6x^4y^4}}$ 53. $\sqrt{\dfrac{8r^2s^3}{2r^3s^2}}$ 54. $\sqrt{\dfrac{10abc^2}{2a^2b^3c^4}}$

Adding and Subtracting Radical Expressions

Only add or subtract radical expressions with *like terms*, that is, whose radicals are the same. To compute: $6\sqrt{5} + 11\sqrt{5} = \underline{}$

| Same radicals = Like terms |

- Factor out the like radicals. $(6 + 11)\sqrt{5}$
- Simplify, if necessary. $= 17\sqrt{5}$ Sum

$3a\sqrt{2} + 9a\sqrt{2} = \underline{}$	$16\sqrt{10} - 7\sqrt{10} = \underline{}$	$5\sqrt{11a} - 12\sqrt{11a} = \underline{}$
$(3a + 9a)\sqrt{2} = 12a\sqrt{2}$	$(16 - 7)\sqrt{10} = 9\sqrt{10}$	$(5 - 12)\sqrt{11a} = {}^-7\sqrt{11a}$
Sum	Difference	Difference

Some radicals can be simplified to make their radicals the same. Then they can be added or subtracted if their radicals are the same.

| $7\sqrt{5} + 13\sqrt{7} = \underline{}$ |
| Radicals are different. They cannot be added or subtracted. |

$9\sqrt{3} + 8\sqrt{12} = \underline{}$	$6\sqrt{2a^2} - 3a\sqrt{2} = \underline{}$	$36\sqrt{b} + 18\sqrt{9b} = \underline{}$
$= 9\sqrt{3} + 8\sqrt{4} \cdot \sqrt{3}$	$= 6\sqrt{2} \cdot \sqrt{a^2} - 3a\sqrt{2}$	$= 36\sqrt{b} + 18\sqrt{9} \cdot \sqrt{b}$
$= 9\sqrt{3} + 8 \cdot 2 \cdot \sqrt{3}$	$= 6\sqrt{2} \cdot a - 3a\sqrt{2}$	$= 36\sqrt{b} + 18 \cdot 3 \cdot \sqrt{b}$
$= 9\sqrt{3} + 16\sqrt{3}$	$= 6a \cdot \sqrt{2} - 3a\sqrt{2}$	$= 36\sqrt{b} + 54\sqrt{b}$
$= (9 + 16)\sqrt{3} = 25\sqrt{3}$	$= (6a - 3a)\sqrt{2} = 3a\sqrt{2}$	$= (36 + 54)\sqrt{b} = 90\sqrt{b}$

Simplify, if possible.

1. $20\sqrt{11} - 35\sqrt{11}$

2. $\sqrt{21} + 6\sqrt{21}$

3. $19\sqrt{b} + 18\sqrt{b}$

4. $5x\sqrt{2} - 29x\sqrt{2}$

5. $16\sqrt{3} + 8\sqrt{75}$

6. $7\sqrt{25b} + 12\sqrt{4b}$

7. $^-2\sqrt{500} - 4\sqrt{45}$

8. $6\sqrt{b^3} - 15b\sqrt{b}$

9. $^-19a^2\sqrt{72} + 3a^2\sqrt{128}$

10. $3y\sqrt{98} + 15y\sqrt{2}$

11. $17\sqrt{6a^2} - 4a\sqrt{6}$

12. $12k\sqrt{48k^2} - 9k\sqrt{27}$

13. $6\sqrt{300b^3} + 8\sqrt{75b^3}$

14. $\sqrt{96y^4} - \sqrt{150y^4}$

15. $61\sqrt{9x^3} + 28\sqrt{x}$

16. $29\sqrt{3} + 18\sqrt{9}$

17. $2\sqrt{64a} + 17\sqrt{16a}$

18. $32\sqrt{45b^2} - 19b\sqrt{80}$

19. $\sqrt{200} - \sqrt{72} + 3\sqrt{32}$

20. $5\sqrt{4b^3} - 6b\sqrt{9b}$

21. $3\sqrt{45n^2} + 2\sqrt{5} - \sqrt{5n^2}$

22. $4y\sqrt{147} + 11y\sqrt{75}$

23. $17\sqrt{50a^3} - \left(\sqrt{2a} + \sqrt{a^2}\right)$

24. $\sqrt{48n^3} + 3\sqrt{3n} - 7\sqrt{9n}$

25. $\sqrt{\dfrac{7}{16}} + 2\sqrt{\dfrac{7}{16}}$

26. $5\sqrt{\dfrac{3}{a^2}} - \sqrt{\dfrac{6}{a^2}}$

27. $7\sqrt{\dfrac{10}{2y^4}} - 3\sqrt{\dfrac{40}{2y^4}}$

Using Radicals

Find the hypotenuse for these right triangles. (Look for the pattern.)

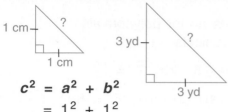

$c^2 = a^2 + b^2$
$\quad = 1^2 + 1^2$
$c^2 = 2$
$c = \sqrt{2}$ cm

$c^2 = a^2 + b^2$
$\quad = 3^2 + 3^2$
$c^2 = 18$
$c = \sqrt{18}$
$c = 3\sqrt{2}$ yd

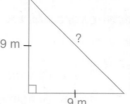

$c^2 = a^2 + b^2$
$\quad = 9^2 + 9^2$
$c^2 = 162$
$c = \sqrt{81} \cdot \sqrt{2}$
$c = 9\sqrt{2}$ m

Can you write a formula for the ratio of the sides?
The ratio is: $1a : 1a : 1a\sqrt{2}$, where a = the leg.

Study the bisected equilateral triangles. (Can you find the pattern?)

$\overline{DB} = \dfrac{?}{} $ m
$\overline{DB} = \dfrac{1}{2} \times 2$ m
$\overline{DB} = 1$ m

$c^2 = a^2 + b^2$
$2^2 = 1^2 + b^2$
$4 = 1 + b^2$
$3 = b^2$
$\sqrt{3} = b$

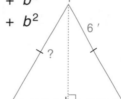

$c^2 = a^2 + b^2$
$6^2 = 3^2 + b^2$
$36 = 9 + b^2$
$27 = b^2$
$\sqrt{27} = b$
$\sqrt{9} \cdot \sqrt{3} = b$
$3\sqrt{3} = b$

$\overline{DB} : \overline{DC} : \overline{CB} = 1 : \sqrt{3} : 2$
(Pattern $= 1a : 1a\sqrt{3} : 2a$)

Solve for the missing dimension of these figures.

28.

29.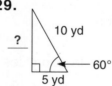

30.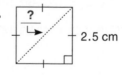

31.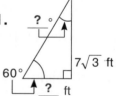

32. Find the perimeter of the triangles in exercises 28 to 31.

33. Find the diagonal of a square having a perimeter of 40 dm.

34. Find the hypotenuse of an isosceles right triangle if each leg is $3\frac{1}{3}$ yd long.

35. If the legs of a right triangle each measure $2\sqrt{5}$ in., what is the hypotenuse?

36. What is the length of the hypotenuse of a right triangle if one leg is 8 cm and the other is 16 cm?

37. Find the diagonal of a rectangle 10 m long and 20 m wide.

38. What is the perimeter of a right triangle whose legs each measure 11 in.?

16-6 Multiplication and Division of Radical Expressions

To multiply radical expressions: Use the same rules as for polynomials and the rules for radicals.

$6\sqrt{3} \cdot 4\sqrt{5} = \underline{\ ?\ }$

$= (6 \cdot 4) \cdot \left(\sqrt{3} \cdot \sqrt{5}\right)$

$= 24\sqrt{3} \cdot \sqrt{5}$

$= 24\sqrt{15}$

- Cluster similar terms.
- Simplify.
- Use the Product Rule for Radicals.

$3a\sqrt{8} \cdot 2a\sqrt{2} = \underline{\ ?\ }$

$(3a)(2a)\sqrt{8} \cdot \sqrt{2} = 6a^2\sqrt{8} \cdot \sqrt{2}$

$6a^2\sqrt{16} = 6a^2 \cdot 4 = 24a^2$

$^-9\sqrt{10b} \cdot 7\sqrt{2b} = \underline{\ ?\ }$

$= (^-9)(7)\left(\sqrt{10b} \cdot \sqrt{2b}\right) = {}^-63\sqrt{20b^2}$

$= {}^-63\sqrt{20} \cdot \sqrt{b^2} = {}^-63\sqrt{5} \cdot \sqrt{4} \cdot b$

$= (^-63)(2)\sqrt{5}\, b = {}^-126b\sqrt{5}$

Remember how to multiply two binomials?

$(2 + \sqrt{3})(5 + \sqrt{3}) = \underline{\ ?\ }$

| ① $(2 \cdot 5)$ |
| $+$ ② $2\sqrt{3}$ |
| $+$ ③ $(\sqrt{3})(5)$ |
| $+$ ④ $\sqrt{3} \cdot \sqrt{3}$ |

$= 10 + \underbrace{2\sqrt{3} + 5\sqrt{3}}_{\text{combine}} + \sqrt{9}$

$10 + 7\sqrt{3} + 3 = 10 + 3 + 7\sqrt{3} = 13 + 7\sqrt{3}$

True or false. Explain.

1. The product of two irrational numbers can be a rational number.

2. The product of an irrational number and a rational number is never a rational number.

3. The set of irrational numbers is closed under multiplication.

4. The set of irrational numbers is closed under division.

Simplify. (Hint: Remember to use the distributive property in exercises 17–19.)

5. $^-2\sqrt{5} \cdot 17\sqrt{2}$

6. $20\sqrt{3} \cdot 6\sqrt{3}$

7. $8\sqrt{2} \cdot 3\sqrt{30}$

8. $a\sqrt{6} \cdot 11a\sqrt{2}$

9. $9x\sqrt{5} \cdot 6x\sqrt{8}$

10. $18\sqrt{5b} \cdot 2\sqrt{b}$

11. $10\sqrt{6} \cdot 7\sqrt{6a}$

12. $3y\sqrt{y^3} \cdot {}^-2y\sqrt{y}$

13. $\frac{1}{5}\sqrt{2y} \cdot {}^-60\sqrt{2y}$

14. $9k\sqrt{48} \cdot k\sqrt{3}$

15. $6\sqrt{10a^3} \cdot 6\sqrt{8a}$

16. $3\sqrt{2} \cdot 7\sqrt{5a} \cdot \sqrt{10a}$

17. $2\sqrt{3}\left(7 + \sqrt{3}\right)$

18. $\sqrt{11}\left(9 - 2\sqrt{11}\right)$

19. $\sqrt{3}\left(\sqrt{12} + \sqrt{27}\right)$

20. $\sqrt{a}\left(\sqrt{2a} + \sqrt{14a}\right)$

21. $\sqrt{x^2y}\left(\sqrt{2xy} - \sqrt{6y}\right)$

22. $2\sqrt{ab}\left(\sqrt{5a} - \sqrt{5b}\right)$

23. $\sqrt{m^3}\left(\sqrt{6mn} + \sqrt{9mn^2}\right)$

24. $^-\sqrt{3b}\left(\sqrt{18b^3} - \sqrt{6b}\right)$

25. $^-2\sqrt{c}\left(\sqrt{50cd^3} - \sqrt{80c^2d^2}\right)$

Dividing Radical Expressions: Divide radical expressions as polynomials are divided. Where necessary, rationalize the denominator.

$\dfrac{\sqrt{5}}{\sqrt{15}} = $?

$\dfrac{\sqrt{5}}{\sqrt{15}} \cdot \dfrac{\sqrt{15}}{\sqrt{15}} = \dfrac{\sqrt{75}}{15} = \dfrac{\sqrt{25 \cdot 3}}{15}$

$= \dfrac{\sqrt{25} \cdot \sqrt{3}}{15} = \dfrac{5\sqrt{3}}{15} = \dfrac{\sqrt{3}}{3}$

OR $\dfrac{\sqrt{5}}{\sqrt{15}} = \sqrt{\dfrac{5}{15}} = \sqrt{\dfrac{1}{3}}$

$= \dfrac{\sqrt{1}}{\sqrt{3}} \cdot \dfrac{\sqrt{3}}{\sqrt{3}} = \dfrac{\sqrt{3}}{3}$

$\dfrac{\sqrt{2a^3}}{\sqrt{3a}} = $?

$\dfrac{\sqrt{2a^3}}{\sqrt{3a}} \cdot \dfrac{\sqrt{3a}}{\sqrt{3a}} = \dfrac{\sqrt{6a^4}}{3a} = \dfrac{\sqrt{6}\sqrt{a^2 \cdot a^2}}{3a}$

$= \dfrac{\sqrt{6}\,a \cdot a}{3a} = \dfrac{\sqrt{6}\,a}{3} = \dfrac{a\sqrt{6}}{3}$

OR $\dfrac{\sqrt{2a^3}}{\sqrt{3a}} = \sqrt{\dfrac{2a^3}{3a}} = \sqrt{\dfrac{2a^2}{3}} = \dfrac{a\sqrt{2}}{\sqrt{3}} \cdot \dfrac{\sqrt{3}}{\sqrt{3}}$

$= \dfrac{a\sqrt{2 \cdot 3}}{3} = \dfrac{a\sqrt{6}}{3}$

Choose a, b, c or d to rationalize the denominator; then simplify.

a. $\sqrt{5}$ **b.** $\sqrt{2}$ **c.** $\sqrt{6}$ **d.** $\sqrt{3}$

26. $\dfrac{3\sqrt{8}}{2\sqrt{3}}$

27. $\dfrac{\sqrt{5a^2}}{\sqrt{10a}}$

28. $\dfrac{6\sqrt{35m^3}}{\sqrt{21m^2}}$

29. $\dfrac{3\sqrt{2}}{4\sqrt{8}}$

30. $\dfrac{y\sqrt{18y^3}}{\sqrt{45y}}$

31. $\dfrac{\sqrt{16a^3}}{\sqrt{24}}$

32. $\dfrac{3\sqrt{7m^5}}{\sqrt{42m}}$

33. $\dfrac{7\sqrt{3n^3}}{\sqrt{15n}}$

Simplify.

34. $\dfrac{\sqrt{90}}{\sqrt{10}}$

35. $\dfrac{8\sqrt{3}}{4\sqrt{2}}$

36. $\dfrac{9}{3\sqrt{10}}$

37. $\dfrac{10\sqrt{2}}{\sqrt{50}}$

38. $\dfrac{20\sqrt{b^3}}{\sqrt{2b}}$

39. $\dfrac{a^2\sqrt{3}}{\sqrt{8a^2}}$

40. $\dfrac{^-15\sqrt{50}}{\sqrt{5}}$

41. $\dfrac{r\sqrt{27}}{\sqrt{3r}}$

42. $\dfrac{2\sqrt{500}}{7\sqrt{10}}$

43. $\dfrac{\sqrt{27b^2}}{\sqrt{3b}}$

44. $\dfrac{36}{\sqrt{12}}$

45. $\dfrac{3\sqrt{200m^5}}{\sqrt{20m^3}}$

46. $^-3\sqrt{5} \cdot {}^-6\sqrt{10}$

47. $\sqrt{x^2y^3} \cdot \sqrt{xy}$

48. $3t\sqrt{2} \cdot 8t\sqrt{18}$

49. $\dfrac{^-7\sqrt{a^2b} \cdot {}^+2\sqrt{ab}}{2\sqrt{ab^2}}$

50. $\dfrac{3\sqrt{8} \cdot 4\sqrt{6n}}{2\sqrt{2n}}$

51. $\dfrac{5\sqrt{5a} \cdot {}^-2\sqrt{15b}}{10\sqrt{20ab}}$

Solve.

52. $(6 + \sqrt{3})(^-2 + \sqrt{3})$

53. $(3 + \sqrt{5})(3 - \sqrt{5})$

54. $(4 - \sqrt{6})(3 - \sqrt{6})$

55. $(a + \sqrt{7})(3a + \sqrt{7})$

56. $(12 + \sqrt{x})(6 + \sqrt{x})$

57. $(9 + 2\sqrt{3})(4 - \sqrt{3})$

58. $(2 + \sqrt{x^2})(3 + \sqrt{x^2})$

59. $(5 + 4\sqrt{a})(3 + \sqrt{a})$

60. $(2 + 3\sqrt{n})(5 - \sqrt{n})$

Solving Quadratic Equations by Factoring

Quadratic Equation is an equation that can be written in this form:

$$ax^2 + bx + c = 0 \quad \text{where} \quad (a \neq 0)$$

Quadratics:

$2x^2 + 11x - 7 = 0$ where	$x^2 - 16 = 0$ where	$5x^2 + 6x = 0$ where
$a = 2, b = 11, c = {}^-7$	$a = 1, b = 0, c = {}^-16$	$a = 5, b = 6, c = 0$

▶ **Zero-Product Property:** The product of two terms is 0 when *either* of the factors is 0. This property is often used to solve quadratic equations.

If $ab = 0$, then $a = 0$ or $b = 0$. **Example:** If $5a = 0$, then $a = 0$.

▶ **To solve a quadratic equation:**

$x^2 - 9x = {}^-20$

- Bring all terms to the same side of the equation; the other side will equal 0.

  $x^2 - 9x + 20 = 0$

- Factor completely the polynomial side of the equation.

  $(x - 4)(x - 5) = 0$

- Use the **Zero-Product Property:** let each factor equal 0 and solve for the value of the variable. These values will form the solution set.

  Let $(x - 4) = 0$ Let $(x - 5) = 0$
             $x = 4$ $x = 5$

  Solution Set (SS): $\{4, 5\}$ or $x = 4$ or 5

  Check:

- Check. Substitute each value of x to see if it makes the quadratic equation true.

  For $x = 4$:   **For $x = 5$:**

  $x^2 - 9x = {}^-20$ $x^2 - 9x = {}^-20$

  $4^2 - 9(4) = {}^-20$ $5^2 - 9(5) = {}^-20$

  $16 - 36 = {}^-20$ $25 - 45 = {}^-20$

          ${}^-20 = {}^-20$ ${}^-20 = {}^-20$

$3x^2 + 9x = 0$	$x^2 - 16 \quad = 0$	$2x^2 + 9x = 5$
$3x(x + 3) = 0$	$(x + 4)(x - 4) = 0$	$2x^2 + 9x - 5 = 0$
Let $3x = 0 \longrightarrow x = 0$	Let $(x + 4) = 0 \longrightarrow x = {}^-4$	$(2x - 1)(x + 5) = 0$
and $(x + 3) = 0 \rightarrow x = {}^-3$	and $(x - 4) = 0 \rightarrow x = 4$	Let $(2x - 1) = 0 \rightarrow 2x = 1$

$3x^2 + 9x = 0$

$3x(x + 3) = 0$

Let $3x = 0 \longrightarrow x = 0$

and $(x + 3) = 0 \rightarrow x = {}^-3$

    SS: $\{0, {}^-3\}$

Check:

$3(0)^2 + 9(0) = 0$

    $0 + 0 = 0 \rightarrow 0 = 0$

$3({}^-3)^2 + 9({}^-3) = 0$

  $27 - 27 = 0 \rightarrow 0 = 0$

$x^2 - 16 \quad = 0$

$(x + 4)(x - 4) = 0$

Let $(x + 4) = 0 \longrightarrow x = {}^-4$

and $(x - 4) = 0 \rightarrow x = 4$

    SS: $\{{}^-4, 4\}$

Check:

$({}^-4)^2 - 16 = 0$

$16 - 16 = 0 \longrightarrow 0 = 0$

$(4)^2 - 16 = 0$

$16 - 16 = 0 \longrightarrow 0 = 0$

$2x^2 + 9x = 5$

$2x^2 + 9x - 5 = 0$

$(2x - 1)(x + 5) = 0$

Let $(2x - 1) = 0 \rightarrow 2x = 1$

                 $x = \frac{1}{2}$

and $(x + 5) = 0 \rightarrow x = {}^-5$

    SS: $\left\{\frac{1}{2}, {}^-5\right\}$

Check:

$2\left(\frac{1}{2}\right)^2 + 9\left(\frac{1}{2}\right) = 5$

$2({}^-5)^2 + 9({}^-5) = 5$

Find the solution set for each of the factored equations.

1. $(x - 4)(x - 2) = 0$ **2.** $(x + 6)(x - 6) = 0$ **3.** $x(x + 10) = 0$

4. $(x + 11)(x + 1) = 0$ **5.** $(x - 5)(x - 5) = 0$ **6.** $(3x + 1)(x - 7) = 0$

Solve.

7. $x^2 + 6x + 8 = 0$ **8.** $x^2 - 100 = 0$ **9.** $y^2 - 15y + 56 = 0$

10. $4x^2 + 12x = 0$ **11.** $x^2 + 18x + 81 = 0$ **12.** $x^2 - 6 = 5x$

13. $k^2 + 14k = {}^-40$ **14.** $t^2 - 8t = 33$ **15.** $9s^2 - 3s = 0$

16. $x^2 + 6x = 72$ **17.** $r^2 - 11 = 10r$ **18.** $7p^2 + 35p = 0$

19. $3x^2 - 16x - 12 = 0$ **20.** $5x^2 + 41x + 8 = 0$ **21.** $4x^2 = 1$

22. $6x^2 - 19x = 20$ **23.** $7x^2 - 8 = 10x$ **24.** $12b^2 = 7b + 10$

Choose the correct solution set for each equation.

25. $x^2 - 11x = {}^-30$
     a. $\{5, 6\}$ **b.** $\{{}^-5, {}^-6\}$ **c.** $\{3, 10\}$ **d.** $\{{}^-3, {}^-10\}$

26. $3x^2 + 17x - 6 = 0$
     a. $\left\{\frac{1}{6}, 3\right\}$ **b.** $\{1, {}^-6\}$ **c.** $\left\{\frac{1}{3}, {}^-6\right\}$ **d.** $\left\{-\frac{1}{6}, {}^-1\right\}$

27. $6x^2 = 11x + 10$
     a. $\left\{\frac{2}{5}, -\frac{3}{2}\right\}$ **b.** $\left\{\frac{5}{2}, -\frac{2}{3}\right\}$ **c.** $\{5, {}^-2\}$ **d.** $\{2, {}^-3\}$

28. $4x^2 + 17x + 4 = 0$
     a. $\{2\}$ **b.** $\left\{\frac{1}{4}, 4\right\}$ **c.** $\{4, 1\}$ **d.** $\left\{-\frac{1}{4}, {}^-4\right\}$

29. $x^2 - 20x = {}^-100$
     a. $\{10\}$ **b.** $\{10, {}^-10\}$ **c.** $\{{}^-10\}$ **d.** $\{{}^-2, {}^-50\}$

Solve.

30. The product of 2 consecutive positive integers is equal to 8 more than the product of 6 and the larger integer. What are the integers? (Hint: There will be two sets of answers.)

Two consecutive integers

$x(x + 1) = 6(x + 1) + 8$ ← 8 more than the product of 6 and the larger integer

31. When the product of 9 and a number is subtracted from the square of that number, the result is 10. Find the number. (Hint: There are two possible answers.)

32. The length of a rectangular herb garden is 1 meter less than twice its width. What is the width of the garden if the area is 28 square meters? (Hint: Width cannot be a negative number.)

33. Twice the product of 2 consecutive positive integers is 7 more than 7 times the sum of the same integers. Find both integers.

16-8 Completing the Square

Completing the square makes a quadratic equation into a perfect square trinomial by adding a term to the given equation:

$$x^2 + bx = c$$

To solve a quadratic equation by completing the square: Solve: $x^2 + 6x - 7 = 0$

- Transfer all terms containing "x" to the left side and all other terms to the right side of the equation.

$$x^2 + 6x - 7 = 0$$
$$x^2 + 6x \quad = 7$$

- Find one half of the coefficient of x. Square the result and add it to *both* sides of the equation.

$$6x \rightarrow \tfrac{1}{2} \text{ of } 6 = 3$$
$$3^2 = 9$$
$$x^2 + 6x + 9 = 7 + 9$$

- Rewrite the left side as the square of a binomial.

$$(x + 3)^2 = 16$$

- Take the square root of each side of the equation and solve for x.

$$\sqrt{(x + 3)^2} = \sqrt{16}$$
$$(x + 3) = \pm 4$$
$$x + 3 = {}^+4 \quad AND \quad x + 3 = {}^-4$$
So, $\quad x = {}^+1 \quad AND \quad\quad\quad x = {}^-7$

- Check by substituting each value in the original equation. **Check:**

$$x^2 + 6x - 7 = 0$$

When $x = 1$	When $x = {}^-7$
$(1)^2 + 6(1) - 7 = 0$	$({}^-7)^2 + (6)({}^-7) - 7 = 0$
$7 \quad - 7 = 0$	$49 - 42 - 7 = 0$

Solutions for $x^2 + 6x - 7 = 0$ are: $x = 1 \quad AND \quad x = {}^-7$

Give the number to be added to both sides of each equation.

1. $x^2 - 2x - 5 = 0$ **2.** $x^2 + 4x - 3 = 0$ **3.** $x^2 - 8x - 10 = 0$

4. $x^2 + 5x - 7 = 0$ **5.** $x^2 - 3x - 8 = 0$ **6.** $x^2 - 6x - 4 = 0$

7. $x^2 - x - 7 = 0$ **8.** $x^2 + x - 2 = 0$ **9.** $x^2 - 7x + 5 = 0$

Solve each equation by completing the square.

10. $x^2 + 4x - 21 = 0$ **11.** $x^2 - 3x + 2 = 0$ **12.** $x^2 - 4x - 45 = 0$

13. $x^2 + 5x - 14 = 0$ **14.** $x^2 - 2x - 3 = 0$ **15.** $x^2 - x - 12 = 0$

16. $x^2 + 7x + 12 = 0$ **17.** $x^2 - 3x - 18 = 0$ **18.** $x^2 + x - 20 = 0$

19. $x^2 + 6x - 8 = 0$ **20.** $x^2 + 14x - 11 = 0$ **21.** $x^2 - x - 3 = 0$

Completing the Square If x Has a Coefficient

If x has a coefficient, divide both sides of the equation by this coefficient before completing the square. Study this example.

Solve: $2x^2 - 4x - 8 = 0$ ⟶ $2(x^2 - 2x - 4) = 0$

- Divide by 2. ⟶ $\dfrac{2(x^2 - 2x - 4)}{2} = \dfrac{0}{2}$

  $x^2 - 2x - 4 = 0$

- Rewrite. ⟶ $x^2 - 2x = 4$
- Add $\left(-\dfrac{2}{2}\right)^2 = 1$. ⟶ $x^2 - 2x + 1 = 4 + 1$

  $(x - 1)^2 = 5$

- Find the square root and solve. ⟶ $x - 1 = {}^+\sqrt{5}$ AND $x - 1 = {}^-\sqrt{5}$

  $x = 1 + {}^+\sqrt{5}$ AND $x = 1 + {}^-\sqrt{5}$

Solve each equation by completing the square.

22. $3x^2 - 9x - 6 = 0$ **23.** $4x^2 - 8x + 4 = 0$ **24.** $3x^2 - 12x + 1 = 0$

25. $4x^2 - 24x + 16 = 0$ **26.** $5x^2 - 10x - 10 = 0$ **27.** $7x^2 - 35x + 21 = 0$

28. $8x - x^2 = 3$ **29.** $6x^2 + 24 = 36x$ **30.** $8x^2 - 32 = {}^-4x$

31. $2x^2 + 18x = {}^-5$ **32.** $2x^2 + 8x = {}^-8$ **33.** $3x^2 - 30 = 18x$

34. $5x^2 + 60 = 50x$ **35.** $6x^2 - 12x = {}^-6$ **36.** $2x^2 + 12x = 30$

37. $4x^2 - 24 = 20x$ **38.** $x^2 - 6x = 0$ **39.** $3x^2 - 24x = 0$

Solve. (The first one is done.)

40. The product of two *positive* numbers is 117. The larger number is 4 more than the smaller number. Find the numbers.

Let: x = smaller number Equation: $x(x + 4) = 117$

  $x + 4$ = larger number $x^2 + 4x = 117$

  $x^2 + 4x + 4 = 117 + 4$

  $(x + 2)^2 = 121$

So, $x + 2 = {}^+11$ and $x + 2 = {}^-11$

  $x = {}^+9$ and $x = {}^-13$ ⟵ Not a solution

The numbers are ${}^+9$ and $({}^+9 + 4)$ or ${}^+13$.

41. If a positive number is increased by three times its square, the result is 14. Find the number.

42. If twice the square of a positive number is decreased by the number, the result is 28. Find the number.

43. The square of a positive number decreased by 18 is equal to twice the sum of the number and 15. Find the number.

44. Find two consecutive even numbers whose product equals 288.

471

The Quadratic Formula

The **Quadratic Formula** is used to solve any quadratic equation.

If $ax^2 + bx + c = 0$, and a, b, and c are real numbers and $a \neq 0$, then:

$$x = \frac{^-b \pm \sqrt{b^2 - 4ac}}{2a}$$

Solve: $3x^2 - 5x - 2 = 0 \longrightarrow a = 3$, $b = {}^-5$, and $c = {}^-2$

- Substitute the values for **a, b,** and **c** in the **Quadratic Formula** and solve for **x**.

$$x = \frac{^-b \pm \sqrt{b^2 - 4ac}}{2a}$$

$$x = \frac{^-({}^-5) \pm \sqrt{({}^-5)^2 - 4(3)({}^-2)}}{2(3)} = \frac{5 \pm \sqrt{25 - (4)({}^-6)}}{6} = \frac{5 \pm \sqrt{25 + 24}}{6}$$

Two roots

$$x = \frac{5 \pm \sqrt{49}}{6} \longrightarrow x = \frac{5 + \sqrt{49}}{6} \text{ and } x = \frac{5 - \sqrt{49}}{6}$$

$$x = \frac{5 + 7}{6} = \frac{12}{6} = 2 \text{ and } x = \frac{5 - 7}{6} = \frac{^-2}{6} = \frac{^-1}{3}$$

Solution Set: $\left\{ 2, \dfrac{^-1}{3} \right\}$ or $x = 2$ and $x = \dfrac{^-1}{3}$

- **Check:** For $x = 2$ **AND**   For $x = \dfrac{^-1}{3}$

$3x^2 - 5x - 2 = 0$	$3x^2 - 5x - 2 = 0$
$3(2^2) - 5(2) - 2 \overset{?}{=} 0$	$3\left(\dfrac{^-1}{3}\right)^2 - 5\left(\dfrac{^-1}{3}\right) - 2 \overset{?}{=} 0$
$12 - 10 - 2 = 0$	$3\left(\dfrac{1}{9}\right) + \dfrac{5}{3} - 2 = 0$
	$\dfrac{3}{9} + \dfrac{5}{3} - 2 = 0$
	$\dfrac{1}{3} + \dfrac{5}{3} - 2 = \dfrac{6}{3} - 2 = 0 \rightarrow 2 - 2 = 0$

Use the Quadratic Formula to solve these equations.

1. $3x^2 + x - 2 = 0$
2. $x^2 - 4x - 5 = 0$
3. $6x^2 + x - 2 = 0$
4. $2x^2 - 5x + 2 = 0$
5. $2x^2 + 5x - 3 = 0$
6. $12x^2 + 11x - 15 = 0$
7. $3x^2 - 16x + 5 = 0$
8. $14x^2 - x - 3 = 0$
9. $25x^2 - 10x + 1 = 0$
10. $x^2 - 4x - 45 = 0$
11. $6x^2 - 7x = 0$
12. $49x^2 - 35x + 4 = 0$
13. $x^2 - 11x + 30 = 0$
14. $n^2 - 7n = 0$
15. $a^2 - 6a + 6 = 0$
16. $d^2 - 5d - 3 = 0$
17. $r^2 - 2r - 20 = 0$
18. $y^2 - 18 = 0$

Irrational Numbers as Roots

Some quadratic equations have irrational numbers as solutions or roots.

Solve: $2x^2 + 3x = 1$ $\quad$ Rewrite in quadratic form. $\quad$ $2x^2 + 3x - 1 = 0$

$a = 2$, $b = 3$, $c = {}^-1$

$$x = \frac{{}^-b \pm \sqrt{b^2 - 4ac}}{2a}$$

$$x = \frac{{}^-3 \pm \sqrt{3^2 - 4(2)({}^-1)}}{2 \cdot 2} = \frac{{}^-3 \pm \sqrt{9 + 8}}{4} = \frac{{}^-3 \pm \sqrt{17}}{4} \quad \text{Irrational number}$$

Solution Set: $\left\{ \dfrac{{}^-3 + \sqrt{17}}{4}, \dfrac{{}^-3 - \sqrt{17}}{4} \right\}$ or $x = \dfrac{{}^-3 + \sqrt{17}}{4}$ AND $x = \dfrac{{}^-3 - \sqrt{17}}{4}$

Solve.

19. $x^2 - 4x + 2 = 0$
20. $x^2 - 2x - 10 = 0$
21. $x^2 + 2x - 1 = 0$
22. $9x^2 - 12x + 1 = 0$
23. $x^2 + 5x + 1 = 0$
24. $2x^2 + 7x + 4 = 0$
25. $3x^2 + 2x - 2 = 0$
26. $4x^2 - 12x + 9 = 0$
27. $4x^2 - 4x - 1 = 0$
28. $3x^2 + 2x - 3 = 0$
29. $4x^2 - 2x - 3 = 0$
30. $3x^2 - 4x - 1 = 0$
31. $6x^2 - 8x - 5 = 0$
32. $9x^2 - 6x - 1 = 0$
33. $2x^2 + 10x - 3 = 0$

Solve. (Quadratic equations are not always expressed in terms of x.)

34. $a^2 + 6a - 7 = 0$
35. $3c^2 - 4c - 1 = 0$
36. $x^2 - 8x + 15 = 0$
37. $2g^2 - 2g - 5 = 0$
38. $r^2 + 7r + 12 = 0$
39. $b^2 + 12b + 36 = 0$
40. $d^2 - 3d - 1 = 0$
41. $2v^2 - 5v + 3 = 0$
42. $4a^2 - 2a - 25 = 0$
43. $^-5 = n^2 + 5n$
44. $d^2 - 2d = 9$
45. $2y^2 - 6y + 3 = 0$
46. $2m^2 + 3m - 9 = 0$
47. $3y^2 - 6y + 2 = 0$
48. $2b^2 - 2b = 3$

CHALLENGE

49. The difference between the square of a number and 3 times that number is 4. Find the number. (Hint: Express this as a quadratic equation and solve.)

50. Find two consecutive integers such that twice the square of the first is equal to 4 less than 9 times the second. (Hint: Not every root is usable in the solution of a problem.)

Problem: Sue and Gina live 30 km away from each other. They both leave home at 3:00 PM and bicycle toward each other. If Sue's rate of speed is 20 km/hr and Gina travels at 16 km/hr, at what time will they meet?

Sue   3:00 PM

20 km/hr

30 km   ?

16 km/hr

Gina   3:00 PM

1 IMAGINE   Visualize, then draw and label, two people 30 km away from each other traveling toward each other at different rates.

2 NAME   *Facts:*   30 km — total distance
20 km/hr — rate of speed for Sue
16 km/hr — rate of speed for Gina
3:00 PM — starting time

Question: __?__ hr — for their meeting (implied)
__?__ — time of meeting (stated)

3 THINK   Use the *distance* formula: *distance* = rate × time.

The information given can be organized in a chart. Let x = the time they travel.

The total distance is 30 km.

Sue's distance + Gina's distance = 30 km
     $20x$ + $16x$ = 30 km

Name	Rate	Time	Distance
Sue	20	x	$20x$
Gina	16	x	$16x$

4 COMPUTE   Solve the equation.
$20x + 16x = 30 \longrightarrow$ Add like terms.
     $36x = 30 \longrightarrow$ Divide by 36.
       $x = \dfrac{30}{36} = \dfrac{5}{6}$ hr

Sue and Gina will travel for $\dfrac{5}{6}$ hr, or 50 minutes, before they meet. If they left their homes at 3:00, they will meet at 3:50 PM.

5 CHECK   Substitute $\dfrac{5}{6}$ for x.
     $20x + 16x = 30 \longrightarrow 20\left(\dfrac{5}{6}\right) + 16\left(\dfrac{5}{6}\right) \overset{?}{=} 30$

                           $\dfrac{100}{6} + \dfrac{80}{6} = \dfrac{180}{6} = 30 \longrightarrow 30 = 30$

Make a chart and solve.

1. The Capital City Local leaves the train station at 9:00 AM and averages 40 mph. The Capital City Express leaves the same station at 9:45 and travels at 60 mph. At what time will the express train overtake the local? (Hint: The distance of the local train will equal the distance of the express train.)

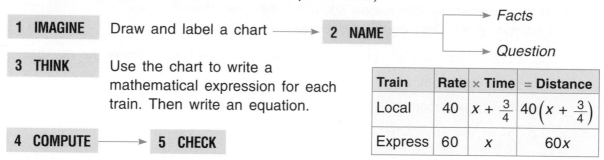

Train	Rate	× Time	= Distance
Local	40	$x + \frac{3}{4}$	$40\left(x + \frac{3}{4}\right)$
Express	60	x	$60x$

2. A round-trip to a wildlife refuge took $16\frac{1}{2}$ hours. If Kim averaged 36 mph going and 30 mph returning, how far away is the refuge? (Hint: The distances are the same.)

Direction	Rate	× Time	= Distance
To	36	x	
From	30	$16\frac{1}{2} - x$	

3. Two campers set out from their tent in opposite directions. Carlos travels due east at 16 km/hr and Juan travels due west at 14 km/hr. Each carries a 2-way radio that has a range of 40 km. For how long will they be able to contact each other by radio? (Hint: The total distance is 40 km.)

4. At the beginning of track season Tina's average time for 1 lap was 55 seconds. At the end of the season her average time for one lap was 49.5 seconds. If her average speed increased by 0.8 m/sec, how long is one lap? (Hint: Let x be Tina's rate at the beginning of the season.)

5. Mrs. Lee left for work at 7:00 AM, she drove at about 30 mph. Twenty minutes later, her husband discovered that she had forgotten her office keys. He got in his car and followed her at 40 mph. How long will it take him to catch up with her? What time will it be?

6. Ken inherited $6000. He would like to invest some of the money at 6% interest and some at 10% interest to yield an annual interest income of $500. How much should he invest at each rate? (Hint: Total interest is $500.)

Investment	× Rate	= Interest
$ x	0.10	?
$6000 − x	0.06	?

7. How many pounds of a Colombian coffee that sells for $5 a pound should be combined with 4 lb of a Brazilian coffee that sells for $4.25 a pound to obtain a blend that sells for $4.75 a pound? (Hint: Total cost = $5x + $17 = $4.75 (4 + x).)

Type	Amount	× Cost/lb	= Total Cost
Colombian	x	$5.00	$5x$
Brazilian	4	$4.25	$17
Blend	$4 + x$	$4.75	$(4 + x)\ $4.75

Number Problems

Find the *positive number* whose square is 45 more than 4 times the number. (Hint: Only one root satisfies this problem.)

Let x equal the number and $4x + 45$ equal 45 more than 4 times the number.

- Write the equation. ⟶ $x^2 = 4x + 45$
- Set the equation equal to 0. ⟶ $x^2 - 4x - 45 = 0$
- Factor the equation. ⟶ $(x - 9)(x + 5) = 0$

$$x - 9 = 0 \text{ and } x + 5 = 0$$
$$x = 9 \qquad\qquad x = -5$$

This is **not** a solution
The solution is a
positive number.

- Check: $x^2 = 4x + 45$
$$(9)^2 \stackrel{?}{=} 4(9) + 45$$
$$81 = 36 + 45$$

Solve.

1. Find two consecutive positive integers whose squares when added equal the sum of 61.

2. Find two consecutive negative integers such that twice the first increased by the square of the second is 46.

3. Two equals twice the square of a certain positive number decreased by 3 times the number. What is the number?

4. The square of a certain positive integer is 21 more than 4 times that integer. What is the integer?

5. If 5 times a certain positive number is increased by the square of the number, the sum is 126. What is the number?

6. When twice the square of a number is decreased by 3 times the number, the result is nine. What is the number?

7. Find two consecutive positive odd numbers whose product is 143.

8. The product of two consecutive even positive integers is 168. What are the integers?

9. Find two consecutive odd integers such that the sum of their squares is 130.

10. Twice the first of two consecutive integers increased by the square of the second is 78. What are the two integers?

11. If 3 times a number is increased by the square of that number, the result is 40. Find the number.

12. Of three consecutive negative integers the square of the smallest is 8 less than twice the square of the largest. What are these integers? (Hint: largest = x, smallest = $x - 2$.)

13. Of three consecutive positive integers the square of the largest is 12 less than the sum of the squares of the two smaller integers. Find the smallest integer.

Geometry Problems

The hypotenuse of a right triangle measures 10 ft. One leg is 2 ft longer than the other leg. Find the length of each leg.

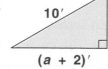
10′   (a)′   (a + 2)′

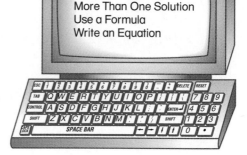
USE THESE STRATEGIES:
Use a Model/Drawing
Logical Reasoning
More Than One Solution
Use a Formula
Write an Equation

- Draw and label the figure.

- Use the Pythagorean theorem to write the equation. $\quad c^2 = a^2 + b^2$

- Substitute and solve.
$$10^2 = a^2 + (a + 2)^2$$
$$100 = a^2 + (a^2 + 4a + 4)$$
$$96 = 2a^2 + 4a$$

- Set the equation equal to 0. $\quad 2a^2 + 4a - 96 = 0$

- Factor completely.
$$2(a^2 + 2a - 48) = 0$$
$$2(a + 8)(a - 6) = 0$$

- Solve for the two values of **a**.
$$(a + 8) = 0 \longrightarrow a = {}^-8$$
$$(a - 6) = 0 \longrightarrow a = {}^+6$$

- Length, a, can only be a positive number. Choose the positive root. $\quad a = {}^+6$

- Now find the value of $(a + 2)$, the other leg. $\quad (a + 2) = 6 + 2 = 8$

- Check by substituting values in $c^2 = a^2 + b^2$
$$c^2 = a^2 + b^2$$
$$(10)^2 \overset{?}{=} (6)^2 + (8)^2 \longrightarrow 100 = 36 + 64$$

14. A rectangle is 5 inches longer than it is wide. The area is 126 square inches. Find the dimensions of the rectangle.

15. A square and rectangle are equal in area. If the length of the rectangle is 3 cm longer than the side of the square and the width is 14 cm less than 3 times the side of the square, what is the area of the square? What are the dimensions of the rectangle?

16. What are the altitude and base of parallelogram WXYZ if its area is 91 cm^2?

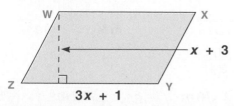
x + 3   3x + 1

17. The height of a parallelogram is 2 in. longer than 3 times its base. If its area is 56 in.^{2}, what are the lengths of its altitude and base?

18. The length of a rectangle is 3 in. more than its width. The area is 54 square inches. Find the length of its diagonal.

19. If the area of trapezoid RSTU is 49 ft^2, what are the lengths of its parallel sides? Of its height?

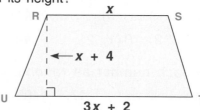
x   x + 4   3x + 2

20. The area of a rectangle is 70 cm^2. Its length is equal to 24 cm decreased by twice its width. Find its dimensions.

21. What are the dimensions of rectangle MNOP if the area is 63 sq in.?

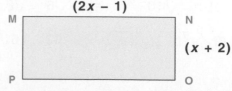
(2x − 1)   (x + 2)

477

More Practice

Identify the slope of each line given two of its points.

1. $C(3, ^-2)$ $D(6, ^-1)$
2. $R(4, 0)$ $S(^-2, 3)$
3. $T(^-1, ^-2)$ $U(^-2, ^-1)$
4. $X(4, ^-3)$ $Y(2, ^-3)$
5. $A(0, 5)$ $B(^-2, 1)$
6. $E(2, ^-1)$ $F(2, 4)$
7. $M(^-4, ^-1)$ $P(0, 1)$
8. $G(^-1, 4)$ $H(1, 6)$
9. $B(^-7, ^-3)$ $R(^-3, 7)$

Express each equation as y in terms of x.

10. $3x + y = 10$
11. $2x - 4y = 10$
12. $y - \dfrac{x}{2} = 3$
13. $5(x - y) = 15$
14. $y - 2 = 3x$
15. $2y - 1 = 3x$
16. $6x + 2y - 8 = 0$
17. $5x - 2y - 4 = 0$
18. $\dfrac{y}{2} + x + 3 = 0$

Identify the slope and y-intercept of each line.

19. $x + y = 3$
20. $x - y = ^-2$
21. $2y = 8 - x$
22. $y = 2 + \dfrac{x}{3}$
23. $3x + y = 4$
24. $2x + 5 = y$
25. $4(x + y) = ^-1$
26. $^-3(x - y) = ^-2$
27. $\dfrac{x + y}{4} = 1$

Tell whether the slope is positive, negative, zero, or undefined.

28. $2x - y = 4$
29. $\dfrac{x}{4} + y = 2$
30. $x = ^-3$
31. $^-5(x - y) = 10$
32. $y = ^-5$
33. $y - x = 7$

Write the equation of each line. Graph each.

34. $m = 2$; $b = ^-3$
35. $m = 3$; $b = 5$
36. $m = \dfrac{1}{2}$; $b = 1$
37. $m = ^-1$; $X(2, 1)$
38. $m = ^-2$; $P(4, 2)$
39. $m = \dfrac{^-1}{3}$; $R(^-2, 4)$
40. $b = 1$; $Y(2, 5)$
41. $b = 0$; $Z(1, 5)$
42. $b = ^-2$; $T(^-1, ^-1)$
43. $A(3, ^-2)$; $B(1, 2)$
44. $L(4, 6)$; $M(2, 0)$
45. $N(^-1, 3)$; $O(3, ^-1)$

Identify each number as *rational* or *irrational*.

46. $\sqrt{40}$
47. $\sqrt{400}$
48. $\sqrt{144}$
49. $\sqrt{120}$

Simplify.

50. $\sqrt{60}$
51. $\sqrt{x^2 y^3}$
52. $\sqrt{75 r^2}$
53. $\sqrt{200a^2 b}$
54. $\dfrac{2\sqrt{8}}{\sqrt{2}}$
55. $\dfrac{\sqrt{20d^2}}{\sqrt{5d}}$
56. $\sqrt{\dfrac{6}{24}}$
57. $\sqrt{\dfrac{mn}{2n}}$
58. $\sqrt{10} \cdot \sqrt{40}$
59. $\sqrt{6} \cdot \sqrt{8}$
60. $\sqrt{3n} \cdot \sqrt{6nt}$
61. $(\sqrt{12m^3}) \cdot (\sqrt{8m})$
62. $(2\sqrt{a^2 b^3})(\sqrt{5a^2 b^3})$
63. $(6\sqrt{5m})(\sqrt{10m^3})$
64. $\sqrt{3c^5} \cdot \sqrt{27c^2}$

Compute.

65. $3\sqrt{2} + 6\sqrt{2}$ **66.** $12\sqrt{6} - 4\sqrt{6}$ **67.** $4\sqrt{2a} + 5\sqrt{2a}$

68. $19\sqrt{8} - 5\sqrt{32}$ **69.** $8\sqrt{27} + 5\sqrt{12}$ **70.** $\sqrt{98} - 7\sqrt{2}$

71. $\sqrt{3}(\sqrt{6} + 4\sqrt{3})$ **72.** $\sqrt{5}(\sqrt{10} + \sqrt{40})$ **73.** $5\sqrt{a}(\sqrt{2a} - \sqrt{3b})$

74. $\sqrt{8}(\sqrt{6m^3} + \sqrt{24m})$ **75.** $\sqrt{a^2b} - a\sqrt{b} + \sqrt{4a^2b}$

76. $(3\sqrt{3} + \sqrt{2})(3\sqrt{3} - \sqrt{2})$ **77.** $(5\sqrt{a} - \sqrt{5})(2\sqrt{a} - \sqrt{5})$ **78.** $(\sqrt{6} + \sqrt{n})^2$

79. $(\sqrt{27} - \sqrt{3})^2$ **80.** $(\sqrt{c} - \sqrt{3b})(2\sqrt{c} + \sqrt{27b})$ **81.** $(\sqrt{m} - 3\sqrt{m})^2$

82. $\sqrt{\dfrac{5}{15a}}$ **83.** $\sqrt{\dfrac{2n}{6n^3}}$ **84.** $\sqrt{\dfrac{3a^3}{8a}}$

85. $\dfrac{5\sqrt{st^2} \cdot 2\sqrt{st}}{4\sqrt{s^2t}}$ **86.** $\dfrac{4\sqrt{6} \cdot r\sqrt{8r}}{3\sqrt{2r}}$ **87.** $\dfrac{8\sqrt{ab} \cdot {}^-4\sqrt{12a}}{2\sqrt{3bc}}$

88. $\dfrac{2\ell}{\sqrt{4\ell^2 + 12\ell + 9}}$ **89.** $\dfrac{3x^2 - 6x}{\sqrt{x^4 - 4x^3 + 4x^2}}$ **90.** $\dfrac{\sqrt{6a} \cdot \sqrt{2a}}{\sqrt{a^3 + 3a}}$

91. $\dfrac{2n\sqrt{12n}}{\sqrt{2n^2}}$ **92.** $\dfrac{3}{\sqrt{a+b}}$ **93.** $\dfrac{n}{\sqrt{m^2 + 2mn + n^2}}$

94. $\sqrt{\dfrac{d^2 + 4d + 4}{d + 2}}$ **95.** $\sqrt{\dfrac{b + c}{b^2 - c^2}}$ **96.** $\sqrt{\dfrac{h^2 - 6h + 9}{h - 3}}$

97. $\dfrac{\sqrt{5a} + \sqrt{10a}}{\sqrt{5a^2}}$ **98.** $\dfrac{\sqrt{24} - \sqrt{6n}}{\sqrt{6n}}$ **99.** $\dfrac{\sqrt{a^3} - \sqrt{ab^2}}{\sqrt{ab^2}}$

Solve using the quadratic formula.

100. $x^2 - 7x + 12 = 0$ **101.** $2x^2 - 5x - 7 = 0$ **102.** $x^2 - 10x = 24$

103. $2x^2 - 4x = 10$ **104.** $2x^2 - 9 = 3x$ **105.** $4x^2 + 4x = {}^-1$

106. $x^2 - 81 = 0$ **107.** $x^2 - 20 = 0$ **108.** $x^2 - 2x - 1 = 0$

Solve by completing the square.

109. $x^2 - 16x - 7 = 0$ **110.** $x^2 - 6x + 2 = 0$ **111.** $x^2 + 2x - 3 = 0$

112. $x^2 - 8x = 0$ **113.** $x^2 + 10x = 0$ **114.** $x^2 + 2x - 4 = 0$

115. $2x^2 + 12x + 8 = 0$ **116.** $3x^2 - 3x - 9 = 0$ **117.** $5x^2 + 35x = {}^-10$

Solve each equation.

118. $3x^2 = 432$ **119.** $x^2 + 3x - 28 = 0$ **120.** $x^2 + 2x = 35$

121. $x^2 - 6x = 0$ **122.** $x^2 - 6x = {}^-7$ **123.** $x^2 - 8x = 18$

124. $x^2 = 24$ **125.** $\dfrac{25}{4} + 5x + x^2 = 0$ **126.** $5x^2 - 1 = 2x$

More Practice

Mixture Problems

Solve. (The first one is done.)

127. A solution of salt water is 8% salt. How much water must be added to the 10 L solution to make it a 5% salt solution?

Let w = the amount to be added. Use this chart.

	Amount	×	Rate	=	Percentage
Original solution	10	×	0.08	=	0.8
New solution	(10 + w)	×	0.05	=	0.5 + 0.05w

Write and solve an equation.

$$0.8 = 0.5 + 0.05w$$
$$100[0.8 = 0.5 + 0.05w]$$
$$80 = 50 + 5w$$
$$80 - 50 = 50 - 50 + 5w$$
$$30 = 5w$$
$$6 = w \quad \text{So, 6 L of water must be added.}$$

128. A party mix is made of pretzels costing $2 a pound and cereal costing $2.40 a pound. If the total mixture costs $2.15 a pound and 4 pounds of party mix were made, how many pounds of each ingredient were bought?

129. A chemist needs 600 ml of a 7.5% solution of acid. There are in the lab 6% and 8% acid solutions. How many ml of each solution should be mixed to make the 7.5% solution?

130. The smaller of 2 pipes takes 3 hours longer than the larger to fill a tank. If both pipes are used, the job can be done in 2 hours. How long will it take the smaller pipe to fill the tank alone?

131. What is the length of the diagonal of a rectangle whose length is 2 cm longer than its width, and whose area is 48 cm^2?

132. A 17-ft ladder leaning against a building reaches a point 15 ft above the ground. How far is the foot of the ladder from the foot of the building?

133. A chemist mixes 10 lb of salt with 40 lb of water. How many pounds of a 50% salt solution must be added to end with a 30% solution?

134. Jose rowed north on a lake for 8 miles. Then he rowed west for 3 miles. How far was he then from his starting point? (Round to nearest tenth of a mile.)

135. A chemist has some 20% salt solution and some 36% salt solution. How many ounces of each should be mixed to produce 160 oz of a solution whose concentration is 30%?

Math Probe

TANTALIZING TAUTOLOGY

> A **tautology** is any compound statement that is
> *always* true, no matter what the truth
> values of the individual statements.

Use a truth table to determine if the following *conditional statement*
is a tautology. Refer to pages 140–143 for help.

$$(p \wedge q) \rightarrow [(p \vee q) \leftrightarrow (p \rightarrow q)]$$

p	q	$(p \wedge q)$	$(p \vee q)$	$(p \rightarrow q)$	$[(p \vee q) \leftrightarrow (p \rightarrow q)]$	$(p \wedge q) \rightarrow [(p \vee q) \leftrightarrow (p \rightarrow q)]$
T	T	T	T	T	T	T
T	F	F	T	F	F	T
F	T	F	T	T	T	T
F	F	F	F	T	F	T

The final column shows that $(p \wedge q) \rightarrow [(p \vee q) \leftrightarrow (p \rightarrow q)]$ is always true.
It is a tautology.

Copy and complete. Tell whether or not each statement is a tautology.

1. $\sim (p \rightarrow \sim q) \leftrightarrow (p \wedge q)$ (Biconditional)

p	q	$\sim q$	$p \rightarrow \sim q$	$\sim(p \rightarrow \sim q)$	$p \wedge q$	$\sim(p \rightarrow \sim q) \leftrightarrow (p \wedge q)$
T	T					
T	F					
F	T					
F	F					

2. $[p \wedge (p \rightarrow q)] \rightarrow q$ (Conditional)

p	q	$p \rightarrow q$	$p \wedge (p \rightarrow q)$	$[p \wedge (p \rightarrow q)] \rightarrow q$
T	T			
T	F			
F	T			
F	F			

3. $[(p \vee q) \wedge (\sim p)] \rightarrow q$ (Conditional)

p	q	$p \vee q$	$\sim p$	$(p \vee q) \wedge (\sim p)$	$[(p \vee q) \wedge (\sim p)] \rightarrow q$

4. $(q \rightarrow p) \wedge (\sim p \rightarrow \sim q)$ (Conjunction)

p	q	$q \rightarrow p$	$\sim p$	$\sim q$	$\sim p \rightarrow \sim q$	$(q \rightarrow p) \wedge (\sim p \rightarrow \sim q)$

Advanced Placement Practice

Choose the correct answer.

1. $\sqrt{20} + 7\sqrt{5}$ can be written in the form $x\sqrt{5}$. Find the value of x.
   a. $11\sqrt{5}$ b. 9 c. 2 d. $5\sqrt{9}$

2. The slope of the line $y = \frac{1}{4}x + 3$ is:
   a. 3 b. 4 c. $\frac{1}{4}$ d. none of these

3. The y-intercept of the graph of the equation $y = 3x - 2$ is:
   a. $^-2$ b. 3 c. 2 d. $^-3$

4. If the sum of $\sqrt{75}$ and $x\sqrt{3}$ is $8\sqrt{3}$, what is the value of x?
   a. 5 b. $\sqrt{25}$ c. 7 d. 3

5. The solution set of the equation $x^2 - 9x + 20 = 0$ is:
   a. $\{^-5, 4\}$ b. $\{^-4, ^-5\}$ c. $\{4, 5\}$ d. $\{^-4, 5\}$

6. The expression $5\sqrt{6}$ is equivalent to:
   a. $\sqrt{30}$ b. $\sqrt{60}$ c. $\sqrt{120}$ d. $\sqrt{150}$

7. $\sqrt{63} - 2\sqrt{7}$ is equivalent to:
   a. $5\sqrt{7}$ b. $\sqrt{7}$ c. $^-\sqrt{7}$ d. none of these

8. What is the slope of the line whose equation is $y - 3x = 5$?
   a. 3 b. $^-3$ c. 5 d. $^-5$

9. The expression $\dfrac{1}{x^2 - 2x - 3}$ is undefined if x is equal to:
   a. $^-3$ and 1 b. $^-1$ and 3 c. 3 d. $^-1$ and $^-3$

10. Which is equivalent to $4\sqrt{3}$?
    a. $\sqrt{12}$ b. $\sqrt{46}$ c. $\sqrt{19}$ d. $\sqrt{48}$

11. What is the positive root of the equation $5x^2 - 45 = 0$?
    a. 9 b. 4 c. 3 d. $\sqrt{50}$

12. The graph of the line passing through $(^-2, ^-4)$ and $(^+3, ^+6)$ has a slope of:
    a. $\dfrac{^-2}{3}$ b. $^+2$ c. $^+\dfrac{1}{2}$ d. $^-3$

13. The lengths of the legs of a right triangle are 6 and 4. Find the length of the hypotenuse.
    a. $2\sqrt{13}$ b. $4\sqrt{13}$ c. $4\sqrt{6}$ d. $2\sqrt{6}$

14. The product of $\sqrt{18}$ and $\sqrt{2}$ is:
    a. $3\sqrt{2}$ b. $9\sqrt{2}$ c. 6 d. $3\sqrt{3}$

15. Which is an irrational number?
    a. $\dfrac{^-1}{6}$ b. $\sqrt{16}$ c. $\sqrt{5}$ d. none of these

16. The sum of the square of a positive integer and 5 is 30. Find the positive integer.
    a. 35 b. $\sqrt{\dfrac{25}{2}}$ c. 5 d. $\sqrt{36}$

17. What is the diagonal of a square whose side equals 4 cm?
    a. $4\sqrt{2}$ b. 8 c. $16\sqrt{2}$ d. $2\sqrt{8}$

Advanced Placement Practice

18. Which line has a negative slope?

    a. $y = {}^-3$ **b.** $x = {}^-3$ **c.** $x + y = {}^-3$ **d.** $x - y = 3$

19. Which line has a slope of 0?

    a. $y = {}^-3$ **b.** $x = {}^-3$ **c.** $x + y = {}^-3$ **d.** $y = 3 + x$

20. Given $m = \dfrac{1}{2}$ and $b = 3$, write the equation of the line.

    a. $2y + x = 6$ **b.** $2y - x = 6$ **c.** $2y - 6x = 1$ **d.** $2y + 6x = 1$

21. Find the slope of $\overline{AB}$ given $A(3, {}^-2)$ and $B(1, 1)$.

    a. $^-1\dfrac{1}{2}$ **b.** $\dfrac{^-2}{3}$ **c.** $1\dfrac{1}{2}$ **d.** 5

22. Which line is parallel to $y = 2x + 3$?

    a. $y = 2x - 8$ **b.** $4 = \dfrac{1}{2}x - 8$ **c.** $y = \dfrac{1}{2}x + 8$ **d.** $y = {}^-2x + 8$

23. Which line is perpendicular to $y = \dfrac{^-1}{3}x + 2$?

    a. $y = \dfrac{1}{3}x + 4$ **b.** $y = 3x - 2$ **c.** $y = {}^-3x - 2$ **d.** none of these

24. When 8 is divided by $\sqrt{2a^2}$ the quotient is:

    a. $\dfrac{4\sqrt{2}}{a}$ **b.** $\dfrac{8\sqrt{2a^2}}{a^2}$ **c.** $\dfrac{8\sqrt{2a^2}}{a}$ **d.** $\dfrac{4\sqrt{2a}}{a}$

25. The product of $\sqrt{3} \cdot 5\sqrt{k}$ is 30. Find the value of k.

    a. 12 **b.** 36 **c.** $2\sqrt{3}$ **d.** $4\sqrt{3}$

26. The product of $\sqrt{3}$ and $7 + \sqrt{3}$ is:

    a. $16\sqrt{3}$ **b.** $7\sqrt{3} + 3$ **c.** $7\sqrt{3} + 6$ **d.** $7\sqrt{3} + 9$

27. Find the solution set for $x^2 - 4x = 21$.

    a. $\{7, {}^-3\}$ **b.** $\{3, 7\}$ **c.** $\{3, {}^-7\}$ **d.** $\{^-3, {}^-7\}$

28. What is the solution set for $x^2 - 5x + 2 = 0$?

    a. $\dfrac{^-5 \pm \sqrt{17}}{2}$ **b.** $\dfrac{5 \pm \sqrt{21}}{2}$ **c.** $\dfrac{^+5 \pm \sqrt{17}}{2}$ **d.** $\dfrac{^+5 \pm \sqrt{33}}{2}$

29. Which points form a line having a slope that is undefined?

    a. $({}^-4, {}^-3)(4, 2)$ **b.** $({}^-2, 4)({}^-3, 4)$ **c.** $(0, {}^-1)({}^-1, 0)$ **d.** $(4, {}^-3)(4, 2)$

Write the equation of each line in exercises 30–35.

30. $m = \dfrac{1}{5}; b = 3$ **31.** $m = {}^-3; b = 0$ **32.** $m = \dfrac{^-2}{3}; b = {}^-1$

33. $m = \dfrac{^+1}{2}; b = {}^-2$ **34.** $m = \dfrac{^-1}{4}; b = 1$ **35.** $m = 2; b = {}^-3$

Compute.

36. $\dfrac{6}{\sqrt{3}}$ **37.** $\dfrac{8}{\sqrt{2n}}$ **38.** $\dfrac{26x^2}{\sqrt{2x}}$ **39.** $\sqrt{\dfrac{2}{3}}$

40. $\sqrt{\dfrac{m^4}{49}}$ **41.** $\sqrt{\dfrac{25}{3}}$ **42.** $2\sqrt{6} + \sqrt{150}$ **43.** $\sqrt{98} - 3\sqrt{2}$

44. $3\sqrt{3b^3} + 2\sqrt{3b}$ **45.** $\sqrt{48} - 2\sqrt{3} + \sqrt{75}$ **46.** $4\sqrt{3} \cdot {}^-2\sqrt{6}$

47. $\sqrt{8} \cdot 3\sqrt{2}$ **48.** $\sqrt{5}\,(16 - \sqrt{5})$ **49.** $\sqrt{7}\,(\sqrt{28} - \sqrt{7})$

Advanced Placement Practice

50. $\dfrac{\sqrt{6m^2}}{\sqrt{12m}}$

51. $\dfrac{5\sqrt{3a^3}}{\sqrt{6a}}$

52. $(3 + \sqrt{2})(4 + \sqrt{2})$

53. $(8 - \sqrt{5})(8 + \sqrt{5})$

54. $(2 + 3\sqrt{7})^2$

55. $(2 - \sqrt{3})(3 + \sqrt{27})$

Find the solution set of each equation.

56. $x^2 - 3x = 0$

57. $n^2 - 6n + 9 = 0$

58. $m^2 - 36 = 0$

59. $9y^2 = 100$

60. $4a^2 + 5a = 6$

61. $10n^2 = 11n - 3$

62. $2m + 8 = m^2$

Solve using the quadratic formula.

63. $n^2 - 6n + 7 = 0$

64. $b^2 - 6b - 6 = 0$

65. $y^2 - 4y + 2 = 0$

66. $2r^2 - 12r + 3 = 0$

67. $x^2 - 5x - 6 = 0$

68. $4a^2 + a = 1$

Solve by completing the square.

69. $a^2 - 20a + 19 = 0$

70. $r^2 - r - 3 = 0$

71. $m^2 + 8m - 3 = 0$

72. $d^2 + d - 7 = 0$

73. $2n^2 - 6n - 8 = 0$

74. $7r^2 + 21r - 42 = 0$

Solve.

75. Of three consecutive *positive* numbers the square of the largest is 18 more than 9 times the smallest. Find the numbers.

76. The sum of the squares of two consecutive positive odd numbers is 34. Find both numbers.

77. The length of a rectangle is 5 cm longer than its width. If the area is 84 cm², find both dimensions.

78. The height of a triangle is 5 ft longer than its base. If its area equals 52 ft², what is the length of its height? (Hint: $A = \dfrac{bh}{2}$.)

79. Find the following for $\triangle STU$:
   a. the base
   b. the altitude
   c. the area

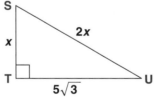

80. The area of a right triangle is 960 cm². If the height is 60 cm, what is the hypotenuse?

81. One leg of a right triangle is 17 cm less than the other. If the hypotenuse is 25 cm, what is the length of each leg?

82. The length of $\overline{RX}$ is 5 cm. What is the area of each shaded region in π units?

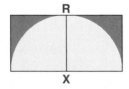

83. The hypotenuse of $\triangle KAR$ is $(7a)$ in. The base is $(3a)$ in. Express the height in radical form, then find the perimeter.

84. Complete, if possible.

a.
p	q	$\sim p \rightarrow q$
T	?	F

b.
p	q	$p \wedge \sim q$
?	F	T

c.
p	q	$p \leftrightarrow q$
?	F	T

Advanced Placement Practice

Advanced Placement-Type Test II

Choose the correct answer.

1. The slope of the line $y = \frac{1}{3}x + 2$ is:

   a. 2   **b.** $\frac{-1}{3}$ **c.** $\frac{1}{3}$ **d.** none of these

2. If the sum of $\sqrt{50}$ and $x\sqrt{2}$ is $9\sqrt{2}$, what is the value of x?

   a. 4   **b.** $\sqrt{6}$ **c.** 9   **d.** 10

3. The expression $6\sqrt{5}$ is equivalent to:

   a. $\sqrt{180}$ **b.** $2\sqrt{60}$ **c.** $\sqrt{30}$ **d.** $\sqrt{60}$

4. What is the slope of the line whose equation is $y - 4x = {}^-1$?

   a. $^-4$ **b.** 4   **c.** $^-1$ **d.** $\frac{1}{4}$

5. Which is equivalent to $\sqrt{147}$?

   a. $7\sqrt{21}$ **b.** $3\sqrt{21}$ **c.** $3\sqrt{7}$ **d.** $7\sqrt{3}$

6. The graph of the line passing through $(^-1, 3)$ and $(^+2, {}^-9)$ has a slope of:

   a. $^-4$ **b.** 4   **c.** $\frac{-1}{4}$ **d.** $\frac{1}{4}$

7. The product of $\sqrt{3a}$ and $\sqrt{12ab}$ is:

   a. $6\sqrt{ab}$ **b.** $\frac{1}{2\sqrt{b}}$ **c.** $\sqrt{36ab}$ **d.** $6a\sqrt{b}$

8. The sum of the square of a positive integer and $^-2$ is 62.
   Find the positive integer.

   a. $\sqrt{60}$ **b.** $2\sqrt{15}$ **c.** 8   **d.** none of these

9. Which line has a negative slope?

   a. $y = {}^-2$ **b.** $x = 2$ **c.** $x + y = {}^-2$ **d.** $x - y = {}^-2$

10. Given $m = \frac{1}{4}$ and $b = 3$, which is the equation of the line?

    a. $\frac{1}{4}y + x = 3$ **b.** $y + \frac{x}{4} = 3$ **c.** $\frac{1}{4}y - x = 3$ **d.** $4y - x = 12$

11. Which line is parallel to $y = 3x + 2$?

    a. $3y = x$ **b.** $y = {}^-3x + 1$ **c.** $y = 3x - 1$ **d.** $y = x + 2$

12. When $3n$ is divided by $\sqrt{12n^3}$ the quotient is:

    a. $\frac{\sqrt{3n}}{2n}$ **b.** $\frac{\sqrt{3}}{2}$ **c.** $\frac{\sqrt{3}}{2n^2}$ **d.** $\frac{\sqrt{3n}}{12n^2}$

13. The product of $\sqrt{12n^3}$ and $\sqrt{2n}$ is:

    a. $2n\sqrt{6n}$ **b.** $2n^3\sqrt{6}$ **c.** $2n^2\sqrt{6}$ **d.** $2\sqrt{6n^4}$

14. What is the solution set for $x^2 - 6x - 5 = 0$?

    a. $3\pm\sqrt{14}$ **b.** $6\pm\sqrt{5}$ **c.** $3\pm\sqrt{4}$ **d.** $\frac{\pm\sqrt{11}}{2}$

15. $\sqrt{27} + 2\sqrt{3}$ can be written in the form $x\sqrt{3}$. Find the value of x.

    a. 3   **b.** $\sqrt{9}$ **c.** 6   **d.** 5

16. The y-intercept of the graph of the equation $y = \frac{1}{2}x - 4$ is:

    a. $^-4$ **b.** $\frac{1}{2}$ **c.** 4   **d.** 2

17. The solution set of the equation $x^2 - 11x = {}^-24$ is:

    a. $\{3, 8\}$ **b.** $\{^-3, {}^-8\}$ **c.** $\{3, {}^-8\}$ **c.** $\{^-2, {}^-12\}$

18. $\sqrt{54} - 2\sqrt{6}$ is equivalent to:

    a. $3\sqrt{6}$ **b.** $\sqrt{42}$ **c.** $\sqrt{6}$ **d.** $3\sqrt{42}$

Advanced Placement-Type Test II

19. The expression $\dfrac{1}{x^2 - 3x - 18}$ is undefined if x is equal to:
    a. 3 and $^-3$ b. 6 and $^-3$ c. $^-3$ and $^-6$ d. 3 and 6

20. What is the positive root of the equation $3x^2 - 48 = 0$
    a. 4   b. $2\sqrt{9}$ c. 8   d. $4\sqrt{6}$

21. The lengths of the legs of a right triangle are both 4 cm.
    Find the length of the hypotenuse.
    a. $4\sqrt{2}$ cm   b. $2\sqrt{2}$ cm   c. $16\sqrt{2}$ cm   d. none of these

22. What is the diagonal of a square whose side equals 6 cm?
    a. $6\sqrt{6}$ cm   b. $6\sqrt{2}$ cm   c. $12\sqrt{3}$ cm   d. $2\sqrt{6}$ cm

23. Which line has a slope of 0?   a. $y = {}^-2$ b. $x = {}^-4$ c. $x - y = 0$ d. $x = 2$

24. What is the y-intercept of $\overleftrightarrow{AB}$ given $A(^-4, 2)$ and $B(1, {}^-8)$.
    a. 2   b. $^-8$ c. $^-6$ d. $^-2$

25. Which line is perpendicular to $y = 3x + 4$?
    a. $y = \dfrac{x}{3}$ b. $y = \dfrac{x}{4} - 4$ c. $y = \dfrac{x}{3} + 4$ d. $y = \dfrac{^-x}{3} + 4$

26. The product of $\sqrt{20} \cdot 3\sqrt{k}$ is 30. Find the value of k.
    a. 5   b. 10   c. $\sqrt{5}$ d. $\sqrt{10}$

27. Find the solution set for $x^2 - 5x = 24$ a. $\{8, {}^-3\}$ b. $\{3, {}^-8\}$ c. $\{^-3, {}^-8\}$ d. $\{8, 3\}$

28. Which points form a line having a slope that is undefined?
    a. $(3, 4)(3, 5)$ b. $(2, 3)(4, 3)$ c. $(^-4, 0)(0, 0)$ d. none of these

29. What value for k will complete the square of the equation: $x^2 - 6x + k = 0$?
    a. 36   b. 9   c. $^-9$ d. 24

30. Which set is a Pythagorean triple?   a. 1, 2, 3   b. 3, $3\sqrt{3}$, 6   c. 7, 7, $\sqrt{3}$ d. all of these

31. What is the square root of $50m^5$?
    a. $250{,}000m^{10}$ b. $5m\sqrt{2m^3}$ c. $5m^2\sqrt{2m}$ d. $10m\sqrt{m^3}$

32. What is the square root of $4a^2 - 20a + 25$?
    a. $2a + 5$ b. $2a - 5$ c. $2a^2 - 5$ d. none of these

33. Find the product of $\sqrt{2}\,(6 + 3\sqrt{2}\,)$.
    a. $6\sqrt{2} + 6$ b. $12\sqrt{2}$ c. $6\sqrt{2} + 3\sqrt{2}$ d. $6\sqrt{2} + 12$

34. Between what two positive integers does $4\sqrt{3}$ lie?
    a. 6 and 7   b. 3 and 4   c. 4 and 5   d. 7 and 8

35. What is the height of an equilateral triangle 8 cm on each side?
    a. $8\sqrt{2}$ cm   b. $4\sqrt{3}$ cm   c. $4\sqrt{2}$ cm   d. $8\sqrt{3}$ cm

36. Find the area of a square $3\sqrt{5}$ cm on each side.   a. 15 cm^2 b. 75 cm^2 c. 30 cm^2 d. 45 cm^2

37. Select the missing head for this table.

p	q	?
T	T	T
T	F	T
F	T	T
F	F	F

    a. $\sim p \wedge q$
    b. $p \longleftrightarrow q$
    c. $p \vee q$
    d. $p \rightarrow q$

Advanced Placement-Type Test II

38. For what value of n will the fraction $\dfrac{7}{3n-6}$ be undefined?

    a. $^-2$ **b.** 2 **c.** 3 **d.** $^-3$

39. Express the difference between $(r-2)^2$ and $2r(3-r)$ as a trinomial.

    a. $^-r^2 + 2r + 4$ **b.** $r^2 - 10r - 4$ **c.** $^-r^2 + 2r$ **d.** $3r^2 - 10r + 4$

40. The expression $\dfrac{3}{(x+2)(x-1)}$ is undefined if x equals:

    a. $(2, 1)$ **b.** $(^-2, ^-1)$ **c.** $(2, ^-1)$ **d.** $(^-2, 1)$

41. If a equals the largest of 3 consecutive integers, which expression represents the smallest?   **a.** $a+2$ **b.** $a-1$ **c.** $a+1$ **d.** $a-2$

42. Which expression is a perfect square trinomial?   **a.** $4m^2 - 49$
    b. $4m^2 - 28m + 49$ **c.** $2m^2 - 14m - 49$ **d.** none of these

43. The product is $10a^2 + ab - 126b^2$. If one factor is $5a + 18b$, what is the other?
    a. $2a - 7b$ **b.** $2a + 7b$ **c.** $2a + 6b$ **d.** $2a - 2b$

44. The sum is $\dfrac{3m+2n}{9}$. If one addend is $\dfrac{5m-n}{15}$ what is the other?

    a. $\dfrac{13n}{45}$ **b.** $\dfrac{^-13n}{45}$ **c.** $\dfrac{30m+13n}{45}$ **d.** none of these

45. If $4s + t$ represents the width of a rectangle and $6s$ represents the length, which binomial represents the perimeter?
    a. $10s + 6st$ **b.** $20s + 2t$ **c.** $20t - 2s$ **d.** $24s^2 + 6st$

46. If $7n - 1$ represents the radius of a circle, which binomial represents the circumference?
    a. $(14n - 2)\pi$ **b.** $(7n - 1)\pi$ **c.** $(14n^2 - 2)\pi$ **d.** $(14n - 1)\pi$

Solve.

47. Working alone a printer completed a job in 20 minutes. A better printer could have done the same job in 12 minutes. How long would it take both printers working together?

48. The sum of the reciprocals of two positive numbers is $\dfrac{7}{24}$. One number is 2 less than the other. Find the numbers.

49. The side of a larger square is 1 m less than twice the side of a smaller square. If the area of the smaller square is 33 m^2 less than the area of the larger square, find the sides of each square.

50. The area of a square is 20 cm^2 less than the area of a rectangle whose length is 2 cm longer than the side of the square and whose width is 5 cm less than twice the side of the square. Find the dimensions of the rectangle.

51. The base of a right triangle is $2\sqrt{23}$ cm. Its hypotenuse is $8\sqrt{2}$ cm. Find its height.

52. Complete the truth table for: $[q \wedge (p \rightarrow q)] \rightarrow p$.

p	q	$p \rightarrow q$	$q \wedge (p \rightarrow q)$	$[q \wedge (p \rightarrow q)] \rightarrow p$
T	T			
T	F			
F	T			
F	F			

Logic Enrichment for Advanced Placement*

Logical Equivalences

Logical Equivalences are two statements that are *always* either both true or both false.

Statement	Symbol		Truth Value
Given Conditional	$p \longrightarrow q$	If the figure is a square, the polygon is a quadrilateral.	True
Converse	$q \longrightarrow p$	If the polygon is a quadrilateral, the figure is a square.	False (not always)
Inverse (negative of conditional)	$\sim p \longrightarrow \sim q$	If the figure is NOT a square, the polygon is NOT a quadrilateral.	False (not necessarily)
Contrapositive (negative of converse)	$\sim q \longrightarrow \sim p$	If the polygon is NOT a quadrilateral, the figure is NOT a square.	True

Logically Equivalent (" $\longleftrightarrow$ " Reads: "if and only if")

Conditional $(p \longrightarrow q)$ $\longleftrightarrow$ Contrapositive $(\sim q \longrightarrow \sim p)$
   Always have the same truth value.

Converse $(q \longrightarrow p)$ $\longleftrightarrow$ Inverse $(\sim p \longrightarrow \sim q)$
   Always have the same truth value.

Biconditionals: statements formed by the conjunction ($\wedge$) of
   the conditionals $p \longrightarrow q$ AND $q \longrightarrow p$.
   These are equivalent when p and q are BOTH true or BOTH false.
   This expressed as:

   $p \longleftrightarrow q$ Read: p if and only if q.

Biconditional	Truth Value	Equivalent Expression	
$p \longrightarrow q \wedge q \longrightarrow p$	T	$p \longleftrightarrow q$	Yes
$p \longrightarrow q \wedge q \longrightarrow p$	F	$p \longleftrightarrow q$	Yes

Let **p** represent "There are 26 letters in the alphabet" and
   q represent "$(2a)(3a) = 5a^2$."

Write a statement for each conditional.

1. $p \longrightarrow q$ 2. $p \longrightarrow \sim q$ 3. $\sim p \longrightarrow q$ 4. $\sim p \longrightarrow \sim q$

5. Name the truth value of each of the conditionals in exercises 1–4.

6. Which exercises 1–4 are logical equivalents? (Hint: Both are true or both are false.)

   Let **p** represent "There are 100 centimeters in 1 meter" and
      q represent "$32°F = 0°C$."

Write the biconditional statement represented by each of the following.

7. $p \longleftrightarrow q$ 8. $p \longleftrightarrow \sim q$ 9. $\sim p \longleftrightarrow q$ 10. $\sim p \longleftrightarrow \sim q$

11. Name the truth value of each statement in exercises 7–10.

Write each statement in symbolic form using the given letters. (The first one is done.)

12. Venus is a planet if and only if the sun is a star. (V, S) $V \leftrightarrow S$

13. Venus is not a planet if and only if the square root of 2 is a rational number. (V,R)

14. Venus is a planet *and* the sun is a star if and only if the square root of 2 is not a rational number. (V, S, R)

15. The square root of 2 is a rational number if and only if Venus is not a planet *and* the sun is not a star. (R, V, S)

Which statement is logically equivalent to each statement given?

16. If I do not study, then I will not do well in school.
   a. If I do not study, then I do well in school.
   b. If I do well in school, then I do study.
   c. If I do not do well in school, then I do study.

17. If a polygon has 4 right angles, then it is a rectangle.
   a. If a polygon does not have right angles, then it is a rectangle.
   b. If a polygon does not have 4 right angles, then it is a rectangle.
   c. If a polygon is not a rectangle, then it does not have 4 right angles.

Copy and complete each truth table.

	p	q	$q \rightarrow p$	$\sim p$	$\sim q$	$\sim p \rightarrow \sim q$
18.	T	T				
19.	T	F				
20.	F	T				
21.	F	F				

22. Which statement is logically equivalent to "If 17 is not a prime number then $|{}^-4| \neq 4$?"
   a. If $|{}^-4| \neq 4$ then 17 is a prime number.
   b. If $|{}^-4| = 4$ then 17 is a prime number.
   c. If $|{}^-4| = 4$ then 17 is not a prime number.

	p	q	$\sim p$	$\sim p \rightarrow q$	$p \lor q$	$\sim p \rightarrow q \leftrightarrow (p \lor q)$
23.	T	T				
24.	T	F				
25.	F	T				
26.	F	F				

27. Which statement is logically equivalent to "If a pentagon does not have 4 sides then a liter equals 10^3 mL?"
   a. A pentagon has 4 sides and a liter equals 10^3 mL.
   b. If a liter does not equal 10^3 mL, then a pentagon does have 4 sides.
   c. A liter does not have 4 sides or a pentagon has 4 sides.

Logic Enrichment for Advanced Placement

Write each statement in symbolic form using the given letters.

28. Ten is not a prime number *or* Ohio is a state if and only if the square of a negative number is negative. (T, O, S)

29. Perpendicular lines form 90° angles if and only if Spain is not in Europe *and* Hawaii is an island. (P, S, H)

Let **p** represent "Two is a prime number,"
  q represent "Two is an odd number," and
  r represent "| $^-2$ | = | $^+2$ |."

Write a statement for each symbol and tell its truth value.

30. $q \longrightarrow p$	**31.** $\sim p \longrightarrow q$	**32.** $(p \land r) \longrightarrow q$
33. $\sim p \longrightarrow \sim r$	**34.** $(p \lor q) \longrightarrow r$	**35.** $(p \land q) \longrightarrow \sim r$
36. $p \longrightarrow (q \land \sim r)$	**37.** $r \longrightarrow (p \land \sim q)$	**38.** $q \longrightarrow (\sim p \lor r)$
39. $\sim p \longrightarrow (r \land p)$	**40.** $(\sim r \longrightarrow p) \land q$	**41.** $(p \lor r) \longrightarrow \sim q$
42. $\sim q \longrightarrow \sim(r \lor p)$	**43.** $r \longrightarrow \sim(p \lor q)$	**44.** $q \longrightarrow \sim(\sim r \lor q)$

Complete the last column of each truth table.

Disjunction

	p	**q**	**?**
45.			
46.	T	T	
47.	T	F	
48.	F	T	
49.	F	F	

Conditional

	p	**q**	**?**
50.			
51.	T	T	
52.	T	F	
53.	F	T	
54.	F	F	

Equivalence

	p	**q**	**?**
55.			
56.	T	T	
57.	T	F	
58.	F	T	
59.	F	F	

Complete each truth table.

60.

p	**q**	$p \lor q$	$p \longrightarrow (p \lor q)$
T	T		
T	F		
F	T		
F	F		

61.

p	**q**	$\sim q$	$p \land \sim q$	$\sim(p \land \sim q)$
T	T			
T	F			
F	T			
F	F			

62.

p	**q**	$\sim p$	$p \land q$	$\sim p \lor (p \land q)$
T	T			
T	F			
F	T			
F	F			

63.

p	**q**	$\sim p$	$\sim p \lor q$	$(\sim p \lor q) \longleftrightarrow p$
T	T			
T	F			
F	T			
F	F			

Logic Enrichment: Advanced Placement Practice

Let p represent "$4 > 8$" and q represent "$12 \leq 15$."
What is the truth value of each of the following?

1. $\sim p$ 2. $\sim q$ 3. $p \wedge q$ 4. $p \vee q$ 5. $p \longrightarrow q$

6. $\sim p \vee q$ 7. $\sim p \wedge q$ 8. $\sim p \longrightarrow q$ 9. $\sim(p \wedge q)$ 10. $\sim(p \vee q)$

Let p represent "$x \cdot x = x^2$"; q represent "$x + x = x^2$."
What is the truth value of each of the following?

11. p 12. q 13. $\sim p$ 14. $\sim q$ 15. $p \longrightarrow q$

16. $p \vee q$ 17. $p \longrightarrow \sim q$ 18. $p \longleftrightarrow q$ 19. $q \longrightarrow \sim p$ 20. $\sim(p \wedge \sim q)$

Choose the correct answer.

21. The symbol for a conjunction is:
    a. $\vee$ b. $\wedge$ c. $\sim$

22. The symbol for a disjunction is:
    a. $\vee$ b. $\wedge$ c. $\sim$

23. The converse of $p \longrightarrow \sim q$ is:
    a. $\sim q \longrightarrow p$ b. $q \longrightarrow \sim p$ c. $\sim p \longrightarrow q$

24. The inverse of $\sim p \longrightarrow q$ is:
    a. $\sim p \longrightarrow \sim q$ b. $p \longrightarrow \sim q$ c. $\sim q \longrightarrow p$

25. The contrapositive of $p \longrightarrow \sim q$ is:
    a. $\sim p \longrightarrow q$ b. $\sim q \longrightarrow p$ c. $q \longrightarrow \sim p$

26. If $p \longrightarrow q$ is false then:
    a. both p and q are true   b. both p and q are false
    c. p is true but q is false

27. If $q \vee \sim p$ is false then:
    a. q is false and $\sim p$ is true   b. both q and $\sim p$ are false
    c. q is true and $\sim p$ is false

28. If p is true and q is false then:
    a. $p \wedge q$ is true   b. $p \wedge q$ is false   c. $p \vee q$ is false

29. Which is logically equivalent to $p \longleftrightarrow r$?
    a. $(r \longrightarrow p) \vee (p \longrightarrow r)$ b. $(p \longrightarrow r) \wedge (r \longrightarrow p)$ c. $(p \longrightarrow r) \wedge (\sim p \longrightarrow r)$

30. Let p represent "x and y are supplementary angles" and q represent "x is an acute angle." Which statement represents "If x and y are supplementary angles, then x is not an acute angle?"
    a. $p \longrightarrow q$ b. $p \longrightarrow \sim q$ c. $\sim(p \longrightarrow q)$

31. Let p represent "$\sqrt{9}$ = a rational number"; q represent "Pi is a rational number" and r represent "3.14 is an irrational number." Which statement represents "$\sqrt{9}$ is a rational number if and only if pi is not a rational number or 3.14 is not an irrational number?"
    a. $p \longleftrightarrow (\sim q \vee \sim r)$ b. $p \longleftrightarrow \sim(q \wedge r)$ c. $p \longleftrightarrow (\sim q \wedge \sim r)$

Logic Enrichment: Advanced Placement Practice

Complete the table for the missing truth value if it can be determined.
a. T **b.** F **c.** can not tell

32.

p	q	p↔q
F	?	F

33.

p	q	p ∨ q
?	T	T

34.

p	q	p→q
F	?	T

35.

p	q	~(p ∨ q)
F	F	?

36.

p	q	~(p ∧ q)
T	?	F

37.

p	q	~p ∨ ~q
?	T	F

Label each truth table: converse, inverse, or contrapositive of $p \rightarrow q$.

38.

p	q	~p	~q	
T	T	F	F	T
T	F	F	T	T
F	T	T	F	F
F	F	T	T	T

39.

p	q	~p	~q	
T	T	F	F	T
T	F	F	T	F
F	T	T	F	T
F	F	T	T	T

40.

p	q	
T	T	T
T	F	T
F	T	F
F	F	T

Complete the heading for the unknown column.

41.

p	q	~q	?
T	T	F	F
T	F	T	T
F	T	F	F
F	F	T	F

a. $p \wedge {\sim}q$
b. $p \rightarrow {\sim}q$
c. $p \vee {\sim}q$

42.

p	q	~p	?
T	T	F	F
T	F	F	T
F	T	T	T
F	F	T	F

a. ${\sim}p \wedge q$
b. ${\sim}p \leftrightarrow q$
c. ${\sim}p \rightarrow q$

43.

p	q	~p	~q	?
T	T	F	F	T
T	F	F	T	T
F	T	T	F	F
F	F	T	T	T

a. ${\sim}p \wedge {\sim}q$
b. ${\sim}p \vee {\sim}q$
c. ${\sim}p \rightarrow {\sim}q$

44.

p	q	~q	?
T	T	F	T
T	F	T	T
F	T	F	T
F	F	T	T

a. ${\sim}q \vee p$
b. $q \vee {\sim}q$
c. ${\sim}(p \vee {\sim}q)$

45.

p	q	~p	p ∨ ~p	?
T	T	F	T	T
T	F	F	T	T
F	T	T	T	T
F	F	T	T	T

a. $q \leftrightarrow (p \vee {\sim}p)$
b. $(p \vee {\sim}p) \leftrightarrow p$
c. $q \rightarrow p \vee {\sim}p$

46.

p	q	~p	?
T	T	F	F
T	F	F	F
F	T	T	T
F	F	T	F

a. ${\sim}p \wedge q$
b. ${\sim}p \vee q$
c. ${\sim}p \rightarrow q$

Final Advanced Placement-Type Test

Choose the correct answer.

1. Solve for n: $37 = 6n - 5$.   **a.** $^-7$ **b.** $^-5$ **c.** 7   **d.** 5

2. Solve for a: $3a - 8 = 5a + 20$.   **a.** $^-14$ **b.** 6   **c.** 14   **d.** $^-6$

3. The perimeter of a square is 20 cm. Find its area.
   a. 16 cm^2 **b.** 400 cm^2 **c.** 25 cm^2 **d.** 10 cm^2

4. Solve for t: $0.06t - 0.3 = 1.2$
   a. 2.5   **b.** 0.25   **c.** 25   **d.** 15

5. If $a = 4$ and $b = {}^-3$, find the value of $\dfrac{2a^2b}{^-6}$.
   a. $^-16$ **b.** 8   **c.** $^-8$ **d.** 16

6. For which inequality is this graph the solution?

   a. $^-4 < 2x < 2$ **b.** $x > {}^-2$ **c.** $x \le 1$ **d.** $x \ge 2$

7. The conditional is always logically equivalent to its:
   a. contrapositive   **b.** converse   **c.** inverse   **d.** none of these

8. From $2ab - 3b^2$ take $7b^2 - 3ab + 1$.   **a.** $10b^2 - 5ab + 1$
   b. $^-10b^2 + 5ab - 1$ **c.** $10b^2 + 5ab + 1$ **d.** $4b^2 - 5ab + 1$

9. Which is a rational number?   **a.** $\sqrt{60}$ **b.** π **c.** 3.14   **d.** none of these

10. What is the value of $\dfrac{6!}{4!}$?   **a.** 30   **b.** 2   **c.** 3   **d.** 20

11. What is the median of: 16, 18, 14, 15, 18, 13?
    a. $15.\overline{6}$ **b.** 18   **c.** 15   **d.** 15.5

12. For what value of b will the expression $\dfrac{8}{3b - 12}$ be meaningless?
    a. $^-4$ **b.** $^-3$ **c.** 4   **d.** 3

13. The expression of $\sqrt{300}$ is equal to:
    a. $3\sqrt{10}$ **b.** $10\sqrt{3}$ **c.** $100\sqrt{3}$ **d.** $3\sqrt{100}$

14. The circumference of a circle is 6π ft. Find the area.
    a. 9π ft^2 **b.** 36π ft^2 **c.** 12π ft^2 **d.** 6π ft^2

15. The product of $6a^2b$ and $^-3ab^2c$ is:
    a. $18a^2b^2c$ **b.** $^-18a^2b^2c$ **c.** $^-18a^3b^3c$ **d.** $18a^3b^3c$

16. The y-intercept of the equation $3x - y + 3 = 0$ is:
    a. 3   **b.** $^-3$ **c.** 2   **d.** $^-2$

17. Solve for c: $\dfrac{c + 4}{16} = \dfrac{2c - 1}{20}$.   **a.** 8   **b.** $^-8$ **c.** 4   **d.** $^-4$

18. Biconditional statements are equivalent when:
    a. p is true and q is false.   **c.** p is false and q is true.
    b. p and q are both true or both false.   **d.** none of these

19. Select the missing head for this table.

p	q	?
T	T	F
T	F	T
F	T	F
F	F	F

    a. $\sim p \wedge q$
    b. $p \wedge \sim q$
    c. both a and b
    d. none of these

Final Advanced Placement-Type Test

20. What is the largest integer that satisfies the inequality $2x - 1 < {}^-3$?
    a. $^-1$ **b.** $^-2$ **c.** 0   **d.** 1

21. Sneakers come in 3 colors and 2 styles. How many different purchase options are available?
    a. 6   **b.** 5   **c.** 3   **d.** 8

22. What is the slope of the graph of the equation $2x - y = 4$?
    a. 2   **b.** 4   **c.** $^-1$ **d.** $^-2$

23. Solve for y: $x + y = 8$ and $x - y = 2$.
    a. 3   **b.** $^-3$ **c.** 5   **d.** $^-5$

24. Solve the inequality $2m - 7 \leq {}^-1$ for m if the replacement set is the set of integers.
    a. $m \leq 4$ **b.** $m \leq 3$ **c.** $m \leq {}^-4$ **d.** $m \geq {}^-3$

25. From four cards labeled NINE a card is drawn and returned, and then another card is drawn. Find $P(\text{N}, \text{E})$.
    a. $\dfrac{1}{8}$ **b.** $\dfrac{1}{6}$ **c.** $\dfrac{2}{8}$ **d.** $\dfrac{2}{6}$

26. Solve this system of equations for y: $2x + 4y = 7$ and $2x + 6y = 19$
    a. 6   **b.** $^-13$ **c.** $^-6$ **d.** 13

27. If all entries under the column heading $(p \wedge q) \longrightarrow (q \vee \sim q)$ are true, then this statement is:
    a. a conjunction   **b.** biconditional   **c.** a tautology   **d.** none of these

28. Which of the following is the graph of a parabola?
    a. $y = x^2 + 3$ **b.** $y = 3x - 2$ **c.** $y = 3x + 2$ **d.** $y = \dfrac{x}{2} - 3$

29. Factor: $x^2 + 2x - 24$.
    a. $(x - 6)(x - 4)$ **b.** $(x - 6)(x + 4)$ **c.** $(x + 6)(x + 4)$ **d.** $(x + 6)(x - 4)$

30. Find the positive root of $3n^2 - 75 = 0$.
    a. 25   **b.** $^-5$ **c.** 5   **d.** $5\sqrt{3}$

31. Factor: $16 - a^2b^2$.
    a. $(8 - ab)^2$ **b.** $(8 + ab)(8 - ab)$ **c.** $(4 + ab)(4 - ab)$ **d.** $(4 - ab)^2$

32. Find the sum in simplest form: $\dfrac{2d}{3} + \dfrac{4d}{6}$.
    a. $\dfrac{4d}{3}$ **b.** $\dfrac{8d}{6}$ **c.** $\dfrac{4d}{6}$ **d.** $\dfrac{6d}{9}$

33. The difference of $\sqrt{48}$ and $\sqrt{27}$ is:
    a. $\sqrt{21}$ **b.** $\sqrt{9}$ **c.** $\sqrt{3}$ **d.** $\sqrt{6}$

34. Which of the following is not the graph of a straight line?
    a. $y = x^2$ **b.** $4x + 6 = 12$ **c.** $2x + 4 = 8$ **d.** $3x - y = 4$

35. One angle of a triangle is $40°$. Another is one third the largest. Find the largest.
    a. $105°$ **b.** $35°$ **c.** $120°$ **d.** $110°$

36. If $83\frac{1}{3}\%$ of a number is 25, what is the number?
    a. 1.2   **b.** 36   **c.** 20.8   **d.** 30

37. Solve for x: $7x + 4y = 10$ and $6x + 4y = 3$.
    a. 7   **b.** 14   **c.** 13   **d.** 0

Final Advanced Placement-Type Test

38. Find the product of $(3x + 4)(2x - 5)$.   **a.** $6x^2 - 23x + 20$
   b. $6x^2 - 7x - 20$ **c.** $6x^2 - 23x - 20$ **d.** $6x^2 + 7 - 20$

39. A team won 9 games and lost 3. What is the ratio of wins to games played?
   a. $\dfrac{1}{3}$ **b.** $\dfrac{3}{4}$ **c.** $\dfrac{4}{3}$ **d.** $\dfrac{3}{1}$

40. In which set of data are mean and mode the same?
   a.   18, 16, 16, 17   **b.**   16, 18, 17, 18   **c.**   16, 17, 17, 18   **d.**   none of these

41. Which equation is the graph of a horizontal line?   **a.** $x + 1 = 7$
   b. $y - 2 = 4$ **c.** $y^2 = 36$ **d.** $x^2 = 36$

42. What is the solution set of $x^2 - x - 12$?   **a.** $\{^-3, {}^-4\}$
   b. $\{3, {}^-4\}$ **c.** $\{3, 4\}$ **d.** $\{^-3, 4\}$

43. Find $m\angle MXR$ if $\overline{XM} \parallel \overline{SR}$.   **a.** $110°$
   b. $120°$ **c.** $30°$ **d.** $130°$

44. Two complementary angles have a ratio of 4 : 1. Find the smaller angle.
   a. $18°$ **b.** $36°$ **c.** $72°$ **d.** $20°$

45. What is the result of $45m^3n^5$ divided by $3mn^3$?
   a. $15m^2n$ **b.** $15m^3n^2$ **c.** $15m^2n^2$ **d.** $15m^4n^8$

46. The expression $\dfrac{1}{x^2 + x - 30}$ is undefined for what values?
   a. $^-5$ and 6 **b.** $^-5$ and $^-6$ **c.** 5 and 6 **d.** 5 and $^-6$

47. The sum of $\sqrt{50}$ and $n\sqrt{2}$ is $11\sqrt{2}$. Find n.
   a. 11 **b.** 6 **c.** $^-14$ **d.** $^-6$

48. For which inequality would the boundary line be a dotted line?
   a. $y - 4x \leq 7$ **b.** $7x - 3y \leq 2$ **c.** $y - 4x > 7$ **d.** $x + 4y \geq {}^-2$

49. $WXYZ$ is a square. The coordinates of two of its vertices are $W(^-1, {}^-2)$, $X(^-1, 3)$. What is its perimeter?
   a.   16 units   **b.**   25 units   **c.**   18 units   **d.**   20 units

50. What is the graph of $3x - 5 < 1$?   **a.**
   b.   **c.**   **d.**   none of these

51. If 0.0000365 is written as 3.65×10^n, what is the value of n?
   a.   5   **b.** $^-6$ **c.** $^-5$ **d.** $^-6$

52. If $12m - 3$ represents the perimeter of an equilateral triangle, which expression represents one side?
   a. $4m + 1$ **b.** $4m - 1$ **c.** $24m - 9$ **d.** $36m - 9$

53. Divide $18c^3d^2 + 24c^2d^3 - 9d^4$ by $3d^2$.   **a.** $6c^3d + 8c^2d^2 - 3d^2$
   b. $6c^3 + 8c^2d - 3d^2$ **c.** $6c^3 + 8c^2d^2 - 3d^2$ **d.** $6cd + 8cd^2 - 3d^2$

54. If y varies directly as x and $y = 36$ when $x = 9$, find y when $x = 7$.
   a.   28   **b.**   63   **c.**   21   **d.**   11

55. From five cards labeled EIGHT a card is drawn and not returned, and then another card is drawn. What is $P(T, \text{a vowel})$?
   a. $\dfrac{1}{10}$ **b.** $\dfrac{2}{25}$ **c.** $\dfrac{3}{5}$ **d.**   none of these

Final Advanced Placement-Type Test

Answer 9 questions from this part. Show all the work.

56. Solve algebraically and graph the equations
$x = 3y + 4$ and $x + y = {}^-8$.

58. The square of a negative number increased
by twice that number is 35. Find the number.

59. Graph the solution set of $2x - y > 5$
and $x + \dfrac{y}{2} \leq 3$.

60. Solve and graph: ${}^-3 < 2x + 1 < 5$.

62. One painter takes twice as long as another
to paint a room. Together they could have
painted the room in $2\dfrac{2}{3}$ hours. How long
would it take each painter working alone?

64. In a video game for a hit 25 points are
gained and for a miss 10 points are lost.
If out of 20 shots 45 points were scored
how many hits were made?

65. The area of a trapezoid $PQRS$ is
16 cm² less than the area
of square $WXYZ$. What is the area
of each figure?

57. A purchase totalling $\$2.55$ was paid for
in coins. There were some nickels, 1 less
dime than nickels, and 1 more quarter
than nickels.
   a. How many nickels were there?
   b. What was the total number of coins?

61. The legs of a right triangle are 4 cm
and 12 cm.
   a. Find the hypotenuse.
   b. Find the perimeter.

63. $CDEF$ is a square. The coordinates of
two of its vertices are $C({}^-1, {}^-2)$
and $D({}^-1, 3)$.
   a. Find its perimeter.
   b. Find the length of $\overline{CE}$.
   c. Find its area.

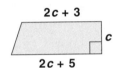

66. An isosceles right triangle ABC is inscribed
in circle P. The circumference is $8\sqrt{2}\,\pi$ cm.
   a. Find the length of $\overline{AB}$.
   b. Find the length of $\overline{AC}$.
   c. Find the area of $\triangle ABC$.
   d. Find the perimeter of $\triangle ABC$ in radical form.
   e. Find the area of the shaded region.

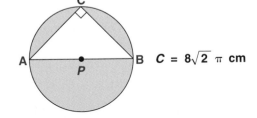

$C = 8\sqrt{2}\,\pi$ cm

67. The perimeter of this parallelogram is 48 inches.
   a. Solve for r.
   b. Find its dimensions.
   c. Find the length of $\overline{DF}$.
   d. Find its area.

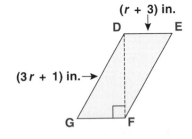

68. A solution of cooking oil contains 25% saturated fat.
How many milliliters of unsaturated fat can be added
to 120 mL of the solution to get a mixture which is
only 20% saturated fat?

69. Complete each truth table by choosing one of these answers:
T (True)   F (False)   Cannot be determined.

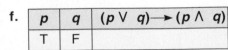

a.

p	q	$\sim p \rightarrow q$
?	T	F

b.

p	q	$p \leftrightarrow q$
T	?	F

c.

p	q	$\sim p \vee q$
T	?	F

d.

p	q	$\sim (p \vee q)$
F	?	T

e.

p	q	$p \wedge \sim q$
?	T	F

f.

p	q	$(p \vee q) \rightarrow (p \wedge q)$
T	F	

Final Advanced Placement-Type Test

Still More Practice

CHAPTER 1

Practice 1-1

Give the place value of the underlined digit.

1a. 2<u>6</u>,847,500   **b.** 0.062<u>4</u>

Compare. Write <, =, or >.

2a. 38,454 <u> ? </u> 38,545

 b. 0.173 <u> ? </u> 0.317

Order from least to greatest.

3a. 0.207, 0.2, 0.027, 0.127

 b. 3.064, 3.64, 3.604, 3.416

4a. 73,289 + 9,981   **b.** 27,683 + 6,104

5a. 49.3 + 13.05   **b.** 104 + 9.7

6a. $6.74 + $3.95   **b.** $32.04 + $58.67

7. Through the resourcefulness of the mayor, a city saved $16,867,304. Round this number to the nearest million.

8. How much less than 340,569 is 330,569?

9. In 1980 the population of a city was 6,974,755; in 1990 the population increased by 102,328. What was the 1990 population?

10. Pamela cut three pieces 10.4 m, 12.6 m, and 8.5 m long from a bolt of material. How much fabric did she use?

Practice 1-2

1a.   6,401,362
     − 832,549

b.   2,000,000
     − 989,123

2a. 42,107 − 29,658   **b.** 804,720 − 1,867

3a.   9.786
      −7.893

b.   8.7014
      −2.6538

4a. 100.4 − 23.6   **b.** 8 − 2.7

 c. $50 − $23.69   **d.** $80.25 − $62.07

5a. 5092 × 608   **b.** 32,108 × 260

6a.   0.005
       × 0.83

b.   9.8
       ×0.5

 c. 0.17 × 67   **d.** 2.8 × 4.8

7. The morning volume of stock exchanged was 1,340,582. At noon, it dropped 25,479 shares, then increased 305,353. What was the closing volume?

8. At a sporting goods store, Tom bought items priced at $34.95, $14.75, $2.69, and $5.35. Round the numbers to estimate his bill.

9. Ralph made four trips. He recorded these distances: 0.6 km, 1.4 km, 2.5 km, and 0.8 km. Estimate the total distance.

10. Tim is 162.5 cm tall. How much shorter is he than John, who is 168.04 cm tall?

Practice 1-3

Estimate. Write < or >.

1a. 2068 ÷ 47 <u> ? </u> 40

 b. 1840 ÷ 1000 <u> ? </u> 2

 c. 56 ÷ 0.07 <u> ? </u> 80

2a. 6300 ÷ 70   **b.** 1224 ÷ 40

3a. 47,606 ÷ 79   **b.** 86,112 ÷ 416

4a. 64)‾1536   **b.** 0.05)‾0.385

5a. 13,566 ÷ 1.9   **b.** 1722 ÷ 0.42

6a. 0.389 ÷ 0.08   **b.** 85.2 ÷ 0.6

7. Estimate the cost of 32 hamburgers at $1.85 each.

8. Which is greater: 0.05 × 0.3 or 0.3 × 0.5?

9. Multiply 0.078 by 10 and add 0.06.

10. A package of 8 lamb chops weighs 5.42 kilograms. What is the average weight of 1 lamb chop?

CHAPTER 2

Practice 2-1

Give an equivalent fraction.

1a. $\frac{5}{7} = \frac{?}{35}$ **b.** $\frac{3}{4} = \frac{27}{?}$

Change to a whole or mixed number.

2a. $\frac{36}{8}$ **b.** $\frac{60}{5}$

Write each fraction as a decimal.

3a. $\frac{7}{20}$ **b.** $\frac{2}{9}$

Compare. Write <, =, or >.

4a. $\frac{3}{5}$? $\frac{1}{3}$ **b.** $\frac{1}{4}$? $\frac{2}{9}$

List the prime numbers.

5a. 2, 7, 8, 19   **b.** 23, 24, 27, 29

Write the factors.

6a. 18   **b.** 48   **c.** 72

Write the prime factors, using exponents.

7a. 64   **b.** 108

8a. 200   **b.** 120

9. Dan used $\frac{3}{8}$ yd of tape on a ball. Peter used $\frac{5}{16}$ yd. Who used more tape?

10. Which of these fractions is in simplest form: $\frac{18}{36}$ or $\frac{17}{33}$?

Practice 2-2

Find the LCD.

1a. $\frac{1}{18}, \frac{1}{24}$ **b.** $\frac{1}{6}, \frac{1}{9}$

Write the least common multiple.

2a. 10, 12   **b.** 8, 9

c. 9, 15, 30   **d.** 21, 63, 126

Add or subtract.

3a. $\frac{1}{4} + \frac{2}{5}$ **b.** $\frac{5}{12} - \frac{1}{18}$

4a. $4\frac{2}{5} + 7\frac{1}{6}$ **b.** $13\frac{5}{6} - 7\frac{2}{5}$

5a. $3\frac{1}{3} - 1\frac{1}{8}$ **b.** $7\frac{4}{5} - \frac{2}{3}$

6a. $12 - \frac{3}{8}$ **b.** $20 - 9\frac{3}{4}$

7. How much less than $8\frac{1}{7}$ is $4\frac{3}{5}$?

8. From 12, subtract the sum of $2\frac{1}{2}$ and $4\frac{3}{4}$.

9. Increase $12\frac{7}{9}$ by $4\frac{2}{3}$.

10. How much greater is $10\frac{2}{9}$ than $4\frac{4}{5}$?

Practice 2-3

Write the common factors.

1a. 16, 24   **b.** 36, 54

Write the greatest common factor.

2a. 16, 48   **b.** 18, 36

c. 15, 32   **d.** 42, 24

Multiply.

3a. $8 \times 1\frac{3}{4}$ **b.** $4\frac{2}{5} \times 15$

4a. $3\frac{2}{9} \times 2\frac{4}{7}$ **b.** $1\frac{1}{6} \times 1\frac{5}{7}$

Write the reciprocal.

5a. $\frac{5}{6}$ **b.** $\frac{9}{7}$

6a. $\frac{1}{3} \div \frac{1}{6}$ **b.** $\frac{3}{8} \div \frac{1}{4}$

7a. $3\frac{9}{11} \div \frac{6}{7}$ **b.** $\frac{3}{8} \div 4\frac{1}{2}$

c. $6 \div 2\frac{1}{4}$ **d.** $\frac{6}{7} \div 12$

Estimate and compare. Write <, =, or >.

8a. $6 \div 2\frac{1}{2}$? $2\frac{1}{2} \div 6$

b. $1 \div 2\frac{1}{2}$? $1 \div \frac{1}{2}$

9. Subtract $4\frac{9}{10}$ from the quotient of $2\frac{1}{2}$ divided by $\frac{1}{10}$.

10. Multiply $4\frac{1}{3}$ by 12 and divide the product by $\frac{2}{3}$.

CHAPTER 3

Practice 3-1

Simplify. Follow the order of operations.

1a. $16 + 4 \times 3 + 4$ **b.** $7 + 7 \div 7 - 7$

2a. $(7 - 0.3) \times (4.1 + 0.6)$

  b. $6 + 2.3 \times 4$

3a. $30(5 - 2) + 10$

  b. $3(28 - 17) - 15 \div 5$

4a. $\dfrac{24 - 8}{50 - 46} + 9 \times 0 + 3$

  b. $\dfrac{36 + 14}{18 + 7} + 7 \times 6 - 4$

5a. $3[9(42 - 38) - 3 \times 6]$

  b. $4[(16 - 4) + 3(8 + 9) - 50]$

Write a mathematical expression for each of the following:

6a. 7 more than a number

  b. a number decreased by 3

7a. 5 times a number increased by 6

  b. the quotient of a number and 9

Find the value of the expression when $a = 6$, $b = 7$, $c = 4$.

8a. $a + 18$ **b.** $24 - b$

9a. $4a - b + 5c$ **b.** $\dfrac{1}{2b} \div a$

10. When $n = 3$ and $p = 6$, evaluate $9n - 20 + 9p$.

Practice 3-2

Solve and check.

1a. $4 + x = 13$ **b.** $n + 5 = 14$

2a. $s - 16 = 11$ **b.** $t - 8 = 9$

3a. $c + 20 = 32$ **b.** $d - 12 = 8$

4a. $y - 25 = 5$ **b.** $r + 16 = 24$

5a. $14 = 6 + a$ **b.** $8 = n - 7$

Write an equation and solve.

6. Seven more than a number is 13. What is the number?

7. A number decreased by 12 is 32. What is the number?

8. The sum of 46 and a number is 69. What is the number?

9. Six less than a number is 91. What is the number?

10. A number increased by 21 is 50. What is the number?

Practice 3-3

Solve the equation and check.

1a. $8n = 72$ **b.** $4x = 120$

2a. $\dfrac{t}{4} = 6$ **b.** $\dfrac{s}{25} = 4$

3a. $7 + 8n = 55$ **b.** $2n - 8 = 100$

4a. $\dfrac{n}{5} + 6 = 14$ **b.** $6 + \dfrac{n}{12} = 14$

5a. $\dfrac{a - 8}{3} = 5$ **b.** $\dfrac{t + 6}{5} - 3 = 8$

Write an equation and solve.

6. Twice a number is 64. What is the number?

7. The quotient of a number and 4 is 12. Find the number.

8. A number divided by 9 is 6. What is the number?

9. One number is 23 more than 4 times another number. Find the smaller number if the greater number is 51.

10. 8 less than 5 times a number is 22. What is the number?

11. The product of a number and 9 is increased by 16. If the result is 115, what is the number?

Practice 3-4

List the members of these sets:

1a. even numbers between 10 and 20

  b. multiples of 7 less than or equal to 35.

Use {1, 3, 5, 7, ..., 35} as the replacement set to find the solution set:

2a. $m \leq 5$ **b.** $c > 20$

3a. $x \neq 1$ **b.** $a \geq 36$

Solve for the missing variable.

4. $P = 2\ell + 2w$ when $P = 28'$ and $w = 5'$

5. $A = bh$ when $A = 48$ m^2 and $h = 6$ m

6. $C = 2\pi r$ when $r = 14$ cm and $\pi \approx \frac{22}{7}$

Solve using formulas.

7. A high speed French train travels 200 mph. If the distance between two cities is 344 miles, how long will it take the train to travel this distance? ($D = rt$)

8. How long will it take $1106 to earn $300 at 4% a year? ($I = prt$)

Solve using equations.

9. Gonzo the gorilla weighs 85 pounds less than twice the weight of Harry the Hippo. If Gonzo weighs 1010 pounds, how much does Harry weigh?

10. Angie baked 60 brownies for the school fair. She packed 24 of them away before going to the phone. Her little brothers ate $\frac{1}{4}$ of the brownies she left out. How many brownies did Angie have for the fair?

Practice 3-5

Write the opposite of each integer.

1a. $^-4$ **b.** $^-8$

2a. $^-15$ **b.** $^+28$

Compare. Write < or >.

3a. $^-8$ _?_ $^+7$ **b.** $^+4.1$ _?_ $^-1.06$

Add.

4a. $^-8 + {}^+2$ **b.** $^-35 + {}^+16$

5a. $^-25 + {}^-15$ **b.** $^-6 + {}^-3$

6a. $^-6 + {}^-14$ **b.** $^-17 + {}^-9$

Subtract.

7a. $^-7 - {}^-4$ **b.** $^-12 - {}^-6$

8a. $^-15 - {}^-8$ **b.** $^+21 - {}^-14$

9a. $^-7 - {}^+7$ **b.** $^-2 - {}^+4$

Write an equation and solve.

10a. What number is $^-8$ less than $^-15$?

  b. A number added to $^+7$ is $^-13$. Find the number.

Practice 3-6

Multiply.

1a. $^+6 \times {}^+8$ **b.** $^-12 \times {}^+4$

2a. $^-3 \times {}^+10$ **b.** $^-13 \times {}^-5$

3a. $^-26 \times {}^-3$ **b.** $^-25 \times 0$

Divide.

4a. $^+42 \div {}^+7$ **b.** $^+81 \div {}^+9$

5a. $^-56 \div {}^-8$ **b.** $^-70 \div {}^-5$

6a. $^+320 \div {}^-16$ **b.** $^-140 \div {}^+70$

Solve.

7a. $m \div {}^+8 = {}^+3$ **b.** $r \div {}^-2 = {}^-10$

8a. $\frac{d}{^-4} = {}^+11$ **b.** $\frac{x}{^+7} = {}^-3$

9a. $^-4a = {}^-28$ **b.** $^+7n = {}^-35$

10a. $^-3a + 1 = {}^+13$ **b.** $^+2b - 1 = 11$

CHAPTER 4

Practice 4-1

Identify the number property shown.

1a. $4(0.3 + 1.2) = 4(0.3) + 4(1.2)$

b. $5 + (7 + 2) = (5 + 7) + 2$

c. $^-4 \times 1 = ^-4$ **d.** $\frac{1}{5} \times 5 = 1$

Solve. Identify the number property used.

2a. $8.3 + (0.7 + 0.2) = (8.3 + n) + 0.2$

b. $^-7.6 + 4.1 = n + ^-7.6$

c. $n\left(\frac{1}{2} + \frac{^-1}{4}\right) = 6\left(\frac{1}{2}\right) + 6\left(\frac{^-1}{4}\right)$

Name the opposite of each rational number.

3a. $^-5\frac{1}{3}$ **b.** $^-0.2$ **c.** $^+6.4$

Compute.

4a. $^+2.3 + ^-4$ **b.** $^-1.6 + ^-5.7$

5a. $^-0.3 - ^+1.2$ **b.** $^+15 - ^+3.2$

6a. $^+3.8 + ^-4.1 = n$ **b.** $^-6.2 - ^-2.6 = n$

7a. $^-3\frac{1}{4} + ^-1\frac{1}{2}$ **b.** $^+2\frac{1}{3} + ^-4$

8a. $^-7 - ^-3\frac{2}{3}$ **b.** $^+8\frac{4}{5} - ^-1\frac{1}{10}$

9. After falling $3.5°C$ the temperature was $5.3°C$. What was the starting temperature?

10. Stocks worth $^+8\frac{1}{4}$ changed $^-1\frac{3}{8}$ points. What was the final value?

Practice 4-2

1a. $^+6.7 + ^-4.2 = a$ **b.** $^-0.7 - ^+1.2 = r$

2a. $^+3\frac{1}{3} - ^-1\frac{1}{6} = n$ **b.** $^-7 - ^+6\frac{2}{5} = t$

3a. $n + ^+1.4 = ^-0.6$ **b.** $m + ^-2\frac{1}{2} = 5$

4a. $x - ^-4.2 = ^-10$ **b.** $a - ^-4.2 = ^+10$

5a. $d - \frac{3}{4} = ^+2\frac{1}{8}$ **b.** $b - ^-4.1 = ^+5.9$

6a. $20 - x = ^-2.5$ **b.** $x + ^-8 = ^+3.5$

Write an equation and solve.

7. A bookstore sold 515 books last month. 36 books were returned for credit. On how many books did the bookstore actually profit?

8. You deposited $10.60 in the bank, withdrew $4.25, and later withdrew $2.15. What is the net result of these transactions?

9. In 3 successive games, Helen lost 9 points. What was her total number of points lost?

10. Maureen paid $.85 each for 4 felt pens. What did the pens cost her?

Practice 4-3

Multiply.

1a. $^+6 \times ^+8\frac{1}{3}$ **b.** $^-12 \times ^+4\frac{1}{2}$

2a. $^-5 \times ^-7.6$ **b.** $^-20 \times ^+6.5$

3a. $^-3 \times \frac{^-5}{6}$ **b.** $^-2\frac{1}{2} \times ^+2\frac{1}{2}$

4a. $\frac{^+3}{4} \times \frac{^-8}{9}$ **b.** $^-1\frac{1}{3} \times 0$

5a. $^+1.4 \times 9$ **b.** $^-2.2 \times ^-0.2$

6a. $\frac{^-1}{4} \div \frac{^-1}{5}$ **b.** $^+15 \div ^-3\frac{1}{5}$

7a. $^-1\frac{3}{4} \div ^+21$ **b.** $^-7\frac{1}{7} \div ^-7\frac{1}{7}$

8a. $\frac{^+7.2}{^-8}$ **b.** $\frac{^-1.08}{^-12}$

9a. $^+6 \div ^-0.5$ **b.** $^+1.2 \div ^-0.18$

10. A plastics stock dropped $1\frac{1}{4}$ point every day for a week. How many points had the stock dropped at week's end?

Practice 4-4

Solve.

1a. $^-3m = ^-2.7$ **b.** $^+1.5d = ^-4.5$

2a. $\frac{^{+1}}{4}r = \frac{^-2}{9}$ **b.** $^-1\frac{1}{3}n = ^-8$

3a. $\frac{m}{^-2.1} = ^+4$ **b.** $\frac{c}{^+1.2} = ^-0.8$

4. $^-2.5n - ^-1.4 = ^-4.6$

5. $\frac{^-1}{4}d + 2\frac{1}{2} = ^-3\frac{1}{4}$

Evaluate the expression when $n = \frac{^-1}{3}$

6a. $4n$ **b.** ^-9n

7a. $^-6n + ^+14$ **b.** $9(2 + n)$

Solve.

8. $\frac{^-2}{3}(b + 6) = ^-9$

9. $^-0.8(5 - t) = ^-2.4$

Write an equation and solve.

10. Twice a number added to $^-4.75$ is $^-2.5$. Find the number.

CHAPTER 5

Practice 5-1

Write the standard numeral.

1a. 10^4 **b.** 10^6

2a. $3(10^6) + 2(10^2)$ **b.** $7(10^{-1}) + 1(10^{-4})$

Find the product or quotient.

3a. 2.7×1000 **b.** 725×1000

4a. 72×10^3 **b.** 681×10^4

5a. $18.1 \div 10^2$ **b.** $1.23 \div 10^4$

Write as a power of 10.

6a. $10,000,000$ **b.** 0.0001

Write in exponential form.

7a. $405,271,000$ **b.** 0.0056

Write the standard numeral.

8a. 6.74×10^2 **b.** 7.87×10^3

9a. 5.6×10^{-4} **b.** 3.04×10^{-7}

10a. 4.3×10^{11} **b.** 1.65×10^{-4}

Practice 5-2

Express each as a power of ten.

1a. $10^7 \times 10^2$ **b.** $10^3 \times 10^{-5}$

2a. $10^{-4} \times 10^{-2}$ **b.** $10^{-2} \times 10^{-3}$

3a. $10^5 \div 10^2$ **b.** $10^{-4} \div 10^{-6}$

Copy and complete with correct power of ten.

4a. $3,240,000 = 3.24 \times 10^?$

b. $15,670 = 1.567 \times 10^?$

5a. $0.0024 = \underline{\;?\;} \times 10^{-3}$

b. $0.00015 = 1.5 \times 10^?$

Write in scientific notation.

6a. $63,700$ **b.** $92,900,000$

7a. 0.003 **b.** 0.0000082

Compute using scientific notation.

8. $(2.1 \times 10^3) \times (7.2 \times 10^2)$

9. $(7.5 \times 10^5) \div (2.5 \times 10^3)$

10. A satellite travels 4.5×10^8 miles in a 30-day month. How far does it travel each day?

Practice 5-3

Check these numbers for divisibility by 2, 3, 4, 5, 9, and 10.

1a. 29   **b.** 270

2a. 1276   **b.** 345

3a. 48   **b.** 1209

4a. 80,901   **b.** 8341

5a. 9,286   **b.** 2703

Find the next three terms in each sequence.

6a. 1, 5, 9, 13, ...   **b.** 3, 9, 27, ...

7a. 1, 6, 31, 156, ...   **b.** 1, 3, 4, 7, 11, ...

Use p, q, and r to write a statement for each symbol.
p: $^+7$ is an integer. q: 35 is an even number.
r: 51 is a composite number.

8a. $\sim p$ **b.** $p \wedge q$

9a. $\sim q \vee \sim r$ **b.** $q \longrightarrow \sim r$

10. Construct a truth table for $\sim p \vee q$.

CHAPTER 6

Practice 6-1

Express each ratio as a fraction in lowest terms.

1a. 4 : 9   **b.** 0.7 : 5.6

2a. 12 : 36   **b.** 60 : 35

3a. $3\frac{1}{2}$ to $5\frac{1}{4}$ **b.** 0.006 to 1.2

Give an equal ratio.

4a. $\frac{3}{8} = \frac{?}{24}$ **b.** $\frac{2}{9} = \frac{8}{?}$

Compare. Write = or ≠.

5a. $\frac{72}{45}$? $\frac{8}{5}$ **b.** $\frac{48}{54}$? $\frac{8}{11}$

Solve each proportion.

6a. $\frac{n}{5} = \frac{7}{10}$ **b.** $\frac{4}{9} = \frac{6}{x}$

7a. $\frac{6}{12} = \frac{n}{3}$ **b.** $\frac{2}{m} = \frac{14}{16}$

8a. $\frac{12}{21} = \frac{0.3}{y}$ **b.** $\frac{9.6}{n} = \frac{3.2}{4.11}$

Express as a rate.

9a. 4 cans of fruit for $1.20

     b. 100 meters in 12 seconds

10. Jane bought 3 dozen eggs for $2.40. What was the rate per dozen?

Practice 6-2

Write a proportion and solve.

1. Laura can type 325 words in 5 minutes. How long will it take her to type 975 words at the same rate?

2. A tailor hems 14 dresses in 2 hours. At the same rate, how many can he hem in 8 hr?

3. A set of 8 glasses costs $5.67. What is the cost of 1 dozen glasses?

4. Henry can bicycle 0.4 km in 5 minutes. At the same rate, how long will it take him to travel 3 km?

5. The Earth is 93 million miles from the Sun, and Mercury's distance is 16 million miles. On a solar system chart, Earth is 0.9 in. from the Sun. What is Mercury's distance?

On a scale drawing, the dimensions of a house are 21 cm wide and 32.5 cm long. If the scale is 5 cm = 15 m,

6. What is the width of the house?

7. What is the length of the house?

Using a scale of 2 cm = 5 km, find the actual distance when the measurement is:

8a. 8 cm   **b.** 3.5 cm

9a. 6 cm   **b.** 4.8 cm

10a. 7.5 cm   **b.** 9 cm

Practice 6-3

Solve.

1. How long will it take 6 workers to complete a job it takes 4 workers 8 hours?

2. If 12 workers can complete a job in 4 hours, how long will it take 8 workers?

3. How long will 5 workers take to complete a job if 10 workers take $1\frac{1}{2}$ days?

4. If 18 artists make 150 greeting cards in a day, how many artists are needed to make 225 cards?

5. Three volunteers can paint a house in 24 hr. At this rate, how long would it take 4 volunteers to do this job?

Solve.

6. Divide 45 into 3 parts with a ratio of 2 : 3 : 4.

7. Divide 200 into 2 parts with a ratio of 7 to 3.

8. Divide 372 into 3 parts proportioned to 4 : 5 : 3.

9. Jordan mixed 2 liters of pineapple juice for every 3 liters of orange juice to make Island Punch. How many liters of each are needed for 15 liters of punch?

10. Three friends divided 156 baseball cards among themselves in a ratio of 2, 5, and 6. How many cards did each receive?

Practice 6-4

Solve.

1. Peg, Paul, Joe, and Anne picked 6 qt of strawberries in 2 hr. Joe left. How much longer will it take to pick 6 more quarts?

2. If 12 students set up for the school carnival in 3 hr, how long would it have taken 6 students?

3. A job is done by 5 aides in 7 days. How many aides could do it in half that time?

Divide 30 into two parts with a ratio of:

4a. 2 to 3   **b.** 1 to 5

Divide 128 into two parts with a ratio of:

5a. 1 to 3   **b.** 3 to 5

Copy and complete the chart, using the table on page 552.

Angle	Sin	Cos	Tan
6. 87°			
7.	0.883		
8.		0.988	

9. $\triangle ABC$ is similar to $\triangle DEF$.

   a. $\overline{AB}$ is 3 cm and $\overline{BC}$ is 5 cm. If $\overline{DE}$ is 4.5 cm, how long is $\overline{EF}$?

   b. If m $\angle$ ABC is 70° then what is m $\angle$ DEF?

10. A pilot is flying above the town of Summit. At an angle of depression of 15°, he sights the town of Madison, which he knows is 12 miles from Summit. At what altitude is he flying?

CHAPTER 7

Practice 7-1

Solve.

Write each as a percent.

1a. 0.31   **b.** 0.004

2a. 0.05   **b.** 6.66

3a. $\frac{3}{5}$ **b.** $\frac{1}{6}$

4a. $2\frac{9}{10}$ **b.** $\frac{3}{25}$

Write each as a decimal.

5a. 37.5%   **b.** 7%

6a. 400%   **b.** 0.2%

Write each as a fraction.

7a. $14\frac{2}{7}$%   **b.** 85%

Find:

8a. 28% of 96   **b.** 400% of 12

9a. 0.2% of $120   **b.** $83\frac{1}{3}$% of 354

Practice 7-2

Find the value of the variable.

1a. 40% of $a = 60$ **b.** 1% of $x = 3.2$

2a. 90% of $n = 2.0$ **b.** $37\frac{1}{2}$% of $b = 18$

3a. 20% of $r = 1.2$ **b.** 15% of $y = 10.5$

4a. $66\frac{2}{3}$% of $s = 36$ **b.** 32% of $z = 4.8$

5a. 13% of $n = 1.053$ **b.** 60% of $a = 138$

6. Of the total library collection, about 17%, or 140 books, are detective stories. About how many books are in the library?

7. Twelve students in the class prefer skiing as a winter sport. If this is 40% of the class, how many students are in the class?

8. A length of 20 cm is 80% of an adult nighthawk's length. How long is an adult nighthawk?

9. During a recent sale the sports department sold $1\frac{1}{2}$ dozen sleeping bags. This was $37\frac{1}{2}$% of the number to be sold. What was the total number of sleeping bags on sale?

10. The Joyces paid $32,000, or 30% of their mortgage. How much was the mortgage?

Practice 7-3

What percent of:

1a. 28 is 7?   **b.** 48 is 15?

2a. 3 is 7?   **b.** 250 is 5?

3a. 120 is 150?   **b.** 45 is 60?

Find the percent of increase or decrease.

4a. Original: 320   **b.** Original: $2500
New: 400   New: $3800

5a. Original: 80   **b.** Original: $12.50
New: 70   New: $9.75

6. Of the 4200 residents, 1680 attended a town picnic. What percent went to the picnic?

7. Three hundred of the 450 items at a hospital bazaar were handmade. What percent were handmade?

8. In a certain town, 3380 citizens voted in a local election. What percent of the total population of 5200 voted?

9. Mr. Gomez has a small farm of 18 acres. He planted 4 acres in wheat. What percent of the farm was used for other purposes?

10. Of the 140 students in the eighth grade, 34 eat lunch at school. What percent do not eat at school?

Practice 7-4

Compare by writing $<$, $=$, or $>$.

1. 25% of 50 _?_ 30% of 50.

2. 15% of 100 _?_ 15% of 200.

3. $12\frac{1}{2}$% of 80 _?_ $12\frac{1}{2}$% of 40.

4. $37\frac{1}{2}$% of 8 _?_ 75% of 4.

5. $2\frac{1}{2}$% of 100 _?_ $0.2\frac{1}{2}$% of 100.

6. 9 in. is what percent of 2 ft?

7. $8\frac{1}{3}$% of 72 is what percent of 36?

8. Jeff weighs 63 kg. Tony weighs 21 kg. What percent of Jeff's weight is Tony's?

9. 20% of a kilometer is how many meters?

10. After spending 80% of her money, Gail had $4 left. How much money had she at first?

CHAPTER 8

Practice 8-1

Find the profit or loss to the nearest cent.

1a. Cost: $128
Rate of Loss: 2.5%

b. Cost: $80
Rate of Loss: $8\frac{1}{3}$ %

2a. Cost: $516
Rate of Profit: 6.5%

b. Cost: $86.25
Rate of Profit: 3.2%

Find the selling price.

3a. Cost: $92.50
Loss: $5\frac{1}{2}$ %

b. Cost: $190
Gain: 15%

c. Cost: $420
Profit: $8.25

Find the discount and selling price.

4a. Reg. price: $150
Discount: $33\frac{1}{3}$ %

Selling price: _____

b. Reg. price: $60
Discount: 40%

Selling price: _____

Solve.

5. Blank tapes are selling at $3.50 and are reduced $1. What is the rate of discount?

6. A calculator usually sold for $22.50 is on sale at 5% off. How much money would you save?

7. Socks are sold for $2.50 a pair. You get a 10% discount if you buy six pairs. What would the six pairs cost?

8. A video game costs $87.50 on sale at 15% discount. What was the original price?

9. The Waylands sold their home at a 30% loss. The original price was $99,000. How much did they lose?

10. The Baxter tree farm realized a gain of 21% on their original investment of $12,000. How much profit did they make?

Practice 8-2

Add 100% to:

1a. 42%   **b.** 12.5%   **c.** $62\frac{1}{2}$ %

2a. 56%   **b.** $33\frac{1}{3}$ %   **c.** 34%

Round answer to the nearest cent.
Find 4% sales tax on:

3a. $36.59   **b.** $58.85

Find $3\frac{1}{2}$ % sales tax on:

4a. $80.90   **b.** $76.87

Find $6\frac{1}{4}$ % sales tax on:

5a. $96.95   **b.** $260.54

Given a sales tax of 6% find the total cost of:

6a. $49.85   **b.** $426.50

Find the rate of discount, given the list price and discount.

7a. $40; $5   **b.** $550; $165

Solve.

8. A popcorn maker listed at $23.50 was sold at a 20% discount. What did the consumer pay if a sales tax of $6\frac{1}{2}$ % was included?

9. After the sales tax was added to a $12.50 purchase, Rose paid the cashier $13.25. What was the rate of sales tax?

10. What was Sharon's change from $15.00 if she bought a racquet-ball racquet marked $12.88 and paid a sales tax of 4%?

Practice 8-3

1. What is 6.5% of: **a.** $340?   **b.** $52,680?

2a. What percent of $200 is $32?

b. What percent of $1456 is $87.36?

3a. 3.5% of what number is $210?

b. 8% of what number is $1312?

Find the commission, given the amount of sales and the rate of commission.

4a. $1570; 6%   **b.** $82,965; 10%

Find the rate, given the commission and the amount of sales.

5a. $294; $5346   **b.** $7800; $65,000

6. What was Blake's rate of commission if he collected $176.40 on a sale of $840?

7. An agent received $437.50 commission on a sale of $6250. What was her rate of commission?

8. $180 was received for a sale of $3000. What was the rate of commission?

9. If a commission agent received $400 at a rate of 8% commission, what was the amount of the sale?

10. Mrs. Helin sells appliances for a 20% commission. One week she earned $456. What was the amount of sales for that week?

Practice 8-4

Complete the chart.

	Principal	Rate	Time	Interest
1a.	$2000	$8\frac{1}{2}$ %	4 yr	?
b.	$640	?	3 yr	$96
2a.	$5000	6%	?	$1350
b.	?	8%	3 yr 3 mo	$455
3a.	$1200	?	4 yr 6 mo	$216
b.	$8580	12%	1 yr 4 mo	?
4a.	?	5.5%	3 yr	$140.25
b.	$10,000	16%	?	$5600
5a.	$687	12%	?	$41.22
b.	?	6.5%	4 yr	$377

6. Mrs. Alba borrowed $6200 from a bank that charges 12% interest. She repaid the loan at the end of 1 yr 6 mo. What amount did she pay the bank?

7. How long will it take to earn $787.50 on $5000 at $5\frac{1}{4}$%?

8. Susan collected $1.20 interest after 6 months. What was the amount of her deposit if the bank pays 6% interest?

9. Mr. Bradley's investment of $4500 earned him $1800 at the end of 5 years. What rate of interest did he receive?

10. How much must be invested at 6% interest to earn $187.50 in 2 years 6 months?

CHAPTER 9

Practice 9-1

Use the spinner in finding the probability.

1a. P (20) **b.** P (40)

2a. P (even)

b. P (multiple of 7)

3a. P(n > 40) **b.** P (60)

4a. P (factor of 100) **b.** P (50 < n < 70)

5a. P (n = 40, n = 40)

b. P (multiple of 20, factor of 20)

6. A store sells watches having 3 different faces and 5 different watch bands. How many styles of watches can it sell?

7–8. Construct a histogram to show:

Student	Score	Student	Score
Lorraine	88	Dominic	97
Patricia	40	Kris	49
Rose	35	Sam	88
John	45	Mary	53
Terry	75	Steven	91
James	70	Robert	82
Cecilia	100	Frank	73

9. Compute the mean, the mode, and the range of the test scores in exercises 7–8.

10. Find the median of the test scores.

Practice 9-2

What percent of Mr. DeWitt's $5000 check was spent on each item shown on the graph?

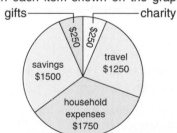

gifts — charity
$250 $250
savings $1500
travel $1250
household expenses $1750

1a. savings **b.** household expenses

2a. charity **b.** travel and gifts

From cards numbered 1–10, choose a card and do not replace it. Find the probability of:

3a. P (1, 3, 5) **b.** P (odd, even)

4–5. Construct a double line graph to show this information:

				Grade			
	K	1	2	3	4	5	6
Girls	13	35	31	25	41	21	19
Boys	10	29	37	22	19	33	18

6–7. Construct a circle graph to show:

Activity	Number of Hours Spent Per Day	Activity	Number of Hours Spent Per Day
Sleeping	8	School	6
Eating	2	Other	3
Playing	3	Studying	2

8–9. Make a bar graph for the following.

Inches of snow fall	14	18	7	23
Year	1st	2nd	3rd	4th

10. Find the value of:

a. $\frac{7!}{5!}$ b. 3!(5! − 2!)

CHAPTER 10

Practice 10-1

Read each symbol.

1 a. $\overleftrightarrow{AB}$ **b.** $\overrightarrow{AB}$

Tell the relation of:

2 a. $\overline{AB}$ to $\overline{CD}$ **b.** $\overline{JK}$ to $\overline{LM}$

Name each angle and give the vertex.

3 a.   **b.**

What kind of angle has a measure of:

4 a. 138°   **b.** 30°

How many angles are within:

5 a. a square   **b.** a hexagon

Find the measure of:

6 a.   **b.**

What is the complement of:

7 a. 30°   **b.** 75°

What is the supplement of:

8 a. 60°   **b.** 135°

9. What is the measure of a straight angle?

10. What is the $m \angle$ N?

Practice 10-2

Complete.

1. A _____ is a flat surface that extends indefinitely in all directions.

2. Lines are _____ if they lie in the same plane and never intersect.

3. A _____ intersects a pair of parallel lines forming interior and exterior angles.

4. _____ triangles have exactly the same size and shape.

5. In congruent triangles their corresponding sides and angles are _____ .

Classify.

6. A triangle with angles of 30°, 60°, and 90°.

7. An angle that measures 90°.

8. A triangle with an angle greater than 90°.

9. A triangle with two congruent sides.

10. Why are these pairs of triangles congruent?

     a.   **b.**

Practice 10-3

1 a. 0.427 m = $\underline{?}$ mm   **b.** 0.007 m = $\underline{?}$ mm

2 a. 9240 mm = $\underline{?}$ m   **b.** 0.0842 m = $\underline{?}$ mm

3 a. 42 m = $\underline{?}$ mm   **b.** 0.806 km = $\underline{?}$ m

4 a. 246 m = $\underline{?}$ km   **b.** 4 m = $\underline{?}$ mm

5 a. 880 yd = $\underline{?}$ mi   **b.** 0.5 mi = $\underline{?}$ ft

6 a. 32 oz = $\underline{?}$ lb   **b.** $1\frac{1}{2}$ lb = $\underline{?}$ oz

7 a. 0.5 qt = $\underline{?}$ pt   **b.** 5 qt 3 pt = $\underline{?}$ gal

Solve.

8. A 40-yd piece of wire can be cut into how many pieces of 1-ft length?

9. Arrange these measurements from least precise to most precise.
   a. 8.13 m, 241.6 m, 8.1247 m
   b. 0.0079 km, 26.34 km, 78.5 km, 98.176 km

10. Give the greatest possible error and interval of measure.

    a. 9.063 cm   **b.** 0.06 km

CHAPTER 11

Practice 11-1

Complete the *perimeter* charts.

	P (Rectangle)	ℓ	w
1a.	70 m	22 m	?
b.	40.4 m	12.1 m	?
2a.	?	8.3 m	5.9 m
b.	1 m	36 cm	?
3.	50.3 m	?	9.4 m

	P (Triangle)	a	b	c
4a.	?	6 cm	8 cm	7 cm
b.	12 cm	4 cm	5 cm	?
5.	?	2.8 m	3.5 m	1.2 m

6. Susan made a quilt 4.4 meters long and 3.1 meters wide. How many meters of binding will she need along the outside of the quilt?

7. The border of a triangular park is to be lined with maple trees every 8 meters. If the sides of the park are 80 meters, 56 meters, and 72 meters long, how many trees are needed?

8. Sally ran 0.34 kilometer around a rectangular field 83 meters long. What is the width?

9. Craig ran around a square enclosure 20 meters on a side. If he ran 250 meters in all, how many times did he pass the beginning point?

10. A rectangle is twice as long as it is wide. If the perimeter is 246 cm, find the other dimensions of the rectangle.

Practice 11-2

Complete the *area* charts.

Rectangle:

	Area	length	width
1a.	?	6 cm	2.3 cm
b.	?	$8\frac{1}{3}$ in.	6 in.
2a.	24 cm^2	12 cm	?
b.	4928 cm^2	?	56 cm
3a.	204 m^2	17 m	?
b.	?	200 m	150 m
4a.	?	9.11 cm	3.24 cm
b.	6375 m^2	?	75 m

Parallelogram:

	Area	base	height
5a.	?	8.1 cm	4 cm
b.	?	6.31 m	5.1 m
6a.	112 m^2	?	8 m
b.	72 cm^2	4.5 cm	?

7. How many square meters of carpet are needed to cover a rectangular room 11 meters by 13 meters?

8. The area of a table top is 3.12 m^2. Find the length if the width is 1.2 meters.

9. A lawn in the shape of a parallelogram has a base of 32 meters and a height of 26 meters. What is the area?

10. How many square tiles 4 cm on an edge are needed to cover a surface 4 m by 5 m?

Practice 11-3

Complete the *area* charts.

Triangle:

	Area	base	height
1.	?	90 in.	42 in.
2.	36 cm^2	8 cm	?
3.	3813 m^2	?	93 m
4.	?	4 ft	2 yd

Trapezoid:

	Area	base$_1$	base$_2$	height
5a.	?	4.5 m	3 m	7.6 m
b.	?	15 cm	19 cm	12.4 cm
6a.	1056 cm^2	50 cm	38 cm	?
b.	207 in^2	10.7 in.	9.3 in.	?

7. A trapezoidal desk top 48 cm in height is covered with stain-resistant plastic. The parallel bases are 55 cm and 50 cm. What is the area?

8. Candace is making a quilt which will include 84 triangular pieces of fabric. If each triangle has a base of 14 cm and a height of 7 cm, what will be the total area of all the triangles?

9. A triangle having a base of 15 cm and a height of 12 cm is cut from a rectangular piece of construction paper 28 cm long and 22 cm wide. What area is wasted?

10. Find the height of a trapezoid that has an area of 100 dm^2 and whose bases are 14 dm and 6 dm.

Practice 11-4

Find the circumference given.

1a. $d = 1.4$ cm   **b.** $d = 4$ in.

2a. $r = 7$ mm   **b.** $r = 3.5$ ft

Given the radius, find the area of the circle.

3a. 7 m   **b.** 10 cm

4a. 25 cm   **b.** 2.1 cm

Given the diameter, find the area of the circle.

5a. 32 ft   **b.** 40 in.

6. A circular pool has a diameter of 15 m. What is the surface area of its cover?

7. What is the area of the largest circle that can be cut from a rectangle 14 cm wide and 20 cm long?

8. The diameter of Mercury is 3100 miles. Find its circumference.

9. A circular garden measures 25 ft in diameter. Find the circumference in yards. (Round to the nearest tenth.)

10. 435 meters of fence enclose a circular field. Estimate the number of meters from the center to a point on the circumference.

CHAPTER 12

Practice 12-1

Classify each number as rational or irrational.

1a. $\frac{4}{7}$ **b.** $\sqrt{17}$ **c.** 0.23

Express each repeating decimal as a fraction.

2a. $0.\overline{5}$ **b.** $0.2\overline{7}$ **c.** $1.8\overline{3}$

Find the squares of each number.

3a. 18   **b.** $^-6.1$

4a. $\frac{^-7}{9}$ **b.** $^+1\frac{1}{2}$

Find the square root of:

5a. 324   **b.** 12.96

6a. 810,000   **b.** $\frac{100}{169}$

Find the square root and round it to the nearest tenth.

7a. 4.8841   **b.** 0.23

Find the square root and round it to the nearest hundredth.

8a. $\sqrt{56}$ **b.** $\sqrt{37}$

Between what two consecutive numbers is each:

9a. $\sqrt{13}$ **b.** $\sqrt{69}$ **c.** $\sqrt{97}$

10. Three times the square root of a number is 48. Find the number.

Practice 12-2

Classify each number as rational or irrational.

1a. $^-9$ **b.** 0.17   **c.** π

2a. $\frac{5}{6}$ **b.** $\sqrt{8}$ **c.** 0.36...

Find a number between:

3a. 2.15 and 2.16

b. $^-2\frac{1}{5}$ and $^-2\frac{1}{4}$

4. Write the inequality shown on the graph.

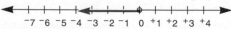

5. Write the inequality shown on the graph.

Find the solution. Graph it on a real number line.

6a. $y + 2 > 6$ **b.** $x + 5 \geq 7$

7a. $x - 3 < 7$ **b.** $y - 3 \leq 0$

8a. $3y \geq 9$ **b.** $\frac{1}{2}x \leq 9$

9a. $\frac{m}{^+3} \geq ^-2$ **b.** $\frac{b}{6} \leq ^-1$

10a. $2c + 1 < 11$ **b.** $^-3n - 2 > 1$

Practice 12-3

Use the Pythagorean theorem to solve.

1.
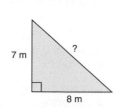

2.
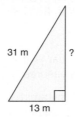

Which sets of measures form right triangles?

3a. 3', 4', 5'   **b.** 7 m, 7 m, 10 m

4a. 12 m, 16 m, 20 m   **b.** 16 m, 30 m, 34 m

5a. 0.3 m, 0.5 m, 0.6 m

  b. 1 ft, $1\frac{1}{3}$ ft, $1\frac{2}{3}$ ft

6. A landscaper plans a path along a diagonal of a rectangular park. Find the length of the path if the park is 30 m long and 16 m wide.

7. Starting from the same position, Karen walked north at 3 km/hr and David east at 4 km/hr. How far apart were they in 2 hr?

8. Find the area of a circular garden with a radius of 10 ft.

9. A flat plastic ring has an outer diameter of 8 cm and an inner diameter of 5 cm. What is the area of the ring?

10. A paperweight has a circular base with a radius of 4 cm. What is the area of the piece of felt needed to cover the base?

CHAPTER 13

Practice 13-1

Find the surface area of each prism.

1.
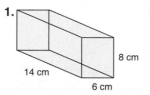

2.
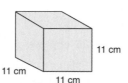

3.
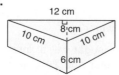

4.

Find the surface area of a cube with an edge of:

5a. 41 in.   **b.** 8.75 ft

Given the radius and height, find the surface area of each cylinder.

6a. r = 12 cm, h = 10 cm **b.** r = 10 in., h = 5 in.

7a. r = 4 cm, h = 7 cm   **b.** r = 7 yd, h = 9 yd

8. A hat box is 34 cm in diameter and 30 cm deep. How many square meters of cardboard were used to make 6 similar boxes? Round to the nearest tenth.

9. How much more bunting was used to drape the sides of a rectangular platform 3 m long, 2.5 m wide, and 110 cm high than a cylindrical one of the same height with a diameter of 3 m? Round to the nearest tenth.

10. Is the entire surface area of a cylinder 30 cm in diameter and 60 cm high more or less than 1 m^2?

Practice 13-2

Find the surface area of each pyramid.

1.
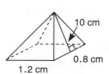

2.

Given the radius and height find the surface area of each cone.

3a. r = 10', h = 10'   **b.** r = 5 ft, h = 7 ft

4a. r = 17 yd, h = 2 yd   **b.** r = 14", h = 14"

Tell the number of faces, edges, and vertices of:

5a. triangular pyramid   **b.** square pyramid

Solve.

6. The base of a rectangular pyramid is 9 cm by 12 cm. The height of each triangular face is 8 cm. What is the surface area?

7. A spherical decoration has a radius of 4.6 in. What is its surface area?

8. How much vinyl is needed to cover a tube 14 inches in diameter and 45 inches high?

9. Find the surface area of a storage tank 15 yards high with a 3.3 yard diameter.

10. The area of the base of the pentagonal pyramid is 339 sq m. If the height of the pyramid is 20 m, find the volume.

Practice 13-3

Find the volume of each.

1.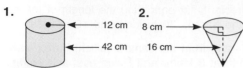

12 cm
42 cm

2. 8 cm
16 cm

Find the volume of:

3 a. a triangular prism
base of triangle = 3.75 yd
height of triangle = 3.33 yd
height of prism = 2 yd

b. a triangular pyramid
height of triangular base = 5 cm
base of triangle = 4.6 cm
height of pyramid = 7.8 cm

4 a. a rectangular prism
ℓ = 8 in.
w = $5\frac{1}{2}$ in.
h = 14 in.

b. a pyramid
ℓ = 6.3 m
w = 4 m
h = 5 m

5 a. a square pyramid
e = 8.3 m
h = 8.3 m

b. a cube
e = $3\frac{1}{3}$ ft

Solve.

6. What is the volume of a shipping crate that measures $5\frac{1}{2}$ ft on each side?

7. A pyramid-shaped tent covers an area of 36 square feet. What is the tent's volume if it is 8.2 feet high?

8. What is the capacity of a water tank that is 51.6 m tall with a diameter of 13.2 m?

9. A circular swimming pool is 21 feet in diameter and 8.5 feet deep. What is its volume?

10. What is the volume of a conical mold if the diameter of its base is 12 in. and its height is 18 in.?

Practice 13-4

Complete.

1 a. 1 000 000 cm^2 = ___ m^2

b. 1 m^2 = ___ dm^2

2 a. 0.056 m^2 = ___ cm^2

b. 0.005 m^2 = ___ cm^2

3 a. 60 000 cm^2 = ___ m^2 **b.** 2450 cm^2 = ___ m^2

4 a. 1 cm^3 = ___ mL **b.** 1 dm^3 = ___ L

5 a. 5.4 dm^3 = ___ L **b.** 0.58 L = ___ cm^3

6 a. 2 dm^3 weigh _?_ kg

b. 26 cm^3 weigh _?_ g

7. Estimate the number of kilograms of candy needed to fill 20 conical party hats 12 cm in diameter and 16 cm high.

8. Will a bucket 28 cm in diameter and 34 cm deep hold 20 liters of water?

9. How many kilograms of sugar will fit into a canister 20 cm in diameter and 24 cm deep? (Round to the nearest tenth.)

10. How many cones 5 cm in radius and 16 cm deep can you fill from a cylindrical container holding 5 liters?

Practice 13-5

Complete.

1 a. 0.6 m^2 = _?_ cm^2 **b.** 10 mm^2 = _?_ cm^2

2 a. 840 cm^2 = _?_ m^2 **b.** 8 cm^2 = _?_ mm^2

3 a. 1 000 000 m^2 = _?_ km^2

b. 1 cm^2 = _?_ mm^2

Compare. Write <, =, or >.

4 a. 1 m^2 _?_ 1 cm^2 **b.** 1 cm^2 _?_ 1 mm^2

5 a. 0.1 m^2 _?_ 1000 cm^2 **b.** 1 km^2 _?_ 1000 m^2

Solve.

6. What volume of oil could be contained in 7

cylinders, each 0.6 m in radius and 3 m high?

7. What is the volume of a cone having the same dimensions as the cylinder in problem 6?

8. How many cubic centimeters of wood are in a tree stump with a radius of 31 cm if the stump is 45 cm high?

9. A 17-cm-high cylinder with a radius of 22 cm is filled with chips. Gary filled a cone 17 cm high and 22 cm in radius with some of them. How many cubic cm remained in the cylinder?

10. A glue stick measures 2.4 cm in diameter and is 8 cm high. What is its volume?

CHAPTER 14

Practice 14-1

Find and graph the solution in the set of integers.

1a. $x + 4 = {}^-2$ **b.** $x - {}^+5 = {}^-2$

2a. $x < 6$ **b.** $x + 3 \geq 1$

3a. $x^2 = 9$ **b.** $x + 2 = 2$

Find and graph the solution in the set of real numbers.

4a. $\dfrac{x}{3} = {}^-2$ **b.** $x > {}^-1$

5a. $x \leq 5$ **b.** $\dfrac{x}{3} \geq 6$

Graph these points.

6a. $A({}^-4, 6)$ **b.** $B(4, {}^-8)$

7a. $C(3, 7)$ **b.** $D({}^-6, 9)$

Complete the function table. Make a graph.

8a. $y = x - 2$ **b.** $y = 3 + x$

x	2	1	0	$^-1$	$^-2$
y					

x	$^-3$	$^-2$	$^-1$	0	1	2
y						

9a. $y = 2x + 3$ **b.** $y = 5x - 6$

x	2	1	0	$^-1$	$^-2$
y					

x	3	2	1	0	$^-1$
y					

10. Graph these equations on the same grid. Determine the point of intersection.
$x + 4 = y$ and $4x + 1 = y$

CHAPTER 15

Practice 15-1

Compute.

1a. $(4x - y) + (2x + 4y)$ **b.** $(t^3 - 5u^2) + (3t^3 + u^2)$

2a. $(3a - 4b) - (2 + 2b)$ **b.** $(r^3 - 2v) - (r^3 + 5v)$

3a. $(x^2)(x^5)$ **b.** $(3y^2)(-4y^3)$

4a. $(2p + 3t)(4p + 5t)$ **b.** $(5x - 2y)(3y + 2x)$

5a. $(2x^2)^3$ **b.** $\dfrac{15y^2z^3}{3xy}$

6a. $(x + 4)(x - 4)$ **b.** $(x - 2)^2$

7a. $(d + 8)^2$ **b.** $(5r + 3s)^2$

8. A change purse has 19 coins in nickels and dimes. If the total value is $1.35, how many dimes are there?

9a. Find the perimeter.

b. Find the area.

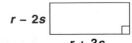

$r - 2s$

$r + 3s$

10. The sum of two numbers is 23. If twice the first is decreased by 4 times the second, the result is 4. Find the numbers.

Practice 15-2

Factor.

1a. $12r - 18s$ **b.** $21abs - 35ab$

2a. $ef - gf$ **b.** $8a^2cd^2 - 4acd^2$

3a. $k^2 + 11k + 28$ **b.** $6t^2 + 17t + 12$

4a. $p^2 - 7p - 60$ **b.** $h^2 - 7h + 10$

5a. $m^2 - n^2$ **b.** $16x^2 - 9y^2$

6a. $x^2 + 6x + 9$ **b.** $9c^2 - 24cd + 16d^2$

7a. $2x^2 + 10x - 28$ **b.** $6t^2 - 44tb^2 + 14b$

8a. Find the perimeter.

b. Find the area.

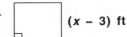

$(x - 3)$ ft

9. The sum of 3 consecutive odd numbers is 321. What is the largest?

10. The second side of a triangle is 7 in. greater than the first. The third side is 6 in. less than twice the first. If the perimeter is 73 in., what is the length of each side?

Practice 15-3

Express in lowest terms.

1a. $\dfrac{56a^2b}{7ab}$

b. $\dfrac{4m^2 - 25n^2}{4mx + 10nx}$

Compute.

2a. $\dfrac{2c^2}{15ab} \cdot \dfrac{20ab^3}{72c^5}$

b. $\dfrac{3(t + c)^2}{15} \cdot \dfrac{5}{t + c}$

3a. $\dfrac{4x^3}{9b^2} \div \dfrac{12x^2}{15b^3}$

b. $\dfrac{x - 2b}{5x^2} \div \dfrac{x^2 - 13xb + 22b^2}{15x^4b}$

4a. $\dfrac{3}{5t} + \dfrac{4}{5t}$

b. $\dfrac{2}{3} - \dfrac{7}{3c}$

5a. $\dfrac{3x - 2}{5} + \dfrac{7x + 3}{8}$

b. $\dfrac{5x - 7}{4} - \dfrac{2x - 3}{6}$

6a. $\dfrac{4}{2x - 6} - \dfrac{3}{4x - 8}$

b. $\dfrac{9a}{4x - 4y} - \dfrac{13a}{4x + 4y}$

7a. $\dfrac{2}{x^2 - 9} - \dfrac{3}{(x + 3)}$

b. $\dfrac{x + 2}{x - 3} - \dfrac{x - 5}{x + 7}$

8. Carly is now 5 times as old as Henri. In 9 years, her age will be twice Henri's age then. How old is Carly now?

9. The larger of two numbers is 18 more than the smaller. When the larger number is divided by the smaller the quotient is $\dfrac{5}{2}$. Find both numbers.

10. One angle of a triangle is 70°. One of the other angles is $\dfrac{2}{3}$ as large as the other. What is the measure of each angle?

CHAPTER 16

Practice 16-1

What is the slope and *y*-intercept of:

1a. $2x + y = 5$

b. $3x - 2y = {}^-1$

2a. $4x + y - 12 = 0$

b. $x + 2y + 3 = 0$

Graph the lines given:

3a. $m = {}^-1; P(4, 3)$

b. $m = 2; P({}^-1, {}^-3)$

Find the slope of the line joining the given points.

4a. $({}^-4, {}^-2), (0, 0)$

b. $({}^-1, {}^+2), ({}^-3, {}^-3)$

5a. $({}^-3, 4)(3, {}^-4)$

b. $(3, 2), (5, 6)$

Given *m* and *b* write the equation of line:

6a. $m = {}^-2; b = {}^-2$

b. $m = 3; b = 0$

7a. $m = \dfrac{{}^-1}{2}; b = 1$

b. $m = \dfrac{1}{4}; b = {}^-1$

8a. Name the *y*-intercept.

b. What is the slope of $\overleftrightarrow{AB}$?

c. Write the equation of $\overleftrightarrow{AB}$.

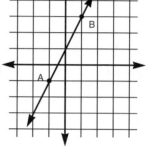

Simplify.

9a. $\sqrt{48}$

b. $\sqrt{2} \cdot \sqrt{3}$

10a. $7\sqrt{2} - \sqrt{2} - 5\sqrt{2}$

b. $2\sqrt{3} - 5\sqrt{2} + 7\sqrt{3} + 8\sqrt{2}$

Practice 16-2

1a. $\sqrt{\dfrac{1}{9}} + 3\sqrt{\dfrac{2}{9}}$

b. $4\sqrt{\dfrac{4}{x^3}} - \sqrt{\dfrac{8}{x^3}}$

2a. $3\sqrt{4} \cdot 16\sqrt{2}$

b. $40\sqrt{6} \cdot 12\sqrt{6}$

3a. $\sqrt{\dfrac{18a^5}{49b^6}}$

b. $\sqrt{\dfrac{2a^3}{4ab}}$

Solve.

4a. $x^2 = 64$

b. $\dfrac{3s^2}{64} = 27$

5a. $x^2 + 2x - 4 = 0$

b. $2y^2 + y - 4 = 0$

6a. $8x^2 - 9x - 2 = 0$ **b.** $4u^2 + u - 1 = 0$

7a. $x^2 = 18$ **b.** $y^2 - 8y = 0$

8. The length of a rectangle is 3 times its width. The area is 48 m². Find its dimensions.

9a. Find the hypotenuse.

b. Find the area.

10. If 3 times a number is increased by the square of that number the result is 40. Find the number.

Problem Solving: Review

Choose one of the problem-solving strategies, page viii, and solve.

1. A teacher is putting 96 crayons into boxes of two different sizes. One holds 5 crayons; the other holds 9. How many of each box must the teacher fill so that no crayons are left over and all the boxes are full?

2. A poll showed that 7 out of 10 students surveyed were planning to go to college. If 350 students were surveyed, how many plan to go to college?

3. The area of Rhode Island is 1214 sq mi, while that of Texas is 267,338 sq mi. About how many times larger than Rhode Island is Texas?

4. This week Luke earned $69, which is 3 times what he earned last week. How much did Luke earn last week?

5. A frieze covered $\frac{3}{4}$ of a wall's width and $\frac{2}{9}$ of its height. What part of the wall did the frieze cover?

6. How many liters of water will be needed to fill $\frac{2}{3}$ of an aquarium 20 cm long, 12 cm wide, and 15 cm deep?

7. Ann swims 200 meters in $7\frac{1}{2}$ minutes. It takes Donna $\frac{2}{3}$ that time to swim the same distance. How far can Ann swim in $12\frac{1}{2}$ minutes?

8. A revolving door at a library entrance revolves over an area 70 inches in diameter. Over how many square feet does the door revolve?

9. Hector has drawn a row of 4 shapes: a square, a circle, a triangle, and a hexagon. Each is a different color: green, red, yellow, or blue. Name the order (left to right) and the color of the shapes, given that: the circle and hexagon are at opposite ends; the red shape is to the right of the circle; the green shape is to the left of the blue shape; the square is not red.

10. The area of a square is 10 sq cm. What is the length of the side?

11. A bag contains 6 black marbles and 9 white marbles. If without looking Li pulls a marble from the bag, what is the probability it will be black?

12. Albert spent exactly $1.00 for pencils and pens at a stationery store. The pencils cost $.15 each and the pens, $.25. How many of each did Albert buy?

13. The gas tank of a car holds 13 gallons. If the car can travel 546 mi on 2 tanks of gas, how many miles per gallon does the car get?

14. Of 205 used books offered at a garage sale, 82 were sold. What percentage were not sold?

15. For a walk-a-thon Chris had 8 sponsors who paid $.15 a mile and 10 sponsors who paid $.25. How much money did Chris earn if she walked 12 miles?

16. If the side of a regular octagon increases by 3 cm, how much does the perimeter increase?

17. Ronald had 60 postcards. He gave 12 to Karen and $\frac{1}{2}$ of those remaining to Louis. How many cards did Ronald have left?

18. Write a number with 3 different digits. Reverse the digits, and subtract the smaller number from the larger. Then divide the difference by 11. Now do the same for a few more 3-digit numbers. What pattern do you find?

19. Wilfred is dividing some trading cards among his friends. He has 3 cards too few to give 4 to each, and if he gives 2 to each there will be 7 cards left over. How many friends does Wilfred have?

20. The area of a square is 256 cm^2. What is its diagonal?

21. Find the base and the perimeter of $\triangle ABC$.

515

Brain Builders

TEST 1

1a. $\frac{2}{8} + \frac{1}{3}$ **b.** $21 \times \frac{3}{7}$

2a. $16\frac{2}{3}\%$ of 3   **b.** $1 - \frac{1}{3} + \frac{1}{2}$

3a. $\frac{5}{9} = $? %   **b.** $15 = $? % of 80

4a. $4700 \text{ cm} = $? m   **b.** $52\frac{1}{3} - 38\frac{1}{4}$

5a. $8\frac{3}{9} + 2\frac{4}{7}$ **b.** 80% of 5

6. A batter made 216 hits in 540 times at bat. What was her batting average?

7. A carpenter cut three boards, 362 m, 234 m, and 5625 m long. What was the total length of the boards?

8. If 7.5 m of lace cost \$16.80, what will 5 m cost?

9. Find the interest on \$500 at $4\frac{1}{2}\%$ for 2 yr 8 mo.

10. Find the cost of ribbon selling at \$1.15 a yard if the seller makes a profit of 20%.

TEST 2

1a. $4 = $? % of 16   **b.** $\frac{0.6}{4} = 0.$?

2a. 15% of 26   **b.** $\frac{7}{8} = 0.$?

3a. $\frac{?}{27} = \frac{1}{3}$ **b.** $0.2125 = \frac{?}{?}$

4a. $\frac{1}{3} + \frac{1}{12}$ **b.** $3\frac{1}{7} \div 7\frac{1}{3}$

5a. $65\frac{2}{7} - 28\frac{3}{4}$ **b.** $6 = 5\%$ of ?

6. Juan had 16 416 g of fudge. He packaged it in boxes of 342 g each. How many boxes did he fill?

7. A radio sells for \$96 on the installment plan. It sells for $12\frac{1}{2}\%$ less if paid for in cash. How much is saved by paying cash?

8. Mr. Toner's salary is \$580 a week plus 6% commission on sales. His sales for four weeks were \$1850. What was his entire pay for the period?

9. Marie received \$651 interest on her savings last year. If the rate of interest was $3\frac{1}{2}\%$, how much did she save in the bank?

10. The shadow cast by a 1 m ruler is 0.4 m long. The shadow cast by a tree at the same time is 1 m long. How tall is the tree?

TEST 3

1a. $\frac{1}{6} + \frac{1}{7}$ **b.** $8\frac{2}{3} \times \frac{9}{2}$

2a. 56% of 10   **b.** $\frac{4.5 \text{ kg}}{3 \text{ kg}}$

3a. $\frac{5}{6} = $? %   **b.** $47\frac{2}{3} - 6\frac{7}{10}$

4a. $9\frac{1}{3} \div 4\frac{2}{3}$ **b.** $12 = $? % of 40

5a. $\frac{1}{2}$ of $12 = 25\%$ of ?   **b.** $4 \text{ m} \div 2.2$

6. Joan bought a used car listed at \$6800. If she received a 15% discount, how much did she pay?

7. If 4251 km is 75% of the air distance from London to a point in North Africa, what is the total distance between the two points?

8. Don borrowed \$5000 at 4% interest. If he paid back the loan 9 months later, how much interest did he pay?

9. The coolant in a radiator is found to contain 1 part alcohol to 4 parts water. If the radiator holds 4 L, how much water is in the radiator?

10. A merchant bought 1500 kg of meat at \$2.30 per kg. If the broker's commission was $2\frac{1}{2}\%$, what was the total price paid by the merchant?

TEST 4

1a. 40% of $\frac{5}{2}$ **b.** $\left(\frac{1}{8} + \frac{2}{9}\right)18$

2a. $\frac{2}{3}$ of $\frac{1}{12}$ **b.** ? % of $2 = \frac{1}{8}$

3a. $\frac{1}{2}\% = 0.$?   **b.** $14 = $? % of 56

4a. $6\frac{1}{4}\%$ of 16   **b.** $22\frac{2}{11} - 3\frac{1}{8}$

5a. $6\frac{1}{2} \div 8\frac{2}{3}$ **b.** $\frac{1}{2}(3.2 - 1.6)$

6. If 3.96 kg of meat cost \$16.80, what will 3.3 kg cost?

7. The discount on a bill was \$33. If the rate of discount was $5\frac{1}{2}\%$, what was the original bill?

8. A TV set sold for 15% more than it cost. If the profit was \$81, what was the original cost of the TV?

9. A car travels at the rate of 80.5 km/hr. How far does it go in 12 min?

10. What is the cost per kg of a coffee blend consisting of 3 kg of coffee at \$4.25 per kg and 2 kg of coffee at \$4.35?

1a. $16 = 5\%$ of $\underline{\ ?\ }$ **b.** $\frac{5}{8} = 0.\underline{\ ?\ }$

2a. 40% of 3.6 **b.** $6\frac{2}{3} - 1\frac{3}{4}$

3a. $80\% = \frac{?}{?}$ **b.** $\frac{1}{2}$ hr $= \underline{\ ?\ }$ day

4a. $\frac{1}{3}\left(16 \div \frac{2}{3}\right)$ **b.** $0.3\,(4.8 - 2.6)$

5a. $910\text{m} = \underline{\ ?\ }$ km   **b.** $3\frac{1}{4} \div 5\frac{4}{7}$

6. Mrs. Logan earns $500 a week and a 5% commission on all sales over $2000. One week her sales amounted to $4225. What were her earnings for the week?

7. A ship's radar picked up an object 0.64 of the distance between the ship and the shore. If the distance from the ship to shore was 5 km, how far was the object from the shore?

8. John won $\frac{2}{5}$ of the games he played. If he won 36 games, how many games did he play?

9. A dealer bought oranges at $3.75 per doz and sold them at $4.00 per doz. What was his rate of gain?

10. What is the ratio of 0.6 m to 12 m?

1a. $\frac{2}{3} \times \frac{3}{6}$ **b.** $18 = \underline{\ ?\ }\%$ of 27

2a. $3.2 - 16\%$ of 20 **b.** $10\left(^+6 + {}^-3\right)$

3a. $24\frac{1}{5} + 35\frac{8}{10}$ **b.** $76\frac{3}{4} + 58\frac{3}{5}$

4a. 20% of 0.025 **b.** $15\frac{1}{2}\%$ of 40

5a. $55\frac{5}{9}\%$ of $11\frac{1}{4}$ **b.** $0.3125 = \underline{\ ?\ }\%$

6. A ship's radar picked up a plane 27.86 km distant. If this was 80% of the distance between the ship and the nearest vessel, how far away was the nearest vessel?

7. A fur coat was marked $1280. What rate of discount was given if it was sold for $1088?

8. A broker receives $525 a week plus 5% commission on all sales over $2000. If her weekly sales last week were $3650, what were her total earnings?

9. A builder uses 1 bag of cement (94 kg each) to 2 bags of sand (100 kg each) to make concrete. What is the ratio of cement to sand?

10. If the cost of an item to a merchant is $36 plus a 5% shipping charge, for how much must it be sold in order to realize a gain of $16\frac{2}{3}\%$?

1a. $3\frac{1}{2} \times \frac{3}{20}$ **b.** 8% of $6\frac{2}{3}$

2a. $18 \div \frac{1}{9}$ **b.** $16\frac{2}{3}\%$ of $9\frac{3}{5}$

3a. $\sqrt{361}$ **b.** $3\frac{1}{8} + 4\frac{7}{16}$

4a. $2^2 + 3^2$ **b.** $3\frac{5}{16} - 2\frac{11}{12}$

5a. $\sqrt{169} - \sqrt{36}$ **b.** $\dfrac{3\frac{1}{8}}{6\frac{1}{4}} \times 2$

6. A furniture dealer bought chairs at $60 each. How much money did she make on a dozen chairs if she sold them at a total profit of 15%?

7. If 65% of Bob's weight is 44.59 kg, what is his weight?

8. What is the ratio of 6 hours to 6 days?

9. Find the interest on $600 at 3% a year for June 20 to September 18.

10. The discount on an item of clothing amounted to $3.20. What was the original price of the article if the rate of discount was 8%?

1a. $\frac{3}{2} \div \frac{3}{4} - 1$ **b.** $14\frac{2}{7}\%$ of 56

2a. $7\frac{1}{2}$ da $= \underline{\ ?\ }$ hr   **b.** $4 + \left(\frac{8}{3} \div 2\frac{2}{3}\right)$

3a. $\sqrt{324} + \sqrt{64}$ **b.** $15\frac{2}{3} - 12\frac{3}{4}$

4a. $15 = \underline{\ ?\ }\%$ of 80 **b.** $32 = \frac{1}{2}\%$ of $\underline{\ ?\ }$

5a. $25\frac{2}{3} - 6\left(3\frac{1}{3}\right)$ **b.** 84% of 35

6. What would it cost to lay a tile floor in a room measuring 12 m × 18 m if tile costs $12 per m^2 ?

7. During September, a farmer paid 64¢ per liter for gasahol for his tractor. The following month, he paid 60¢ a liter. What was the percent of decrease?

8. What part of 1.25 cm is 0.5 cm?

9. A man invested $5000 in a savings account. It earned 4% interest during the first year and $3\frac{1}{2}\%$ during the second year. What (simple) interest did he receive at the end of two years?

10. The area of a triangle is 64 cm^2 and the altitude is 16 cm. Find the base.

1a. $\frac{3}{8} + \frac{3}{9}$ **b.** $16\frac{2}{3}\%$ of ? = 12

2a. $18\frac{3}{4} \div 8\frac{1}{3}$ **b.** 85% of 3

3a. $\left(\frac{9}{8} - \frac{5}{16}\right) \times {}^-4$ **b.** $\sqrt{3025}$

4a. 3 = 15% of ?   **b.** $37\frac{1}{2}\%$ of 56

5a. 36 = 25% of ?   **b.** $15 = \sqrt{?}$

6. A family's income is $2160 a month. They spend $675 on rent, $600 on food, $250 for clothing, $150 for fuel, and $305 on miscellaneous. The rest goes to savings. If these items were plotted on a circle graph, how many degrees would be alloted to savings?

7. An automobile can go 30 km on 4 L of gas. The tax, on gasoline is 3.5¢ liter. What tax is paid by a driver who travels 9600 km a year?

8. Find the area of a trapezoid with parallel sides measuring 12 cm and 14 cm respectively and with a height of 13 cm.

9. How many square meters of ground are in a triangular plot that has a base of 20 m and an altitude of 15 m?

10. Find the area of a circular traffic island whose diameter is 25.2 m.

1a. $\frac{7}{10} + \frac{3}{5} - 1$ **b.** 3% of 6

2a. $87\frac{1}{2}\%$ of 3 = ?   **b.** $\sqrt{9} + 3$

3a. $3\frac{1}{4} \times 84$ **b.** $4\frac{1}{3} - 2\frac{1}{8}$

4a. 40% of 3.4   **b.** 1.101 dm = ? cm

5a. $16(\sqrt{25})$ **b.** 42% of 6.5

6. A package weighing 31 kg is delivered by parcel service. The rates are 90¢ for the first kilogram and 48¢ for each additional kilogram. Find the cost of delivery.

7. Find the total amount of the following bank deposits: four $20 bills; four $10 bills; seven $5 bills; eight $1 bills; five half-dollars; nine quarters; three dimes; seven nickels; and a check for $10.25.

8. Find the perimeter of a field 90 m long and 60 m wide.

9. The base of a triangle is 6 m and the altitude is 48 m. Find the area in m^2.

10. A used automobile was sold for $6450 at a 25% loss. Find the cost.

1a. ? % of 12 = 3   **b.** $9 \div \frac{1}{2} + \frac{3}{4}$

2a. 140 m = ? dm   **b.** $4 = \frac{?}{30}$ of 120

3a. $3\frac{1}{4}\%$ of 50   **b.** $6\frac{1}{4}\%$ of 32

4a. $77\frac{3}{4} - 27\frac{1}{2}$ **b.** $n - {}^+2.1 = {}^-3.5$

5a. $(\sqrt{64})\frac{3}{8}$ **b.** $\sqrt{4225}$

6. Mr. Stone bought a house for $104,500. He paid $58,500 and got a 10-yr mortgage at 6% for the balance. What was his monthly interest payment?

7. A garden measures 12 m by 12 m by 15 m. How many meters of fencing are needed to enclose it?

8. Jane worked from 1:15 PM to 5:35 PM at $3.24 an hr. How much did she earn?

9. About 1 kg of grass seed is required to seed a plot of ground 20 m^2 in area. How many kilograms would be needed to seed a lawn 25 m × 64 m?

10. A ditch has a cross section in the shape of a trapezoid. Its top width is 8 m, the bottom width is 4 m, and the depth is 6.5 m. What is the area of the cross section?

1a. ${}^-5 \div {}^+\frac{1}{5}$ **b.** $8\frac{2}{3} \times \frac{1}{13} + 1$

2a. ? % of 25 = 2   **b.** ${}^+35 + \left({}^-2 \times {}^-2\frac{1}{2}\right)$

3a. $33\frac{1}{3}\%$ of 240   **b.** $3\left(\sqrt{324}\right)$

4a. $\frac{{}^-8}{3} - \frac{{}^-3}{8}$ **b.** $5 = \frac{?}{100}$ of 20

5a. 7.6 − 5.103   **b.** $\sqrt{1225} - \sqrt{100}$

6. The perimeter of a rectangle is 62 m. If its width is 14 m, what is its length?

7. The bottom of a 5.5 m ladder is 3.3 m from the base of a wall, and the top just reaches the bottom of a window in the wall. How high is the window above the base of the wall?

8. Find the area of a parallelogram with a base of 8.6 m and an altitude of 15 m.

9. The diameter of a tank is 7 m and the height is 7 m. Find the surface area.

10. In order to start a business, Hal borrowed $800 at 6% interest for 2 years. How much interest did he pay?

TEST 13

1a. 300 dm = _?_ cm

b. 60% of 0.6

2a. $6 - 3\frac{1}{3}$

b. 49.5 m = _?_ cm

3a. $14 = $ _?_ % of 84

b. $15 = 30\%$ of _?_

4a. $\sqrt{81} + \sqrt{25}$

b. $62\frac{1}{2}\%$ of 8

5a. $17\frac{1}{3} \div 8\frac{2}{3}$

b. XLIV − XXX

6. Vinyl covering for office desks sells at $6.20 per m². Find how much it costs to cover a desk 0.8 m wide and 1.5 m long.

7. A rectangular field is 82.5 m wide and has an area of 16 335 m². What is its length?

8. An airplane propeller spins in a circle with a radius of 2 m. Over what area does it revolve?

9. If 4.5% of a number is 450, what is 25% of $\frac{1}{4}$ the number?

10. Eggs bought at 81¢ a dozen were sold at 90¢ a dozen. Find the percent of gain.

TEST 14

1a. 0.7 kg = _?_ g

b. $52\frac{1}{3} - 10\frac{1}{6}$

2a. $16\frac{2}{3}\%$ of _?_ = 2

b. $0.5625 = \frac{?}{?}$

3a. 24% of 20

b. $\frac{8}{3} \div 2\frac{2}{5}$

4a. $\sqrt{4096}$

b. $\frac{3}{16} = 0.$ _?_

5a. $3\frac{1}{3}\%$ of 33

b. $\sqrt{289} - \sqrt{225}$

6. Find the cost of 9.6 m of carpet if 6.4 m cost $54.70.

7. The stock report showed that East Co. shares were down $\frac{3}{4}$ on Monday, down $\frac{1}{8}$ on Tuesday, but up $\frac{1}{2}$ on Wednesday, Thursday, and Friday. What was the overall change that week?

8. The distance between two towns is 12.85 km. If a car has gone 95% of the way from the first town toward the second, how far is the car from the second town?

9. A manhole lid has a diameter of 80 cm. What is its area?

10. The perimeter of a square poster is 96 cm. How many cm² of cardboard did it take to make the poster?

TEST 15

1a. 14% of 25

b. $10^6 \times 10^3$

2a. $2.4 = 20\%$ of _?_

b. $10 = $ _?_ % of 80

3a. $8 - \left(\frac{3}{4}\text{ of }6\right) + 3$

b. $\frac{4}{9} = $ _?_ %

4a. 6.8×6

b. $\sqrt{169} + \sqrt{49}$

5a. $80 - \left(\frac{3}{4} \times 12\right) - (3\% \text{ of } 100)$

b. $\sqrt{1024} - 16$

6. A jacket was sold for $18 at a loss of $4.50. What was the percent of loss?

7. If a 60-L tank is to be filled with a mixture of 2 parts of light oil to 3 parts of heavy oil, how many liters of each type of oil will be needed?

8. If the plan of a room 5 m wide and 10 cm long measures 2 cm × 4 cm, what scale has been used?

9. How many meters long is a rope that fits exactly twice around the rim of a wheel 1.5 m in diameter?

10. The odometer of a car read 16 335.4 km when Ted exited from the turnpike. If he had driven for $3\frac{1}{2}$ hr at an average speed of 90 km/hr, what was the odometer reading when he entered the turnpike?

TEST 16

1a. $\frac{^-5 + {}^-4}{^-3}$

b. $(^+5 - {}^-8)(^-3)$

2a. $0.0325 = $ _?_ %

b. $16\frac{2}{3} \div 3\frac{1}{3}$

3a. $10\frac{1}{4} \times \frac{1}{41}$

b. 1800 cm = _?_ m

4a. $8\frac{5}{6} - 6\frac{7}{8}$

b. $4 - (25\% \text{ of } 16) + 8$

5a. $\frac{3\frac{2}{3}}{7\frac{1}{3}} - \frac{1}{2}$

b. $\sqrt{529}$

6. A rise of 12° in temperature followed by a drop of 7° is the same as a rise or drop of how many degrees?

7. If $6\frac{1}{2}\%$ of a number is 255, what is the number?

8. The width of a flag is $\frac{1}{9}$ times its length. If the flag is 0.81 m long, what is its perimeter?

9. Find the cost of 8,400,000 bricks at $16 per thousand.

10. The top of a bookcase measures 10 in. in width. If the length is 2.4 times the width, how many inches does the diagonal measure?

TEST 17

1a. $16 + {}^-16\frac{1}{2}$ **b.** $36 = \underline{\ ?\ }\%$ of 4

2a. $({}^-4 + {}^+16) - 2$ **b.** 1 gross = $\underline{\ ?\ }$ doz

3a. $84 \times \frac{5}{7} \times \frac{3}{40}$ **b.** $38 = \underline{\ ?\ }\%$ of 76

4a. $5^2 + 5^2$ **b.** $16\frac{1}{3} + 4\frac{2}{15}$

5a. 6% of $16\frac{2}{3}$ **b.** $\dfrac{101\frac{2}{3}}{\frac{5}{12}}$

6. Li has a garden 40 m by 10 m. If she plants 2 melons per m² and sells them at 2 for 95¢, how much will she make?

7. Geri bought a used car for $8400. She put $1400 down and paid the balance, plus 6% interest, over a period of 2 years. What was her monthly payment?

8. The distance between two towns on a road map is 3.5 cm. If the scale of the map is 1 cm = 20 km, how far apart are the two towns?

9. What is the entire surface area of a tank 10 m high and 14 m in diameter? (Use $\frac{22}{7}$ for π.)

10. The eighth grade earned $312 washing cars. If $12\frac{1}{2}\%$ of this was spent for supplies and other expenses, how much money was left?

TEST 18

1a. $\frac{4}{3} \div \frac{3}{4}$ **b.** 48% of 50

2a. 5.89×30 **b.** $91.76 - 10.07$

3a. 110% of $\underline{\ ?\ } = 1045$ **b.** $4\frac{3}{8} \times \frac{3}{5}$

4a. $8.4 = \underline{\ ?\ }\%$ of 420   **b.** $8 \times {}^-4 \div {}^-2$

5a. $({}^-7 \times {}^-8) + {}^-50$ **b.** $6\frac{3}{5} \div 14 \div \frac{22}{7}$

6. A baseball team won 96 games and lost 54 games during the season. What is the percent of games won?

7. On a circle graph, 60° showed the portion of a 24-hr day that a man spent in recreation. How many hours did he spend in recreation?

8. A parallelogram has an area equivalent to the area of a 32-cm square. Its base is 64 cm. What is its altitude?

9. The sum of three consecutive even numbers is 66. What are the numbers?

10. A computer operator ran 18 programs last week. If this is 40% of his library of programs, how many does he have all together?

TEST 19

1a. 28.3×10^2 **b.** $7842 \div 10^3$

2a. $6.3 = \underline{\ ?\ }\%$ of 9.45   **b.** $32 = 200\%$ of $\underline{\ ?\ }$

3a. $({}^-6 \times {}^+4) - {}^-4$ **b.** $32 = 300\%$ of $\underline{\ ?\ }$

4a. $6^2 \times 6^2$ **b.** Estimate: 42.9×9.6

5a. 0.06 km = $\underline{\ ?\ }$ m   **b.** $3n - 2 = 16$
  $n = \underline{\ ?\ }$

6. Susan rides her bicycle 4136 m to and from school every day. How many kilometers does she ride in a 5-day week?

7. A radio listing for $120 was sold at a 20% discount. If the sales tax was 4%, what did the radio cost?

8. Find the area of a triangular banner with a 12 in. base and an 8.2 in. altitude.

9. Lettuce is 80¢ a head. If 3 heads will serve approximately 15 people, what will Mrs. Rippert pay for lettuce for a dinner party of 60 guests?

10. At dawn the temperature was 12°C. By noon it had risen 8°, but by sunset it had dropped 10°. What was the temperature at sunset?

TEST 20

1a. $48\frac{3}{5} - \frac{7}{15}$ **b.** $\sqrt{3^2 + 4^2}$

2a. $3:4 = 6:\underline{\ ?\ }$ **b.** 30.5 cm = $\underline{\ ?\ }$ m

3a. 78.9×10^{-2} **b.** $5a + 7 = 32$
  $a = \underline{\ ?\ }$

4a. $0.9175 = \frac{?}{?}$ **b.** $\dfrac{3(2 + 4)}{2}$

5a. $^-15 - {}^+15 \div {}^-3$ **b.** 1.2×3004

6. Find the length of the diagonal of a rectangle 10 cm wide and 24 cm long.

7. A metal alloy contains 8 parts of zinc to 4 parts of copper. Find the weight of copper in a 3600-kg casting made from this alloy.

8. Find the area in square meters of a parallelogram that has a base of 120 cm and an altitude of 40 cm.

9. How many cm² of paper are needed for a label covering the surface of a can 9 cm in diameter and 15 cm high?

10. A billboard shaped like a trapezoid has bases of 14 ft and 8 ft. The altitude is 6 ft. Find the area of the billboard.

1a. $\frac{2.8}{?} = \frac{0.32}{0.08}$

b. $\frac{5}{8} b = 40$

$b = \underline{?}$

2a. $2\frac{1}{3} - 3\frac{1}{2}$

b. 36% of 5

3a. $6x - 3 = 15$

$x = \underline{?}$

b. $^-8 \div 2 + 4$

4a. $(^-5 \times ^-7) \times ^-2$

b. 25% of 16 − 4

5a. $\sqrt{\frac{4}{9}}$

b. MCDXCII = $\underline{?}$

6. What is the cost of 1.4 kg of beef if 0.7 kg cost \$1.75?

7. 8 increased by a number is 17. What is the number?

8. A forest ranger can see for a distance of 35 km from her tower. How many square kilometers of territory can she observe?

9. 7 less than a certain number is 12. What is the number?

10. Find the length of a pole that has its top resting against the top of a wall 5 m high and its bottom at a point 26 m from the base of the wall.

1a. $0.0306 \div 0.006$

b. $589.64 \div 10^3$

2a. 120 is 40% of $\underline{?}$

b. $^-12 \times ^+4 + ^+40$

3a. $3^2 - 3^2$

b. $28 - 3x = 10$

$x = \underline{?}$

4a. 50 030 cm = $\underline{?}$ m

b. $0.0325 = \frac{?}{?}$

5a. 6.5×0.008

b. $20.04 - 8.765$

6. A certain city block is 133 m by 66.5 m. If Dan walks around it three times, what part of a kilometer will he walk?

7. The length of a rectangle is three times its width. What is the area in m² if the width is 15 m?

8. A field is 48 m long and 36 m wide. What is the difference between the diagonal and $\frac{1}{2}$ the perimeter of the field?

9. 4 increased by 4 times a number is 13. What is the number?

10. Tim's score in a game is $^-16$. If he makes another score of $^-3$, what is his total score?

1a. $0.384 \div 2.4$

b. $\frac{3}{64} = 0.\underline{?}$

2a. 90 is $\underline{?}$ % of 150

b. $(^-21 + ^-16) + ^+7$

3a. $4 - 0.016$

b. $^-8 \times ^-7\frac{1}{4}$

4a. 0.075×0.4

b. $\frac{7.6 \times 3.4}{2}$

5a. $\frac{3}{5} x = 18$

$x = \underline{?}$

b. $\sqrt{225} \div \frac{3}{5}$

6. If a plane can fly 625 km in 2.5 hr, how far will it go in $1\frac{1}{5}$ hr?

7. How many days are there in March, April, and May all together?

8. Kim's watch lost 2 minutes one day but gained 5 minutes the following day. How many minutes off the correct time was the watch at the end of the second day?

9. Tony and Peter collect coins. Tony has three more than twice as many as Peter. Together they have 87 coins. How many coins does Peter have?

10. A scientific encyclopedia listing for \$150 was sold for \$127.50. What was the rate of discount?

1a. $100 - 75.48$

b. $(6 \times ^-9) - ^-4$

2a. $\left(\frac{5}{8} \times \frac{1}{5}\right) + \frac{3}{4}$

b. $\underline{?} - \frac{2}{3} = 3\frac{5}{6}$

3a. $\frac{?}{8} = \frac{1.5}{1.6}$

b. If $n = 3$,

$\left(n - \frac{1}{2}\right) + \frac{3}{4} = \underline{?}$

4a. $\frac{1}{4}$% of 1600

b. $\sqrt{198}$ is between $\underline{?}$ and $\underline{?}$

5a. $\frac{10^5}{10^3} = \underline{?}$

b. 1.7 is $\underline{?}$ % of 34

6. A road 20 m wide was built through the Blanch estate. If the road has an area of 2.9 km², how long is it?

7. If 6 eighth graders can arrange the chairs in an auditorium in 20 minutes, how long will it take 4 of them working at the same rate?

8. Mrs. Brady bought a \$420 microwave oven for \$100 down and \$11.80 per week for 28 weeks. How much more did she pay by using the installment plan?

9. Susan completed 3 times as many art projects as Molly. Together they have completed 12 projects. How many has Molly completed?

10. At his father's car wash, Peter checked in 23 cars the first hour, 18 the second hour, 12 the third hour, and 26 the fourth hour. What was the average number of cars that entered the car wash each hour?

Drill and Mental Math

1 DRILL

1. What is the value of 6 in each numeral:
   6,425,312; 463,289; 33,469; 78,642
2. Round to the nearest thousand:
   62,574; 37,584; 892; 89,492; 79,601
3. Add 100 to: 47; 563; 7643; 83,724;
   423,526; 302,891; 145,960
4. Add: 3 + 4 + 5 + 6, 30 + 40 + 50 + 60,
   300 + 400 + 500 + 600
5. Subtract: 15 − 9, 150 − 90, 1500 − 900

MENTAL

1. Write the standard numeral:
   300,000 + 40,000 + 8000 + 300 + 60 + 5
2. Compare. Use > or <.
   456,789 _?_ 466,789

3. Which names the greatest number?
   36 ÷ 4, 36 × 4, 36 − 4, 36 + 4
4. Which names the least number?
   24 + 4, 24 − 4, 24 ÷ 4, 24 × 4
5. Add: 8405 + 6698 = _?_
6. Find the difference by subtracting and
   adding:
   5467 − 2800 = (5467 − 3000) + _?_ = _?_
7. Find the difference to the nearest thousand:
   49,925 − 25,395
8. Write in expanded form: 30,600,210
9. Find the sum to the nearest thousand:
   2456 + 3815 + 5190
10. A newscaster reported a federal grant for
    $224,500. Actually, the grant was for
    $20,000 more. What was the actual
    amount of the grant?

2 DRILL

1. Round to the nearest hundred:
   860; 592; 1256; 3205; 10,945
2. Round to the nearest tenth:
   0.05, 0.16, 0.370, 4.06, 7.71, 32.03
3. Round to the nearest hundredth:
   4.345, 6.728, 0.582, 0.766, 83.891
4. Add 0.4 to: 0.3, 0.34, 0.033, 3.350
5. Subtract 0.5 from: 1, 3, 0.9, 1.5, 2.3,
   0.74

MENTAL

1. Which is equal to 210 × 398?
   8358; 83,580; 835,800
2. Compare. (Use <, =, or >.)
   45 × 710 _?_ (40 × 710) + (5 × 710)

3. One car weighs 2000 pounds. How much
   do 10 such cars weigh?
4. Which is greater: 50 × 310 or 18,000?
5. Write the standard numeral for:
   (5 × 1,000,000) + (7 × 100,000) +
   (9 × 1000) + (6 × 10)
6. Add 500 to 684.
7. From 6230 subtract 5000.
8. Tim had $648 in the bank. After he
   deposited $200, how much was in his
   savings account?
9. When Adam withdrew $300 from his
   account of $792, how much money had
   he left?
10. One factor of 2400 is 60. What is the other
    factor?

3 DRILL

1. Round to the nearest million: 896,524;
   2,135,673; 7,842,130; 9,520,310
2. Add: 8 + 6, 80 + 600, 800 + 600,
   8000 + 6000, 8 million + 6 million
3. Multiply by 200: 1, 3, 15, 10, 24, 250
4. Divide: 8 ÷ 4, 80 ÷ 4, 800 ÷ 4, 8000 ÷ 4
5. Divide by 50: 50, 500, 300, 3000, 100,
   1000, 200, 2000, 400, 4000, 5000

MENTAL

1. How many 100-lb bags can you fill with
   160 lb + 235 lb + 406 lb of sand?
2. There are 100 centimeters in one meter.
   How many meters is 600 centimeters?
3. What number multiplied by 60 equals
   1800?
4. Write 2 and 2 hundredths.
5. Arrange in order from least to greatest:
   0.1, 0.01, 0.001, 0.16, 0.016
6. Is 0.07 + 0.9 greater or less than 1?
7. At $.90 a dozen, find the cost of 7 dozen.
8. Elena bought 10 hamburgers at $.89 each.
   Was $9.00 enough to pay for them all?
9. 230 boys attended the school picnic. This
   was 60 less than the number of girls. How
   many girls attended?
10. Of 184 parking places, only 70 were filled.
    How many places were not filled?

4 DRILL

1. Express as decimals:
   $\frac{1}{5}, \frac{1}{10}, \frac{1}{100}, \frac{1}{2}, \frac{1}{4}, \frac{3}{4}, \frac{7}{10}, \frac{1}{20}, \frac{3}{10}$
2. What number is named?
   $8 + 4$, $31 - 4$, 4×7, $48 \div 4$
3. Tell the correct operation $(+, -, \times, \div)$:
   $24 \underline{\ ?\ } 4 = 28$ $24 \underline{\ ?\ } 4 = 20$
   $24 \underline{\ ?\ } 4 = 96$ $24 \underline{\ ?\ } 4 = 6$
4. Tell the correct relation $(= \text{ or } \neq)$:
   $29 + 4 \underline{\ ?\ } 30$ $32 \div 4 \underline{\ ?\ } 8$
   $9 \times 4 \underline{\ ?\ } 30$ $44 - 4 \underline{\ ?\ } 40$
5. Tell the correct relation $(<, =, >)$:
   $38 \times 4 \underline{\ ?\ } 160$ $38 + 22 \underline{\ ?\ } 60$
   $38 \div 2 \underline{\ ?\ } 20$ $82 - 38 \underline{\ ?\ } 40$

MENTAL

1. Which is greater: $29 + 4$ or $29 - 4$?

2. If 1 liter costs $.45, about how much will 8.6 liters cost?
3. Multiply 2.45 by 0.2 and add 0.01 to the product.
4. A butcher received 4 shipments of beef. Each shipment weighed 15.5 kg. What was the total weight of the beef?
5. Add 9 to the product of 100×9.
6. From the sum of $82 + 6$ subtract 8.
7. Don filled 67 boxes. Ted filled 14 more than Don. How many boxes did Ted fill?
8. At 200 miles per hour, how far can you go in 4 hours?
9. A plane goes 1400 miles in 4 hours. Find the number of miles per hour.
10. Tim weighs 60 kg, which is 6 kg more than Sue weighs. How much does Sue weigh?

5 DRILL

1. Round to the nearest ten: 42, 68, 258, 387, 1357, 8092, 2096
2. Tell the value of 4 in: 24; 304; 1543; 27,460; 2.4; 3.004; 1.7114
3. Round to the nearest tenth. Subtract.
   $0.8 - 0.03$, $0.25 - 0.05$, $0.65 - 0.6$, $0.75 - 0.57$, $1.24 - 0.78$
4. Tell the correct relation $(<, =, >)$:
   $\frac{5}{6} \underline{\ ?\ } \frac{2}{3}$, $\frac{3}{4} \underline{\ ?\ } \frac{5}{6}$, $\frac{10}{12} \underline{\ ?\ } \frac{5}{6}$,
   $\frac{7}{8} \underline{\ ?\ } \frac{21}{24}$
5. $\frac{2}{3} = \frac{?}{12}$, $\frac{3}{4} = \frac{?}{16}$, $\frac{4}{5} = \frac{?}{25}$, $\frac{3}{8} = \frac{?}{48}$

MENTAL

1. Which is greater: $3.25 + 0.70$ or 4?

2. Which is less: $5.82 - 0.85$ or 5?
3. From a 3-meter length of wire, Fred cut lengths of 0.8 meter, 0.6 meter, and 1.1 meters. How much wire was left?
4. Write the numeral: $7(10) + 2(0.1) + 5(0.001) + 1(0.001)$
5. What fraction added to $\frac{5}{7}$ is equal to 1?
6. How much greater than $\frac{4}{9}$ is 1?
7. Order from least to greatest: $\frac{1}{2}, \frac{1}{5}, \frac{1}{6}, \frac{1}{3}, \frac{1}{10}, \frac{1}{100}$
8. Tom had 100 stamps. He gave $\frac{2}{5}$ of them away. How many stamps did he give away?
9. Mary's allowance was increased from $6 to $8. Express this increase as a fraction in simplest form.
10. Which is greater: $\frac{2}{3}$ of 18 or $\frac{5}{6}$ of 18?

6 DRILL

1. Simplify: $\frac{10}{12}, \frac{8}{16}, \frac{14}{21}, \frac{9}{12}, \frac{6}{24}, \frac{27}{36}$
2. Tell which fraction is greater:
   $\frac{1}{2}$ or $\frac{5}{8}$, $\frac{4}{5}$ or $\frac{11}{15}$, $\frac{11}{20}$ or $\frac{1}{2}$, $\frac{3}{10}$ or $\frac{4}{5}$
3. Subtract: $\frac{5}{8} - \frac{1}{4}$, $\frac{3}{4} - \frac{1}{2}$, $\frac{7}{10} - \frac{1}{5}$, $\frac{8}{9} - \frac{1}{3}$
4. Subtract: $3\frac{3}{5} - 1\frac{1}{5}$, $5\frac{7}{8} - 2\frac{5}{8}$,
   $8\frac{5}{7} - 4\frac{3}{7}$, $6\frac{2}{3} - 1\frac{1}{3}$
5. From 3 subtract: $\frac{1}{2}$, $1\frac{1}{2}$, $\frac{3}{4}$, $2\frac{3}{4}$, $\frac{5}{6}$

MENTAL

1. Write the number that is 1 greater than 56,719.
2. Write the number that is 1 less than 500,010.

3. Compare. (Use $<$, $=$, or $>$.)
   $\left(8 \times \frac{1}{10}\right) + \left(4 \times \frac{1}{100}\right) \underline{\ ?\ } \frac{8}{10} + \frac{4}{100} + \frac{2}{1000}$
4. How much greater than 1 is $\frac{1}{5} + \frac{3}{5} + \frac{2}{5}$?
5. How much would you save on a table that regularly costs $64 if you bought it at a "$\frac{1}{4}$ off" sale?
6. How much change would you receive if you used a $20 bill to pay for a lunch that cost $10.38?
7. At $6.25 a yard, find the cost of $\frac{1}{5}$ yard of lace.
8. Which is greater: $\frac{2}{5} \times \frac{7}{10}$ or $\frac{2}{5} + \frac{7}{10}$?
9. How much greater is $1\frac{1}{4}$ than $\frac{9}{8}$?
10. Eric earned $16.00. If he saved $\frac{2}{5}$ of it, how much did he save?

7 DRILL

1. Change to improper fractions: $6\frac{1}{2}$, $5\frac{2}{3}$, $3\frac{5}{8}$, $1\frac{3}{4}$, $10\frac{1}{5}$, $2\frac{5}{6}$

2. Change to mixed numerals: $\frac{23}{18}$, $\frac{25}{4}$, $\frac{62}{7}$, $\frac{34}{5}$, $\frac{73}{9}$, $\frac{32}{6}$

3. Identify as prime or composite: 3, 13, 15, 18, 43, 63, 51, 9

4. Tell the equivalent fraction that has a denominator of 10: $\frac{1}{2}$, $\frac{2}{5}$, $\frac{5}{5}$, $\frac{10}{50}$, $\frac{5}{25}$

5. Subtract: $\frac{5}{8} - \frac{1}{2}$, $\frac{5}{6} - \frac{1}{3}$, $\frac{7}{9} - \frac{1}{3}$, $\frac{3}{4} - \frac{1}{8}$

MENTAL

1. Write the value of 7 in 0.007.
2. How much greater than $\frac{27}{8}$ is 4?

3. What fraction represents $\frac{1}{8}$ more than the original whole?
4. What fraction added to $\frac{1}{4}$ is equal to $\frac{5}{8}$?
5. Mr. White used $\frac{5}{8}$ of a full tank of gasoline and Mrs. White used $\frac{1}{4}$ of the tank. Did they empty the tank?
6. Write the prime numbers that are greater than 10 and less than 20.
7. What fraction represents $\frac{1}{5}$ less than the original whole?
8. $\frac{2}{5}$ of a number is 30. What is the number?
9. $\left(\frac{3}{7} \div \frac{3}{7}\right) \div \frac{4}{5} = $?
10. Helen earns $40 a week and saves $15 of it. What part of her weekly earnings does she save?

8 DRILL

1. Round to estimate the quotient: $4000 \div 9$, $3000 \div 28$, $20{,}000 \div 49$, $10{,}000 \div 22$, $63{,}000 \div 50$

2. Tell the reciprocal: $\frac{1}{2}$, $\frac{2}{3}$, $\frac{5}{6}$, $\frac{3}{4}$, $\frac{5}{7}$, $\frac{2}{9}$

3. Complete: $8 \div 2 = 8 \times $?, $\frac{1}{2} \div \frac{2}{3} = \frac{1}{2} \times $?, $3 \div \frac{3}{4} = 3 \times $?

4. Divide 10 by: 2, $\frac{1}{2}$, 5, $\frac{1}{5}$, $\frac{2}{5}$, 10, $\frac{1}{10}$, 20

5. Divide: $\frac{1}{4} \div \frac{1}{2}$, $\frac{1}{3} \div \frac{1}{6}$, $\frac{1}{5} \div \frac{1}{10}$, $\frac{1}{8} \div \frac{1}{4}$

MENTAL

1. If $\frac{1}{2}$ watermelon was shared among 8 people, what part of a whole watermelon did each receive?

2. How many $\frac{3}{4}$ in. pieces of paper can be cut from a strip 9 in. long?
3. What fraction added to $\frac{3}{5}$ is equal to 1?
4. $1\frac{1}{6} \times $? $= 1$
5. If $2\frac{1}{2}$ cases of juice cost $20, what is the price of a case?
6. Simplify: $[(6 \times 8) - (40 \div 5)] + 3$.
7. Round $12\frac{5}{8}$ to the nearest whole number.
8. Which is greater: $\frac{1}{2} \div \frac{1}{4}$ or $\frac{1}{3} \div \frac{1}{6}$?
9. How much greater than 10 is $6\frac{1}{2} + 4\frac{3}{4}$?
10. Write the nearest odd number that is less than the product of 8×7.

9 DRILL

1. Read each numeral, changing the fractional part to its equivalent decimal: $0.5\frac{1}{2}$, $0.2\frac{7}{10}$, $12\frac{1}{2}$, $0.08\frac{3}{8}$, $0.4\frac{1}{4}$, $0.04\frac{1}{4}$

2. Add: $\frac{1}{4} + \frac{1}{2}$, $9 + \frac{2}{3}$, $3\frac{1}{2} + \frac{1}{8}$, $2\frac{1}{2} + 4\frac{1}{4}$

3. Subtract: $\frac{1}{2} - \frac{1}{4}$, $8 - \frac{5}{6}$, $6\frac{1}{2} - \frac{1}{4}$, $3\frac{3}{4} - 1\frac{1}{2}$

4. Multiply: $\frac{2}{3} \times \frac{3}{4}$, $\frac{1}{4} \times \frac{4}{5}$, $\frac{3}{4} \times \frac{1}{5}$, $\frac{3}{8} \times 1\frac{1}{3}$

5. Divide: $\frac{5}{8} \div 5$, $\frac{3}{4} \div 6$, $4 \div \frac{1}{4}$, $8 \div \frac{2}{3}$

MENTAL

1. Solve for n: $\frac{2}{3} \times n = 1$
2. Find the value of $\frac{3}{5} \times \frac{1}{3} \times 0$.

3. Write the prime factors of 51.
4. Which represents $4 \div 5$: $\frac{4}{5}$ or $\frac{5}{4}$?
5. Find the difference between $\frac{2}{3}$ and $\frac{3}{4}$.
6. Joe mowed $\frac{1}{4}$ of the lawn yesterday and $\frac{3}{8}$ of it today. How much of the lawn is still to be mowed?
7. Which is less: $\frac{9}{8} - \frac{3}{4}$ or $\frac{9}{8} \div \frac{3}{4}$?
8. To $\frac{3}{8}$ of 64 add 10.
9. If a lawyer's fee is $\frac{1}{8}$ of the money collected on a client's behalf, how much will the lawyer charge for collecting $1200?
10. What number is named? $\left(\frac{1}{3} \div \frac{1}{3}\right) + \left(\frac{1}{3} \times \frac{1}{3}\right) - 1$

10 DRILL

1. Add: 6 + 7, 600 + 700, 6000 + 7000
2. Tell if the sentence is true or false:
   8 + (4 × 3) = 20   16 − (2 × 3) = 12
   (3 × 2) × 8 = 50   (9 − 1) ÷ (2 + 2) = 2
3. Tell which is greater: 9(8) or 70, 6 × 3 or 23 − 6, 24 + 15 or 4 × 9
4. Tell the order for doing the operations:
   3(4 + 6)   [(16 ÷ 2) + 6] − 5
   (5 × 6) + (10 × 3)   4[(2 + 3) + 5]
5. Tell if the sentence is true or false:
   3 + 0 = 3   0 + 7 = 0   8 − 8 = 0
   0 + 7 = 7 + 0   3 − 0 = 0

MENTAL

1. Which is greater: $\frac{5}{6} \times \frac{1}{6}$ or $\frac{5}{6} \div \frac{1}{6}$?

2. Write an open sentence for: the sum of a number plus itself is equal to 12.
3. Which expression shows 2 less than a number? $n + 2$, $n − 2$, $2 \times n$, $n \div 2$
4. Which expression shows a number divided by 6? $n − 6$, $n + 6$, $6 \times n$, $n \div 6$
5. 30 is 25 more than what number?
6. Jane is 6 years older than Paul. If Jane is 20 years old, how old is Paul?
7. If 7 erasers cost 84¢, what will one eraser cost?
8. Find the area of a picture 9 cm by 7 cm.
9. At 30¢ each, how many lemons can be bought for $4.50?
10. Beth bought a dress at $\frac{1}{4}$ off the regular price. If the regular price was $24.00, how much did she save?

11 DRILL

1. Multiply by 7 and add 2 to: 3, 4, 5, 7, 8
2. Solve: $6 + n = 8$ $y + 7 = 9$ $n + 8 = 10$
   $4x = 11$ $8 + n = 16$ $m + 5 = 10$
   $8 + b = 17$ $r + 7 = 15$
3. Solve: $n − 2 = 9$ $a − 7 = 6$ $x − 9 = 20$
   $m − 7 = 6$ $n − 4 = 13$ $y − 6 = 14$
   $x − 7 = 28$ $20 − y = 7$
4. Tell which fractions are a little less than 1:
   $\frac{1}{9}$, $\frac{4}{5}$, $\frac{7}{15}$, $\frac{9}{10}$, $\frac{45}{47}$, $\frac{3}{50}$, $\frac{6}{11}$, $\frac{25}{28}$
5. If $n = 7$, what number is named by:
   $4n + 2$ $5n − 5$
   $42 − n$ $3(n + 4)$

MENTAL

1. What number is named? $[(9 \times 6) + 6] − 9$
2. What number added to 0.07 is equal to 1?
3. How much greater than 0.7 is 1?
4. Write an open sentence for: $\frac{2}{3}$ of a number is less than 60.
5. Write an open sentence for: 4 less than a number is 12.
6. 30 is 25 less than what number?
7. From the sum of 82 + 6 subtract 8.
8. The sum of 12 and a number is 20. What is the number?
9. 4 added to twice a number is 16. What is the number?
10. $60 is $25 less than what amount?

12 DRILL

1. If $n = 6$, what number is named by:
   $76 + n$ (9 × n) + 3
   (46 − n) × 2   (n ÷ 2)15
2. Solve: $8 + x = 17$ $r + 9 = 21$ $13 + c = 43$
   $n − 9 = 13$ $m − 6 = 23$ $s − 7 = 19$
   $c − 23 = 12$
3. Express algebraically: 7 more than y, 6 less than 2, twice c, the product of 7 and n, 8 times a number, a number divided by 8, $\frac{2}{3}$ of a number
4. Solve: $7n = 84$, $6n = 30$, $5n = 75$
5. Solve: $x \div 4 = 7$, $\frac{r}{4} = 15$, $\frac{x}{21} = 7$

MENTAL

1. Write an algebraic expression to show the product of a number and 7.

2. The product of a number and 9 is 27. What is the number?
3. Twice a number is 24. What is the number?
4. Three times a number divided by 8 is 12. What is the number?
5. $\frac{1}{3}$ of what number plus 10 is 30?
6. 35 is the product of what number and 7?
7. The sum of 5 times a number plus 3 is 68. What is the number?
8. Bob is 3 years older than his brother Joe. Joe is 11. How old is Bob?
9. Jean earned $54. If she saved $\frac{1}{3}$ of this, how much did she save?
10. What number is named? $[(8 \times 3) − 3 \div 7]$

13 DRILL

1. Name the opposite integer:
   $^-4$, $^+8$, $^-15$, $^-9$, $^+12$, $^+3$
2. Read in order from least to greatest:
   $^+3$, $^+8$, $^+1$, $^+7$, 0, $^+5$, $^-6$, $^-1$, $^-5$, $^-3$
3. Read in order from greatest to least:
   $^+3$, $^+8$, 0, $^+7$, $^+5$, $^+9$, $^-7$, $^-2$, $^-8$, $^-4$
4. Tell what integer is 1 less than:
   $^+1$, $^-15$, 0, $^-8$, $^-10$, $^+19$
5. Tell what integer is 1 greater than:
   $^+5$, $^+11$, $^-8$, $^-10$, $^+16$, $^-28$

MENTAL

1. Write the numeral that represents negative 4.

2. Write the integer that is the opposite of $^-6$.
3. On a horizontal number line, what integer is two units to the left of negative 3? Write the numeral.
4. On a horizontal number line, what integer is two units to the right of negative 1? Write the numeral.
5. What integer is suggested by a profit of $60 and a loss of $22?
6. What integer is suggested by a temperature of 8 degrees below zero?
7. Write an integer to express the idea of 30 feet below sea level.
8. What operation is suggested by moving on a number line from $^-4$ to $^-1$?
9. Does $(^-5 + 2) + 7$ equal $^-5 + (2 + 7)$?
10. How much less than $^-1$ is $^-9$?

14 DRILL

1. Add: $^-5 + {}^+3$, $^+2 + {}^-7$, $^-1 + {}^-8$, $^-5 + {}^+13$
2. Name the integer that is 2 greater than:
   $^-3$, 0, $^-5$, $^+11$, $^-17$, $^-1$
3. Complete: $^+5 - {}^+4 = {}^+5 + \underline{\ ?\ }$,
   $^+7 - {}^-8 = {}^+7 + \underline{\ ?\ }$, $^-3 - {}^+6 = {}^-3 + \underline{\ ?\ }$
4. Tell the number named:
   $^+7 - {}^+2$, $^+7 - {}^-2$, $^-7 - {}^-2$, $^-7 - {}^+2$,
   $^+3 - {}^+2$, $^+3 - {}^-2$, $^-3 - {}^-2$, $^-3 - {}^+2$
5. Multiply:
   $^-8 \times {}^-7$ $^-6 \times {}^-9$ $^-4 \times {}^-10$
   $^-15 \times {}^-5$ $^+3 \times {}^-8$ $^+5 \times {}^-7$ $^+10 \times {}^-9$

MENTAL

1. On a horizontal number line, what integer is 8 units to the left of zero?

2. What number is 7 greater than $^-3$?
3. What number is 5 less than 0?
4. Compare. (Use < or >.) $^-14$ $\underline{\ ?\ }$ $^-24$
5. One day, the temperature was $^-8°C$. After the temperature rose 10 degrees, what was the new reading?
6. How much less than $9\frac{2}{3}$ is $4\frac{2}{5}$?
7. What number is named? $^-5(^-4 \times {}^+11)$
8. Which is greater: $^+4 - {}^-6$ or $^-4 - {}^+6$?
9. Does $^+3 + (^-2 + {}^+4)$ equal $(^+3 - {}^-2) + {}^+4$?
10. The temperature was 3°C. Then it dropped 10°. What was the new temperature?

15 DRILL

1. Divide: $^-16 \div {}^-4$, $^-20 \div {}^-10$,
   $^-144 \div {}^-12$, $^-9 \div {}^-3$, $^+27 \div {}^-3$,
   $^+36 \div {}^-12$
2. Solve: $a + 7 = 16$, $\frac{d}{6} = {}^-12$,
   $b - 12 = 20$, $^-2w + 7 = 25$
3. Translate and solve: A number and 4 is 16, a number divided by 5 is 25, a number minus 4 is 8.
4. Solve: $12 + e = {}^-19$, $\frac{x}{5} - 3 = {}^-7$,
   $y - 9 = {}^-18$, $2x + 4 = {}^-16$
5. Divide by 10 and then add $^-2$ to:
   $^+100$, $^-100$, $^+50$, $^-50$, $^+40$, $^-40$, $^+200$,
   $^-200$, $^+70$

2. The product of a number and $^-8$ is 56. What is the number?
3. Let $n = {}^-4$. Simplify: $8n - (3n + 5)$
4. $\frac{1}{5}$ of what number minus 3 equals $^-10$?
5. Find the value of x: $^-8x + 6 = 54$
6. Solve for n: $10(n - 4) = {}^-70$
7. In a school of 926 pupils, there are 22 more boys than girls. How many girls are there? How many boys?
8. Let $a = {}^-4$, $b = 5$, and $c = 0$. Evaluate: $2a + 3c - b$
9. Peter gained 9 points, then lost 15 points. What is his score?
10. If 6 is subtracted from a certain number and the difference is multiplied by 10, the product is 70. What is the number?

MENTAL

1. Write the missing factor: $^-15 \div \underline{\ ?\ } = 3$

526

16 DRILL

1. Tell the correct relation (= or ≠):
$^+7 + {}^+5 \underline{\ ?\ } 12$ $^-6 + {}^-9 \underline{\ ?\ } 15$
$^-7 + {}^+3 \underline{\ ?\ } 10$ $^+8 + {}^-3 \underline{\ ?\ } 5$

2. Give the value of n: $^-14 + {}^+2 = 2n$
$^+15 - {}^-3 = 3n$ $^+21 + {}^-1 = 5n$

3. Solve: $^-2n = {}^+12$, $\frac{n}{6} = {}^-3$, $^+5n = {}^-20$,
$^-7n = {}^-42$, $n \div {}^+4 = {}^-7$, $n \div {}^-6 = {}^+4$

4. Add $^-1.1$ to: $^+2.2$, $^-2.2$, $^+5.5$, $^-5.5$,
$^+3.4$, $^-3.4$

5. Subtract $^+1.5$ from: $^+1.5$, $^-1.5$, $^+2$, $^-2$,
$^+3.5$, $^-3.5$

MENTAL

1. Write an open sentence for: a number
minus 4 is equal to 8.5.

---

2. Write the numeral that represents 3 times
negative 2.7.

3. The opposite of one third of a number is
$^-12$. What is the number?

4. What number minus 4 is equal to $^-7.3$?

5. Jane's age 8 years ago was $12\frac{1}{2}$. What is
her present age?

6. From $^-2\frac{3}{4}$ subtract $1\frac{1}{2}$.

7. Double the sum of $^-19.3$ and $^-7.7$.

8. $(^+2)\ (^-3.2)\ (^-2.5)\ (^-0.5)\ (^+4)\ (0) = \underline{\ ?\ }$

9. To $\frac{^-1}{8}$ of 240 add 8.

10. Evaluate the expression $a + b - 2c$ when
$a = {}^+1.4$, $b = {}^+8.6$, and $c = {}^-4$.

---

17 DRILL

1. Add $^+10$ to: $^-1$, $^+3$, $^-8$, $^+11$, $^+2.4$, $^-3.5$,
$^+1.8$, $^-9.5$, $^-2.1$

2. Tell which fraction is less: $\frac{^-5}{8}$ or $\frac{^-8}{5}$, $\frac{^-5}{2}$ or
$\frac{^-2}{5}$, $\frac{^-7}{3}$ or $\frac{^-3}{7}$, $\frac{^-5}{6}$ or $\frac{^-6}{5}$

3. Subtract $^+2.1$ from: $^+2.1$, $^-2.1$, $^+3.5$,
$^-3.5$, $^+4.7$, $^-4.7$, $^+7.9$, $^-7.9$

4. Divide: $^-0.05 \div {}^+5$, $^-1.2 \div {}^-6$,
$^-0.9 \div {}^-0.3$, $^+4.8 \div {}^-0.6$, $^-0.35 \div {}^+7$

5. Multiply by $^-1.2$: 3, 5, 7, 9, 8, 0, 0.03

MENTAL

1. Which is greater: $\frac{1}{2} \div \frac{^-1}{4}$ or $\frac{^-1}{4} \div \frac{1}{2}$?

2. Which is greater: $\frac{^-2}{3}$ or $\frac{^-3}{4}$?

---

3. After John had sold 42 papers, he had 18
papers left. How many papers did he have
at first?

4. The sum of 9 and a number is 15. What is
the number?

5. The sum of 16 and a number is 30. What
is the number?

6. 9 added to twice a number is 19. What is
the number?

7. Use < or > to make the sentence true:
$\frac{^-2}{5} \times {}^+20 \underline{\ ?\ } \frac{^-2}{5} \times {}^+10$.

8. Three times a number divided by 8 is $^-12$.
What is the number?

9. At $1.25 a yard, what is the cost of
4 yards of material?

10. At 250 miles per hour, how long will it take
a plane to go 2500 miles?

---

18 DRILL

1. Add $\frac{^-1}{2}$ to: $^-1$, $^-1\frac{1}{2}$, $^-1\frac{1}{4}$, $^+3$, $^+3\frac{1}{2}$, $^+4$, $^-3\frac{1}{2}$,
$^-5\frac{3}{4}$

2. Multiply by $^-3$: $^+2$, $^+2\frac{1}{3}$, $^-3$, $^-3\frac{2}{3}$, $^+4$, $^+4\frac{1}{9}$,
$^-5$, $^-5\frac{2}{9}$

3. Subtract $^+10$ from: $^+1$, $^-1$, $^+5$, $^+2.5$, $^-3.5$,
$^+6.1$, $^-4.8$, $^+5.3$, $^-1.2$

4. Round to the nearest tenth: $^-1.17$, $^+3.59$,
$^-2.2\frac{3}{4}$, $^+7.8\frac{1}{5}$, $^-9.7\frac{1}{2}$

5. Express as decimals: $\frac{^-1}{5}$, $\frac{^-1}{4}$, $\frac{^-1}{10}$, $^+0.1\frac{1}{2}$,
$^-1.1\frac{2}{5}$, $^-2\frac{3}{4}$, $^+5.2\frac{4}{5}$

MENTAL

1. Which is greater: $0.9 - 0.3$ or
$0.09 - 0.03$?

---

2. Which is greater: $^-0.035 + {}^-0.7$ or $^-1$?

3. Write the equivalent decimal for $\frac{^-5}{8}$.

4. What number will make this equation true?
$^-4 + n = 0$.

5. Compare. (Use <, =, or >.)
$^-4 + {}^-5 \underline{\ ?\ } {}^-9 + {}^+3$.

6. How much less than $^-0.05$ is $^-0.5$?

7. Order from least to greatest: $^-0.4$, $^-0.04$,
$^-0.45$, $^-0.14$, $^-1.4$.

8. Tell the decimal named: $^-16 \div 1000$.

9. Which is closer to $\frac{^-1}{2}$: $\frac{^-5}{9}$ or $^-0.5\frac{1}{4}$?

10. Express the sum as a decimal:
$2.04\frac{3}{5} + 4.1\frac{1}{4}$.

DRILL

1. Tell if the number is divisible by 5: 43, 65, 70, 235, 400, 314
2. Tell if the number is divisible by 2: 64, 73, 228, 357, 601
3. Tell if the number is divisible by 9: 727, 1512, 6381, 3650, 4521
4. What number is named? 10^6, 10^2, 10^4, 10^5, 10^{-1}, 10^0, 10^{-2}, 10^{-3}
5. Name the exponent of 10 for: 100, 1000, 0.1, 1,000,000, 0.0001

MENTAL

1. Jeff weighs 63 kg. This is 3 times his brother's weight. How much does his brother weigh?

2. Write the standard numeral for:
$(7 \times 10^5) + (6 \times 10^4) + (3 \times 10^3) + (5 \times 10^2) + (4 \times 10^1) + (8 \times 10^0)$
3. Which is greater: 2×10^4 or 20×1000?
4. Use exponents to write 43,261 in expanded form.
5. Which is greater: 4×10^5 or 5×10^4?
6. Let $a = 3$ and $b = 4$. Find $a^2 + b^2$.
7. Which is greater: 10^2 or 10^{-2}?
8. Express 0.0000302 in scientific notation.
9. Express 0.208007 in expanded form using exponents.
10. 40 pupils took a test. If 0.9 of them passed, how many pupils passed the test?

20

DRILL

1. Square: 10, 12, 13, 9, 4, 8, 15
2. Express in exponential form: 5×5, $8 \times 8 \times 8 \times 8$, $6 \times 6 \times 6 \times 6 \times 6$, $2 \times 2 \times 2 \times 2 \times 2 \times 2 \times 2$
3. Which is greater: 2^3 or 3^2? 1^8 or 2^4? 5^1 or 7^2? 7^3 or 4^5?
4. Find the product in exponential form: $10^3(10^4)$, $10^4(10^4)$, $(10^1)10^7$, $10^2(10^5)$
5. Find the quotient in exponential form: $10^6 \div 10^2$, $10^5 \div 10^4$, $10^8 \div 10^5$, $10^7 \div 10^3$

MENTAL

1. Write the product as a number with an exponent: $4 \times 4 \times 4 \times 4 \times 4 \times 4$

2. Write the standard numeral: $2^4 \times 2^2$
3. 20 is equal to the sum of the squares of what two numbers?
4. Write this product using an exponent: 40×40
5. Write the standard numeral: 4×10^5
6. Which is greater: 6.2×10^6 or 62,000,000?
7. Which has three identical factors? 12, 16, 27, 21
8. Which is divisible by 6? 99, 84, 963
9. If a man traveled 540 km in 9 hours, at what rate of speed was he traveling?
10. What number is named? 6×10^{-4}

DRILL

1. Name the prime factors of: 4, 6, 8, 10, 25, 9, 15, 18
2. Express in exponential form: 5×5, 4×4, $10 \times 10 \times 10$, $6 \times 6 \times 6$, $2 \times 2 \times 2 \times 2$
3. What number is named? 5^2, 6^2, 8^2, 9^2, 1^2, 3^2
4. Name two equal factors of: 25, 49, 36, 1, 4, 64
5. What number is named? $2^2 \times 3$, 2×5^2, $2^2 \times 5$, $3^2 \times 2$

MENTAL

1. The product of what number and itself is 400?

2. What is one of the two equal factors of 225?
3. Find the area of a square that is 12 centimeters on a side.
4. The area of a square tabletop is 81 square feet. How many yards long is each edge?
5. Which is greater: 12^2 or 12×2?
6. Write the first 6 non-zero multiples of 6.
7. Write the prime factors of 28.
8. Which of these numbers are divisible by 6? 765, 842, 1260, 8088
9. Write the next three numbers in this sequence: 1, 2, 4, 8, _?_, _?_, _?_
10. Which is greater: (6.03×10^0) or $0.0603 \div .001$?

DRILL

1. Write these products in exponential form: $6^2(6)$, $8^2(8)$, $3^2(3)$, $5^5(5)$, $1^2(1)$
2. Read each and then name the factors: 3^3, 4^3, 10^3, 1^3, 2^3, 9^3, 8^3
3. If $a = 2$, what number is named by: $a + 4$, $a \times a$, a^3, $2a - 4$, $4a$, $3a^2$?
4. Express in scientific notation: 13,000; 2700; 450,000; 6,000,000; 9,810,000
5. What number is named? 3×10^3, 5×10^5, 2×10^4, 6.1×10^4, 8.2×10^3, 2.5×10^4, 4.7×10^5

MENTAL

1. Does 4^3 equal 3^4?
2. Which is greater: 6^3 or 3×6?
3. Which quotient is greater than 1000? $5365 \div 55$, $5365 \div 5$, $5365 \div 525$

4. Write the standard numeral: $7(10^2) + 3(10^0) + 2(10^{-3}) + 1(10^{-5})$
5. Which is greater: 200×425 or 2000×45?
6. The product of what number and itself is 900?
7. The number of centimeters in the diameter of an atom is expressed in scientific notation as 1.06×10^{-8}. Write the diameter as a standard numeral.
8. Write in exponential form: 876,505.
9. Which is the best estimate for the quotient of $8.4 \div {}^-3$: between $^-3$ and $^-4$ or between $^-2$ and $^-3$?
10. An airline prepares 5220 meals for 63 flights. On the average, about how many meals are served on one flight?

23

DRILL

1. Write ratios equivalent to 3 to 4: $6:\underline{?}$, $9:\underline{?}$, $12:\underline{?}$, $15:\underline{?}$, $24:\underline{?}$, $30:\underline{?}$
2. Write ratios equivalent to 5:6: $\underline{?}:30$, $\underline{?}:18$, $\underline{?}:60$, $\underline{?}:36$, $\underline{?}:24$
3. Express as fractions in simplest form: 12:20, 4 to 8, 6 to 10, 81:72, 36:27
4. Tell the correct relation (= or ≠): $\frac{6}{7} \underline{\;?\;} \frac{2}{3}$, $\frac{3}{8} \underline{\;?\;} \frac{9}{24}$, $\frac{1}{4} \underline{\;?\;} \frac{8}{2}$, $\frac{25}{45} \underline{\;?\;} \frac{5}{8}$
5. Solve each proportion: $\frac{6}{12} = \frac{n}{2}$, $\frac{3}{4} = \frac{n}{16}$, $\frac{8}{n} = \frac{80}{100}$, $\frac{5}{6} = \frac{25}{n}$

MENTAL

1. Which ratio is greater: $\frac{2}{3}$ or $\frac{3}{5}$?

2. A team won 10 out of 15 games played. What fractional part of the games played did the team win?
3. Solve: $2:15 = 1:n$
4. If 3 pencils cost 45¢, how much will one dozen pencils cost?
5. Find the value of n: $\frac{n}{24} = \frac{6}{4}$
6. Divide 30 into two parts having the ratio of 2 to 3.
7. If lemons sell at 4 for 96¢, will 6 cost more or less than $1.20?
8. If 6 men can do a job in 4 days, will 9 men take more or less time to do the same job?
9. At $2.00 a dozen, what will 4 articles cost?
10. Divide 45 oranges between Leo and Jan so that one share is to the other as 2 is to 3.

24

DRILL

1. Give two ratios equivalent to: $\frac{3}{5}$, $\frac{3}{8}$, $\frac{2}{3}$, $\frac{12}{7}$, $\frac{11}{3}$
2. Tell the ratio in simplest form:
   3 pt to 1 gal   18 in. to 1 yd
   3 da to 1 wk   50 min to 5 sec
3. Tell the value of n: $\frac{n}{9} = \frac{2}{3}$, $\frac{4}{5} = \frac{n}{45}$, $\frac{12}{5} = \frac{n}{25}$, $\frac{8}{4} = \frac{24}{n}$
4. Double each ratio and express as a proportion: 4:5, 6:8, 3:4, 7:12, 1:8
5. 200% of $\underline{?}$ is: 8, 16, 4, 10, 24, 14, 22, 50

MENTAL

1. Solve: $\frac{9}{18} = \frac{n}{10}$
2. When the price of pencils is 3 for $.48, will one pencil cost more or less than $.15?

3. If 3 men can do a job in 5 days, will one man take more or less time to do the same work?
4. If a bus goes 180 km in 2 hours, how far will it go in 5 hours?
5. If Mrs. Lopez drives 348 kilometers in 4 hours, is her rate of speed faster or slower than 90 km/h?
6. If 2.5 kilograms of candy cost $6.60, what will 5 kilograms of candy cost?
7. Subtract 0.009 from 2.
8. Divide 0.816024 by 8.
9. Find the perimeter of a square whose edge is 10.3 cm.
10. Tim measured 3 metal rods. The first measured 3.56 m, the second 4.2 m, and the third 3.3 m. To the nearest 0.1 m, find the combined lengths.

25 DRILL

1. Tell the equivalent fraction that has a denominator of 100: $\frac{9}{10}$, $\frac{2}{5}$, $\frac{13}{20}$, $\frac{3}{25}$, $\frac{3}{4}$, $\frac{9}{50}$
2. Express as percents: 0.05, 0.25, 0.4, 0.5, 0.75, 0.60
3. Express as decimals: 10%, 60%, 72%, 5.5%, 37.5%, 10.4%
4. Express as fractions in simplest form: $12\frac{1}{2}$%, $62\frac{1}{2}$%, $33\frac{1}{3}$%, $66\frac{2}{3}$%, $14\frac{2}{7}$%
5. What is 50% of: 12, 60, 100, 84, 26, 200?

MENTAL

1. The width of a rectangle is 0.4 of the length. What percent of the length is the width?

2. $\frac{2}{3}$ of Bill's money is $8. What percent of his money is $8?
3. Prices on men's shirts are marked $12\frac{1}{2}$% off. What decimal part of the cost is this?
4. Which is greater: $37\frac{1}{2}$% or $\frac{3}{10}$?
5. What is 100% of $100?
6. Is 90% of a number more or less than the number?
7. Divide 1 dozen articles between two boys in the ratio of 4 to 2.
8. $\frac{1}{2}$ a number is 8. What is $\frac{3}{4}$ of the number?
9. If 4 men do a job in 7 hours, how long will it take 2 men to do that job?
10. How much did Ben lose if he bought a book for $2.70 and sold it for $\frac{2}{3}$ of the cost?

26 DRILL

1. Express as decimals: $\frac{6}{10}$, $\frac{3}{100}$, $\frac{8}{1000}$
2. Express as decimals: $\frac{1}{2}$, $\frac{1}{4}$, $\frac{1}{8}$, $\frac{1}{5}$, $\frac{3}{4}$, $\frac{3}{8}$
3. Express as fractions in simplest form: $33\frac{1}{3}$%, 25%, 20%, $16\frac{2}{3}$%, $83\frac{1}{3}$%, $87\frac{1}{2}$%
4. Find $14\frac{2}{7}$% of: 14, 21, 63, 56, 700, 490, 42.7, $1.40
5. Find $87\frac{1}{2}$% of: 24, 64, 16, 40, 4.8, 0.32, 0.88, $2.40

MENTAL

1. Out of 400 children in a school, 30% need dental care. How many students need dental care?
2. An importer received a shipment of 540 oriental rugs. If $83\frac{1}{3}$% of them were sold, how many rugs were sold?
3. There was a reduction of $16\frac{2}{3}$% on a radio listed at $120. What was the amount of the reduction?
4. A survey shows that 9 out of 10 children drink milk at lunch. What percent of the children is that?
5. About $\frac{2}{7}$ of the earth's surface is land. What percent is this?
6. At $1.20 a dozen, how much will 9 eggs cost?
7. Mary earned $48. If she saved $12\frac{1}{2}$% of her earnings, how much did she save?
8. Solve. $8 : n = 2 : 5$.
9. What is the ratio of 2 days to 2 weeks?
10. Compare. (Use $<$, $=$, or $>$.) $66\frac{2}{3}$% of 27 __?__ 75% of 28

27 DRILL

1. What percent of 36 is: 9, 3, 18, 12, 36, 45, 54, 72?
2. What percent of 200 is: 100, 50, 150, 300, 400?
3. Solve: $4 = \frac{4}{5}$ of n, $3 = \frac{1}{9}$ of n, $6 = \frac{2}{3}$ of n
4. Find the number when 10% of it is: 20, 5, 17, 24, 3, 35, 10
5. Solve: 80% of $n = 100$, 25% of $n = 200$, $33\frac{1}{3}$% of $n = 20$, 75% of $n = 6$, 50% of $n = 7$

MENTAL

1. If a team wins 20 out of 30 games, what percent of the games do they win?

2. A farmer picked 60 crates of tomatoes. If he sold 45 crates, what percent were sold?
3. What percent of 90 cents is 75 cents?
4. What percent of a meter is a decimeter?
5. $120 is $\frac{4}{5}$ of what amount?
6. Tony's share of the cost of a trip is $33\frac{1}{3}$%. If his share is $22.50, what is the cost of the trip?
7. Express $2\frac{1}{2}$% as a fraction.
8. $8\frac{1}{3}$% of 72 is what percent of 36?
9. After spending 60% of her money, Rosa had $20 left. How much money did she have at first?
10. Don's weight increased from 72 kg to 78 kg. By what percent did his weight increase?

28

DRILL

1. Express as percents: $1\frac{1}{4}$, $2\frac{3}{4}$, $3\frac{2}{3}$, 3.5
2. Express as percents:
   $\frac{1}{20}$, $\frac{1}{200}$, $\frac{1}{300}$, $\frac{1}{500}$, $\frac{2}{300}$, $\frac{3}{400}$
3. At 10%, find the discount on: $50, $80, $120, $200, $45.50
4. Subtract from 100%: 30%, 42%, 65%, $33\frac{1}{3}$%, 12.5%, $14\frac{2}{7}$%
5. Find the list price when a discount of $20 is: 5%, 10%, 25%, $12\frac{1}{2}$%, 20%

MENTAL

1. A lamp that cost $24 was sold at a gain of $\frac{1}{6}$ of the cost. What was the selling price?
2. A salesperson took a loss of $\frac{1}{3}$ by selling an article at $12 below cost. What was the cost?
3. At 6%, find the commission on $6000.
4. A rug marked $650 was sold for 80% of the marked price. What was the selling price?
5. Ties marked $5.20 were reduced 20%. How much would be saved on two ties?
6. A discount of $1.50 on an item marked $15 is what rate of discount?
7. Find the list price when a discount of $40 is $12\frac{1}{2}$%.
8. A commission of $960 is 8% of the selling price of a camper. What is the selling price of the camper?
9. What is the value of n if $\frac{1}{3n} = 30$?
10. Divide 15 into two parts so that the ratio of one part to the other is 2 to 3.

29

DRILL

1. 10 is what percent of: 20, 100, 40, 60, 90, 10, 50, 80?
2. What is the number if 5% is: 5, 12, 7, 13, 0.2, 0.04, 0.5, 1.2?
3. Find the number: $4 = 12\frac{1}{2}$% of $\underline{\ ?\ }$, $10 = 5$% of $\underline{\ ?\ }$, $150 = 20$% of $\underline{\ ?\ }$
4. Add to 100%: 3%, 8%, 25%, 6.25%, $83\frac{1}{3}$%
5. What percent of 50 is: 5, 10, 2, 25, 100, 75, 11, 21, 40?

MENTAL

1. How much will you save if you get a $12\frac{1}{2}$% discount on an item marked $12.40?
2. How much does 1 lb of veal cost if $\frac{1}{3}$ lb costs $12?
3. Find the total cost of a $40 lamp if the sales tax is 5%.
4. 198% of 65 is about: 33, 13, 130
5. Tom bought a bicycle for $63. If he sold it at a gain of $11\frac{1}{9}$%, what was the gain?
6. 8 in. is what percent of a foot?
7. $16\frac{2}{3}$% of the 1230 tapes in the school learning center were donated. How many tapes were donated?
8. $18 was $66\frac{2}{3}$% of what Ann earned on a job. How much had she earned?
9. What is the sale price of a $36 toaster oven with a 25% discount?
10. After deducting a commission on a $200 chair, a dealer received $160. What rate of commission did he give the agent?

30

DRILL

1. Express as fractions in simplest form: 0.6, 0.30, 0.35, 0.625, 0.125, 0.05, 0.04
2. Find: 15% of 40, $37\frac{1}{2}$% of 32, 75% of 16, $83\frac{1}{3}$% of 36
3. Find a 20% tip on: $10, $5, $2.50, $25, $4.50, $20.25
4. Find the unit price if 4 items cost: $8, $6, $4.80, $2.40, $3.60, $.84
5. Express as a decimal: $3.2\frac{1}{2}$, $45\frac{1}{2}$%, $0.1\frac{1}{4}$, $11\frac{1}{4}$%, $0.2\frac{1}{5}$, $6\frac{1}{5}$%, $2\frac{3}{4}$%

MENTAL

1. Helen has 40 photos in her album. If this is 40% of the number of photos Jane has, how many photos does Jane have?
2. Two partners divided their profit in a 3 to 1 ratio. Find each share if their profit was $20,000.
3. Stan deposited $200 for 3 years at 5% rate of interest. Find his interest.
4. 40% of the class wore braces. If 12 wore braces, how many were in the class?
5. What is the rate of discount on a pair of shoes marked $45 and sold for $5 less than the marked price?
6. What is the amount of sales if the commission of $8\frac{1}{3}$% amounts to $50?
7. Which is greater: 0.14 or $\frac{1}{7}$?
8. George sold 30% of the 200 cards in a box. How many cards were left in the box?
9. How much greater than 2.4 is 4.8?
10. Find the commission when the amount of sales is $200 and the rate of commission is 2%.

31 DRILL

1. Tell the greatest possible remainder when dividing by: 2, 4, 6, 9, 3, 7, 5
2. Find 40% of: $10, $5, $50, 35, 75, 90, 400, $1.75, $600
3. Express as percent: 0.5, 0.35, 0.02, 0.85, 1.1, 0.05, 0.004
4. At $.25 each find the cost of: 3, 5, 10, 6, 7, 12, 40, 100
5. Find the rate of discount if the list price is $40 and the discount is: $4, $10, $5, $2, $6, $8, $1, $3

MENTAL

1. What is the mean of these math tests: 90, 70, 80, 85, 75?
2. What is the range of the tests in exercise 1?
3. What is the mode of the tests in exercise 1?
4. At $7.20 a meter, how much would 5 meters of fabric cost?
5. A coat costs $76.89 and gloves cost $18.59. Will $100 pay for both?
6. A tax collector is paid $60 commission for collecting $1500. Find the rate of commission.
7. Bob spent $1.50 of his $5.00. What fractional part of his money was that?
8. Find the cost of a stereo if Anna paid a $30 down payment and 4 payments of $12.50.
9. The Bloom family drove for 4 hours at a speed of 87 km/h. About how far did they drive?
10. Which is a better buy: 10 oz for 89¢ or 14 oz for $1.40?

32 DRILL

1. Solve each proportion: $\frac{6}{42} = \frac{1}{n}$, $\frac{30}{n} = \frac{6}{5}$, $\frac{35}{7} = \frac{n}{1}$, $\frac{60}{100} = \frac{n}{20}$
2. What percent of 360° is: 60°, 90°, 120°, 180°, 30°, 40°, 300°
3. Express these probabilities as percents: $\frac{3}{4}$, $\frac{5}{6}$, $\frac{1}{3}$, $\frac{2}{5}$, $\frac{7}{10}$
4. Tell about the hats if the probability of selecting a red hat is: $\frac{1}{3}$, $\frac{2}{5}$, $\frac{3}{7}$, $\frac{2}{6}$, $\frac{4}{10}$
5. Cards marked 1 to 9 are in a box. What are the chances of picking a number that is: odd, even, prime, square?

MENTAL

If you toss a cube with faces numbered 1 to 6, what is the probability of:

1. getting a 5 on top?
2. getting a number greater than 5 on top?
3. getting a number less than 6 on top?
4. getting a number greater than 2 on top?
5. getting a number less than 4 on top?

What is the probability of:

6. picking a red item from a bag of 8 items — 4 red, 3 brown, and 1 white?
7. picking a red or tan item from a bag of 10 items — 4 red, 3 tan, and 3 blue?
8. picking a yellow item from a bag of 7 items — 4 gray and 3 yellow?
9. getting heads when you toss a penny 100 times?
10. getting both heads when you toss a penny and a nickel 100 times?

33 DRILL

1. A spinner is labeled 1 to 8. What is P? (odd), (even), (prime number), (multiple of 2), (number less than 1), (number less than 9)
2. In the word PARALLELOGRAM what is P? (E), (R), (L), (A), (vowel), (L or M), (not a vowel)
3. To the nearest penny, find 5% of: 60¢, 80¢, 50¢, 70¢, $1.10
4. Find the number: $\frac{5}{6}$ of $n = 300$, $\frac{2}{3}$ of $n = 66$, 0.5 of $n = 10$, 0.08 of $n = 320$
5. Find the number: 80% of $n = 100$, 25% of $n = 2000$, $33\frac{1}{3}\%$ of $n = 20$

MENTAL

1. A team spent $90 of its $270 budget for referees. What percent is that?
2. What angle on a circle graph would be drawn for exercise 1?

The weekly rainfall was: 2 in., $1\frac{1}{2}$ in., $2\frac{1}{2}$ in., $2\frac{1}{4}$ in., $2\frac{3}{4}$ in., 2 in., 1 in.

3. What is the range in weekly rainfall?
4. What is the mode in weekly rainfall?
5. What is the average rainfall?
6. What is the median rainfall?
7. The range in height for the class is 6 in. If the tallest student is 5 ft 11 in., how tall is the shortest?
8. The daily temperature range was 15°C. If the daily low was ⁻2°C, what was the high?
9. Ed tosses a coin twice. What is the probability of getting H,H?
10. Bart's Bakery sells 3 types of pastry with four toppings. How many different style pastries does the bakery sell?

34 DRILL

1. Complementary or supplementary angles? 24°, 156°; 164°, 16°; 15°, 75°
2. Find the third angle of a triangle if two angles are: 90° and 60°; 82° and 64°
3. Name the number: 5^2, 12^2, 13^2, 20^2, 7^2
4. Name the measure of the supplement of each angle: 40°, 100°, 35°, 60°, 5°, 45°, 120°, 110°
5. How many inches are in: 2 ft, $\frac{1}{2}$ ft, 8 ft, $2\frac{1}{4}$ ft, 1 yd, $1\frac{1}{3}$ yd, 4 ft?

MENTAL

1. What is the Fahrenheit temperature if the Celsius temperature is 50°? ($F = \frac{9}{5} C + 32$)
2. Find the perimeter of an equilateral triangle 30 cm on a side.
3. A rectangle 5 inches wide has a perimeter of 60 in. What is its length?
4. A poster 10 cm long has a perimeter of 30 cm. What is its width?
5. A plant grew to a height of 1 m 34 cm 12 mm. What is its height in meters?
6. One angle in a right triangle measures 40°. Find the measure of the third.
7. The opposite angles of a parallelogram measure 100° each. What does each of the other angles measure?
8. Express the difference as a decimal: $5.1\frac{3}{4} - 4.1\frac{1}{5}$
9. What number is named? $[(2 \times 5) + 8] - (4 \div 1)$
10. The smaller angle of a complementary pair is 25° less than the larger angle. What is the measure of the smaller angle?

35 DRILL

1. Express the ratio in simplest form: 60 mg to 1 g, 200 mg to 1 g, 20 L to 1 kL
2. Find m ∠ ABC if when bisected it equals: 10°, 40°, 90°, 36°, 85°, 91°
3. Find the perimeter of a regular pentagon if each side is: 3 m, 8 m, 2.1 m, 1.2 m, 6.5 m, 4.2 m
4. To 2 ft 4 in. add: 3 in., 1 ft 2 in., 8 in., 2 ft 10 in., 3 ft 4 in.
5. Subtract 1 m 50 cm from: 2 m, 300 cm, 2.7 m, 450 cm, 8.9 m

MENTAL

1. A rectangular plot containing 33 dm^2 is 11 dm long. How wide is it?
2. A trapezoid's bases are 12 ft and 8 ft. Its height is 4 ft. Find the area.
3. The longest chord of a circle is 8 cm. How long is the radius?
4. If a lawn mower uses $9\frac{3}{4}$ liters of gas in an hour, about how many liters of gas are used in $\frac{2}{5}$ hour?
5. A recipe calls for $\frac{2}{3}$ cup of sugar. How many cups of sugar will be used for 6 times the recipe?
6. If $n = 7$, what is the value of $\frac{-3}{5}(n + 3)$?
7. Let $n = 7$. Simplify: $(n^2 + 1) - 10$
8. A bus travels 90 km/h. How far will it go in 3 hr 20 min?
9. Compare. (Use <, =, or >.) 4 hr 20 min + 2 hr 18 min __?__ $6\frac{1}{2}$ hr
10. Compare. (Use <, =, or >.) 10 hr 45 min − 3 hr 30 min __?__ 7 hr

36 DRILL

1. Express in cm: 35 mm, 42 mm, 500 mm, 460 mm, 375 mm, 6 mm
2. Express in m to the nearest 0.1 m: 125 cm, 88.6 cm, 16.4 dm, 23.05 dm
3. Express in liters: 100 mL, 5200 mL, 1460 mL, 500 mL, 250 mL
4. Express in grams: 1000 mg, 2000 mg, 850 mg, 645 mg, 58 mg
5. Express in kilograms to the nearest 0.1 kilogram: 1200 g, 5600 g, 425 g, 750 g, 82 g, 46 g

MENTAL

1. 164 mm is how many centimeters?
2. If an athlete runs 9 m/sec, how many meters will he run in 3.5 seconds?
3. A board that is 0.6 m in length is how many millimeters in length?
4. Which might be the length of a bowling alley? 18 mm, 18 cm, 18 m
5. A giraffe can be 5485 mm tall. Express this in meters to the nearest 0.1 m.
6. A desk top is 60 cm long. What percent of a meter is the length?
7. Express the ratio in simplest form: 30 cm to 1 m
8. Beth cut 4 feet of ribbon from a 2-yard piece. What part of a yard was left?
9. How many kiloliters will it take to fill a tank that holds 50,000 L?
10. 2000 mg of aspirin is equivalent to how many grams of aspirin?

37 DRILL

1. Find the side of a square whose perimeter is: 48 cm, 3.6 cm, 26 ft, 100 in., 12 m, 6.4 m, 2.3 m
2. Subtract 4 from the square of: 5, 7, 8, 20, 9, 4, 11, 15
3. Let $\ell = 12'$. Find the perimeter if w is: 4', 2', 10', 5', 8', 11', 3.5', 6.5'
4. Find the area of a rectangle 10 cm long with a width of: 8 cm, 2.8 cm, 1.2 cm
5. Multiply by $\frac{22}{7}$: 7, 14, 35, 21, 1.4, 3.5, 4.2, 70, 2.8

MENTAL

1. A baseball diamond has an area of 8100 ft^2. Find the perimeter.

2. Find the perimeter of a trapezoid whose sides are 30 m, 50 m, 90 m, and 40 m.
3. Express the ratio of 250 cm to 1 m.
4. A square measures 0.3 km on a side. Find the perimeter in meters.
5. The perimeter of a rectangle is 84 cm. The width is one half the length. Find the dimensions.
6. What number is named? $(8 - 6)^3 + (3 + 5)^2 - 3^2$
7. Find the circumference of a circular flower bed that is 2.1 m in diameter.
8. What is the perimeter of a merry-go-round 28 ft in diameter? (Use $\frac{22}{7}$ as π.)
9. Find the diameter of a pipe whose circumference is 44 cm. (Use $\frac{22}{7}$ as π.)
10. What is the area of a circle having a radius of 10? (Use 3.14 as π.)

38 DRILL

1. What number is named? 7^2, $\left(\frac{1}{2}\right)^2$, 0.9^2
2. Find the perimeter of a square if a side is: 10 cm, 12 cm, 1.4 cm, $4\frac{1}{2}$ ft
3. Find the radius if the diameter is: 3 m, 5 m, 2.2 cm, 1.8 m, 0.2 m
4. Find the area of a square if one side is: 8 cm, 10 cm, 1.2 m, 6 yd, 2.5 yd
5. Find the side of a square if the area is: 100 cm^2, 64 cm^2, 1.44 m^2, 256 ft^2

MENTAL

1. How much greater is the perimeter of a square that measures 4 in. on each side than the perimeter of a square containing 4 in.^{2}?

2. If the perimeter of a square is 32 dm, what is the length of each side?
3. Find the perimeter of a square field that has an area of 1600 m^2.
4. If the perimeter of a square is 28 cm, what is its area?
5. The circumference of a wheel is 44 cm. What is the radius? (Use $\frac{22}{7}$ as π.)
6. Michael has 2 square tabletops to cover. If a side of each tabletop is 40 cm, how many cm^2 must he cover?
7. Is 9^2 greater or less than 2^9?
8. Write the product as a standard numeral: $2^3 \times 2^2$
9. Write the quotient as a standard numeral: $10^6 \div 10^2$
10. What is the area of a circular tabletop having a diameter of 1.4 m?

39 DRILL

1. Find the circumference of a circle when the diameter is: 14 cm, 2.1 m, 28 in., 3.5 ft, 4.9 yd, 70 mm, 1.4 m
2. Find the area of a triangle with a base of 8 cm and a height of: 14 cm, 8.8 cm, 4.6 cm, 12.2 cm
3. Find the area of a circle whose radius is: 10 cm, 1 m, 2 m, 20 m
4. What fraction equals: $\sqrt{\frac{1}{4}}$, $\sqrt{\frac{9}{16}}$, $\sqrt{\frac{25}{49}}$, $\sqrt{\frac{1}{64}}$, $\sqrt{\frac{16}{49}}$
5. Square each fraction: $\frac{1}{3}$, $\frac{2}{5}$, $\frac{5}{9}$, $\frac{7}{10}$, $\frac{4}{11}$, $\frac{6}{7}$, $\frac{8}{15}$

MENTAL

1. Find the hypotenuse of a right triangle with a height of 3 in. and a base of 4 in.

2. Find the diagonal of a rectangle with a length of 0.8 m and a width of 0.6 m.
3. Find the hypotenuse of a right triangle whose base is 1.5 m and height is 2 m.
4. A tree broke 12 ft above its base. The top hit the ground 16 ft from the base. How long was the fallen part?
5. How long is the diagonal brace on a gate that measures 4 ft by 3 ft?
6. Subtract 4 m^2 from an area of 9 m × 8 m.
7. Two angles of a triangle measure 28° and 62°. What kind of triangle is it?
8. Divide 18^2 into two parts with a ratio of 4 to 5.
9. $12 is $66\frac{2}{3}$% of what number?
10. Find the number: $\sqrt{256} + 2\sqrt{16}$

40 DRILL

1. Find the circumference in π units when the radius is: 5 m, 7 in., 1.1 cm, $3\frac{1}{2}$ ft, 2.3 m, 12 in.
2. Find the area in π units when the diameter is: 8 m, 2 cm, 3 m, 4 in., 10 ft., 1.2 yd, 2.2 m
3. Name the measure of the complement of each angle: $60°$, $40°$, $35°$, $5°$, $45°$, $76°$, $20°$, $80°$
4. What is the reciprocal of: $\frac{22}{7}$, 4, $\frac{1}{2}$, 8, $\frac{3}{4}$, 0.3, $^-6$, $\frac{^-2}{3}$
5. Divide $^-24$ by: 4, $\frac{1}{2}$, 8, $\frac{3}{4}$, $^-0.3$, $^-6$, $\frac{^-2}{3}$, $\frac{^-4}{5}$

MENTAL

1. Add: $(2.0 \times 10^2) + (5.0 \times 10^4)$.
2. Subtract: $(6.5 \times 10^3) - (5 \times 10^2)$.
3. What is the area of a parallelogram if the base is 9 m and the height is 4 m?
4. Find the area of a 9-ft long rectangle whose perimeter is 26 ft.
5. Divide 36 m^2 into two parts whose ratio is 4 to 5.
6. Divide $14 into two parts whose ratio is 4 to 3.
7. A rectangle 5 inches wide has a perimeter of 60 in. What is its length?
8. Solve for n: $\frac{n+2}{8} = \frac{6}{12}$
9. The circumference of a circle is 66 in. Find its radius.
10. The area of a circle is 154 cm^2. Find its diameter.

41 DRILL

1. Name the next 2 digits: $1.1\overline{5}$, $0.\overline{3}$, $0.\overline{15}$, $0.3\overline{6}$, $1.0\overline{9}$, $1.\overline{302}$
2. Round to the nearest hundredth: $1.0\overline{7}$, $0.24\overline{5}$, $0.1\overline{53}$, $0.\overline{15}$, $3.\overline{82}$
3. Name the 2 whole numbers closest to: $\sqrt{5}$, $\sqrt{15}$, $\sqrt{27}$, $\sqrt{91}$, $\sqrt{80}$, $\sqrt{111}$
4. Name the number: $\sqrt{9+16}$, $\sqrt{41+40}$, $\sqrt{500+400}$, $\sqrt{90+54}$
5. Multiply by 4: $\sqrt{121}$, $\sqrt{169}$, $\sqrt{81}$, $\sqrt{25}$, $\sqrt{400}$, $\sqrt{256}$, $\sqrt{900}$, $\sqrt{64}$

MENTAL

1. If an object 0.035 cm long was magnified 10 times, what length would it appear to be?
2. What is 20% of $\sqrt{100}$?
3. Compare. (Use $<$, $=$, or $>$.) $\frac{4}{9}$? $0.\overline{45}$
4. What is the hypotenuse of a right triangle when $a = 6$ in. and $b = 8$ in.?
5. Solve for h: $^+7 + h + {}^-3 = {}^+12.4$.
6. Solve for n: $2n + \sqrt{49} = 11$.
7. Write in increasing order: $0.\overline{2}$, 0.2, $0.2\overline{1}$, $0.2\overline{3}$, $0.\overline{23}$.
8. Solve. $2n - 1 \leq 7$.
9. Solve. $\frac{n}{5} + 3 > 5$.
10. $\sqrt{12}$ is between what two whole numbers?

42 DRILL

1. Give the square root of: 4, 16, 81, 9, 25, 49, 121, 144, 225, 0.36
2. Express as a fraction: $^-1\frac{1}{2}$, $^+2.5$, $^+4\frac{1}{5}$, $^-1.2$, $^-0.8$, $^+5.1$
3. Solve: $\sqrt{169} - \sqrt{49}$; $\sqrt{64} - \sqrt{25}$; $\sqrt{225} - \sqrt{100}$; $\sqrt{144} - \sqrt{9}$; $\sqrt{81} - \sqrt{4}$
4. Name the number: $6^2 + 6^2$; $24^2 + 7^2$
5. Name the number: $\left(\frac{1}{2}\right)^2 + \frac{3}{4}$; $\frac{1}{9} + \left(\frac{2}{3}\right)^2$; $\left(\frac{1}{5}\right)^2 + \frac{1}{100}$; $\left(\frac{1}{2} + \frac{1}{4}\right)^2$; $\left(\frac{1}{6} + \frac{1}{2}\right)^2$

MENTAL

1. Does this set of measures form a right triangle? 3 cm, 3 cm, 5 cm
2. Does this set of measures form a right triangle? 0.6 m, 0.8 m, 1 m
3. Write in increasing order: π, $3.\overline{2}$, $3\frac{1}{5}$, $\sqrt{3}$, 2^2
4. Simplify: $5^2 + (10 - 2^2)$
5. A number squared added to the number doubled is 18. What is the number?
6. The square of a number is 1.21. Find the number.
7. Between what two whole numbers is $\sqrt{200}$: 13 – 14; 14 – 15; 15 – 16?
8. Choose the best estimate for $\sqrt{57}$: 7.1; 7.3; 7.5
9. $\frac{n+1}{6} = \frac{1}{2} \longrightarrow \frac{1}{2} = \frac{?}{6}$
   So, $\frac{n+1}{6} = \frac{?}{6}$ and $n = \underline{\quad?\quad}$
10. Solve for n: $n^2 - 4 = 60$

43 DRILL

1. What number is named? 4^3, 7^3, 10^3, 3^3, 1^3, 5^3, 6^3, $(0.1)^3$
2. What number is named? $\sqrt[3]{1000}$, $\sqrt[3]{27}$, $\sqrt[3]{1}$, $\sqrt[3]{216}$, $\sqrt[3]{0.008}$
3. Find the cube of each fraction: $\frac{1}{3}$, $\frac{2}{5}$, $\frac{1}{4}$, $\frac{2}{7}$, $\frac{1}{10}$, $\frac{3}{10}$
4. Tell the number of faces: cube, rectangular prism, triangular prism
5. Find the rate when a discount of $20 is given on: $80, $100, $160, $200, $1000

MENTAL

1. A sandbox 80 cm by 40 cm is filled to a depth of 30 cm. Find the volume.

2. The edge of a cube is $\frac{2}{3}$ in. Find the volume.
3. A 96 cm^3 box is 8 cm × 4 cm × ___?___ cm.
4. Find the volume of a rectangular pyramid with the same dimensions as a prism that measures 6 m × 3 m × 10 m.
5. The cube of 2 is what percent of 32?
6. Find the edge of a cubical box that holds 64 cm^3.
7. Which holds more: a cubical bin 5 m on each edge or a bin 4 m × 5 m × 6 m?
8. What is the missing factor: $7 \times 7 \times$ ___?___ $= 343$
9. What number is named? $6\left(2^3\right) - \sqrt{16}$
10. Mark caught 6 fish weighing 21 lb 4 oz in all. What was the average weight of the fish?

44 DRILL

1. Tell the volume of a cube when each edge measures: 5 in., 6 ft, 1 yd, 8 cm, 20 cm, 30 cm
2. Tell the volume of a rectangular prism when the edges measure: 4 in. × 4 in. × 10 in.; 3 ft × 5 ft × 2 ft; 4 m × 3 m × 8 m; 2 m × 15 m × 4 m
3. Tell the volume in π units of a cylinder with a radius of 10 cm and a height of: 2 cm, 4 cm, 10 cm, 5 cm, 2.5 cm
4. Find the surface area of a cube whose edge is: 3 in., 5 ft, 10 dm, 4 m
5. Find the surface area of a rectangular prism if the height is 9 cm and the base is: 6 cm × 4 cm; 8 cm × 7 cm

MENTAL

1. The edges of a box measure 7 in. by 9 in. by 4 in. Find the volume.

2. Which has the greater volume: a can 10 cm high with a radius of $3\frac{1}{2}$ cm or a can 10 cm high with a 7-cm diameter?
3. What is the depth of a chest that is 10 ft long and 6 ft wide and occupies 480 ft^3 of space?
4. How many cubes that measure 2 inches on each edge will fill a box 12 in. by 6 in. by 4 in.?
5. A box that occupies 350 cm^3 is 7 cm high. Find the area of its base.
6. How many cubic feet is a wooden beam that is 20 ft × 14 ft × 10 ft?
7. Find the volume of a prism 6 ft high with a base having an area of 25 ft^2.
8. Find the volume of a pyramid 9 m high having a base with an area of 36 m^2.
9. Simplify: $\sqrt[3]{27} + (10^3 - 5^3)$.
10. Find the value of $a^3 + a^2b^2 + b^3$ given $a = 2$ and $b = 10$.

45 DRILL

1. In which quadrant is each? $(7, {}^-2)$; $({}^+7, {}^-2)$; $({}^-7, {}^-2)$; $({}^-2, {}^+7)$
2. On which axis does each lie? $(0, {}^+3)$; $({}^-7, 0)$; $(0, {}^-2)$; $({}^-4, 0)$; $(0, 0)$
3. $y = 3x - 1$: What is the y-coordinate? $(7, y)$; $(3, y)$; $(0, y)$; $({}^-1, y)$; $(2, y)$; $({}^-3, y)$
4. $x - 2y = 10$: What is the x-coordinate? $(x, 1)$; $(x, 0)$; $(x, {}^-1)$; $(x, 2)$; $(x, {}^-3)$
5. Which points lie on the line $2x + y = 13$? $(0, 13)$; $(2, 9)$; $(6, 0)$; $({}^-1, 10)$; $(5, 3)$

MENTAL

1. Solve: $1 \div \left(1 + \frac{1}{2}\right)$
2. Solve: $1 + \dfrac{1}{1 + \frac{1}{3}}$

3. Write y in terms of x: $2x + y = 7$
4. Which equation is the graph of a straight line? $x + y = 1$; $x^2 + y = 1$
5. A certain number plus 3 times that number is 56. What is the number?
6. Let $b = {}^-3$ and $a = {}^-2$. Simplify: $(a^2b^3) + 10$.
7. Simplify: $1 + \dfrac{1}{\sqrt{16} - \sqrt{4}}$
8. A taxi driver covered 238 km on Monday, 365 km on Tuesday, and 297 km on Wednesday. About how many kilometers was that altogether?
9. There are 362 pages in a book. Nancy read 106 pages. Estimate the number of pages she has left to read.
10. At a busy airport, an airplane lands every 15 seconds. How many planes land during a 3-hour time span?

536

46

DRILL

1. Solve for y. Let $x = {}^-3$. $x + y = 3$, $x - y = 3$, $xy = 6$, $x + 2y = 3$, $x - 2y = 3$
2. Solve. Let $a = 4$, $b = 3$, and $c = 6$. $b^2 + 6$, $2a - 1$, $a^2 + 3$, $16 + b^2$, $20 + 2c$
3. Tell whether the line is straight or curved. $x^2 - y = 5$, $2x - y = 5$, $2xy = 5$, $x^2 - y^2 = 5$, $2x = y$
4. Write y in terms of x.
   $2y - x = 6$ $\qquad$ $3y + x = 9$
   $y - x = 7$ $\qquad$ $y - x = {}^-2$
5. Solve. Let $x = 2$, $y = 3$, and $z = 4$. x^2, y^2, z^2, x^3, y^3, z^3, $x + y$, $2y + z$, $3x + y$, $16 - x^2$

MENTAL

1. What number is named by $(0.4)^3$?

2. Solve: $2x + 7 + x = 19$
3. In which two quadrants do the coordinates have the same signs?
4. When graphed, these points lie on a line parallel to what axis? $({}^-3, 2)$; $({}^-1, 2)$; $(4, 2)$
5. What are the coordinates of the origin?
6. When graphed, these points lie on a line parallel to what axis? $({}^-4, 5)$; $({}^-4, 1)$; $({}^-4, {}^-1)$
7. The sum of two numbers is 5; their difference is 1. What are the numbers?
8. Ana and Beth sold 115 tickets. Ana sold 4 more than twice as many as Beth. How many did each girl sell?
9. Find x: $x + 3x = 204$
10. Subtract 6 from a number and double the result. The answer is 12. What is the number?

47

DRILL

1. Add 10 to: $a + 1$; $b + 3$; $c + 10$; $d - 10$; $e - 5$; $a^2 - 20$; $ab - 7$.
2. Subtract b from: b, $10b$, $3b$, $7b$, $a + b$, $a + 4b$, $a^2 - 2b$, $a^2 - 5b$.
3. What number is named? $2^2 \times 3$, $3^2 \times 2$, $3^2 \times 7$, $7^2 \times 2$, $5^2 \times 3$, $3^2 \times 2^2$, $5^2 \times 2^2$
4. If $a = {}^-1$ and $b = {}^+2$, solve: $a + b$, ab, $b - a$, $a - b$, $\frac{a}{b}$, $2a + b$, $2b + a$.
5. What value of a makes each meaningless? $27 \div (2 - a)$; $8 \div (3 + a)$; $10 \div (a - 5)$; $9 \div (a + 6)$; $15 \div (6 + 2a)$

MENTAL

1. Solve for n: $2n + 4 - 5n = {}^-11$
2. Simplify: $3a - 4a + 7a$
3. True or False: ${}^-8(2a - 3b) = 16a + 24b$
4. Simplify: $2(a + b) + 3a$
5. What is the GCF of 42, 72, and 18?
6. From $5b + 2c$ take $3b - 2c$.
7. The sum of two numbers is 15. Their difference is 4. Find the numbers.
8. Divide 33 in the ratio of 4 to 7.
9. The cube of 3 is what percent of 9?
10. A day is what percent of a week?

48

DRILL

1. What values of n makes each meaningless? $\frac{10}{n - 2}$; $\frac{12}{4n}$; $\frac{8}{n + 3}$; $\frac{5}{6 - n}$; $\frac{9}{7 + n}$
2. Multiply by a^2: a^3, $2a$, ab, a^2, $4ab^2$, $5a^2b^2$, a^3, $3a^3b^3$
3. Solve: $a^4 \div a^2$, $a^5 \div a^3$, $a^7 \div a^6$, $30a^2 \div 2a$, $8a^3 \div 2a^2$, $24a^6 \div 8a^3$
4. Prime factor: 9, 10, 15, 20, 45, 50, 12, 27
5. Divide by $2a$: $18ab$, ${}^-6a^2b$, $20a^2b^2$, ${}^-8a^3bc$, $24ab^2$, $4a^2 + 2a$, $6a + 10ab$

MENTAL

1. If 1 more than twice a number is subtracted from 6 times the number, the result is 21. What is the number?

2. The length of a rectangle is 2 ft longer than its width. The perimeter is 16 ft. What is the length?
3. The area of a rectangle is 48 m². The length is 3 times the width. What is the width?
4. Find the sum of $3x + 2y$ and $4(x + y)$.
5. Find the difference between $7x + 4y$ and $4(x - y)$.
6. The product of two numbers is 24. Their sum is 10. What are the numbers?
7. The product of two numbers is 36. Their difference is 5. Find the numbers.
8. The width of a garden is $\frac{1}{4}$ of its length. The area is 36 ft². What is the width?
9. What is the product of a and $(b + c)$?
10. Solve: $1.5(3 - 2a) = {}^+0.3$

GLOSSARY

The glossary lists in alphabetical order significant and recurring mathematical terms that appear throughout the text. It is intended not so much as a memorization device but as a quick and simple reference tool for the students.

A

absolute value   The distance that a number is from zero on the number line. The absolute value of a positive number or a negative number is always positive. The absolute value of zero is 0.

acute angle   An angle measuring less than 90°.

addend   Any one of a set of numbers to be added.

angle   Two rays with a common endpoint, called the vertex.

area   The number of square units a region contains.

associative property of addition   The grouping of the addends does not change the sum. For all numbers, a, b, and c, $a + (b + c) = (a + b) + c$.

associative property of multiplication   The grouping of the factors does not change the product. For all numbers a, b, and c, $a \times (b \times c) = (a \times b) \times c$.

B

binomial   A polynomial with two terms. $3x + 4y$ is a binomial.

bisect   To divide a segment or an angle into two congruent parts.

boundary line of half-plane   The line that separates two half-planes is the boundary of each half-plane.

box-and-whisker plots   A graph used to show the division of data into fourths. It also shows the range and median.

C

cancellation   The dividing of both the numerator and the denominator of a fraction by any common factors before multiplying.

Celsius scale   The scale used to measure temperature in the metric system in which 0° is the freezing point of water and 100° is the boiling point. The symbol is C.

centimeter   A unit of length in the metric system equal to 0.01 meter.

checking account   One type of bank account that usually does not pay interest.

circle   A closed plane figure all of whose points are equidistant from a point within called the center.

circle graph   A type of graph used to display information based on percentages rather than frequencies.

circumference   The distance around, or the perimeter of, a circle.

commission   Money earned equal to a percent of the selling price of items sold.

common denominator   A multiple of the denominators of two or more fractions.

common factor   The set of common factors of 8 and 20 is {1,2,4} because each number is a factor of 8 and 20.

common multiple   The set of common multiples of 3 and 4 is {0,12, 24, . . .} because each number is a multiple of 3 and 4.

commutative property of addition   The order of the addends does not change the sum. For all numbers a and b, $a + b = b + a$.

commutative property of multiplication   The order of the factors does not change the product. For all numbers a and b, $a \times b = b \times a$.

complementary angles   Two angles the sum of whose measure is 90°.

complex fraction   A fraction having a fraction in the numerator, the denominator, or both.

composite number   A whole number greater than 1 that has more than two factors.

compound event   In probability, when one event follows another.

compound interest   Interest found by calculating interest for each period and adding it to the principal from the previous period. The interest for the next period is calculated by using this new principal. The interest may be compounded annually, semiannually, quarterly, monthly, or daily.

conditional   A compound statement in the form: "if p, then q" or "p implies q," symbolized by ($p \rightarrow q$). The first statement, p, is called the hypothesis or antecedent, and the second, q, is called the conclusion or consequent.

cone   A solid figure having one circular base and a curved surface.

congruent figures   Figures having the same size and shape.

conjunction   A compound statement formed by joining two statements with the connective **AND**. "p and q" is symbolized by $p \wedge q$.

constant   A certain number by which the terms in a sequence are created.

converse   A new conditional formed by switching the antecedent and consequent in a conditional.

coordinate plane   A grid divided into four quadrants used to locate points by naming ordered pairs.

coordinates   Ordered pair of numbers used to locate a point on a grid.

corresponding parts   Matching sides or angles of a figure.

cosine   In a right triangle, the ratio that exists between the measure of the side adjacent to the given angle and the measure of the hypotenuse.

credit buying   Purchasing goods or services without paying the entire cost at once.

cube   A rectangular prism with six congruent faces.

customary system of measurement   The system of measurement based on foot, pound, quart, and Fahrenheit measures.

cylinder   A solid figure having two parallel, congruent, circular bases and a curved surface.

D

decimal   A numeral that includes a decimal point, which separates the ones place from the tenths place.

decimeter   A unit of length in the metric system equal to 0.1 meter.

degree of polynomial   The highest degree of any of the terms of a polynomial.

dekameter   A unit of length in the metric system equal to 10 meters.

denominator   The denominator of a fraction names the total number of congruent or equal parts.

dependent events   In probability, when the second event is affected by the first.

diameter   A segment passing through the center of a circle with both endpoints on the circle.

difference of two squares   The product of two binomials that are the sum and difference of the same two numbers.
Example: $a^2 - b^2 = (a + b)(a - b)$

digits   The mathematical symbols used to express a standard numeral: 0, 1, 2, 3, 4, 5, 6, 7, 8, 9.

discount   A reduction on the regular, or list, price of an item.

disjunction   A compound statement formed by joining two statements with the connective **OR**. "p or q" is symbolized by $p \vee q$.

distributive property of multiplication over addition   The product of a factor times a sum can be written as the sum of the two products. For all numbers a, b, and c, $a \times (b + c) = (a \times b) + (a \times c)$.

dividend   The number to be divided.

divisible   A number (n) is divisible by another number (a) if there is no remainder when n is divided by a.

divisor   The number by which the dividend is divided.

double bar graph   A bar graph that displays two sets of related data for comparison purposes.

double line graph   A line graph that displays two sets of related data for comparison purposes.

E

edge   The line segment formed by the intersection of two faces of a polyhedron.

empty set   A set having no elements (0 or { }).

equally likely outcomes   In probability, when the chance is the same of getting any one of the desired outcomes.

equation   A mathematical sentence expressing equality.

equilateral triangle   A triangle with three congruent sides.

equivalent fractions Fractions that name the same number: $\frac{2}{3}$ and $\frac{4}{6}$ are equivalent fractions.

estimate To round one or more numbers in an operation to determine an approximate answer.

evaluate To evaluate a mathematical expression, replace the variable with a number, then simplify.

expanded numeral A numeral expressed in terms of the place value of each digit: 324 means $(3 \times 100) + (2 \times 10) + (4 \times 1) =$
 300 + 20 + 4

exponent A number that tells how many times the base is to be used as a factor. In 6^3 the exponent is 3 and the base is 6.

expression An open mathematical phrase or sentence containing one or more variables. The value of the expression depends upon the value given the variable.

extremes In the proportion $a:b = c:d$, the terms a and d are the extremes.

F

faces The sides that make up a solid figure.

factor One of two or more numbers that are multiplied to form a product.

Fahrenheit A scale used to measure temperature. The symbol is F.

finance charge The interest paid to a store for delaying total payment for the item purchased.

formula A general fact or rule expressed by using symbols. Example: $A = \ell w$

fraction Part of a region, an object, or a set; any number $\frac{a}{b}$ where $b \neq 0$.

frequency distribution A chart that records the number of times an event or response occurs.

front-end estimation A method of estimation using the first digits of numbers.

function A quantity that depends on a second quantity.

G

gram The basic unit of mass in the metric system.

graph A point or a collection of points on a line or a coordinate plane.

greatest common factor (GCF) The greatest factor that is common to two or more numbers.

greatest possible error (GPE) One half of any given unit of measure. **(GPE)** indicates the degree of precision of measurement.

H

half-plane The region formed when a boundary line divides a plane.

hectometer A unit of length in the metric system equal to 100 meters.

hexagon A polygon with six sides.

histogram A type of bar graph that shows the number of results that occur within an interval.

hypotenuse The side opposite the right angle in a right triangle.

I

identity element of addition Zero is the identity element in addition because adding zero to a number does not change its value. For any number a, $a + 0 = a$.

identity element of multiplication One is the identity element in multiplication because multiplying a number by 1 does not change its value. For any number a, $a \times 1 = a$.

improper fraction A fraction having its numerator equal to or greater than its denominator.

independent events In probability, when the first event does *not* affect the second event.

inequality A mathematical sentence using an inequality symbol. The symbols used are $<$, $>$, $\neq$.

integers Numbers that are either positive or negative and 0.

interest The amount paid by the borrower for the use of the principal for a stated period of time.

intersection of sets The intersection of two sets is the set of all the elements common to both sets.

interval The constant difference between numbers, such as on a scale or graph.

inverse A new conditional formed by negating both the antecedent and the consequent of a conditional.

inverse property The sum of a number (a) and its opposite ($-a$) is zero. The product of a number and its reciprocal is one.

inverse relationships   Opposite operations: addition and subtraction are inverse relationships; multiplication and division are inverse relationships.

irrational number   A number that cannot be expressed as a rational number in the form $\frac{a}{b}$, where $b \neq 0$. As a decimal, it is a nonrepeating, nonterminating decimal.

isosceles triangle   A triangle having two opposite sides and two opposite angles congruent.

K

kilo-   A prefix meaning thousand.

kilogram   A unit of mass in the metric system equal to 1000 grams.

kiloliter   A unit of capacity in the metric system equal to 1000 liters.

kilometer   A unit of length in the metric system equal to 1000 meters.

L

least common denominator (LCD)   The least common multiple of the denominators of two or more fractions.

least common multiple (LCM)   The least number other than 0 that is a common multiple of two or more numbers.

like terms   The variable part of each term is the same. Example: $2x$ and $4x$.

line   A set of points in order extending indefinitely in opposite directions.

linear equation   An equation whose graph is a straight line.

line of symmetry   A line that divides a figure into two congruent parts.

liter   The basic unit of capacity in the metric system.

M

mean   The average of a set of numbers.

means   In the proportion $a:b = c:d$, the terms b and c are the means.

median   The middle number in a set of numbers arranged in order. If there is an even number of entries, the median is the average of the two numbers in the middle.

meter   The basic unit of length in the metric system.

metric system   The system of measurement based on meter, gram, liter, and Celsius measures.

metric ton   A unit of mass in the metric system equal to 1 000 000 grams.

milli-   A prefix meaning thousandth.

milligram   A unit of mass in the metric system equal to 0.001 gram.

milliliter   A unit of capacity in the metric system equal to 0.001 liter.

millimeter   A unit of length in the metric system equal to 0.001 meter.

mixed number   A number having a whole number part and a fraction part.

mode   The number that appears most frequently in a set of numbers.

monomial   An algebraic expression consisting of a single term that may be a product of numbers and variables.

multiple   The product of a given number and any whole number. Some multiples of 3 are 0, 3, 6, 9, 12, ...

N

negation   If a statement is represented by p, then *not p* is the negation of that statement. The symbol is $\sim p$.

net   A flat pattern for a solid figure.

numerator   The numerator of a fraction names the number of parts being considered.

O

obtuse angle   An angle measuring greater than 90°, but less than 180°.

octagon   A polygon with eight sides.

ordered pair   A pair of numbers that locate a point in a coordinate plane. The first number tells how far to move right or left on the x-axis. The second number tells how far to move up or down on the y-axis. (4,6) and (⁻3,5) are ordered pairs.

order of operations   The order in which mathematical operations must be done when more than one operation is involved.

origin   The point (0,0) in the coordinate plane where the x-axis and the y-axis intersect.

P

parabola A smooth curve resulting from graphing an equation in the form: $y = x^2 + a$.

parallel lines Lines in a plane that never intersect.

parallelogram A quadrilateral with two pairs of parallel sides.

partitive proportion A proportion used when a total amount is distributed into unequal parts.

pentagon A polygon with five sides.

percent The ratio or comparison of a number to one hundred.

percentage Parts per hundred.

perfect square A number whose square root is an integer.

perimeter The measure of the distance around a figure.

period The name given to every group of three places in a numeral. The periods are called ones, thousands, millions, ...

perpendicular lines Lines in a plane that intersect to form right angles.

pi The ratio of the circumference to the diameter of any circle. The symbol for this constant ratio is π. ($\pi \approx 3.14$ or $\frac{22}{7}$)

pictograph A graph using a picture to represent a given quantity.

pi units A way of expressing circumference or area in terms of π.

place value The value of a digit depending upon its position or place in a standard numeral. In 843, the 4 is in the tens place and means 4 tens or 40.

plane A flat surface that extends indefinitely in all directions.

point A location or position on a plane usually named by a capital letter.

polygon A simple closed figure with sides that are line segments.

polyhedron A space figure having polygons as faces.

polynomial Any mathematical expression of two or more terms.

power of a number The result of using a number as a factor a given number of times. An exponent is used to express the power. $10^3 = 10 \times 10 \times 10$, or 1000.

precision A property of measurement based on the size of the unit of measure. The smaller the unit, the more precise the measure.

prime factorization Expressing a composite number as the product of two or more prime numbers.

prime number A whole number greater than 1 that has only two factors, itself and 1.

principal The amount of money borrowed from a bank.

prism A polyhedron having one pair of parallel faces for which the prism is named. The other faces are polygons.

probability A branch of mathematics that analyzes the chance that a given outcome will occur. The probability of an event is expressed as the ratio of a given outcome to the total number of outcomes possible.

product The result of multiplying two or more factors.

proportion An equation stating that two ratios are equal.

protractor An instrument for measuring the number of degrees in an angle.

pyramid A polyhedron having one base for which the pyramid is named. The other faces are triangular and meet at a common vertex.

Pythagorean Theorem Theorem that states that *the sum of the squares of the legs of a right triangle equals the square of the hypotenuse.*

Q

quadrant One of four sections into which the coordinate plane is divided.

quadrilateral Any four-sided polygon.

quotient The answer that results from the division of the dividend by the divisor.

R

radius A segment from the center of a circle to a point on the circle.

random sample A subgroup or part of a total group, each of which or whom has an equally likely chance of being chosen.

range (interval of measure) The given measure plus or minus the greatest possible error.

rate of commission The percent of the total amount of goods or services sold that is earned by the seller.

rate of discount The percent taken off the original, or list, price.

rate of interest The percent paid to the depositor on the principal.

rate of sales tax The percent of the list, or marked, price levied as a tax.

ratio A comparison of two numbers by division.

rationalizing the denominator Simplifying a fraction with a radical in the denominator by multiplying both numerator and denominator by a number that will make the denominator a whole number.

rational number A number that can be written in fractional form $\frac{a}{b}$ where a and b are integers and $b \neq 0$. Zero, the positive and negative whole numbers, the positive and negative fractions, and repeating or terminating decimals make up the set of rational numbers.

ray Part of a line with one endpoint.

real-number system The system made up of all rational and irrational numbers.

reciprocal The product of a number and its reciprocal is 1. 4 and $\frac{1}{4}$ are reciprocals since $4 \times \frac{1}{4} = 1$.

rectangle A quadrilateral with all angles congruent and two pairs of congruent sides.

rectangular prism A prism with six rectangular faces.

rectangular pyramid A pyramid with a rectangular base.

regular polygon A polygon having all sides and angles congruent.

regular price The original, or list, price of an item; the price before a discount has been given.

relation set A set of one or more pairs of ordered numbers.

repeating decimal A decimal in which the last digit or group of digits of the quotient repeats.

replacement set The set of numbers from which the variable can be replaced.

rhombus A parallelogram with all sides congruent and opposite angles congruent.

right angle An angle measuring exactly 90°.

right triangle A triangle with a right angle.

rotation symmetry Symmetry about a point. The figure appears the same after rotating through a specific number of degrees.

S

sale price The difference between the list price and the discount.

sales tax The amount added to the marked price of an item and collected as tax.

scale The ratio of a pictured measure to the actual measure.

scalene triangle A triangle with no congruent sides.

scientific notation The expression of a number as the product of a power of 10 and a number greater than or equal to 1 but less than 10.

segment A part of a line with two endpoints.

sequence A list of numbers written in order.

set A collection of elements having something in common.

significant digits The number of digits in a number, excluding zeros (unless the zeros are between nonzero digits).

similar figures Figures having the same shape but varying in size. The corresponding sides of similar figures are in proportion.

simple interest The amount paid by a bank to a depositor only on the principal for a stated period of time.

sine In a right triangle, the ratio that exists between the measure of the side opposite a given angle and the measure of the hypotenuse.

slope The coefficient of x when an equation is solved for y.

slope-intercept form A linear equation in the form $y = mx + b$, where m is the slope of the line and b is the y-intercept.

solution set The set of numbers that make an equality or an inequality true.

sphere A curved space figure having all points equidistant from the center.

square A rectangle with four sides of the same measure.

square root A number which when multiplied by itself gives the original number (radicand).

standard numeral The name given to a number as it is written or read.

straight angle An angle measuring exactly 180°.

subset A set with elements that belong to another set.

supplementary angles Two angles the sum of whose measures is 180°.

surface area The sum of the areas of all the faces of a solid figure.

T

tangent The ratio that exists in a right triangle between the measure of the side opposite a given angle and the measure of the side adjacent to the same angle.

tautology A compound statement which is true regardless of the truth values of the statements of which it is composed.

term Each number in a sequence.

terminating decimal A decimal which has no remainders. 0.05 is a terminating decimal.

trapezoid A quadrilateral with one pair of parallel sides.

tree diagram A diagram showing all possible outcomes of an event or of more than one event.

triangle A polygon with three sides.

triangular prism A prism having two parallel triangular faces.

triangular pyramid A pyramid with a triangular base.

trinomial A polynomial with three terms.

U

union of sets A set made up of the combination of all the members of two or more sets.

V

variable A letter of the alphabet that stands for a number value in a mathematical expression or equation.

Venn diagram A special diagram using overlapping circles to show how data are related.

vertex The common endpoint of two rays in an angle, two line segments in a polygon, or three or more edges in a polyhedron.

vertical angles Opposite angles (nonadjacent) formed by two intersecting lines.

volume The number of cubic units of space a figure contains.

W

whole number Any of the numbers 0, 1, 2, 3, 4, 5, 6, ….

X

x-axis The horizontal number line in a coordinate plane.

Y

y-axis The vertical number line in a coordinate plane.

y-intercept The y-coordinate of the point where a graph crosses the y-axis.

Index

Table of Trigonometric Ratios

Angle	Sin	Cos	Tan	Angle	Sin	Cos	Tan
0°	0.000	1.000	0.000	45°	0.707	0.707	1.000
1°	0.017	1.000	0.017	46°	0.719	0.695	1.036
2°	0.035	0.999	0.035	47°	0.731	0.682	1.072
3°	0.052	0.999	0.052	48°	0.743	0.669	1.111
4°	0.070	0.998	0.070	49°	0.755	0.656	1.150
5°	0.087	0.996	0.087	50°	0.766	0.643	1.192
6°	0.105	0.995	0.105	51°	0.777	0.629	1.235
7°	0.122	0.993	0.123	52°	0.788	0.616	1.280
8°	0.139	0.990	0.141	53°	0.799	0.602	1.327
9°	0.156	0.988	0.158	54°	0.809	0.588	1.376
10°	0.174	0.985	0.176	55°	0.819	0.574	1.428
11°	0.191	0.982	0.194	56°	0.829	0.559	1.483
12°	0.208	0.978	0.213	57°	0.839	0.545	1.540
13°	0.225	0.974	0.231	58°	0.848	0.530	1.600
14°	0.242	0.970	0.249	59°	0.857	0.515	1.664
15°	0.259	0.966	0.268	60°	0.866	0.500	1.732
16°	0.276	0.961	0.287	61°	0.875	0.485	1.804
17°	0.292	0.956	0.306	62°	0.883	0.469	1.881
18°	0.309	0.951	0.325	63°	0.891	0.454	1.963
19°	0.326	0.946	0.344	64°	0.899	0.438	2.050
20°	0.342	0.940	0.364	65°	0.906	0.423	2.145
21°	0.358	0.934	0.384	66°	0.914	0.407	2.246
22°	0.375	0.927	0.404	67°	0.921	0.391	2.356
23°	0.391	0.921	0.424	68°	0.927	0.375	2.475
24°	0.407	0.914	0.445	69°	0.934	0.358	2.605
25°	0.423	0.906	0.466	70°	0.940	0.342	2.747
26°	0.438	0.899	0.488	71°	0.946	0.326	2.904
27°	0.454	0.891	0.510	72°	0.951	0.309	3.078
28°	0.469	0.883	0.532	73°	0.956	0.292	3.271
29°	0.485	0.875	0.554	74°	0.961	0.276	3.487
30°	0.500	0.866	0.577	75°	0.966	0.259	3.732
31°	0.515	0.857	0.601	76°	0.970	0.242	4.011
32°	0.530	0.848	0.625	77°	0.974	0.225	4.332
33°	0.545	0.839	0.649	78°	0.978	0.208	4.705
34°	0.559	0.829	0.675	79°	0.982	0.191	5.145
35°	0.574	0.819	0.700	80°	0.985	0.174	5.671
36°	0.588	0.809	0.727	81°	0.988	0.156	6.314
37°	0.602	0.799	0.754	82°	0.990	0.139	7.115
38°	0.616	0.788	0.781	83°	0.993	0.122	8.144
39°	0.629	0.777	0.810	84°	0.995	0.105	9.514
40°	0.643	0.766	0.839	85°	0.996	0.087	11.430
41°	0.656	0.755	0.869	86°	0.998	0.070	14.301
42°	0.669	0.743	0.900	87°	0.999	0.052	19.081
43°	0.682	0.731	0.933	88°	0.999	0.035	28.636
44°	0.695	0.719	0.966	89°	1.000	0.017	57.290
45°	0.707	0.707	1.000	90°	1.000	0.000	———

Answers to Selected Odd-Numbered Exercises

1 Whole Numbers and Decimals

Page 2 1. $(8 \times 10,000) + (4 \times 1000) + (2 \times 100)$ $+ (1 \times 10) + (9 \times 1)$ **3.** $(4 \times 1,000,000)$ **5.** $(9 \times 1,000,000) + (6 \times 100,000) + (2 \times 10,000) + (7 \times 1000) + (9 \times 100)$ **7.** $(6 \times 1,000,000,000) + (7 \times 100,000,000) + (2 \times 10,000,000) + (1 \times 1,000,000) + (8 \times 100,000) + (9 \times 1000) + (5 \times 10)$ **9.** $(7 \times 1,000,000,000,000) + (6 \times 100,000,000,000) + (4 \times 10,000,000,000) + (3 \times 1,000,000,000)$ **11.** 7 tenths **13.** 2 millionths **15.** 4 tenths **17.** 2 ten millionths

Page 3 19. 90,503 **21.** 4,009,080 **23.** 60.0015 **25.** 0.8007 **27.** 3,000,000 **29.** 81,000,000,000,000 **31.** 1,500,000 **33.** 3,750,000,000 **35.** 8.400507 **37.** 0.527004 **39.** 0.270400005 **41.** 530.02 **43.** 27.6009 **45.** 0.012345 **47.** 0.000001 **49.** d

Page 4 1. ones **3.** hundred thousands **5.** tenths **7.** hundred thousandths **9.** 3 **11.** 8 **13.** 4

Page 5 15. < **17.** > **19.** = **21.** < **23.** > **25.** > **27.** < **29.** > **31.** 60,969,721; 60,961,721; 60,901,721 **33.** 0.64988, 0.64987, 0.0698 **35.** 49.006, 46.069, 4.606 **37.** 0.0201, 0.0021, 0.00201 **39.–43.** Answers will vary. **39.** 0.46, 0.47 **41.** 0.001, 0.0011 **43.** 0.01001, 0.010015

Page 7 1. 19,607,258,321,900 **3.** 19,607,000,000,000 **5.** 20,000,000,000,000 **7.** 19,607,258,300,000 **9.** 19,600,000,000,000 **11.** 246.8 **13.** 246.803146 **15.** 200 **17.** 24,000,000 **19.** 27,000,000 **21.** 6,000,000 **23.** 107,000,000 **25.** 8.030 **27.** 10.288 **29.** 21.008 **31.** 6.325 **33.** credit cards **35.** computers

Page 8 1. 878,289 **3.** 3,221,904 **5.** 80,930 **7.** 57,692

Page 9 9. 1,273,879 **11.** 6,779,123 **13.** 34,076,059 **15.** 3.189 **17.** 21.41 **19.** 29,000,000 **21.** 156,000 **23.** 6.430 **25.** \$103.60 **27.** \$3.25

Page 10 1. 6,012,512 **3.** 2,045,767 **5.** 165,787 **7.** 2,765,732 **9.** 3,290,108 **11.** 412,977,369 **13.** 28.33 **15.** 0.0864 **17.** 49.155 **19.** 0.573 **21.** 1.47 **23.** 5.16

Page 11 25. 60,000 **27.** 100,000 **29.** 2; 2.328 **31.** 57; 56.734 **33.** 19–11.1; 7.91 **35.** 0.3–0.2; 0.117 **37.** 7.0–1.0; 6.032 **39.** 6.6–0.8; 5.8217 **41.** 6.56 **43.** 19.5 **45.** 1.28 **47.** 44; 44 **49.** 1; 7; 9; 1; 0

Page 12 1. 138,272 **3.** 193,440 **5.** 307,230 **7.** 824,618 **9.** 6,039,915 **11.** 0.7408 **13.** 2.5221 **15.** 2.781 **17.** 0.1648 **19.** 0.00206

Page 13 21. 50; 400; 20,000 **23.** 40; 8000; 320,000 **25.** 50; 20,000; 1,000,000 **27.** 10; 6; 60 **29.** 30; 9; 270 **31.** 7; 1; 7

Page 14 1. 107 **3.** 2004 **5.** 400 R67 **7.** 102 **9.** 801 **11.** 4016 R27 **13.** 75 R145 **15.** 74 R102

Page 15 17. 0.6 **19.** 0.07 **21.** 0.28 **23.** 2.44 **25.** 2.04 **27.** 0.982 **29.** 0.51 **31.** 4.69 **33.** 2.53 **35.** 0.51

Page 16 1. 10; 20.1 **3.** 10; 1.25 **5.** 10; 0.05 **7.** 100; 200 **9.** 100; 40 **11.** 100; 31 **13.** 90 **15.** 120 **17.** 710 **19.** 0.03

Page 17 21. 3.6 **23.** 7.1 **25.** 4.88 **27.** 2.25 **29.** 7.55 **31.** 7.78 **33.** 6.94 **35.** 20.26 **37.** 20

39. 35 **41.** 50 **43.** 2 **45.** 0.2 divided by 0.25 **47.** 15 **49.** 12 **51.** 60 **53.** 0.08 **55.** 0.006

Page 18 1. 56,000 **3.** 180 **5.** 82 **7.** 0.05

Page 19 9. = **11.** = **13.** < **15.–35.** Answers will vary. **15.** 7,900,000 **17.** 10 **19.** 41,200 **21.** 2 **23.** 150,000 **25.** 32,000 **27.** 60 **29.** 200 **31.** 3 **33.** 700 **35.** 8 **37.** R **39.** R **41.** U **43.** R **45.** U

Page 21 1. identity of addition; 0 **3.** associative; 1.8 **5.** associative; 1.2 **7.** associative; 6.7 **9.** 168; commutative; associative **11.** 57; commutative; associative; identity of addition **13.** 41.3; distributive; identity of multiplication **15.** 84; distributive **17.** 319; commutative; associative **19.** 17.04; commutative; associative **21.** 902; commutative; associative; identity of addition **23.** 6.7; identity of multiplication

2 Fractions

Page 32 1. $\frac{1}{2}$ **3.** $3\frac{1}{2}$

Page 33 5. $2\frac{2}{3}$ **13.** $\frac{41}{8}$ **15.** $\frac{19}{4}$ **17.** $\frac{19}{4}$ **19.** $\frac{11}{2}$ **21.** $\frac{15}{4}$ **23.** $\frac{17}{3}$ **25.** $\frac{29}{12}$ **27.** $\frac{38}{3}$ **29.** $\frac{17}{16}$ **31.** $\frac{339}{11}$ **33.** $\frac{151}{7}$ **35.** $\frac{7199}{73}$ **37.** $1\frac{2}{5}$ **39.** $3\frac{1}{2}$ **41.** $2\frac{1}{8}$ **43.** $14\frac{1}{8}$ **45.** $19\frac{2}{3}$ **47.** $9\frac{1}{10}$ **49.** $7\frac{1}{9}$ **51.** $8\frac{5}{9}$ **53.** $3\frac{3}{25}$ **55.** $27\frac{3}{5}$ **57.** $195\frac{1}{2}$ **59.** $37\frac{1}{3}$ **61.** $129\frac{1}{2}$ **63.** $146\frac{4}{7}$ **65.** $672\frac{5}{6}$ **67.** $\frac{9}{2}$ hr **69.** $\frac{125}{8}$ yd

Page 34 1. 3, 4 **3.** $\frac{6}{21}, \frac{8}{28}$ **5.** $\frac{15}{18}, \frac{20}{24}$

Page 35 7. $\frac{3}{4}$ **9.** $\frac{3}{7}$ **11.** $\frac{7}{14}$ **13.** $\frac{4}{6}$ **15.** $\frac{3}{4}, \frac{3}{7}, \frac{9}{11}$ **17.** 18 **19.** 6 **21.** 21 **23.** 9 **25.** $\frac{1}{12}$ **27.** $\frac{1}{2}$ **29.** $\frac{6}{7}$ **31.** $\frac{2}{5}$ **33.** $\frac{3}{5}$ **35.** $\frac{1}{8}$ **37.** $\frac{1}{3}$ **39.** $\frac{1}{2}$ **41.** $\frac{1}{9}$ **43.** $\frac{1}{4}$ **45.** $\frac{1}{9}$ **47.** $\frac{9}{28}$ **49.** $\frac{5}{8}$ in. **51.** $12\frac{1}{6}$ hr

Page 36 1. 1, 2, 3, 4, 6, 9, 12, 18, 36 **3.** 1, 2, 4, 5, 10, 20, 25, 50, 100 **5.** 1, 2, 4, 5, 8, 10, 16, 20, 40, 80 **7.** 1, 2, 3, 4, 6, 8, 9, 12, 18, 24, 36, 72 **9.** 1, 2, 3, 4, 6, 8, 12, 24 **11.** true **13.** true; 1 and 2 are only factors **15.** false; 1, 2, 3, 6 **17.** composite **19.** prime **21.** prime **23.** composite **25.** composite

Page 37 1. $2 \times 3 \times 3 \times 5$ **3.** $3 \times 3 \times 7$ **5.** $2 \times 2 \times 2 \times 7$ **7.** $2 \times 2 \times 2 \times 3 \times 3$ **9.** $2 \times 2 \times 3 \times 7$ **11.** $2 \times 2 \times 3$ **13.** $3 \times 3 \times 3$ **15.** $2 \times 2 \times 2 \times 2 \times 5$ **17.** 3^2 **19.** 3×5 **21.** 2^6 **23.** 2^5 **25.** $2^5 \times 3$ **27.** $2^2 \times 3$ **29.** 5^3 **31.** a **33.** c

Page 38 1. 2 **3.** 9 **5.** 1 **7.** 15 **9.** 5 **11.** 3 **13.** 18 **15.** 9 **17.** 3

Page 39 1. 520 **3.** 24 **5.** 30 **7.** 180 **9.** 180 **11.** 450

Page 40 1. 0.8 **3.** 0.125 **5.** 0.875 **7.** 0.65 **9.** 0.22 **11.** $0.2\overline{4}$ **13.** 2.25 **15.** $11.0\overline{1}$ **17.** 5.5

Page 41 19. $0.\overline{21}$ **21.** $0.1\overline{8}$ **23.** $1.0\overline{1}$ **25.** 0.375 **27.** $0.\overline{7}$ **29.** $0.\overline{6}$ **31.** 0.4 **33.** $0.\overline{2}$ **35.** 0.15 **37.** $0.\overline{190476}$ **39.** 0.3 **41.** 0.225 **43.** 4.4 **45.** $5.\overline{142857}$ **47.** $1.\overline{2}$ **49.** $8.1\overline{6}$ **51.** $4.\overline{307692}$ **53.** $3.\overline{571428}$ **55.** $6.\overline{1}$ **57.** $1.3\overline{6}$ **59.** $6.\overline{2}$ **61.** 0.75 **63.** 0.85 **65.** 0.625

Page 42 1. < **3.** < **5.** > **7.** > **9.** > **11.** >

Page 43 13. > **15.** > **17.** > **19.** = **21.** < **23.** < **25.** < **27.** > **29.** < **31.** > **33.** < **35.** < **37.** $\frac{3}{4}, \frac{2}{3}, \frac{1}{5}$ **39.** $\frac{5}{6}, \frac{4}{5}, \frac{1}{3}, \frac{2}{7}$ **41.** $2\frac{3}{7}, 1\frac{5}{8}, 1\frac{4}{9}, \frac{8}{9}$

Page 45 1. $\frac{1}{2}$ **3.** $\frac{1}{2}$ **5.** $\frac{1}{3}$ **7.** $\frac{2}{3}$ **9.** $\frac{11}{12}$ **11.** $\frac{5}{8}$ **13.** 18 **15.** $9\frac{2}{7}$ **17.** $4\frac{5}{6}$ **19.** $7\frac{2}{9}$ **21.** $17\frac{5}{6}$ **23.** $11\frac{3}{10}$

25. $10\frac{11}{12}$ **27.** $6\frac{8}{21}$
Page 46 **1.** $\frac{1}{17}$ **3.** $\frac{1}{21}$ **5.** $\frac{1}{3}$ **7.** $\frac{3}{10}$ **9.** $\frac{3}{7}$ **11.** $\frac{2}{5}$
Page 47 **13.** 9 **15.** 5 **17.** $3\frac{1}{2}$ **19.** $2\frac{1}{4}$ **21.** $4\frac{1}{2}$
23. $5\frac{17}{18}$ **25.** $4\frac{8}{9}$ **27.** 1 **29.** 1 **31.** 11 **33.** 8
Page 49 **1.** $\frac{9}{40}$ **3.** $\frac{2}{9}$ **5.** $\frac{2}{21}$ **7.** 6 **9.** 2 **11.** $1\frac{2}{3}$
13. 4 **15.** $\frac{4}{7}$ **17.** $5\frac{5}{24}$ **19.** $23\frac{1}{5}$ **21.** 30 **23.** $15\frac{1}{5}$
25. $12\frac{1}{2}$ **27.** 116 **29.** $1\frac{1}{4}$ **31.** $34\frac{1}{5}$ **33.** 3 **35.** $\frac{1}{2}$
37. 201 **39.** $1\frac{9}{14}$ **41.** 1 **43.** $3\frac{7}{9}$ **45.** 6 **47.** 20
49. 24 **51.** 81
Page 50 **1.** $\frac{8}{7}$ **3.** $\frac{1}{7}$ **5.** $\frac{10}{1}$ **7.** $\frac{7}{9}$ **9.** $\frac{5}{7}$ **11.** $\frac{5}{14}$
Page 51 **13.** $\frac{2}{3}$ **15.** $\frac{7}{10}$ **17.** $\frac{15}{22}$ **19.** $1\frac{1}{2}$ **21.** $\frac{12}{35}$
23. $1\frac{1}{4}$ **25.** 21 **27.** 72 **29.** 20 **31.** 14 **33.** 10
35. 8 **37.** $\frac{2}{21}$ **39.** $\frac{1}{6}$ **41.** $1\frac{7}{17}$ **43.** $3\frac{7}{17}$ **45.** $\frac{6}{7}$
47. $1\frac{5}{7}$ **49.** 12 **51.** $\frac{1}{14}$ **53.** $1\frac{8}{27}$ **57.** $6\frac{1}{2}$ **59.** $1\frac{3}{4}$
61. $1\frac{1}{7}$ **63.** $12\frac{3}{8}$ **65.** 51
Page 53 **1.** 11 **3.** 16 **5.** 2 **7.** 10 **9.** 6 **11.** 2
13. 3 **15.** 12 **17.** 30 **19.** $\frac{2}{3}$ **21.** $\frac{2}{25}$ **23.** 4 **25.** 7
27. $3\frac{1}{6}$ **29.** $2\frac{2}{21}$ **31.** $4\frac{1}{5}$ **33.** $12\frac{1}{10}$ **35.** $20\frac{5}{12}$ **37.** $7\frac{1}{6}$

3 Equations, Inequalities and Integers
Page 64 **1.** 10 **3.** 10 **5.** 11 **7.** 45
9. 8 **11.** 0 **13.** 9 **15.** 105
Page 65 **17.** 148 **19.** 288 **21.** 1 **23.** 444
25. 0 **27.** 131 **29.** 0 **31.** 15 **33.** 80
35.–47. Answers will vary. **35.** + 92 or × 47 **37.** + 94
or × 48 **39.** + 116 or × 59 **41.** + 2 or × 2 **43.** (144
÷ 8) − [(2 + 5) × 2] = 4 **45.** [144 ÷ (8 − 2) + 5] × 2
= 58 **47.** 144 ÷ [(8 − 2) + (5 × 2)] = 9
Page 66 **1.** $n + 5$ **3.** $t - 4$ **5.** $10w$ **7.** $15 + \frac{n}{2}$
9. $15 - z$ **11.** $a + b$ **13.** $c - 10$ **15.** $\frac{j}{6}$ **17.** $\frac{20}{a}$
19. $2q - 3$ **21.** $o + p$ **23.** $\frac{54}{x}$
Page 67 **27.** $2n - 6$ **29.** $n + 2(3)$ or $n + 6$ **31.** $\frac{2n}{7}$
33. $n + 10 - 2$ **37.** $2p$ **39.** $1.07p$ or $p + 0.07p$
41. $\frac{7}{8} p$
Page 68 **1.** 6 + 1 = 7 P.M.; 6 − 1 = 5 P.M. **3.** 1 + 2
= 3 P.M.; 1 + 1 = 2 P.M.; 1 − 1 = 12 P.M. **5.** 10 + 2
= 12 P.M.; 10 + 1 = 11 A.M.; 10 − 1 = 9 A.M.
Page 69 **7.** 28 **9.** 81 **11.** 150 **13.** 9 **15.** 7
17. 5 **19.** 680 **21.** 110 **23.** 0 **25.** 6 **27.** 112
29. 96 **31.** 46 **33.** 2 **35.** 4 **37.** 76.5 **39.** 76
41. 10 **43.** 6
Page 70 **1.** $6n = 42$ **3.** $\frac{n}{3} = 10$ **5.** $3n = 18$
7. $n - 6 < 20$ **9.** $n - 17 \neq 18$
Page 71 **11.** $\frac{n}{3} \neq 17$; inequality **13.** $17 + n = 34$;
equation **15.** $8 + n \geq 20$; inequality **17.** $6n + 4 = 40$;
equation
Page 72 **1.** true **3.** true **5.** false **7.** true **9.** true
11. false
Page 73 **13.** 30 **15.** any whole number ≥ 1 **17.** 11
19. 30 **21.** 5 **23.** any whole number except 36
25. any whole number > 19 **27.** any whole number > 6
29. r **31.** $5b$ **33.** 1 **35.** 0 **37.** =
Page 74 **1.** c **3.** a **5.** a
Page 75 **7.** 4 **9.** 17 **11.** 71 **13.** 11 **15.** 201
17. 220 **19.** 215 **21.** 46 **23.** 406 **25.** 11 **27.** b;
$a = 45$ **29.** c; $x = 22$
Page 76 **1.** c **3.** c
Page 77 **7.** 4 **9.** 375 **11.** 6 **13.** 1800 **15.** 14

17. $\frac{1}{3}$ **19.** 132 **21.** 1.8 **23.** 825 **25.** 8.4 **27.** a;
$n = 8$ **29.** c; $n = 150$ **31.** b; $x = 45$
Page 78 **1.** e **3.** d **5.** a **7.** a **9.** d
Page 79 **11.** 3 **13.** 25 **15.** 1 **17.** 11 **19.** 4
21. 342 **23.** 68 **25.** 9 **27.** b; $n = 8$
Page 80 **1.** 7 **3.** 0 **5.** 14 **7.** 50 **9.** 4 **11.** 9
13. 8 **15.** 12 **17.** 11
Page 81 **19.** 16 **21.** 18 **23.** 9 **25.** 26 **27.** 7
29. 33 **31.** 5 **33.** 4
Page 82 **1.** even whole numbers greater than 0
3. whole numbers between 20 and 26 **5.** whole numbers
between 99 and 200
Page 83 **7.** {11, 12, 13, 14, 15, 16, 17, 18, 19}
9. {0, 4, 8, 12, 16, 20, 24, 28, 32, 36, 40, 44, 48}
11. {7, 9, 11, 13, ...} **15.** {10, 11, 12, 13, 14, 15,
16, 17, 18, 19, 20, 21, 22, 23, 24, 25} **17.** {25, 30,
35, 40, 45, 50} **19.** {17, 21, 23, 25, 27, 29, 31, 33}
21. {0, 1, 2, 3} **23.** {20, 10} **25.** ϕ **27.** {20}
29. ex. 20, 23, 25, 27 **31.** ex. 19, 25 **33.** yes; ex. 25
Page 84 **1.** area of triangle; b = base, h = height
3. volume of rectangular prism; ℓ = length, w = width,
h = height **5.** circumference of circle; d = diameter
7. area of square; s = side **9.** $A = 75 \text{ ft}^2$ **11.** $V =$
162 ft^3 **13.** $s = 15 \text{ yd}$ **15.** $V = 216 \text{ ft}^3$ **17.** $\ell = 10 \text{ ft}$
Page 85 **19.** $C = TS \times R$ of C **21.** $T = MP \times R$ of T
23. $P = \frac{I}{rt}$
Page 86 **1.** $^+3$ **3.** $^+7$ **5.** $^-2$ **7.** G **9.** J **11.** L
13. $^-2$ **15.** $^+9$ **17.** $^-15$ **19.** $^+15$ **21.** 0 **23.** $^+81$
25. $^-42$ **27.** $^+21$ **29.** $^-31$ **31.** ex. 13, 14, 17, 18,
21, 22, 25, 26, 29, 30
Page 87 **33.** $^+6$ **35.** $^-8$ **37.** $^+5$ **39.** $^-7$ **41.** 0
43. > **45.** > **47.** > **49.** < **51.** > **53.** > **55.** =
57. = **59.** =
Page 88 **1.** $^+7$ **3.** $^+2$ **5.** $^-2$ **7.** $^-1$ **9.** 0 **11.** $^+12$
13. $^-4$ **15.** $^+11$ **17.** $^-4$ **19.** $^-21$ **21.** $^-6$ **23.** $^+13$
25. $^+4$ **27.** 0
Page 89 **29.** $^+77$ **31.** $^+18$ **33.** $^-42$ **35.** $^-56$
37. $^+25$ **39.** 0 **41.** $^+9$ **43.** $^+6$ **45.** $^+9$ **47.** $^-2$
49. $^-9$ **51.** $^-8$ **55.** $^+8$ **57.** $^+5$ **59.** $^+13$ **61.** $^-10$
63. $^-3$ **67.** $^-9$ **69.** $^+1$ **71.** $^+120$ **73.** $^+81$

4 Rational Numbers
Page 100 **1.** $^-9.14$ **3.** $^+\frac{9}{2}$ **5.** $^+2.8$ **7.** $^-4\frac{1}{5}$ **9.** 0;
integer **11.** $^+100$; integer **13.** $^+\frac{5}{8}$ **15.** $^+4.0\overline{1}$
17. $^+5.\overline{75}$ **19.** $^-2.\overline{6}$ **21.** $^-5\frac{1}{2}$ **23.** $^-42.\overline{1}$ **25.** $^-\frac{21}{7} =$
$^-3$; integer **27.** $^-2.3$ **29.** $^+0.2$
Page 101 **41.** > **43.** < **45.** < **47.** = **49.** <
51. < **53.** $^-\frac{9}{2}$, $^-3$, $^-2.5$, $^-0.3$, 0, $^+1\frac{1}{2}$, $^+3\frac{3}{4}$ **55.** $^-3$,
$^-\frac{9}{4}$, $^-0.5$, 0, $^+1\frac{1}{3}$, $^+2.75$ **57.** T **59.** F **61.** T **63.** F
65. $^+\$9.25$ **67.** $^-3\frac{1}{8}$ **69.** $^-10.5°$
Page 103 **5.** commutative of addition **7.** identity of
multiplication **9.** associative of multiplication
11. commutative of multiplication **13.** inverse of
multiplication **15.** 0; identity of addition **17.** $^-5$;
commutative of multiplication **19.** $^+\frac{1}{2}$; inverse of addition
21. 0; commutative of addition **23.** 0.5; distributive
27. $^+0.5$ **29.** $^+1\frac{1}{5}$ **31.** $^+3.1$ **33.** $^-4.\overline{6}$
Page 104 **1.** $^+12$ **3.** $^-10$ **5.** $^-2$ **7.** $^+2$ **9.** $^+1.9$
11. $^+0.6$ **13.** $^-0.1$ **15.** 0 **17.** $^-1.2$ **19.** $^-2.7$
21. $^+2.8$ **23.** $^+0.13$ **25.** 0 **27.** $^-0.34$ **29.** $^+6.8$
31. $^-46.4$ **33.** $^-19.8$ **35.** $^-10$
Page 105 **37.** 0 **39.** $^-\frac{5}{9}$ **41.** $^-\frac{3}{4}$ **43.** $^-\frac{2}{11}$ **45.** $^+\frac{3}{4}$

47. $^-5\frac{3}{4}$ **49.** $^-4\frac{7}{8}$ **51.** $^+7\frac{9}{10}$ **53.** 0 **55.** $^+15$
57. $^-11$ **59.** $^-13.9$ **61.** $^+1.1$ **63.** $^-\frac{5}{7}$ **65.** $^-2\frac{5}{8}$
67. $^-\frac{5}{6}$ **69.** $^+6$ **71.** $^-8$ **73.** $^+11$ **75.** $^-13$
77. $^-12.5$ **79.** a
Page 106 **1.** $^-13$ **3.** $^-5$ **5.** $^+13$ **7.** $^-23.2$ **9.** 0
11. $^-2.3$ **13.** $^+4.18$ **15.** $^+3.37$ **17.** $^-2.44$
19. $^+2.25$ **21.** $^-4.8$ **23.** $^+0.28$ **25.** $^-17.8$
27. $^-4.85$ **29.** $^+77.77$ **31.** $^-4.172$
Page 107 **33.** $^-1\frac{1}{8}$ **35.** $^-\frac{5}{8}$ **37.** $^-\frac{29}{24}=^-1\frac{5}{24}$
39. $^-2\frac{1}{8}$ **41.** $^-1\frac{17}{20}$ **43.** $^+7\frac{1}{12}$ **45.** $^-3$ **47.** $^+5$
49. $^-19.7$ **51.** $^-3.22$ **53.** $^+26.17$ **55.** $^+0.2$
57. $^-1\frac{7}{8}$ **59.** $^+\frac{11}{15}$ **61.** $^-3$ **63.** $^+1.5$ **65.** $^+5.5$
Page 108 **1.** c **3.** c **5.** c
Page 109 **7.** 10 **9.** $^-7.8$ **11.** $^-13.4$ **13.** $^+\frac{1}{6}$
15. $^-5\frac{5}{8}$ **17.** $x-^-20=^-2.5;^-22.5$ **19.** $(x+^-2.3)$
$-^-4.1=^+10;^+8.2$ **21.** $x+\frac{^-4}{5}+^-1\frac{3}{10}+^+4\frac{1}{5}=^-2;$
$^-4\frac{1}{10}$ **23.** $^-11$ **25.** $^+6.9$ **27.** $^-6.7$ **29.** $^-7$
31. $^+10.7$ **33.** $^+1.8$ **35.** $^+\frac{3}{10}$ **37.** $^+6\frac{1}{6}$ **39.** $^+14\frac{1}{9}$
41. $^-1\frac{2}{15}$

Page 110 **1.** $^+24$ **3.** $^-42$ **5.** $^-2.2$ **7.** 0 **9.** $^+8$
11. $^-70$ **13.** $^-9$ **15.** $^+24$ **17.** $^+\frac{3}{10}$ **19.** $^-2\frac{4}{5}$
21. $^-12$ **23.** $^+6$ **25.** $^+34.5$ **27.** 0
Page 111 **29.** $^+70$ **31.** $^+6$ **33.** $^+2.5$ **35.** $^-4$
37. $^-2$ **39.** positive **41.** positive **43.** opposite **45.** a
47. d **49.** a
Page 112 **1.** $^-7;^-7$ **3.** $^-1;^-1$ **5.** 0; 0 **7.** $^+8$
9. $^-12$ **11.** $^+5$ **13.** $^-\frac{9}{10}$ or $^-0.9$ **15.** $^+91$ **17.** $^+\frac{151}{10}$
or $^+15.1$ **19.** $^+\frac{1}{5}$ **21.** $^-\frac{1}{4}$ **23.** $^-\frac{22}{25}$ **25.** $^-\frac{201}{1}$
Page 113 **27.** $^+19$ **29.** $^-1$ **31.** $^-0.61$ **33.** $^-0.8$
35. $^+900$ **37.** $^-8$ **39.** $^+1\frac{2}{3}$ **41.** $^-\frac{1}{9}$ **43.** $^-1$
45. $^+2\frac{1}{6}$ **47.** $^+30$ **49.** $^+5.5$ **51.** $^-8.64$ **53.** $^+0.5$
55. $^-\frac{7}{9}$ **57.** $^-1\frac{1}{7}$ **59.** $^-8.4$ **61.** $^-\frac{1}{5}$ **63.** $^-0.9$
65. $^+\frac{9}{20}$ **67.** c; $^-24$
Page 114 **1.** divide; $^-1.2$ **3.** $\frac{t}{3}=^-20; t=^-60$
5. $^-2.5n=^-30; n=^+12$ **7.** $^-3\frac{1}{3}n=^+20; n=^-6$
Page 115 **9.** $^-14$ **11.** $^+16$ **13.** $^-7$ **15.** $^+9$
17. $^-0.7$ **19.** $^-4\frac{1}{2}$ **21.** $^-90$ **23.** $^+448$ **25.** $^+1.6$
27. $^+7.7$ **29.** $^-5.7$ **31.** $^-13.5$ **33.** c **35.** c
37. $^-16\frac{1}{5}$ **39.** $^+2$ **41.** $^+5.5$
Page 117 **1.** 10; $^-9$ **3.** 100; $^-7$ **5.** 100; $^+1.5$ **7.** 4;
$^-1.25$ **9.** 4; $^+\frac{9}{10}$ **11.** a; $n=7$ **13.** a; $r=12$
15. b; $e=12$ **17.** $^-4$ **19.** $^+1.3$ **21.** $^+5$ **23.** $^+3.6$
25. $^+2\frac{2}{3}$ **27.** $^+9$

5 Number Theory

Page 128 **1.** 10 **3.** 1,000,000 **5.** 1 **7.** 100
9. 1,000,000,000 **11.** 10^7 **13.** 10^4 **15.** 10^6 **17.** 10^3
19. 10^0
Page 129 **21.** 96.3 **23.** 215 **25.** 43.15
27. 0.0182519 **29.** 8295 **31.** 900,000 **33.** 0.246
35. 0.004 **37.** 0.007 **39.** 0.011 **41.** 58 **43.** 0.09
45. 49.1 **47.** 0.01 **49.** 241 **51.** 0.002 **53.** 6
55. 9.63 **57.** $0.273\times10^2; 0.0681\times10^3; 0.00901$
$\times10^4; 43.115\times10^1; 77.833\times10^1; 0.42151\times10^5$
59. 8 mm; 0.8 mm
Page 130 **1.** 4, $^-4$ **3.** 3, $^-3$ **5.** $^-6$ **7.** 2
Page 131 **9.** 9223.25 **11.** 0.343 **13.** 720.050706
15. 60.090337 **17.** 9×10^{-3} **19.** $(7\times10^0)+$

$(5\times10^{-1})+(6\times10^{-4})$ **21.** $(4\times10^0)+(2\times10^{-1})+$
$(9\times10^{-2})+(3\times10^{-3})+(5\times10^{-4})+(6\times10^{-5})$
23. $(1\times10^2)+(1\times10^1)+(3\times10^0)+(1\times10^{-2})+$
(3×10^{-3}) **25.** $(2\times10^0)+(7\times10^{-1})+(9\times10^{-2})+$
$(6\times10^{-5})+(6\times10^{-7})$ **27.** $(9\times10^{-3})+(8\times10^{-5})+$
(7×10^{-8}) **29.** c **31.** 4 **33.** $2^5; \frac{1}{32}$
Page 132 **1.** 6 **3.** $^-2$ **5.** $^-4$
Page 133 **7.** 1.23 **9.** 7.0 **11.** 1.3 **13.** 2.2×10^3
15. 8.03×10^5 **17.** 2.871×10^6 **19.** 1.5×10^3
21. 3×10^{-3} **23.** 1.7×10^{-4} **25.** 1.9707×10^8
27. 8.006×10^{-1} **29.** 7×10^{-9} **31.** 2.0202×10^9
33. 5.201×10^9 **35.** 7×10^{-8} **37.** 563
39. 0.00056 **41.** 481,000 **43.** 0.00000000203
45. 0.000000085 **47.** 6,540,000,000,000 **49.** 160
51. 134,000,000,000 **53.** 5030
55. 6,100,000,000,000 **57.** 0.00007208
59. 811,000,000 **61.** 2.01×10^5 **63.** 8.4×10^4
65. 9.04×10^{-2} **67.** 5.4×10^{-2}

Page 134 **1.** 10^{11} **3.** 10^9 **5.** 10^3 **7.** 10^3 **9.** 10^6
11. 10^8 **13.** 10^{10} **15.** 10^2
Page 135 **17.** 918,000,000 **19.** 18,560
21. 0.000000001326 **23.** 2000 **25.** 25,000
27. 2400 **29.** 0.0006 **31.** 1.6074×10^{13} **33.** 6.75
$\times10^{22}$ **35.** 2.7×10^1 **37.** 5.4×10^3 **39.** $1.3\times$
10^{-2} **41.** 4.5×10^{-6} **43.** 5×10^0
Page 136 **1.** 2, 3, 4 **3.** 2, 4 **5.** 2, 3, 4, 5, 8, 10
7. 2, 3, 5, 9, 10 **9.** 2, 3 **11.** 5 **13.** 8 **15.** 10
Page 137 **17.** no, yes, no, no **19.** yes, no, no, yes, no, no, yes **21.** yes, yes, yes, yes, yes, yes, yes **23.** no, no, no, no, no, no, no **25.** yes, yes, yes, yes, no, yes, yes
Page 138 **1.** 20, 24, 28 **3.** 68, 60, 52 **5.** 29, 25, 21 **7.** 80, 87, 94 **9.** 8.3, 8.6, 8.9 **11.** $5\frac{1}{3}, 6\frac{1}{3}, 7\frac{1}{3}$
13. 18, 17, 11; pattern: $-1, -6$ **15.** 10, 20, 18; pattern: $-2, \times2$ **17.** 41, 50, 60; pattern: $+n, +n+1$
19. 256;1024;4096 **21.** 19,683; 531,441; 14,348,907
23. 81;243;729 **25.** 625; 3125; 15,625
Page 139 **1.** The sky is not blue. **3.** Apples are not round. **5.** Michigan is not a city. **7.** Broccoli is not good for you. F **9.** Potatoes have eyes. T **11.** Lemons are not sweet. T **13.** p; T, F; $\sim p$; F, T **15.** r, T, F $\sim r$, F, T
Page 140 **1.** $p \wedge q$ **3.** $q \rightarrow r$ **5.** $\sim p \wedge \sim r$
7. $r \rightarrow p \wedge q$ **9.** $\sim(p \wedge q)$ **11.** Silence is golden and knowledge is power. **13.** Silence is golden or time does not fly. **15.** It is not true that silence is golden or time flies. **17.** If knowledge is power, then time flies. **19.** If silence is golden, then time flies. **21.** It is not true that if silence is golden and knowledge is power, then time flies.
Page 141 **23.** $\sim q$; F, T, F, T; $p \wedge \sim q$; F, T, F, F **25.** $\sim p$; F, F, T, T; $\sim p \longleftrightarrow q$; F, T, T, F **27.** $\sim p$; F, F, T, T; $\sim q$; F, T, F, T; $\sim p \wedge \sim q$; F, F, F, T **29.** $p \rightarrow q$; T, F, T, T; $\sim(p \rightarrow q)$; F, T, F, F **31.** F, F, T
Page 142 **1.** If it is summer, then it is July; If it is not July, then it is not summer; If it is not summer, then it is not July. **3.** If a number is divisible by 3, then it is divisible by 9; If a number is not divisible by 9, then it is not divisible by 3; If a number is not divisible by 3, then it is not divisible by 9. **5.** If I go to the park, then it does not rain; If it does rain, then I do not go to the park; If I do not go to the park, then it does rain. **7.** $\sim w \rightarrow \sim q$
9. $\sim q \rightarrow p$ **11.** $t \rightarrow \sim r$ **13.** $q \rightarrow p$ **15.** If a polygon is a triangle, then it has exactly three sides.
17. If you passed the test, then you studied and did your homework.

Page 143 19. a 21. d 23. a 25. $(p \rightarrow q)$ T, F, T, T; $(q \rightarrow p)$; T, T, F, T; $(p \rightarrow q) \rightarrow (q \rightarrow p)$; T, T, F, T

6 Ratio and Proportion

Page 155 1. $\frac{2}{5}$ 3. $\frac{1}{7}$ 5. $\frac{5}{2}$ 7. $\frac{4}{3}$ 11. $\frac{\$15}{2}$ or $7.50 for 1 13. $\frac{90 \text{ km}}{1 \text{ hr}}$ 15. $\frac{1}{\$.70}$ 17 $\frac{\$1.40}{1 \text{ gal}}$ 21.–25. Answers will vary. 21. $\frac{6}{8}, \frac{9}{12}, \frac{12}{16}$ 23. $\frac{2}{3}, \frac{4}{6}, \frac{6}{9}$ 25. $\frac{2}{5}, \frac{4}{10}, \frac{6}{15}$ 27. $\frac{1}{3}$ 29. $\frac{9}{2}$ 31. $\frac{1}{2}$ 33. $\frac{4}{3}$ 35. $\frac{1}{2}$ 37. $\frac{28}{5}$ 39. $\frac{1}{2}$ 41. $\frac{6}{1}$

Page 157 1. 16 3. 30r; 3 5. 60 7. 2 9. $\neq$ 11. $\neq$ 13. $\neq$ 15. = 17. $\neq$ 19. $\frac{50}{100} = \frac{22.5}{45}$ 21. $\frac{2.7}{0.3} = \frac{90}{10}$ 23. $\frac{3}{17} = \frac{96}{544}$ 25. $\frac{3}{10} = \frac{30}{100}$ 27. 3 29. 2 31. $\frac{10}{21}$ 33. 0.16 35. $18 37. 4 kg 39. 28 km

Page 159 1. $\frac{6}{360} = \frac{2}{120}$; $\frac{6}{2} = \frac{360}{120}$ 3. $\frac{45}{25} = \frac{18}{10}$; $\frac{45}{18} = \frac{25}{10}$ 5. true

Page 160 1. 16 km 3. 192 km
Page 161 5. 180 cm 7. 22.8 km 9. 10 cm 11. 0.78 km 13. 16.8 mi 15. 12.6 mi 17. 450 cm 19. 2250 cm 21. 1 mi = 1250 km
Page 162 1. $\frac{9}{12} = \frac{x}{6}$; 4.5 days 3. $\frac{5}{x} = \frac{1\frac{1}{6}}{3\frac{1}{2}}$; 15 editors
Page 164 1. 120; 180 3. 40; 60; 80 5. 1600; 2400; 3200

Page 166 1. $\angle H \cong \angle K$, $\angle F \cong \angle L$, $\angle G \cong \angle J$; $\frac{HF}{KL} = \frac{2}{4} = \frac{1}{2}$, $\frac{FG}{LJ} = \frac{3}{6} = \frac{1}{2}$, $\frac{GH}{JK} = \frac{4}{8} = \frac{1}{2}$ 3. $\angle B \cong \angle E$, $\angle A \cong \angle D$, $\angle C \cong \angle F$; $\frac{AB}{DE} = \frac{1}{5}$, $\frac{BC}{EF} = \frac{1.4}{7} = \frac{1}{5}$, $\frac{AC}{DF} = \frac{1}{5}$

Page 167 5. $\overline{HK}$ 7. 7.5 9. $\frac{11}{22} = \frac{5}{d}$, 10; $\frac{11}{22} = \frac{8}{c}$, 16

Page 168 1. 0.8 3. $1.\overline{3}$ 5. 0.8
Page 169 9. 0.259; 0.966; 0.268 11. 0.993; 0.122; 8.144 13. 0.070; 0.998; 0.070 17. 0.883; 28° 19. 0.471; 62°

7 Percent

Page 180 1. 62% 3. 302% 5. 30% 7. 12.5% 9. $16\frac{2}{3}$% 11. 6.25% 13. 3% 15. 175% 17. 310% 19. 0.1% 21. 1.2% 23. 502%
Page 181 25. 23% 27. 125% 29. 24% 31. 85% 33. $11\frac{1}{9}$% 35. $58\frac{1}{3}$% 37. 110% 39. 300% 41. 212% 43. 34% 45. 24% 47. 79% 49. 7% 51. 1.6% 53. 263% 55. 517% 57. 10.3% 59. 340% 61. F; 5% 63. T 65. T 67. T 69. F; 30% 71. F; 0.7%
Page 182 1. $\frac{1}{5}$ 3. $\frac{7}{20}$ 5. $\frac{3}{2}$ 7. $\frac{18}{25}$ 9. $\frac{15}{4}$ 11. $\frac{5}{8}$ 13. $\frac{7}{8}$ 15. $\frac{19}{500}$ 17. $\frac{1}{500}$ 19. 0.06 21. 0.61 23. 0.05 25. 0.21 27. 0.13 29. 1.43 31. 0.08 33. 0.049 35. 1.529
Page 183 37. 0.375, 37.5% 39. $\frac{1}{25}$, 0.04 41. $\frac{5}{16}$, 31.25% 43. 0.9, 90% 45. $4.66\overline{6}$, $466.\overline{6}$% or $466\frac{2}{3}$% 47. 5, 5.0 49. $\frac{1}{250}$, 0.4% 51. $0.44\overline{4}$, $44.\overline{4}$% or $44\frac{4}{9}$% 55. 0.004 57. 0.00125 59. 0.00625
Page 184 1. 18 3. 4 5. 70 7. 90 9. 78 11. 21.6 13. 12.75 15. 12 17. 480 19. 0.1 21. 8.5 23. 210
Page 186 1. 20% 3. $6\frac{2}{3}$% 5. 150% 7. $33\frac{1}{3}$% 9. 180% 11. $33\frac{1}{3}$% 13. 45%

Page 187 15. 4%, 2500% 17. 40%, 250% 19. 75%, $133\frac{1}{3}$% 21. 20%, 500%
Page 188 1. 100 3. 160 5. 120 7. 75 9. 36 11. 3.2 13. 200 15. 512 17. 162
Page 189 19. $166\frac{2}{3}$ 21. 7 23. 15% 25. 1280 27. 1.25 29. 4.4% 31. 750 33. $11\frac{1}{9}$%
Page 191 1. $\frac{1}{3}$ 3. $\frac{1}{10}$ 5. $\frac{3}{10}$ 7. $\frac{5}{8}$ 9. $\frac{1}{7}$ 11. $\frac{1}{6}$ 13. $8\frac{1}{3}$% × 60; 5 15. 50% × 64; 32 17. 70% × 50; 35 19. 90% × 30; 27 21. 10% × 10; 1 23. 40% × 15; 6 25. b; $16\frac{2}{3}$% 27. a; 30% 29. c; 50% 33. 75%; 15; 20 35. $66\frac{2}{3}$%; 30; 45 37. 45; 90%; 50 39. 18; 60%; 30
Page 192 1. $33\frac{1}{3}$% 3. 40% 5. 500% 7. 22.2%
Page 193 9. increase; $3600; 13.0% 11. increase; $2600; 40.6% 13. increase; $2100; 28% 15. decrease; $3300; 34.7%

8 Consumer Mathematics

Page 204 1. $25 3. $16.50 5. $701.67 7. $1.64 9. $2.69
Page 205 13. $173.25 15. $147.42 17. $331.50
Page 206 1. $9; $51 3. $2.52; $33.48 5. $.76; $24.49 7. $1.13; $5.62
Page 207 9. a; $168.30 11. a; $97.60 13. 85%; $21.25 15. 90%; $17.01
Page 208 1. 10% 3. 16% 5. $300
Page 209 7. $\frac{1}{7}$ or $14\frac{2}{7}$% 9. 4% 11. $52 13. $65 15. $11
Page 210 1. $.48; $10.08 3. $4.73; $94.73 5. $5.64; $92.39 7. $2.04; $44.94 9. $24.83; $416.93
Page 211 11. $.16; $2.13 13. $.78; $10.28
Page 212 1. $120 3. $53.40 5. $295.80 7. $42.59 9. $271.95 11. $413.83
Page 214 1. 12.5% 3. 2.5% 5. $7600 7. $1450 9. 3%
Page 215 11. $6600 13. 7.5% 15. $135 17. $12,666.67 19. 3.5%
Page 216 1. $80.75 3. $3777.75 5. $36.18
Page 217 7. $1908 9. $9330.33 11. $5286.33 13. $3561.50 15. $80,906.25 17. $1272
Page 218 1. $5.13, $210.13, $5.25, $215.38; $5.38, $220.76, $5.52, $226.28; $26.28, 226.28
Page 219 3. $262.66; $12.66 5. $1125.51; $125.51 7. $441.53; $41.53
Page 220 1. $.60 3. $5.58 5. $2.19 7. $172.38 9. $123.08
Page 222 1. nineteen and $\frac{35}{100}$ 3. four hundred thirty-nine and $\frac{90}{100}$ 5. one thousand twelve and $\frac{0}{100}$ 7. three thousand seventy-five and $\frac{57}{100}$
Page 223 13. $568.32; + $50.75; $619.07; − 75.40; $543.67; − 48.00; $495.67; − 29.95; $465.72; + 150.50; $616.22 15. $75.40
Page 225 1. $15.17 3. 7.5% 5. $700.00; $136.50; $52.50; $511.00
Page 227 1. $1350 3. $2505 5. $3375 7. $4414 9. $7410 11. $11,890

9 Probability and Statistics

Page 240 1. $\frac{1}{6}$ 3. 1 5. 0 7. $\frac{1}{2}$ 9. $\frac{1}{3}$
Page 241 11. $\frac{3}{26}$ 13. 0 15. $\frac{2}{13}$ 17. $\frac{3}{20}$ 19. $\frac{1}{2}$ 21. $\frac{1}{2}$ 23. $\frac{2}{3}$ 25. $\frac{1}{3}$ 27. 0 29. 0 31. $\frac{1}{3}$ 33. $\frac{1}{3}$ 35. $\frac{1}{3}$

37. $\frac{2}{3}$ **39.** $\frac{1}{6}$ **41.** 0 **43.** $\frac{1}{6}$ **45.** $\frac{1}{4}$ **47.** $\frac{5}{6}$ **49.** $\frac{1}{2}$

Page 242 **1.** $\frac{1}{16}$ **3.** $\frac{1}{64}$ **5.** $\frac{1}{12}$ **7.** $\frac{1}{24}$

Page 243 **9.** $\frac{1}{20}$ **11.** $\frac{3}{100}$ **13.** $\frac{1}{10}$ **15.** $\frac{1}{90}$ **17.** $\frac{1}{18}$

19. $\frac{1}{45}$ **21.** (H, 4), (T, 2), (T, 3), (T, 4) **25.** $\frac{1}{4}$ **27.** $\frac{1}{2}$

29. $\frac{1}{4}$, the same **31.** $\frac{4}{45}$ **33.** $\frac{1}{18}$ **35.** $\frac{2}{5}$

Page 244 **1.** 120 **3.** 24 **5.** 144 **7.** 744 **9.** 714 **11.** 210

Page 245 **13.** 24 **15.** 360 **17.** 40,320 **19.** 60 **23.** 5040 **25.** 2520 **27.** 120 **29.** 360,360 **31.** 7980 **37.** 15 **39.** 70 **41.** 84

Page 247 **1.** 20% **5.** 30%, 60%, 52%, 36%; 44.5%; 7012 people

Page 248 **1.** 325 **3.** 300 **5.** August 10

Page 251 **1.** $200 **3.** 8 ft

Page 252 **1.** 55 students **3.** Today's World; News **5.** 200 subscriptions

Page 254 **1.** $33\frac{1}{3}$% **3.** $16\frac{2}{3}$%; 60°

Page 256 **1.** 13; 27; 28; 29

Page 257 **3.** $58; $64.25; $57.50; $45 **7.** Lauren; L:94 min; E:90 min **9.** 75, 105; 75, 90 **11.** 24.74 sec

Page 258 **1.** negative **3.** positive **5.** positive **7.** positive **9.** negative

Page 260 **3.** triangle; triangle

Page 261 **7.** 34; 51; 38 and 72 **9.** 40; 41; 30 and 70

10 Geometry and Measurement

Page 272 **1.** false; a line contains an infinite number of points **3.** true; definition of how lines are named **5.** false; H is the vertex **7.** false; a ray has only one endpoint **9.** false; parallel lines do not intersect, they are everywhere equidistant

Page 273 **11.** $\overline{AB}$ **13.** $\angle EFG$ **15.** K **17.** $\overrightarrow{NO}$ **19.** $\overrightarrow{ST}$ **21.** $\overrightarrow{BA}$ **23.** Z **25.** $\overline{LM}$ **27.** $\angle NJK$ **29.** $\overrightarrow{FA}$, $\overrightarrow{FD}$, $\overrightarrow{FJ}$, $\overrightarrow{FK}$ **31.** $\overline{AB}$, $\overline{BF}$, $\overline{FH}$, $\overline{HJ}$, $\overline{GH}$, $\overline{KG}$, $\overline{FG}$ **33.** $\overline{HB}$ **35.** ΔHGF, ΔFHG

Page 274 **1.** true; sum is 180° (90° + 90°) **3.** false; obtuse $\angle > 90°$ **5.** false; obtuse $\angle > 90°$

Page 275 **7.** 60° **9.** 70° **11.** acute; 40° **13.** acute; 26° **15.** acute; 30° **17.** obtuse; 120° **19.** 83° **21.** 72° **23.** 59° **27.** 172° **29.** 34° **31.** 95° **33.** $\angle LPM$ **35.** 23°; 113° **37.** 8.1° **39.** 89.2° **41.** 26.7° **43.** 12.3°

Page 278 **1.** $\angle K$, $\angle N$; $\angle L$, $\angle M$ **3.** $\angle H$, $\angle M$; $\angle K$, $\angle O$; $\angle J$, $\angle N$; $\angle L$ $\angle P$ **5.** alternate interior

Page 279 **7.** $\overrightarrow{MS}$ **9.** corresponding; right **11.–15.** Answers will vary. **11.** $\angle AEF$, $\angle CEB$; $\angle FEB$, $\angle AEC$ **13.** $\angle$'s: AEG, FCD, BEG; HCF **15.** $\angle$'s: AEF, HCF; HCG, AEG; GCD, GEB; FEB, FCD

Page 280 **1.** true; equilateral Δ has 3 60° angles **3.** true; definition of scalene Δ **5.** false; sum of $\angle$'s: of Δ is 180°, third $\angle$ is 100°

Page 281 **7.** 50°; 90° **9.** obtuse; 123° **11.** acute; 60° **13.** 60°; 90° **15.** obtuse; 8° **17.** $\angle 10$ **19.** 180°, they are $\angle$'s: of ▲ **21.** 360° **23.** 180° **25.** 180° **27.** 180° **29.** 180° **31.** 180°

Page 282 **1.** $\overline{ED}$ **3.** $\overline{CA}$ **5.** $\angle E$

Page 283 **7.** yes; yes; yes **9.** yes **11.** SAS **13.** SAS **15.** SAS

Page 284 **1.** 6 **3.** 40 **5.** 20 **7.** 5 **9.** $1\frac{2}{3}$ **11.** 63,360 **13.** 96 **15.** 73 **17.** 152 **19.** 2640 **21.** 7

Page 285 **23.** 9; 12 **25.** 2000 **27.** 4050 **29.** 9 ft **31.** 1 qt 3 c **33.** 2 c 4 fl oz **35.** 2 ft 5 in. **37.** 7 gal

39. 7 c **41.** 41 oz or 2 lb 9 oz

Page 286 **1.** a **3.** c **5.** a **7.** c **9.** a

Page 287 **21.** 3 cm **23.** 1 cm **25.** 20 mm **27.** 33 mm **29.** c or cm **31.** d or mm **33.** c or cm

Page 288 **1.** 0.08; 0.8; 80; 8000 **3.** 0.00207; 0.0207; 0.207; 2.07; 20.7; 2070 **5.** 4.9; 490; 4900; 49 000; 490 000; 4 900 000 **7.** 0.005; 0.05; 5; 50; 500; 5000

Page 289 **9.** 5000 **11.** 0.3 **13.** 0.042 **15.** 0.05 **17.** 120 **19.** 20 000 **21.** 0.0053 **23.** 27 000 **25.** 4200 **27.** 0.04016 **29.** a **31.** a **33.** c **37.** 7004 m; 7.004 km. **39.** 12 177 mm; 12.177 m **41.** 61 mm; 6.1 cm **43.** 500 803 cm; 5.00803 km **45.** > **47.** > **49.** <

Page 290 **1.** 92.1 cm **3.** 199 cm **5.** 11 000 m **7.** mi, yd, ft, in. **9.** mo, wk, d, min, s

Page 291 **11.** 1 m, 0.1 m, 0.01 m, 0.001 m **13.** 1 km, 0.1 km, 0.01 km, 1 m **15.** 0.5 cm **17.** 0.05 cm **19.** 1 m, 0.5 m, 7 ± 0.5 m **21.** 0.1 mm, 0.05 mm, 0.6 ± 0.05 mm **23.** 0.5 cm **25.** 2 ± 0.5 cm **27.** 0.32 cm **29.** 14.8 m **31.** 59.02 m **33.** 427 mm **35.** 33 mm **37.** 3150 m

Page 292 **1.** c **3.** b **5.** b

Page 293 **7.** 25° C **9.** ⁻20° C **11.** 18.$\overline{3}$ °C **13.** 10° C **15.** ⁻3.$\overline{3}$° C **17.** 77° F **19.** 14° F **21.** 98.6° F **23.** 32° F **25.** 24.8° F

11 Perimeter and Area

Page 304 **1.** 37.5 cm **3.** 101 m **5.** 38 in.

Page 305 **7.** 66.6 dm **9.** 14 ft **11.** 120 in. **13.** 6.4 m **15.** $9\frac{1}{2}$ yd **17.** 70 in. **19.** 22 ft **21.** 210 mm **23.** 30 mm

Page 306 **1.** 210 cm² **3.** 81 mm² **5.** 384 in.²

Page 307 **7.** 31.36 m² **9.** 780 mm² **11.** $2\frac{1}{2}$ in.² **13.** $58\frac{1}{2}$ ft² **17.** 0.13122 ca

Page 308 **1.** 56 cm² **3.** 182 mm² **5.** 30.53 m² **7.** 26 yd² **9.** $1\frac{1}{6}$ ft² **11.** $1\frac{1}{4}$ yd²

Page 310 **1.** 18 cm² **3.** 75.2 dm² **5.** 115 200 cm² **7.** 174 ft² **9.** 18 ft²

Page 311 **13.** 27 in.² **15.** 7.5 m² **17.** 74.7 cm²

Page 312 **1.** 69.08 cm **3.** 8.792 m **5.** 43.96 cm **7.** 21.98 cm **9.** 69.08 in. **11.** 6.3742 m **13.** 19.80398 cm **15.** $25\frac{2}{3}$ in. **17.** 78.5 mm **19.** 62.8 mm

Page 314 **1.** 254.34 cm² **3.** 1384.74 m² **5.** 78.5 yd² **7.** 19.625 cm²

Page 315 **9.** 452.16 mm² **11.** 154 in.² **13.** 530.66 in.²

Page 316 **1.** 9.14 cm² **3.** 1016 mm² **5.** 6.5158 cm²

Page 317 **9.** 36 cm² **11.** 51.875 m² **13.** 33.28 cm²

Page 318 **1.** 90 mL **3.** 44 mL **5.** 70 mL

Page 319 **7.** 4 **9.** 2 **11.** 2 **13.** 5 **15.** 1 **17.** 4 km² **19.** 900 000 m² **21.** 444 m² **23.** 7.1 km² **27.** 3.5 cm

Page 320 **1.** 7 m **3.** 10 m **5.** $14\frac{1}{2}$ ft

12 Real Numbers

Page 332 **1.** $\frac{-16}{1}$ **3.** $\frac{1}{4}$ **5.** $\frac{9}{7}$ **7.** $\frac{0}{1}$ **9.** $\frac{29}{20}$

Page 333 **11.** 9; 6; $\frac{2}{3}$ **13.** $\frac{9}{9} = 1$ **15.** $\frac{94}{99}$ **17.** $\frac{1}{33}$ **19.** $\frac{182}{999}$ **21.** $\frac{2}{333}$ **23.** $\frac{1426}{9999}$ **25.** $\frac{32}{9999}$ **27.** 900; $\frac{29}{900}$ **29.** $\frac{19}{30}$ **31.** $\frac{37}{450}$ **33.** $\frac{329}{990}$ **35.** $\frac{1498}{495}$ **37.** $\frac{1062}{495}$ **39.** $\frac{10,118}{4995}$ **41.** $\frac{62,513}{9990}$ **43.** ⁻14.0 **45.** 0.0625

47. $0.2\overline{3}$ **49.** $^+0.0\overline{6}$ **51.** $^-1.\overline{1}$
Page 334 **1.** 0.16 **3.** 1.69 **5.** 0.0036 **7.** 81
9. $\frac{9}{25}$

Page 335 **11.** 5 **13.** 11 **15.** $\frac{3}{4}$ **17.** $\frac{2}{3}$ **19.** 1.7
23. 13, 14 **25.** 8, 9 **27.** 12, 13 **29.** 13, 14 **31.** 19, 20 **33.** 8.485 **35.** 6.245 **37.** 12.247 **39.** 19.391 **41.** 24.900

Page 336 **1.** 4, 4
Page 337 **3.** 5; 1225 **5.** 29 **7.** 24 **9.** 37 **11.** 54 **13.** 97 **15.** 121 **17.** 259 **19.** 201 **23.** 3.2 **25.** 8.2 **27.** 25.1 **29.** 25.7 **31.** 0.31 **33.** 0.45 **35.** 1.23 **37.** 3.01

Page 338 **1.** true **3.** false **5.** true **7.** true **9.** true
Page 339 **11.** rational **13.** irrational **15.** rational **17.** rational **19.** rational **21.** irrational **23.** rational **25.** rational **37.** ±6 **39.** ±9 **41.** 0.55 **43.** $\frac{1}{2}$
45. $11\frac{7}{12}$ **47.** 0.0065 **49.** 7.0895

Page 340 **1.** $\{r:r > 7\}$ **3.** $\{r:r < 30\}$ **5.** $\{r:r < 16\}$ **7.** $\{r:r > {}^-2\}$ **9.** $\{r:r > 2\}$
Page 341 **11.** $\{n:n < 5\}$ **13.** $\{t:t < 4\}$ **15.** $\{t:t \ge 20\}$ **17.** $\{x:x > 20\}$ **19.** $\{r:r \ge 6\}$ **21.** $\{b:b \le {}^-6\}$ **23.** $\{x:x \le 24\}$ **25.** $\{s:s \ge 90\}$ **27.** $\{m:m \le {}^-3\}$ **29.** $\{n:n < {}^-4\}$ **31.** $\{t:t \le {}^-4\}$ **33.** $\{d:d \le {}^-12\}$ **35.** $\{a:a < {}^-10\}$ **37.** $\{t:t > {}^-5\}$ **39.** $\{y:y \ge {}^-6\}$ **41.** $\{c:c \ge {}^-1\}$

Page 342 **1.** yes **3.** no **5.** yes **7.** no **9.** no **11.** yes
Page 343 **13.** 24 m **15.** 36 km **17.** 2 m **19.** 0.8 cm **25.** $3\sqrt{2}$ cm or 4.243 cm **27.** $2\sqrt{2}$ in. or 2.828 in. **29.** $7\sqrt{2}$ m or 9.899 m

13 Surface Area and Volume
Page 354 **1.** 170 m² **3.** 88 ft²
Page 355 **5.** 96 cm² **7.** 312 m² **9.** 5766 in.² **11.** 2.16 yd² **13.** $253\frac{1}{2}$ ft² **15.** 1188 ft²
17. 106.68 cm²
Page 356 **1.** two triangular bases in prism, one triangular base in pyramid
Page 357 **3.** 364.56 cm² **5.** 110.4 ft² **7.** 79.5 m² **11.** 5; 9; 4; 6 **13.** 7; 10; 10; 6
Page 358 **1.** 200.96 ft² **3.** 125.6 m²
Page 359 **5.** 98.4704 yd² **7.** 119.7125 ft² **9.** 38.6848 ft² **11.** 68.6875 m² **13.** 486.7 in.² **15.** 128.6144 ft²
Page 360 **1.** 24 units³ **3.** 36 units³
Page 361 **5.** 54 units³ **7.** $V = \ell \times w \times h$ **9.** 8 **11.** $4^3 = 4 \times 4 \times 4$; 64 **13.** $6^3 = 6 \times 6 \times 6$; 216 **15.** $8^3 = 8 \times 8 \times 8$; 512 **17.** $10^3 = 10 \times 10 \times 10$; 1000 **19.** $20^3 = 20 \times 20 \times 20$; 8000 **21.** $40^3 = 40 \times 40 \times 40$; 64,000 **23.** 110.592 cm³ **25.** 1728 in.³ **27.** 216 in.³ **29.** 8365.427 cm³
Page 362 **1.** rectangular prism; 2205 ft³ **3.** rectangular pyramid; 1200 m³
Page 363 **5.** pentagonal pyramid; $757.\overline{3}$ ft³ **7.** 312 in.³ **9.** 221,760 ft³ **11.** $46.8693\overline{3}$ m³ **13.** 24 yd³
Page 364 **1.** 769.3 ft³ **3.** 522,527.4 in.³ **5.** 94,200 yd³ **7.** 1205.8 ft³
Page 365 **9.** 847.8 in.³ **11.** 4396 dm³ **13.** 3799.4 yd³ **15.** 480.7 cm³
Page 366 **1.** L **3.** kL **5.** L **7.** L **9.** mL
Page 367 **11.** 0.425 **13.** 2.4 **15.** 2.57 **17.** 230 **19.** 0.291 **21.** 7.6 **23.** 460 **25.** 0.07 **27.** 3 150 000 **29.** 7 kL **31.** 14 kL **33.** 2.6 kL **35.** 0.2 L **37.** 1.1 L **39.** 3 L

Page 368 **1.** kg **3.** kg **5.** t **7.** g **9.** g
Page 369 **11.** 7000 **13.** 0.00035 **15.** 16 500 **17.** 3.6 **19.** 4730 **21.** 560 **23.** 6500 **25.** 5.6 **27.** 1900 **29.** 1 kg **31.** 5 mL; 5g **33.** 5.7 dm³; 5.7 kg **35.** 8 dm³; 8 kg

14 Coordinate Geometry
Page 380 **1.** $^-5$ **3.** 0 **5.** $^-7$
Page 381 **7.** 6 **9.** $^-2$ **11.** $x < 3$ **13.** $x \ge 6$ **15.** $x > 4$ **17.** $x \le {}^-4$ **19.** $x < 3$ **21.** $x \ge {}^-2$ **23.** $x \ge 3$ **25.** $x < 3$ **27.** $x < 4$ **29.** $x \ge {}^-5$ **35.** a **37.** b; d
Page 382 **1.** (1, 5) **3.** (1, 2) **5.** (5, 1) **7.** (3, 0) **9.** (0, 3)
Page 383 **11.** K **13.** D **15.** J **17.** C **19.** H **21.** F **35.** polygon or letter C
Page 384 **1.** $(^-3, 1)$ **3.** $(4, {}^-1)$ **5.** (2, 1) **7.** $(^-2, 0)$ **9.** $(2, {}^-2)$
Page 385 **11.** L **13.** A **15.** B **17.** E **19.** C **21.** H **23.** E,F **25.** G,H **43.** origin **45.** III **47.** line segment parallel to y-axis **49.** line segment bisecting quadrant II
Page 386 **1.** 8 **3.** $^-24$ **5.** $^-8$ **7.** $^-16$
Page 387 **9.** $y = {}^-3x + 9$ **11.** $y = {}^-4x + 12$ **13.** $y = {}^-2x + 5$ **15.** $^-5, {}^-1, 3, 7, 11, 15, 19, 23$ **17.** $3x + 8$; $^-1, 5, 8, 11, 17, 23, 29, 35$ **19.** 14; 13; 10; 9 **21.** 14; 10; 6; 2 **23.** $^-2$; 3; 8; 13 **25.** 4; 3; 2; 1
Page 388 **1.** $^-1\text{-}5$; $^-6$; 0-5; $^-5$; $(0, {}^-5)$; 1-5; $^-4$; $(1, {}^-4)$; 2-5; $^-3$; $(2, {}^-3)$
Page 389 **3.** $^-3$; 0 + 3; 3; (0, 3); 2 + 3; 5; (1, 5); 6 + 3; 9; (3, 9); 10 + 3; 13; (5, 13) **5.** b, c **7.** d **9.** a, b **11.** $^-8, {}^-2, 4, 10$ **13.** 0, 2, 4, 8
Page 391 **1.** 3, 4, 5, 6, 7 **3.** $^-8, {}^-5, {}^-2, 1, 4$ **5.** 10, 9, 8, 7, 6 **7.** 12, 9, 6, 3, 0 **9.** 3, $2\frac{1}{2}$, 2, $1\frac{1}{2}$, 1 **11.** d **13.** (4, 3) **15.** (2, 6) **17.** no solution
Page 392 **1.** $y = {}^-x + 5$ **3.** $y = {}^-x + 2$ **5.** $y = x - 5$ **7.** $y = x - 5$ **9.** $y = x - 3$ **11.** (3, 9) **13.** $(1, {}^-3)$ **15.** $(^-1, 0)$ **17.** $(^-6, {}^-2)$
Page 393 **19.** $2x = 6$; $(3, {}^-6)$ **21.** $4y = 8$; (1, 2) **23.** $5y = 10$; $(^-5, 2)$ **25.** $^-x = 2$; $(^-2, {}^-6)$ **27.** $x = 2$; $(2, {}^-4)$ **29.** $x = 1$; $(1, {}^-10)$
Page 394 **1.** b **3.** a, b **5.** b **7.** $y > {}^-x + 2$; dotted **9.** $y > x - 5$; dotted **11.** $y < 3x + 1$; dotted **13.** $y < 2x - 3$; dotted
Page 395 **15.** (0,0); true; shade below **17.** $y = x - 3$; solid **19.** $y = x + 4$; solid **21.** $y = x - 5$; dotted **23.** $y = 2 + x$; solid **25.** $y = 1 - x$; solid **27.** $y = 4 - x$; dotted
Page 396 **13.** $y < 3 - x$; $y < 2$; $x > {}^-1$; $x + y < 5$; $y > 4x$; $x + y < 3$; $x > 0$; $y > {}^-2x$; $y < 0$
Page 397 **15.** a, c **17.** a
Page 399 **1.** (0, 4) **3.** $(0, {}^-4)$ **5.** (0, 3) **7.** $(0, {}^-2)$ **13.** 18, 8, 2, 0, 2, 8, 18 **15.** 17, 12, 9, 8, 9, 12, 17 **17.** $4\frac{1}{2}$, 2, $\frac{1}{2}$, 0, $\frac{1}{2}$, 2, $4\frac{1}{2}$
Page 400 **1.** $^-9, 6$ **3.** 0, $^-6$ **5.** $1\frac{1}{2}$, 3 **7.** 0, 2 **9.** $^-1\frac{1}{2}$, 3 **11.** $^-5, 0$
Page 401 **23.** $\frac{1}{2}$ **25.** $\frac{1}{2}$ **27.** $^-6$ **29.** ex. 27, 28 **31.** b

15 Polynomials and Rational Expressions
Page 416 **1.** binomial; 2 **3.** binomial; 1 **5.** trinomial; 2 **7.** binomial; 1 **9.** monomial; 0 **11.** trinomial; 3
Page 417 **13.** 100 **15.** 29 **17.** 25 **19.** $^-43$ **21.** $^-35$ **23.** 1 **25.** $\frac{1}{16}$ **27.** $1\frac{1}{16}$ **29.** b; c **31.** a; c **33.** a; c
Page 419 **3.** $23a^2b^2$ **5.** $^-2x + 24y$ **7.** $13r + 3s$

9. $^-6b^2 - 6c$ **11.** $^-2x^2 - 6$ **13.** $32xy - 7y$
15. $2k^2 - 5$ **17.** $4a^2 - 12a + 7$ **19.** $^-3x^2 + 5xy + 5y^2$
21. $62x^3 - 5x - 3$ **23.** $61x^2 + 44x - 111$ **25.** $14x^2 -$
$47x + 64$ **27.** $8 - 9x^2 + 2x^3$ **29.** $xy^2 + x^2y + x^3$
31. $6t^3 + t^2 - 20t$

Page 420 **1.** t^7 **3.** r^7 **5.** m^{13} **7.** y^6 **9.** 1 **11.** a^8
13. y^{14} **15.** x^{12} **17.** a^2b^2 **19.** $64a^6$

Page 421 **1.** $^-72y^7$ **3.** $^-28c^2d^2$ **5.** $^-60r^3s^2$ **7.** $48c^4d$
9. $16m^2$ **11.** $6x^3 + 24x^2 + 27x$ **13.** $^-36t^4 + 28t^3 + 40t^2$
15. $30r^2t - 48rt^2$ **17.** $12a^3b - 8a^2b^2$ **19.** $^-42b^3 + 6b^4$
21. $^-72k^3 - 153k^2$ **23.** $d^8e^4f^{16}$ **25.** $^-3r^3y^2$ **27.** 18
29. $^-7k^2m^4$

Page 422 **1.** $x^2 + 16x + 63$ **3.** $y^2 + 11y + 28$ **5.** $x^2 -$
$14x + 48$ **7.** $x^2 - 2x - 24$ **9.** $m^2 - 2m - 8$ **11.** $x^2 +$
$9x + 18$ **13.** $d^2 + 5d - 50$ **15.** $d^2 - 15d + 50$
17. $p^2 + 5p - 14$

Page 423 **19.** $2x^2 + 11x + 12$ **21.** $3m^2 - 25m + 28$
23. $6c^2 - c - 35$ **25.** $12a^2 - 7a - 10$ **27.** $3z^2 - 27z$
$+ 42$ **29.** $6x^2 + 14x - 132$ **31.** $49d^2 - 16$ **33.** $36n^2$
$+ 12n + 1$ **35.** b **37.** c **39.** $10x^2 - 27xy + 18y^2$
41. $2c^2 + 3cd - 44d^2$ **43.** $7a^2 + 32ab - 15b^2$ **45.** $x^3 +$
$5x^2 + 11x + 15$ **47.** $2y^3 - 8y^2 + 5y + 3$ **49.** $^-m^3 +$
$5m^2 - 10m + 8$

Page 425 **1.** $3x$ **3.** $35x^2$ **5.** x^2y **7.** $10a^2$ **9.** $4y^2z$
11. $10y^3$ **13.** $10y^3(2 + y^2)$ **15.** $3a^4(3 + 4a)$
17. $a^2b^3(a^2 + b)$ **19.** $3m^4n(m^3 - 3n^5)$ **21.** $x^2(1 - 3x)$
23. $cd(cd - 1)$ **25.** $9m^4(2 + 3m^2 + 5m^4)$ **27.** $6xy(1 -$
$2xy + 3x^2y^2)$ **29.** $2a^4(8 - 12a^2 + 9a^4)$ **31.** $2n(8n^2 - 9n$
$- 10)$ **33.** $2(x^2 + 9x - 12)$ **35.** $r^2s^3(1 + rs + r^2s^2)$
37. $7xz(7y - 8xz^2)$ **39.** $16a^3b^5(2a^2 + 3b^4 - 1)$

Page 426 **1.** 2 **3.** 5 **5.** 3; 1

Page 427 **7.** c **9.** c **11.** $(x + 6)(x + 2)$
13. $(z - 3)(z - 7)$ **15.** $(a + 11)(a - 3)$
17. $(m - 10)(m - 3)$ **19.** $(a - 9)(a + 7)$
21. $(m + 5)(m + 4)$ **23.** $(b + 1)(b + 5)$
25. $(m + 10)(m - 1)$ **27.** $(n + 6)(n - 3)$
29. $(n - 6)(n + 2)$ **31.** $(x + 7)(x - 2)$
33. $(y - 8)(y + 2)$ **35.** $(x + 4)(x + 4)$
37. $(b - 11)(b + 3)$ **39.** $(s + 7)(s - 5)$
41. $(n - 6)(n - 7)$ **43.** $(n - 2)(n - 8)$
45. $(x + 2y)(x - y)$ **47.** $(x^2 + 2y^2)(x^2 - 5y^2)$

Page 429 **1.** $4x$ **3.** $6x; 2x$ **5.** $4; 2$ **7.** $3y; 4$
9. $4x; 4x$ **11.** $(2x + 1)(x + 1)$ **13.** $(3y - 1)(y - 3)$
15. $(3x + 2)(x + 3)$ **17.** $(5x + 1)(x + 2)$
19. $(7y + 1)(y + 2)$ **21.** $(7a - 4)(a - 1)$
23. $(11a + 5)(a + 1)$ **25.** $(7x + 2)(x + 3)$
27. $(3m + 2)(2m - 5)$ **29.** $(7x + 2)(5x - 4)$
31. $(2m - 1)(11m - 3)$ **33.** $(6n + 5)(3n - 1)$
35. $(2x^2 + 1)(x^2 + 3)$ **37.** $(3c^3 + 1)(c^3 + 2)$
39. $(2c + 3d)(3c + d)$ **41.** $(7a - 2)(2a + 4)$
43. $(5c - 2)(2c + 3)$ **45.** $(3b - 7)(b - 4)$
47. $(4s - 3t)(s - 2t)$ **49.** $(6x + 5y)(2x - 3y)$
51. $(8r - 3)(2r + 5)$ **53.** $(10d + 7e)(3d - 2e)$
55. $(5b - 4c)(4b + 5c)$ **57.** $(2a^2 - 9)(a^2 + 7)$
59. $(3a + 2b)(2a - 3b)$ **61.** $(3c^2 + 4d^4)(5c^2 - 7d^4)$
63. $(5e^3 - f)(e^3 - 4f)$ **65.** $(7 - 5m^2)(1 - 3m^2)$
67. $(4 + 7h^2)(2 - 5h^2)$

Page 430 **1.** $x^2 - 6x + 9$ **3.** $z^2 + 10z + 25$ **5.** $y^2 - 8y$
$+ 16$ **7.** $4x^2 + 4x + 1$ **9.** $9a^2 - 12a + 4$ **11.** $36x^2 +$
$12x + 1$ **13.** $4a^2 + 4ab + b^2$ **15.** $25y^2 - 20yz + 4z^2$
17. no **19.** $(y - 6)^2$ **21.** $(z - 7)^2$ **23.** $(3x + 1)^2$

25. $(9a + 2)^2$ **27.** $(3c - 2)^2$ **29.** $(m - n)^2$
31. $(4 - 3y)^2$ **33.** $(10 + 3m)^2$ **35.** $(x - 3y)^2$
37. $(7r - s)^2$ **39.** $(3mn - 4)^2$ **41.** $\left(\frac{1}{3}b - 6\right)^2$

Page 431 **1.** $x^2 - 9$ **3.** $x^2 - 121$ **5.** $4x^2 - 9$ **7.** $9y^2$
$- 16$ **9.** $4m^2 - 49$ **11.** $16t^2 - 25s^2$ **13.** $49x^2 - 4y^2$
15. $x^4 - 1$ **17.** $(y + 5)(y - 5)$ **19.** $(2a + b)(2a - b)$
21. $(3m + 1)(3m - 1)$ **23.** $(y + 10)(y - 10)$
25. $(2m + 3)(2m - 3)$ **27.** $(x + 20)(x - 20)$
29. $(7 - t)(7 + t)$ **31.** $(15 + 4x)(15 - 4x)$

Page 432 **1.** $2(3x + 7)$ **3.** $3(y^2 + 2y + 2)$ **5.** $x(3x - 2)$
7. $2(x - 7)(x + 4)$ **9.** $(a - 5)(a - 9)$ **11.** $2(m + 6)(m + 4)$
13. $(2x + 3)(x - 5)$ **15.** $(5a - 4)(2a + 3)$
17. $(6y - 1)(y - 2)$ **19.** $2(x + 4)^2$ **21.** $3(x - 5)^2$
23. $x(x + 1)^2$ **25.** $(5a - 2b)^2$ **27.** $8(x - 2y)(x - y)$
29. $3(2n + 1)(2n - 1)$ **31.** $am^3(m + 6)(m - 6)$
33. $2d(2e + 5f)(2e - 5f)$

Page 433 **35.** $4(x - 1)^2$ **37.** $4(x + 2)(x - 1)$
39. $2(x + 7)^2$ **41.** $(b + 10)(b - 6)$ **43.** $(y - 11)^2$
45. $3(x + 4)(x - 4)$ **47.** $2x(3y - 4)$ **49.** $2(3y + 1)(y - 1)$
51. $(10 + 9d)(10 - 9d)$ **53.** $(z + 9)(z - 9)$
55. $(7y + 2)(4y - 1)$ **57.** $(2x + 5)(2x - 5)$ **59.** $(y + 9)^2$
61. $8(m + 2)(m - 2)$ **63.** $(3x + 2y)(x - 4y)$
65. $3a(a - 4b^2)$ **67.** $3(y - 1)^2$ **69.** $(r + 4)(r - 7)$
71. $3(1 + 4n)(1 - 2n)$ **73.** $(5y + 2)(3y - 1)$
75. $(7r - 2)(r - 3)$ **77.** $3(x + 2y - 3z)$
79. $5(x + 2)(x - 2)$ **81.** $(e^2 + 8d)(e^2 - 8d)$
83. $5n(n^6 + 25)$ **85.** $am^3(1 - 6m^2)(1 + 6m^2)$
87. $2(e^2 + 4)(e + 3)(e - 3)$ **89.** $2x(4x + 3)$
91. $(b - 1)(b - 5)$ **93.** prime **95.** prime
97. $14x(x + 2)(x - 2)$ **99.** $(a + 3)(a - 3)(a^2 + 4)$
101. $(3x - 4y)^2$ **103.** $(7s^3 + 18)(7s^3 - 18)$ **105.** prime
107. $(3cd - 2)^2$ **109.** $9(d^2 - 2e^2)$
111. $(2c + 3)(2c - 3)(4c^2 + 9)$ **113.** $3(3m - 2n)(2m + 3n)$
115. $(x + 3)(x - 10)$ **117.** $7(t + 2)(t + 1)$
119. $[(a + b) + (c + d)] \times [(a + b) - (c + d)]$

Page 434 **1.** m^6 **3.** $4x^6$ **5.** x^7 **7.** $4x^2 - 2x^5$
9. $3a^3b$ **11.** $4m^3 - 2$ **13.** b^5 **15.** $2c - 4d$ **17.** $^-1c^5$
19. $2ab - 5a^2$

Page 435 **21.** $x + 3$ **23.** $2x - 5$ **25.** $2a + 1$

Page 436 **1.** 0 **3.** $^-2$ **5.** $\frac{2}{5}$ **9.** 3 **11.** $\frac{5}{x - 5}$ **13.** $\frac{1}{x + y}$

Page 437 **15.** $\frac{8}{5}$ or $1\frac{3}{5}$ **17.** $\frac{1}{t^2 - 6t + 5}$ **19.** $\frac{r^2 + r - 2}{r - 3}$
21. $\frac{18k^2 + 12k}{k - 4}$ **23.** $\frac{a + 4}{10a + 5}$ **25.** $\frac{x^3}{3}$ **27.** $\frac{1}{3x - 15}$
29. $\frac{5s + 20}{4s}$ **31.** $5t + 15$ **33.** $\frac{1}{y^2 + 3y - 10}$

Page 438 **1.** $\frac{11}{2y}$ **3.** $\frac{3x - y}{x - y}$ **5.** $\frac{1}{x - 2}$ **7.** $\frac{5}{k}$ **9.** $\frac{^-5x + 17}{3x + 2}$
11. $\frac{1}{s - 4}$ **13.** $\frac{a^2 + 5a - 3}{a^3}$ **15.** 3 **17.** 1 **19.** $\frac{a + 6}{a + 3}$
21. $\frac{^-11x + 24}{3x - 4}$ **23.** $\frac{4}{s - 3}$ **25.** $\frac{a + 3b}{4a + 3b}$

Page 439 **1.** 40 **3.** $3k^2 - 3k$ **5.** $9a^2$ **7.** $4a$
9. $y^2 + 3y$

Page 440 **3.** $\frac{^-13}{20x}$ **5.** $\frac{a^2 - 4a - 10}{a^2 - 11a + 30}$ **7.** $\frac{10k - 27}{3k^2}$
9. $\frac{^-a}{4a + 2}$

Page 441 **11.** $\frac{x^2 + 11x - 28}{x^2 - 49}$ **13.** $\frac{5 + 20x}{x^2y}$ **15.** $\frac{^-11b}{3b - 18}$
17. $\frac{49t}{12t - 6}$ **19.** $\frac{148}{15x}$ **21.** $\frac{x^2 + 11x - 46}{x^2 - 25}$ **23.** $\frac{^-9x^2 + 93x + 1}{2x - 20}$
25. $\frac{^-p}{2p^2 + 2}$ **27.** $\frac{9m^2 + 56m - 7}{81m^2}$ **29.** $\frac{^-4r - 104}{r^2 - 16}$
33. $\frac{7}{5 - a}$ **35.** $\frac{6n}{m - 8}$ **37.** $\frac{1}{b - 5}$ **39.** $\frac{2mn}{3n - m}$ **41.** $\frac{m^2 + n^2}{m - n}$
43. $\frac{c - d}{c - 4d}$

16 Linear and Quadratic Equations

Page 457 **1.** $a = 2$; $b = 0$ **3.** e is undefined; $f = \frac{-1}{3}$
5. $\frac{1}{8}$ **7.** 6 **9.** 0 **11.** $^-1$ **13.** 3 **15.** 0 **17.** $\frac{1}{5}$
19. undefined **21.** negative **23.** positive **25.** undefined
27. E **29.** B **31.** D **33.** A

Page 459 **1.** $m = 3$, $b = ^-7$ **3.** $m = \frac{-1}{3}$, $b = ^-2$
5. $m = \frac{3}{4}$, $b = ^-1\frac{7}{8}$ **7.** $m = 3$, $b = 9$ **9.** $m = \frac{1}{2}$, $b = 4$
11. $m = \frac{1}{6}$, $b = 1\frac{1}{2}$ **19.** $2y - x = ^-4$ **21.** $2x + 5y = ^-20$
23. $y = ^-4$ **25.** $2x - 7y = 0$ **27.** $x - 4y = 20$
29. $x + 4y = 3$ **31.** $x + 2y = ^-2$ **33.** $2x + 6y = 3$
35. parallel **37.** perpendicular

Page 460 **1.** $^-1$ **3.** $^-4$ **5.** 0 **7.** $3x + 2y = ^-2$
9. $3x + 2y = 12$ **11.** $x - y = 0$ **13.** $4x - y = 0$
15. $x - 5y = 0$ **17.** $3x - y = 0$ **19.** $x + y = 4$
21. $x - 2y = 4$

Page 461 **23.** $7x + 9y = ^-24$ **25.** $x + 4y = 24$
27. $x + 7y = 3$ **29.** $5x - y = 11$ **31.** $3x - y = ^-3$
33. $y = \frac{2}{3}x - 6$ or $2x - 3y = 18$ **35.** $x + y = 0$
37. $2x - 3y = 0$ **39.** $3x - 2y = 1$ **41.** $2x - y = ^-1$
43. $2x - 5y = 1$ **45.** $2x + 3y = 9$

Page 463 **1.** rational **3.** rational **5.** irrational
9. $6\sqrt{3}$ **11.** $10\sqrt{5}$ **13.** $3y\sqrt{11}$ **15.** $y^2\sqrt{y}$ **17.** $3\sqrt{6}$
19. $7ab\sqrt{2a}$ **21.** $5\sqrt{2}$ **23.** $15x\sqrt{2}$ **25.** $\frac{56\sqrt{11}}{11}$
27. $\frac{11a\sqrt{6}}{3}$ **29.** 10 **31.** $\frac{1}{4}$ **33.** $\frac{10\sqrt{3}}{3}$ **35.** $\frac{2x}{3}$ **37.** $\frac{y^3}{4}$
39. $\frac{x\sqrt{15}}{8}$ **41.** $\frac{6\sqrt{5}}{5}$ **43.** $n\sqrt{2n}$ **45.** $n\sqrt{30}$ **47.** $\frac{5\sqrt{6}}{n}$
49. $\frac{4d^2\sqrt{3}}{3}$ **51.** $\frac{3m\sqrt{2mn}}{8n^2}$ **53.** $\frac{2\sqrt{rs}}{r}$

Page 464 **1.** $^-15\sqrt{11}$ **3.** $37\sqrt{b}$ **5.** $56\sqrt{3}$ **7.** $^-32\sqrt{5}$
9. $^-90a^2\sqrt{2}$ **11.** $13a\sqrt{6}$ **13.** $100b\sqrt{3b}$ **15.** $183x\sqrt{x}$
$+ 28\sqrt{x}$ **17.** $84\sqrt{a}$ **19.** $16\sqrt{2}$ **21.** $8n\sqrt{5} + 2\sqrt{5}$
23. $85a\sqrt{2a} - \sqrt{2a} - a$ **25.** $\frac{3\sqrt{7}}{4}$ **27.** $\frac{\sqrt{5}}{y^2}$

Page 465 **29.** $5\sqrt{3}$ yd **31.** $30°$; 7 ft **33.** $10\sqrt{2}$ dm

35. $2\sqrt{10}$ in. **37.** $10\sqrt{5}$ m

Page 466 **1.** true; $\sqrt{6} \cdot \sqrt{6} = \sqrt{36} = 6$ **3.** false;
$\sqrt{6} \cdot \sqrt{6} = \sqrt{36} = 6$ **5.** $^-34\sqrt{10}$ **7.** $48\sqrt{15}$
9. $108x^2\sqrt{10}$ **11.** $420\sqrt{a}$ **13.** ^-24y **15.** $144a^2\sqrt{5}$
17. $14\sqrt{3} + 6$ **19.** 15 **21.** $xy\sqrt{2x} - xy\sqrt{6}$
23. $m^2\sqrt{6n} + 3m^2n$ **25.** $^-10cd\sqrt{2d} + 8cd\sqrt{5c}$

Page 467 **27.** b; $\frac{\sqrt{2a}}{2}$ **29.** b; $\frac{3}{8}$ **31.** d; $\frac{a\sqrt{6a}}{3}$
33. a; $\frac{7n\sqrt{5}}{5}$ **35.** $\sqrt{6}$ **37.** 2 **39.** $\frac{a\sqrt{6}}{4}$ **41.** $3\sqrt{r}$
43. $3\sqrt{b}$ **45.** $3m\sqrt{10}$ **47.** $xy^2\sqrt{x}$ **49.** ^-7a
51. $\frac{-\sqrt{15}}{2}$ **53.** 4 **55.** $3a^2 + 4a\sqrt{7} + 7$ **57.** $30 - \sqrt{3}$
59. $15 + 17\sqrt{a} + 4a$

Page 469 **1.** $\{4, 2\}$ **3.** $\{0, ^-10\}$ **5.** $\{^+5\}$ **7.** $\{^-4, ^-2\}$
9. $\{7, 8\}$ **11.** $\{^-9\}$ **13.** $\{^-4, ^-10\}$ **15.** $\{0, \frac{1}{3}\}$
17. $\{^-1, 11\}$ **19.** $\{6, \frac{-2}{3}\}$ **21.** $\{\frac{1}{2}, \frac{-1}{2}\}$ **23.** $\{2, \frac{-4}{7}\}$
25. a **27.** b **29.** a

Page 470 **1.** 1 **3.** 16 **5.** $\frac{9}{4}$ **7.** $\frac{1}{4}$ **9.** $\frac{49}{4}$ **11.** $x = 1$,
$x = 2$ **13.** $x = 2$, $x = ^-7$ **15.** $x = 4$, $x = ^-3$ **17.** $x = 6$,
$x = ^-3$ **19.** $x = ^-3 \pm \sqrt{17}$ **21.** $x = \frac{1 \pm \sqrt{13}}{2}$

Page 471 **23.** $x = 1$ **25.** $x = 3 \pm \sqrt{5}$ **27.** $x = \frac{5 \pm \sqrt{13}}{2}$
29. $x = 3 \pm \sqrt{5}$ **31.** $x = \frac{-9 \pm \sqrt{71}}{2}$ **33.** $x = 3 \pm \sqrt{19}$
35. $x = 1$ **37.** $x = ^-1$, $x = 6$ **39.** $x = 0$, $x = 8$

Page 472 **1.** $\{^-1, \frac{2}{3}\}$ **3.** $\{\frac{+1}{2}, \frac{-2}{3}\}$ **5.** $\{^-3, \frac{1}{2}\}$
7. $\{5, \frac{1}{3}\}$ **9.** $\{\frac{1}{5}\}$ **11.** $\{0, \frac{7}{6}\}$ **13.** $\{5, 6\}$
15. $\{3 \pm \sqrt{3}\}$ **17.** $\{1 \pm \sqrt{21}\}$

Page 473 **19.** $2 \pm \sqrt{2}$ **21.** $^-1 \pm \sqrt{2}$ **23.** $\frac{-5 \pm \sqrt{21}}{2}$
25. $\frac{-1 \pm \sqrt{7}}{3}$ **27.** $\frac{1 \pm \sqrt{2}}{2}$ **29.** $\frac{1 \pm \sqrt{13}}{4}$
31. $\frac{4 \pm \sqrt{46}}{6}$ **33.** $\frac{-5 \pm \sqrt{31}}{2}$ **35.** $c = \frac{2 \pm \sqrt{7}}{3}$
37. $\frac{1 \pm \sqrt{11}}{2}$ **39.** $b = ^-6$ **41.** $v = 1$; $1\frac{1}{2}$
43. $\frac{-5 \pm \sqrt{5}}{2}$ **45.** $\frac{3 \pm \sqrt{3}}{2}$ **47.** $\frac{3 \pm \sqrt{3}}{3}$

Tables for Measures

Metric Units

Length

1 millimeter (mm) = 0.001 meter (m)

1 centimeter (cm) = 0.01 meter

1 decimeter (dm) = 0.1 meter

1 dekameter (dam) = 10 meters

1 hectometer (hm) = 100 meters

1 kilometer (km) = 1000 meters

Mass

1 milligram (mg) = 0.001 gram (g)

1 kilogram (kg) = 1000 grams

1 metric ton (t) = 1000 kilograms

Capacity

1 milliliter (mL) = 0.001 liter (L)

1 kiloliter (kL) = 1000 liters

Temperature

0° Celsius (C) .... Water freezes.

100° Celsius (C) .... Water boils.

Customary Units

Length

1 foot (ft) = 12 inches (in.)

1 yard (yd) = 36 inches

1 yard (yd) = 3 feet

1 mile (mi) = 5280 feet

1 mile (mi) = 1760 yards

Weight

1 pound (lb) = 16 ounces (oz)

1 ton = 2000 pounds

Capacity

3 teaspoons (tsp) = 1 tablespoon (tbsp)

1 cup (c) = 8 fluid ounces (fl oz)

1 pint (pt) = 2 cups

1 quart (qt) = 2 pints

1 quart (qt) = 4 cups

1 gallon (gal) = 4 quarts

Temperature

32° Fahrenheit (F) ... Water freezes.

212° Fahrenheit (F) ... Water boils.

Percent Table

$25\% = \frac{1}{4}$ $70\% = \frac{7}{10}$ $66\frac{2}{3}\% = \frac{2}{3}$

$50\% = \frac{1}{2}$ $80\% = \frac{4}{5}$ $16\frac{2}{3}\% = \frac{1}{6}$

$75\% = \frac{3}{4}$ $90\% = \frac{9}{10}$ $83\frac{1}{3}\% = \frac{5}{6}$

$10\% = \frac{1}{10}$ $12\frac{1}{2}\% = \frac{1}{8}$ $9\frac{1}{11}\% = \frac{1}{11}$

$20\% = \frac{1}{5}$ $37\frac{1}{2}\% = \frac{3}{8}$ $11\frac{1}{9}\% = \frac{1}{9}$

$30\% = \frac{3}{10}$ $62\frac{1}{2}\% = \frac{5}{8}$ $14\frac{2}{7}\% = \frac{1}{7}$

$40\% = \frac{2}{5}$ $87\frac{1}{2}\% = \frac{7}{8}$ $12\% = \frac{3}{25}$

$60\% = \frac{3}{5}$ $33\frac{1}{3}\% = \frac{1}{3}$ $5\% = \frac{1}{20}$

$15\% = \frac{3}{20}$ $3\frac{1}{3}\% = \frac{1}{30}$ $1\% = \frac{1}{100}$

$6\frac{1}{4}\% = \frac{1}{16}$ $6\frac{2}{3}\% = \frac{1}{15}$ $2\% = \frac{1}{50}$

$8\frac{1}{3}\% = \frac{1}{12}$ $8\% = \frac{2}{25}$ $4\% = \frac{1}{25}$

$\frac{1}{2}\% = \frac{1}{200}$

Problem-Solving Handbook

▼

The *Problem-Solving Handbook* provides additional word problems for all the math skills presented in your textbook. Included are problems from different areas such as science, history, and the arts, as well as non-routine problems and challenging puzzlers. Applying math skills to different real-life situations will improve your understanding of concepts and also help you remember key procedures.

The *Problem-Solving Handbook* is also preparation for taking state and national achievement tests. Read the *Test-Taking Checklist* on the following page and apply the tips whenever you are assigned new word problems. If possible, share your answers and explain them to other students. Good problem-solving and test-taking strategies, together with lots of practice, will help you succeed on the standardized test that follows each chapter of word problems.

✓ The Problem-Solver's Test-Taking Checklist

Did you know that you can become a better problem-solver? For greater success on tests with word problems, including standardized tests, keep in mind the following tips. Review the tips from time to time to be sure you are taking advantage of all the test-taking and problem-solving skills available to you.

Before the Test

Have I...

✓ gotten plenty of rest the night before?

✓ asked if I can use a calculator during the test?

✓ asked if I need to bring scrap paper, or if it will be provided? Am I expected to hand in my scrap paper to support my solutions?

During the Test

Have I...

✓ understood what is being asked by the test administrator?

✓ paid attention to the written directions, which may change from section to section in the test?

✓ scanned the page so I have a feeling for all the tasks being examined?

✓ skipped items that are difficult for me and returned to them after I've completed the other questions?

✓ considered all of the problem-solving strategies I know to solve a challenging problem?

✓ repeated numbers, directions, or key words softly to myself to get a better understanding of a question?

✓ checked if the computed answer is reasonable when compared to my estimated answer?

✓ determined which of my computed answer or estimated answer is correct, if the two solutions do not agree?

✓ considered whether there is an alternative method I can use to solve the problem?

✓ estimated to determine the answer without doing the actual computation?

✓ eliminated as definitely wrong one or more choices for the answer?

✓ chosen the most probable correct answer from the remaining choices?

✓ reread each direction to be sure that I have answered the question?

✓ written legibly, especially when work involved erasing and reworking, or where answers were derived from intermediate steps?

✓ clearly labeled polygons or other figures with letters positioned in their proper places?

✓ double-checked that my fraction answers are in simplest form, since answers not in lowest terms are often considered incorrect?

✓ checked my solutions by substituting each answer in the original expression or equation?

✓ used number sense or measurement benchmarks to check that answers seem reasonable?

✓ checked solutions by reworking a problem without looking at my first answer, only then comparing and adjusting the solution as necessary?

Solve each problem. Name any strategy or strategies you used.

1. **Astronomy** At the farthest point in its orbit, Jupiter is 507.4 million miles from the Sun. At the nearest it is 460.1 million miles from the Sun. Express these two distances as standard numerals, then in expanded form.

2. **Astronomy** At the farthest point in its orbit, Mars is 249 million miles from Earth. Neptune is 2913 million miles from Earth. Express these distances as standard numerals. For each, write the place value of the digit 2.

3. In 1998 the gross domestic product (GDP) of Portugal was 144.8 billion dollars; Vietnam's GDP was 134.8 billion dollars and Greece's was 143.0 billion dollars. Express each amount as a standard numeral.

4. Using the numbers in problem 3, order the GDPs of Portugal, Vietnam, and Greece from greatest to least. What is the difference in dollars between the GDP of Portugal and that of Vietnam? Write the short word name for the difference in billions of dollars.

5. Great Britain consists of England, Scotland, and Wales. Estimate the total population of Great Britain if the populations are as follows: England: 59,508,382; Scotland: 5,111,000; and Wales: 2,927,000.

6. The state of Hawaii is made up of five counties. Hawaii county has a population of 142,390; Honolulu's population is 864,571; Kalawao's is 58; Kauai's is 56,539; and Maui's is 121,939. Estimate, then find, the state's total population.

7. Jess, Ona, and Simka are in a contest to write the smallest decimal. Jess writes a 13-digit decimal, Ona's is 9-digits, and Simka's is 20 digits. Assuming they each wrote the smallest possible decimal, who wins the contest?

8. **Astronomy** Jupiter has a diameter of 89,000 miles, more than 10 times greater than the diameter of Earth. Use what you know about place value to estimate Earth's diameter.

9. **Geography** The Great Lakes, Superior, Michigan, Huron, Erie and Ontario, and their connecting channels form the largest fresh surface water system on Earth. Lake Superior is about 22,000 sq mi larger than Lake Erie in water surface area, which is about 3000 sq mi larger than Lake Ontario. Lake Ontario is about 15,000 sq mi smaller than Lake Michigan in surface area, which is about 1000 sq mi smaller than Lake Huron. Lake Huron is about 23,000 sq mi in water surface area. Estimate the water surface area of each Great Lake, then order them from greatest to least.

10. Kirsten is making 3 gallons of vegetarian chili. An 8-oz can of beans costs $0.89 and a 12-oz can costs $1.09. Which is the better buy?

11. **Physics** The speed of light through air is 299,792.458 km per second. Light travels through water 25% more slowly than through air. What is the speed of light through water?

12. The average water depth of Lake Superior is 601.10 ft. The average water depth of Lake Ontario is 243.30 ft. How many times deeper is Lake Superior than Lake Ontario?

13. **Geography** The Caspian Sea has an area of 143,244 square miles. Using the formula *area = length × width*, determine the width of this 760-mile long sea.

14. Would $(a \times b) \times c = (c \times a) \times b$? Explain your answer using properties of multiplication. Then substitute any set of whole numbers to check your thinking.

15. **Geography** Gannett Peak in Wyoming has an altitude of 13,804 ft. That is 2.84 times higher than Spruce Knob in Kentucky. What is the altitude of Spruce Knob?

16. In 1999, 10,283,598 people visited the Great Smoky Mountains National Park. Estimate both the number of visitors per week and the number of visitors per day.

17. The Vietnam Veterans Memorial in Washington, DC, was visited by 4,442,238 people in 1999. On average how many people visited per week? per day?

18. At 20°C, 13.45 gallons of water weigh 112.0 pounds. How much does 1 gallon of water weigh?

19. **Science** At 20°C, 35.96 cubic feet of water weigh 2240 pounds. How much does 1 cubic foot of water weigh?

20. **Chemistry** One atom of chlorine has an atomic weight of 35.453. What is the atomic weight of 14 atoms of chlorine?

21. The population of Alabama in 1999 was 4,369,862, which was an 8.2% increase from 1990. What was the population of Alabama in 1990?

22. Use the chart to the right to order the states by area from greatest to least. Find the total area.

State	Area in sq mi
Alabama	50,750
Alaska	570,374
Arkansas	52,075

Solve each problem. Name any strategy or strategies you used.

1. For their birthdays Phoebe and Raoul each got a round 12 in. cake. Phoebe's mother cut her cake into twelfths, Raoul's mother cut his cake into sixteenths. Phoebe ate three pieces of her cake. How many pieces of his cake will Raoul need to eat to have eaten an equal amount?

2. In liquid measure 2 pints equal 57.75 in.³ In dry measure, 2 pints equal $\frac{69,006}{10,000}$ in.³ Can you use mental math to determine which has the greater measure? Rewrite the amounts as fractions in simplest form and compare them. Which is greater?

3. **Social Studies** California is home to $\frac{3}{5}$% or $\frac{3}{5}$ of 1% of the Native Americans living in the U.S. Washington state is home to 1.8% of the Native Americans in the U.S. Which state has more Native Americans? How many times more?

4. **Social Studies** Of all Native Americans living in the U.S., 2.8% are Apache, and $1\frac{1}{2}$% or $1\frac{1}{2}$ of 1% are Chippewa. Are there more people of Chippewa or Apache descent living in the U.S.? About how many times more?

5. **Architecture** The distance from the foundation of the pedestal to the tip of the torch of the Statue of Liberty is 305′1″. The distance from the base of the statue to the tip of the torch is about half that height and about $6\frac{1}{2}$ times longer than the height of the tablet the statue holds. Estimate the height of the tablet.

6. Fran has a gardening job that is going to take 45 hours to complete. She needs to figure out how many people to hire and for how many hours. Write all the possible combinations of people hired and hours worked, assuming everyone she hires will work an equal number of whole hours.

7. A tablespoon holds 4 fluid drams, while a teaspoon holds $1\frac{1}{3}$ fluid drams. How many teaspoons of fluid does a tablespoon hold?

8. One square millimeter is equal to 0.002 in.² Is a 100 square-millimeter microchip greater, less than, or equal to a microchip measuring $\frac{1}{5000}$ in.²?

9. Julia wants a tiler to come in and replace $\frac{1}{5}$ of her 70 ceiling tiles. He tells her the cost will be $2.60 per tile. What will be the total cost of the job?

10. An average strand of Franny's hair is $35\frac{3}{18}$ cm long. An average strand of Esme's hair is $21\frac{1}{9}$ cm long. Who has longer hair?

11. Walensa is putting up drapes in his bedroom. His window is $3\frac{3}{16}$ ft wide. If the drapes he wants are each $1\frac{5}{8}$ ft wide, will two of them cover the entire window? Explain.

12. **Social Studies** In 1983 the unemployment rate in the U.S. was $9\frac{3}{5}$%. In 1993 it was $6\frac{9}{10}$%. How much did the unemployment rate decrease in those 10 years?

13. **Social Studies** In Ecuador $10\frac{3}{4}$% of the population is of African descent, $12\frac{3}{8}$% is of Spanish descent, and $23\frac{1}{2}$% is of Native American descent. Are there more people of Native American descent in Ecuador than of Spanish and African descent combined? Explain.

14. Bhundi needs tablecloths to cover the 9-foot long table she has borrowed for her garden party. The three tablecloths she has are $3\frac{1}{4}$ ft, $2\frac{5}{7}$ ft, and $3\frac{1}{8}$ ft long. Estimate whether Bhundi has all the tablecloths she needs.

15. **Social Studies** The average German worker earns almost $31\frac{9}{10}$ dollars per hour. If a German household has two wage earners, what is the average amount of money that household earns per hour?

16. **Biology** The average gestation of a black rhinoceros is 450 days. If a rhinoceros is $\frac{1}{2}$ through the first $\frac{1}{3}$ of gestation, how many more days will it be before she gives birth?

17. Raheeda and Julius are trying to answer a problem that requires adding two fractions. One of the fractions has a denominator of 4 and the other had a denominator of 14. Raheeda says the LCD is 56. Julius disagrees. Who is correct? What is the LCD?

18. Chinua, Feng, and Judy are running for student council president. For a winner to be declared, he or she must receive at least half of the votes cast. Chinua received $\frac{1}{3}$ of the votes, Feng received $\frac{1}{4}$ of the votes, and the rest of the votes went to Judy. Did Judy receive enough votes to win?

19. Magid grew 8 inches last year. His brother Jonah grew $\frac{1}{2}$ foot less than Magid. How much did Jonah grow last year? Express your answer in feet and in lowest terms.

20. The Marichal Boating Company has decided to build a boat that is $2\frac{1}{4}$ times larger than any boat it has ever built. If its largest boat until now is $22\frac{2}{3}$ ft long, how long will the company's new boat be?

21. Ms. Kraske is making punch. Her recipe calls for $\frac{1}{2}$ gallon of lemonade, $\frac{2}{3}$ gallon of cranberry juice, $\frac{1}{4}$ gallon of rainbow sherbet, $\frac{1}{5}$ gallon of cherry juice, and $2\frac{5}{6}$ gallons of club soda. How many gallons of punch is Ms. Kraske making?

22. Rasheed gets a bonus check from his job if he averages working more than 8 hours a day in any week. If he worked $34\frac{1}{2}$ hours over four days, does Rasheed get his bonus? What is the length of his average workday?

23. Robert divides his coin collection equally among himself and 8 friends to play a game. What fractional portion of Robert's coin collection does each person receive?

24. A class has 30 students. If $\frac{2}{5}$ of the students are girls, how many students are boys?

25. A technician installs adjustable keyboard trays on desks. It takes him $\frac{1}{3}$ hour to install a tray. How many trays can he install in $7\frac{1}{2}$ hours?

26. Margaret is decorating a float in a parade. She has $8\frac{1}{2}$ feet of ribbon she is cutting into $4\frac{1}{4}$-inch strips to tie onto the edges of the float. How many strips of ribbon will Margaret have? Express the equation as a complex fraction.

27. Jamal and Jared need to park their cars in Jared's driveway, which is about 12 feet wide. If Jared's car is $6\frac{1}{2}$ feet wide and Jamal's car is $6\frac{3}{4}$ feet wide, will the two cars fit in the driveway? Use rounded numbers to solve.

28. Joely collects insects in her backyard. On Saturday, she caught four batches of insects that weigh $\frac{3}{4}$ oz, $\frac{5}{8}$ oz, $\frac{13}{16}$ oz, and $\frac{7}{10}$ oz, respectively. About how much do these insects weigh altogether? Use clustering to solve, identifying the value you clustered around.

29. Hector worked two days last week at his father's store. For each week Hector worked, his father gave him $284 dollars. About how much money did Hector earn in those two days? Use compatible numbers to solve.

30. Marisol uses $\frac{1}{4}$ gallon of gas to drive to her brother's house. If the $13\frac{1}{2}$ gallon tank was $\frac{3}{4}$ empty when Marisol started driving, how much gas was left when she arrived at her brother's house? What fractional portion of the gas tank did she use in her drive?

31. Naseer Ahmaad Soomo is a Pakistani man reputed to be the tallest living man in the world. He is approximately $2\frac{2}{5}$ meters high. If a meter is about $39\frac{1}{3}$ inches, about how tall is Mr. Soomo in feet and inches? Use compatible numbers to solve.

Test for Chapters 1 and 2

This chapter's skills might appear on a standardized test.

1. **Social Studies** In 1987 the number of licensed drivers between the ages of 20 and 24 in the United States was 17,657,000. In 1997 there were 15,300,293 licensed drivers in that age group. Rounding to the nearest thousand, how many more drivers ages 20 to 24 were there in 1987 than in 1997?

   a. 2 million, 350 thousand
   b. 2 million, 400 thousand
   c. 2 million, 356 thousand
   d. 2 million, 357 thousand

2. **Astronomy** Compared to the mass of Earth, the masses of Mercury, Venus, Mars, and Pluto are 0.0553, 0.815, 0.107, and 0.0021 times as great, respectively. Which two planets have the smallest combined mass?

   f. Mercury and Pluto
   g. Venus and Mars
   h. Venus and Pluto
   j. Mars and Pluto

3. **Economics** The average annual exchange rate for buying US dollars with Canadian dollars was 1.0103 in 1970, 1.0175 in 1975, 1.1693 in 1980, and 1.1668 in 1990. Between which years was the difference in the annual exchange rate greatest?

   a. between 1970 and 1980
   b. between 1975 and 1990
   c. between 1975 and 1980
   d. between 1970 and 1990

4. **Social Studies** The percentages of U.S. workers who belonged to unions in 1985, 1986, 1987, 1988, and 1989 were 18.0, 17.5, 17.0, 16.8, and 15.4 respectively. To the nearest tenth of a percent what was the average percentage of union workers during the years 1985 to 1989?

   a. 17 percent **b.** 16.9 percent
   c. 17.4 percent **d.** 16.94 percent

5. Which of the following does not illustrate the distributive property?

   f. $8 \times 658 = (8 \times 600) + (8 \times 50) + (8 \times 8)$
   g. $8 \times (65 + 8) = (8 \times 65) + (8 \times 8)$
   h. $86 \times (5 \times 8) = (86 \times 5) \times 8$
   j. $(86 + 5) \times 8 = (86 \times 8) + (8 \times 5)$

6. Which of these numbers has the greatest number of prime factors?

   a. 175 **b.** 176 **c.** 135 **d.** 136

7. Which of these numbers has the greatest number of *different* prime factors?

   f. 205 **g.** 176 **h.** 185 **i.** 195

8. **Banking** On February 1, 1995, the Federal Reserve discount interest rate for member banks was $5\frac{1}{4}$ percent, but on January 31, 1996, it fell to 5 percent. On October 15 of 1998, it was $4\frac{3}{4}$ percent, and on November 17 of the same year it was lowered again to $4\frac{1}{2}$ percent. What was the average discount rate for these four periods?

   a. $4\frac{3}{4}$ percent **b.** $4\frac{1}{2}$ percent
   c. 4 percent **d.** $4\frac{7}{8}$ percent

CHAPTER 3   Equations, Inequalities, and Integers

Solve each problem. Name any strategy or strategies you used.

1. Write a mathematical expression and then simplify it: A stadium seats 6,200 people. A recent series of concerts was sold out for three nights. If the cost of a ticket was $16.50, how much money did the stadium take in?

2. Write a mathematical expression and then simplify it: In Ms. Cuardo's nursery there are gardenias in 12 rows of 6 and ivy in 15 rows of 12. What is the total number of gardenias and ivy plants?

3. In the figure, algebraic expressions for finding the side lengths of a right triangle are $2mn$, $m^2 - n^2$, and $m^2 + n^2$ where m and n are positive whole numbers and $m > n$. Find the side lengths of a right triangle if $m = 2$ and $n = 1$.

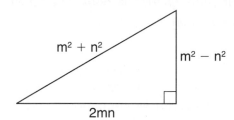

4. Write an algebraic expression and then evaluate it: Harold has d dimes and n nickels in his pocket. Find the total value of the coins in cents if $d = 4$ and $n = 7$.

5. Write an algebraic expression and then evaluate it: A car service charges a basic fee of $3 and $2 for each mile m. Find the cost of a 7-mile ride.

6. Write an algebraic expression and then evaluate it: Joanna has q quarters and p pennies in her change purse. Find the total value of the coins in cents if $q = 5$ and $p = 3$.

7. A deluxe computer monitor is at least $450 more expensive than a standard monitor. Write a mathematical sentence for this situation. Let d represent the price of the deluxe monitor and s represent the price of the standard monitor.

8. Jean Paul repairs refrigerators. He charges $45 to make a house call and $20 per hour. The equation for what he charges is $C = 45 + 20h$ where C is the total charge and h is the number of hours he works. If the total charge was $145, did he work 4, 5, or 6 hours?

9. In 2001 the postage for mailing a first-class letter was 34¢ for the first ounce and 21¢ for each additional ounce. This is given by the equation $P = 34 + 21w$ where P is the amount of postage and w is the number of additional ounces. If the total postage for mailing a letter is 97¢, how much does the letter weigh?

10. An equation for finding the admission price for one student in a class of eighth graders attending an amusement park is $T = 18a$ where T is the total admission for the whole class, 18 is the number of students in the class, and a is the admission price for one student. If the total admission price for the class is $468, is the admission price for one student $26, $27, or $28?

11. An equation relating a child's dosage of medicine to an adult dosage of the same medicine is $d = \left(\dfrac{c}{c + 12}\right) a$ where d is the child's dosage, c is the child's age in years, and a is the adult dosage. If the adult dosage is 3 teaspoons and the child's dosage is 1 teaspoon, is the child 4, 5, or 6 years old?

Use after Lesson 3-5.   H – 9

12. Every day Philip's father eats three meals totaling 1600 calories. He eats a total of 750 calories for breakfast and lunch. Write an equation for finding how many calories he eats at dinner. Then solve the equation.

13. Rachel received a $25 rebate on her recent purchase of a DVD player. With the rebate, she spent $185.95. Write an equation for finding the original cost of the DVD player. Then solve the equation.

14. During a five-day work week, Brian earned $145 per day as a substitute teacher. Write an equation for finding his total earnings for the week. Then solve the equation.

15. The cost of heating the Seto home with natural gas for 3 months during the winter was $284.31. Write an equation for finding the average cost per month for heating the home. Then solve the equation.

16. The perimeter of a rectangular plot of land is 19.2 m. The length of the lot is twice the width. Write an equation for finding the width. Then solve the equation and find the dimensions of the plot.

17. Jorge bought 3 CDs, each with the same price, and a set of earphones with a price of $10. The total cost before tax was $34. Write an equation for finding the cost of each CD. Then solve it.

18. In the county where Pat lives, the fine for driving over the speed limit is determined by the speed limit plus $5 for each mile per hour over the speed limit. If Pat paid a fine of $125, how many miles over the speed limit of 50 mi per hour was she driving?

19. Tickets for a minor league baseball game for an adult and two children cost a total of $21. The adult ticket is $3 more than a child's ticket. Write and solve an equation to find the cost of a child's ticket and an adult's ticket.

20. Raymond's age plus his sister Janice's age is 48 years. Janice's age is half Raymond's age plus 6 years. How old is Raymond? How old is Janice?

21. Using n, $n + 2$, and $n + 4$ to represent three consecutive odd numbers, write and solve an equation to find the three consecutive odd numbers whose sum is 237.

22. Lina is 6 years younger than Kyle. When you multiply her age by 9, the product is 81. Find Kyle's age and Lina's age.

23. Let n, $n + 2$, and $n + 4$ represent three consecutive even numbers. The quotient of the second even number and 8 is 24. Find the three consecutive even numbers.

24. A school administrator used the inequality $s \leq 28$ to determine the number of students to assign to each class. If the administrator also wants each class to have at least 16 students, what are the possible numbers of students for a class?

25. Myrna uses the inequality $y < 12$ inches to sort lengths of yarns for her art project. She rejects lengths that make the inequality true. If she measures lengths of 10, 11, 12, 13, and 14 inches, which lengths will she keep?

26. A tank is 60 cm long, 30 cm wide and 40 cm high. How many cubic cm of water are in the tank if the surface of the water is 4 cm from the top?

27. A square plot of land had a perimeter of 36.4 m. The plot was enlarged by making each side 1 meter longer. Find the area of the enlarged plot of land.

28. A diver descended 67 ft below the surface of the water to observe the lower part of a coral formation. She then ascended 42 feet to look at the top of the formation. Write an expression involving integers to show her movements. Then write an integer to indicate her location when looking at the top of the formation.

29. A football team lost 2 yards on the first down and gained 11 yards on the second down. Write an expression involving integers to show the team's progress. Then simplify the expression to find the total number of yards gained or lost.

30. During a lab experiment, a chemical substance was heated so that its temperature rose 8°C. The temperature at the end of the experiment was 3°C. Write and solve an equation to find the temperature of the substance at the beginning of the experiment.

31. Over a period of time the average change in the price of a stock was $^-$$3 per week. Write and solve an equation to find how many weeks it would take for the change in the price of the stock to be $^-$$39.

32. When a number is divided by $^-$15, the quotient is 20. Write and solve an equation to find the number.

33. When a number is multiplied by $^-$16, the product is $^-$96. Write and solve an equation to find the number.

34. The table shows the average surface temperature of planets that are nearest the Sun in our solar system.

    a. Which of the planets has the lowest average surface temperature? Which has the highest?

    b. Which planet's surface area temperature is closest to the surface temperature of Earth?

    c. List the planets in order from warmest surface temperature to coolest surface temperature.

Average Surface Temperatures	
Planet	**Temperature (°C)**
Earth	7
Mars	-53
Mercury	177
Venus	457

35. The three states of matter are solid, liquid, and gas. The temperature change from solid to liquid is called the *melting point* and the temperature change from liquid to gas is called the *boiling point*. The table shows the approximate melting points and boiling points at sea level for some selected substances. Write an integer to represent the change from boiling point to melting point of oxygen; the change from boiling point to melting point of mercury.

Melting and Boiling Points (°C)		
Substance	**Melts at**	**Boils at**
Water	0°	100°
Oxygen	$-219°$	$-184°$
Nitrogen	$-210°$	$-195°$
Mercury	$-39°$	357°

Test for Chapter 3

This chapter's skills might appear on a standardized test.

1. At a football game half-time show, the marching band was in 3 sections, each with 8 rows of 8 players. The dancers were in 2 sections, each with 6 rows of 7 dancers. Which expression could you use to find the total number of band members and dancers in the half-time show?

   a. $3(8 + 8) + 2(6 \times 7)$
   b. $3 \cdot 8^2 + 2(6 \times 7)$
   c. $3 \cdot 8^2 \times 2(6 \times 7)$
   d. $(3 + 2)(8^2 + 6 \times 7)$

2. If n represents the position of a number in the sequence, which expression gives the rule for this sequence?

   $$8, 11, 14, 17, \ldots$$

   f. $n + 3$ **g.** $8 + n$
   h. $3n + 5$ **j.** $2n - 5$

3. Find the value of the expression $\dfrac{4(a - b)}{3c}$ when $a = 6$, $b = 3$, and $c = 2$.

   a. 6   **b.** 12
   c. 2   **d.** 3

4. The floor of a rectangular storage room measures 6 ft by 9 ft. How many square tiles, each 9 inches on a side, are needed to cover the floor?

   f. 96   **g.** 54   **h.** 48   **j.** 192

5. The sum of two integers is 3. When the lesser integer is subtracted from the greater integer, the difference is 9. What are the integers?

   a. 9 and $^-6$ **b.** $^-6$ and 3
   c. $^-6$ and $^-3$ **d.** 6 and $^-3$

6. Which mathematical sentence can be used to describe this situation?

   Karen is no older than 12 years old.

   f. $k \neq 12$ **g.** $k \geq 12$
   h. $k > 12$ **j.** $k \leq 12$

7. Which set of values for x will make the following sentence true?

   $$5(x - 3) \geq 15$$

   a. $\{1, 2, 3\}$ **b.** $\{3, 4, 5\}$
   c. $\{5, 6, 7\}$ **d.** $\{6, 7, 8\}$

8. Which equation has the same solution as $d - 7 = 3$?

   f. $d \div 2 = 5$ **g.** $4d = 16$
   h. $100d = 10$ **j.** $32 = 8d$

9. A cab ride costs \$5 for the first mile and \$3 for each additional mile. An equation for this situation is $C = 5 + 3(m - 1)$ where C is the total cost of the ride and m is the number of miles traveled. If a cab ride costs \$23, how many miles was the ride?

   a. 7   **b.** 6
   c. 8   **d.** 9

10. Find two integers whose product is $^-36$ and whose sum is $^-9$.

11. The number of square units in the area of a rectangle is the same as the number of units in its perimeter. The width of the rectangle is 3 in. Find the length. Explain how you found the answer.

CHAPTER 4 Rational Numbers

Solve each problem. Name any strategy or strategies you used.

1. One week a certain stock closed at $22\frac{1}{4}$ per share. The next week it closed at the opposite of the opposite of that price. What was its closing price the second week?

2. One metal was at a temperature of $-7\frac{5}{18}$°C. A second metal was at a temperature of $-20\frac{5}{9}$°C. Which metal was cooler?

3. A geothermal steam well is at a depth of -1.73 miles. Additional drilling makes the well -0.15 miles deeper. How deep is the well after the drilling?

4. A ship set sail from Honolulu, whose latitude is 20°N. The ship sailed 15°S, then 8°N, and then 59°S. What was the latitude of the ship at that point?

5. When the stock market opened a certain stock was priced at $32\frac{1}{8}$. By noon the stock had risen $2\frac{1}{4}$ points. At 3 P.M. it had fallen $1\frac{7}{8}$ points from the new price. When the market closed the stock had fallen another $1\frac{3}{4}$ points. What was the price of the stock at noon? at 3 P.M.? at closing time?

6. Ferdinand's bank permits an overdraft of up to $50 before it returns a check because of insufficient funds. Ferdinand had $85 in his account. He deposited $45. Then he wrote checks for $25, $58, and $76. Did Ferdinand have enough money in his account to cover these checks? If not, did his bank return any of these checks because of insufficient funds? Explain your answer.

7. At the beginning of the day, the prices of stocks A and B are the same. At the end of the day, the change in the price of stock A is $-\frac{5}{12}$, and stock B's new price is $\frac{7}{12}$ greater than the new price of stock A. What is stock B's change for the day?

8. The greatest depth that a human being has reached underground is -2.23 miles. The greatest depth that a human being has reached under the ocean's surface is -4.55 miles deeper than the greatest depth that a human being reached underground. How far below the ocean's surface have human beings gone?

9. A company earns -3.62 million dollars in 2000 and 4.5 million dollars in 2001. How much does the company earn in all during the two years?

10. A diver was at a depth of $-90\frac{1}{4}$ ft. She rose $40\frac{3}{4}$ ft to where another diver was. At what depth were the two divers?

11. A wooden stick measuring 7.1 cm when left in water increased in length. If its final measurement was 7.34 cm, find its increase in length.

12. What rational number must be added to the sum of $\frac{1}{2}$ and $\frac{1}{3}$ for the three numbers to have an average of $\frac{1}{6}$?

13. In one year, a company earned a total of $^-8.35$ million dollars. Of that amount, $^-2.5$ million dollars was for a defective product that needed to be recalled. What were the company's earnings if the loss caused by the defective product is not counted in the total earnings?

14. Thea's metal rod when left in the freezer decreased $\frac{3}{8}$ in. in length. If the new length measured $8\frac{1}{4}$ in., what was the initial length of the rod?

15. Find two rational numbers that have a sum of $^-0.1$ and a product of $^-0.42$.

16. What is three times the sum of $^-1.5$ and $3\frac{1}{2}$?

17. Six times a certain number decreased by 13 is $^-16\frac{2}{5}$. What is the number?

18. When $^-12\frac{9}{10}$ is subtracted from my number, the answer is $^-0.43$. What is my number?

19. During a drought the water level of a river changes $^-\frac{1}{4}$ ft each week. After 5 weeks of drought, how much must the water level change to return to its original level?

20. The highest and lowest temperatures recorded are 57.8°C in Africa and $^-88.3$°C in Antarctica. How much greater is the highest temperature than the lowest temperature?

21. Ms. Ramos bought $4\frac{1}{2}$ lb of apples at $.78 per pound, a bag of oranges for $2.29, $2\frac{1}{3}$ lb of bananas at $.39 per pound, and $10\frac{2}{3}$ lb of melon at $.27 per pound. If Ms. Ramos paid with a $10 bill, what was her change?

22. A cat climbs 30 ft at the beginning of each hour and falls 20 ft during each hourly period. If the cat begins its climb at 8:00 A.M., at what time will it make contact with a point 120 ft from the ground?

23. The changes in stock over a 5-day period were: $+1\frac{1}{4}$, $+\frac{5}{8}$, $-\frac{3}{4}$, $-1\frac{7}{8}$, and $-1\frac{1}{2}$. Find the net change for the week.

24. A deep sea diver found sunken treasure at a depth of $^-110\frac{3}{4}$ ft. He rose $28\frac{5}{8}$ ft where he had left his camera. At what depth was his camera?

25. When placed in liquid nitrogen a chemical changes in temperature $^-5.2$°C every second. What is the overall change in temperature after a minute?

26. Twice a number subtracted from 36 is equal to 15 more than one third of the number. What is the number?

27. In the last hour, the temperature dropped $2\frac{3}{8}°$ to reach $-5\frac{5}{16}°$. What was the temperature an hour ago?

28. Migration across an ocean current caused a net loss of -13.02 mi in a fish's forward progress in 4.2 h. Find the net loss per hour.

29. The class kept a 5-day record of the water-table level. The record read: 15 in., -2 in., 3.4 in., 10.9 in., and $-4\frac{1}{2}$ in. What was the average water-table level during this time period?

30. When 300 students are in the school auditorium, only $\frac{2}{3}$ of the seats are occupied. How many seats are in the auditorium?

31. Last week 274 people attended the school concert. This number was 14 fewer than twice the number of people who attended the last school concert. How many people attended the last school concert?

32. The maximum depth of a minisub is 3,945 ft. A trip calls for the minisub to descend to a depth of 1,745 ft and then to descend another 2,090 ft. Will the sub descend to within 200 feet of its maximum depth?

33. A store received a shipment of books. Twenty were sold and $\frac{2}{5}$ of those remaining were returned to the publishing company. If 48 books were returned, how many books were in the original shipment?

34. The world's largest moth has a wingspread of $10\frac{1}{2}$ in. that is $4\frac{1}{2}$ in. more than half the wingspread of the world's largest butterfly. What is the wingspread of the world's largest butterfly?

35. The quotient of a number and $-\frac{9}{10}$ is $3\frac{3}{5}$. What is the number?

36. What is half the sum of $-1\frac{1}{4}$, 2.3, and $-3\frac{1}{4}$?

37. James is $\frac{1}{4}$ as old as Ms. Bustos, his grandmother. James sister, Lisa, is $\frac{3}{8}$ as old as her grandmother. If the sum of the ages of James and Lisa is decreased by 6, the result is 39. How old is Ms. Bustos?

38. Rowena keeps a record of time she spends practicing piano. On Monday she spends $1\frac{1}{4}$ h, on Tuesday and Wednesday, she spends 2 h each day, and on Thursday she spends $1\frac{3}{4}$ h. How many hours will she have to spend practicing for the rest of the week in order to have an average of exactly 90 min each day?

Test for Chapter 4

This chapter's skills may appear on a standardized test.

1. One half of the student population of Kennedy School takes allied arts courses and one third of the others take advanced placement courses. The remaining 300 students do not take any of these courses. How many students are in Kennedy School?

   a. 1800 **b.** 1350
   c. 900 **d.** 550

2. Three fourths of a gasoline storage tank is emptied by filling each of five buses with the same amount of fuel. What part of the total capacity of the storage tank did each bus receive?

   f. $\frac{1}{5}$ **g.** $\frac{1}{10}$
   h. $\frac{2}{15}$ **j.** $\frac{3}{20}$

3. Of Sally's salary, $\frac{1}{10}$ is spent for clothing and $\frac{1}{3}$ is for food and rent. What part of the salary is left for other expenditures and savings?

   a. $\frac{17}{30}$ **b.** $\frac{3}{5}$
   c. $\frac{2}{3}$ **d.** $\frac{7}{10}$

4. After reading a low of $-16°F$ at 10 P.M., the temperature began rising an average of 3 degrees an hour. What was the thermometer reading at 1 A.M.?

   f. $-25°F$ **g.** $-7°F$
   h. 7°F **j.** 9°F

5. One positive rational number is 2 more than another. The sum of their squares is 34. Find the smaller number.

   a. -5 **b.** -3
   c. 5 **d.** 3

Write your answers to the following. Be accurate and thorough in your explanation.

6. At the stationery store Ann bought three items priced $.65, $1.49, and $.35. She had a coupon for $1 off the total price. Explain which properties of rational numbers Ann can use to simplify adding her total bill. How much did she pay?

7. In a class with the same number of boys and girls, $\frac{1}{8}$ of the girls and $\frac{5}{6}$ of the boys are school athletes. What part of the class consists of boys who are not school athletes?

8. The stock market has the following record of gain or loss for the week:

   $-5\frac{4}{5}$, 7.25, -4.3, $2\frac{1}{8}$, $-3\frac{1}{3}$

   Order these rational numbers from least to greatest.

9. If a river rises 6 inches, its water level changes $\frac{1}{2}$ ft. If the level changes $-1\frac{1}{2}$ ft, has the river risen or fallen? Explain your answer.

10. During a drought the water-table level changed -0.45 m per day. If the drought lasted $1\frac{1}{7}$ weeks, express the overall change in the water-table level using a rational number.

11. A number is divided by 5 and then decreased by -3. The result is 8.9. What is the number?

CHAPTER 5 Number Theory

Solve each problem. Name any strategy or strategies you used.

1. A sheet of construction paper is 0.06 mm thick. How thick will a stack of 1000 sheets of construction paper be?

2. Paving bricks are 21.2 cm wide. If the builder places 1000 of these bricks side-by-side to make a path, how many meters long will the path be?

3. An old computer can execute a command in 2.3 seconds. A new computer can execute the same command 1000 times faster. How long does it take the new computer to execute the command?

4. Paper is often packaged in amounts called "reams." A ream usually consists of 500 sheets. A stack of 20 reams of paper is 38 inches high. How thick is one sheet of paper?

5. **Geography** The area of Alaska is about 1,480,000 square kilometers. Express this area in scientific notation.

6. **Geography** The area of New York City is about 206,000 acres. Express the area in scientific notation.

7. **Social Studies** New Jersey is the most densely populated state in the United States. The population of New Jersey is about 8,500,000 and its land area is about 19,200 km². What is the population density of New Jersey?

8. **Social Studies** Alaska is the least densely populated state in the United States. The population of Alaska is about 630,000 and its land area is about 1,480,000 km². What is the population density of Alaska?

Chemistry Chemists use units called "moles" to measure amounts of chemicals. One mole is the amount of a substance that contains the same number of basic entities (atoms, molecules, or radicals) as there are atoms in 12 grams of carbon-12: 6.023×10^{23} atoms.

9. If you have 3.49334×10^{25} carbon-12 atoms, how many moles do you have?

10. How many atoms are there in 600 moles of carbon-12?

Physical Science Some units for measuring very short periods of time are milliseconds, microseconds, and nanoseconds. A millisecond is one thousandth of a second, a microsecond is one millionth of a second, and a nanosecond is one billionth of a second.

11. Express one millisecond as a part of a second using a power of 10.

12. Express one microsecond as a part of a second using a power of 10.

13. Express one second in nanoseconds using a power of 10.

14. How many nanoseconds are in a microsecond? in a millisecond?

15. Which is a longer period of time, 0.025 microseconds or 2.5 nanoseconds?

16. Which is a shorter period of time, 50 microseconds or 0.25 milliseconds?

A leap year is any year whose number is divisible by 4. The only exceptions are centesimal years that are not divisible by 4, such as 900, 1800, and 2200.

17. Every leap year includes the date February 29. Did the month of February have 29 days in 1932?

18. History Abraham Lincoln won the presidential election in 1860. Was 1860 a leap year? Explain.

19. Science A comet passes near Earth every year that is divisible by 9. Will the comet pass near Earth in the year 2178? Explain.

20. Eight people buy a lottery ticket as a group. The grand prize is $888,772. If they win, will the 8 people be able to share the prize equally? Explain.

21. George has two plants in the lot next to his house. He claims that each year the number of plants will double. If that is true, how many plants will he have at the end of 10 years?

22. A fan club for a country singer began with just three members. The club hopes to triple its size each month. If that happens how many members will there be at the end of one year?

23. If a commuter bus picks up 5 people on the first stop, 8 people on the second stop, 11 people on the third stop, and so on, how many people will get on at the seventh stop?

24. A tank contains 15,360 gallons of water. At the end of each day, one half of the water is removed and not replaced. How much water is left in the tank after 10 days?

25. Mr. Posio is planning to fence a 1-meter wide strip of land for a nursery. To order materials, he needs to know how the amount of fencing will increase if the length of the nursery increases while its width remains the same.

Length (in meters)	1	2	3	4	5	6	7	8
Perimeter (in meters)	?	?	?	?	?	?	?	?

a. Copy and complete the table.
b. As the length increases, what happens to the perimeter?
c. What is the rule for finding perimeter as the width increases?
d. Find the perimeter if the length of the strip of land is 10m; 12m.

In the Fibonacci sequence {1, 1, 2, 3, 5, 8, 13, . . .} each term after the first two terms is obtained by adding certain numbers.

26. Find the pattern in the Fibonacci sequence and use it to write the next three terms.

27. Use the Fibonacci sequence rule to find the missing terms in the sequence 3, ?, ?, 9, ?, ?.

28. Write the negation for this statement: Eleven is a prime number.

29. Write the negation of this statement: The sum of 8 and 5 is not 13.

30. Let p represent the statement "I eat lunch," and q represent the statement "I go for a walk."

    a. Write a statement for $p \wedge q$.
    b. Write a statement for $p \vee q$.
    c. Write a statement for $p \rightarrow q$.
    d. Write a statement for $p \leftrightarrow q$.

31. Use the biconditional "I am on time if and only if my alarm clock works."

    a. Write the related conditional statement.
    b. Write the related disjunction.
    c. Write the related conjunction.

32. **Writing** The truth table at the right shows the truth values for conditional statements based on all possible combinations of truth values for statements p and q. Verify the table by doing the following: For each row create statements for p and q that reflect the truth values shown. Then write the conditional for each row and check its truth value.

Conditional		
p	q	$p \rightarrow q$
T	T	T
T	F	F
F	T	T
F	F	T

33. This statement is a contrapositive that is related to a certain conditional statement: *If it is not winter, then it is not January.* Write the conditional statement.

34. This statement is the converse that is related to a certain conditional statement: *If I go to the beach, then it is a sunny day.* Write the conditional statement.

35. This statement is the inverse that is related to a certain conditional statement: *If you go to the park, then I do not go to the park.* Write the conditional statement.

36. This statement is the contrapositive that is related to a certain conditional statement: *If the weather is not cold, then it is not snowing.* Write the inverse that is related to the original conditional statement.

37. Use this conditional statement: *If a number is divisible by 9, then it is divisible by 3.* Write the converse, inverse, and contrapositive, and give the truth value of each.

38. Use this conditional statement: *If a number is even, then it is divisible by 2.* Write the converse, inverse, and contrapositive and give the truth value of each.

39. **Writing** Do a conditional statement and its inverse always have the same truth value? Explain using examples.

40. **Writing** Do a conditional statement and its converse always have the same truth value? Explain using examples.

Test for Chapter 5

This chapter's skills might appear on a standardized test.

1. A concert at a park was attended by 1000 people. When the concert ended, the crowd in the park decreased by half every five minutes. After 15 minutes, how many people had left the park?

   a. 875   **b.** 750
   c. 250   **d.** 125

2. What is the missing term in this sequence?

   4, 12, ?, 108, . . .

   f. 20   **g.** 48
   h. 36   **j.** 60

3. The rule for a sequence is $8 - 3n$, where n = number of the term. What are the first four terms of the sequence?

   a. 5, 2, $^-$1, $^-$4   **b.** 8, 5, 2, 0
   c. 8, 11, 14, 17   **d.** 5, $^-$2, 1, $^-$4

4. Jamal has 9 CDs. He plans to buy an average of 3 CDs a month. Which of the following represents the number of CDs Jamal will have 6 months from now?

   f. 12   **g.** 18   **h.** 27   **j.** 3^6

5. The Chinese calendar assigns animal names to years according to an addition sequence. 1956 and 1992 were Years of the Monkey. There were two Years of the Monkey between 1956 and 1992. What were those years?

   a. 1968 and 1980
   b. 1972 and 1986
   c. 1970 and 1980
   d. 1972 and 1984

6. In 1850 the world's population was estimated to be 1 billion. In 1930 it was estimated to be 2 billion. In 1975 it was estimated to be 4 billion. What would be the next number in the sequence of populations?

   f. 5 billion   **g.** 6 billion
   h. 8 billion   **j.** 16 billion

7. The average distance of the planet Jupiter from the Sun is 778,000,000 km. What is this distance expressed in scientific notation?

   a. 778×10^6 **b.** 7.78×10^7
   c. 7.78×10^8 **d.** 0.778×10^9

8. Which of the following numbers is divisible by 5, 8, and 9?

   f. 636,120   **g.** 567,890
   h. 754,720   **j.** 902,680

9. Which is the inverse of this statement: If a number is divisible by 6, then it is divisible by 3.

   a. If a number is divisible by 3, then it is divisible by 6.
   b. A number is divisible by 6 if and only if it is divisible by 3.
   c. If a number is not divisible by 3, then it is not divisible by 6.
   d. If a number is not divisible by 6, then it is not divisible by 3.

Open-Ended Response Question

Write your answers to the following. Be as accurate and thorough in your explanation as you can.

10. Test the following conjecture and explain in your own words why it is true or false: If a number is divisible by both 3 and 4, then it is divisible by 12.

Solve each problem. Name any strategy or strategies you used.

1. Riza has 27 CDs and 36 tapes. What is the ratio of the number of her CDs to the total number of her CDs and tapes?

2. Pete drove 156 mi and used 6 gal of gasoline. At this rate, can he drive 561 mi on a full tank of 21 gal of gasoline? Explain.

3. In a firm of 294 employees, the ratio of full-time employees to part-time employees is 5 : 2. How many part-time employees are in the firm?

4. A tower casts a shadow of 9 m and a tree next to the tower casts a shadow of 0.6 m. If the tower is 18 m tall, how tall is the tree?

5. A snack food mixes 3 parts of peanuts for every 8 parts of popcorn. How many pounds of peanuts would be mixed with 30 lb of popcorn?

6. One store sells 3 cans of fruit cocktail for $0.79. Another store sells fruit cocktail at 2 cans for $0.55. Which is the better buy? Explain your answer.

7. Two numbers are in the ratio 2 : 5. If 6 is subtracted from their sum, the result is 50. Find the larger number.

8. A 0.5 kg bag of mixed nuts costs $1.35. At the same rate, how much would a 2.3 kg bag of mixed nuts cost?

9. Bob paints 15.08 yd of fence in 5.2 h, and Jake paints 19.72 yd in 6.8 h. Each feels that the other is not doing a fair share of the work. Prove that they are doing proportional amounts of painting.

10. A poster that Leila likes costs $6.50. The store is running a sale of 2 posters for $12.00. How much money will Leila save by buying 10 posters, 2 at a time, instead of at $6.50 each?

12. Bananas cost $0.48 per pound. Roy bought $1.20 worth.

11. A freight train can travel 504 miles in 6 hours. At the same rate, how far can the train travel in 10 hours?

14. The ratio of advertising time to total air-time of a weekly TV show is 3 : 16. If a weekly TV show is 60 minutes long, how much time is devoted to advertising?

13. Students in an art class are in the ratio of 5 girls to 4 boys. Can there be 20 students in the class? What is the largest class size with fewer than 40 students? Explain your answers.

15. Mr. Santos paints $\frac{3}{4}$ of a house in 3 days. If he continues to work at the same rate, how much more time will he need to paint the rest of the house?

16. The scale of a map is $\frac{3}{4}$ in. = 12 mi. What is the area, in square miles, of a park represented on this map by a square whose side is 1 inch?

17. If 4 men can clear the snow near a church in 6 hours, how many hours will it take 12 men working at the same rate to perform this task?

18. A school club includes students from grades 6, 7, and 8 in the ratio of 1 : 3 : 2. If the school club has 54 members, how many grade 8 students are members of the club?

19. A bag of cat food will feed 18 cats for 54 days. For how many days will that bag of cat food feed 12 cats?

20. What is the scale of a drawing in which a jar 28 cm tall is drawn 1.75 cm high?

21. Three boys have baseball cards in the ratio of 19 : 5 : 3. If the boy with the least number has 9 baseball cards, how many baseball cards does the boy with the greatest number have?

22. On a map, 1.5 cm represents a distance of 45 km. If two points on the map are 0.8 cm apart, how many kilometers apart are these points?

23. A dietician has sufficient food to feed 13 patients for 4 weeks. How many days will this supply last if 13 more patients are added?

24. A $300,000 inheritance is to be divided among three people in the ratio 2 : 3 : 5. What is the value of the smallest share?

25. A scale drawing of a house has the scale 2 cm : 1.5 m. If the house has a length of 16 cm on the drawing, what is its actual length?

26. Two boys can paint a fence in 5 hours. How many hours will it take 3 boys working at the same rate to paint the fence?

27. Each of boxes A, B, and C contains 8 bars of chocolate. What is the minimum number of bars that can be transferred among the boxes so that the ratio of the number of bars in box A to box B to box C is 1 : 2 : 3? Explain your answer.

28. On a map, a line segment $\frac{1}{2}$ inch long represents a distance of 250 miles. Using the same scale, how many miles long is a road that is $5\frac{1}{4}$ inches on the map?

29. If the degree measures of three angles of a triangle are in the ratio of 1 : 3 : 5, what is the degree measure of the smallest angle?

30. On a map, 1 cm represents 100 km. If two cities are 275 km apart, how many centimeters apart are they on the map?

31. A rectangular photograph 3.5 inches by 5 inches is to be enlarged so that its shorter dimension will be 10.5 inches. Find the larger dimension of the enlargement.

32. From the top of a school building 60 feet high, the angle of depression to the road in front of the school is 38°. Find the distance from the road to the school to the nearest foot.

33. A 10-ft ladder and a 15-ft ladder are placed against the same wall and make congruent angles with the ground as shown in the diagram below. If the 10-ft ladder reaches a height of 6 ft against the wall, how much farther up the wall does the 15-ft ladder reach?

34. Jan is holding his kite string 3 ft above the ground as shown in the diagram below. The distance between his hand and a point directly under the kite is 95 ft. If the angle of elevation to the kite is 50°, find the height, *h*, of his kite to the nearest foot.

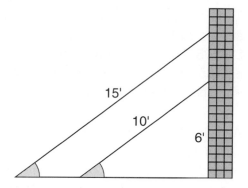

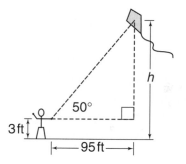

35. A man 5 ft 8 in. tall casts a shadow of 8 ft. What is the height of a pole that casts a shadow of 96 ft at the same time?

36. How long is the shadow of a 35-ft tree if a 98-ft tree casts a 42-ft shadow at the same time?

37. A tower standing on level ground casts a shadow 21 ft long at the same time that another tower 75 ft high casts a shadow of 25 ft long. Find the height of the first tower.

38. **Challenge** A 20-ft ladder leans against a building. If the foot of the ladder is 8 ft from the building, find, to the nearest degree, the measure of the angle that the foot of the ladder makes with the ground. (Use the Table of Trigonometric Ratios on page 552 in your textbook.)

39. Henry was sighting the height of a kite over the park. He used a baseline of 200 ft. The angle formed by the baseline and the sighting of the kite was 11°. How high was the kite?

40. From the top of a 120-ft lighthouse, the angle of depression of a boat out at sea is 26°. Find, to the nearest foot, the distance from the boat to the foot of the lighthouse.

Test for Chapter 6

This chapter's skills may appear on a standardized test.

1. Two numbers are in the ratio of 3 : 4. If 9 is subtracted from their sum, the result is 40. What is the larger number?

   a. 35   **b.** 21
   c. 28   **d.** 49

2. In a molecule of water, there are two atoms of hydrogen and one atom of oxygen. How many atoms of hydrogen are in 36 molecules of water?

   f. 18   **g.** 44
   h. 37   **j.** 72

3. Sterling silver is made of an alloy of silver and copper in the ratio of 37 : 3. If the mass of a sterling silver ingot is 800 grams, how much silver does it contain?

   a. 660 g   **b.** 740 g
   c. 640 g   **d.** 700 g

4. If on a scale drawing 48 ft are represented by 12 inches, then $\frac{1}{4}$ inch represents how many feet?

   f. 8 ft   **g.** 4 ft
   h. 2 ft   **j.** 1 ft

5. A baseball team played x games, losing four of them and winning the rest. What is the ratio of games won to games lost?

   a. $\frac{x}{4}$ **b.** $\frac{4}{x}$
   c. $\frac{4}{x-4}$ **d.** $\frac{x-4}{4}$

Open-Ended Response Questions

Write your answers to the following. Be as accurate and thorough in your explanation as you can.

6. At one store, 0.5 kg of lettuce cost $0.79. At another store, lettuce sells for $1.55 per kilogram. Which is the better buy? Explain your answer.

7. The profits from an investment are to be shared by three friends in the ratio of 3 : 2 : 5. The profit for the year was $1,765. Determine the amount of profit each is to receive. Explain your answer.

8. A 10-ft ladder is to be placed against a wall. The base of the ladder must be placed at an angle of 72° with the level ground for secure footing. Find, to the nearest inch, how far the base of the ladder should be from the wall and how far up the wall the ladder will reach? Explain your answers.

9. At the same time of day a cable pole and a yardstick cast shadows of 20 ft and 4 ft, respectively, as shown in the diagram below. If the angle of elevation of the Sun is the same for both the cable pole and the yardstick, determine the height of the cable pole.

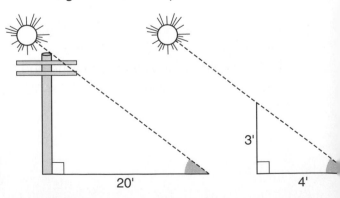

Solve each problem. Name any strategy or strategies you used.

1. A survey revealed that nine tenths of the people surveyed preferred Flossy White Toothpaste. What percent of the people surveyed preferred Flossy White Toothpaste?

2. A survey revealed that 4 out of 9 people felt stressed while at their jobs. What percent of the people surveyed felt stressed while at their jobs?

3. Tod spends 0.006 of each day brushing his teeth. What percent of a day does he spend brushing his teeth?

4. Rhonda said that she spends 0.042 of each day eating meals. What percent of a day does she spend eating meals?

5. **Business** One music store offers a discount of $\frac{3}{8}$ off all merchandise while another music store offers a discount of 35% off all merchandise. Which store offers a greater discount? Explain.

6. **Business** One clothing store marks up the merchandise it receives by $\frac{5}{8}$. Another clothing store marks up its merchandise by 60%. Which store does a greater markup? Explain.

7. A florist received a shipment of 10 vases. Three of them were cracked. She called the shipper and complained that one third of the vases shipped were damaged. Was she correct? Explain.

8. In a certain school 200 out of 250 eighth-grade students passed a state math test. The newspaper reported that 80% of the students passed. Was the newspaper report correct? Explain.

9. A flood destroyed 0.025 of the merchandise in a warehouse. The foreman declared that 25% of the merchandise had been destroyed. Was the foreman correct? Explain.

10. The price of a certain kind of writing pen rose from $1.00 to $1.25, an increase of $\frac{1}{4}$. A salesperson said that the price increased $\frac{1}{4}$%. Was the salesperson correct? Explain.

11. In February the number of books withdrawn was 300% of the number withdrawn in January. Write this percent as a decimal.

12. In March the number of books withdrawn was $66\frac{2}{3}$% of the number withdrawn in February. Write this percent as a decimal.

Books Withdrawn from the School Library

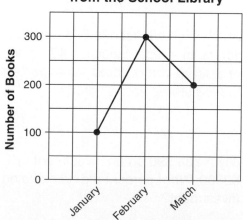

13. The American Discovery Trail from Delaware to California is 6356 miles. If the Gomez family walked 1.25% of the trail on their vacation, how far did they walk?

14. A gallon of gas costs $1.85 at Gabe's Gas Station. Of that amount 30% goes to state, local, and highway taxes. How much money per gallon goes to taxes?

15. The sales tax in a certain state is 8%. The Nelson family bought a washing machine for $699. How much sales tax did they pay?

16. A local middle school has an enrollment of 1300 students. Fifty-five percent of the students are females. How many of the students are males?

17. In a middle school with an enrollment of 1300 students, 34% are in the sixth grade, 30% are in the seventh grade, and the rest of the students are in the eighth grade. How many students are there altogether in the seventh and eighth grades?

18. From a sales tax of 8%, 3% goes to the local government, 1% goes to the county government, and 4% goes to the state government. If a computer costs $800, how much of the sales tax will go to the local government? to the county? to the state?

19. A market research company sent survey forms to 1200 people. Four hundred fifty completed forms were returned. What percent of the forms were returned?

20. At a certain school 80% of the 200 eighth graders play on a sports team. If 24 eighth graders withdraw from sports teams, what percent would then be on sports teams?

21. On a state highway 40% of the 40 rest areas offer food services. If 8 more of the rest areas add this feature, what percent of the rest areas will offer food services?

22. One hundred sixty people make a cross-country biking trip. Twenty-five percent of the people are first timers. If 8 of the first timers are women, what percent of the first timers are men?

23. An election district has 688 registered voters. In a recent election 430 of the registered voters voted. What percent of the registered voters voted?

24. A company predicts that its earnings this year will be 120% of last year's earnings. If last year's earnings were $525,000, how much does the company predict it will earn this year?

25. Jay made $90 on an investment of $2000. What percent did he make on his investment?

26. Nori's investment of $2000 lost $250. What percent of his investment did he have after the loss?

27. Hiram hiked 30% of a canal towpath along the American Discovery Trail. If he hiked 6 miles, how long is the canal towpath section of the trail?

28. Karen puts aside $500 of her monthly salary to pay her rent. This represents $37\frac{1}{2}\%$ of her monthly salary. What is her monthly salary?

29. A blend of coffee beans requires 15% Kenyan coffee beans. If 30 ounces of Kenyan coffee beans are available, how many pounds of the blend can be made?

30. On the first day of a week-long fundraising drive, a charity collected $250. This represented $16\frac{2}{3}\%$ of the goal for the entire drive. What was the goal of the drive?

31. A theater has 875 seats. At last night's performance, 658 of those seats were filled. About what percent of the seats were filled?

32. Myrna deposited $795 in a new savings account that has an annual yield of 2.15%. About how much will her account earn in interest in the first year?

33. Census figures for the year 2000 revealed that a town had a population of 2956. This was 148% of the town's 1990 population. About how many people lived in the town in 1990?

34. A freight elevator has a weight capacity of 5 tons. A shipment of 3156 lb was loaded onto the elevator. About what percent of the elevator's weight capacity was used by the shipment?

The graph shows the average normal monthly temperatures in Burlington, Vermont, from April through October. Use the graph for problems 35–38. Express all answers to the nearest tenth of a percent.

35. By what percent does the temperature normally increase from May to June?

36. By what percent does the temperature normally decrease from September to October?

37. By what percent does the temperature normally increase from April to July?

38. By what percent does the temperature normally decrease from July to October?

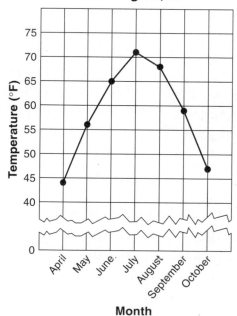

Normal Monthly Temperatures Burlington, VT

Test for Chapter 7

This chapter's skills might appear on a standardized test.

1. Which is another name for 0.040?

   a. 40%   **b.** 0.4%

   c. $\frac{1}{25}$ **d.** $\frac{2}{5}$

2. Which list shows the numbers in order from least to greatest?

   f. 0.6, 6%, $\frac{2}{3}$, $\frac{5}{8}$

   g. 0.6, 6%, $\frac{5}{8}$, $\frac{2}{3}$

   h. 6%, $\frac{2}{3}$, $\frac{5}{8}$, 0.6

   j. 6%, 0.6, $\frac{5}{8}$, $\frac{2}{3}$

3. Ms. Grey earned $37,500 this year. She received a raise of 4.5%. How much will she earn next year?

   a. $1687.50
   b. $16,875
   c. $54,375
   d. $39,187.50

4. A survey of 1100 people showed that 83% of those surveyed disapproved of using a cellular phone while driving a car. How many people surveyed did not disapprove of using a cellular phone while driving?

   f. 187   **g.** 913
   h. 1017   **j.** 831

5. What percent of an hour is 12 minutes?

   a. 12%   **b.** 10%
   c. 20%   **d.** 40%

6. A restaurant bill came to $60.80. Tax and tip added 22.5% to the bill. Which is the best estimate of the final bill?

   f. $82   **g.** $72
   h. $120   **j.** $48

7. The sales tax on a new refrigerator came to $44.80. The sales tax rate is 8%. What is the total cost of the refrigerator including tax?

   a. $560   **b.** $604.80
   c. $515.20   **d.** $358.40

8. Kyle earned $6 per hour last year at his summer job. This summer he earned $6.72 per hour. Which describes the change in his hourly earnings?

   f. an increase of 72%
   g. an increase of 12%
   h. an increase of 6%
   j. a decrease of 12%

Open-Ended Response Question

Write your answers to the following. Be as accurate and thorough in your explanation as you can.

9. You have two options for buying a ministereo system that has a price tag of $300 before tax.

   Option 1: You can pay the 8% sales tax on the original price and then take a $100 rebate.

   Option 2: You can take a $100 rebate first and then pay the 8% sales tax.

   Which option would you choose? Explain your reasoning.

Solve each problem. Name any strategy or strategies that you used.

1. The Friedmans sold their house, which cost them $125,000 three years ago, at a gain of 20%. How much money did the Friedmans gain from the sale of their house?

2. Mr. Black bought a refrigerator on sale at a 10% discount. The list price was originally $1,790. If he paid $3\frac{1}{4}$% sales tax and a delivery fee of $50, what was his total expenditure?

3. By what rate were bicycle helmets discounted?

Sale		
	List Price	Sale Price
Cycling Shorts	$25.00	$20.00
Bicycle Helmets	$47.50	$28.50
Cycling Shirts	$18.00	$13.06

4. Greg bought a pair of in-line skates on sale. How much did he pay for the skates if the sales tax was $5\frac{1}{2}$%?

35% off List Price	
	List Price
Skateboards	$89.70
In-line Skates	$139.00
Roller Skates	$78.45

5. Noelle lives in a state in which there is no sales tax on individual clothing items less than $50. Otherwise the sales tax is 6%. She bought 2 sweaters for $25 each and boots that were originally $52 but were discounted 10%. She also bought a winter coat, originally listed at $160 and discounted 20%. To the nearest cent, what was Noelle's total expenditure?

6. The Johnson Oil Company gives a 15% discount on each home delivery if payment is received within 15 days. The company delivered 230 gallons of oil to the Wu household on October 29. If the cost of oil is $1.80 per gallon, and Johnson Oil Company received payment on November 12, how much did Mr. Wu pay for the oil delivery?

7. The Boys Club earned $278 from its recycling drive. Of the amount earned, 22% was used for supplies and snacks. How much money did the Boys Club have left?

8. A $50 item went on sale. Each week for three weeks the price was discounted 10%. David said that the total discount was 30%, or $15. Was David correct? Explain.

9. The cost of an exercycle was originally listed at $280 and was reduced 20%. The following week the price was discounted another 10%. Finally another 25% reduction was made. What was the final price of the exercycle?

10. During a closeout sale, Phil's Photo advertised all items at 25% off. An additional discount of 10% would be given to any customer who paid cash. Rodney paid cash for a camera that originally sold for $350. If sales tax was 5%, how much did Rodney pay for the camera? What was his total savings?

11. Mr. Watanabe earns a base salary of $250 per week and a commission of 2% of the price of any car he sells. Last week he sold 4 cars for $74,650 in total. How much did Mr. Watanabe earn last week?

12. Khalil opened a savings account with a deposit of $150. The account earns interest at a rate of 3%, compounded monthly. What was the total balance in his account after 5 months?

13. Mrs. Graham earns $2\frac{1}{2}$% of her total sales at Colony Furniture. In order to earn $400 in commission, what would her total sales have to be?

14. What rate of commission does Ms. Wong receive if she sells 5 television sets at $350 each and earns $70 in commission?

15. Mr. Edwards earns a base salary of $18,200 per year. He earns a commission of $1\frac{1}{2}$% of total sales up to $500,000 and 2% commission on total sales over $500,000. Last year his total sales were $3,750,000. What did he earn last year?

16. The Wilsons want to have $155,000 after they make improvements to their home and sell it. They have spent $25,000 on improvements. The listing real estate agency charges a 6% commission for selling their home. For how much money must the Wilsons sell their home?

17. Pio borrowed $2,500 from his father. Pio agreed to repay his father, including 5% annual simple interest. If Pio repays the loan in 9 months, how much money will he pay?

18. Pedro claims that if he lends $900 at a simple interest rate of 7% for 3 years, he will receive the same amount of interest as if he lent $1,800 at a simple interest rate of $3\frac{1}{2}$% for 18 months. Is Pedro correct? Explain.

19. Amelia made two investments. In the first, she invested $1,500 at a simple interest rate of $4\frac{1}{2}$% for 10 months. In the second, she invested the same amount at a simple interest rate of $2\frac{1}{2}$% for 18 months. Which investment will earn Amelia more money? How much more?

20. Mr. Lee lends Mr. Ali $15,000 at a simple interest rate of 12% for 5 years to start a new Internet company. If Mr. Ali repays the principal before the 5 years are up, he must also include a $2,000 pre-payment penalty. Mr. Ali wants to repay the loan in 3 years. How much would he pay Mr. Lee?

21. Lia's father invested $5,000 in a trust fund for her the day she was born. The fund earned 6% interest, compounded annually. Lia withdrew the money on her 18th birthday to pay for college. College costs are $7,000 per year. How many years of college will the trust fund pay for?

22. Ben has $7,000 that he can invest for 2 years. He is trying to decide whether to deposit the money in a savings account that pays $3\frac{1}{4}$%, compounded monthly, or in a certificate of deposit that has an annual percentage yield of $7\frac{1}{4}$%. With which investment would Ben earn more interest? How much more?

23. Ms. Garcia earned $725 last week. If 12% was deducted for taxes, 5% was deducted for savings, and 6% was deducted for her retirement fund, how much money did Ms. Garcia take home?

24. Ms. Umeki bought $210 worth of clothing using her credit card. She paid $100 at the end of the first month and $25 at the end of each of the next three months. She then paid the balance. If the finance charge was 1% per month, how much did the clothing actually cost her?

25. Mr. Alomar used his credit card to make purchases totaling $520 in May. He paid $200 the first month and paid the balance the second month. After the first month, the finance charge was 1% on the unpaid balance. How much could he have saved if he had paid cash for his purchases?

26. Mr. Curry bought an armchair for $650 plus 4% sales tax. He agreed to pay for the chair in equal installments every month for a year, including finance charges. The store's finance charge is based on an annual percentage rate of 18%. To the nearest cent, what was the amount of each of Mr. Curry's monthly payments?

The table below shows the 1999 basic state income tax rates for New Mexico and Oklahoma that apply to taxable income for married persons filing a joint return. Use the table to solve problems 27–28.

New Mexico		Oklahoma	
Not over $8,000	1.7%	First $2,000	0.5%
$8,001 to $16,000	3.2%	Next $3,000	1.0%
$16,001 to $24,000	4.7%	Next $2,500	2.0%
$24,001 to $40,000	6.0%	Next $2,300	3.0%
$40,001 to $64,000	7.1%	Next $2,400	4.0%
$64,001 to $100,000	7.9%	Next $2,800	5.0%
Over $100,000	8.2%	Next $6,000	6.0%
		Remainder	6.75%

27. Mr. and Mrs. Martinez live in Santa Fe, New Mexico. They had a taxable income of $57,000. How much did they pay in state income tax?

28. Mr. and Mrs. Slocum live in Tulsa, Oklahoma. Mrs. Slocum worked part time and earned $8,000. Mr. Slocum earned $20,000. If they filed a joint tax return, how much did they pay in state income tax?

29. Ms. Daly uses the circle graph at the right to show her deductions from her gross pay and her net pay for a month. If Ms. Daly's gross pay for the month was $5,256.00,

   a. how much was deducted for state tax? social security? federal income tax? other deductions?
   b. how much was her net pay?

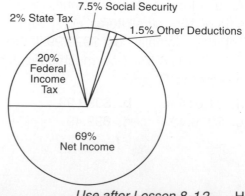

7.5% Social Security
2% State Tax
1.5% Other Deductions
20% Federal Income Tax
69% Net Income

Test for Chapter 8

This chapter's skills might appear on a standardized test.

1. Gail paid $36 for a blouse that was on sale for 25% of the original price. What was the original price of the blouse?

   a. $48　　　　**b.** $ 60
   c. $72　　　　**d.** $144

2. Members of the Harvest Glee Club wear identical red blazers. The list price of each blazer is $42.50. If the director buys a blazer for all 15 members of the club at a discount of 10%, what is the total in savings?

   f. $42.50　　　**g.** $46.75
   h. $63.75　　　**j.** $93.50

3. Last year Ms. Teves earned $37,346.20. The amount withheld for state taxes was $1,867.31. What percent of her gross pay went to state taxes?

   a. 0.5%　　　**b.** 1.5%
   c. 5%　　　　**d.** 15%

4. Ms. Prince bought a $1,200 refrigerator on credit. She paid $150 per month for 5 months and paid the balance the sixth month. What was the actual cost of the refrigerator if the monthly finance charge after the first month was 0.75%?

   f. $1,203.38　　**g.** $1,209.00
   h. $1245.00　　**j.** $2,100.00

5. An electronics store is having a weekend sale of 10% off all items. Jeric buys a TV set that originally cost $999.99. If the sales tax is 8.5%, how much does Jeric pay for the TV set?

   a. $1,014.99　　**b.** $999.99
   c. $976.49　　　**d.** 899.49

Write your answers to the following. Be as accurate and thorough in your explanation as you can.

6. An investment is expected to yield a profit of 98% per year. If the investment is $2,500, what is the approximate profit for the year?

7. Jenny has $1,000 that she wants to invest for one year. She can invest the money at a simple interest rate of 9% or at a rate of 6%, compounded quarterly. Which would be the better investment? Explain your answer.

8. Will had $2,500 invested for 2 years at an interest rate of 4%, compounded quarterly. If he withdraws all the accumulated funds after two years, for how many months can he spend $250 of the funds each month? Explain your answer.

9. Some stores charge a 10% service charge on all payments received after 30 days in addition to the regular interest charges and penalties. Sophie is 61 days late in paying a $708 bill. Calculate how much service charge Sophie has to pay.

10. During a special promotion at a music store, Wendy was able to buy $50 worth of CDs for $30 and $100 worth of CDs for $80. Was either rate of discount 20%? Explain your answer.

PROBLEM-SOLVING HANDBOOK

Solve each problem. Name the strategy or strategies that you used.

1. Suppose you want to play a game in which picking a 1, 2, or 3 is equally likely. You have already made number cards labeled 1, 2, 3, 2, and 3. What number card would you have to add to that set in order to play your game?

2. You play a game using the set of number cards created for problem 1. Suppose you pick a card. Give an example of an impossible event. Then give an example of a certain event.

3. A bag contains the letter tiles *a, e, f, e, g, m, z,* and *n.* You pick a tile without looking. What is the probability that you will pick a vowel?

4. You play a game in which you roll two 1–6 number cubes at a time. Make a table that gives all of the possible sums for a single roll of the two cubes. Then use that table to find the probability of rolling a sum of 10 or more.

5. A drawer has 3 blue socks, 4 black socks, 2 gray socks, and 1 white sock. Two socks are picked without replacing either. What is the probability of picking a pair of black socks?

6. You have a 1–4 spinner and a number cube that has the numbers 2, 2, 3, 3, 4, and 4. You spin the spinner and roll the cube. What is the probability of getting a pair of twos?

7. Bess, Sarah, and 14 other classmates write their names on cards. To choose two team captains, the teacher picks two cards without looking. What is the probability that Bess and Sarah will both be chosen to be captains?

8. There are 10 finalists in a science contest that has 4 prizes. In how many different ways can the finalists win 1st, 2nd, 3rd, and 4th prizes?

9. A disk jockey plans to play a set of 6 songs. In how many different orders can he play the 6 songs?

10. A random sample of 500 people were asked if they felt that long-distance phone rates were too expensive. Eighteen people said yes. What percent of people said yes?

11. In a random sample of 400 people, 68 said that they had traveled overseas at least once last year. If 5,000 people were surveyed, how many would probably say that they had traveled overseas at least once last year?

12. **Challenge** Robert prints a 5-page list. The pages are unnumbered. Robert drops the list and the pages are scattered. If Robert picks up the pages at random, what is the probability that the pages are in the correct order?

PROBLEM-SOLVING HANDBOOK

For problems 13–15, use the pictograph below.

13. Which country had the most computers? How many computers was that?

14. What was the difference between the number of computers in Germany and the number of computers in the United Kingdom?

15. Use the data in the pictograph to construct a bar graph. What scale did you use? Why?

For problems 16–19, use the table States Visited by More Than 500,000 Travelers from Overseas, 1997.

16. How many states are not in the table? How many visitors from overseas did these states receive in 1997?

17. Use the data from the table to make the following histograms:
    - one with intervals of 500,000 visitors,
    - one with intervals of 1,000,000 visitors.

18. What fraction of the states had 500,000 or fewer visitors from overseas? What fraction of the states had fewer than 1,000,000 visitors from overseas?

19. Which of your two histograms gives a more detailed picture of the data? Explain your answer.

For problems 20–21, use the table Why Americans Exercise.

20. Which kind of graph would you choose for the data: a circle graph, a double-line graph or a double-bar graph? Why? Make the graph.

21. What kind of data about exercise would be better displayed using a line graph?

Countries with the Most Computers in 2000	
Country	**Number of Computers**
France	▢
Germany	▢ ▢
Japan	▢ ▢ ▢
United Kingdom	▢ ▢
United States	▢ ▢ ▢ ▢ ▢ ▢ ▢ ▢ ▢

Key: ▢ = 20,000,000 computers
      ▢ = 15,000,000 computers
      ▢ = 10,000,000 computers
      ▢ = 5,000,000 computers

States Visited by More Than 500,000 Travelers from Overseas, 1997	
State	**Number of Visitors**
California	6,436,000
Florida	6,073,000
New York	5,274,000
Hawaii	3,073,000
Nevada	2,202,000
Massachusetts	1,210,000
Illinois	1,137,000
Texas	1,040,000
Arizona	968,000
New Jersey	726,000
Georgia	653,000
Pennsylvania	629,000
Washington	581,000
Colorado	532,000

Why Americans Exercise	
To stay healthy:	65%
To look good:	7%
To lose weight:	18%
To have fun:	10%

22. During one week in 2001, Broadway theaters charged the following top ticket prices: $90, $85, $85, $80, $90, $85, $85, $65, $90, $90, $85, $85, $65, $60, $70, $84, $85, $95, $85, $75, $85, $99, $69, $80, $80, $85, $70, and $70. Find the range, mean, median, and mode for this set of data.

23. The employees at Chex.Com have the following weekly salaries: $4,500, $1,200, $1050, $1000, $1000, $800. $800, $800, $750, and $700. Find the range, mean, median, and mode for this set of data. Which measure would you use if you wanted to describe the typical salary? Explain your answer.

24. The mean number of lunches served at Max's during the last four days is 50. Max's lunch totals for three days were 48, 52, and 46. How many lunches did Max's serve on the fourth day?

25. You have quiz scores of 80, 85, 78, 75, 80, 87, and 85. What score do you need on your next quiz to raise the median to 82?

26. Draw a scatter plot for the set of data below. Tell whether the scatter plot shows a positive correlation, a negative correlation, or no correlation. Then use the data to predict the height of a person with a foot length of 11 inches.

Foot Length (in inches)	8.5	9.5	9	8	9.75	10	8.25	7.5
Height (in inches)	59.5	65.5	63	58	68	70	57.75	52.5

For problems 27–29, use the double stem-and-leaf plot below.

27. Which race had a greater range of winning speeds? How much greater?

28. Make a box-and-whisker plot for the Indianapolis 500 and for the Daytona 500. For which race was the median of the winning speeds greater? What was the difference between the two median winning speeds?

29. In which race was the middle 50% of the winning speeds clustered more closely to the median? Explain your answer.

Winning Speeds in the Daytona 500 and the Indianapolis 500, 1986–2000

Indianapolis 500 Leaves	Stem	Daytona 500 Leaves
4	13	8
8 6 5 5	14	2 8 8 8 8
7 7 3	15	4 5 6 7
8 8 2 1	16	0 2 7
6 1	17	3 6
6	18	

Key: 1 | 17 | = 171 miles per hour
| 17 | 3 = 173 miles per hour

Test for Chapter 9

This chapter's skills might appear on a standardized test.

1. A juice manufacturer creates a game in which each bottle cap has one of the following symbols: star, circle, triangle, square, pentagon, crescent. There are an equal number of caps with each symbol. When you collect five of one symbol, you get a prize. What is the probability that you will be able to get a prize after buying only five juice bottles?

   a. $\frac{1}{46,656}$ **b.** $\frac{1}{7,776}$

   c. $\frac{1}{30}$ **d.** $\frac{1}{6}$

2. A deck of 6 cards has the numbers 5–10. Two cards are picked without replacing either. What is the probability of picking two multiples of 2?

   f. $\frac{1}{6}$ **g.** $\frac{1}{5}$

   h. $\frac{1}{4}$ **j.** $\frac{1}{2}$

3. A club has 8 members. In how many different ways can they elect a president, vice president, and treasurer?

   a. 3   **b.** 8
   c. 336   **d.** 40,320

4. Maria makes a circle graph that shows the data from the table. When she draws the part of the graph that represents "They are a necessity," what measure should she use for the central angle?

How People Feel About Cellular Phones	
They are a necessity:	22%
They are a convenience:	59%
They are basically a status symbol:	17%
Don't know:	2%

   f. 22°   **g.** 59°
   h. 79.2°   **j.** 144°

5. Students recorded the number of minutes of commercials on 20 radio stations in each hour. The results are shown below. What is the median for the set of data?

   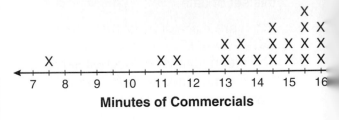
   Minutes of Commercials

   a. 7.5   **b.** 14.5   **c.** 15.5   **d.** 16

6. Which graph would you choose for the data below: a double-line graph or a circle graph? Why? Make that graph.

Motion Picture Receipts (in billions of dollars)		
Year	Theaters	Video Rental
1995	6.5	7.4
1996	7.0	7.0
1997	7.6	7.2

7. Ten college seniors graduated at the following ages: 22, 22, 22, 22, 21, 22, 88, 22, 21, and 22. Find the mean and mode for this set of data. Which would give you a better description of the age of a typical graduate, the mean or the mode? Why?

8. In a random sample of 300 people, 75 said they ate out at least once a week. If 10,000 people were surveyed, how many people would probably say that they ate out at least once per week?

Solve each problem. Name any strategy or strategies that you used.

1. What are the greatest and least whole-number measures possible of an acute angle? an obtuse angle?

2. How many angles are formed when a transversal cuts through any two parallel lines? Draw a picture to justify your answer.

3. What are three different ways to name the angle below?

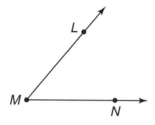

4. Trace the angle below. Then construct an angle congruent to it.

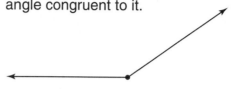

5. Ray *MA* is an angle bisector of ∠*TMH*. If the measure of ∠*TMA* is 26°, what are the measures of ∠*AMH* and ∠*TMH*?

6. Draw acute angle *ABC*. Then bisect it. Label the bisector *BD*. What are the measures of ∠*ABC*, ∠*ABD*, and ∠*DBC*?

7. What is the measure of an angle if 5° is subtracted from twice the complement and the result is 65°?

8. If the measure of ∠*A* is three times that of ∠*B*, find the measure of ∠*A* when angles *A* and *B* are supplementary.

9. **Critical Thinking** Without using a protractor, determine the measure of the smallest angle formed by bisecting an 80° angle and then bisecting the resulting angles.

10. **Challenge** What is the least number of distinct lines in a plane that can be drawn so that the total number of points of intersection is 6?

11. Measure the angle below. Use a protractor to draw its supplement. Then use a compass and a straightedge to construct another angle congruent to its supplement.

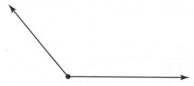

12. **Critical Thinking** Without using a protractor, draw an angle that is about 40° and an angle that is about 140°. Explain how you drew each angle. Then find the actual measure of each angle. How do the measures of the angles compare with 40° and 140°? Are they close?

13. If two angles are both complementary and congruent, what is the measure of each angle?

14. If two angles are supplementary and one angle is less than 90°, what can be said about the measure of the other angle?

15. In the figure below, the m∠BCA is 120°. The m∠BDF is 110°. What is the m∠CBD?

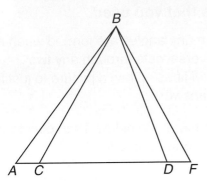

16. In the figure below, explain why triangle BAC is congruent to triangle EDC.

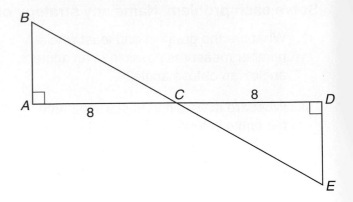

17. Reasoning In the figure below, explain why triangle ABC is congruent to triangle ADC.

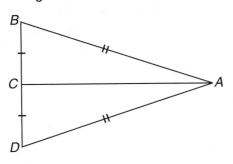

18. In the figure below, what is the measure of ∠x?

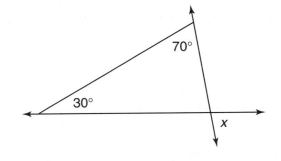

19. Can a right triangle have congruent angles? If so what is the greatest number of congruent angles? What would be their measures?

20. How many congruent angles are there in an equilateral triangle? in an isosceles triangle?

21. What corresponding congruent parts do you need to know to prove that two triangles are congruent?

22. For two non-right triangles how many pairs of corresponding congruent parts do you need to know to prove that the triangles are congruent?

23. Use the figure at the right for problems *a–e*.

   a. Name the transversal.
   b. Name all pairs of alternate interior angles.
   c. Name all pairs of alternate exterior angles.
   d. Name all pairs of corresponding angles.
   e. Name all pairs of adjacent angles.

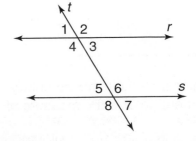

24. Two babies, Juan and Kate, are born on the same day. Juan weighs 8 lb 6 oz, Kate weighs 7 lb 14 oz. What is the difference in their weights?

25. A gas tank that holds 20 gallons of gas contains 2 gallons 3 quarts of gas. How much gas will it take to fill the tank? If gas costs $2.63 a gallon, how much will it cost to fill the tank?

26. To make curtains for his bedroom, Kimanzi needs 4 pieces of fabric that are 42 in. long. He has 4 yd of fabric. How many more yards does he need?

27. Irina is training to run a 14 km race. The racetrack at her school is exactly 3 km 5 hm. How many complete laps must she make to run 14 km?

28. Josef is 124 cm tall. His friend James told him that that means he is over 10 meters tall. Is James right? What is Josef's height in meters?

29. Cristi measured her math book and found its length to be 25.5 centimeters. Use the GPE of the measurement to write the interval of measure for the length of her math book.

30. Mrs. Daniel's recipe for cherry punch, which serves 6 people, calls for 3 c seltzer, 6 c cherry juice, and $\frac{1}{2}$ c lime juice. If she is making punch for 20 people, how much of each ingredient would she need? If Mrs. Daniel can only buy ingredients in quarts or gallons, how much of each would she need to buy?

31. Extra water is given to the Riverdale biking team when the temperature is over 34°C. If the three-day forecast predicts that it will be 89°F on Tuesday, 96°F on Wednesday, and 97°F on Thursday, for which days should the coach buy extra water?

32. Lake Moosetail is safe for ice-skating if it has been 29°F or colder for more than a week. The official temperature has averaged ⁻2°C for the last ten days. Is it safe to go ice-skating? Explain your reasoning.

33. The reading on the thermometer at your school is 68°F. Use the GPE of the temperature reading to determine the range of measure for the current temperature.

34. James and Josef are comparing the lengths of their mountain bikes. James' bike is 49 in. long. Josef's bike is 122 cm long. One inch equals about 2.54 centimeters. Whose bike is longer?

35. Points *A*, *B*, *C*, *D*, and *E* lie in order on a straight line. The distance between points *A* and *E* is 40 cm. The distance between points *A* and *D* is 300 mm. The distance between points *B* and D is 20 cm. Point *C* is halfway between points *B* and D. What is the distance between points *B* and *C* in millimeters?

Test for Chapter 10

This chapter's skills might appear on a standardized test.

1. Perpendicular lines intersect to form _____ angles.

   a. acute
   b. complementary
   c. right
   d. straight

2. The supplement of a 12° angle is _____.

   f. 78°
   g. 168°
   h. an acute angle
   j. a right angle

3. How many exterior angles are formed when two parallel lines are intersected by a third line?

   a. 2   b. 4   c. 6   d. 8

4. How many congruent sides does a scalene triangle have?

   f. 2   g. 3   h. 0   j. 4

5. How many congruent angles does an isosceles triangle have?

   a. 2   b. 3   c. 0   d. 4

6. The supplement of the complement of an angle is 100°. What is the measure of the angle?

   f. 10°   g. 90°   h. 180°   j. 80°

7. Which of the following is not equal to 0.078 km?

   a. 78 m
   b. 0.78 dm
   c. 78,000 mm
   d. 7,800 cm

8. 98°F is about how many degrees Celsius?

   f. 37°C   g. 47°C
   h. 107°C   j. 67°C

9. Angle x is 6 less than twice its complement. What are the measures of both angles?

   a. 62°, 18°
   b. 58°, 90°
   c. 32°, 58°
   d. 62°, 118°

10. What is the measure of angle x?

    f. 90°   g. 138°
    h. 42°   j. 48°

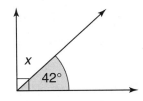

Write your answers to the following. Be as accurate and thorough in your explanation as you can.

11. Explain how you can tell if two triangles are congruent. You may use drawings to justify your answer.

12. Mark's goal is to run 20 miles in one week. The track he uses is 1500 yd long. Create a running schedule for Mark so that he can reach his goal.

13. Can the supplement and complement of a given angle ever be the same? Explain your reasoning. You may use drawings to justify your answer.

Solve each problem. Name any strategy or strategies you used.

1. A flower bed has the shape of an equilateral triangle. One side of the flower bed measures $3\frac{1}{6}$ ft. What is its perimeter?

2. Sandy Real Estate company bought 30 hectares of land in Ontario. The company's plan is to divide the land into 50-are plots for building homes. There are 100 ares in a hectare. How many plots can the company make?

3. **History** The Hanging Gardens of Babylon, one of the Seven Wonders of the Ancient World, were thought to be in the shape of a square 400 ft long by 400 ft wide. What is the area of a garden with those measurements?

4. **History** When Robert Koldewey excavated the site of the Hanging Gardens in 1899, he found they were actually 100 ft by 150 ft. What is the area of the gardens he found?

5. **History** The Great Pyramid at Giza is another of the Seven Wonders of the Ancient World. Each triangular face of the pyramid has a 756-ft base and a height of 612 ft. Find the area of one face.

6. **History** The floor of the King's Chamber in the Great Pyramid is in the shape of a rectangle 34 ft long and 17 ft wide. Find its perimeter and area.

7. Apartments at 245 Boardwalk Avenue rent for $3 per square foot. The rectangular penthouse measures 85 ft by 22 ft. How much does it cost to rent this penthouse?

8. Apartments at 3572 North Avenue rent for $6 per square foot. Apartment #3 is rectangular and measures 52 ft by 12 ft. How much does it cost to rent apartment #3?

9. The Zieglers want to build a fence around their hexagonal lot. Fencing costs $4.27 per yard. If two sides of the lot are 22 ft long, two sides are 33 ft long, and two sides are 20 ft long, how much will the fence cost?

10. **Critical Thinking** What is the length of a side of a square whose area is 16 square inches?

11. **Sports** Lambeau Field, where the Green Bay Packers play football, is 120 yd long and 53 yd 1 ft wide. What is the perimeter of the field? What is its area?

12. **Sports** In metric units a football field is 110 m long and 48.8 m wide. Find its perimeter in meters and its area in square meters.

13. The area of a rectangle is 36 square inches. Find three possible sets of dimensions for the rectangle.

14. The perimeter of a rectangle is 24 inches. Find three possible sets of dimensions for the rectangle.

15. A trapezoid has bases measuring 9 in. and 14 in. and a height measuring 5 in. Find its area.

16. The radius of a pizza is 10 cm. Find its diameter, circumference, and area.

17. Big Ben is a bell that sits in a very large clock tower in London, England. The tower has 4 clock faces, each with a diameter of 23 ft. What is the total area of the clock faces?

18. A car's windshield wiper is 16 in. long. What is the length of the semicircle made by the windshield wiper? How many square inches of windshield does it wipe?

19. Ralph took the subway uptown 6 miles, then across town 3 miles, then downtown 6 miles. What is the least number of miles he will have to travel to get back to where he started? How many miles will Ralph travel altogether?

20. The next day Ralph took the same trip, but traveled downtown 10 miles instead of 6 miles. From there he traveled 5 miles back to his starting point. The path for his entire trip formed a trapezoid. Find the area of this trapezoid.

21. Mrs. Crosby needs new felt for the base of her lamp so that it will not scratch her desk. The base is circular and has a radius of 9 cm. How much felt should she buy?

22. While at the fabric store, Mrs. Crosby decides to buy lace to go around the base of her lamp. (See problem 21.) How many centimeters of lace should she buy?

23. Mr. Singh's garden is a quadrilateral. The east edge is 7 ft wide, the west edge is 16 ft wide, the south edge is 15 ft long, and the north edge is 12 ft long. The northeast and northwest corners are right angles. How many square feet of plastic does Mr. Singh need to cover his entire garden for winter?

24. Mr. Singh's roses grow along the entire north edge of his garden in a rectangular plot that takes up 48 square feet of garden space. What are the dimensions of his rose garden?

25. A circular pond has a radius of 10 ft. There are plans to build a paved path around the pond. If the path is to be 2 ft wide, how many square feet of paving are needed?

26. The radius of a pizza is 7 in. It is divided into 8 equal slices. What is the area of each slice?

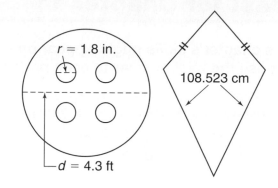

27. At the kite show second place went to a diamond-shaped kite with a perimeter of 362 cm. Two sides of the kite measure 108.523 cm each. Find the length of the remaining congruent sides of the kite.

28. The first-place kite is a circle with a diameter of 4.3 ft, with a pattern of four circles cut out around the center. Each of these circles has a radius of 1.8 inches. How many square inches of fabric comprise the first-place kite?

29. Grutz Flooring is replacing the rectangular gymnasium floor at Hartford Avenue School. The gym is 96 ft long, and has an area of 5200 square feet. How wide is the floor?

30. Grutz is also replacing the wooden hallway floor. It is a rectangular hallway, 12 ft by 23 ft. At its center is a marble circle 4 ft in diameter showing the school seal. How many square feet of wood will Grutz Flooring need for the hallway?

31. Emily is making circular campaign badges that have a diameter of 3.2 in. for a student council race. How many sq. in. of cardboard will she need to make badges for 26 students?

32. Gillian is making triangular election badges. The badges have a 3.75 in. base, and an area of 7.5 sq. in. Find the height of each badge.

33. Caitlin is going to sew an 8.5 ft by 11 ft American flag. The blue field will be a 4.5-ft square. How much red fabric will Caitlin need to buy?

34. Caitlin decides to sew a Japanese flag, too. It will be a 5 ft by 7 ft white field with a red circle sewn in the middle. The circle's diameter will be 3 ft. How much red fabric will she need? How much white fabric will show?

35. For Remy's flag project, he will need 14.732 sq yd of fabric. Standard Notions sells fabric by the half yard. Wendy's Yarns sells fabric by the quarter yard. Where should Remy buy his fabric? Explain your thinking.

36. Rohanna has a 123 square foot rectangular piece of carpeting that is 12.687 ft long. One side of her square living room is 11.327 ft. Does she have enough carpeting to completely cover her living room floor?

This chapter's skills might appear on a standardized test. Choose the best answer to each problem.

1. What is the perimeter of a regular pentagon with one side that is 7.09 m?

    a. 35.45 m   **b.** 45.35 m
    c. 14.18 m   **d.** 50.27 m

2. A rectangular barn is 40 ft long and 19 ft wide. Next to it is a silo with a radius of 4 ft. What is the area of the ground covered by the barn and silo together?

    f. 760 sq ft
    g. 772.56 sq ft
    h. 810.24 sq ft
    j. not enough information

3. The Yorko tiger cage needs a new floor because the Bengal tiger chewed a hole in the old one. Flooring costs $9.85 per square yd. How much will it cost to cover the 10 yd by 8 yd cage?

    a. $80.00   **b.** $788.00
    c. $868.00   **d.** $98.50

4. The Statue of Liberty holds a tablet that is 23'7" long and 13'7" wide. What is the area of the face of the tablet?

    f. 46,129 sq in. **g.** 299 sq ft
    h. 46,129 sq ft   **j.** 29,990 sq in.

5. Sam and Daniel both bought 729 sq ft of carpeting for their living rooms. Sam's living room is square; Daniel's living room is rectangular and half as wide as Sam's. What are the dimensions of Daniel's living room?

    a. 32 ft by 12 ft
    b. 27 ft by 27 ft
    c. 13.5 ft by 54 ft
    d. not enough information

6. Sam is giving his old carpet (see problem 5) to a roofer who uses it to patch leaks. He is working on a roof that needs an 18 ft by 4 ft patch. How much of the old carpet will be left over when the carpenter is done?

    f. none
    g. 592 sq ft
    h. 72 sq ft
    j. 657 sq ft

Open-Ended Response Questions

Write your answers to the following. Be as accurate and thorough in your explanation as you can.

7. If you know the radius of a circle that is inscribed in a square, can you determine the area of that square? Its perimeter? Use formulas for area and perimeter to explain your answer.

8. Suppose you double each dimension of a given rectangle. How does the perimeter of the larger rectangle compare with the perimeter of the original rectangle? How does the area of the larger rectangle compare with the area of the original rectangle? Use several examples to illustrate your answer.

9. A trapezoid has an area of 48 square inches. Find a set of possible dimensions (base length and height) for the trapezoid.

PROBLEM-SOLVING HANDBOOK

Solve each problem. Name the strategy or strategies that you used.

1. Batting average is found by dividing the number of hits by the number of at bats. A batter has a batting average of 0.333 . . . , or 0.$\overline{3}$. If the batter has 450 at-bats, how many hits does the batter have?

2. Nicole changes 0.$\overline{7}$ to fractional form. What number does Nicole find?

3. Morris designs two posters. The first is a rectangle that is 4.5 ft by 2 ft. The second poster is a square that has the same area as the first poster. What are the dimensions of the square?

4. Nicole buys ceramic floor tile for a square room that has sides of 15 ft. In order to buy enough tile to cover the room, Nicole has to spend $335.25. What is the cost per square foot?

5. Two square numbers have a sum of 181 and a difference of 19. What are the two numbers?

6. A square carpet has an area of 144 square feet. How many square yards is the carpet?

7. Mr. Brown's square garden has an area of 625 square feet. Mr. Brown wants to put a fence around the garden. How many feet of fencing does Mr. Brown need?

8. Five times the square root of a number is $^-35$. What is the number?

9. Between what two whole numbers is $\sqrt{925}$? Is $\sqrt{925}$ a rational number?

10. A number is squared, then tripled. The result is 48. What is the number?

11. The diagram to the right shows a circular field enclosed by a square fence. The area of the square is 400 yd². The area of a circle is given by the formula $A = \pi r^2$. What is the area of the circle?

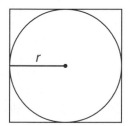

12. A square reflecting pool has a perimeter of 51.2 m. What is the area of the reflecting pool?

13. Nadine says that the sum of the square roots of a number is always zero. Do you agree with Nadine? Explain your answer.

14. George buys 450 tiles. Each tile is 1 ft by 1 ft. Is it possible for George to use exactly 450 tiles to cover the floor of a square room? Explain your answer.

15. Critical Thinking In calculations the fraction $\frac{22}{7}$ is sometimes used as an approximate value of the number π. The number π is an irrational number. Is $\frac{22}{7}$ also an irrational number? Explain your answer.

16. Critical Thinking Is the midpoint between $\sqrt{10}$ and $\sqrt{5}$ on a number line the graph of a rational number or an irrational number? Explain your answer.

17. Critical Thinking Is the midpoint between $\sqrt{\frac{9}{4}}$ and $\sqrt{\frac{9}{16}}$ on a number line the graph of a rational number or an irrational number? Explain your answer.

18. Use your calculator to find $\frac{1}{51}$ in decimal form. Can you tell whether the decimal terminates or repeats? Explain your answer.

19. The Talon Corporation hires Nicole to create a database. Nicole's rate of pay is $15 per hour. The Talon Corporation has budgeted for a maximum of $600 worth of Nicole's time (t) The inequality $15t \le 600$ gives the number of hours the Talon Corporation expects Nicole to work. How many hours does the Talon Corporation expect Nicole to work?

20. A sign in a nightclub says that a maximum of 1,250 people can be in the club. Between 8:00 P.M. and 10:00 P.M., the club lets people in but does not exceed the maximum. At 10:00 P.M., the club stops letting people in. At 11:00 P.M. the club lets 120 people in without exceeding the limit. Write and solve an inequality that shows how many people (p) were in the club just before the club admitted people at 11:00 P.M.

21. Half of a number a increased by 7 is greater than 8. Write and solve an inequality that finds the value of a.

22. Roland hikes at an average rate of 2.75 miles per hour. He knows from his map that Blixen's Bluff is at least 11 miles away. Write and solve an inequality that give the number of hours (h) it will take for Roland to hike to Blixen's Bluff.

23. The product of a number b and -7 is less than 42. Write and solve an inequality that finds the value of b.

24. The Boathouse rents sailboats for $6 per hour plus a $12 fee. Suppose you have $30. Write and solve an inequality that gives all of the possible amounts of time (t) in hours for which you can rent a sailboat.

25. Challenge The area of the rectangle to the right is greater than or equal to 34 square inches. Write and solve an inequality that gives the value of n. Then give the width of the rectangle.

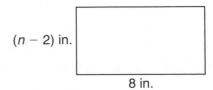

$(n-2)$ in.

8 in.

26. The world's longest aerial tramway takes passengers to the top of Sandia Peak in Albuquerque, New Mexico. The tram climbs a vertical distance of 0.76 mi as it covers a horizontal distance of 2.6 mi. To the nearest hundredth of a mile, what is the diagonal distance of the tram wires?

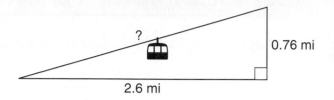

27. The diagram at the right shows a rectangular park. A diagonal path cuts across the park. To the nearest meter, What is the length of the path?

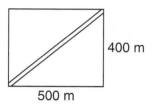

28. <mark>Critical Thinking</mark> Can you make a right triangle with sides of 9 in., 12 in., and 15 in.? Use the Pythagorean theorem to explain your answer.

29. <mark>Critical Thinking</mark> Can you make a right triangle with sides of 10 in., 6 in., and 4 in.? Use the Pythagorean theorem to explain your answer.

30. George flies a kite. He has let out all 100 ft of his kite string. The kite is flying next to the top of a 60 ft-high flagpole. How many feet away from George is the flagpole?

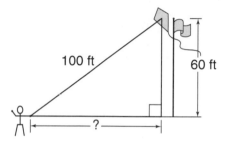

31. Ned hikes 4 miles east. He then hikes 2.7 miles north. How many miles to the nearest tenth is Ned from the point at which he started?

32. Julie hikes 3 km north, then 4 km west, and then 3 km north. How many kilometers to the nearest tenth is Julie from the point at which she started?

33. Firemen use a 40-ft ladder to rescue someone who is 30 ft above the ground. To the nearest foot how many feet away from the building is the ladder?

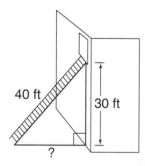

34. A 50-ft ladder is placed 16 ft away from a building. Will the ladder be able to reach the fourth floor, which is 48 ft above the ground? Explain your answer.

35. The bottom of a 35-ft ladder is 10 ft away from a building. To the nearest foot how far up the side of the building is the top of the ladder?

Test for Chapter 12

This chapter's skills might appear on a standardized test.

1. A square painting has an area of 400 square inches. How many inches of metal will be needed to frame the poster?

   a. 20 in.   **b.** 80 in.
   c. 100 in.   **d.** 1,600 in.

2. A square garden has a perimeter of 68 ft. What is the area of the garden?

   f. 272 ft²   **g.** 289 ft²
   h. 4,624 ft²   **j.** none of these

3. Which of the following is an irrational number?

   a. $\sqrt{\dfrac{16}{100}}$ **b.** 0.5959 . . .
   c. $\sqrt{84.64}$ **d.** none of these

4. Five decreased by one third of a number n is greater than or equal to 3. Which of the following statements is true?

   f. $n \geq {}^-2$ **g.** $n \geq {}^-6$
   h. $n \leq 2$ **j.** $n \leq 6$

5. A boat leaves a dock and travels 3 mi. north. The boat then travels 2.5 mi. west. To the nearest tenth how many miles from the dock is the boat?

   a. 1.7 mi.   **b.** 2.3 mi.
   c. 3.9 mi.   **d.** 15.3 mi.

6. A square has an area of 81 square centimeters. What is the length of a diagonal of the square?

   f. $\sqrt{81} - \sqrt{18}$
   g. $\sqrt{81}$
   h. $\sqrt{162}$
   j. none of these

Write your answers to the following. Be as accurate and thorough in your explanation as you can.

7. The diagram below shows one end of a folding table. The width of the table is 36 in. The length of one leg of the folding table is 48 in. To the nearest inch what is the height of the table?

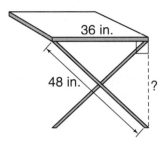

8. Ralph works at Mad Martin's Music Mall. He receives a salary of $200 per week plus 4% of his sales. Last week Ralph's total earnings were less than $500. Write and solve an inequality that tells for what amounts of weekly sales (s) Ralph will earn less than $500.

9. Three less than the square root of a number is $^-7$. What is the number?

10. A ski lift climbs a vertical distance of 0.8 km. The cables from which the lift hangs cover a diagonal distance of 2.2 km. To the nearest tenth of a kilometer what horizontal distance does the ski lift cover?

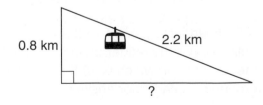

Solve each problem. Name the strategy or strategies you used.

1. Keiko is making a hexagonal prism out of paper. She is going to use one piece of red paper for each side and blue paper for each of the bases. How many pieces of red and blue paper will she need?

2. Each lateral, or rectangular, face of Keiko's hexagonal prism is 8 cm by 5 cm. What is the lateral area of the prism? What are the two possible perimeters of the base?

3. The Great Pyramid of Giza in Egypt has a square base with sides of 756 ft. Each of the pyramid's triangular faces has a height of 612 ft. What is the surface area of the pyramid?

4. Suppose you build a scale model of the Great Pyramid in problem 3. The base is a square with sides 18.9 in. What is the height of each triangular face? What is the surface area of the model?

5. Neil builds a pyramid with a rectangular base that is 3 in. by 5 in. Each of the triangular faces of the pyramid has a height of 7 in. What is the surface area of the pyramid?

6. **Challenge** A rectangular prism has a base that is 4 in. by 5 in. If the prism has a surface area of 148 in.², what is the height of the prism?

7. A can of black beans has a diameter of 4.8 in. and a height of 4.52 in. A can of garbanzo beans has a radius of 3.33 in. and a height of 4.5 in. Which has the greater surface area?

8. Which has a greater surface area, a cone with a radius of 9.18 cm and a slant height of 1.6 m or a cylinder with a radius of 9.18 cm and a height of 1.6 m? What is the difference in square centimeters?

9. **Challenge** Farmers use silos to store grain and other products. A typical silo is a cylinder capped with a dome, or half sphere. What is the surface area of a silo 42.3 ft high that has a diameter of 12 ft?

10. An ice sculptor has bought a block of ice that is half as tall as he is, and is shaped like a cube. If he is 6′3″, what is the surface area of the ice block?

11. A swimming pool is 50 m by 8 m by 1.5 m. How many cubic meters of water does it hold? Will a swimming pool that is 25 m × 4 m × 0.75 m hold half as much water? Explain your thinking, then find the volumes to check your theory.

12. Chandra holds a cylinder and a cone. They are both 10 cm in height, and their bases have the same diameter. If the cylinder is $\frac{1}{3}$ filled and the cone is filled to the rim, which holds the greater volume of water?

13. Mrs. Walther packed all her belongings in boxes to fill a storage space that is 14 ft by 12 ft, with a 9-ft ceiling. If the moving truck is 7 ft high, 7 ft wide, and 16 ft long, at least how many trips will it take to move her belongings?

14. Jungi has two candles shaped like rectangular pyramids. The red candle has a base of 1 square foot and a height of 2 in. The blue candle has a volume of 10 cubic inches. Which candle has the greater volume?

15. A cylinder is 14 in. high and has a diameter of 4 in. Estimate the volume of a rectangular box into which the cylinder would just fit.

16. Sheryl says that she can reach things that are 10 ft above the ground. If she is in a rectangular room that is 25 ft by 15 ft and that has a volume of 3375 cubic feet, can she touch the ceiling?

17. Botha stores his poster in a box shaped like a triangular prism. The box is $4\frac{1}{2}$ in. longer than the poster, which is 17.5 in. long. If the area of the triangular base is 6 square inches, what is the volume of the box?

18. Marjorie is building a footstool in the shape of a rectangular prism. If its length is 2 ft, its height is 2 ft, and its volume is 6 cubic feet, what is the width of the stool?

19. A cylindrical glass is half-filled with water. If the glass is 12 cm tall and has a volume of 150.72 cubic centimeters, what is the diameter of the base? (Use $\pi = 3.14$.)

20. A cylinder fits exactly inside a square prism that has a base area of 16 square inches. What is the volume of the cylinder?

21. A 1 lb 4 oz box of oat cereal is 7.3 cm by 24 cm by 34 cm. How many ounces of cereal per cubic centimeter does the box hold?

22. Miguel is using a conical cup to scoop water out of a clogged sink. The cup has a diameter of 6 cm and a height of 4 cm. After 10 scoops, how much water has Miguel removed?

23. The petri dishes in Alfonso's science class have a diameter of 4 cm and a depth of 1 cm. If he has two dishes, can they together hold 20 mL of rainwater?

24. A pan measuring 20 cm by 3 dm by .04 m is filled with water. What is the mass of the water in grams?

25. Shinjo has a box for collecting rainwater on his roof that is 10 cm tall, 2 dm wide, and .5 m long. If the box is 30% full after a storm, what is the liquid volume of the rainwater Shinjo has collected?

26. Wai reports that a large truck weighs about 2 t. Brian says it weighs 2 000 000 mg. Ricardo says it weighs 20 000 hg. Only one of them is correct. Which one?

27. A water tank is 6.2 m in diameter and 9 m deep. How many kiloliters of water does it hold when it is 0.7 full?

28. An ice tray holds 12 ice cubes, each of which has a capacity of 2 cubic centimeters. How many mL of water does the ice tray hold?

29. Three brothers, Raja, Sunil, and Vikram, pour glasses of lemonade from a bottle. Raja gets 300 mL, Sunil gets 0.3 L, and Viram gets 3 cL. Did the brothers all get the same amount of lemonade?

30. Sunil drinks from a glass that is 6 cm in diameter. How tall must each glass be to hold the volume of lemonade described in problem 29?

31. Ms. Ngele drinks 4 megacups of coffee each day. Her megacup holds 0.6 L of coffee. How much coffee did Ms. Ngele drink in November?

32. If Ms. Ngele's cup is 11 cm high, what is its diameter? (See problem 31.) If you wanted to put all the coffee she drinks in a week into a jar with an 8 cm lid, what would be the minimum height of the jar?

33. The average offensive lineman in the National Football League weighs 141 kg. The average jockey weighs about 52 kg. Express the difference in their weights in centigrams.

34. Arlene is trying to catch rain in a glass that is 4 cm tall and has a diameter of 2 cm. If she catches 1.5 mL of water a minute, how long will it take for her to fill the glass?

35. An average bathtub holds about 40 000 mL of water. What is the mass of that water in kg?

36. Powdered chai tea from India comes in a rectangular tin that is 13 cm by 8 cm by 6.2 cm. If the tin is completely full, what is the mass of the tea?

Test for Chapter 13

This chapter's skills might appear on a standardized test.

Choose the best answer to each problem.

1. A vat is 9.2 ft by 8.4 ft by 47.3 ft. What is its volume?
   a. 3655.344 ft³
   b. 3655.344 ft²
   c. 1819.52 ft²
   d. 1819.52 ft³

2. A solid cone has a slant height of 5 in. and a radius of 0.9 in. What is its surface area? Use 3.14 for π.
   f. 16.6734 in.²
   g. 28.26 in.²
   h. 25.434 in.²
   j. 10.182 in.²

3. A sphere has a diameter of 2.3 in. What is its surface area? Use 3.14 for π.
   a. 66.44 in.²
   b. 33.25 in.²
   c. 14.45 in.²
   d. 16.61 in.²

4. Some barns in rural Wisconsin are octagonal. If 1 gallon of paint covers 100 square feet of barn, how many gallons of paint are needed to cover all sides of a barn each side of which measures 8.6 ft by 34 ft?
   f. 239.2   g. 23.392
   h. 292.4   j. 2.924

5. St. Bernards are among the largest breeds of dog. Which of these is a reasonable estimate of the weight of an adult St. Bernard?
   a. 200 kg   b. 88 000 g
   c. 0.3 t   d. 10 000 dg

Write your answers to the following. Be as accurate and thorough in your explanations as you can.

6. A rectangular pyramid and a rectangular prism are both 10 in. tall. The prism has a base of 2 in. by 4 in. and the pyramid has a base of 3 in. by 8 in. What is the difference in volume between the two figures?

7. If a cylinder fits exactly inside a rectangular prism, which will have the greater volume? Use your understanding of the formula for determining volume to explain your answer.

8. A cylinder has a radius of 3 cm and a height of 8 cm. If there are three containers of water, one containing 0.2 L, one holding 20 dL, and another holding 0.2 dL, which of these glasses could be emptied into the cylinder without spilling over the cylinder's edge? Explain.

9. A triangular pyramid and a triangular prism have bases whose area is the same. However, the pyramid is twice as tall as the prism. Which figure has the greater volume? Explain why you do not need measurements to answer the question.

10. The dimensions of a glass block, in inches, are 9 by 9 by 4. How many glass blocks are needed to make up a wall that is 4 in. thick, 6 ft high, and 9 ft long?

Solve each problem. Name the strategy or strategies that you used.

1. Shamir has to graph the solution of the equation $x + 5 = {}^-4$ on a number line. Does his graph use an open or a closed circle? Is the solution a positive or negative integer?

2. Itzahk is graphing the compound inequality $^-4 < x < {}^-2$ on a number line. What are the boundary points of his graph?

3. Joanne tells Mrs. Robinson, her teacher, that she has graphed the equation $x - 3 = {}^-4$ on a number line. Mrs. Robinson corrects Joanne's terminology. What incorrect term did Joanne use?

4. Roland is graphing the ordered pair (5, 2) on a coordinate plane. He places the point 5 units up from the origin and 2 units to the right of the origin. Did he correctly graph the ordered pair? Explain.

5. Shauna graphs the ordered pair (6, 0) on a coordinate plane. She tells her teacher that the point is on the *x*-axis. Is she correct? Explain.

6. Jose graphs (4, 3) and (6, 1) on the coordinate plane. Which point is farther from the *y*-axis? Why?

7. Luann has to graph an ordered pair with a *y*-value of $^-3$ and an *x*-value of 2 on a coordinate plane. What is the ordered pair? In what quadrant of the coordinate plane does it lie?

8. Molly is solving the equation $y - 3x = 8$. If *y* is a negative integer, will the value for *x* be positive or negative? Explain.

9. Tad is graphing an ordered pair in quadrant III of the coordinate plane. Samantha is graphing an ordered pair in quadrant II of the coordinate plane. If Tad and Samantha multiply the coordinates in their ordered pairs, which product is negative?

10. Ichiro is graphing an ordered pair that is 4 units from the *x*-axis and 5 units from the *y*-axis on a coordinate plane. The point lies in quadrant II. What is the ordered pair?

11. Renaldo wrote $8x + 2y = 24$ and Henry wrote $2x + y = 6$ as equivalent equations to $4x + y = 12$. Which of these equivalent equations is correct? Explain.

12. Using integer values for *x* from $^-2$ to 1, Katia solved the equation $y = x - 2$. If those *x* and *y* values formed ordered pairs and were graphed, which point would lie in quadrant IV?

13. The formula for the perimeter of a square is $P = 4s$. Make a table of values and then graph the ordered pairs. Is the relationship a function? If yes, is it a linear function? (*Hint:* Graph s as the x coordinate and P as the y coordinate.)

14. As a salesman Wyclef could earn 6% commission on total weekly sales or $500 plus 1% commission on total sales per week. At what amount of weekly sales would his income for a week be the same under both conditions? Let y = weekly income and x = total weekly sales.

15. According to a recent survey, 35% of adults are concerned about poverty as a problem. Using x = number of adults surveyed, and y = adults concerned about poverty, write an equation that represents the result of the survey.

16. Use the equation in problem 15 to graph the result of the survey. Does the equation represent a linear function? Using the graph determine how many adults out of 500 surveyed are concerned about poverty.

17. Piedmont Paving, a highway paving company, can pave 6 miles of road in three 8-hour shifts. Find the number of miles it can pave in one hour.

18. Piedmont Paving has been hired to pave 50 miles of road at a rate of $125 an hour. Use the information from problem 17 to determine how much money Piedmont Paving will bill for this job.

19. Two puppies weigh 12 and 14 ounces, respectively. The heavier puppy is gaining an ounce a week while the other puppy is gaining two ounces a week. In how many weeks will the puppies' weight be the same?

20. Ruby took an aptitude test consisting of two parts: verbal and math. Her total score was 1240. She scored 120 points more on the math section than on the verbal section. Write and solve a pair of equations to determine Ruby's math and verbal test scores.

21. A store owner has 24 lb of pasta worth $.70 a pound. She wants to mix it with pasta worth $.45 a pound so that the resulting mixture can be sold for $.55 a pound. How much of the $.45-pasta must she use?

22. A farmer mixes cream that is 32% fat with milk that is 2% fat to make 50 gallons of milk that is 5% fat. How many gallons of cream and milk must he use?

23. The perimeter of an isosceles triangle is 34 inches. The base is 2 inches shorter than the length of each of the other two sides. Find the length of the sides and the base of the triangle.

24. The sum of the digits of a 2-digit number is 16. The number is 11 times the value of its ones digit. What is the number?

25. Kenji and his brother share a telephone. They are allowed to use it for up to 90 minutes a day altogether. Write a linear inequality and graph it to show how they can share the time.

26. Alonzo has 40 feet of materials to fence off his rectangular vegetable garden. Write and graph an inequality to show the possible dimensions of the garden.

27. When the tens digit of a two-digit number is added to three times the ones digit, the sum is 29. If the digits are added, the sum is 15. What is the original number?

28. Nate made a design on his computer. He used the line $y = x$ as the boundary and colored it red. He shaded the region $y > x$ green and the region $y < x$ blue. Make and color a drawing of his design.

29. Sweaters priced from $20 to $39 are on sale for $15. Sweaters priced from $40 to $69 are on sale for $35. Is the relation between the regular price and the sale price a function? Explain.

30. Trina saves some of her $10 allowance and spends the rest on movies and treats. Write and graph an equation to show the possible amounts she spends on movies and treats.

31. The southwest corner of Abraham Lincoln Park houses a right triangular monument with an area of 13,500 sq ft. The monument's south border is 125 ft long and the monument's perimeter is 590 ft. How long are the other two sides?

32. Jack and Pele earned $20 for baby-sitting. Two times what Jack earned equals three times what Pele earned. How much did each make for baby-sitting?

33. Find two positive numbers whose sum is 20 such that their product is as large as possible. (*Hint:* let x be one number and $20 - x$ be the other number. Then graph the equation $y = 20x - x^2$ to answer.)

34. A ball is thrown up at a speed of 32 ft/sec. The path of the ball is modeled by the equation $h = {}^-16t^2 + 32t$ where h = the height of the ball in feet and t = the time in seconds. Make a table of values using values of t as integers from 0 to 8. Then graph the equation to show the path of the ball. Determine how many seconds later the ball hits the ground.

35. A group of 20 people are packing food for the needy. An adult can pack 5 boxes an hour while a young person can pack 3 boxes an hour. If the group must pack at least 76 boxes an hour to meet its shipping schedule, what is the least number of adults that must be among the packers?

Test for Chapter 14

This chapter's skills might appear on a standardized test.

1. In graphing the solution of the inequality $-2x > 6$ on a number line, which of the following would be part of the graph?

   a. -4
   b. 2
   c. -3
   d. 4

2. Ragib graphs the ordered pair $(-6, 0)$ on a coordinate plane. In which quadrant does this ordered pair lie?

   f. quadrant I
   g. quadrant III
   h. quadrant IV
   j. none of the above

3. Find the common solution for $y - x = 5$ and $y = 3x + 3$.

   a. (5, 0)
   b. (6, 1)
   c. (1, 6)
   d. (0, 5)

4. Which of the following ordered pairs satisfies the equation $y = x + -5$?

   f. (6, 1)
   g. $(-2, 7)$
   h. $(2, -7)$
   j. $(-1, -6)$

5. Lucille graphs the ordered pair (6, 3) on a coordinate plane. Which of the following points is closer to the x-axis than (6, 3)?

   a. (3, 6)
   b. (5, 3)
   c. (3, 3)
   d. (5, 2)

6. Which of the following is an equivalent equation to $y - 2x = 13$?

   f. $y = 13 - 2x$
   g. $y = 2x - 13$
   h. $y = 13 + 2x$
   j. $2x = 13 - y$

7. Paulette has to graph the equation $1 - 3x = y$. Which ordered pair is on the graph?

   a. $(5, -2)$
   b. (2, 5)
   c. $(-2, -5)$
   d. $(2, -5)$

8. Which of the following ordered pairs makes the inequality $y \le x - 5$ true?

   f. $(2, -4)$
   g. (6, 1)
   h. $(-1, -7)$
   j. all of the above

Write your answers to the following. Be as accurate and thorough in your explanation as you can.

9. A small farm sells fresh herbs for $1.50 per 1– ounce bunch. The cost of preparing the growing area is $500 plus $.25 per 1– ounce bunch. How many ounces must be sold to break even? What is the break-even amount of revenue?

10. Louis hand decorates wooden boxes to sell at craft fairs. He sells the boxes for $15 each. He calculates a cost of $10 for supplies plus $10 in labor per box. How many boxes must he sell to break even?

11. How many integers are common to the solution sets of $2x + 3 > -5$ and $x - 5 < 3$? Explain how you found your answer.

Solve each problem. Name any strategy or strategies you used.

1. The diagram to the right shows a cylindrical fountain with a statue in the middle of it. The statue stands on a cylindrical base with a diameter of 6 ft. The entire fountain has a diameter of 16 ft. The volume of a cylinder is given by the equation $V = \pi r^2 h$. What volume of water is needed to fill the fountain?

3 ft

2. Which of the two polynomials below is written in descending order? Explain your answer.

   a. $x^3 + 9x^2 + 10x + 5$
   b. $5 + 4s + 2s^2 + s$

3. A number a subtracted from the cube of a number a is equal to 60. Write an equation to represent this situation. Then use the *Guess and Test* strategy to find the value for a that makes the equation true.

4. Find the perimeter of the rectangle shown below.

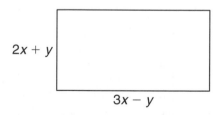

$2x + y$

$3x - y$

5. In terms of a and b, find the perimeter of the right triangle shown below. Explain how you found your answer.

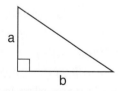

a

b

6. The sum of two polynomials is $3x^2 - 2xy + 6$. One of the polynomial addends is $x^2 + 3xy + 4$. What is the other addend?

7. **Critical Thinking** Traci used the laws of exponents to find that $\frac{n^{12}}{n^4} = n^3$. What mistake did Traci make? What is the correct answer?

8. Find the area of the rectangle shown below.

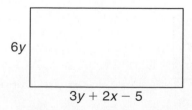

$6y$

$3y + 2x - 5$

9. Find the area of the square shown below.

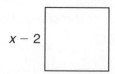

$x - 2$

10. The area of a rectangle is $(8x^2 - 4x)$ square units. Find as many possible pairs of dimensions of the rectangle as you can. Write each pair of dimensions as a product of length times width. For example, one possible pair of dimensions is $x(8x - 4)$.

11. **Science** Lydia launches a model rocket. The height in feet of the model rocket at any given time is given by the equation $128t - 16t^2$, where t represents the time in seconds after the launch. Write the expression in factored form. Then find the height of the rocket after 2 seconds.

12. **Science** To represent the height of any object that has been dropped, thrown, or launched into the air, you can use the Vertical Motion Formula, which is shown at the right. Suppose a ball is thrown straight up in the air with a velocity of 36 ft per second and that the thrower's hand is 4 ft above the ground when the ball is thrown. Write an expression in factored form that gives the height of the ball.

Vertical Motion Formula

$h = -16t^2 + vt + s$, where
h is the height in feet
v is the upward speed in feet per second when the object is released
t is the time since the object was released
s is the starting height of the object in feet

13. Use the expression that you wrote in problem 12. At what height will the ball be after 2 seconds? after 9 seconds? In this problem what does it mean when the Vertical Motion Formula gives a negative number as an answer?

14. The surface area of a cylinder is given by the expression $2\pi r^2 + 2\pi rh$. Write the expression in factored form. Then use the expression to find the amount of aluminum that is needed to make the can that is shown at the right.

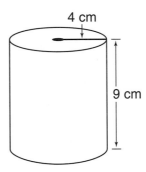

4 cm

9 cm

15. Find the width of a rectangle that has an area of $(y^2 - 16)$ square units and a length of $(y + 4)$ units.

16. Find the altitude to the base of a parallelogram that has an area of $(6x^2 - 2x - 20)$ square units, and a base of $(2x - 4)$ units.

17. Write the expression in factored form that gives the area of the shaded part of the figure to the right.

f

f 5

5

18. Find the area of the rectangle shown below.

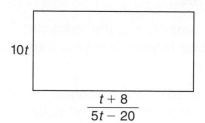

$10t$

$$\frac{t+8}{5t-20}$$

19. The area of the rectangle shown below is $\left(\dfrac{3s-4}{s-2}\right)$ square units. Find the width.

$$\frac{3s-4}{s^2-16}$$

20. Find the perimeter of the rectangle shown below.

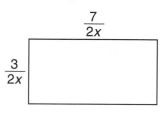

$$\frac{7}{2x}$$

$$\frac{3}{2x}$$

21. The triangle below is an equilateral triangle. Find the perimeter of the triangle.

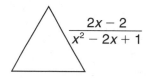

$$\frac{2x-2}{x^2-2x+1}$$

22. Find the perimeter of the rectangle shown below.

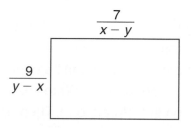

$$\frac{7}{x-y}$$

$$\frac{9}{y-x}$$

23. Find the perimeter of the trapezoid shown below.

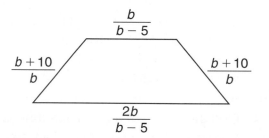

$$\frac{b}{b-5}$$

$$\frac{b+10}{b}$$

$$\frac{b+10}{b}$$

$$\frac{2b}{b-5}$$

24. **Challenge** Find the volume of the rectangular prism shown below.

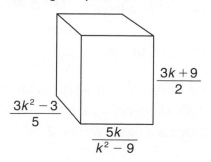

$$\frac{3k+9}{2}$$

$$\frac{3k^2-3}{5}$$

$$\frac{5k}{k^2-9}$$

25. **Challenge** Find the volume of the rectangular prism shown below.

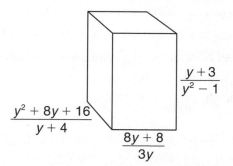

$$\frac{y+3}{y^2-1}$$

$$\frac{y^2+8y+16}{y+4}$$

$$\frac{8y+8}{3y}$$

Test for Chapter 15

This chapter's skills might appear on a standardized test.

1. Which of the following polynomials is written in descending order?

   a. $9 + 2v^2 + v$
   b. $6s^3 + 5s^2 + 4 + 3s$
   c. $2m^6 + 4m^2 + 6m + 8$
   d. none of these

2. Choose the set of values of x and y that will make the equation $2x^2 + xy - y^2 = 0$ true.

   f. $x = 2, y = 4$
   g. $x = 4, y = -2$
   h. $x = {}^-2, y = 4$
   j. none of these

3. The area of a rectangle is $(4f^2 - 20f)$ square units. Which of the following could *not* be the dimensions of this rectangle?

   a. 4 units by $(f^2 - 5f)$ units
   b. $2f$ units by $(2f - 10)$ units
   c. $4f$ units by $(f - 5)$ units
   d. none of these

4. Find the length of a rectangle that has a width of $(3g + 2)$ units and an area of $(6g^2 + 16g + 8)$ square units.

   f. $(g + 4)$ units   **g.** $(3g + 2)$ units
   h. $(2g + 4)$ units   **j.** none of these

5. Find the perimeter of a rectangle that has a length of $\frac{10x}{x^2y}$ units and a width of $\frac{20x}{3y}$ units.

   a. $\frac{60x}{3x^2y}$ units

   b. $\left(60x + \frac{40x^2y}{3x^2y}\right)$ units

   c. $\left(60x + \frac{40x^2y}{3y}\right)$ units

   d. none of these

Write your answers to the following. Be as accurate and thorough in your explanation as you can.

6. The surface area of a cone is given by the expression $\pi r^2 + \pi r\ell$. Write the expression in factored form. Then use the expression to find the amount of paper that is needed to make the drinking cup shown below.

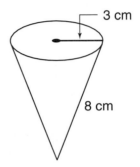

7. The Highway Code of Great Britain uses the expression $\frac{x^2}{20} + x$, where $x =$ speed in miles per hour, to find the stopping distance in feet of a car. Write this expression in factored form. Then use the expression to find the stopping distance of a car that is traveling at 30 miles per hour.

8. A rectangle has a length of $\left(\frac{20f + 20}{f^2}\right)$ units and a width of $\left(\frac{f^3}{f^2 + 4f + 3}\right)$ units. Find the area of the rectangle.

9. A plane travels at a rate represented by $(x + 100)$ kilometers per hour. Represent the distance it can travel in $(2x + 5)$ hours.

10. Express in simplest form the cost of one pencil if $3x$ pencils cost $(18x^2 - 6x)$ cents.

Solve each problem. Name any strategy or strategies you used.

1. **Science** The U.S. Department of Energy recommends air-conditioner sizes based on the size of the room that the air conditioner will cool. The relationship between room size and recommended air-conditioner size is given in the table at the right. Find the slope of the line that relates room size, (*x*), to air-conditioner size, (*y*). [*Hint:* Think of each pair of numbers in the table as coordinates of a point (*x, y*).]

Room Size in Square Feet (*x*)	Air Conditioner Size in BTUs (*y*)
400	8,000
500	10,000
600	14,000
800	16,000

2. Use the data and your results from problem 1 to find the equation of the line that relates room size, (*x*), to air-conditioner size, (*y*). Then graph this line. According to your results, how many BTUs are needed to cool a room that is 300 square feet?

3. **Problem Formulation** Use the data about room size and air-conditioner size to write your own problem. Include an answer. Then exchange problems with a classmate and solve each other's problems.

4. **Challenge** There are two boat rental services at Loon Lake. Each service charges a fixed starting fee and an hourly fee. The graph at the right shows the total cost in dollars, (*y*), for renting a boat for a given number of hours, (*x*), at each service. Only values for *x* > 0 are shown, since a boat cannot be rented for a negative number of hours. Based on the graph, which one of the following statements is true? Explain your answer.

   a. The fixed fee is the same at both boat rental services.

   b. The hourly fee is the same at both boat rental services.

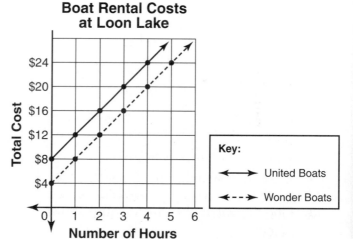

Boat Rental Costs at Loon Lake

Total Cost / Number of Hours

Key:
←→ United Boats
←--→ Wonder Boats

5. Bill rents studio time to record a CD. The studio charges a flat fee of $75 plus a charge of $50 per hour. Write an equation to find the total rental charge, (*y*), for a given number of hours, (*x*). Then make a graph of the equation.

6. A health insurance company charges a fixed monthly fee, (*x*), and a fee, (*y*), for each doctor's visit. In April Shari paid a total of $230 for 2 doctor's visits and the monthly fee. In June Shari paid a total of $245 for 3 doctor's visits and the monthly fee. Write two equations, in terms of *x* and *y*, to represent these 2 monthly payments.

PROBLEM-SOLVING HANDBOOK

7. Find the perimeter of the rectangle shown below.

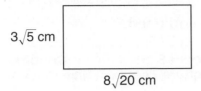

$3\sqrt{5}$ cm

$8\sqrt{20}$ cm

8. Find the perimeter of the trapezoid shown below.

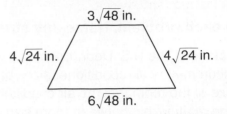

$3\sqrt{48}$ in.

$4\sqrt{24}$ in. $4\sqrt{24}$ in.

$6\sqrt{48}$ in.

9. Find the hypotenuse of the right triangle shown below.

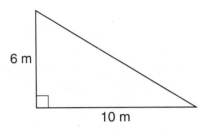

6 m

10 m

10. Find the diagonal of the rectangle shown below.

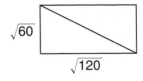

$\sqrt{60}$

$\sqrt{120}$

11. Find the volume of the figure shown below.

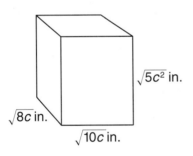

$\sqrt{5c^2}$ in.

$\sqrt{8c}$ in.

$\sqrt{10c}$ in.

12. The diagram below shows a rectangular park. A fence will enclose the shaded area of the park. Write an expression that gives the perimeter of the fence in terms of a.

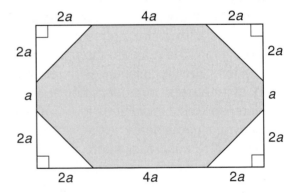

$2a$ $4a$ $2a$

$2a$ $2a$

a a

$2a$ $2a$

$2a$ $4a$ $2a$

13. Find the value of m in the figure shown below.

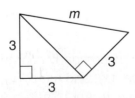

m

3

3

3

14. Find the area of the rectangle shown below.

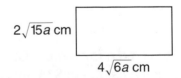

$2\sqrt{15a}$ cm

$4\sqrt{6a}$ cm

15. Find the area of a rectangle that has a length of $(a + \sqrt{3})$ units and a width of $(a - 3\sqrt{3})$ units.

16. Find the area of a square that has sides of $3\sqrt{n} + 4$ units.

17. **Science** A fireworks display with an initial velocity of 30 meters per second is launched from the ground. The approximate height, (h), of the display in meters at any given point in time, (t), in seconds after the launch is given by the formula $h = -5t^2 + 30t$. At what time will the display first reach a height of 40 m? Explain how you can use factoring to find the answer.

18. **Science** A soccer ball is kicked in the air with an initial velocity of 48 feet per second. The approximate height, (h), of the ball in feet at any given point in time, (t), in seconds after the kick is given by the formula $h = -16t^2 + 48t$. At what time will the ball be at a height of 32 ft? Explain how you found your answer.

19. The product of 2 consecutive positive odd integers is equal to 5 more than the product of 6 and the smaller integer. What are the 2 consecutive positive odd integers?

20. The length of a rectangular patio is 5 feet less than three times its width. The area of the patio is 50 square feet. What are the dimensions of the patio?

21. The product of two positive numbers is 247. The larger number is 6 more than the smaller number. Find the numbers.

22. If twice the square of a number is increased by four times that number, the result is 30. Find that number.

23. A mural has an area of 108 square feet. The length of the mural is 12 feet greater than the width. What are the dimensions of the mural?

24. A rectangular room has an area of 336 square feet. The length of the room is 4 feet less than twice the width. What are the dimensions of the room?

25. Challenge Mia has a can of varnish that will cover 4000 square inches of wood. She wants to make a box with a square base and a height of 12 in. If Mia wants to varnish the outside of the box, what is the length of the side of the largest base that Mia can make and still cover the entire box with varnish? (*Hint:* Express the surface area of the box as a quadratic equation and solve.)

26. On the 18th hole of the Fairview Golf Course, the ground slopes downward from the tee so that the fairway is 10 ft lower than the tee. When Ted hits a golf ball from the 18th tee, the height of the golf ball, (h), in feet above the fairway at any given time, (t), in seconds is given by the equation $h = -16t^2 + 60t + 10$. How many seconds after Ted hits the ball will the ball hit the ground?

27. Find two consecutive positive integers such that 3 times the square of the first is equal to 3 greater than 15 times the second.

28. Three times the square of a certain positive integer is 2 less than 7 times that integer. What is the integer?

Test for Chapter 16

This chapter's skills might appear on a standardized test.

1. The weather service records snowfall during a blizzard. The results are given in the table below.

Hours, (x)	2	3	4
Inches of Snow, (y)	4	6	8

Suppose you graph the data. What is the slope of the line that relates time, (x), in hours to snowfall, (y), in inches?

a. $\frac{1}{2}$
b. 2
c. 4
d. none of these

2. For each ride a taxi company charges a flat fee of $0.50 plus a charge of $0.80 per mile. Which of the following equations gives the total cost in dollars, (y), for a ride of a given number of miles, (x)?

f. $y = x + 0.8$
g. $y = 0.5x + 0.8$
h. $y = 0.8x + 0.5$
j. $x = 0.5y + 0.8$

3. A right triangle has legs of 8 in. and 12 in. What is the length of the hypotenuse?

a. $4\sqrt{5}$ in.
b. $4\sqrt{13}$ in.
c. $16\sqrt{13}$ in.
d. none of these

4. Find the area of a rectangle that has a length of $3\sqrt{10a}$ units and a width of $2\sqrt{8a}$ units.

f. $6a\sqrt{5}$ square units
g. $6\sqrt{18a}$ square units
h. $24\sqrt{5a}$ square units
j. $24a\sqrt{5}$ square units

5. A flare is launched into the air with an initial velocity of 80 feet per second. The approximate height, (h), of the flare in feet at any given point in time, (t), in seconds after the launch is given by the formula $h = -16t^2 + 80t$. At what time will the flare first reach a height of 64 ft?

6. The difference between the square of a number and 4 times that number is 12. What is the number?

7. A charter sailboat company charges a fixed fee plus a daily charge. One group arranges for a 3-day sailing trip and pays a total of $1400. Another group takes a 5-day trip and pays a total of $2200. A third group takes a 7-day trip and pays a total of $3000. Graph a line that shows the relationship between the total charge, (y), for a sailing trip and the number of days in a sailing trip, (x). Then write the equation of the line.

8. Find the perimeter of the rectangle shown below.

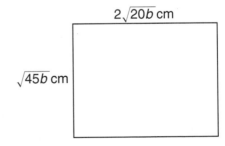

$2\sqrt{20b}$ cm

$\sqrt{45b}$ cm

9. A rectangle and a square have the same area. The length of the rectangle is 3 cm more than twice the length of a side of the square. The width of the rectangle is 2 cm less than the length of a side of the square. Find the length of the side of the square.

10. If 10 times a number is added to the square of that number, the result is 75. Find the number.